HANDBOOK
OF EMPLOYMENT
DISCRIMINATION RESEARCH

HANDBOOK OF EMPLOYMENT DISCRIMINATION RESEARCH

Rights and Realities

Edited by

LAURA BETH NIELSEN

and

ROBERT L. NELSON

American Bar Foundation and Northwestern University
Chicago and Evanston, USA

Springer

A C.I.P. Catalogue record for this book is available from the Library of Congress.

ISBN-10 1-4020-3370-2 (HB)
ISBN-13 978-1-4020-3370-4 (HB)
ISBN-10 1-4020-3455-5 (e-book)
ISBN-13 978-1-4020-3455-8 (e-book)

Published by Springer
P.O. Box 17, 3300 AA Dordrecht, The Netherlands.

www.springeronline.com

Printed on acid-free paper

Printed in the Netherlands.

This book is dedicated to our children
Ben, Hannah, Ian, Skyler, Willy, and Zach

Table of Contents

Acknowledgements xi
Introduction xiii
Laura Beth Nielsen and Robert L. Nelson

Section I
Overview: Socio-Legal Approaches to Anti-Discrimination Law

Chapter 1
Scaling the Pyramid: A Sociolegal Model of Employment Discrimination Litigation 03
Laura Beth Nielsen and Robert L. Nelson

Chapter 2
Law's Role in Addressing Complex Discrimination 35
Susan Sturm

Chapter 3
What We Know About the Problem of the Century: Lessons from Social Science to the Law, and Back 59
Susan T. Fiske

Section II
Debating the Prevalence and Character of Descrimination

Chapter 4
Including Mechanisms in Our Models of Ascriptive Inequality 75
Barbara F. Reskin

Chapter 5
Understanding the Sources of Ethnic and Racial Wage Gaps and Their Implications for Policy 99
Pedro Carneiro, James J. Heckman and Dimitriy V. Masterov

Chapter 6
Discrimination in Consummated Car Purchases 137
Ian Ayres

Chapter 7
Racial Equality Without Equal Employment Opportunity? Lessons from a Labor Market for Professional Athletes 149
William Bridges

Chapter 8
Employment Discrimination Based on Sexual Orientation: Dimensions of Difference 167
Kathleen E. Hull

Chapter 9
Occupational Mobility Among African-Americans: Assimilation or Resegregation 189
Sharon M. Collins

Section III
Changing Boundaries: Historical and Social Development of Anti-Discrimination Law

Chapter 10
Discrimination and Diplomacy: Recovering the Fuller National Stake in 1960s Civil Rights Reform 203
Mary L. Dudziak

Chapter 11
Sowing the Dragon's Teeth: Materialization in Lesbian and Gay Anti-discrimination Rights 219
Jonathan Goldberg-Hiller

Chapter 12
Rights or Quotas? The ADA as a Model for Disability Rights 237
Katharina Heyer

Section IV
Mobilizing Law: Rights Consciousness, Claiming Behaviour, and the Dynamics of Litigation

Chapter 13
The Evolution of Employment Discrimination Law in the 1990s: A Preliminary Empirical Investigation 261
John J. Donohue III and Peter Siegelman

Chapter 14
Perceiving and Claiming Discrimination 285
Brenda Major and Cheryl R. Kaiser

Chapter 15
Mobilizing Employment Rights in the Workplace 301
Catherine R. Albiston

Chapter 16
The Intersectionality of Lived Experience and Anti-Discrimination Empirical Research 325
Tanya Katerí Hernández

Chapter 17
Law at Work: The Endogenous Construction of Civil Rights 337
Lauren Edelman

Chapter 18
Discrimination Against Caregivers? Gendered Family Responsibilities, EmployerPractices, and Work Rewards 353
Erin L. Kelly

Section V
Social Psychology of Bias

Chapter 19
Aversive Racism: Bias Without Intention 377
Samuel L. Gaertner, John F. Dovidio, Jason Nier, Gordon Hodson and Melissa A. Houlette

Chapter 20
Applying Social Research on Stereotyping and Cognitive Bias to Employment Discrimination Litigation: The Case of Allegations of Systematic Gender Bias at Wat-Mart Stores 395
William T. Bielby

References 409
About the Authors 451
Index 453

Acknowledgements

This collection would not have been possible without the efforts of many individuals and the support of the American Bar Foundation.

The project began as a conference we organized, which was primarily funded by the American Bar Foundation with help from Stanford Law School. The success of the conference itself, and this volume, is due in large part to the efforts of the conference planning group, which consisted of Lawrence Bobo, John Donohue III, Linda Krieger, Lauren Edelman, Barbara Reskin, Peter Siegelman, and Claude Steele.

For their participation at the conference and their inspiration in the study of antidiscrimination law, we also thank the conference participants: Kathryn Abrams, Catherine (KT) Albiston, Ian Ayres, Mahzarin Banaji, William Bielby, James Boddy, William Bridges, Thomas Burke, Pedro Carneiro, Bliss Cartwright, Ruth Colker, Sharon Collins, Tucker Culbertson, Kay Deaux, Theresa Demchak, John Donohue III, Mary Dudziak, Lauren Edelman, Susan Fiske, Sam Gaertner, Jon Goldberg-Hiller, James Heckman, Tanya Hernandez, Katharina Heyer, Kathleen Hull, Cheryl Kaiser, Erin Kelly, Linda Krieger, Richard Lempert, Samuel Lucas, Glenn Loury, Brenda Major, Dmitriy Masterov, Michael McCann, Robert Nelson, Laura Beth Nielsen, David Oppenheimer, Barbara Reskin, Deborah Rhode, John Ricca, Patricia Schaeffer, Brad Seligman, Peter Siegelman, Claude Steele, and Susan Sturm.

We were assisted ably by Eric Bennett, Aaron Beim, Adriene Hill, Miriam Parrish, Anne Godden-Segard, and Lucinda Underwood with the conference and in the preparation of the manuscipt for publication.

This collection also represents the initial project of the Discrimination Research Group. The Discrimination Research Group is an effort to bring together scholars from a variety of disciplines to study employment discrimination and law and is supported by the American Bar Foundation, the Center for Advanced Study in the Behavioral Sciences, and The Ford Foundation.

Introduction

This volume contains a collection of original papers by leading legal scholars and social scientists that develop new perspectives on anti-discrimination law, with an emphasis on employment discrimination. The articles were written for a conference held at Stanford Law School in Spring 2003 that was sponsored by the American Bar Foundation and Stanford Law School. The purpose of that conference, this volume, and ongoing work by the Discrimination Research Group based at the American Bar Foundation and the Center for Advanced Study in the Behavioral Sciences is to advance the social scientific understanding of employment discrimination and the operation of employment discrimination law as a social system, and to consider the legal and policy implications of this emerging body of social science.

Now is a pivotal moment for an attempt at a deeper understanding of discrimination and law. After three decades of theoretical development and empirical research on employment discrimination and its treatment in law, it is crucial that lawyers, social scientists, and policymakers assess what we know and do not know about employment discrimination and its treatment by law. To date, there are several streams of active research that only occasionally engage with each other. Economists and sociologists continue to debate the extent to which women, minorities, and other traditionally disadvantaged groups face discrimination in labor markets and organizations. Organization scholars and legal scholars have begun to map the effect of anti-discrimination law on organizational structures and processes, and to raise questions about the extent to which the legalization of organizational employment systems represents symbolic or substantive changes in employment practices. Psychologists continue to develop and test theories about implicit bias and stereotyping by decision-makers in organizations, as well as the effects of differential treatment on groups which may be the target of such treatment. Students of social movements and social change analyze the rise of rights consciousness among traditionally disadvantaged groups, and the degree to which public opinion is sympathetic to remedial regimes such as anti-discrimination law and affirmative action.

At the center of these social scientific inquiries is employment discrimination law, which is itself a complex, changing, and incompletely understood social system. In the last decade, we have seen considerable expansion in the scope of formal statutory and judge-made rights—as discrimination based on age, disability, and sexual harassment have been added to longer standing protections against racial and gender discrimination. As a result, there has been a very significant growth in the number of complaints filed with the EEOC and in federal courts (filings tripled from 8,000 in 1989 to almost 24,000 in 1998). Yet, we also have seen significant judicial retrenchment on some theories of discrimination and on affirmative action, and low success rates for plaintiffs (estimated at less than 20% for federal cases with opinions). And there is evidence that many victims of discrimination take no action on their grievance, either informally, through workplace mechanisms, or through law. Thus, while employers perceive a growing threat from employment discrimination litigation, others suggest that employment discrimination law may have greater symbolic, than real effect.

Thus, there is still much to learn about fundamental aspects of employment discrimination law as a social system. The chapters in this volume grapple with many of these issues. What drives the growing demand for litigation? How does the mobilization of formal law compare to the use of organizational dispute resolution mechanisms? To what extent does discrimination continue in subtle but pervasive forms, and what explains variation in the amount and character of discrimination across organizational and market contexts? How do different groups of workers perceive the extent to which they are discriminated against and what if anything do they do about it? How have the courts responded to different types of employment discrimination claims, and what explains variation in the outcomes of litigated cases? How have employers responded to discrimination law? How does the mobilization of law vary across different sub-fields of discrimination law? How is employment discrimination law affected by broader political and legal currents, such as the erosion of affirmative action through public initiatives and judicial rulings or the new jurisprudence of federalism? In this changing political environment, will social movements, such as the campaign for gay and lesbian employment rights, continue to pursue legal avenues for social change? These specific questions relate to matters of broader theoretical importance. What is the relationship between anti-discrimination law and patterns of social inequality? What priority should anti-discrimination law have in efforts to ameliorate the unequal position of traditionally disadvantaged groups?

Questions of this scope require interdisciplinary scholarship. This collection includes original contributions from many of the legal scholars, economists, psychologists, sociologists, political scientists, and historians who are at the forefront of new research on discrimination and law. In this volume, as in the conference that brought these scholars together, we see discussion across different social science disciplines, as well as between legal scholars and social scientists. As a collection, these chapters suggest a broad reconsideration of employment discrimination and its treatment in law. Although the chapters offer a range of perspectives, they suggest that employment discrimination remains a pervasive problem that is not effectively redressed through law. Thus, despite the growth of anti-discrimination law as a field, there is a persistent gap between rights and realities in the workplace.

Overview of Sections

Introductory chapters. The volume is introduced by three papers that broadly analyze anti-discrimination law and its relationship to existing social science. In our own contribution, we write as lawyer-sociologists attempting to advance a socio-legal understanding of employment discrimination law. We examine the debate among competing conceptions of the anti-discrimination law which argue that the law has become too expansive, is too weak, or is too reliant on litigation. After reviewing doctrinal developments in the law and trends in claiming behavior before the EEOC and the federal courts through the 1990s to present, we apply the concept of the pyramid of disputes to discrimination claims to assess the ongoing debate. Although the analysis demonstrates that there are significant gaps in our knowledge of how employment discrimination claims arise and are dealt with, it also suggests that the current system is dramatically under-inclusive of potential claimants. We assert that the dramatic rise in court filings in the last decade can be explained by a modest growth in the percentage of potential plaintiffs who take formal legal action. We conclude that rather than ask why there are so many discrimination lawsuits, it may be more appropriate to ask why there are so few.

Susan Sturm, a leading legal scholar writing on discrimination, advances a new perspective on the role that anti-discrimination law can play in the workplace. She contends that in the new era of complex and subtle forms of discrimination, the law must move away from a litigation-oriented effort to punish violations to problem-solving approaches that give employers incentives to rid their organizations of discrimination. She cites examples of how these new approaches have been successful in some organizations and of court decisions that encourage employer innovations.

Susan Fiske, a noted social psychologist who gained prominence for her role in the amicus brief written on behalf of the American Psychological Association in the Supreme Court case, *Price Waterhouse v. Hopkins* (1989), reviews advances in psychological literature on prejudice that demonstrate two forms of bias that operate in human society: (1) unconscious, unexamined bias, that produces discrimination in the workplace because individuals feel more comfortable with members of their in-group and tend to exclude and avoid members of out-groups; and (2) the more extreme out-group bias that a small minority of individuals possess, which leads to blatant discrimination, even hate crimes. While these two forms of bias are embedded in deep social and psychological processes, Fiske asserts that they are not completely immune from treatment. She sketches how psychology can inform law's response to bias and discrimination.

The prevalence and character of discrimination. Much social scientific research addresses the basic question of whether discrimination, and of what kind and against what groups, remains prevalent in American society. The chapters in this section move this discussion in novel, important directions.

Barbara Reskin, a leading scholar of gender inequality, argues that social scientists too often have limited their analyses of inequality to questions of motive, rather than seeking to develop theories about the mechanisms that produce inequality throughout the social system. After critiquing prior research on ascriptive inequality that focuses on motives, she draws on research on labor markets and the sociology of the workplace to outline a new research program that attempts to explain how ascriptive inequality operates. She describes research that highlights mechanisms that operate at four levels: intrapsychic mechanisms; interpersonal mechanisms; societal mechanisms; and organizational mechanisms. And she suggests that these mechanisms can be studied in at least four useful approaches: studies of contexts with variable inequality (such as across communities); studies of variation in inequality across organizations; case studies of organizations; and studies based on discrimination lawsuits. Through these new efforts, Reskin asserts that sociologists can go beyond documenting that race and gender disparities exist and begin to explain how they come to exist.

James Heckman, a Nobel Laureate economist, has made very significant contributions to the literature on the positive effects of law on the economic progress of African-Americans. He demonstrated that Title VII had sudden, dramatic effects on the Black–White wage gap in the southern textile industry (Heckman and Payner, 1989). He and Donohue found similar evidence of "discontinuous" patterns of relative Black progress (1991), and thus argued against Richard Epstein (1992) and others who doubted the ability of anti-discrimination law to effect improvement in Black economic well being. In the paper in this volume, Carneiro, Heckman, and Masterov move to a different position in the debate. Through an ambitious examination of multiple datasets they assert that the roots of the disadvantaged labor market position of minorities in the labor market of the 21st century run to early childhood differentials between African-Americans, Hispanics and Whites. Racial disparities in various measures of achievement and ability are associated with differences in early childhood environments, such as the well being of parents. They draw the inference that discrimination in the labor market in the modern era cannot play an important role in producing Black–White wage gaps and urge that policy approaches seek to close the gap at an early age rather than strengthen anti-discrimination law.

Ian Ayres contributes to this debate by reviewing the literature on discrimination in the car buying market. In the early 1990s, Ayres and his colleagues aroused controversy through a set of audit studies that found significant discrimination against women and minorities in bargaining for new cars. Here, Ayres examines criticisms of those initial studies, as well as recently published research that raises questions about the original findings. He concludes that the weight of the research supports the view that women and minorities are not treated fairly in the car buying market.

William Bridges performs an analysis of racial differences in compensation for major league baseball players, a context which presents an unusual opportunity to examine productivity and wages. Bridges finds that Black athletes tend not to appear in certain highly paid positions (notably pitching), but that in the more recent "free agency" period, Blacks actually obtain a premium over Whites, controlling for output. He concludes that in some markets, race can generate premiums for historically disadvantaged groups.

Susan Collins reports a different fate for African-American managers in American corporations. She documents that African-Americans continue to lag behind White workers in major corporations. Indeed, in the mid-1970s, as new anti-discrimination laws went into effect, African-Americans began to enjoy new opportunities in business.

Yet many were channeled into affirmative action offices, which typically did not lead to significant promotions in other areas in the organization. Thus, corporate opportunities were simultaneously created and constrained.

Kathleen Hull breaks new ground by bringing together research on the prevalence and effect of workplace discrimination on gays and lesbians in the workplace, trends in public attitudes about homosexuals and legal protections for their employment rights, and the scope and effectiveness of collective action in the legal arena. Hull cites research that reveals that many gays and lesbians experience workplace discrimination and are forced to develop strategies for hiding their sexual orientation or coming out in safe ways. A majority of the American public holds hostile attitudes toward homosexuals, although there are surprisingly high levels of support for non-discrimination laws in employment. Anti-discrimination laws with respect to sexual orientation are now in effect in jurisdictions (all local and state) that encompass 48% of Americans. Several thousand employers, including the majority of Fortune 500 companies, embrace anti-discrimination policies covering sexual orientation or provide same-sex partner benefits. Hull concludes from her analysis that discrimination on the basis of sexual orientation is different from other forms of discrimination, in its effects in the workplace, in how it is viewed by the public, and in the contours of the political battles it has generated. She takes this as evidence of the need for discrimination research to pay attention to variations in how different kinds of discrimination operate and are treated in law.

Social psychology of bias. The two chapters in this section move from a synthesis of social psychological research on bias in general to an expert report of how unchecked gender stereotyping produced gender inequality in America's largest retailer, Walmart. Gaertner and Dovidio are notable in the psychology of bias for their work on aversive racism, a form of bias which is unintentional, but which can be documented through experimental manipulation. Here they team with Nier, Hodson, and Houlette to synthesize the research on how aversive racism operates between Blacks and Whites and discuss a psychological model that can be employed to combat it—the Common Ingroup Identity Model. Experiments document that White people, both conservatives and liberals, discriminate against African-Americans, although in different ways and not in all circumstances. (There is no discrimination when outcomes are clear, such as with strong job applicants of both race. Bias appears only when there is ambiguity about the credentials of candidates.) Their research suggests that tendencies toward biased decision-making can be modified, however, by creating a racially integrated decision-making group who are given a common goal. Thus, integrated interviewing or selection teams are likely to reduce racial bias in ratings of candidates.

William Bielby's chapter is a shortened version of the expert witness account he filed in the *Dukes v. Walmart* litigation, which, since the writing of Bielby's report has become the largest class certified in an employment discrimination lawsuit. As this book goes to press, the case is pending trial. Bielby's report is interesting for the substance of the expert opinion he offers and as an example of how social science is being deployed in the courts. Following the literature set out by many of the authors in this volume, Bielby argues that the disparities in the proportion of women employed in upper management at Walmart, compared to their percentage representation in positions from which management jobs are recruited, reflects the operation of gender bias in a selection system without adequate standards or safeguards against bias.

Mobilizing law: Rights consciousness, claiming behavior, and the dynamics of litigation. Having considered the underpinnings of discrimination, the chapters in this section consider whether, why, and how law becomes mobilized through litigation. Donohue and Siegelman, who did pathbreaking work on trends in employment discrimination litigation in the 1970s and 1980s, revisit the hypothesis of an earlier article with data on litigation trends in the 1990s. The earlier article (Donohue and Siegelman, 1991) asserted that litigation rates followed unemployment rates. As unemployment went down, discrimination lawsuits also decline because workers have more opportunities in the labor market and have smaller damages. This model no longer works in the 1990s, which saw both declines in unemployment and dramatic increases in litigation. Donohue and Siegelman argue that changes in the civil rights laws, and in particular the growth in the potential for non-compensatory damages, fed the surge in litigation behavior.

Major and Kaiser summarize major findings on the psychology of perceiving and claiming discrimination. The research they cite (much of it their own) reveals that individuals resist seeing themselves as the target of discrimination, even in the face of direct evidence, and even when they see other members of their group as victims of discrimination. Moreover, they report that individuals who do raise claims of discrimination are subjected to scorn by fellow workers and managers, even in cases in which the allegations are true. Their research may help explain why relatively few potential victims of discrimination seem to do anything about it.

Catherine Albiston's chapter examines the consequences of the Family and Medical Leave Act (FMLA) in the workplace. Albiston identifies several obstacles to invoking FMLA, including workplace ideologies of "the good worker," the family wage, and managerial control of work schedules. Yet, Albiston found that FMLA operated as a cultural resource, that gave workers a sense of power to invoke a different, legal set of norms. Albiston's research exemplifies new efforts to empirically study legal consciousness, and how employment laws may have important mobilizing effects in the workplace, even though they do not necessarily spur an increase in formal legal action.

Lauren Edelman's chapter develops a general framework for examining the interaction between law and organizations. Edelman argues that employment discrimination law is endogenous to organizations, meaning that employment discrimination law "takes shape within the social fields it seeks to regulate." Edelman traces how legal mandates create imperatives in organizations to achieve symbolic compliance with law, but that for many reasons symbolic compliance often fails to eliminate discrimination. The gap between symbolic change and real change may be exacerbated by two related phenomenon: organizations increasingly "managerialize" rights protection machinery in the workplace; and courts exhibit an increasing tendency to excuse employers from liability if they have adopted certain organizational forms, such as internal complaint mechanisms for sexual harassment.

Tanya Hernandez, a legal scholar known for her expertise in critical race theory, provides an empirical illustration of intersectionality theory in the context of employment discrimination complaints. She cites her own research and other published data that establishes that African-American women are more likely than their White female counterparts to file charges of sexual harassment at work. What is not clear, but which Hernandez begins to explore, is whether the difference is attributable to different levels in amount or severity of harassment against Black women. Hernandez calls for more research that addresses the lived experience of women who make harassment claims, both women of color and other groups.

Erin Kelly examines the distinct employment disadvantages that part-time earners face. Part-time workers, who overwhelmingly are women, are subject to lower earnings than full-time workers (on a per hour basis) and enjoy no legal protection based on their part-time status, as such. Indeed, Kelly is skeptical that the law is prepared to expand its protection to this large, growing group of workers. Kelly's research demonstrates the limits of employment discrimination law with respect to certain forms of inequality. "Part-time work" is not itself a protected category. As a result, the gender inequality that follows from the disproportionate presence of women in part-time work is not actionable under law.

Changing boundaries: Historical and social development of anti-discrimination law. The three chapters in this section push the boundaries of history, perspective, and nation state in the consideration of anti-discrimination laws. Mary Dudziak makes the historical connection between the needs of American foreign policy in the Cold War and the passage of the Civil Rights Act of 1964. She offers convincing evidence that foreign policy leaders were deeply concerned about the damage to the image of the United States from official resistance to civil rights demonstrations in the South. She further asserts that the growing perception that discrimination was a national problem shaped the jurisprudence of federalism through which the courts legitimated new forms of Congressional legislation concerning civil rights.

Jonathan Goldberg-Hiller examines the discourse around lesbian and gay rights, in particular the theme invoked by opponents that gays and lesbians are seeking "special rights." Drawing on the theory of materialization developed by Judith Butler, he suggests that opponents of extending anti-discrimination law to same sex marriage and partnership benefits have tried to paint the demands of gays and lesbians as examples of the excesses of contemporary anti-discrimination law. Because large segments of the American public continue to regard gays and lesbians with suspicion, arguments for equal treatment in courts and legislatures are recast as attacks on conventional morality and social institutions. In this way, "materializing" gays and lesbians as a threat to the social fabric works to limit the reach of anti-discrimination law.

Katharina Heyer analyzes the Americans with Disabilities Act as an international model of disability rights. She examines the impact of the American "rights-based" approach on disability law in Japan and Germany, two societies with strong social welfare orientations. She finds that despite the catalyzing effects of the American model of rights on disability rights movements in Japan and Germany, these societies retained their emphasis on quotas as the principal mechanism for protecting the employment needs of the disabled. The reasons are the cultural significance of work (for which quotas act as a "foot in the door"), constitutional mandates that require the state to offer positive rights to employment (as opposed to negative rights to be free from discrimination), and continuing tensions between an individualized rights model and, on the one hand, German society's commitment to labor and welfare traditions, and on the other, Japanese society's commitment to communitarian values. In all three societies, the disabled continue to face high unemployment rates. Heyer suggests that it is difficult to determine which system has the greatest potential to improve the working lives of the disabled, but that it will be interesting to see the competition between rights and welfare models play out in these three societies in the years ahead.

CONCLUSION

The chapters in this volume show the breadth and richness of research on employment discrimination and law. Here we see research from different disciplines and legal scholars about different forms of discrimination in different historical and social contexts. The amount of research in this area reflects the centrality of concerns for justice and equality in contemporary law and society and the widespread efforts that are being undertaken to pursue justice claims by lawyers, activists, and others. As promising as this work is, it only begins to develop the kind of systematic understanding of discrimination and law that is needed to form the basis for new theories of the relationship between law and inequality or to chart future directions in anti-discrimination policy. We hope this volume inspires more research of the kind exemplified here.

Laura Beth Nielsen and Robert L. Nelson, editors

SECTION I

Overview: Socio-Legal Approaches to Anti-Discrimination Law

CHAPTER 1

Scaling the Pyramid: A Sociolegal Model of Employment Discrimination Litigation

Laura Beth Nielsen and Robert L. Nelson

ABSTRACT

This chapter develops a sociolegal model of employment discrimination law in the United States. It addresses two competing characterizations of employment discrimination law: that it is an increasingly powerful and costly system of enforceable rights, on one hand, or a weak system that has largely symbolic effects, on the other. After articulating a legal constructionist framework for a systemic analysis of discrimination law, we summarize key developments in formal law, synthesize research on workplace discrimination, and analyze filings and dispositions data on discrimination litigation in federal courts from 1990–2001. When we apply Miller and Sarat's concept of the pyramid of disputes (1981) to these data we see the system of discrimination litigation differently. While the most visible aspects of the system sustain an expansive view of discrimination law, the vast gulf between the base of potential discrimination claims and the small proportion of cases that receive favorable legal treatment supports the opposite view. A sociolegal model thus raises important avenues for new empirical study and begins to redefine the current debate. Rather than ask why there are so many discrimination claims, perhaps we should ask why there are so few?

INTRODUCTION

Employment discrimination law is subject to two very different characterizations in the United States. On the one hand, employment discrimination laws can be characterized as an increasingly powerful system of enforceable rights. Federal, state, and municipal laws offer formally broad legal protections from workplace discrimination for minorities, women, the disabled, working parents, and the aged, among others. Individual complainants, government agencies, and plaintiffs' lawyers are increasingly active in seeking to enforce these protections in public agencies and the courts. Charges of discrimination made to the Equal Employment Opportunity Commission increased 14% between 1992 and 2002 (EEOC, 2003a). Employment discrimination lawsuits filed in federal court rose 161% between 1990 and 2001 (AO annual). As the number

L. B. Nielsen and R. L. Nelson (eds.), Handbook of Employment Discrimination Research, 3–35.

of claims has grown, the variety of types of discrimination alleged also has increased. Whereas charges of racial and gender discrimination in hiring and promotion predominated in the early years of the Civil Rights Act, the current set of claims includes large numbers of allegations of discriminatory firing, sexual harassment, age discrimination, and disability discrimination (Donohue and Siegelman, 1991; Donohue and Siegelman, 2002).

The expanding scale and diversity of employment discrimination claims has produced a backlash of criticism against employment discrimination laws by some members of the employment defense bar (see Bisom-Rapp, 1999) and conservative commentators (Howard, 1994; Howard, 2001; Olson, 1991; Olson, 1997). Often focusing on media reports of major awards, critics assert that anti-discrimination law has become a "windfall for plaintiffs" (Colker, 1999; Olson, 1997). The insurance industry attempts to capitalize on perceptions of a growing risk of employment discrimination litigation by offering insurance against such claims (Bielby and Bourgeois, 2002). In the marketing of the new products, insurance companies have repeated the most dramatic stories of employer liability in discrimination suits (Bielby and Bourgeois, 2002; Nielsen and Beim, 2004). An increasingly critical tone about these trends also appears in academic discussions. In a recent paper, Donohue and Siegelman (2003) assert that the Civil Rights Act of 1991, which gave plaintiffs additional remedies and more frequent access to jury trials, combined with an increasingly entrepreneurial plaintiffs' bar, has generated more lawsuits and larger awards, even though the underlying phenomena of workplace discrimination may actually be declining (Bisom-Rapp, 1999, pp. 960–961, n. 4; Donohue and Siegelman, 2002, p. 15, n. 27).

Anti-discrimination law is characterized by many social scientists, legal scholars, and potential plaintiffs as largely ineffective in redressing employment discrimination. Or worse, some see anti-discrimination law as providing legitimation for workplace inequality (Nelson and Bridges, 1999). Social scientists point to the relative lack of progress in recent decades (that is, after major gains in the early years following the passage of the Civil Rights Act of 1964) for women and minorities in closing the earnings gap and for overcoming patterns of occupational segregation by sex and race (Jacobs, 2001; Reskin, 1998). Research on the prevalence of discrimination in the workplace shows a striking disjuncture between the perceptions of white women and people of color in the workplace, and their white male colleagues and supervisors (Dixon, Storen, and Horn, 2002).

Moreover, other research finds that significant barriers confront plaintiffs. Potential plaintiffs are reluctant to complain (Bumiller, 1988). Those who do complain seldom succeed within their own organization (Edelman, 1992; Edelman, Erlanger, and Lande, 1993; Edelman and Suchman, 1997), before the EEOC (2003a), or in the courts (Clermont and Eisenberg, 2000; Colker, 1999; Eisenberg, 1989; Litras, 2000; Litras, 2002; Morgan, 1999).

In this chapter, we seek to explain these conflicting images by reconceptualizing employment discrimination law in sociolegal terms. Our objective is to develop a model that raises theoretical questions about the operation of employment discrimination law as a social system, and to assess what we know and do not know about those questions. The empirical focus of the chapter is the claiming process within employment discrimination law: who has potential legal grievances, do they do anything about it, and with what likely result?

Much of the debate about anti-discrimination law takes place over what is characterized as a dramatic rise in employment discrimination complaints, lawsuits, and awards. This chapter sheds new light on this debate by bringing together a review of doctrinal and statutory developments in employment discrimination law, a summary of literature on discrimination in the workplace, and an analysis of the most comprehensive data available about employment discrimination litigation in the federal courts from 1990 to 2001. We utilize Miller and Sarat's (1981; see also Galanter 1983) pyramid of disputes to inform our analysis and empirical inquiry into these apparently contradictory characterizations of employment civil rights.

This sociolegal approach helps us begin to make sense of the divergent accounts of employment discrimination law. In many ways, the symbolic and actual reach of employment discrimination law has grown in the last decade. Statutory rights and remedies have expanded. There has been a significant rise in the amount of litigation and the emergence of larger awards in a small, unusual set of cases. But, we also find that the expansion of rights and remedies has been undercut in more subtle ways by countervailing judicial development. Moreover, the empirical data suggest that anti-discrimination law does not offer an effective remedy for many people who perceive themselves to be the target of workplace discrimination. Perhaps most importantly, our empirical analysis suggests that the dramatic rise of employment discrimination claiming that occurred in the 1990s can be attributed to a relatively small increase in the rate of claiming by aggrieved individuals. Given some important gaps that remain in the socio-legal understanding of employment discrimination litigation, we suggest directions for future research.

We proceed in five parts. First, we put this analysis in the context of current debates about the relationship between inequality, discrimination, and rights. Second, we sketch a legal constructionist framework for analyzing anti-discrimination law, a framework that takes legal developments seriously, but locates legal development within particular fields of social action. Third, we review major developments over the last two decades in federal law on employment discrimination. These developments create the appearance of significant expansion in anti-discrimination law, but also entail less visible shifts that may limit plaintiffs' ability to litigate successfully. These trends in formal law lead to conflicting expectations about trends in discrimination litigation. Fourth, we examine the claiming system of anti-discrimination law—reviewing social scientific data on the incidence of perceived discrimination, the likelihood that targets of discrimination will seek redress, and the likely outcome of these efforts. In the final section of the chapter, we perform a rough analytic exercise which compares estimates of the incidence of discrimination against one particular group (full time African-American workers), the likelihood that they will file a complaint with the EEOC or in court, and the likely size of their recovery.

1. INEQUALITY, DISCRIMINATION, AND THE RISE IN CLAIMING

A sociolegal analysis of employment discrimination litigation must begin with a discussion of the relationship between employment discrimination and inequality, because current debates about anti-discrimination law are very much anchored in questions about this relationship. It is widely recognized that racial minorities, women, and other groups protected by anti-discrimination laws are significantly disadvantaged in outcomes relating to education, employment, health, wealth accumulation, criminal justice, and housing (Conley, 1999; Oliver and Shapiro, 1997; Sampson and Lauritsen, 1997; Smedley, Stith, and Nelson, 2002; Squires and O'Connor, 2001). For example, in 2000, the median full-time earnings of African-American males were 77% of white male workers. Women full-time workers made 74% as much as full-time male workers[1] and 71% of white male workers.[2] Yet there is active debate about the source of differential outcomes and in particular the role that discrimination plays in producing inequality.

One camp in this debate is skeptical about the significance of discrimination as a source of labor market outcomes. The skeptics point to the historical decline in measures such as the wage gap, cite public opinion data that show a decline in racist and sexist attitudes (see, e.g., Donohue and Siegelman, 1991, p. 1001 n. 69–70, citing), assert that blatant barriers for the hiring and promotion of women and minorities no longer exist, and argue that non-discriminatory factors, such as differences in amount and quality of schooling (and other human capital variables) and different worker preferences (Heckman, 1998; Mincer and Ofek, 1982; Nelson and Bridges, 1999), explain differential outcomes. They argue that policy tools other than anti-discrimination efforts will be more useful in closing differential outcomes. Moreover, if one assumes that there is now less labor market discrimination than in the past, at the same time there is significantly more litigation, it suggests that the rise in litigation might be due to frivolous claims.

Indeed, the skeptical view can be seen in judicial opinions that shape current discrimination litigation. In a district court opinion denying class certification to African-American employees at Lockheed Martin Aeronautics, the court observed:

> In the initial days after the enactment of Title VII, class action law in the employment discrimination context developed in a culture where many employers completely excluded members of minority groups from positions and job benefits at all but the lowest levels of the company ... In contrast to the early days of Title VII, it is now more uncommon to find an employer that overtly encourages wholesale discrimination on the basis of race; race discrimination today usually comes in more subtle forms (*Reid v Lockheed Martin Aeronautics* at 660, 2001).

[1] Calculated from the 2000 census data, available at www.census.gov/hhes/income00. White men's median income in this category is $40,350 and African-American men's is $30,893.

[2] Calculated from the 2000 census data, available at www.census.gov/hhes/income00. Women's income in this category (without regard to race) is $28,823 and African-American women's income is $25,745.

As a result of this changed "culture," the court said the law now demanded more proof of company-wide discrimination before it would allow plaintiffs to proceed as a class. After reviewing statistics concerning racial disparities from different departments, jobs, and locations of the defendant employer, the court left the plaintiffs to pursue claims as individuals (*Reid v Lockheed Martin Aeronautics*, 2001).

The other side in this debate sees discrimination as pervasive in labor markets, employing organizations, and other contexts that shape differential outcomes. The "discrimination-as-pervasive" camp interprets the historical trends as slowing in the contemporary period and therefore no guarantee that differential outcomes will continue to decline (Grodsky and Pager, 2001; Jacobs, 2001; Nelson and Bridges, 1999). It suggests that much of the movement in public opinion measures of racism and sexism are superficial, and do not fully reflect deeper, more complex attitudes that tend to support the hierarchical position of traditionally dominant groups (Bobo, 2000; Sidanius, Singh, Hetts, and Federico, 2000). It asserts that blatant forms of discrimination have been replaced by subtle forms of bias and stereotyping that have negative effects on outcomes for traditionally disadvantaged groups,[3] and cites studies that find racial and gender-based differentials remain unexplained even after introducing extensive controls for non-discriminatory factors (Reskin, 2001).

Our approach to the debate about the centrality of discrimination to inequality is not so much to choose sides as to recognize the complexity of the issue, suggest that no one can definitively state the extent to which discrimination is implicated in unequal outcomes, and move beyond the debate to explore alternative empirical and theoretical approaches to understand anti-discrimination law as a social system. We acknowledge that discrimination as defined by law is only one source of differential outcomes among groups. Many aspects of inequality by race, gender, and other protected characteristics are structural in nature, rooted in historical disadvantage and hierarchical relationships among groups. Because many forces contribute to differential outcomes, it is difficult in the aggregate to neatly decompose inequality into that which is attributable to ongoing discrimination and other sources. If we could flip a switch tomorrow and end all employment discrimination, then it would not immediately eliminate labor market inequality.

Nonetheless, it also is not clear that the elimination of all forms of employment discrimination would have only a trivial effect. While the skeptics assert much of the wage gap between races and genders can be explained by non-discriminatory factors, there is no simple formula to determine what we would expect to find in terms of relative pay for different groups in the absence of workplace discrimination. For example, in their review of the literature on the gender gap in wages, Nelson

[3] Several kinds of evidence are cited, including audits of employers (Neckerman and Kirschenman, 1991; Neumark, 1996), self-reports of being the target of discrimination (Dixon, Storen, and Van Horn, 2002), and considerable psychological research on implicit bias of various kinds (Banaji, Hardin, and Rothman, 1993; Banaji and Hardin, 1996; Deaux, 1995; Deaux and Kile, 1991; Dovidio, Brigham, Johnson, and Gaertner, 1996; Dovidio and Gaertner, 1996; Fiske, 1998; Fiske, Bersoff, Borgida, Deaux, and Heilman, 1991; Fiske, Cuddy, Glick and Xu, 2002; Pettigrew and Martin, 1987).

and Bridges concluded that efforts to decompose the wage gap based on aggregate data into such basic categories as within-job vs. between-job wage differences proved highly speculative (1999, pp. 59–65). As a result, they questioned the conclusion of some analysts that pay discrimination litigation could do little to close the wage gap. "Rather than characterizing the gains from eliminating unjustified between-job wage gains as being small or nearly insignificant, we think that the evidence could just as easily be used to describe the effects as positive but indeterminate in size" (Nelson and Bridges, 1999, p. 65).

Necessary as the debate about discrimination and inequality is, much can be gained by moving beyond it. Philosophical, political, and policy debates about discrimination law are largely uninformed about how anti-discrimination law operates as a social system. We do not understand such basic issues as the incentives that motivate lawyers and parties to use or avoid the law in various ways or the ways courts and employers resolve claims of discrimination (see, for example, notable research in other fields of law by Kritzer (1990) and Macaulay (1979)). Without empirical research on these issues, we cannot judge whether the gains produced by the system are "symbolic" or "real." In this chapter, we attempt to advance this systemic understanding by looking at the relationship between developments in formal law, research on the prevalence of employment discrimination, and the claiming system.[4]

2. THE LEGAL CONSTRUCTION OF DISCRIMINATION

We suggest that it is valuable to conceive of employment discrimination law in a "legal constructionist" framework. The core principles of this framework will be familiar to sociologists and law and society scholars. But they bear restating as applied to the specific context of employment discrimination law.

A *legal* constructionist approach is important for three reasons. First, discrimination is intimately connected to justice norms and expectations. Whether people perceive that they have a discrimination claim (or, for employers and managers, whether they are subject to a discrimination claim) depends both on how they define "fair treatment" and "responsibility in law" (Friedman, 1987; Lind and Tyler, 1988; Sanders and Hamilton, 2001). Second, the legal actors who interpret and apply anti-discrimination law do so through the distinctive logic and procedure of the law. Thus, decisions about whether illegal discrimination took place will be influenced by the specialized jurisprudence of anti-discrimination law (e.g., the language of statutes and prior decisions that define

[4] In a normative sense, we assert that the right to be protected from discrimination is important and valuable in itself, even if the broader economic impact of anti-discrimination law is unclear. Fair treatment in the workplace, without regard to group membership, is fundamental to a system of workplace justice (Selznick, 1969). For the society as a whole, but especially for the members of traditionally disadvantaged groups, rights at work reaffirm principles of justice and personhood. The sheer number of individuals who currently avail themselves of making claims under anti-discrimination law suggests that it is a vital institution.

burdens of proof, etc.) and general evidentiary and procedural rules. Laypersons do not necessarily understand whether they have valid legal claims of discrimination (Marshall, 2003); but employing organizations often have well scripted routines for dealing with potential discrimination claims based on the perceived legal risk (Bisom-Rapp, 1999; Nielsen, 1999). Third, legal institutions and actors (the courts, regulatory agencies, employment law specialists) have distinctive features (such as those detailed by Galanter (1974), Kagan (2001), and Burke (2002)) that will shape discrimination law, just as they shape other kinds of law. American anti-discrimination law is, in Burke's terms, a litigious policy, in the sense that it primarily relies for enforcement on statutory rights recognized through litigation (or the threat of litigation), rather than through a strong regulatory regime. Thus, while large organizations and government contractors have some affirmative obligations to report data bearing on compliance with equal opportunity rules, litigation by private parties is the predominant source of compensation for discrimination and the most significant force motivating compliance. As such, the social organization of discrimination litigation, including the ideologies, practices, and incentives of plaintiff and defense lawyers, are very important to how the system actually operates.

A legal *constructionist* approach is crucial for four reasons. First, the definition of discrimination is a social and cultural production. For example, forms of sexual harassment that are now clear violations of the law were not seen as legally problematic before MacKinnon's path breaking work that led to a new consensus in law. Second, as such, the "law" against discrimination is an indeterminate system, which is subject to re-interpretation and maneuver. Third, because the meaning of discrimination in the law is a historical and institutional production, its meaning is path dependent. The definition of discrimination or the jurisdiction of anti-discrimination law may change, but not in ways that ignore the doctrinal or legislative events leading to the decision in question. Fourth, by identifying anti-discrimination law as a construction, it becomes important to identify who work as the "agents of construction"—that is, which groups (employment lawyers, human resource managers, civil rights advocates, etc.) attempt to define the law in specific ways in specific contexts.

The legal construction of discrimination occurs in distinct, but overlapping and interpenetrated fields (Bourdieu, 1977). The field concept calls for treatment of particular arenas and institutions as social systems that involve competition among professional, business, and political actors, who deploy different ideologies and practices of law. The field concept also allows for external analyses of the individual fields as entities that may be moving in certain ways (for example, pro-plaintiff or pro-defendant). We can think of anti-discrimination law as being produced in at least six distinct fields that are worthy of analysis in their own right. The fields include: (1) the judicial field, which consists of the federal and state courts that interpret anti-discrimination law; (2) the legislative field, which includes the United States Congress; (3) the regulatory field, including the Civil Rights Commission, the EEOC, and the Office of Federal Contract Compliance Programs (OFCCP); (4) employing organizations; (5) the academic field; and (6) politics and public attitudes.

The study of each of the individual fields is important for our understanding of employment discrimination, but without an understanding of the places where these fields come together, affect one another, and shape what is happening in one another, we cannot gain a full picture of the shape of anti-discrimination law as a social system.

There are several exemplars of scholarship that theorize about employment discrimination law as a social system and are built on the inter-field study of anti-discrimination law. Most notably, perhaps is that of Edelman (1992), who studied the processes by which equal employment opportunity structures are diffused through organizations. In a recent work, Edelman has examined the relationship between organizational EEO practices and judicial rulings, a relationship she terms as the endogeneity of law (2002). This line of research, documents how the courts (judicial field) sometimes excuse employers (organizational field) from liability based on the presence of an affirmative action program or an articulated policy on sexual harassment, etc. When courts take such organizational practices into consideration in determining liability, they further encourage organizations to adopt such practices. As Edelman rightly points out, these trends raise serious questions about what the "legalization" of the workplace means for employee rights. Is legalization primarily a symbolic shift in managerial practices or does it represent enhanced rights for workers? (See also Bisom-Rapp, 1999).

Barnes' recent work on legislative overrides of judicial decisions that discusses the origins and impact of the Civil Rights Act of 1991 (forthcoming) is another example of inter-field research. Barnes shows that the impetus for this legislation was a series of federal court decisions that were seen as seriously cutting back on employment discrimination law, including most prominently the Supreme Court's decision in *Wards Cove v. Atonio*, which limited disparate impact theories of discrimination. The first Bush administration was under considerable pressure from civil rights groups in the wake of the Clarence Thomas-Anita Hill hearings and the victory of Ku Klux Klan leader David Duke in the Louisiana Republican primary. After first vetoing one version of the legislation, Bush signed a bill that contained several compromises between business and civil rights groups. Indeed, Barnes uses the Civil Rights Act of 1991 as an exemplar of "hyperpluralism" in which Congress purposefully passed a bill containing terms that were sure to generate litigation over their meaning.

Another example is Sturm's argument about "second-generation" discrimination in which she sets forth a framework linking (1) employing organizations; (2) the evolving jurisprudence of courts; and (3) regulatory processes (2001). Sturm largely adopts the view of recent psychological and sociological research that discrimination continues within employing organizations, but in a more subtle fashion than in the past. She suggests that to deal with this more subtle form of discrimination, it is necessary to move away from "command and control" regulation or punitive litigation, in the direction of organizational problem-solving. She finds in some recent sexual harassment law cases, an indication that the courts are also moving in this direction: they judge the liability of employers based on what steps employers have taken to deal with such problems. Citing examples of organizations which have attempted to solve problems of discrimination through voluntary efforts, Sturm sees promise in a new regime of anti-discrimination law that urges this kind of organizational problem solving. We do not necessarily agree with Sturm's meta-narrative about what is going on in these fields—either in employing organizations or in the tendency of courts to excuse employers from liability. Yet what is important to recognize is that it is possible to join issue in empirical debates about these fields and their relationships and then refine the theory about the system as a whole.

In what follows, we consider the relationship between events in the legislative and judicial fields and the claiming process in employment discrimination law. The claiming process spans several fields, as individuals come to see themselves as experiencing discrimination in the workplace, and then make decisions about how to proceed within the employing organization or to seek redress through the EEOC and the courts.

3. EXPANSION AND RETRENCHMENT IN EMPLOYMENT DISCRIMINATION LAW: LEGISLATIVE AND JUDICIAL DECISIONS

In the 40 years that followed the passage of the Civil Rights Act of 1964, employment discrimination law has been a dynamic and conflictual field, in both legislative and judicial arenas. The outcomes of legislative and judicial contests have a direct bearing on the claiming process, as these shape what constitutes an actionable claim, whether actionable claims are worth pursuing for lawyers and their clients, and what burden of proof must be met to prevail. In this section, we provide a brief synopsis of recent legislative and judicial changes that affect the substance of employment discrimination law.

Our review suggests that there has been a recurring pattern of expansion and retrenchment in legislative and judicial mandates on employment discrimination. A series of Supreme Court decisions in the 1970s and 1980s, as well as new legislation in the 1990s, significantly expanded rights and protection for employees. But as the federal judiciary became more politically conservative from the 1980s onward, there has been significant retrenchment in what constitutes an actionable employment discrimination claim. The expansion of rights through legislation and landmark judicial innovations is perhaps the more visible kind of change in the system while the elements of retrenchment by the courts are more technical and less visible in character.

3.1. Expansion: Major Statutory and Judicial Developments Encouraging Employment Discrimination Litigation

In the late 1980s and 1990s, Congress appeared to be the champion of the underrepresented. When the Supreme Court issued a number of pro-employer/defendant decisions that restricted protections for employee/plaintiffs (*Wards Cove v. Atonio*, 1989; *Price-Waterhouse v. Hopkins*, 1989; *Martin v. Wilkes*, 1989), Congress responded with the Civil Rights Act of 1991, which overrode the increasingly conservative jurisprudence on a variety of issues. President Bush signed the Americans with Disabilities Act

(ADA) into law in 1990 and the first bill that President Clinton signed into law was the Family and Medical Leave Act (FMLA) in 1993. Each of these legislative actions represented a significant expansion of employee rights in the workplace.

The Civil Rights Act of 1991 in some respects was the most sweeping legislative change in the period (Barnes, forthcoming; Note, 1996). For plaintiff/employees alleging discrimination on grounds other than race prior to the Civil Rights Act of 1991, Title VII provided only equitable remedies and primarily was limited to back pay (Cox, 1987). Plaintiffs alleging racial discrimination could obtain additional remedies only if they were eligible to and were successful in a jointly filed §1981 claim. The Civil Rights Act of 1991 allowed those not previously eligible under §1981 to also make claims for compensatory damages (for psychological distress), although the amount of the potential award is capped according to the size of the organization/defendant. Statutory provision for compensatory damages not only allowed plaintiffs greater potential awards, but also triggered the 7th Amendment right to a jury trial in a civil action, meaning that plaintiff/employees can now insist that their cases be heard by a jury (Estreicher and Harper, 2000).

The 1990s also saw passage of the Americans with Disabilities Act (ADA), which protects employees from discrimination based on disability (with damages similar to those provided under the Civil Rights Act of 1991) and requires employers of people with disabilities to make "reasonable accommodations" for their employees with disabilities. (Burke, 2002). The Family and Medical Leave Act of 1993 (FMLA) provides employees with up to 12 weeks of unpaid leave due to their own illness, a close family member's medical need, and/or birth or adoption of a child. FMLA prohibits mistreatment, including firing or demotion, of an employee who uses family leave.

The most significant judicially constructed theory of discrimination in the period was the emergence of sexual harassment as a cause of action in Title VII jurisprudence. In *Meritor Savings Bank v. Vinson* (1986), the Supreme Court acknowledged that quid pro quo sexual harassment constitutes discrimination "on the basis of sex" and therefore is prohibited by Title VII. Since *Meritor*, sexual harassment claims have become an important category of sex discrimination cases (EEOC, 2003a; EEOC, 2003b).

3.2. Retrenchment: The Jurisprudence of Anti-discrimination Law

During the same period in which we see the expansion of statutory rights against discrimination, the Supreme Court and other appellate court decisions began to limit the scope of anti-discrimination law in a variety of ways. Compared to the newsworthiness of legislation, judicial changes are less publicly visible, but no less important in the determination of whether an employment discrimination claim is viable or not. In what follows, we trace how the courts have limited the scope of anti-discrimination law by making it more difficult to prove discrimination, by interpreting the 11th Amendment as a limit on Congressional power to pass anti-discrimination statutes, by ratcheting up the requirements for what an organization or state must prove before it may lawfully engage in affirmative action, by providing increasingly minimalist burdens on employer/defendants facing sexual harassment claims, and by limiting the scope of disparate impact theories of discrimination.

3.2.1. Making Employment Discrimination More Difficult to Prove in Court

As the courts have moved in the direction of requiring direct proof of discriminatory intent, of limiting the scope of disparate impact theories of discrimination, and of finding voluntary efforts at affirmative action to be illegal and unconstitutional, the jurisprudence of employment discrimination law is characterized by what Freeman referred to as the "perpetrator model" of discrimination (Freeman, 1982; Freeman, 1998). In the perpetrator model, anti-discrimination law has the more limited purpose of remedying specific intentional wrongs, rather than redressing systemic aspects of discrimination and inequality that are not so clearly linked to intentional decisions.

In *Griggs v. Duke Power Co.* (1971) the Supreme Court, with Chief Justice Burger writing for the majority, allowed plaintiffs to prevail in a showing of discrimination without proof of discriminatory intent. The high court recognized that "practices that are fair in form, but discriminatory in operation," should be illegal. *Griggs* represented the Court's willingness to accept disparate impact theories of discrimination. *Wards Cove Packing v. Atonio* (1989) significantly eroded the *Griggs* standard and represents the perpetrator model in the extreme. In *Wards Cove*, the Court emphasized that employers should not be held liable for their actions unless the employee/plaintiffs could demonstrate individual animus on the part of the employer. *Wards Cove* was partially overturned by the Civil Rights Act of 1991 discussed above.

Similarly, difficult cases in the early period of the ADA have led to jurisprudence which rejects protection for people with a number of disabilities (Bellinger, 2000; Krieger, 2000). As a result, courts have accepted narrow definitions of the crucial statutory term "reasonable accommodation."

3.2.2. 11th Amendment Bars to Congressional Authority to Pass Anti-discrimination Legislation

Perhaps the most significant doctrinal development in recent years is the U.S. Supreme Court's decisions limiting Congressional authority to pass laws designed to remedy discrimination. This resurgence of federalism began with decisions that did not affect employment discrimination at all, as the Supreme Court began eroding Congressional authority by narrowing down the scope of constitutionally regulable activities under the commerce clause.[5]

[5] For a more comprehensive discussion of this trend, see Post and Siegel (2000) or *United States v. Lopez* (1995) (striking down the Federal Gun Free School Zone Act because it exceeded Congressional authority to regulate interstate commerce) and *United States v. Morrison* (2000) (striking down the Violence Against Women's Act because Congress did not have the authority to create a federal civil remedy for victims of gender based violence under either the Commerce Clause or Section 5 of the 14th Amendment).

Despite nearly 100 years of Supreme Court deference to Congressional power via the Commerce Clause, this new theory of federalism was brought to bear on employment discrimination in *Kimel v. Florida Board of Regents*, in which the Supreme Court struck down Congress' extension of ADEA protections to state employees as not permissible under section 5 of the 14th Amendment. Finally, in *Alabama v. Garrett*, the Supreme Court invoked its increasingly expansive vision of the 11th Amendment to strike down the application of the Americans with Disabilities Act to the states.

3.2.3. Affirmative Action More Difficult to Legally Justify

Affirmative action in employment became nearly impossible to practice in the period. For a government employer (or government contractor) to practice affirmative action, they must meet the constitutional standard for making a race-based distinction including a formal finding of past discrimination by the body (*Wygant v Jackson*, 1986). Any racial distinction, whether or not designed to favor a traditionally underrepresented group, has been judicially determined to amount to a racial classification, triggering strict scrutiny, and may not be used to remedy general or societal discrimination or inequality (*City of Richmond v. Croson*, 1989).

The Title VII standard for race or gender classifications (for private employers) is only slightly less burdensome. It requires that the employer makes a showing of past discrimination, proposes a plan to remedy a "manifest imbalance" along race or gender lines in a "traditionally segregated job category," and does not employ quotas or otherwise unnecessarily "trammels the rights" of the majority group.[6]

3.2.4. Minimalist Burdens on Employer/Defendants Facing Sexual Harassment Claims

Sexual harassment under Title VII, which increasingly had become a source of discrimination claims since 1986, has become easier to defend against as a result of recent decisions. In *Faragher v. City of Boca Raton* (1998), the Supreme Court announced that while employers can be held vicariously liable for the actions of employees who create a hostile work environment, the employer may offer an affirmative defense that they, the employer, had a reasonable policy on sexual harassment, and that the target of the harassment failed to act reasonably to end the harassment. And, lower courts have begun to interpret nearly any policy as a "reasonable" one (Marks, 2002).

3.2.5. Limiting the Scope of Disparate Impact Theories of Discrimination

The Civil Rights Act of 1991 restored disparate impact to its pre-*Wards Cove* status, but recent Supreme Court and appellate court opinions limit the scope of disparate impact theories, albeit not in Title VII cases. In *Adams v. Florida Power Corp.* (2002), the 11th circuit joined other circuits in denying disparate impact theories for ADEA

[6] See *Steelworkers v. Weber* (1979) and *Johnson v. Santa Clara County* (1987).

claims. And, in *Alexander v. Sandoval* (2001), the Supreme Court held that Title VI of the Civil Rights Act does not allow a private right of action to enforce disparate impact regulations under Title VI.

Age discrimination in employment is prohibited by the Age Discrimination in Employment Act (ADEA). Although the ADEA does not specifically allow for disparate impact theories, federal courts disagree as to whether an ADEA claim can be brought using a disparate impact theory. In the 1990s, the Supreme Court decided *Hazen Paper v. Biggins*, which did not specifically address the disparate impact theory. Nevertheless, a number of Appellate Courts took the language in *Hazen* to mean that disparate impact would not be permissible under the ADEA. There is a circuit court split on the issue, with the 1st, 2nd, 6th, 7th, 10th, and 11th circuits denying claims of disparate impact under the ADEA (*Adams v. Florida Power Corp.*, 2001, *Ellis v. United Airlines Inc.*, 1996).

4. THE CLAIMING SYSTEMS OF EMPLOYMENT DISCRIMINATION LAW

These statutory and judicial developments lead to conflicting expectations about trends in complaints and lawsuits. On the one hand, the addition of new rights for the aged, the disabled, and for women who are sexually harassed, as well as expanded remedies and rights to jury trial under the Civil Rights Act of 1991, would lead one to expect a rise in claiming behavior. But judicial retrenchment on the allowable scope of anti-discrimination law, as well as an increasingly skeptical judicial stance towards plaintiffs' claims, might offset this rise. Moreover, changes in law are not the only factors that might affect claiming behavior. Donohue and Siegelman argued that discrimination claims throughout the 1970s and 1980s responded to the economic cycle. When the economy was strong, few lawsuits were filed; when the economy was bad, more employees sued (Donohue and Siegelman, 1993). After a recession in the early 1990s, the economy experienced steady growth until 2000. If the economic account holds, then we would expect less claiming behavior, ceteris paribus.

But what do we observe about trends in claiming? While we already have alluded to general statistics about the rise in employment discrimination lawsuits, and how this rise has been interpreted as evidence of anti-discrimination law exceeding its legitimate function, statistics on lawsuits and media reports of big cases may be misleading indicators on the claiming process as a whole (Nielsen and Beim, 2004). It is necessary to investigate trends in claiming behavior from the bottom–up (so to speak), starting with what we know about the number of potential grievances in the workplace and moving to a critical examination of the best empirical data available on litigation filings and outcomes.

We do so by applying Miller and Sarat's "Pyramid of Disputes" to the claiming systems of employment discrimination law. After summarizing their concept, we review the existing literature on the stages of the system, summarize data from the EEOC on trends in discrimination complaints from 1992 to 2001, and present an analysis of data obtained from the Administrative Office of the Federal Courts on filings and dispositions of employment discrimination lawsuits in federal district courts from 1990 to 2001. The literature and data allow us to portray the broad contours of change in discrimination claims, but also reveal critical gaps in our knowledge about the claiming system. As we suggest in the title, we will attempt to scale the pyramid of employment discrimination claims from the bottom up.

4.1. The Pyramid of Disputes

In a classic article, Miller and Sarat (1981) develop the concept of the dispute pyramid to provide an overview of the processes that lead from perceived injuries to formal claiming behavior. The concept can be readily applied to claims arising from anti-discrimination law.

At the base of the dispute pyramid are *perceived injurious experiences*—the broad mass of injuries that people recognize. Some proportion of these experiences become *grievances*: injuries that involve a violation of right or entitlement. Grievances can be thought of as 100% of potential claims, for without a violation of right or entitlement individuals will not seek redress. Only some grievances become *claims*: when an individual contacts the party responsible for the grievance. Fewer still are *disputes*: when the party allegedly responsible for an individual's claim initially denies their responsibility. Some number of disputes result in *filings*: a formal complaint (in a litigation model, a court filing) and the smallest category of all is made up of *trials*: cases that are adjudicated.

Drawing on data from their study of middle range claims by individuals (over $1,000 by individuals in the late 1970s), Miller and Sarat demonstrate that cases drop out of the dispute pyramid at a rapid rate. Only 70% of people with grievances press them to a claim, only 46% pursue a grievance to the level of dispute, only 5% of grievances lead to filing a lawsuit, and only 0.06% of grievances end up in trial.[7] Galanter (1983) summarizes other literature about the variables that affect this pyramid of probabilities: the wealthier and better educated are more likely to make claims and pursue them to court, as are those individuals who have terminated their relationship with the party with whom they have a grievance.

A comprehensive understanding of trends in employment discrimination litigation requires comprehensive data on all the stages of the dispute pyramid. That is, what is the likelihood that individuals will have grievances stemming from perceived employment discrimination, complain about discrimination, engage in disputes with employers, file formal complaints outside the organization (with the EEOC, an equivalent state agency, or a federal or state court), and adjudicate their claim?

[7] It is important to note that these data are drawn from all civil cases and are not specific to anti-discrimination claims.

4.2. Personal Experiences of Discrimination in the Workplace

Galanter observed that the base of the dispute pyramid—whether one perceives oneself as injured and thus as someone who might have a legal claim—is the most difficult to analyze and the least understood aspect of disputing systems. In some respects, these problems are especially vexing in efforts to define the baseline of personal experiences with discrimination. As Smith notes in his critical review of the literature prepared for the National Academy of Sciences panel on measuring racial discrimination (Smith, 2002), a target of discrimination may not even know they have been discriminated against for a variety of reasons.

Individuals may be uncertain as to what qualifies as employment discrimination (e.g., epithets, jokes, verbal assaults, etc.?) (Marshall, 2003). They may have different propensities to report that they feel discriminated against, with some "over-reporting" discrimination because they attribute their frustrations to racial disadvantage (Harrell, 2000; Lucas, 1994), while others "under-report" perceived discrimination due to a sense of shame or their rejection of victimhood (Bobo and Suh, 2000; Feagin, 1991; Suh, 2000), because friends, family, and coworkers discourage them from thinking they were victims of discrimination (Suh, 2000), or due to the interpersonal costs associated with making a discrimination claim (Kaiser and Miller, 2001a; Kaiser and Miller, 2001b; Kaiser and Miller, 2003). Responses about experience with discrimination vary with question formats (e.g., explicitly race-focused vs. open-ended, venue-specific vs. general, time-specific vs. ever, etc.).

Despite these problems, a considerable body of empirical research on experiences with discrimination exists (Smith, 2002). Many researchers find self-reports to be meaningful measures of experience with discrimination (Bobo and Suh, 2000; Landrine and Klonoff, 1996). And there are several clear patterns in the survey data that inspire confidence about the validity and reliability of the data. Smith's study of self-reported discrimination found that some 95% of respondents reporting discrimination could provide highly specific descriptions of the circumstances in follow-up questions (Smith, 2000).

With these comments as methodological background, what do the survey data on personal experiences with employment discrimination indicate? African-Americans consistently report the highest levels of discrimination; whites report the least; and Asians and Hispanics fall in between (Smith, 2002, p. 16). The percentage of African-Americans reporting that they were discriminated against "at [their] place of work" within "the last 30 days" varied between 21% and 18% for years 1997–2001 in national Gallup polls (Smith, 2002, p. 26). The percentage rises with longer time horizons. Some 33% of blacks and Hispanics reported that they "ever" were "not offered a job that went to a white" because of racial discrimination; 31% reported being "passed over for a promotion which went to a white" because of racial discrimination (Smith, 2002, p. 28). The data also show that better educated and more race conscious respondents report higher levels of experience with discrimination than other respondents (Bobo and Suh, 2000).

These data on self-reports of discrimination are consistent with other studies that focus specifically on claiming behavior. Using data from a national survey of over 2,000 adults conducted in 1972, Curran found that 9% of respondents said that they had experienced job discrimination at least once in the last year (Curran, 1977, p. 103). Similarly, based on the data from the Civil Litigation Research Project (CLRP), Kristin Bumiller reported that about 11% of those surveyed had experienced illegal or unfair treatment because of their race, age, sex, handicap, union membership, or other things"[8] (Bumiller, 1988, p. 424). These percentages are for the entire sample of respondents. When the samples are broken down by race, the results are quite similar to the studies cited above.

A recent study of discrimination in the workplace conducted by researchers at Rutgers University deserves special consideration, given its focus on employees, the detailed nature of the questions it employed about the experience of workplace discrimination, and its nationwide sample. The Rutgers study found that 10% of respondents said that they had been "treated unfairly at [their] workplace because of their race or ethnicity" (Dixon et al., 2002, p. 11). Over half of the African-Americans surveyed "knew of" discrimination in the workplace in the last year and more than one-quarter (28%) had themselves experienced discrimination due to race in the last year (Dixon et al., 2002). In contrast, only 6% of whites had themselves been treated unfairly due to their race in the previous year (Dixon et al., 2002). More generally, when asked if the practice of determining promotions is unfair, only 6% of whites said yes, while almost half (46%) of African-Americans answered yes, and 12% of workers of other races said yes (Dixon et al., 2002, p. 14). When asked what type of discrimination they face in the workplace, those who report being treated unfairly most commonly report being passed over for promotion (28%), being assigned undesirable tasks (21%), and hearing racist comments (16%) (Dixon et al., 2002).[9]

4.3. Making Complaints

Deciding whether or not one should make a complaint internally within the organization, to a Federal Agency, to a lawyer, or even to one's friends and family involves complicated processes. In this section of the chapter, we review the literature on whether people who think they have been the target of discrimination do something about it.

[8] This question is not limited to the workplace—the "illegal" or "unfair" treatment could be racial profiling by police, discrimination in housing, or some other form of unfair treatment than in the workplace.
[9] The Rutgers study is based on a nationwide sample of 1000 employed workers weighted to match the presence of selected groups in the census data. The sample is 12% African-American, 72% White, 5% Hispanic, 2% Asian, 1% Native American, 1% Bi-racial, and 3% other. The response rate for the survey is not reported in the research report.

4.3.1. Extra Legal and Informal Complaints

In the Rutgers study described in the previous section, more than a third (34%) of those who reported unfair treatment in the workplace did not do anything (Dixon et al., 2002, p. 15). Although they also may complain to friends, family members, or even co-workers, some 29% said that they "reported the incident to a supervisor;" 19% "filed a complaint according to company procedures;" 10% "avoided certain areas or people in the office;" 4% "quit;" and 2% "confronted the person." Only 3% said they "sued" the company or their co-worker.[10]

4.3.2. Internal Organization Complaint Handling

Case law mandates that prior to filing a formal complaint with the EEOC, a worker exhausts her internal remedies within the employing organizations. Most large employers have policies and departments in place to handle such complaints. But what is the nature of the internal complaint process?

The passage and enforcement of the Civil Rights Act of 1964 resulted in corporate actions regarding anti-discrimination law. Organizations instituted formal internal procedures and departments to track developments and resolve disputes (Edelman, 1992), although these offices may be more of a symbolic signal that the corporation is complying with the law than an internal structure that actually produces good results for complaining employees (Edelman, 1992). In response to their inaccurate perceptions about the actual risks of being on the losing end of an anti-discrimination lawsuit (Edelman, Erlanger, and Abraham, 1992), employing organizations operate to "managerialize" the process of complaining. Edelman and her colleagues have shown that internal processes seek to de-emphasize and de-politicize incidents of workplace discrimination. While the courts have encouraged these processes by citing the presence of internal complaint structures as evidence against the inference of discrimination (Edelman, 2002), by redefining possible incidents of discrimination as "misunderstandings," internal processes may operate to deflect employees from pursuing their claims as matters of rights (Edelman et al., 1993).

These data demonstrate that even those employees who take formal actions inside their company are likely to confront a corporate culture with a vested interest in transforming their claim from discrimination to something else.

4.3.3. Trends in Formal Complaints: Federal Agency and Court Statistics

The components of the disputing system of anti-discrimination law about which we have some direct measures are those for which the government collects and reports statistics: discrimination charges filed with the EEOC and federal district court filings

[10] As we demonstrate in what follows, if 3% of African-Americans who thought they were treated unfairly on the basis of race or ethnicity in the past year in fact sued their employer, we would see vastly more lawsuits than are filed. The 3% figure in the Rutgers report may include EEOC complaints as well as state and federal lawsuits. It also may also be rounded up from a smaller fraction.

of employment related civil rights cases. Data on state agencies and courts are more fragmentary and for purposes of this chapter, we focus on the federal case (for more on state court verdicts, see Oppenheimer, 2003).

The broad contours of formal complaints over time are straightforward. Employment related civil rights cases filed in federal district court grew from 336 in 1970 to 7,613 in 1989 (Donohue and Siegelman, 1991, p. 989); by 1994 the number reached 15,965; by 1998 filings reached 23,735 (AO annual). By 2001, the number of filings had declined slightly to 21,157 (AO annual; see also Litras, 2000; Litras, 2002). One limitation of the Administrative Office (hereafter AO) data is that they do not categorize cases by type of discrimination alleged. For some insight into changes in the nature of allegations, we must consult data from the EEOC.

Table 1 reports EEOC charge statistics for the years 1992–2002 (EEOC, 2003a). The total number of individual charge filings (which may include multiple types of discrimination) rose sharply in the first four years of this period, 1992–1995, largely in response to the addition of disability cases starting in 1993. Hence, in 1992, 77,302 individual charges of discrimination were filed with the EEOC; in 1993, 87,942 complaints were filed; in 1994 the total number of complaints reached the high watermark for the EEOC, with 91,189 complaints; but then began to recede, with 87,529 in 1995, and then dropped dramatically to 77,990 in 1996, before rebounding to 80,680 in 1997 and staying in the range of 77,000–81,000 between 1998 and 2001. They rose above 84,000 in 2002.

Figure 1 presents the same data graphically. Two types of discrimination clearly rise in prominence over the period: retaliation—which grows from 15.3% of individual complaints to 27.5% of individual complaints—and disability—which the EEOC began to enforce in July 1992 and immediately jumps to 17.4% of complaints in 1993. Thereafter, disability claims vary between 20% and 23% of complaints. Complaints about other types of discrimination are quite stable over the time period. Race remains the most frequent type of discrimination charge (although it declines from 41% to 36% of charges in the period), followed closely by sex (which rises from 30% to 31%), age (which declines from 27% to 22%), national origin (which begins and ends the period at 10%), religion (1–3%), and equal pay act claims (1–2%).

The rise in disability claims appears to be a simple reflection of the impact of the ADA. The reason for the rising number of retaliation charges is less obvious. It may reflect the rising proportion of charges that involve dismissal, a finding documented by Donohue and Siegelman for the period 1965–1989 (Donohue and Siegelman, 1991). It may also reflect an increasing tendency for plaintiffs (and their lawyers) to add retaliation as a claim in discrimination disputes. It may reflect more retaliatory behavior by employers. Without in-depth analysis of claims over time and the employment contexts that produce them, we are left to speculate about the reasons for this shift.

We also know from EEOC data that the character of sex discrimination charges has changed significantly in the last 15 years. Sexual harassment was first recognized as actionable under Title VII in 1986. By 1992, the EEOC and state Fair Employment agencies received 10,532 sexual harassment claims (EEOC, 2003b). This number rose

Table 1. EEOC charge statistics, fiscal year 1992–2002[12]

	1992	1993	1994	1995	1996	1997	1998	1999	2000	2001	2002
Total charges	72,302	87,942	91,189	87,529	77,990	80,680	79,591	77,444	79,896	80,840	84,442
Race	29,548	31,695	31,656	29,986	26,287	29,199	28,820	28,819	28,945	28,912	29,910
	40.90%	36.00%	34.80%	34.30%	33.80%	36.20%	36.20%	37.30%	36.20%	35.80%	35.40%
Sex	21,796	23,919	25,860	26,181	23,813	24,728	24,454	23,907	25,194	25,140	25,536
	30.10%	27.20%	28.40%	29.90%	30.60%	30.70%	30.70%	30.90%	31.50%	31.10%	30.20%
National origin	7,434	7,454	7,414	7,035	6,687	6,712	6,778	7,108	7,792	8,025	9,046
	10.30%	8.50%	8.10%	8.00%	8.60%	8.30%	8.50%	9.20%	9.80%	9.90%	10.70%
Religion	1,388	1,449	1,546	1,581	1,564	1,709	1,786	1,811	1,939	2,127	2,572
	1.90%	1.60%	1.70%	1.80%	2.00%	2.10%	2.20%	2.30%	2.40%	2.60%	3.00%
Retaliation											
All statutes	11,096	13,814	15,853	17,070	16,080	18,198	19,114	19,694	21,613	22,257	22,768
	15.30%	15.70%	17.40%	19.50%	20.60%	22.60%	24.00%	25.40%	27.10%	27.50%	27.00%
Title VII	10,499	12,644	14,415	15,342	14,412	16,394	17,246	17,883	19,753	20,407	20,814
	14.50%	14.40%	15.80%	17.50%	18.50%	20.30%	21.70%	23.10%	24.70%	25.20%	24.60%
Age	19,573	19,809	19,618	17,416	15,719	15,785	15,191	14,141	16,008	17,405	19,921
	27.10%	22.50%	21.50%	19.90%	20.20%	19.60%	19.10%	18.30%	20.00%	21.50%	23.60%
Disability	1,048*	15,274	18,859	19,798	18,046	18,108	17,806	17,007	15,864	16,470	15,964
	1.40%	17.40%	20.70%	22.60%	23.10%	22.40%	22.40%	22.00%	19.90%	20.40%	18.90%
Equal pay act	1,294	1,328	1,381	1,275	969	1,134	1,071	1,044	1,270	1,251	1,256
	1.80%	1.50%	1.50%	1.50%	1.20%	1.40%	1.30%	1.30%	1.60%	1.50%	1.50%

U.S. Equal Employment Opportunity Commission.

*EEOC began enforcing the Americans with Disabilities Act on July 26, 1992.

[12]The number for total charges reflects the number of individual charge filings. Because individuals often file charges claiming multiple types of discrimination, the number of total charges for any given fiscal year will be less than the total of the eight types of discrimination listed. The data are compiled by the Office of Research, Information, and Planning from EEOC's Charge Data System—quarterly reconciled Data Summary Reports, and the national database.

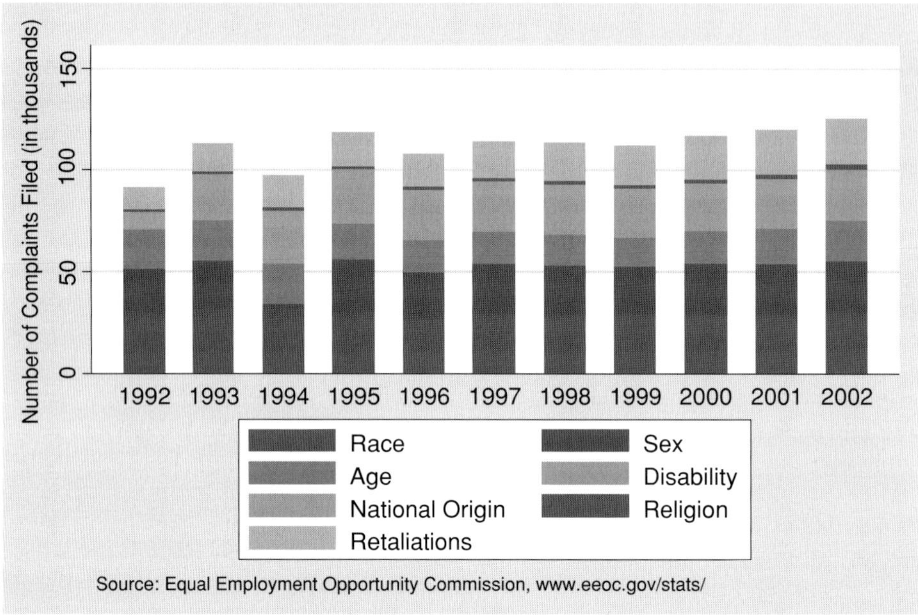

Figure 1. EEOC complaints filed by type of claim, 1992–2002.

to 15,549 in 1995, where it remained relatively stable through 2001. In 2002, there was a decline in sexual harassment charges and an increase in the number of male workers making harassment charges (EEOC, 2003b). Thus, sexual harassment charges equal 56% of the total sex discrimination charges filed with the EEOC in 2002 (EEOC, 2003b).

Data on the rate at which plaintiffs succeed in discrimination cases after they make formal complaints is less comprehensive than data on formal complaints themselves. The EEOC reports "resolutions" by type of discrimination claim each year. In 2001, 8% were resolved by "settlements," 4% were "withdrawn with benefits" (presumably also favorable to the complaining individual), and in 10% the EEOC made a finding of "reasonable cause" that discrimination occurred, which is followed by efforts at conciliation. Most cases end in a finding of "no reasonable cause" (57%), which means that the agency does not find the case meritorious and the individual may pursue a private cause of action, or are closed administratively (21%), which means the case is closed without any remedy or finding for the charging party. In 2001, the EEOC reported obtaining $247.8 million in monetary benefits for charging parties, a figure which does not include monetary benefits won through litigation. The EEOC itself directly litigates a relatively small number of cases per year. It filed between 193 and 481 cases per year between 1992 and 2001. Hence, if we look only at the EEOC, we see that most complainants (78% in 2001) obtain no relief from the EEOC and very few are directly represented by the agency in court. If we divide the monetary

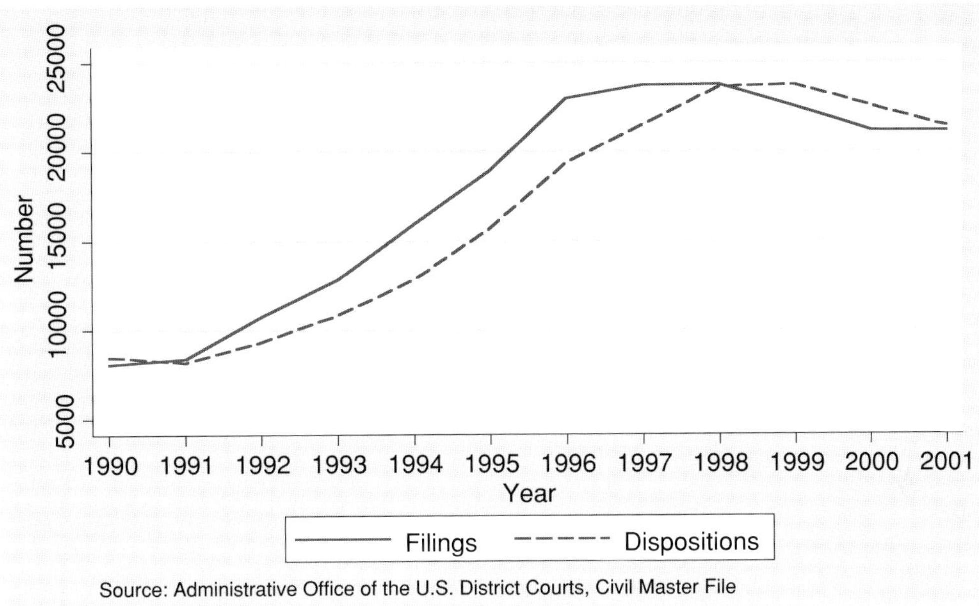

Figure 2. Number of employment discrimination lawsuits, filed and disposed of in U.S. district courts, 1990–2001.

benefits procured by the number of complaints that survive administrative closures and no reasonable cause findings, complainants obtain an average of less than $14,000 per complaint.

The Administrative Office of the U.S. Courts reports annual data on filings and dispositions in federal district courts, including the category "employment discrimination claims" (AO annual). These data have not been extensively analyzed before, with the exception of some government reports (Litras, 2000; Litras, 2002) and the paper by Donohue and Siegelman (2002) referred to above. The data are based on forms that plaintiffs' attorneys are required to fill out at the time of filing and disposition of a lawsuit. As we discuss below, some aspects of the data are subject to error. Nonetheless, they offer a reasonably comprehensive view of aggregate trends in federal discrimination litigation.

Figure 2 displays the number of lawsuits filed and disposed of from 1990 to 2001. Here is graphic evidence of the rise in employment discrimination litigation, as filings rise dramatically from 1990 to 1997, roughly tripling in the time period, before leveling off and declining slightly from 1998 to 2001. Dispositions follow a similar pattern lagged by about one year. Indeed, the median number of months between filing and disposition of these cases hovers between 11 and 12 months. The government is a plaintiff in a declining proportion of filings over this period. In 1990, the government was a plaintiff in 7% of cases; by 2001 the government acts as plaintiff in 2% of cases,

Table 2. Disposition of employment civil rights complaints in U.S. district courts, 1990–2001

Year	Number of employment civil rights complaints disposed*	Percent of cases disposed dismissed						Judgment		
		Total (%)	Settled (%)	Voluntary (%)	Lack of jurisdiction (%)	Want of prosecution (%)	Other (%)	Total (%)	Trial† (%)	Other‡ (%)
1990	8,205	67.2	35.0	8.8	7.0	5.1	11.3	32.8	8.7	24.2
1991	7,911	67.3	36.4	9.2	2.9	5.2	13.6	32.7	9.2	23.5
1992	8,924	67.2	35.1	11.1	1.4	5.1	14.5	32.8	8.4	24.3
1993	10,305	69.6	37.0	11.5	1.2	4.4	15.5	30.4	7.8	22.6
1994	12,232	70.9	39.4	12.6	1.0	3.3	14.5	29.1	7.5	21.6
1995	14,967	72.1	39.9	13.4	1.0	3.5	14.3	27.9	6.8	21.1
1996	18,456	72.0	39.0	13.2	0.8	3.4	15.6	28.0	6.0	22.0
1997	20,564	72.6	39.0	13.8	0.8	3.8	15.2	27.4	5.7	21.7
1998	22,570	72.4	39.3	13.9	0.9	3.8	14.7	27.6	4.8	22.8
1999	22,701	73.1	40.5	13.2	0.9	3.3	15.1	26.9	4.5	22.4
2000	21,524	73.1	41.5	12.6	1.0	3.6	14.4	26.9	4.3	22.6
2001	20,345	74.0	42.5	13.2	0.9	3.6	13.8	26.0	3.8	22.2

Percentages may not sum to total due to rounding.
Administrative office of the U.S. Courts, civil master file, annual.
*Excludes transfers, remands, and statistical closures.
†Trial includes cases disposed of by jury verdict, directed verdict, or bench trial. In some cases, the parties may have settled before the completion of the trial.
‡Includes judgments by default, consent, a motion before trial, judgment of arbitrator, or by some other final judgment method.

albeit roughly the same absolute number of cases. As other commentators have noted, class actions make up a small fraction of filings. Only 20 cases were filed as class actions in 1990, 0.25% of filings; in 2001, some 73 cases were filed as class actions, or 0.35% of filings.

Table 2 reports data on case dispositions by year. Consistent with Galanter's depiction of civil litigation, a small and declining proportion of cases are resolved through a trial. At the beginning of the period, in 1990, two thirds of cases are dismissed without judgments, and only 8.7% go to trial. By 2001 almost three-quarters of cases are dismissed without judgments, and only 3.8% go to trial. The largest single category of dismissal is through settlement. Because we have virtually no information on how favorable settlements are for plaintiffs, this represents an enormous gap in our knowledge about discrimination litigation. The significance of settlements is underscored in figures 3 and 4, which respectively graph the number and percentage of different types of dispositions over the decade. From 1998 onwards, more than 8,000 cases per year are settled. As figure 4 shows, settlements are a slowly rising percentage of dispositions, from 35% in 1990 to 43% in 2001. The next most frequent outcomes are dismissals without judgments, which make up about 30% of dispositions throughout

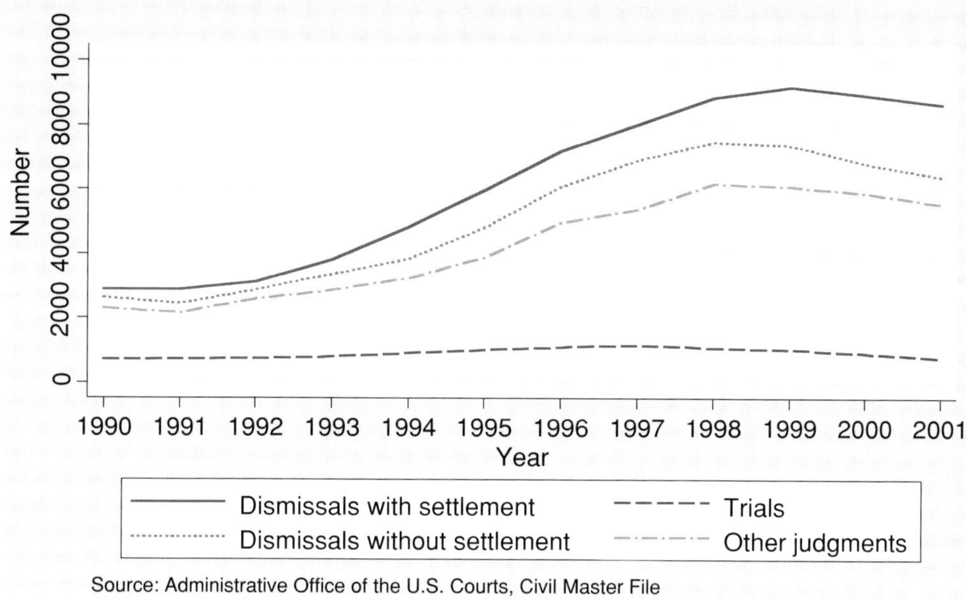

Figure 3. Dispositions of employment discrimination complaints in U.S. district courts by type of disposition, 1990–2001.

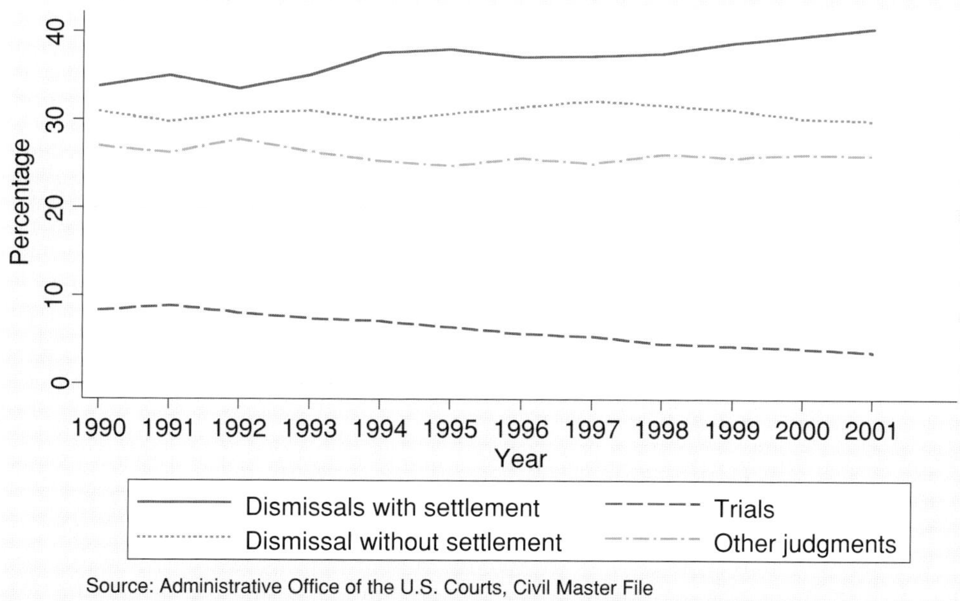

Figure 4. Dispositions of employment discrimination complaints in U.S. district courts by type of disposition, 1990–2001.

Table 3. Plaintiff winners and awards in employment civil rights complaints terminated by trial in U.S. district courts, 1990–2001

						Award amount			
Year	Number of cases terminated by trial verdict*	Percent plaintiff winners (%)	Number of plaintiff winners	Monetary awards Percent	Monetary awards Number	Median ($)	million Less than $500,000 (%)	$1 million or more (%)	$10 or more (%)
1990	709	24.4	173	84.4	146	248,500	54.1	40.4	1.4
1991	728	26.9	196	82.7	162	127,000	65.4	32.1	1.2
1992	752	27.8	209	80.9	169	151,000	66.9	26.0	5.3
1993	803	25.7	206	82.0	169	62,000	85.8	8.3	2.4
1994	916	30.9	283	88.3	250	89,500	87.6	7.6	3.6
1995	1,015	26.5	269	85.1	229	116,000	80.8	13.5	8.7
1996	1,106	32.6	361	82.8	299	125,000	78.6	14.7	8.4
1997	1,167	34.4	401	81.0	325	125,000	78.8	13.5	10.2
1998	1,083	35.5	384	78.6	302	137,000	77.8	14.2	10.6
1999	1,029	34.9	359	83.6	300	150,000	82.0	12.3	6.0
2000	921	35.4	326	80.7	263	156,000	81.4	10.6	5.3
2001	780	38.1	297	80.8	240	130,500	77.9	13.8	7.5

Administrative office of the U.S. courts, civil master file.
*Number of trial cases disposed for which a judgment was known. Includes jury trials, bench trials, and directed verdicts.

the period, and other judgments (such as judgments by default, consent, motion before trial, etc.), which make up just under a quarter of dispositions in most years. The latter two types of dispositions more clearly benefit defendants.

Trials make up a relatively small percentage of case dispositions, but are especially interesting because they are coded for plaintiff wins and award amounts. These data are presented in tables 3 and 4.

Table 3 reveals that the number of cases terminated by trial varies within a limited range by year: In 1990 there were 709 employment discrimination trials terminated by verdict, a number which rises to as high as 1,167 in 1997, but then recedes to 780 in 2001. The plaintiff win rate rises from 24% in 1990 to 38% by 2001, but the percentage of winners who obtain monetary awards declines slightly from 1990 to 2001.

The reported amounts of plaintiff awards must be interpreted cautiously. As Donohue and Siegelman (1993) explained in detail, some award amounts are inflated because the attorneys filling out the case disposition forms did not follow the instruction to report the award "in thousands." If a plaintiff was awarded $9,000 after a trial, then the attorney should have written "9" in the award amount field. However, if the attorney wrote $9,000, the award amount would be set at 9,000 one thousands or $9 million. If anything, then, there is an upward bias in reported awards.

With this danger in mind, table 3 suggests that most plaintiffs win modest awards at trial. The median award in all but 1990 falls between $62,000 and $156,000. While

Table 4. Plaintiff winners and awards in employment civil rights cases terminated in U.S. district courts by type of trial, 1990–2001

			Plaintiff winners in Jury trials						
							Award amount		
Year	Number of cases terminated by Jury trial*	percent plaintiff winners (%)	Number of Plaintiff Winners	Monetary awards Percent	Monetary awards Number	Median ($)	million Less than $500,000 (%)	$1 million or more (%)	$10 or more (%)
1990	254	40.9	104	95.2	99	440,000	51.5	42.4	2.0
1991	241	42.3	102	92.2	94	198,500	61.7	35.1	–
1992	257	43.6	112	92.9	104	319,000	58.7	31.7	7.7%
1993	316	36.7	116	89.7	104	92,500	80.8	10.6	2.9%
1994	464	43.1	200	90.0	180	110,000	85.0	8.3	3.9%
1995	598	35.8	214	86.4	185	150,000	81.1	13.0	9.2%
1996	758	38.5	292	83.9	245	146,000	77.1	15.5	9.4%
1997	877	40.9	359	82.5	296	128,000	78.4	13.5	9.8%
1998	845	40.4	341	79.5	271	139,000	77.9	13.7	10.0%
1999	810	39.3	318	83.6	266	168,500	81.2	12.8	6.4%
2000	748	38.0	284	83.5	237	150,000	82.3	10.5	4.6%
2001	633	40.6	257	81.7	210	141,500	77.6	14.3	7.1%

			Plaintiff winners in bench trials						
							Award amount		
Year	Number of cases terminated by Jury trial†	Percent plaintiff winners (%)	Number of Plaintiff Winners	Monetary awards Percent	Monetary awards Number	Median ($)	million Less than $500,000 (%)	$1 million or more (%)	$10 or more' (%)
1990	410	16.3	67	68.7	46	114,000	58.7	37.0	–
1991	440	19.1	84	75.0	63	69,000	69.8	28.6	3.2
1992	449	21.4	96	66.7	64	43,000	79.7	17.2	1.6
1993	444	19.6	87	74.7	65	35,000	93.8	4.6	1.5
1994	408	19.9	81	84.0	68	43,500	94.1	5.9	2.9
1995	364	14.0	51	82.4	42	45,000	81.0	14.3	4.8
1996	285	22.8	65	78.5	51	71,000	86.3	9.8	2.0
1997	219	18.7	41	68.3	28	84,500	85.7	10.7	10.7
1998	168	24.4	41	73.2	30	141,000	76.7	20.0	16.7
1999	170	22.9	39	82.1	32	54,000	87.5	9.4	3.1
2000	138	26.8	37	64.9	24	183,500	70.8	12.5	12.5
2001	111	33.3	37	75.7	28	112,500	78.6	10.7	10.7

Administrative office of the U.S. courts, civil master file.

– No cases recorded.

*Number of jury trial cases disposed for which a judgment was known.

†Number of bench trial cases disposed for which a judgment was known. Directed verdicts not included.

there appear to be relatively large percentages of plaintiff winners getting more than $1 million in 1990–1992, between 8% and 15% of plaintiff winners obtain awards of more than $1 million from 1993 to 2001. However, if the numbers in table 3 are to be believed, between 5% and 10% of plaintiff winners, or 15–30 plaintiffs, obtain awards of $10 millions or more per year.

Table 4 divides cases decided at trial by jury and bench trials which may be important because the Civil Rights Act of 1991 had the effect of extending the right to jury trial for plaintiffs who claimed compensatory damages or who claimed to be victims of intentional discrimination. The percentage of trials before juries rather than judges rises significantly from 1992 onwards. Jury trials increase from 254 in 1990 to 633 in 2001, while bench trials decline from 410 in 1990 to 111 in 2001. Plaintiffs enjoy higher rates of success before juries than before a judge. In every year, the plaintiff success rate before juries is higher (ranging from 36% to 44%) than the success rate before judges (which ranges from 14% to 33%). Median awards also typically are modestly higher for cases tried to a jury than those tried to a judge. The median awards for jury cases hover around $150,000; median awards in bench trials fall below $100,000 for 8 of 12 years.

After trial, plaintiffs fare poorly. Eisenberg (1989) demonstrate that defendants are extremely likely to have their trial successes preserved after appeal, while more than one-third of plaintiff trial victories are reversed on appeal. The plaintiff success rate after appeal is 11% in bench trial cases, 25.2% in jury trial cases, or 16.9% overall. Colker's (1999) analysis of disability cases from 1992 to 1998, in which she examined both published and unpublished opinions, found that defendants prevailed 93% of the time at the trial level and 84% of the time upon appeal.

These data indicate that most discrimination lawsuits have very different outcomes from the image of major plaintiff victories in highly publicized settlements or trial victories, such as those involving Texaco, Mitsubishi, or Home Depot. Most plaintiffs who file federal suit never reach trial. If they do go to trial, then they lose more than 60% of the time. If they win, then they get relatively modest awards. Perhaps what we know the least about are settlement figures in the large number of lawsuits settled each year.

Yet the number of cases and the size of some awards have generated considerable fear among employers and spawned a new line of insurance against employment liability (Bielby and Bourgeois, 2002). A presentation by the executive of an insurance company that sells employment practice liability insurance warned of "Escalating Exposures." (Presentation given June 19, 2001; on file with authors). Citing many of the same EEOC statistics we cited above, this insurance representative reported that discrimination claims are becoming more frequent and more severe. Without disclosing the source, he reported that in 1999 there were 12 settlements or verdicts of $100 million or more, 135 settlements or verdicts over $15 million, and 101 settlements or verdicts below $15 million. These figures represented more than a doubling of cases in each category of award size from 1997. The presentation goes on to report that there are more than 22,000 labor and employment lawyers in the ABA, that employment issues now make up 30% of all civil litigation in the United States, and that the average verdict in employment liability cases now exceeds $ 450,000.

Many of these insurance industry assertions seem dubious. Yet they are interesting because they portray the system of anti-discrimination law as though it is expansive and costly for employers. Employers, their lawyers, and their insurers may indeed see discrimination law as more costly than in earlier years.

For example, Nielsen and Beim (2004) demonstrate that the information that employers, lawyers and insurers may glean from the media about employment discrimination litigation overstate the risks posed by litigation. Using national and local media coverage of employment cases, Nielsen and Beim demonstrate that newspapers report a plaintiff win-rate nearly three times the actual win-rate of 32%. Moreover, this analysis shows that newspaper accounts of awards in such cases have a median value well over $1million, a figure nearly six times greater than the actual median award of $150,000 in such cases (Nielsen and Beim, 2004).

The popular image of a plaintiff-oriented system stands in marked contrast to how most victims of discrimination and most plaintiffs' lawyers view the system. They think the system heavily favors employers. Bisom-Rapp's analysis of employer and defense attorney responses to employment discrimination law, especially in the area of dismissals, finds that employer defendants have considerable advantages in contests over discrimination claims (1999). Employers, human resource professionals, and defense lawyers have developed effective techniques for minimizing the legal threat posed by discrimination lawsuits in the dismissal context, even though it is not clear that their techniques in fact reduce the amount of discriminatory behavior taking place in the workplace. Her survey of plaintiffs' lawyers finds that they too recognize the distinct advantages that employer-defendants possess, and hence are reluctant to take cases unless they contain particularly powerful evidence of discrimination. Even then, plaintiffs apparently do not have a strong chance of success.

Thus, the empirical data examined so far present no easy answer regarding the competing images of employment discrimination law. One could say that plaintiffs are winning more often than they used to and that large awards are more frequent than they used to be. On the other hand, fewer plaintiffs get to trial, the percent of plaintiff winners who receive any monetary award is down, and the median monetary award is lower than it was 10 years ago. The data we have analyzed thus far represent only the middle and top of the dispute pyramid. By traveling to the base, a different picture of the pyramid begins to emerge.

5. SCALING THE PYRAMID OF EMPLOYMENT DISCRIMINATION CLAIMS: AN ANALYTIC EXERCISE

While there obviously has been extraordinary growth in the number of discrimination lawsuit filings and EEOC complaints, what percentage of possible claims of discrimination are entering the system? Perhaps we would arrive at a different perspective on claiming tendencies if we put the data on formal complaints together with data on the reported prevalence of discrimination among protected groups.

Consider just one category of protected employees for whom we have such data: African-American workers. The survey research cited above contained several different estimates of how many African-Americans had experienced discrimination at work in the last year. The high estimate was 46%, the average was 33%, and the low figure, in the Rutgers study, was 28%. To be conservative, we will use the Rutgers finding as the basis for our estimate. According to U.S. census reports, the number of African-Americans working full-time, year-round in the United States in the year 2000 was 12,197,000 (Census, 2000). Although the Rutgers study found that most African-Americans reported two incidents of discrimination in the last year, we, again conservatively, assume that individuals will file only one discrimination claim. Using the 28% figure from the Rutgers study, we would estimate that 3,415,160 African-American workers perceived that they were the targets of workplace race discrimination in 2000. To be sure, this number of perceived discriminatory incidents must include misperceptions (when the target attributes a decision to discrimination when that is not the motivation of the decision-maker) and unfair treatment that does not meet the legal standard for employment discrimination. But it also excludes discrimination that goes on unnoticed by its targets. Nonetheless, this estimate is a rough approximation for the pool of individuals who feel they have been a target of discrimination. This group approximates the bottom of the dispute pyramid for African-Americans with a claim of racial discrimination.

What percentage of this group starts a claiming process? The EEOC reports that 28,912 individuals filed complaints of racial discrimination in the year 2001. An EEOC charge is only one avenue of formal complaint, yet it probably is the most common nationally. Using this estimate, less that 1% (0.85%) of African-Americans who felt they were discriminated against filed an EEOC complaint.

As we already have seen, this remaining 1% faced further attrition before receiving any remedy. In 2001, the EEOC obtained settlements in 7.9% of the cases it resolved, another 3.8% of complainants withdrew their complaints "with benefits," and 7.5% of cases were determined to have "reasonable cause" and were sent to conciliation. Of the cases sent to conciliation, less than one-third (or 2.2% of resolved cases) ended in "successful conciliations," the remainder were "unsuccessful." If we divide the monetary benefits the EEOC reports for race-based cases among the some 4,443 who obtain relief, they each received on average $19,469. Some 63.3% of cases resulted in a finding of "no reasonable cause," which left the charging party with the right to pursue a private remedy. (The number of "disputes" in figure 5 is the percentage of EEOC complainants given a disposition of "no reasonable cause" or 18,215.) "Administrative closures," which appear largely to provide no relief for the complaining party, made up 17.5% of resolutions. Thus, about four in five EEOC complainants receive no relief from the EEOC, while at least 63% can sue in federal court.

Here we reach a disjuncture in official statistics. We cannot directly determine from federal court or EEOC statistics how many federal lawsuits allege racial discrimination

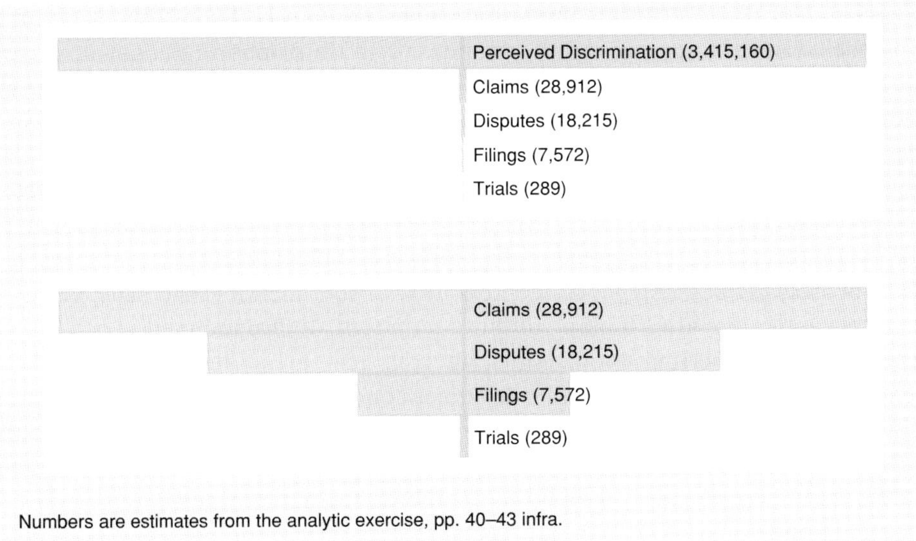

Figure 5. Dispute pyramid of employment discrimination for African-Americans, 2001.

in employment. The best estimate we can make of the number of race-based claims is to assume that the proportion of race cases filed in federal court is the same as the proportion of race charges in the EEOC charge statistics.

By this estimate, 35.8% of the 21,151 employment discrimination cases filed in federal court in 2001 are race cases, or 7,572 lawsuits filed. To estimate what happens to these 7,572 cases, we rely on what we saw in table 2, about the dispositions of all employment discrimination cases. In 2001, 74% of dispositions were dismissals without a judgment. Of these, we expect 42.5% (or 3,218) to settle, while the others are dismissed without relief. Of the 26% of cases that proceed to judgment (or 1,969 cases), 3.8% (or 289) go to trial. Then, as we would project from table 3, of the cases that go to trial, plaintiffs win 38.1% (or 110), and obtain monetary relief in 80.8% of the winning cases (or 89 cases). If the race case awards mirror the overall pool of awards, then the median monetary award is $130,500.

To summarize, of 3.4 million potential race claimants, only 28,912 file an EEOC complaint and only about 7,500 file a federal lawsuit. Of these charging parties and plaintiffs, about 7,771 receive some kind of conciliation or award: 4,443 through EEOC action; 3,218 through litigated settlement; and 110 through litigated victories at trial. That amounts to 28% of those who complain starting with the EEOC or 0.23% or 23 in 10,000 of the potential pool of 3.4 million self-identified targets of racial discrimination in employment.[11]

[11] A replication of this exercise conducted for the population of disabled workers can be found in Burke (2003).

This analytical exercise is admittedly crude. To gain better estimates about the prevalence of discrimination and the propensity to do something about it, it would be necessary to collect survey data from larger samples, as well as data from state agencies and courts. We have treated the cases as though only one individual plaintiff were involved. While this is largely correct, we do know that at least some cases (73 overall in 2001, not just in race-based cases) include classes of plaintiffs. Yet this simple exercise reveals that a very small percentage of African-Americans who feel that they are discriminated against in the workplace take a grievance to the EEOC or the courts. If larger percentages of workers took action, then it could have a dramatic impact on caseloads. After looking at these numbers, we are inclined to ask not why there are so many discrimination claims, but why there are so few?

The answer to that question may lie in studies conducted about rights claiming by sociolegal scholars. In addition to the standard cost/benefit calculations that economists typically consider, sociolegal scholars have begun to identify a number of factors that influence decisions about disputing, including the material resources required to pursue a claim (Curran, 1977), the relationship of the parties to one another (Yngvesson, 1985; Yngvesson, 1988), resistance to being classified as "victim" (Bumiller, 1988), conceptions about other powerful social institutions such as work and family (Albiston, 2000; Albiston, 2001; Morgan, 1999), and resistance to law on ideological grounds (Nielsen, 2000), to name just a few.

The answer to that question may also be suggested in the statistics we have gathered here. The exercise suggests that only little more than one quarter of cases will yield awards for plaintiffs. Most complainants will receive an average of a little more than \$19,000; the median awards in cases that go to trial and win are \$130,000. When these awards are weighed against the difficulties of bringing a complaint, and the social opprobrium such an action typically provokes (Kaiser and Miller, 2001a; Kaiser and Miller, 2001b; Kaiser and Miller, 2003; Major, Kaiser, and McCoy, 2003), it is hardly surprising that so few targets of discrimination take formal action to obtain redress.

6. CONCLUSION

Our preliminary forays into a systemic analysis of anti-discrimination law suggest that it is a system whose symbolic presence is more powerful and pervasive than its practical effect. People of color, white women, those living with disabilities, and people with other protected characteristics have more statutorily protected rights to equal treatment in the workplace than was the case 15 years ago. Changes in the economy and cultural norms about work and the social status of protected groups have wrought significant changes in patterns of employment, so that members of protected groups are employed in jobs today that they could not have held before the beginning the contemporary civil rights era. As a result of changes in education and the dissemination of information about employment rights, protected groups no doubt are more aware of their rights than in the past. As a result, there are many more claims of discrimination than in the early 1970s and 1980s. Yet, it appears to remain the case that workers who feel subjected to discrimination seldom take formal actions within their organization or in court to achieve redress. If they do, they face a daunting array of challenges, are unlikely to obtain a remedy, and, if they do, they are unlikely to obtain a substantial recovery. The settlements announced against companies such as Texaco and Mitsubishi are as rare as they are large.

As employers become more sophisticated about defending their employment practices against legal challenge, and as the law shifts from becoming a force in support of affirmative action to a limitation on affirmative action, the gap between rights of protected groups and the realities they face in the workplace is likely to grow. And yet, the competing images of anti-discrimination law as a social system likely will persist, with those who believe that discrimination is pervasive seeking more law, tougher enforcement of those laws, and "liberal" justices to interpret the laws in ways that favor employees. Those who believe that greedy plaintiffs and unscrupulous lawyers are filing frivolous anti-discrimination lawsuits will argue that new laws are too burdensome on employers, that enforcement activities should be limited to "real" cases, and that legal burdens should be high for proving discrimination.

The competing images of anti-discrimination law as a system are buttressed by selected empirical data on both the sides. But, the sociolegal approach we have sketched here may provide a way to move beyond these conflicting characterizations. First, by taking the law seriously, a sociolegal account can show how the competing narratives about anti-discrimination law can be told from formal legal developments. Second, by scaling the pyramid from the bottom—all of those people who think they were the target of employment discrimination—we reveal that the dramatic rise in employment discrimination claiming can be attributed to a very small increase in the proportion of those who make up the bottom level advancing up the pyramid. Third, this model suggests the need for a program of empirical research on discrimination law as a social system. In the analysis of the claiming system we offered here we found several lacunae. For example, what kinds of claims are brought to court after the EEOC issues a right-to-sue letter? What is the nature of the cases that settle before trial, with what kinds of awards to plaintiffs? What are the factors that predict plaintiff success or failure before and during trial? Questions of similar importance have been raised in research on other fields of anti-discrimination law.

The pyramid is a particularly compelling metaphor for the analysis of the social significance of contemporary anti-discrimination law. The pyramids of ancient civilizations were both real and mythical in character. From a distance, they appear as smooth and inviting inclines upward. Up close they are revealed as consisting of jagged edges made up of formidable steps which were impossible to climb except using hidden stairways available only to some. The pyramids were built as symbols on a grand scale, as critical elements in a system of beliefs. Yet for the workers who slaved to make them, and for the royalty and priests who hoped to gain from them, they were brutally real.

So too, contemporary anti-discrimination law appears from a distance as an imposing edifice of rights. It is only up close in the observation of how these rights are translated into the practices of employing organizations or the claims of workers that we see the jagged edges and formidable obstacles to using these rights. Anti-discrimination law is both real and symbolic. The task for future research is to more fully address the relationship between rights and reality.

CHAPTER 2

Law's Role in Addressing Complex Discrimination

Susan Sturm

ABSTRACT

This essay demonstrates the importance of making explicit and critically assessing assumptions about judicial role that run through antidiscrimination scholarship. A formalistic conception of the judiciary operates as an uninterrogated baseline even for scholars who employ an institutional and cultural analysis of the problems law and courts address. The rule-enforcement conception of law and courts is, however, vastly over-simplified, as both a descriptive and normative matter. Its formalism clashes with the rich, interdisciplinary, and structural analyses that characterize scholars' critique of formal equality doctrine. This essay sketches the outlines of an under-acknowledged but widely practiced and legitimate judicial role: facilitating the elaboration and implementation of public law norms. Legal norms develop not only through liability determinations, but also through legally structured occasions for deliberating about the relationship between norms and practice. Within the context of judicial decision making, norm elaboration occurs in less formal settings that more directly facilitate data gathering and deliberations by relevant stakeholders and experts. These processes generate learning and outcomes that are more generally applicable, even if they have less formally binding effect than a formal adjudication. This analysis cast courts in a crucial but limited role in addressing problems that implicate public norms but are insufficiently understood or resistant to centralized rule enforcement. They emphasize law's role in structuring focal points of normative activity within and across institutions. This role, as an important concomitant of the court's more traditional rule elaboration and enforcement function, enables the judiciary to participate in addressing complex patterns of interaction that produce group-based exclusion without compromising its legitimacy or overstepping its capacity. It would also highlight and create accountability for the many occasions beyond formal liability adjudication in which courts prompt elaboration of equality norms under conditions of uncertainty.

INTRODUCTION

For years, scholars have challenged the dominant legal paradigm for addressing employment discrimination. They have criticized its formalistic, intent-based doctrinal framework as insufficiently descriptive of the dynamics that produce inequality;

L. B. Nielsen and R. L. Nelson (eds.), Handbook of Employment Discrimination Research, 35–59.

insufficiently explanatory of what judges actually do; and insufficiently robust as a normative theory of equality. Viewed in the light of recent interdisciplinary scholarship, the formal equality account—its prime protagonists, its plot, its problematic, and its prognosis—is an easy target.

Recent interdisciplinary scholarship shows that workplace bias often operates as a set of social practices: a dynamic interaction among culture, cognition, and context (Charny and Gulati, 1998, p. 57; Krieger, 1995, p. 1761; Lawrence, 1997, p. 122; Post, 2000, pp. 1, 30; see also Sturm, 2001, p. 458). For example, Lawrence and Krieger have drawn on cognitive and Freudian psychology to debunk conscious intent as an adequate explanation of racial and gender influence on employment decision-making (Krieger, 1995, pp. 1161, 1217; Lawrence, 1997, p. 122). Schultz has criticized courts' failure to consider how organizational and cultural factors, often sustained by employers, shape employees' interest and success in non-traditional jobs (Schultz, 1998, p. 1683). Charny, Gulati, and Wilkins have shown that the dearth of black corporate lawyers results not primarily from overt racism or the lack of qualified candidates. Instead, the tournament system of advancement, cognitive bias, and group dynamics, in combination, cause much of the underparticipation by black lawyers in firms (Wilkens and Gulati, 1996, p. 496; Charny and Gulati, 1998, p. 57). Minow has exposed the implicit, baseline assumptions that normalize a world organized around the values and practices of dominant groups (Minow, 1987, p. 10. See also Yoshino, 2002, pp. 769, 781; Post, 2000, pp. 1, 30).

The inequality stories anchoring these rich accounts convey a flavor of complexity and, to varying degrees, uncertainty. They are descriptively and normatively far more complicated than the stock story of deliberate discrimination. The problematic activities they target are embedded in institutional structures, group interactions, and cultural stereotypes. Their exclusionary character is not intuitively obvious, and sometimes emerges only from analyzing problematic patterns and their potential causes in particular contexts. These dynamics trigger equality concerns, although the precise character of the harm and the contours of the particular norm can be hard to pin down.

What is law's role in addressing these complex problems? How do and should courts elaborate and enforce ambiguous norms? What legitimate repertoires are available to courts for addressing complex discrimination consistent with the rule of law? How do they construct the relationship between the articulation of rights and the enforcement of remedies? What is and should be the nature of judicial interaction with other normative actors? Generally stated, what are the implications of the sociological/institutional/contextual/interdisciplinary analysis of legal problems for judicial participation in the reconstruction of institutional practices?

The answers to these questions are often taken for granted in the discussions about legal doctrine and remedies for workplace discrimination. When grappling with law's response to complex and subtle discrimination, many employment scholars fall back on a surprisingly formalistic conception of law. Their punch line is often a new legal rule that better reflects current understandings of the problem. Some scholars propose doctrinal standards that reflect more complex and dynamic accounts of workplace inequality (Schultz, 1998, p. 1683; Lawrence, 1997, p. 122; Oppenheimer, 1993, p. 899). Yet another approach offers a different cognitive or decisional framework to shape judges' reasoning process as courts address cases involving discrimination (Minow, 1987, pp. 88–89; Post, 2000). A final set of responses considers the implications of this complexity for courts' capacity to address the problem at all. These scholars advocate private or market solutions as better suited to this type of complex, interactive problem (Wax, 1999, p. 1129). Others more modestly counsel against judicial incorporation of cognitive bias insights until sufficient evidence develops to permit articulation of a clear and workable rule (Krieger, 1995).

These responses take for granted a formalistic conception of legal norm elaboration. This conception presumes that "law" emerges from formal adversary process producing post-liability judicial decisions that interpret loosely worded civil rights statutes. The function of legal rules is to dictate the boundaries between legal and illegal conduct. Courts affect informal workplace norms by the "shadow" their decisions (and the costs of generating them) cast over informal decision-making (Mnookin and Kornhauser, 1979, p. 950). Law and legal process operate as a decontextualized process detached from the dynamics by which norms develop and influence practice.

This formalistic judicial conception shapes and constrains scholars' substantive responses to complex discrimination. It influences the proposed content of legal norms, the judicial strategies chosen to address complex problems, and the perceived legitimacy of these choices. The rule-enforcement conception of law and courts is, however, vastly over-simplified, as both a descriptive and normative matter. It fails to incorporate law and society's well-developed insights about legal pluralism, rights consciousness, and legal mobilization (McCann, 1994, p. 6; Merry, 1990). Its legal formalism clashes with the rich, interdisciplinary, and structural analyses that characterize scholars' critique of formal equality doctrine. Indeed, public law scholars' blanket commitment to a rule-enforcement conception of law and law-making seems surprising when compared to the more dynamic and reflexive accounts in international law and human rights scholarship and in the commercial and business domain (Cain, 1994, p. 15; Sugarman, 1994, p. 115).

As a descriptive matter, the judiciary's current dispute processing repertoire includes a much richer set of legal norm elaboration practices than the dominant narrative acknowledges. Within the context of judicial decision-making, norm elaboration occurs in less formal settings that more directly facilitate data gathering and deliberations by relevant stakeholders and experts. These processes generate learning and outcomes that are more generally applicable, even if they have less formally binding effect than a formal adjudication. They involve proceedings about class certification, discovery, and expert witnesses, as well as proceedings about settlement and remedy. Outside the formal law-making and enforcement process, actors participate in norm elaboration that directly contributes to the content of formal legal norms, and courts sometimes actively shape the contours of that informal norm elaboration process.

As a normative matter, the facilitative role that courts, sometimes apologetically, perform is in fact an important, legitimate, and under-theorized aspect of judicial participation in norm elaboration and implementation. It connects the use of coercive state power to provide significant, legally mandated occasions for those directly affected by or responsible for the conduct at issue to participate in evaluating the relationship between current and desired practice. This role encourages a collaborative, deliberative, and accountable problem-solving process that can be linked to collective learning and norm generation. It permits judicial involvement in addressing problems for which some state intervention is warranted to legitimate norms and prompt corrective action, even though coercion through rule enforcement may not be justified or workable. I take the less familiar position of advocating greater use of the nonformal or interactive—within courts and outside—to develop norms specifically to deal with a problem that otherwise resists redress: complex discrimination.

I am not suggesting that courts give up their formal rule elaboration role under the right circumstances. The hammer of rule enforcement is a necessary backdrop, both substantively and procedurally, for the judiciary's facilitative role. I instead suggest that scholars and judges explicitly tailor the relationship between dispute processing institutions and the development of substantive norms. The overarching insistence on judicial imposition of the "right" legal rule places considerable strain on both the law and the courts. As I have discussed elsewhere (Sturm, 2001, p. 458; Sturm, 2002) the complex problems revealed by institutional and behavioral analysis of discrimination resist resolution by either generally applicable rules or private, decentralized norms. Relying on purely private solutions suffers from the mirror image of these problems.

This seemingly intractable dilemma—legal intervention as both necessary and problematic—hinges on shared premises about law and judicial role. I want to step back from the substantive equality debate to examine these unarticulated yet foundational conceptions of the law and the judiciary. This analysis builds on the observation that a significant portion of legitimate "law-making" results from much more dynamic and judicially de-centered interactions than accounted for by the conventional narrative, both within the workplace context and between formal and informal legal actors (Suchman and Edelman, 1996, p. 903). Moreover, I argue that law's role should include creating occasions and incentives for non-state actors to deliberate about norms in context, and to construct conditions of permeability between legal and non-legal actors so that formal law can legitimately and effectively take account of informal normative activity and vice versa. This expansion in conceptions of law's role holds considerable promise in resolving the regulatory dilemma posed by complex discrimination.

This chapter begins by demonstrating the formalistic conception of judicial process and role that recurs in discrimination scholarship. It then briefly discusses the limitations of this conception of the judiciary, drawing on the interdisciplinary insights used by scholars to critique anti-discrimination doctrine. Finally, building on earlier work, it suggests a conception of the judiciary role that emphasizes creating spaces for normative engagement and acting as a catalyst for effective norm elaboration and remediation.

1. UNPACKING THE IMPLICIT ASSUMPTIONS ABOUT LAW AND LEGAL PROCESS

1.1. The Form and Function of Equality Norms

Scholars disagree about the judiciary's proper response to complex and structural discrimination. Their proposals run the gamut, from assuming direct managerial responsibility (Selmi, 2003) to reformulating legal rules (Oppenheimer, 1993, p. 899; Schultz, 1998, p. 1693) to refraining from ruling at all (Wax, 1999, p. 1129). Despite these profound differences, many intellectual adversaries become fellow travelers when it comes to their implicit view of a legal equality norm's form and function. They agree that legal equality norms are, or at least should be, rules that establish boundaries between lawful and unlawful conduct. These rules must be sufficiently clear, consistent, and general to justify attaching coercive consequences to the rule's violation.

An example demonstrates the rule-enforcement conception's centrality in equality scholarship. In her important article, *The Content of Our Categories*, Linda Krieger embraces a rule-enforcement/boundary-setting definition of legal equality norms. She expresses skepticism about proposals that would impose a duty upon employers to reduce "cognitively based judgment errors." Her reservations stem from the current lack of certainty or clarity about how to understand and remediate the problem. Krieger concludes that courts should not intervene until "we know enough about how to reduce cognition-based judgment errors to enable us to translate such a duty into workable legal rules . . . If our goal is to reduce race, gender, and ethnicity-based categorical responses, the imposition of a duty of care without defining what specific actions an employer should undertake to fulfill that duty could prove counterproductive" (Krieger, 1995, pp. 1245, 1247. For other examples, see Schultz, 1998, p. 1683, Post, 2000, pp. 1, 17, 30).

Even scholars analyzing legal equality norms operating outside of courts and inside organizations employ a formalistic conception of legal norms. For example, *Internal Dispute Resolution: The Transformation of Civil Rights in the Workplace,* explores the tension between legal and organizational norms and practices in complaint handlers' approaches to resolving discrimination complaints (Edelman, Erlanger, and Lande, 1993, p. 497). The authors conclude that law plays a very peripheral role in complaint handlers' orientation toward discrimination. The formalistic conception of law they apply in evaluating complaint handlers' approaches plays a critical role in reaching their conclusion. For them, "a major goal of legal forums is to define and announce the boundaries of compliance" (Edelman, Erlanger, and Lande, 1993, p. 511). They posit that "claims framed in terms of rights are often absolute" (Edelman, Erlanger, and Lande, 1993, p. 505). If law is ambiguous or procedurally oriented, it departs from the ideal of "law." Moreover, formal legal standards constitute key indicators of law's presence (Edelman, Erlanger, and Lande, 1993, p. 513). When complaint handlers construe anti-discrimination law as requiring fair, unbiased treatment, rather than "adopting the calculus of the courts and EEO agencies," the authors interpret their conduct to signal a shift from law to management (Edelman, Erlanger, and Lande, 1993, p. 513).

A legal norm thus operates under this view as a code of conduct that gives rise to clear obligations to address well-understood problems with clear normative implications. Legal pronouncements should settle disagreements or uncertainties about the nature and scope of problematic activity and its relationship to the generally articulated constitutional or statutory principles calling for judicial interpretation. Less formal and definitive norms, such as those produced through judicially accountable agreements or emerging from administrative- or expert-facilitated problem solving, do not count as legal norms. Nor do the processes requiring parties to generate information and engage in self-assessment about whether legal norms have been violated. Legal norms are the substantive product of post-adjudicatory deliberation by a court, adoption of enforceable regulations by an administrative agency, or statutory enactment by the legislature. Given the EEOC's current inability to promulgate binding regulations and the legislature's enactment of predominantly open-ended statutes, development of legal equality norms for many scholars thus depends on judicial elaboration.

This type of equality norm presupposes the judiciary's capacity to define and redress the problem through centralized articulation of an appropriate legal rule. Complex, poorly understood or normatively uncertain problems strain judicial capacity to craft and justify robust legal rules. These attributes underlie the queasiness apparent in many scholars' efforts to craft rule-based solutions for complex discrimination. The worry is that courts will get it wrong or, in getting it right, compromise their legitimacy as principled elaborators of public norms.

1.2. The Role of the Judiciary

The picture of a court that emerges from the anti-discrimination literature is that of a unilateral norm elaborator and enforcer. The judicial task is to figure out what abstract legal norms mean in particular contexts, and then to determine what to order others to do to comply with those more fully elaborated norms (and compensate those injured by noncompliance). The judge's defining role is to produce certain and specific outcomes that will differentiate lawful from unlawful conduct and dictate effective remedies for the latter. Through adjudication, judicial participation in law-making achieves legitimacy: it is public, norm- or precedent-generating, and accountable. Settlement necessarily removes a dispute from the realm of public law and potential norm generation. Underlying much scholarship is the assumption that, when courts deviate from formal adjudication of liability (which they do frequently), they no longer engage in norm elaboration and they depart from their core competency (Molot, 2003).

Judicial decisions resulting from formal adversary process are the hallmark of legitimate and effective judicial action. They receive inputs (evidence and arguments) and produce outputs (legal rules, judgments, and sanctions for noncompliance).

Paradigmatic judicial involvement takes place in the courtroom through receiving evidence and argument, and in chambers through detached deliberation and unilateral judgment. The judicial role in discovery and pre-trial motion practice is to narrow and properly frame the issues requiring judicial decision through adjudication and to eliminate issues for which adversary process is unnecessary or inappropriate. Remedial determinations are subsidiary to and in service of the core function of liability determination. Experts and affected stakeholders do not participate in elaborating norms; their role is to supply facts, interpretations, and legal arguments, which are then processed by the judicial decision-maker. Interactions outside of those stylized spaces and forms lack the imprimatur of the adversary process, and thus adjudication's presumption of accountability, transparency, and legitimacy.

Owen Fiss has perhaps the most romantic articulation of this directorial conception of judicial role. The central task of the judiciary is to give operative meaning to constitutional values by searching for "what is true, right or just" (Fiss, 1979, pp. 1, 9). Although Fiss' faith in judicial truth-telling makes him somewhat of an outlier, his basic conception of the judge as unilateral decision-maker is more widely shared. Often, this conception operates implicitly, cropping up in the section of the article that proposes doctrinal reform. This scholarship does not necessarily focus on the court's role in addressing discrimination. Its emphasis, instead, is on demonstrating (quite effectively, I might add) that prevailing doctrinal categories distort or misdirect judges' analyses of employers' decision-making processes (Krieger, 1995; Schultz, 1998, p. 1683; Oppenheimer, 1993, p. 899) or that unstated norms and empirical assumptions dictate judicial outcomes in discrimination cases (Minow, 1987, pp. 88–89; Post, 2000, pp. 1, 17, 30). Relying on insights drawn from psychology, organizational theory, sociology, and critical theory, these scholars show how prevailing doctrinal fails to account for the role of cognitive bias, dominant value structures, and the practices of racial and gender conventions. When it comes to proposing remedies for these empirical and conceptual blind spots, all eyes turn to the judge, or more precisely, to the judge's capacity to craft new rules or frameworks that are adequately sensitive to the complexities of race, gender, and other "practices" of difference. Does the court have the right operative framework for understanding and explaining the social practices of gender and race? (Post, 2000, pp. 1, 17, 30; Schultz, 1998, p. 1683). Do "we know enough about how to reduce cognition-based judgment errors to enable us to translate such a duty into workable legal rules"? (Krieger, 1995, p. 1245).

These questions lead one to ask how courts elaborate specific standards, particularly when they are interpreting ambiguous legal texts. Again, Fiss is perhaps the most didactic in his discussion of method. Particularly in cases involving injunctive relief, judges use intuition, logic, and analogy to apply general law to specific facts and then to issue pronouncements. "The text clothes the court with the authority to give specific meaning to the ideal of equity—to choose among the various subgoals contained within the ideal" (Fiss, 1979b, p. 173). What is needed is just the right rule. If judges get good enough information through the adjudicative process, processed through the right cognitive frame, they can provide just that.

Other scholars have taken a less sanguine view of purely intuitive, logical, and textual methods for developing and applying discrimination doctrine. They challenge the capacity of judges to stand outside the practices they must assess, showing instead that "anti-discrimination law always begins and ends in history, which means that it must participate in the very practices that it seeks to alter and to regulate" (Post, 2000, p. 17). They strive to expand judges' capacities to identify their own preconceptions and stereotypes, and to learn from experts presenting current empirical understandings of discrimination and from those with unfamiliar and suppressed perspectives. Acknowledging that judges, as humans, cannot self-identify the range of perspectives that they are failing to see or the preconceptions that are influencing their decision-making, these scholars gesture toward expanding participation by experts (Krieger, 2003, p. 7) amici, and parties in the adjudicative process (Minow, 1987, p. 88–89).

Yet, these scholars seem to accept the hegemony of a rule elaboration and enforcement regime, with judges developing norms exclusively by imposing a decision, after full consideration of competing perspectives and data. According to this conception, judges dictate the details of legal norms as they apply to new circumstances. For norm elaboration to occur, they assume that the judiciary must choose among competing views about how to give concrete meaning to ambiguous standards, rather than facilitate a participatory process of public, accountable, informed, and principled norm elaboration.[1] Even in cases involving other public bodies involved in some norm-generating role, such as administrative agencies, the focus is primarily on evaluating whether the agency got it right, or at least whether they acted within their authority in interpreting and enforcing the applicable norm. Once a court rules on the applicability of legal norms in a particular case, extended interaction (either with the court or within the relevant institution) questioning the meaning and implementation of the legal norm suggests failure—failure to articulate a precise enough rule, failure to embody the ideal of dispassionate adjudication, or failure to achieve compliance with the applicable rule.

This formalistic conception of law may explain why some discrimination scholars question the legitimacy and desirability of more interactive, consent-based resolutions of conflicts involving public norms. Scholars like Fiss are "against settlement" because they assume that resolution by agreement necessarily detracts from the judiciary's core function of articulating public values (Fiss, 1984, p. 1073). Conflict resolution that takes place outside of formal adjudication is "bargaining in the shadow of the

[1] For example, Linda Krieger's remedy for the current gap between Title VII doctrine and current psychological theory is to have legal actors "accurately and completely specify the various ways in which race can adversely skew an employment decision maker's perception and judgment of a particular applicant or employee and adversely affect his or her employment opportunities." (Krieger, 2003). The adversarial, jurocentric method for revising legal norms remains uninterrogated, but the substance of current doctrine is "naturalized" to reflect developments in empirical social science. Krieger acknowledges the promise of soft law such as jury instructions and advocate argumentation, but seems to value these legal forms as avenues leading to a fully elaborated, judicially imposed specification of desired norms, behaviors, levers, and doctrinal models, rather than as appropriate sites for ongoing and contingent norm elaboration.

law,"—at best a distant and non-binding approximation of public values and more likely a product of personal preferences discounted by bargaining power. Settlement and internal dispute resolution (IDR) are taken necessarily to mean the inevitable privatization and managerialization of law, thereby undermining its normative force (Edelman, Uggen, and Erlanger, 1999, pp. 406, 442).

This view of judicial role, method, and relationship places employment discrimination remedies involving institutional redesign in an uneasy relationship to the articulation of rights. Remedies for complex discrimination often involve redesigning systems, transforming institutional culture, and realigning incentives—practices that connect to but extend beyond the conduct constituting the legal violation. The liability norm does not provide criteria for choosing among those values unrelated to the legal violation itself, although it does shape the definition of the problem to be remedied. For example, a legal violation may consist of maintaining an arbitrary selection system that fosters decision-making biased against women. A non-arbitrary system could take a variety of forms, depending on considerations unrelated to bias minimization (such as efficiency and consistency with organizational culture). Why should judges make these decisions, if judicial legitimacy depends upon adversary process designed to interpret constitutional or statutory principles, and these principles do not govern remedial decision-making? The judiciary as rule-elaborator and enforcer thus faces a legitimacy deficit when it unilaterally imposes remedial choices (Fiss, 1984, p. 1073).

Remedial solutions developed by intermediaries, such as monitors, masters, and experts employed by the judiciary to shore up their remedial design capacity, are similarly suspect. Intermediaries who facilitate the participatory formulation of remedies by affected parties do not invite the same legitimacy problems, but their role tends to be viewed as expedient rather than principled, designed to settle particular disputes and not to generate public norms.

1.3. The Relationship between Legal and Workplace Norms

How does (and should) law interact with organizational and cultural norms to reshape the conditions and practices constituting complex discrimination? This law–norm interaction is quite important to the identification and remediation of complex discrimination. The question, for example, of whether reasonable people would experience conduct as hostile and abusive involves an inquiry into the relevant expectations, power relationships, and gender patterns (*Harris v. Forklift Systems, Inc.*, 1993). Professional norms about effective management and grievance processing may affect judicial allocation of legal responsibility for detecting and responding to exclusionary practices (*Faragher v. City of Boca Rotan*, 1998; Edelman, Uggen, and Erlanger, 1999). Effective remedial decision-making also depends on successfully negotiating the relationship between law and norms. Complex bias reflects and is sustained by organizational norms, incentives, and practices. Changing exclusionary practices requires addressing the interaction of identities such as gender and race with power, merit, and status within particular normative communities (Minow, 1987, pp. 88–89; Post, 2000, p. 17; Sturm, 2001, p. 478).

Scholars (and courts) have long recognized law's influence, as well as its dependence upon cultural and social norms (See Engel and Munger, 1996; Yngvesson, 1988; McCann 1994). Indeed, employment discrimination law's paramount aim has often been described as fostering informal norms of equal participation in the workplace, and its primary obstacle as the resistance of informal normative systems to formal legal intervention. But formal conceptions of law permeate public law scholars' analysis of *how* law influences informal norms: the stock story emphasizes the output of formal legal process determined by judges. Law influences norms, if at all, by judicial calibration of the rules and the remedial consequences of their violation. Law is produced in the courthouse and the legislature by formal state actors with official power to generate and enforce law. Non-judicial actors operate in the world of cultural and social norms, and as consumers, manipulators, or resistors of these legal products. The impact of the processes producing legal outcomes, and of the interactions of formal legal actors with stakeholders outside the domains producing formal legal outputs, does not figure into the law–norm relationship.

In the "law and norms" literature, for example, the law–norm relationship has often been posed as a choice: are the courts (through the imposition of legal rules) better at formulating the appropriate across-the-board norm, or are private actors operating through market interactions, custom and practice more able to develop workable norms? (Rock and Wachter, 1996, p. 1913). Will coercive enforcement disrupt prevailing norms and incentives of non-legal actors or simply underscore their legitimacy? (Bernstein, 1996, 1769; Charny, 1996, pp. 1841, 1852). Depending upon the answer to these questions, many scholars recommend a legal outcome: the law should incorporate, supplant, or defer to informal norms. Thus, the question of whether courts should intervene to address complex discrimination would be cast in terms of whether courts have the capacity to figure out what informal norms or processes are and should be. If so, the courts will tailor a legal rule based on that correct understanding. If not, they will stay out.

The concept of "bargaining in the shadow of the law," coined by Robert Mnookin and Louis Kornhauser in a much-cited article (Mnookin and Kornhauser, 1979, p. 950) acknowledges that law and norms interact, but this analysis focuses on law's formalistic aspects. Law casts a shadow on negotiations and decisions that take place outside of formal legal process. Legal rules establish the range within which informal settlements operate, and can even influence the terms governing informal agreements by legitimating particular principles dictating how the case would come out in court. Non-legal actors take law into account as the outer boundary of their private conflict resolution. If law does migrate into the language of organizational culture, some commentators treat this translation process as necessarily denoting privatization and managerialization (not internalization or elaboration) (Edelman, Uggen, and Erlanger, 1999, pp. 406, 442). Nor does the "shadow of the law" metaphor take account of any impact that non-legal norms have on the development of the legal principles.

As Edelman, Uggan, and Erlanger have shown, the causal arrows can go in both directions: the results of the norm generation process in each domain influence the substantive calculus in the other (Edelman, Uggen, and Erlanger, 1999, p. 406). Edelman and co-authors point out the "endogeneity" of legal norms: courts sometimes incorporate the norms of regulated groups into the judicial formulation of the legal rules. This work also documents the important role of norm intermediaries—lawyers, human resource professionals, organizational consultants—in transporting norms between legal and organizational domains (Edelman, Uggen, and Erlanger, 1999, p. 406). Their account, however, emphasizes law's formal dimensions—adversary process and the legal rules it produces. Intermediation of formal law takes place outside legal process, in informal, professional or managerial networks. In this narrative, courts act as passive consumers of normative outputs produced by non-legal actors outside of the legal domain. The judiciary does not actively shape how local or professional norms take account of existing legal norms, or the circumstances under these informal norms will influence public and enforceable legal norms.

2. THE VALUE OF BRIDGING LAW AND NORMS

It is striking to contrast scholars' static paradigm of judicial role with their dynamic analysis of discrimination that drives the critique of the dominant doctrinal paradigm. Formalism is problematic as a method of norm elaboration for complex discrimination. General rules do not really tell you much about how structural bias operates in particular settings, or why challenged decisions or processes are exclusionary. Detailed prescriptions are problematic because, as detached, centralized adjudicators, the judiciary lacks the deep knowledge of local circumstance or the occasions for ongoing adaptation to context needed to solve local problems. Judicial mastery of a particular workplace dynamic does not get around the dilemma of generalizability; moreover, it will likely trigger concerns about judicial legitimacy and competence, not to mention questions about judicial resources.

Yet, complete privatization abandons the law's role in generating public norms. It would also relegate the intended beneficiaries of employment discrimination laws to the informal norms, power dynamics, and problem solving capacities of their particular workplace. For this reason, many scholars worry about the trend to encourage informal resolution of employment discrimination disputes (Silbey and Sarat, 1989; Delgado et al. 1985; Grillo, 1991). Insistence on rule elaboration and enforcement as the preferred mode of judicial interaction thus disables courts in responding to conditions that implicate publicly articulated values.

Identification, definition, and remediation of group-based inequality require a process of problem solving. Situated knowledge generated through reflective interaction may be more productive than detached logical consideration in identifying the normative significance of challenged practices, what sustains them, and how they can be changed. It may be important to know how particular practices affect members of identified groups, how and why those patterns persist over time, what they mean for the status of group members, and whether alternatives exist that could minimize exclusion. That process identifies the structural dimensions of a problem through an insistent inquiry of tracing back to root causes. It enables participants to articulate norms in context as part of the process of determining why particular circumstances pose a problem requiring remediation. It encourages organizations to gather and share information enabling that analysis to proceed. It emphasizes developing individual and institutional capacity and incentives to respond to problems thus revealed. It fosters the design, evaluation, and comparison of solutions that involve the stakeholders who participate in the day-to-day patterns that produce bias and exclusion. It also entails reframing the aspirations motivating change to reflect these interlocking problems and constituencies. Legal rules resulting from logical analysis do not elucidate the aims, scope, and strategies of this essential problem solving.

As a practical matter, judges and litigants resist participation in rule-enforcement type judicial regulation of complex discrimination. Courts have been extremely reluctant to assume direct responsibility for constructing managerial solutions for subtle bias, based on concerns about institutional competence, resource constraints, and uncertainty about the problem itself. Employees are reluctant to utilize formal process to complain about practices that they are not sure count as discrimination. Employers resist identifying problems within their workplace if they perceive that doing so will essentially do plaintiffs' counsel's work for them. In fact, the formalistic, adjudicatory, rule-enforcement paradigm does not fully describe how judges in fact fulfill their norm elaboration function. The prospect of continued judicial involvement in addressing complex discrimination thus necessitates surfacing these less formal judicial modes and expanding law beyond the model of judiciary as a rule-enforcer.

3. LAW AS CATALYST OF NORMATIVE ELABORATION AND PROBLEM SOLVING

3.1. Expanding the Form and Function of Equality Norms

Rules enforced by sanctions remain as an important backstop and platform for normative elaboration in the area of equality jurisprudence. Some conduct violates clear and well-understood principles. At this point in our history, deliberate exclusion based on race, sex, religion or age is a normatively easy case, as is quid pro quo sexual harassment. (*Burlington Industries, Inc. v. Ellerth, Inc.*, 1998). Rules solidify and preserve well-established baseline norms and aspirations. They also legitimate normative discourse about the domains they regulate. Rules dictating that defendants "stop doing that!" can effectively remedy deliberate discrimination. Compensation to those harmed by intentional discrimination seems directly connected to the wrongful conduct and important to law's purpose and legitimacy. Moreover, the hammer of substantial compensatory damages and coercive sanctions may be necessary as a first step toward an effective problem solving approach. This approach depends on the presence of some company insiders who assume responsibility for interpreting law to prompt internal norm elaboration and implementation. Coercion is sometimes needed to bring companies to the point where they take equity problems seriously, particularly in companies that have denied the existence of or resisted to addressing pervasive discrimination. Courts' facilitative role depends for its legitimacy and effectiveness on the continued operation of legal rules backed by coercive sanctions in areas of normative consensus and simplicity.

What about the role of equality norms in addressing more complicated, less well-understood bias—problems that cannot be isolated to a particular act or actor, that involve dynamics of interaction and evaluation producing marginalization or exclusion, or that are inextricably linked with activities that we actually value? Is there any way for courts to participate in norm elaboration for problems that resist resolution through rules? Can equality norms be dynamic, responsive, and contextually contingent and still robust, in the sense of influencing private actors to engage in normatively desirable conduct?

A facilitative, reflexive, and structural conception of law's form and function (building on such conceptions developed in international human rights and corporate governance domains) offers a way forward (Scott and Trubek, 2002). In areas of normative and remedial uncertainty and complexity, the function of judicially articulated legal norms is not to establish definitive boundaries of acceptable conduct which, if violated, warrant sanction. It is instead to prompt—and create occasions for—normatively motivated inquiry and remediation by non-legal actors in response to signals of problematic conditions or practices. This legal equality norm is one of inquiry, analysis, reflection, and remediation. Law imposes an obligation to inquire upon a showing of an unexplained pattern of bias. The legal consequence of exposing a discrimination problem through this normative inquiry is not the imposition of a sanction; it is instead the imposition of a legally enforceable obligation to correct the problem. This attenuation (but not elimination) of coercion relieves the pressure for a clear, before-the-fact rule (which is needed to justify sanctions for failure to comply) and still maintains incentives and opportunities to elaborate robust norms in context.[2]

Law's involvement sustains the normative dimension as a relevant and legitimate part of the problem solving process. It creates occasions and incentives for parties to convene, thereby solving collective action problems. It introduces "rule of law" values (such as participation, transparency, and reasoned decision-making) to deliberations by non-judicial actors. Courts and other public institutions also provide the architecture to compare and build on the outcomes of this contextual problem solving. Over time, this process promotes the development new legal norms when clear, recurring patterns and normative consensus emerge.

[2] In a similar vein, Silbey and Sarat show that because informal conflict resolution does not require violation of the law to trigger action and does not stigmatize participants, intervention can be earlier and unconstrained by jurisdictional boundaries (Silbey and Sarat, 1989).

There is a procedural dimension to this substantive responsibility to inquire about identified and unexplained problems. What if we think about the exercise of judicial power to prompt inquiry on a continuum? Each phase of the conflict resolution process offers an occasion for bringing together affected and potentially responsible stakeholders to deliberate, albeit with different levels of legal obligation to take action on what is learned from that inquiry.

What makes a condition or practice sufficiently "problematic" to trigger an obligation to correct? More specifically, how would a plaintiff make prima facie showing that a condition or practice sufficiently implicates constitutional or liability concerns? Congress has articulated general, ambiguous equality norms that potentially comprise a variety of equality theories, or mediating principles, such as anti-subordination, equal access, or equal treatment. Individuals or groups affected by these conditions would offer evidence permitting the conclusion that a condition or pattern of exclusion, unequal treatment, or subordination exists. This could be done through statistical evidence, through benchmarking the conditions in a particular firm against other comparable organizations with more inclusive practices, or through methodologically accountable expert testimony.

A signal of problematic conditions or conduct is an identifiable set of circumstances that give reason for concern about compliance with equality norms. Courts and administrative agencies can and indeed have begun to identify indicators of potentially discriminatory conditions or practices. Enduring and unexplained patterns of lower promotion rates by members of particular groups, accompanied by arbitrary and highly decentralized decision-making practices, are one such signal. Unequal participation by the targeted group in informal networks or unequal access to mentors and training is another. Conduct or comments of a sexual or gendered nature, but that are susceptible of multiple interpretations, are the third. These practices may not alone signify gender or racial bias. But in some contexts and circumstances, they do, particularly in the absence of investigation and institutional response (*Dukes v. Wal-mart Stores, Inc.*, 2004). When the problem is complex and contextually contingent, the court lacks an adequate basis for imposing a unitary, overarching mediating principle. It is in a position, however, to trigger attention to a potential problem, and to stimulate problem solving that engages with the normative significance of this potentially problematic activity.

One interesting aspect of these signals is that they demonstrate the role of remedy in defining the normative significance of complex bias. An uninterrogated pattern of exclusion or subtle harassment often looms larger and may produce greater inequality than that same conduct when followed by prompt investigation, analysis, and change. The institution's failure to respond contributes to and indeed, can become a crucial element of the discrimination experience. This is in part because of the incremental, cumulative, and systemic causes of much complex discrimination (Cole, 1991). In these areas, inequality can result from the interaction of micro-level interactions and inadequate structural responses that interrupt these cumulative patterns. Conversely, prompt inquiry into and remediation of problematic conditions or practices can affect whether that pattern ultimately produces, and is experienced as producing, discrimination. The capacity to identify and respond to problems is thus integrally related to the normative significance of the underlying conditions. Process becomes part of the substantive meaning of equality. Elaborating a general norm in context is crucial to formulating a remedial response, which in turn deepens and even alters the understanding of the aspirational norm. This dynamic relationship between problem identification and remediation provides further support for expanding beyond rules for complex discrimination.

3.2. The Role of the Judiciary

Is there a role for the judiciary in this norm elaboration and capacity building process? More precisely, is there a role that is consistent with the judiciary's practices, competencies, self-conceptions, and institutional role? Are there ways, in addition to formal adjudication, for courts to participate in public, accountable norm elaboration? Can they engage in a less directorial relationship to non-legal actors in the norm generation process and still act like judges?

Crafting a workable judicial role is doable. But it requires expanding our analytical lens beyond liability decisions. It also entails generating judicial legitimacy theories that are grounded in a critical examination of actual judicial practices that intervene in and influence workplace norms. This inquiry moves beyond formalistic notions of law and judicial role, just as more nuanced understanding of discrimination resulted from a functional and institutional methodology. The full range of norm-generating activity in which the courts and legal actors participate must be included, as well as the array of actual and potential channels for making that normative activity transparent, public, and precedential.

This pragmatist analysis also takes seriously the impact of courts' concurrent and, for many judges, core function as adjudicators on their non-adjudicatory activities, and how that identity constrains judicial role development. In this sense, this approach differs from the position articulated by Feeley and Rubin that judges are just like other public actors in their role as implementers of public policy. Feeley and Rubin advocate that we "assign the judge the same range of tasks that are assigned to other administrators" (Feeley and Rubin, 2002, pp. 249, 262). Their analysis of judicial legitimacy and efficacy lumps together distinct forms of judicial problem solving activity, from director to broker to catalyst (Sturm, 1990, p. 305). This blanket acceptance of judicial managerialism glosses over valid concerns about certain types of judicial intervention. The legitimacy (and, in my view, long term efficacy) of a judge who assumes direct responsibility for institutional redesign differs markedly from that of a judge who uses the tools and processes of the judiciary to prompt responsible actors to engage in effective problem solving. Judges' willingness to participate in problem solving under conditions of complexity turns on the availability of a role that is consistent with their tools, practices, and relationships.

I have identified three related judicial roles that operate in this intersection of efficacy and legitimacy:

1. Structuring occasions for collective norm development and problem solving in the penumbra of formal judicial process;
2. Increasing non-legal actors' capacity to conduct conflict resolution and problem solving that generates and institutionalizes efficient, fair, and workable norms; and
3. Developing the capacity of mediating actors, such as experts and administrative agencies, to connect the domains of formal and informal norms.

Legal norms thus develop not only through liability determinations, but also through legally structured occasions for deliberating about the relationship between norms and practice. These practices cast courts in a crucial but limited role in addressing problems that implicate public norms but are insufficiently understood and/or resistant to centralized rule enforcement. They emphasize law's role in structuring focal points of intra- and inter-institutional normative activity (Charny, 1996, p. 1841). Each of these roles could be (and will be) the subject of its own article. I undertake here only to give enough concrete meaning to these roles to allow a discussion about their viability and desirability as role conception for addressing complex discrimination.

3.2.1. Norm Generation in the Penumbra of Formal Adjudication

Discussions of courts' role in elaborating equality norms typically involve liability determinations (or, in the critiques of alternative dispute resolution, the absence thereof): Have courts rendered a published opinion determining whether liability does or could flow from the application of legal norm to a particular set of facts? (Albiston, 1999, p. 869). This focus on liability determinations and rule-making as the location of normative elaboration is understandable. These determinations produce a public norm in the form of a published opinion, which is widely available and serves as a guide or binding precedent for future decisions. Published opinions are the result of a formal process designed to enable participation and principled decision-making. This process also incorporates caution, certainty, and predictability that justify the state's imposition of coercive authority.

Liability determinations are not, however, the most frequent or necessarily the preferred occasions for judicial participation in norm elaboration about complex discrimination. Courts regularly participate in deliberations about the meaning and scope of norms as a necessary part of reaching other decisions that are less directly tied to coercive imposition of rules or liability. They do this both by assessing the potential viability of discrimination theories in pre-liability (and sometimes post-liability) decisions and by structuring occasions for parties to deliberate about the normative implications of complex discrimination and strategies for their remediation as part of moving a case forward. In both the roles, courts can participate in and foster normative development in a more open-ended and exploratory posture. Judicial involvement can also influence the way non-legal actors negotiate and deliberate, by focusing on the methods of inquiry and governance structures that produce informal norms and agreements, and by weighting more heavily those outcomes that result from principled, accountable, and participatory practices. Courts could also encourage and facilitate sharing the results of less formal norm elaboration in its penumbra to encourage public norm development, by discouraging confidential settlements, publishing opinions concerning informal agreements implicating public norms, and maintaining a publicly accessible database containing court-approved settlements. These steps would and increase the legitimacy and accountability of informal norm elaboration.

It is important to emphasize that this does not mean necessarily requiring processes that mirror the features of formal adjudication. As Winston has argued, "the form due process should take depends crucially on the setting in which it finds its application. Specific norms or rules should depend on the purpose of the enterprise and even its stage of development" (Winston, 2002, pp. 389, 392). Indeed, under some circumstances, insisting on adversary process as the measure of fair and effective process would defeat the deeper values motivating due process, such as participation, information generation, and effective problem solving, by importing the previously discussed limitations of a rule-enforcement approach into the informal arena. Courts would instead encourage parties to develop (and the court would then assess the adequacy of) functional criteria of adequate process in light of the purposes and attributes of the particular project. Processes or outcomes could be precedential (in the sense of providing a normative or remedial solution that others can learn from) even if they are not formally binding. Parties' full and fair participation could be achieved through creative institutional design and governance, even if they are not represented by counsel. Decisions could be public and norm generating, even if they are not published by Westlaw and Lexis. Courts could develop standards for evaluating informal agreements and expert opinions, and validate those that give general legal norms concrete meaning in the particular context, articulate criteria by which their agreements can be evaluated, and generate the information needed to evaluate resulting normative assessments and agreements.

The judicial process builds in a variety of decision points that invite less binding norm elaboration. Norm elaboration occurs as part of a decision about whether to keep the judicial machinery open as a public forum for engaging with a particular type of problem. One could look at decisions denying summary judgment in the same light (Albiston, 1999, p. 869). The decision at stake may also involve the question of who can legitimately participate in the problem-solving process. It sometimes entails assessments of the type and quality of information needed to participate in the problem solving process or to justify reaching a particular outcome. These types of questions cast the court in a role beyond determining whether to impose liability for violation of a rule. Courts either consciously or unwittingly craft process frameworks that potentially shape the capacity and incentives of non-legal actors to engage in effective problem solving and accountable norm elaboration. These non-binding occasions for normative elaboration have the potential to be public, norm generating, accountable, and precedential, if these terms are given principled rather than formalistic meaning. If, for example, consent decrees are published and used as benchmarks of new normative understandings and remedial responses, they can have general and precedential value even if they are not binding (Galanter, 1988, p. 55). Web publication and developing professional practice networks make possible the dissemination of informal normative activity.

A few examples might help clarify the meaning of norm elaboration in the penumbra of judicial rule enforcement. Class certification decisions require courts to assess plaintiffs' theory of discrimination in deciding whether there are questions of law and fact common to the class, that the representative claims are typical, and that remediation would warrant an injunction affecting the class as a whole (Rule 23, F.R.C.P.). Class certification decisions frequently discuss in some detail the types of problems asserted as discriminatory by plaintiffs and whether they are sufficient systemic to warrant class treatment (*Dukes v. Wal-mart Stores, Inc.*, 2004; *Latino Officers Association City of New York v. City of New York*, 2002; *Webb v. Merck & Co.*, 2002; *Beck v. Boeing*, 2001; *Butler v. Home Depot, Inc.*, 1996). This is not a determination of the likelihood of success at trial (Bone and Evans, 2002, p. 1251), but rather one of whether the case is in a posture to warrant group-based resolution. Class certification also can create a framework for assessing whether participants engage in legitimate and effective information gathering, problem solving, and norm generation once a class is certified. It functions as a focal point for defining the contours of a conflict, identifying the participants (including employees, key company officials, and outside experts) who should be involved, developing the data needed to understand if and why systemic problems persist, and creating ground rules for effective and accountable participation. Class certification is thus an occasion to establish a governance structure that can produce fair, effective, and principled norm generation (Issachoroff, 1999, pp. 337, 367). It is particularly important because most cases settle following class certification.

Similarly, the decision to approve a class action settlement, if taken seriously by the court, involves an assessment of the adequacy of the process that produces the settlement as well as the reasonableness of the settlement itself. Judicial opinions evaluating the adequacy of settlements also address the plaintiffs' theories of discrimination and remediation as part of the process of determining whether the proposed settlement is reasonable. Although this inquiry is too often a judicial rubber stamp, it need not be. It does offer an occasion for the court, which some courts have taken seriously, to review the adequacy of the governance process and the resulting agreement. Courts could develop criteria for evaluating settlements that would take seriously the norm elaboration function of consent decrees, even if the terms of the agreement do not constitute precedent in the formal sense of the word. They could pay attention to the process by which decrees are formulated, the adequacy of participation, and the sufficiency of the information generated through the problem solving process. This type of process review might remedy the legitimacy deficit courts face in monitoring and enforcing consent decrees by offering a process-based justification for backing a private agreement with state enforcement resources and authority. The prospect of a robust process evaluation could induce parties to develop meaningful ways of including affected stakeholders, to develop a workable problem solving process as part of the negotiations, and to elaborate the equality theory underlying the settlement, whether it would in fact present a viable claim at trial (*Molski v. Gleich*, 2000). They may also spell out the parties' remediation theories and strategies.

Decisions about the admissibility and weight of expert testimony also require courts to assess the adequacy and viability of plaintiffs' discrimination theories (*Butler v. Home Depot, Inc.*, 1997; *Collier v. Bradley University*, 2000). A relevancy determination necessarily involves consideration of the relationship between the expert evidence and an underlying theory of discrimination (Walker and Monahan, 1988, p. 877; Meares and Harcourt, 2000, p. 733). For example, as part of its consideration of the admissibility of expert testimony, the court in *Butler v. Home Depot* articulated several possible discrimination theories that would support the relevance of expert testimony "as to the causes, manifestations, and consequences of gender stereotyping as well as the organizational circumstances which allow such stereotypes to flourish" (Meares and Harcourt, 2000, p. 1264). These included the failure of Home Depot to take steps to correct stereotyped decision-making, notwithstanding its awareness that the problem existed and that current practices were inadequate to remedy the resulting gender bias.

Broadening conceptions of judicial role to include prompting and keeping open normative deliberation could provide a workable framework for courts' pre- and post-liability involvement with complex discrimination. Decisions about discovery, party and expert participation, settlement, and out-of-court problem solving would be seen as occasions to (1) bring together those with responsibility for, knowledge of, concern about, and expertise in the potentially problematic conditions; (2) establish the heightened authority and validity of non-adjudicatory deliberations that functionally satisfy core legitimacy and accountability concerns; (3) create incentives for non-judicial actors to develop and demonstrate the capacity to solve problems and to identify the norms and criteria by which those problem solving practices should be evaluated; and (4) share and evaluate the results of this problem solving and conflict resolution. Courts would focus less on getting it right all by themselves and more on determining whether there is sufficient reason to be concerned about complex discrimination to warrant sustained and publicly accountable problem solving by non-legal actors.

Moreover, there are some potential advantages to norm elaboration in the penumbra of judicial power that critics have not taken into account. Courts are more likely to remain involved in addressing complex discrimination if they are not imposing a general rule or assuming direct responsibility for institutional problem solving. They are also constructing an interactive relationship with those responsible for addressing complex discrimination, without actually administering private institutions. This view of judicial role enables courts to avoid the dilemmas facing courts operating solely within the rule-enforcement conception.

3.2.2. Shaping Non-Legal Actors' Participation in Effective Normative Elaboration and Remediation

Courts also shape norms for addressing complex discrimination by creating the architecture to prompt effective problem solving and conflict resolution by non-legal actors, and then developing points of permeability between legal and non-legal arenas so that public norms can emerge out of that local norm generation process. (See Sturm, 1990, p. 305). The judiciary becomes involved in addressing complex discrimination when there is a strong indication that particular systems and practices are failing in ways that fall within the purview of generally articulated equality aspirations. In contexts that resist resolution by a clearly defined rule, judicial intervention supply incentives for employers to implement effective internal problem solving and conflict resolution mechanisms, to evaluate their effectiveness, and to learn from the efforts of others facing similar problems. Coercion is used to induce employers to develop robust internal problem solving mechanisms to address and prevent structural bias, and to sanction failure to take steps needed to address identified. They do this by insisting that employers, with the help of inside and outside collaborators, develop and justify working criteria for evaluating the effectiveness of informal mechanisms. Courts are then in a position to assess employers' justification for and compliance with their effectiveness criteria. This enables courts to function as a catalyst, rather than as a de facto employment director or a deferrer to employers' unaccountable choices.

This structural role has assumed heightened significance because of the explosion of interest in ADR as a way of resolving employment discrimination disputes. Judicial doctrine has encouraged employers to develop IDR and problem solving mechanisms (*Faragher v. City of Boca Rotan*, 1998; *Burlington Industries v. Ellerth*, 1998; *Gilmer v. Interstate/Johnson Lane Corporation*, 1991). The Equal Employment Opportunity Commission has embraced mediation as a method resolving discrimination charges (McDermott, O'Barr, Jose, and Bowers, 2000; EEOC's ADR Policy Statement, 1995). Employers have instituted a wide range of dispute resolution processes, including ombuds officers, mediation, peer review, open door policies, and arbitration (Van Wezel Stone, 2001, pp. 467, 480; Sturm, 2001).

The move to ADR has raised concern among scholars and practitioners who value the judiciary's role in elaborating and holding employers accountable for compliance with public norms. The worry is that ADR (or IDR when it takes place inside an organization) is necessarily private, non-norm generating, and unaccountable. (Abraham, 2003; Edwards, 1986; Fiss, 1984, p. 1073). As David Charny put it, reliance on informal systems is problematic "because one loses the 'public goods' associated with more formal litigation: development of a set of precedents, public revelation about information about important policy matters . . . and the use of judicial decision to propagate and reinforce social norms" (Charny, 1996, p. 1852). Scholars have also expressed concern that the processes used to produce settlements may be unfair, particularly for addressing zero-sum problems involving disputants with unequal power (Abraham, 2003; Grillo, 1991; Van Wezel Stone, 2001, pp. 467, 480; Fiss, 1984, p. 1073).

This critique assumes that the move to IDR necessarily displaces judicial involvement in norm generation processes and outcomes. It also assumes that IDR is by definition individualistic (not systemic) in its orientation, private (not transparent) in its operation, instrumental (not normative) in its analysis, ad hoc (not precedent-setting) in its results, and unaccountable in its process and implementation (Edelman, Erlanger, and Lande, 1993; Grillo, 1991). To the extent that informal processes currently fit this description, these concerns are well-founded. Indeed, research shows that these processes are sometimes used to "bullet-proof" a company rather than remedy problems (Bisom-Rapp, 1999, pp. 959, 967–971; Edelman, Erlanger, and Lande, 1993). However, it is important to separate critiques of current practice from normative theories about the appropriate relationship between courts and informal conflict resolution. The judiciary can and sometimes does play a role in shaping the terms under which informal systems operate to address discrimination. Courts do have the opportunity to assess the adequacy of the processes and to consider the normative outcome of the results. When executed in keeping with this role, judicial introduces a level of accountability and genuine participation that is absent from ADR involving purely contractual norms. Judges can evaluate whether a system is sufficiently robust, accountable, and norm generating to justify private involvement in publicly relevant norm elaboration.

With judicial involvement in assessing and publicizing adequacy criteria, IDR has the potential to be norm generating, transparent, and accountable, at least at the systemic level. These systems build in a process of gathering data about recurring patterns that trigger concern about systemic problems; provide a regular mechanism for reflecting about those patterns, use employee and expert participation in designing and monitoring the system to assure its fairness and legitimacy, and institutionalize opportunities to develop and revise institutional norms and practices that respond to the problems identified through data analysis. Intel's conflict resolution system, described in *Second Generation Employment Discrimination: A Structural Approach*, has built in many of these features (Sturm, 2001, p. 489). So has the National Institute of Health in designing its Center for Cooperative Resolution, which is the subject of a current study (Center for Cooperative Resolution, 2001, Annual Report).

Courts could, and in some instances, have evaluated IDR systems with criteria that relate to the legitimacy and efficacy of the conflict resolution or problem solving process. Sexual harassment and judicial evaluation of subjective employment systems are two areas where courts have made gestures in this direction. Thus far, the criteria have been unevenly developed, without an explicit emphasis on building the capacity and incentives of non-legal actors to engage in norm elaboration and problem solving. Broadening the court's conception of its role to include this crucial function could shore up the lower courts' spotty performance to date in enforcing the Supreme Court's embrace of a structural role that measures decision-making processes in relation to their effectiveness in preventing and addressing problems. This role is also sensitive to judicial competency concerns. Courts are not themselves developing the criteria and architecture for these processes, but rather they are insisting that those who use these processes develop and justify effectiveness criteria.

3.2.3. Promoting Mediating Actors' Capacity to Bridge Legal and Non-Legal Normative Practice

Finally, courts play an important role in influencing how governmental actors (such as the Equal Employment Opportunity Commission) and non-governmental actors (such as experts and lawyers) mediate the relationship between formal law and informal norms and practices. These mediating actors play a normative role within both the judicial and workplace domains. They translate legal norms to non-legal actors, and they educate courts about non-legal normative activity. These mediating actors can play an ongoing role of: (1) building the capacity and constituencies needed to operate effective, accountable systems within organizations; (2) pooling and critically assessing examples across institutions; (3) generating and revising norms that emerge from that reflective practice; and (4) constructing communities of practice to sustain this ongoing reflective inquiry.

Courts review the activities and outcomes of these mediating actors who participate in normative elaboration and capacity building. This review affords the opportunity to prompt the development of standards and processes of accountability governing the role of these norm intermediaries. An example will help illustrate the idea. I have already discussed evaluations of expert testimony as a site for norm elaboration outside the context of rule enforcement. There is also a structural reason to pay attention to the role of experts as participants in norm elaboration. Experts play a crucial intermediary role in the formation and translation of norms. Many of the experts who appear in employment discrimination litigation also conduct research and consult with organizations about the adequacy of their workplace practices (www.bendickegan.com). They play a key role in translating legal principles into organizational norms and vice versa (Edelman, Uggen, and Erlanger, 1999). They are repeat players who work across the boundaries of legal regulation and workplace practice. It is crucial, and not always the case, that these professional intermediaries articulate and satisfy criteria of methodological and process accountability.

Courts can structure processes for the admissibility and evaluation of expert testimony that foster transparency and professional accountability for these norm intermediaries. Courts evaluating expert evidence must assess its persuasiveness, methodological validity, and generalizability (Walker and Monahan, 1988, p. 877; Meares and Harcourt, 2000, pp. 733, 1264). They also consider the degree to which expert evaluation develops replicable methodologies that receive review and validation within the relevant professional community. This review could be conducted with more explicit attention to the crucial intermediary role being played by experts. Ideally, courts could also review administrative agency decision-making with this concern about effective norm intermediation and capacity building as a guiding principle (Dorf and Sabel, 1998, pp. 267, 348).

4. CONCLUSION

This chapter emphasizes the importance of extending the interdisciplinary and constructivist understandings of discrimination to the formulation of the judiciary's role in addressing inequality. It questions the adequacy of rule enforcement as a unitary theory of law's role in addressing complex discrimination. It also critiques the "shadow of the law" image as an adequate guide for shaping the relationship between law and norms. The catalyst judicial role developed here requires a new metaphor that captures the dynamic and interactive relationship between informal norms and formal law. Courts can and should actively participate in structuring the relationship between law and norms, between non-legal and legal actors. Courts are not the only or necessarily the primary site for generating effective problem solving approaches to complex discrimination. But they continue to play a crucial legitimating and boundary-setting function, along the facilitative role that this essay has elaborated. This facilitative role conception opens up new possibilities for legitimate and effective judicial participation in normative elaboration that can respond to complex and subtle forms of discrimination.

CHAPTER 3

What We Know about the Problem of the Century: Lessons from Social Science to the Law, and Back

Susan T. Fiske

ABSTRACT

Social scientists have learned a lot about the American dilemma of discrimination, notably how unexamined and unconscious it can be, the varieties of guises it takes, the surprising importance of ingroup loyalty and perceived threat to the ingroup, as well as the functions it serves for individuals, groups, and society. After nearly a century's study, social psychologists now know that intergroup bias and conflict come in two primary kinds. Most people reveal unconscious, unexamined biases—relatively automatic, cool, indirect, ambiguous, and ambivalent. Unexamined biases predict ordinary discrimination: comfort with own ingroup, plus exclusion and avoidance of outgroups. Much workplace discrimination takes this form. Such biases result from internal conflict between cultural ideals and cultural biases. A small minority, the extremists, harbor a second kind of bias: blatant biases that are more conscious, hot, direct, and unambiguous. Blatant biases predict aggression, including hate crimes and probably the most overt kinds of harassment in the workplace. Such biases result from perceived intergroup conflict over economics and values, in a world perceived to be hierarchical and dangerous. All this makes systems of discrimination hard to change, but not intractable. Reduction of both unexamined and blatant bias results from education, economic opportunity, and constructive intergroup contact. The law–psychology interplay can potentially operate to clarify several issues: intent with regard to unexamined biases, previously neglected categories of discrimination, dangers from ingroup advantage, and even the functions of both unexamined and blatant discrimination for individuals and social systems.

INTRODUCTION

People typically seek similar others, being comfortable with people they perceive as members of their own ingroup. From comfort follows, at best, neglect of people from outgroups and, at worst, murderous hostility toward outgroups perceived as threatening the ingroup. Biases do vary by degree, and the psychologies of moderate and extreme biases differ considerably. Well-intentioned moderates reveal bias more subtle and less examined than the rants and rampages of extremists. By some

L. B. Nielsen and R. L. Nelson (eds.), Handbook of Employment Discrimination Research, 59–73.

counts, 80% of Western democratic populations intend benign intergroup relations but display unexamined biases. In contrast, blatantly biased extremists are completely outfront. Although estimated to be a minority (perhaps 10%), they are salient, vocal, and dangerous.

Social psychology knows a lot about both forms of bias. Some helpful distinctions: stereotyping, prejudice, and discrimination reflect, respectively, people's cognitive, affective, and behavioral reactions to people from other groups (Fiske, 1998). All constitute *bias*, reacting to a person on the basis of perceived membership in a particular human category, ignoring other category memberships and other personal attributes—therefore a narrow, potentially erroneous reaction, compared to individuated impressions formed from personal details.

1. UNEXAMINED BIAS AMONG WELL-INTENTIONED MODERATES

1.1. Automatic, Unconscious, and Unintentional

The big news from two recent decades of research on bias: It is most often underground (Dovidio and Gaertner, 1986). Sparked by findings that even for relatively unprejudiced people, racial category labels automatically prime stereotypes, as indicated by accessibility, scores of studies now support the essential automaticity of stereotypes (for reviews, see Fiske, 1998; 2000b; Macrae and Bodenhausen, 2000). For example, even subliminally presented outgroup category labels activate stereotypic associations in lexical decision tasks. That is, people judge a series of letter-strings, some of which are words and some nonwords. People first primed with an outgroup category label (e.g., for White respondents, *Black* or *Harlem*) respond faster in judging outgroup-related words, stereotypic associations such as *hostile* or *lazy* (e.g., Devine, 1989; Dovidio, Evans, and Tyler, 1986). In a more affective vein, outgroup cues (such as words, faces, or names) easily activate negative evaluative terms such as *bad* or *unpleasant* (e.g., Blair and Banaji, 1996; Greenwald, McGhee, and Schwartz, 1998).

Relatedly, brain imaging shows amygdala activation consistent with primitive emotional prejudices to outgroup faces (Hart, Whalen, Shin, McInerney, Fischer, and Rauch, 2000; Phelps, O'Connor, Cunningham, Funayama, Gatenby, Gore, and Banaji, 2000). Furthermore, automatic activation of outgroup categories and power relations leads to behavior stereotypically associated with that group (e.g., Bargh, Chen, and Burrows, 1996; Bargh, Raymond, Pryor, and Strack, 1995; Dijksterhuis and Bargh, 2001; Dovidio, Kawakami, and Gaertner, 2002). Brain and behavior work both constitute the cutting edge here.

Automatic reactions to outgroup members matter in everyday behavior. Awkward social interactions, embarrassing slips of the tongue, unchecked assumptions, stereotypic judgments, and spontaneous neglect all exemplify mundane automaticity, which creates a subtly hostile environment for outgroup members. The apparent automaticity of routine biases corroborates Allport's (1954) provocative early insights about the inevitability of categorization. Automaticity also shocks well-intentioned people who assume prejudice is conscious and controllable.

All is not lost for the well-intentioned. Category activation is not *unconditionally* automatic. Although people can instantly identify another's category membership (especially gender, race, and age), they may not always activate associated stereotypes (see Fiske, 1998, for a review). Sufficient overload blocks activation (Gilbert and Hixon, 1991). People's long-term attitudes also moderate access to biased associations: Lower levels of chronic prejudice can attenuate stereotype activation (e.g., Monteith, 1993; Moskowitz, Gollwitzer, Wasel, and Schaal, 1999). Temporary goals matter, too: Category activation depends on short-term motivations, including self-enhancement, accurate understanding, and temporary egalitarian goals (e.g., Fein and Spencer, 1997; Moskowitz, Salomon, and Constance, 2000; Neuberg and Fiske, 1987).

Promising as they are, these findings remain controversial. For example, they depend on the nature of the stimuli: Ease of category activation differs depending on whether perceivers encounter verbal labels (easy), photographs (harder), or real people (hardest). Some researchers believe that social categories inevitably activate associated biases, whereas others believe activation depends entirely on short-term goals and long-term individual differences (for a review, see Devine, 2001).

Whether bias is conditionally or unconditionally automatic, people's long- and short-term motives do matter. Even if category activation is entirely automatic, less prejudiced perceivers still can over-ride their automatic associations with subsequent controlled processes. If category activation is conditionally automatic, then people may be able to inhibit it in the first place. Both require motivation.

What's more, even if people do *activate* biases associated with a category, they may not *apply* (or use) those biases (Gilbert and Hixon, 1991). For example, once the category is activated, other information may be consistent or inconsistent with it, and perceivers have to decide what to do about the conflicting information. Inconsistency resolution and subsequent individuation of the other person require resources, which are allocated according to the perceiver's motivation and capacity. Over-riding category use depends on meta-cognitive decisions and higher-level executive functions, not just brute attentional capacity. Other qualifications to using activated categories go beyond the perceiver's motivation and capacity: For example, category use depends on the stimuli (abstractions encourage assimilation, whereas exemplars encourage contrast; Dijksterhuis, Spears, and Lepinasse, 2001) and the perceiver's theory about whether people's dispositions are fixed entities or flexible states (Levy, Plaks, Hong, Chiu, and Dweck, 2001). Psychologists continue to debate automaticity.

Inhibition of both category activation and category application challenges even the most determined moderate. Direct suppression sometimes causes only a rebound of the forbidden biases (Monteith, Sherman, and Devine, 1998; Wegner, 1994). Depending on cognitive capacity, practice, age, and motivation, people can inhibit many effects of social categories (see Fiske, 1998, for a review). Indeed, even amygdala activation to cross-race faces vanishes when people adopt goals forcing them to treat the other as a unique individual or not even as a social object (Wheeler and Fiske, 2005). The take-home message: Bias is more automatic than you think, but less automatic than we thought.

1.2. Cool, Indirect, and Ambiguous

The biases of the moderate, well-intentioned majority not only live underground; they also wear camouflage. Consistent with people's biases reflecting ingroup comfort at least as much as outgroup discomfort, bias often consists in withholding positive emotions from outgroups. Moderates rarely express open hostility toward outgroups, but they may withhold basic liking and respect; hence, their responses represent cool neglect. People more rapidly assign positive attributes to the ingroup than the outgroup, but negative attributes often show at best weak differences (Fiske, 1998). People withhold rewards from outgroups, relative to the ingroup, reflecting favoritism. But they rarely punish or derogate the outgroup (Brewer and Brown, 1998). The damage is relative.

Moderate biases are indirect, relying on norms for appropriate responses. If norms allow biases, they flourish. Biases appear most often when people have unprejudiced excuses (Crosby, Bromley, and Saxe, 1980; Gaertner and Dovidio, 1986). If some people neglect outgroup members, then everyone does, for example, in discretionary contact or helping (Pettigrew, 1998a). If the outgroup member behaves poorly, providing an excuse for prejudice, then the resulting exclusion is more swift and sure than for a comparable ingroup member (Katz and Hass, 1986; Taylor, Fiske, Etcoff, and Ruderman, 1978). Biases also appear in political policy preferences where one might have principled reasons (excuses), but one also just happens to have a series of opinions that all disadvantage the outgroup relative to the ingroup (McConahay, 1986; Pettigrew, 1998b). Excuses for bias fulfill the social norm requiring rational, fair judgments, but controlled comparisons reveal greater bias than toward comparable ingroup members. Researchers debate the meaning of these biases.

People also engage in attributional tricks that discourage sympathy by blaming the outgroup for their own unfortunate outcomes: The outgroup should try harder, but at the same time they should not push themselves where they are not wanted (Catch 22; Pettigrew, 1998b). The blame goes further. Where the ingroup might be excused for its failures (extenuating circumstances), the outgroup brought it on themselves (unfortunate dispositions) (Deaux and Emswiller, 1974; Hewstone, 1990; Pettigrew, 1979). People often attribute the outgroup's perceived failings to their essence: innate, inherent, enduring attributes, perhaps biological, especially genetic, define category distinctiveness (e.g., Yzerbyt, Corneille, and Estrada, 2001).

In making sense of outgroup members, people exaggerate cultural differences (in ability, language, religious beliefs, sexual practices; Pettigrew, 1998b). The mere fact of categorizing into ingroup *us* and outgroup *them* exaggerates intercategory differences and diminishes intra-category differences (Tajfel and Turner, 1979; Taylor, 1981). They all are alike and different from us, besides (Mullen and Hu, 1989). In short, moderates' bias is cool, indirect, and ambiguous.

1.3. Ambivalent and Mixed

Besides being underground and camouflaged, moderate biases are complex. Ambivalent racism entails, for moderate Whites, mixed "pro-Black" pity and anti-Black resentment, which tips over to a predominantly positive or negative response, depending on circumstances (Katz and Hass, 1986). As another example, ambivalent sexism demonstrates two correlated dimensions that differentiate hostile sexism (toward nontraditional women) and subjectively benevolent sexism (toward traditional women) (Glick and Fiske, 1996; Glick and Fiske, 2001a). In both the cases, ambivalence indicates mixed forms of prejudice more subtle than unmitigated hostility.

Mixed biases turn out to be the rule, rather than the exception. Although various outgroups all are classified as *them*, they form clusters (see figure 1; Fiske, Cuddy, Glick, and Xu, 2002). Some elicit less respect, and some elicit less liking. Not only is the bias of well-intentioned moderates of the cool variety (withholding the positive, rather than assigning the negative; Pettigrew, 1998b), but it is not even uniformly lacking in positive views. Specifically, some outgroups (Asians, Jews, career women, Black professionals, rich people) are envied and respected for their perceived competence and high status, but they are resented and disliked as lacking in warmth because they compete with the ingroup. Other outgroups (older people, disabled people, housewives) are pitied and disrespected for their perceived incompetence and low status, but they are nurtured and liked as warm because they do not threaten the ingroup. Only a few outgroups (primarily homeless and poor people of any race) receive contempt, both dislike and disrespect, because they are seen as simultaneously low status and exploiting the ingroup.

Ambivalent, mixed biases justify the status quo. Subordinated, pitied groups have an incentive to cooperate because they receive care, in return for not challenging the hierarchy. Conversely, dominant groups use subordinated groups to maintain their own relative advantage. Envied, competitive groups have an incentive to support the system because they are perceived to be succeeding, even if the culturally dominant group socially excludes them. For dominant groups, respecting envied groups acknowledges the ground rules for competition (which favor them also), but disliking justifies social exclusion (Glick and Fiske, 2001b).

Moderate biases predict exclusion: Unexamined biases predict personal interactions that reek of discomfort and anxiety. Nonverbal indicators (distance, posture, voice tone) and self-reports all reveal interactions that are anything but smooth, mostly due to inexperience with the outgroup (e.g., Crosby et al., 1980; Dovidio et al., 2002).

Moreover, people mentally and behaviorally confirm their biased expectations, leading both parties to maintain their distance. The self-fulfilling prophecy, expectancy effects, and behavioral confirmation all name related phenomena, whereby biased perceivers bring about the very behavior they anticipate, usually negative (e.g., Darley and Fazio, 1980; Rosenthal, 1994; Snyder, 1984). These interpersonal processes result in subsequent avoidance, whenever people can choose the company they keep (Pettigrew, 1998a). Discretionary contact is minimized.

Furthermore, exclusion and avoidance extend to employment, housing, education, and justice that tend to favor ingroup and disadvantage the outgroup (Smelser, Wilson, and Mitchell, 2001). Ample evidence indicates that relatively automatic, cool, indirect, ambiguous, and ambivalent biases permit allocation of resources to maintain ingroup advantage.

1.4. How Do Moderate Biases Originate?

Unexamined prejudice comes from people's internal conflict between ideals and biases, both acquired from the culture (e.g., Devine, 1989), especially the media. Direct, personal experience with outgroup members may be limited (Pettigrew, 1998a). Given substantial de facto residential and occupational segregation (Smelser et al., 2001), people lack experience in constructive intergroup interactions. Cultural media, then, supply most information about outgroups, so people easily develop unconscious associations and feelings that reinforce bias.

Simultaneously, western ideals encourage tolerance of most outgroups (e.g., Bobo, 2001; Gaertner and Dovidio, 1986; Katz and Hass, 1986). Complying with anti-prejudice ideals requires conscious endorsement of egalitarian norms against prejudice. Moderates do endorse anti-prejudice values. The upshot is a conflict between relatively implicit, unconscious biases and explicit, conscious ideals to be unprejudiced. Resulting prejudices are unexamined, modern, and aversive to the people holding them.

2. BLATANT BIAS AMONG ILL-INTENTIONED EXTREMISTS

2.1. Hot, Direct, Unambiguous, and Conscious

In contrast to well-intentioned moderates, extremists openly resent outgroups and reject any possibility of intimacy with them (Pettigrew, 1998b). They resent outgroups—whether racial, cultural, gender, or sexual—as holding jobs that ingroup should have and (paradoxically) living on welfare unnecessarily. They believe that outgroups and the ingroup can never be comfortable together. Extremists are particularly upset by intergroup intimacy. They report that they would be bothered by having a mixed grandchild, that they are unwilling to have sexual relations with outgroup members, and that they are unwilling to have an outgroup boss.

Extreme biases run in packs; people biased against one outgroup tend to be biased against others (Altemeyer, 1996). Ethnocentrism shows reliable individual differences, measured by old-fashioned prejudice scales assessing self-reported attitudes toward racial, ethnic, gender, and sexual outgroups.

2.2. Extreme Biases Predict Aggression

The result is as simple as it is horrible. Because of hot, direct, unambiguous prejudices, extremists advocate segregation, containment, and even elimination of outgroups. Strong forms of bias correlate with approval of racist movements. Hate-crime perpetrators and participants in ethnic violence, not surprisingly, endorse attitudes (prejudices and stereotypes) that fit extreme forms of discrimination (Green, Glaser, and Rich, 1998; Green, Strolovitch, and Wong, 1998).

Aggression takes two main forms: preserving hierarchies and preserving values perceived to be traditional (Duckitt, 2001). Blatant prejudice first predicts approving aggression to maintain the status quo, viewing current group hierarchies as inevitable and desirable (Sidanius and Pratto, 1999). Highly prejudiced people gravitate toward jobs that enhance group hierarchy and defend the status quo (police officer rather than social worker; businessperson rather than educator). Blatant prejudice also predicts self-righteous aggression against non-conformers and others who threaten core values (Altemeyer, 1996). If outgroups deviate and threaten traditional values, then they become legitimate targets of aggression.

2.3. How Do Extreme Biases Originate?

Whether extremists are domestic or international, they endanger those they hate. People become biased extremists because they perceive threats to their ingroup. Thus, extreme bias parallels the ingroup favoritism of biased moderates who also protect the ingroup. Differences lie in the perceived nature and degree of threat.

Threat to economic standing has long been implicated in intergroup bias. Although still controversial, the most convincing but counterintuitive lesson here is that personal economic deprivation is *not* the culprit (Kinder, 1998). People's own wallets do not predict their degree of prejudice. Instead, the most reliable indicators are perceived threat to one's ingroup. Group threat (e.g., high local unemployment) predicts extreme biases against outgroups perceived to be responsible. The causal sequence seems to run from subjective identity (e.g., social class) to perceived group deprivation to prejudice.

Perceived threat to ingroup economic status correlates with worldviews that reinforce a zero-sum, dog-eat-dog perspective. Tough-minded competition reflects the state of intergroup relations. Economic conservatism results. Overall, blatant prejudice correlates with high social dominance orientation (Sidanius and Pratto, 1999), endorsing views that superior groups should dominate inferior groups, using force if necessary, and group equality is neither desirable nor realistic.

Perceived threat to traditional values is the other prong of blatant bias. Extremists view the world as dangerous, with established authority and conventions in collapse. Social conservatism correlates with this origin of extreme bias (Altemeyer, 1996). Such people move in tight ethnic circles and endorse right-wing authoritarian views: old-fashioned values, censorship, mighty leaders who fight evil, and suppression of troublemakers, free-thinkers, women, and homosexuals.

The background of people who become extremists features limited intergroup contact—few outgroup neighbors, acquaintances, and friends. Nor do they value such contact. Extremist bias also correlates with less education, for reasons not fully clear.

3. WHAT REDUCES BIAS?

Given unexamined biases that are unconscious and indirect, change is a challenge, resisting frontal assault. Similarly, given blatant biases rooted in perceived threat to group interest and core values, direct confrontation will likely fail again. Instead, more nuanced means do work.

Education can help. Economic opportunity can help. Moreover, for decades, social psychologists have studied constructive intergroup contact, increasing mutual appreciation (Pettigrew, 1998a): (a) equal status within the immediate setting, (b) shared goals, (c) cooperation in pursuit of those goals, and (d) authorities' support. Under these conditions, contact provides a basis for (e) intergroup friendship. Genuine intergroup friendships demonstrably do reduce stereotyping, prejudice, and discrimination of whatever sort.

4. INTERPLAY BETWEEN LAW AND SOCIAL SCIENCE

The law can potentially clarify issues of intent, categories of discrimination, ingroup advantage, and even the functional level of perceived threat.

4.1. Intent: Not Guilty, by Reason of Automaticity?

One legal interpretation of automatic, unconscious, unintentional bias might apparently imply that it need not be proscribed because the individual does not intend to discriminate. Absent intent, disparate treatment may not fit some legal definitions of discrimination. This interpretation gives one pause, at first, but evidence of intent, organizational responsibility, and conditional automaticity provide some basis for determining the state of mind of the actor accused of discrimination and a deeper understanding of intent, eliminating the trap of "not guilty by reason of automaticity."

4.1.1. Evidence of Intent

Lay people, legal analysts, and social psychologists share some definitions of intentionality (Fiske, 1989). Observers infer intent when the actor had a clear choice and control over choosing. Observers are especially confident in judging intent when someone picks the harder, less typical alternative. And observing the actor's focus of attention also enables observers to infer intent. These three factors—having options, making the hard choice, and paying attention—have potential implications for the law–psychology interface in discrimination.

When do actors have a choice about so-called automatic, unconscious, unintentional stereotyping, one precursor to discrimination? If roughly 80% of respondents are vulnerable to unexamined forms of bias, as we have seen, then how would observers know whether they have a choice when they disadvantage the outgroup? First, one could apply a form of reasonable person standard, assessing whether the typical person can overcome the apparently automatic, unexamined forms of stereotyping. Evidence that similarly situated others could overcome a presumably similar vulnerability to such category-based responses would constitute evidence that a reasonable person indeed would have options.

Psychological research amply indicates, first, that individual motivation, based on personal values, can motivate people to pay attention and to make the hard choice (see Fiske, 1998, for a review). As we have seen, people with intrinsic, egalitarian values that form a core part of their identity demonstrably do show less bias, even of the allegedly automatic kinds. Moreover, people's values stem from the norms in the immediate environment. Individuals can also absorb what I would call ambient values as personal guides for action. Second, motivation based on an interdependent relationship with the target, needing the person to accomplish a common goal, can motivate people to pay attention and to make the hard choice (Fiske, 2000). This implicates the importance of intergroup teams that require everyone's input in order to succeed. Third, motivation can result from accountability to a third party for the quality of interactions with the other (Tetlock, 1992). The role of authorities, as noted in research on intergroup contact, and the role of third-party judges both undercut even the subtle, unexamined forms of bias.

Demonstrably, then, previous research indicates that people can go beyond the initial, unexamined gut-level bias, if sufficiently motivated. Clearly, when people are motivated, they are making the hard choice to go beyond unexamined category-based responses. If, on the other hand, they fail to do so, they nevertheless had a choice. In a legal setting, then, they may be held responsible for not making the effort to go beyond unexamined, superficial factors in judging others.

4.1.2. Organizational Responsibility

A reasonable organization would or should know, at this point in our history, that bias looms as a realistic possibility to taint the decision-making of its agents. Although lay people may disagree about whether discrimination has been eliminated from the current scene, social science data indicate that discrimination is a continuing fact of 21st century employment, housing, and health care (Smelser et al., 2001). For organizations operating in this environment, the safeguards to discourage decision-makers from making the easy choice are obvious. Organizations can structure several factors just noted: Ambient values, teamwork, authority sanctions, and accountability all matter to successful intergroup relations (Fiske and Glick, 1995). One particular concern is group distributions.

From the stereotyping literature, we know that solos operate at a disadvantage. Solos, sometimes called tokens, constitute less than about 20% of a given group. Solos are vulnerable on several counts (Kanter, 1977; Fiske, Bersoff, Borgida, Deaux, and Heilman, 1991; Lord and Saenz, 1985; Mullen, 1991; Taylor, 1981). First, their distinctiveness makes them targets of probable stereotyping. Their social category becomes their most salient feature, and observers consequently organize their impressions around the category. Second, solos are subject to more intense pressure because they attract attention on the basis of their distinctive category. Observers erroneously attribute events in the group to the presence of the solos, and ingroup favoritism suggests those attributions will primarily take the form of blame for negative events. Third, because of the exaggerated attentional focus, solo's performance is judged more extremely. An error becomes a disaster. Sometimes a success becomes a triumph, but ingroup favoritism again suggests that the negative exaggerations will be more common. Thus, attention to solos results in less forgiving scrutiny than members of a subgroup constituting at least 20% of the larger group. Solos suffer anxiety accordingly, and this can undermine their performance, which creates a self-fulfilling prophecy. Moreover, attrition increases among members of underrepresented groups.

Given these well-established patterns, solo structures within organizations present a red flag. A genuine predicament confronts organizations faced with a small pool of employees from an underrepresented group. If the relevant employees are spread evenly throughout the organization, then they are more likely to be situated as solos in any given setting. If they are clustered in particular areas of the organization, reaching critical mass in some sectors and complete absence in others, then they appear to be ghettoized. To the extent the organization can demonstrate that this is a transitional phase, with recruiting trends demonstrating a remedy in process, then that would diminish the attribution of reckless neglect. Overall, organizations clearly can structure and monitor themselves to encourage decision-makers to make the harder choice.

4.1.3. Conditional Automaticity

Up until the last half-dozen years, that was all we knew. In effect, category-based responses were inevitable from responses in the first few milliseconds of an encounter. The variation (the hard choice) came in the decision to go beyond the initial judgment and add more information, enabling the judge to individuate the target.

More recently, social psychologists have learned even the apparently automatic stage of decision-making falls under the influence of individual and social motivation. As we have seen, individual values influence the deployment of automatic stereotypes. Social context does, too. The name for this flexibility where we thought there was inevitability, as noted earlier, is conditional automaticity.

The implication for a legal analysis, it seems to me, is profound. All the questions of intent and responsibility move back a notch to even earlier stages of information gathering and response. People are even more in control of their rapid first responses than psychologists had imagined. However, they still may not examine their initial automatic responses, unless motivated to do so. In the default case, then, people's decisions are likely to follow the easy choice. Thus, the concern about the cognitive monster completely driven by its automatic responses (Bargh, 1999), with no recourse to more controlled over-rides, seems to be over-stated. This takes the legal analysis back from a precipice whereby actors would not be liable for their unexamined biases, not guilty by reason of automaticity.

4.2. Ingroup Advantage: Sabotage by Neglect

Most fundamental to making the easy, biased choice is decision-makers' spontaneous comfort with the ingroup, as we have seen. Much discrimination results from advantaging the ingroup rather than explicitly disadvantaging the outgroup. The implication for a legal analysis is that many forms of discrimination will result from reckless neglect, a failure to benefit the outgroup to the same extent as the ingroup. Withholding benefits, favors, courtesies, advice, and support can destroy a career as surely as the application of negative sanctions. Sensitivity to such sabotage by neglect would surely show the unexamined but destructive form of much everyday discrimination.

This ingroup advantage results from an absence of behavior toward outgroup members. As such, it is indirect and often unexamined. The burden falls on the outgroup member to know and notice the absence of behavior. Psychologists know that noticing an absence is more difficult than noticing a presence. Moreover, events happening to others are harder to identify than events (not) happening to self. Finally, negative events elicit more notice than positive events. For all these reasons, then, the absence of positive benefits provided to self will be harder to detect and to demonstrate. The most typical form of unexamined bias, indirect sabotage by neglect, will require particular legal scrutiny.

4.3. Kinds of Discrimination: Beyond Antipathy

Earlier, we described not only how indirect and automatic bias can be, but also how ambiguous. Dozens of social categories from more than a dozen countries, including varied US samples, show that social groups come in predictable types, from the perspective of cultural biases (Cuddy, Fiske, Kwan, Glick, et al., 2005). And our research indicates that discrimination comes in predictable kinds that follow from the stereotypes and prejudices directed toward different kinds of outgroups (Cuddy, Fiske, and Glick, 2005). Harm comes in more than one kind, that is, *passive harm* (demean, exclude, hinder, derogate) versus the more obvious *active harm* (fight, attack, sabotage). And earlier I noted that important kinds of discrimination result from withholding positive behavior, such as *cooperation* among equals (cooperate, unite, associate). A more subtle kind of positive behavior could be directed downward: *help* (assist, protect, help).

The most notorious kind of bias, pure antipathy, and the most consistent kind of discrimination, both active and passive harm, turn out to be the exception, rather than the rule. Across cultures, the main targets of unadulterated prejudice are poor people of any race, the homeless, the unemployed, and (especially in the US) welfare recipients. Such groups elicit contempt and disgust. They are neither respected nor liked. This kind of prejudice elicits predictable kinds of discrimination, the classic kinds: active harm (fighting, attacking, sabotaging) and passive harm (demean, exclude, hinder, derogate).

As noted earlier, other groups systematically elicit grudging respect, but dislike: envied for their accomplishments, they are viewed as exploiting the rest of society or competing unfairly. Groups that are seen as competent but not warm include professionals from otherwise disadvantaged groups, for example, Black and female professionals, Asians, and Jews. They also include traditionally powerful groups such as men and rich people. These groups elicit cooperation because of their perceived competence, but simultaneously active harm. This paradoxical pattern fits the idea of cooperation under stable social conditions, but active harm under social breakdown. Extreme cases would include group internment or even genocide.

A final cluster of groups elicits paternalistic liking but not respect: Pitied for their incompetence, they are viewed as harmless and subordinate. Groups that are seen as incompetent but warm include, as noted earlier, the elderly, housewives, and disabled people. Their perceived warmth but incompetence elicits predictable kinds of discrimination, ambivalent and paternalistic: helping but not cooperation among equals, passive harm but not active harm.

We would expect the ingroup to receive the most helping and cooperation, and the least harm, in general. Overall, perceived lack of warmth predicts active harm, whereas perceived warmth predicts help. And perceived incompetence predicts passive harm, whereas perceived competence predicts cooperation. The point is that discrimination comes in many guises, but they are predictable.

4.4. Functions of Bias

4.4.1. Individuals

Unexamined bias allows people to function, albeit imperfectly, in a complex world. Cognitive shortcuts maintain efficiency, as Allport famously noted: People cannot function without categories; orderly living depends on it. Maintaining ties with the ingroup also affords a degree of personal comfort, validating one's identity, keeping to familiar norms, controlling resources, enhancing self-esteem, and creating a trusted circle (for a review, see Fiske, 2004, Chapter 11). Also, sometimes stereotypes co-vary with social structure (e.g., fewer men stay home with children that women do, even though most women are not stay-at-home mothers; Eagly, 1987). This co-variation can give people a sense of good-enough accuracy, especially if they are in positions of power (Fiske, 1993).

The implications are that individuals will resist giving up their ways of structuring the world in terms of ingroups and outgroups, as well as the stereotypes about those outgroups. Biases may well be the default position, given their functions for the individual. This suggests that organizations and individual decision-makers must assume that their biases will intrude, if not monitored. Safeguards to make oneself unaware of the target's social category can help sometimes. For example, I grade all coursework blind to the identity of the student. Where that is not possible, individual values, teamwork, and accountability all can help undercut default biases. It puts the burden of prevention on those who hold power. Moreover, those who supervise others must be aware that peers will hold biases against each other unless those biases are checked and replaced by motivations to treat people as individuals.

4.4.2. Society

At a societal level, biases serve the often-observed functions of maintaining the status quo, providing legitimating myths, social ideologies that justify status hierarchies and power relations (Jost and Banaji, 1994; Jost and Major, 2001). As such, they provide stability, at the price of maintaining vested interests and blocking mobility. A full analysis of the societal functions lies outside our current scope, but the point is that the entrenched nature of the intergroup biases stems partly from their societal functions.

5. CONCLUSIONS

Social biases intermingle with basic human tendencies to a surprising degree: categorization, ingroup comfort, social convenience, the status quo all conspire to keep people tied to and favoring others like themselves. This is the bad news from nearly a century of social psychology. This suggests the importance of legal remedies that reinforce our better natures, our aspirations for a free and just society. Social psychology's good news is that we have also learned what motivates people to go beyond their default, protective responses to a genuine interest and knowledge of others, resulting in potential friendship, enthusiasm, and profit from the variety of people in our families, schools, and workplaces.

Author's Note

The initial review of the social psychological literature on bias appeared first as an article in *Current Directions in Psychological Science* (Fiske, 2002). It is reproduced here by permission of the publishers.

SECTION II

Debating the Prevalence and Character of Discrimination

CHAPTER 4

Including Mechanisms in our Models of Ascriptive Inequality*

Barbara F. Reskin

ABSTRACT

Sociologists' principal contribution to our understanding of ascriptive inequality has been to document race and sex disparities. We have made little headway, however, in explaining these disparities because most research has sought to explain variation across ascriptive groups in more or less desirable outcomes in terms of allocators' *motives*. This approach has been inconclusive because motive-based theories cannot be empirically tested. Our reliance on individual-level data and the balkanization of research on ascriptive inequality into separate specialties for groups defined by different ascriptive characteristics have contributed to our explanatory stalemate. Explanation requires including mechanisms in our models–the specific processes that link groups' ascribed characteristics to variable outcomes such as earnings. I discuss mechanisms that contribute to variation in ascriptive inequality at four levels of analysis—intrapsychic, interpersonal, societal, and organizational. Redirecting our attention from motives to mechanisms is essential for understanding inequality and—equally important—for contributing meaningfully to social policies that will promote social equality.

INTRODUCTION

In one of the Britain's most celebrated 19th century murder trials, Adelaide Bartlett was charged with killing her husband, Edwin. The post-mortem revealed the presence of chloroform, a corrosive poison, in his stomach. Reverend George Dyson, Adelaide's intimate companion and Edwin Bartlett's decreed successor for Adelaide's

* I thank Dorothy Friendly for superbly organizing my research materials and Beth Hirsh for research assistance. I am grateful to Edgar Kiser and Michael Hechter whose disagreements with my thesis have helped me to clarify it. Marilyn Read came up with the example with which this essay begins. Finally, I am indebted to Charles Camic, Joan Huber, Rachel Kuller, Franklin Wilson, and especially to Lowell Hargens whose comments on earlier drafts helped me to refine my argument. None of these colleagues bears any responsibility for any remaining problems.

L. B. Nielsen and R. L. Nelson (eds.), Handbook of Employment Discrimination Research, 75–99.

hand, testified that he had purchased the chloroform at Adelaide's request. Thus, the evidence showed both motive for Adelaide—a younger and more desirable spouse—and means—death by chloroform. But the prosecution could not offer convincing evidence showing how the chloroform got into Bartlett's stomach. It is all but impossible to swallow because it causes vomiting. And if chloroform had been poured down Edwin's throat while he was unconscious, traces would have been found in his mouth, throat, and lungs—and none were. In view of the lack of evidence as to *how* the chloroform got in Edwin's stomach, the jury acquitted Adelaide. After the verdict, Sir James Paget, founder of modern pathology, appealed publicly for the truth: "In the interest of science," he implored, "she should tell us how she did it" (Fordham, 1951; Farrell, 1994).

In this essay, I argue that although we have been studying ascriptive inequality in employment for over 30 years with increasingly sophisticated techniques, we have made little headway in explaining it.[1] We have failed to progress because most of our research has focused on *why* ascriptively defined groups vary on their access to societies' rewards, rather than on *how* variation is produced in ascriptive groups' access to opportunities. In other words, our stumbling block is the same one that confronted the jurors in Adelaide Bartlett's murder trial: Until we determine how events occur or are prevented, we cannot satisfactorily explain them. Following Sir Paget, I appeal, in the interests of science and justice, for research on *how* people come to be stratified at work on the basis of their ascribed characteristics.

In the social sciences, "why" explanations tend to attribute variation across ascriptive groups in more or less desirable outcomes to actors' *motives*—the factors that prompt an individual to take a particular action (Black, 1979, p. 727). Conflict theories of ascriptive inequality, which contend that dominant groups use their monopoly over resources to maintain their privileges, exemplify motive-based explanations. "How" explanations for varying levels of inequality, in contrast, spell out the *mechanisms* that produce that variation. By mechanisms, I mean specific processes that link individuals' ascriptive characteristics to workplace outcomes. Mechanism-based theories, which tend to be less general than motive-based theories, specify the practices whose presence and implementation influence the level of inequality in a work setting. Theories about the effects of formalization, transparency, and accountability, which I discuss below, are mechanism-based theories.

I argue below that deriving research questions from motive-based theories without also investigating the mechanisms through which motives operate has precluded advances in explaining ascriptive inequality, both because motive-based theories are all but impossible to test empirically and because they ignore the proximate causes of variability in ascriptive inequality. There is, of course, nothing wrong with asking why; our lack of progress lies in our failure to ask how. We can neither explain ascriptive stratification nor generate useful prescriptions for policies to reduce it until we

[1] Ascriptive inequality refers to inequality across groups defined by some ascriptive characteristic, such as sex, race, or age.

uncover the mechanisms that produce the wide variation in the social and economic fates of ascriptively defined groups.

I first review explanations for ascriptive inequality that focus solely on motives and outline their limitations. I then discuss theoretical and empirical research that focuses on mechanisms. Although I draw examples from research on labor markets and the world of work, my thesis holds more generally for ascriptive stratification in other domains such as education, criminal justice, and health care. For convenience, I call groups defined on the basis of an ascriptive characteristic "ascriptive groups." When I talk about inequality across ascriptive groups, I mean groups categorized by the *same* ascriptive characteristic, such as color. A final prefatory note: Although I am critical of much of the research in stratification, I ask readers to bear in mind that I reached this critical stance primarily from reflecting on the shortcomings in my own work.

1. MOTIVE-BASED EXPLANATIONS: EXPLAINING ASCRIPTIVE INEQUALITY BY ASKING "WHY"

Motives—the purposes prompting our actions—are often seen in the industrialized world as the cause of human behavior. As Tilly (1998, pp. 36–37) observed, our reliance on motives to explain behavior reflects a narrative mode in which people's motives cause events. Thus, it is not surprising that many theories invoke motives to explain ascriptive inequality without addressing the mechanisms through which motives hypothetically operate.[2]

1.1. Some Examples of Motive-Based Explanations

The attention that researchers in ascriptive inequality give to "why" can be seen in theories that view inequality as the result of separate individuals acting to advance their own interests. In these theories, any aversion toward members of a different group might make intergroup contact psychically costly to prejudiced actors. This reasoning led Becker (1971) to formulate one of the first systematic theories of employment discrimination. He claimed that the strength of employers' *taste* for race or sex discrimination is expressed in the above-market wages they pay Whites or men to avoid having to employ minorities or women. Likewise, customers' prejudices motivate them to demand a discount for dealing with members of a group against whom they are prejudiced, and coworkers' prejudices allegedly prompt them to insist on a bonus, thereby motivating nonprejudiced employers to pay equally productive workers unequal wages (Blau, Ferber, and Winkler, 2001, pp. 219–221).

More generally, motive-based accounts of employment disparities across ascriptive groups derived from neoclassical economic theory make two important assumptions.

[2] While working on this chapter, I had to fight the impulse to speculate on *why* sociologists are predisposed to ask "why" rather than "how."

First, the desire for maximal profits hypothetically prompts firms to employ the most productive workers available at the lowest possible wage. Second, firms that discriminate suffer a competitive disadvantage that is a disincentive to discriminate. Given these assumed motives, any difference across ascriptive groups in job opportunities or rewards must stem from group differences on productivity-related characteristics such as skills and turnover (Haagsma, 1998). Economists also point to profit-motivated employers' desire to minimize the costs of labor market transactions, including information costs. Theoretically, employers try to reduce the cost of information by using ascriptive group membership as a proxy for individuals' likely productivity or employment costs. This profit motive should give rise to ascriptive inequality regardless of the accuracy of employers' beliefs about group differences on these characteristics (Blau et al., 2001, pp. 227–228; England, 1994; Phelps, 1972).

Sociological explanations of ascriptive inequality also assign causal status to the motives (or needs) of corporate entities that lead to ascriptive behavior by their agents. Consider, for instance, Kanter's (1977, pp. 48, 63) explanation for women's absence from managerial positions before the 1980s. In filling jobs involving uncertainty, she argued, corporate managers—virtually all White men—preferred "ease of communication and hence social certainty over the strains of dealing with persons who are 'different'" (pp. 49, 58). In short, Kanter theorized that managers' desire for informal communication *motivated* them to exclude members of some ascriptively defined groups.

Conflict theory also often implicates motives in explaining ascriptive inequality. For instance, Blalock (1956) theorized that when minority groups become large enough to threaten Whites, Whites respond by relegating minorities to bad jobs. This thesis has spawned numerous studies on the impact of racial composition on Black–White labor market inequality (e.g., Beggs, Villemez, and Arnold, 1997; Burr, Galle, and Fossett, 1991; Cassirer, 1996; Cohen, 1998; McCall, 2001a; 2001b). None of these researchers addressed the mechanisms through which Whites' hypothesized fears lower Blacks' relative earnings, however, so a half century after Blalock proposed this hypothesis, we still do not know *how* the racial composition of labor markets affects pay gaps between racial groups.

More generally, conflict theory's assumption that people seek to protect, if not increase, their share of scarce resources grants motives such overwhelming force that motives obscure the importance of the mechanisms through which motives might operate (e.g., Collins, 1975, p. 232; Tilly, 1998, p. 11; Tomaskovic-Devey, 1993, p. 10). In 1988, for example, I argued that the basic cause of occupational sex segregation was men's desire to preserve their advantages by maintaining sex differentiation in a variety of spheres, including the workplace. I claimed that men—like other privileged groups—protect their privileged status by making sure that the "rules" for distributing rewards give them the lion's share (Reskin, 1988, p. 60). While I still believe this is true, I wish I had spent more of the intervening 15 years investigating *how* specific workplace mechanisms favor members of dominant groups to varying degrees, and *how* extra-workplace factors lead organizations to alter or maintain those rules.

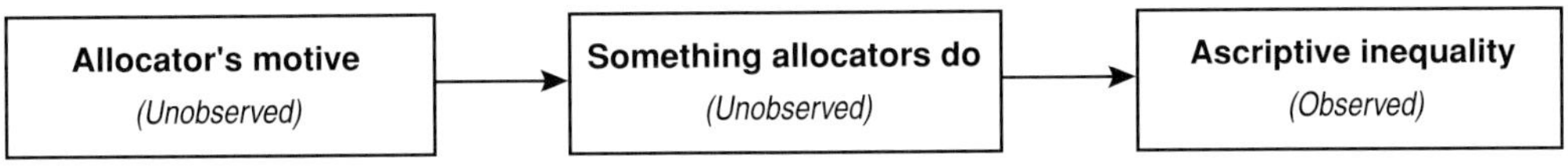

Figure 1. Causal model linking allocator's motive to ascriptive inequality.

The causal model underlying the theoretical approaches to stratification discussed above appears in figure 1. All these approaches attribute ascriptive inequality[3] to the motives of "allocators"—those actors who distribute scarce goods or opportunities among competitors; none specifies the mechanisms through which actors' motives produce more or less ascriptive inequality.[4]

1.2. Theoretical Limitations of Motive-Based Explanations

Motive-based explanations for ascriptive inequality are deficient primarily because they are immune to direct empirical verification. Five problems undermine motive-only explanations of inequality. First and foremost, researchers cannot observe the theoretical cause—allocators' motives. Motives are mental states, and mental states can rarely be directly observed. Indeed, some cognitive psychologists question whether people can really know even their own motives (Wilson and Brekke, 1994).[5] "The peculiar feature of the imputation of motives," as MacIver ([1942] 1964, p. 203) pointed out, "is that we are asserting a nexus between an overt action and a purely subjective factor that cannot be exposed to direct scrutiny and that is not as such manifest in the action." We cannot test, for example, whether corporate managers select subordinates who resemble them because they prefer social clones in certain posts, or whether Blacks' share of a metropolitan labor force affects how much (if at all) White pay-setters are threatened by their presence. Our inability to observe motives means that we cannot know which (if any) motives preceded an outcome. This is an important problem given that disparate motives can produce the same result (Schelling, 1978; Wilson and Brekke, 1994).

Second, ascribing motives to individuals based on their group membership assumes within-group homogeneity on the causal variable. Explanations that attribute motives to groups do not lend themselves to empirical verification because they ignore variation within the ascriptive group from which the allocators are drawn. Theories that assume *group*-based motives preclude the investigation of within-group covariation in, for example, the preference for socially similar subordinates and specific hiring and

[3] Ascriptive inequality, the dependent variable in figure 1, is seen in the strength of the association between an ascribed characteristic and some outcome.

[4] Note that this discussion does not apply to motive-centered models that specify causal mechanisms, such as efficiency theories (discussed below), which specify the employment practices that contribute to ascriptive inequality.

[5] Even if we could be certain of allocators' motives, treating them as causal agents involves a large leap of faith given how seldom people achieve their explicit goals (Tilly, 1998, p. 17).

promotion decisions, or in Whites' perceptions of threat and the actions they might take to reduce Blacks' relative pay.

Third, motive-based theories are limited in scope, applying only to ascriptive inequality stemming from the actions of entities that can engage in purposive behavior. These theories cannot address inequality stemming from the actions of allocators whose motives are directed toward entirely different goals or from practices implemented in the past that persist in the present. As I show below, both inequality and equality can result from neutral mechanisms or structures that have disparate or identical impacts on ascriptive groups (Stryker, 2001). Given the staying power of existing organizational policies and practices (Carroll and Hannan, 2000; Stinchcombe, 1965), the effects of these practices may bear no relationship to the reasons they were originally implemented.

Fourth, the causal priority of motives over outcomes cannot be assumed. As Elster (1989, p. 16) observed, the best way to change people's minds may be to change their circumstances (also see Allport, 1954).

Fifth and finally, disregarding the mechanisms through which motives operate leaves us in the dark as to the immediate causes of variability in ascriptive inequality. In failing to specify the intervening processes that give rise to varying levels of inequality, motive-based theories treat mechanisms as invisible hands. Lacking direct measures of theoretically meaningful explanatory variables, we must treat disparities as evidence for both the hypothesized causal mechanism and its causal effect on the observed group difference. As I argue below, this heavy load of inference is often balanced precariously on a single coefficient.

1.3. Balkanization and Motive-Based Explanations of Inequality

Reinforcing motive-based explanatory theories is the division of stratification scholarship into largely separate specialties that are based on different ascribed characteristics (Reskin and Charles, 1999).[6] This balkanization of scholarship on ascriptive inequality reflects this country's "metanarrative" of discrimination *against* specific groups (Freshman, 2000, p. 428). This metanarrative implies that different explanations hold for different types of ascriptive inequality. Balkanized theories tend to assume that variation in some outcome across ascriptive groups is caused by something related to the particular characteristic that differentiates them.

Balkanization helps preserve the assumption that different motives cause different types of ascriptive stratification. Sex inequality at work, for example, has been attributed to men's hope to maintain their privileged status or to employers' desire to minimize turnover costs. Inequality based on sexual orientation theoretically stems from a different motive—homophobia, itself hypothetically a product of heterosexuals' insecurity regarding their own sexuality. Among motive-based theories advanced

[6] The structure of the American Sociological Association (ASA) mirrors this balkanization. The ASA, which has no section on stratification, has six sections on various bases of *ascribed* inequality.

to explain racial inequality are antipathy or fear by employers, their belief that White customers are reluctant to be served by people of color, or that minorities lack necessary skills (Moss and Tilly, 1996). The exploitation of undocumented immigrant workers hypothetically stems from the xenophobia or fear of competition by native workers (Tilly, 1998, p. 16).

Because different specialties (e.g., gender stratification, race and ethnic stratification) assume that different motives produce different inequalities, different variables appear in analyses of the same outcome—earnings, for example. But if the lack of "soft skills" explains Whites' advantage over Blacks (Moss and Tilly, 1996), why not include soft skills in analyses of sex differences? If employers are compensating something captured by AFQT scores, then why not include this variable in all analyses of earnings? Because we have constructed motive-based stories to account for these differently based expressions of ascribed inequality, and the stories tend to be group-specific. This essentialism reduces the power of theoretical explanations by obscuring the possibility that differential outcomes for each ascriptive divide result from the same general stratification processes. Of course, we cannot dismiss the possibility that some ascriptive characteristics operate differently from others, but we cannot assess the importance of such differences in analyses that are confined to a single group.

1.4. Individual-Level Data and Motive-Based Explanations

Perpetuating the problem of motive-based theories is researchers' heavy use of individual-level data to study ascriptive inequality.[7] In such data, explanatory variables are limited to individuals' characteristics (and the individuals are those allocated *to*, not allocators, the actors whose motives are theoretically relevant in most motive-based theories).[8] As a result, data analysis typically begins by comparing the credentials and "deficiencies" of the ascriptive groups under comparison. Tilly (1998, p. 30) summed up this state of affairs as "habit:"

> [F]aced with male/female differences in wages, investigators look for average human-capital differences among the individuals involved. Noticing that school performances of children correlate with the social positions of their parents, researchers attribute those differences in performance to "family background" rather than considering that teachers and school officials may shape those performances by their own categorical responses to parental social positions. Encountering racial differences in job assignments, researchers ask whether members of distinct racial categories are distributed differently by residential location.

While I agree with Tilly regarding our disposition toward individual-level explanations, it is not simply a matter of habit. Individual-level explanations are the *only*

[7] Although these data are usually analyzed for individuals, they may be aggregated spatially to metropolitan areas or states, or functionally to occupations or industries.

[8] Some readers may object that this assertion denies agency to workers. Certainly, there are workers who can write their own ticket with respect to their occupation, employer, rank, hours, working conditions, benefits, and pay; but they are the exception.

explanations possible with individual-level data, and, like the gambler who keeps returning to a crooked casino because it is the only game in town, many of us turn repeatedly to individual-level data, or direct our students to them, because they are almost the only readily available data.[9]

In quantitative analyses of individual-level data, the conclusions we draw depend on whether or not the partial coefficient for some ascribed status is statistically significant. Although researchers often speak of whether an ascribed characteristic "affects" the dependent variable (Sørensen, 1998, p. 250), whether or not a regression coefficient for an ascriptive characteristic is statistically significant indicates *only* whether there is an association to be explained in a particular data set and given a particular specification of the model. If the partial regression coefficient is significant, we tend to attribute its effect to some unobserved mental states, such as bias or threat, on the part of an allocator. If the partial coefficient is not statistically significant, then we infer different (and exonerating) motives by the allocator—to maximize productivity or reduce turnover, for example.

A case in point is a debate in the *American Sociological Review* over whether the growing wage gap between Black men and White men in the late 1970s and early 1980s reflected increasing wage discrimination. On the basis of an unexplained effect of race on earnings in 1985, but not 1976, Cancio, Evans, and Maume (1996, p. 551) concluded that race discrimination played an increasing role in the wage gap. Farkas and Vicknair (1996) disputed Cancio and her colleagues' conclusion by showing that including a measure of cognitive skill among the regressors wiped out the significant effect of race on the pay gap. They interpreted this result as indicating that employers hired Blacks for lower paying jobs than Whites because Whites had stronger cognitive skills, not because employers were biased against Blacks.[10]

This intellectual skirmish over what belongs on the right-hand side in a regression equation—and the longer-running fight over the role discrimination plays in ascriptive inequality—is inevitable when evidence for or against allocators' hypothesized motives boils down to the statistical significance of the residual effect of an ascribed characteristic. Bearing this in mind, consider a second example. Although male applicants to a high-tech firm were offered significantly higher starting salaries than women were, Petersen, Saporta, and Seidel (2000, pp. 794–795) concluded that the firm had not discriminated against women because, net of age and education, the

[9] This is not the case for the employer data in the National Organizations Study (Kalleberg et al., 1996) or the Multi-City Survey of Urban Inequality. These data sets have made possible important mechanism-based research of ascriptive inequality in the workplace (Baldi and McBrier, 1997; Holzer, 1996; Huffman and Velasco, 1997; O'Connor, Tilly, and Bobo, 2001; Reskin and McBrier, 2000; Tomaskovic-Devey, Kalleberg, and Marsden, 1996).

[10] In response, Maume et al. (1996) challenged Farkas and Vicknair's measure of cognitive skill, the Armed Forces Qualifying Test (AFQT) score, as racially biased and hence an improper control for racial differences in cognitive ability. For discussions of the validity of using AFQT scores to capture racial differences in cognitive skills, see Fischer et al. (1996), Rodgers and Spriggs (1996), Jencks and Phillips (1998), and Raudenbush and Kasim (1998).

sex difference in starting pay disappeared.[11] The firm also made Whites significantly higher final offers than it made to Asians, and it raised its first offer significantly more for Whites than for Blacks. These race differences disappeared when the researchers added two variables to the equation: where applicants were first interviewed (at the firm or on campus), and how applicants had learned of the job (through a classified ad, a headhunter, or a personal contact).

Here too, researchers' conclusions about the reasons for group differences depend on what variables they include on the right-hand side of the regression equation. Although segregation is an important cause of the female–male pay gap (Jacobs, 1999; Petersen and Morgan, 1995), and female and male hires were apparently dissimilarly distributed across jobs (Petersen et al., 2000, p. 795), Petersen and his colleagues did not include in regressions any measure of the jobs applicants were offered. Meanwhile, they inexplicably included the site of the first interview as a determinant of starting pay. For regression analyses to explain group differences in pay, the specifications of earnings regressions must capture the way allocators set pay.

Ultimately, however, the problem in these papers, and in many others (e.g., Kalleberg and Reskin, 1995; Reskin and Ross, 1992), stems from attempts to explain race and sex inequality by workers' personal characteristics. I am not arguing that individual-level analyses add nothing to our understanding of ascriptive inequality. They reveal group differences that require explanation (e.g., Budig and England, 2002; Waldfogel, 1997), and they can rule out individual-level explanations for these differences. Without indicators of the causal mechanisms, however, we cannot discover the causal processes that lead levels of inequality to vary, so the theoretical meaning of the results is inevitably a matter of debate. Instead of enhancing our understanding of how ascriptive groups' outcomes come to be the same or to differ, we embark on a wild-goose chase in which we infer support for or against motive-based models based on whether ascriptive statuses have significant effects on some outcome, net of some set of individual-level control variables.

1.5. Summary

Most of the theories purporting to account for employment inequality emphasize allocators' motives. This approach, I argue, has kept us from being able to explain variation in ascriptive inequality. Motive-based theories cannot be empirically tested because we cannot observe people's motives. Motives do not have an isomorphic relationship to outcomes. Motive-based theories attribute motives wholesale to all members of an ascriptive group, precluding analyses that take advantage of the explanatory power of variation among allocators. And even if we could establish why allocators distribute rewards more or less equally, this knowledge would offer little guidance for

[11] From this and two other studies, Petersen et al. concluded that "women probably face no disadvantage in the hiring process in midsized and large U.S. organizations" (p. 813).

modifying social policies. If we are serious about explaining inequality, our theories and our analytic models must include indicators of causal mechanisms.

2. MECHANISM-BASED MODELS OF ASCRIPTIVE INEQUALITY

Motive-based models of ascriptive inequality consign the processes that convert actors' motives into more or less disparate outcomes to a black box (see figure 1). Inside that black box are mechanisms—the intervening variables that link ascribed characteristics to outcomes of varying desirability. Mechanisms are the processes that convert inputs (or independent variables) into outputs (or dependent variables). Thus, a mechanism is "an account of what brings about change in some variable" (Sørensen, 1998, p. 240). The physical world provides hundreds of examples of mechanisms: gears that convert power into speed and speed into power, circuit breakers that interrupt the flow of electricity, brake pads whose friction against wheels translates pressure on the brake pedal into deceleration.

The social mechanisms I discuss here are social arrangements that link ascriptive group membership to opportunities and rewards.[12] For example, the mechanism that converts workers' hours of work per week into their weekly earnings might be a pre-negotiated agreement that stipulates an hourly wage, a minimum-wage law, or an informal arrangement in which wages are at the discretion of the employer. Many mechanisms can produce or preclude an association between workers' race and their median annual earnings, including those practices governing workers' access to employment and to standard versus nonstandard jobs, and, within firms, access to specific job assignments, as well as the practices that set pay per job or unit of work.[13]

Superficially, a mechanism-based causal model resembles the motive-based model (compare figures 1 and 2). The important difference is that instead of an unobservable causal motive and an unspecified proximate cause ("something allocators do"), in mechanism-based models the proximate cause of ascriptive inequality is specified and observable. Consider, for example, how employers identify prospective workers. Most often allocators—employers or their employees—draw on employees' personal networks (Marsden and Gorman, 1998). Because people's informal networks tend to be homophilous, network hiring links the race, ethnicity, and gender of possible workers to whether and for what job they are hired (Elliott, 2001; Fernandez and Weinberg,

[12] In arguing that social mechanisms are observable, I part company with rational-choice theorists, for whom social mechanisms are *unobserved* theoretical constructs whose high level of abstraction is necessary for broad explanatory power (Hedström and Swedberg, 1998, pp. 10, 13; Kiser and Hechter, 1991).

[13] The mechanisms that cause ascriptive inequality to vary do not include abstract or global phenomena such as devaluation, discrimination, exclusion, exploitation, meritocracy, oppression, and social closure. These describe but do not explain patterns of inequality (e.g., Reskin, 1988; Tomaskovic-Devey, 1993; Weber [1922] 1968).

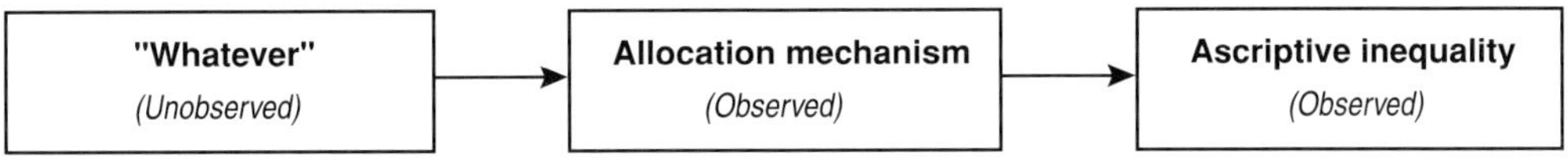

Figure 2. Causal model linking allocation mechanism to ascriptive inequality.

Note: A variety of factors (denoted as "whatever") influence what allocation mechanisms are operative: organizational decisions, economic constraints, or allocators' conscious motives or automatic cognitive biases. Although the influence of these factors on mechanisms deserves study, we can explain the variation in ascriptive inequality without knowing why organizations or individuals implement particular allocation mechanisms.

1997; Lin, 2000). Ethnographic research and case studies point to *why* employers hire through networks—recruiting through informal networks is less costly, creates a richer pool of candidates, allows workers to hoard opportunities, and facilitates excluding workers from discounted groups (Fernandez, Castilla, and Moore, 2000; Fernandez and Weinberg, 1997; Waters, 1999, pp. 105–110). But the difficulty of knowing which if any of these motives prompted a firm to recruit through networks prevents "why" scholarship from explaining variation in ascriptive inequality.

Although a case can be made for giving top priority to identifying organizational-level mechanisms because they are the proximate causes of levels of ascriptive inequality (Reskin, 2000), we must also understand the role of mechanisms that operate indirectly through organizational-level mechanisms, as figure 3 illustrates. Below I discuss mechanisms at the intrapsychic, interpersonal, societal, and organizational levels.

2.1. Intrapsychic Mechanisms

Intrapsychic mechanisms, by definition, involve mental processes and hence are difficult to observe. Nonetheless, social cognition research has experimentally implicated certain intrapsychic mechanisms—automatic cognitive errors—in ascriptive inequality (for summaries, see Brewer and Brown, 1998; Fiske, 1998). The techniques through

Figure 3. Causal model linking distal and proximate allocation mechanisms to ascriptive inequality.

which researchers have observed these mechanisms permit investigation of their impact on workplace inequality, so I focus on them.[14]

Social cognition theory assumes that our brains seek to minimize cognitive effort in part through automatic categorization and association. According to considerable experimental evidence, we automatically categorize people into *ingroups* (people like us), to whom we attribute favorable traits, and *outgroups* (people unlike us), with whom we associate less favorable traits. We prefer members of our ingroup whom we are predisposed to trust, cooperate with, and favor in distributing opportunities (Brewer and Brown, 1998; Fiske, 1998, p. 362). Consider an experiment in which subjects were instructed to distribute rewards between an ingroup member and an outgroup member, either equally or based on performance. Subjects tended to reward the performers equally when the outgroup member did better; when the ingroup member did better, they tended to base the reward on performance (Ng, 1984).

We also automatically link certain traits to social categories. In other words, we stereotype people based on group membership. Moreover, we process information in ways that help to maintain our stereotypes (Brown, 1995; Fiske, 1998, p. 367). Exposure to stereotype-linked activities or traits can activate our stereotypes and thereby affect our behavior (Greenwald and Banaji, 1995). For instance, White subjects subliminally "primed" with (i.e., exposed to) photographs of the faces of young Black men became angrier about a rigged computer glitch than subjects primed with photographs of White men, and White subjects primed with pictures of Black men displayed more hostility toward an unseen partner in a cooperative task than subjects primed with pictures of White men (Chen and Bargh, 1997). This and other research suggest that exposure to stimuli associated with members of a stereotyped group brings to mind the traits stereotypically linked to that group—in this case, the stereotype of young Black men as hostile.

Sociological theories about intrapsychic mechanisms lack the sophisticated measurement techniques that characterize psychological approaches to cognitive bias. For example, Kanter (1977) and Blau (1977, pp. 78–83) each theorized that skewed group composition fosters ascriptive inequality because members of statistical minorities are particularly visible to majority-group members. Majorities hypothetically suffer distorted perceptions of conspicuous minorities, leading to behaviors that disadvantage minority-group members.

Status expectations research has also shown that intrapsychic mechanisms contribute to ascriptive inequality. Theoretically when persons from different status groups interact, members of both groups expect higher-status group members to outperform lower-status group members (Berger, Cohen, and Zelditch, 1972; Ridgeway, 1997). These expectations act as self-fulfilling prophecies, especially when the ascribed status that differentiates the groups is salient. For example, in mixed-sex interaction

[14] Readers can assess their own automatic race, sex, and age stereotypes by taking the Implicit Association Tests at http:/implicit/harvard.edu.

men have more opportunities to perform and others evaluate their performance more positively. Although this approach is better suited to answering "why?" than "how?" (Ridgeway, 1997, p. 223), its systematic theoretical exposition provides a promising foundation for incorporating observable mechanisms.

Intrapsychic mechanisms, although the object of intriguing research, remain largely beyond observation. But sociologists' growing interest in cognitive processes should auger the development of techniques for observing intrapsychic mechanisms that affect our reactions to others, and thereby contribute to explaining variability in ascriptive inequality.

2.2. Interpersonal Mechanisms

Interpersonal mechanisms can affect the amount of ascriptive inequality in the workplace by converting allocators' mental states into differential behavior toward others depending on their ascriptive characteristics. If Kanter (1977) were correct in attributing women's exclusion from managerial jobs to managers' preferences for similar others, this effect would have been brought about through managers' interaction with candidates for managerial posts. The extent to which allocators base personnel decisions on an allocatees' age, sex, color, accent, or perceived sexual orientation obviously contributes to ascriptive inequality in work settings. Innumerable examples of equal treatment and unequal treatment are available; space permits just two. First, according to one of the few studies of employment discrimination against homosexuals, research confederates who portrayed gay or lesbian applicants were treated more negatively during the interview than persons who presented themselves as straight, although they were as likely as straight applicants to get a job offer (Helb et al., 2002). Second, a race discrimination suit against Kansas City Power asserted that managers made special efforts on behalf of White applicants for promotion, but not Black applicants, such as making inquiries when their application did not meet minimum requirements (*Ross v. Kansas City Power and Light,* 293 F. 3d 1041 [2002]).

Importantly, allocators' behavior toward persons from different groups can affect the latter's performance and hence indirectly reduce their relative performance. Such effects often occur in informal interaction. For instance, White experimental subjects who interviewed Black job applicants tended to sit farther from them, made more speech errors, and ended the interviews sooner than those interviewing Whites. White interviewees whose interviewers behaved toward them in ways that interviewers did with Blacks were more nervous and less effective than those treated in ways White interviewers treat White interviewees (Word, Zanna, and Cooper, 1974). Thus, White allocators' differential interaction with Black and White interviewees precipitates poorer interview performance by Blacks that presumably reduces their evaluations relative to those of White interviewees.

Allocators' actions can elicit behavior in others that may culminate in more or less ascriptive inequality (Bargh, 1999, p. 372). In the experiment described above

(Chen and Bargh, 1997), for instance, both the experimenters and the experimental subjects rated the *task partners* of the subjects who had been exposed to Black faces as more hostile than they rated the partners of subjects who had been exposed to White faces.[15] In this case, the non-activation or activation of racial stereotypes by subliminal exposure to pictures of Black or White males affected whether Whites behaved with hostility toward their task partners (an intrapsychic mechanism), and their hostility in turn provoked hostility in their partners (an interpersonal mechanism).

In sum, intrapsychic and interpersonal mechanisms can affect levels of ascriptive inequality, depending on whether organizational mechanisms permit, blunt or eliminate their effects.

2.3. Societal Mechanisms

Whether organizations follow personnel practices that foster or discourage ascriptive inequality depends on external social and economic factors that therefore are mechanisms that indirectly affect ascriptive inequality. Many societal mechanisms affect employers' personnel practices. Among others these include normative considerations within establishments' institutional communities, the expectations of their clientele, collective bargaining agreements, public transportation routes, and public regulations. The impact of Title 7 of the 1964 Civil Rights Act illustrates how societal mechanisms can indirectly affect ascriptive inequality within work settings by influencing what employers do.

Title 7 and its amendments bar employment discrimination based on race, national origin, religion, sex, pregnancy, age, and disability. Of course, outlawing a behavior does not necessarily eliminate it. As Galanter (1974, p. 149) observed, systems can accommodate major changes in the rules without altering everyday practices or redistributing advantage. The impact of laws on workplace mechanisms depends on their implementation. In the case of Title 7, Congress charged the Equal Employment Opportunities Commission (EEOC) and the federal courts with implementation (Blumrosen, 1993; Burstein, 1989; Burstein and Edwards, 1994; Graham, 1990).

The activities of enforcement agencies can affect employers' behavior by challenging or condoning particular personnel actions, by permitting business as usual or by requiring changes in employment structures. Initially, the EEOC had the authority to do just three things: investigate complaints, attempt to conciliate those it deemed valid, and issue regulations (Graham, 1990). In practice, for much of its existence the EEOC has given a free hand to employers. In its handling of complaints, the EEOC signals to the business community what kinds of practices are permissible, and after the 1970s, the message was that employers did not have much to fear (but see Heckman and Payner, 1989).[16] Over the longer run, variation in the agency's resources, political

[15] All the interaction partners had been primed with pictures of White faces.

[16] In the late 1990s, the EEOC has taken to court only a few of the approximately 80,000 complaints it receives annually (Selmi, 1998).

mandate, and specific actions demonstrates its capacity to affect employers' compliance with Title 7 (Blumrosen, 1993). For example, its requirement that large firms report employment breakdowns across broad occupational categories by race and sex compels employers to assemble records in a form in which they and the EEOC can discern inequality. Thus, the extent of enforcement of Title 7 by the EEOC has been an important mechanism, albeit one that has often permitted ascription.

Judicial interpretations of Title 7 have also shaped whether and how firms implement personnel practices that contribute to levels of ascriptive inequality. The direction of the impact of federal courts has varied substantially with shifts in its political makeup. In 1971, the Supreme Court greatly extended Title 7's reach by ruling that neutral employment practices that have a disparate adverse impact on members of protected ascriptive groups are discriminatory, unless justified as a business necessity. By relieving plaintiffs of the near-insurmountable burden of proving intentional discrimination, this decision encouraged employers to alter selection criteria or other practices that contributed to ascriptive inequality. Its effect during the 1970s was to reduce ascriptive inequality by prompting firms to modify employment practices.

But what the courts giveth, the courts can take away. During the 1980s, federal courts chipped away at the disparate-impact doctrine, making it increasingly difficult for plaintiffs to win disparate-impact lawsuits. By 1979, for example, the Supreme Court allowed New York City Transit Authority to exclude participants in a Methadone-treatment program from *all* its jobs, despite the ban's disparate impact on minorities and the Transit Authority's failure to show that a global ban was a business necessity (Lye, 1998). Congress amended Title 7 in 1991 to explicitly ban disparate-impact discrimination, but during the next decade federal courts rarely found practices with a disparate impact in violation of the law.

The right of workers who believe they have experienced discrimination to sue their employers is a third mechanism through which Title 7 has affected employers' practices. But workers' access to the courts has varied over time, as has the pressure on employers to check practices linked to ascriptive inequality. Title 7 initially allowed complainants to sue their employers if the EEOC provided no remedy. Until 1992, however, private attorneys lacked an economic incentive to take discrimination cases, given the low odds of winning (Burstein, 1989; Donohue and Siegelman, 1991; Selmi, 1996; Selmi, 1998). In amending Title 7 in 1991 to give plaintiffs the right to compensatory and punitive damages, Congress strengthened lawsuits as a mechanism to challenge ascriptive inequality—a financial inducement for attorneys to take on discrimination cases. In less than a decade, the annual number of lawsuits tripled from fewer than 7,000 to more than 21,000.

Although employers' litigation victories far outnumber their losses, a few highly visible multi-million-dollar judgments for plaintiffs have influenced employers' practices. Some have done so directly through consent decrees that involve major alterations in employers' personnel practices. For instance, Home Depot revamped its human resources system to conform to a consent decree, developing minimum qualifications for each job and computerizing applications and thereby reducing network hiring (Sturm,

2001). Often the impact of plaintiffs' victories has gone beyond their own employers. After Texaco paid $3 million to settle a sex bias case, a corporate interest group warned its members to carefully review their pay policies.

Finally, corporations' potential legal liability has drawn the attention of entrepreneurs marketing products that may reduce employers' risk of liability. For example, employers can reduce their liability through practices designed to signal nondiscriminatory intent (Bisom-Rapp, 2001). Such "bullet proofing" includes training on diversity and sexual harassment. Discrimination-liability insurance is also being marketed (Bielby and Bourgeois, 2002). The impact of these products on the mechanisms organizations implement that in turn affect levels of ascriptive inequality remains to be seen.

In sum, Title 7's restrictions on employment discrimination created several extra-workplace mechanisms that in turn should influence firm-level mechanisms that affect levels of ascriptive inequality at work. Systematic investigation of the impact of variation in these and other societal-level mechanisms on organizational mechanisms will enhance our ability to explain ascriptive inequality at work.

2.4. Organizational Mechanisms

At the organizational level, mechanisms that affect ascriptive inequality include the practices through which employers and their agents somehow link workers' ascriptive characteristics to work outcomes. Sometimes employers base opportunities and rewards on workers' ascriptive statuses as a matter of policy, favoring some groups and ignoring or harming others. For example, Atlantic Company refused to allow an African-American female manufacturing worker to wear "finger waves" because this hair style was "too different," rejected her request to wear her hair braided, and then told her that her ponytail was "too drastic" although White coworkers wore ponytails (*Hollins v. Atlantic Co.*, U.S. Court of Appeals for the Sixth Circuit 188 F. 3d 652 [1999]). More generally, employers might reserve jobs for co-religionists, give preference to heterosexuals, provide fewer medical benefits for one sex than the other, forbid workers from speaking any language but English while on the job, or use race or gender-conscious practices as part of court-ordered affirmative action. Variation in such policies mandating differential treatment affects levels of ascriptive inequality across firms (e.g., Konrad and Linnehan, 1999; Reskin, 1998; Watkins, 1993).[17] Some superficially neutral practices are designed to disadvantage particular groups. For example, the EEOC sued Alamo Car Rental for enacting a policy prohibiting female employees from wearing head scarves and then firing a Muslim woman for wearing a head scarf during Ramadan (www.eeoc.gov/press/9-30-02f.html).

[17] For example, employers have fired Navajo (*EEOC v. RD's Drive-In*, 2002) and Hispanic workers (*EEOC v. Premier Operator Services*, U.S. District court for the Northern District of Texas 113 F. Supp. 2d 1066 [2000]) for speaking languages other than English while in the workplace. For additional examples of cases involving differential treatment, see www.eeoc.gov/pr.html.

Although personnel practices are unlikely to override organizational policies mandating differential treatment, the personnel practices that organizations implement can check or permit the effects of intrapsychic and interpersonal mechanisms. And societal mechanisms shape organizational practices. Thus, organizational practices are the immediate causes of variation in ascriptive inequality.

One practice that strongly affects whether allocators act on their preference is whether organizations conceal from or make known to decision-makers allocatees' ascriptive characteristics (Wilson and Brekke, 1994). Variation in civil service rules illustrate the impact of revealing or suppressing this information. For several decades in the 20th century, applicants for Civil Service positions were required to attach photographs to their applications: Ensuring that decision-makers knew applicants' race and sex maintained a White Civil Service for decades (Rosenbloom, 1977, pp. 51–58). More recently, changes in the way that major symphony orchestras selected musicians show the impact of evaluators' exposure to allocatees' ascribed characteristics. The introduction of "blind auditions" during the 1970s and 1980s brought female musicians into major symphony orchestras (Goldin and Rouse, 2000). Finally, whether applicants must apply for jobs in person or can conceal their ascribed characteristics through computerized application processes influences ascriptive inequality in hiring through exposure control (e.g., Richtel, 2000; Sturm, 2001).

In many situations in which employers allocate opportunities and rewards, evaluatees' ascriptive characteristics cannot be concealed from allocators. Whether these characteristics influence allocators' decisions depends on how effectively personnel practices check allocators' discretionary behaviors (Bisom-Rapp, 2001; Sturm, 2001). Generally, the more bureaucratized personnel practices are, the less freedom managers have to act on their own stereotypes, biases, or impulses to favor ingroup members. The effects of bureaucratization operate through career ladders, job analysis and compensation systems, collective bargaining agreements dictating working conditions, and the availability of family leave and flexible scheduling, among others (Dobbin et al., 1993; Foddy and Smithson, 1999). Of course, the extent that allocators are bound by these policies will condition their impact (Edelman, 1992; Flack, 1999; Hochschild, 1997; Nelson and Bridges, 1999).

With respect to evaluation processes, the availability of relevant, objective information on evaluatees; the specificity of evaluation criteria; and the extent to which decision-makers are required to use the criteria all matter for levels of ascriptive inequality. In contrast, the more that performance-related information on allocatees is available to evaluators, the less their ascriptive bias (Pugh and Wahrman, 1983; Swim et al., 1989, p. 421). In addition, the vaguer and harder to operationalize the selection criteria are, the more likely that allocators' discretion will affect their decisions (Blalock, 1991).

One mechanism affecting allocators' discretion is the extent to which employers hold allocators accountable for their decisions (Salancik and Pfeffer, 1978; Tetlock, 1992). Accountability exists when allocators anticipate both having to communicate their decisions and having to defend those decisions (Tetlock, 1983). Whether or not allocators anticipate being held accountable for their judgments influences how they mentally encode information, thereby influencing the likelihood of cognitive bias. Accountability is most likely to reduce ascriptive bias when allocators know they must communicate evaluations to candidates and justify them to their superiors (Blalock, 1991, p. 103). In other words, the transparency of allocation processes and their outcomes conditions the impact of accountability on ascriptive bias (Blalock, 1991, p. 41).

Another broad group of mechanisms includes those established to make ascriptive biases visible to employers, workers, and enforcement agencies. Particularly important is whether or not records of employment outcomes are collected and can be examined by ascriptive groups.[18] For example, research subjects examined hypothetical data in which the sexes were equally qualified on average, but men's average pay exceeded women's. When they reviewed one female–male pair at a time, subjects were significantly less likely to detect discrimination and judged any discrimination to be less serious than when they reviewed aggregated data for the hypothetical firm (Clayton and Crosby, 1992, pp. 73–79). In addition, whether earnings were listed by ascriptive group membership influenced whether allocatees noticed and objected to any ascriptive inequality (Major, 1989).

The existence of sanctions exerts an important effect on how firms' personnel practices influence ascriptive inequality. For instance, the California Personnel Board encouraged state agencies to integrate all jobs, but threatened budget cuts for only those agencies that failed to increase women's and minorities' presence in specific targeted jobs. The targeted jobs became more integrated, but the nontargeted jobs became more segregated (Baron, Mittman, and Newman, 1991).

The amount of ascriptive inequality in an organization also depends on whether organizational practices have a *disparate impact* on ascriptive groups. Disparate impact occurs when some neutral mechanism translates group differences on position, experience, or a credential into differential outcomes for ascriptive groups. For example, a nepotism requirement for membership in an all-White union local, although neutral on its face, excluded workers of color from the local (Freshman, 2000, note 142). Whether or not policies have a disparate impact on ascriptive groups depends both on the practice and on whether the groups' members are differentially situated with respect to the practice (Hermes, 1998, pp. 81–82). Whether or not a practice has a disparate impact can depend on whether a firm employs ascriptive groups in different jobs and whether the risk of a layoff, the chance of a promotion, or access to some benefit depends on one's organizational location (e.g., Yamagata et al., 1997).[19]

[18] The Office for Federal Contract Compliance Programs requires contractors to keep such records by race and sex in order to make it easier to employers as well as regulators to detect unequal treatment (Cordova, 1992).

[19] The alternative to disparate impact—identical impact—is likely to be taken for granted and hence is less obvious as a mechanism.

2.5. Summary

The presence and form of organizational practices that require, permit, or foster all differential treatments are the proximate causes of varying levels of ascriptive inequality in places of work. They operate primarily by affecting allocators' access to information about allocatees' ascribed characteristics, controlling whether allocators can act on such information, and the extent to which they make differential outcomes visible. More generally, organizational-level mechanisms influence levels of ascriptive inequality by the extent to which they explicitly treat members of different ascriptive groups differently; the extent to which they mediate the effects of intrapsychic or interpersonal mechanisms by curtailing, allowing, or even encouraging allocators to use discretion in personnel decisions; and the extent to which neutral organizational practices have a different effect on members of different ascriptive groups.

3. IDENTIFYING MECHANISMS FOR STUDY

Here, I suggest ways to identify mechanisms for investigation. A promising approach lies in exploring contextual and structural "effects." *Structure* and *context* are fundamental concepts in sociology because they highlight the importance of setting on social processes. Although structural and contextual effects are not themselves mechanisms (Sørensen, 1998, p. 253), they are proxies for mechanisms that vary across settings. Variation in the association between cities' racial composition and the earnings gap across regions illustrates this point: Racial pay gaps for women are low in midwestern cities with low immigration, high-wage manufacturing, and higher levels of unionization (McCall, 2001, p. 538). Researchers should pursue how collective bargaining and the typical pay of blue-collar jobs penalize minority women for their labor market share. Other promising contextual or structural differences include the smaller racial pay gap in government jobs than in the private sector (Grodsky and Pager, 2001), the difference in White men's promotion rates across work settings varying in their race and sex composition (Baldi and McBrier, 1997), and men's greater advantage in the chance to exert influence over female coworkers when the sexes work in the same rather than in separate establishments (Mueller, Mulinge, and Glass, 2002, p. 176). These and many other structural and contextual effects point to mechanisms for study.

Theory and *research* also can suggest organizational-level mechanisms for study. Research building on Weber's ([1922] 1968) recognition of bureaucracy's constraining impact on managerial discretion has identified several likely mechanisms that affect ascriptive inequality, foremost among them being formalization (Bielby, 2000; Nelson and Bridges, 1999; Perry, Davis-Blake, and Kulik, 1994; Reskin, 2000). Investigating the specific processes that link organizations' sex composition to women's share of top jobs can adjudicate among theoretical interpretations, such as labor supply, institutional norms, and internal pressure groups (Cohen, Broschak, and Haveman,

1998; Konrad and Pfeffer, 1991; Reskin and McBrier, 2000; Tomaskovic-Devey et al., 1996). Given the role of organizational inertia for maintaining inequality, Baron and Pfeffer (1994, p. 205) called for research on its causes. Kim's (1999) account of the effect on the pay gap in 1993 of a 1931 decision by the California Civil Service to pay workers in predominantly female jobs less than comparably qualified workers in male jobs demonstrates this strategy's potential payoff in illuminating the mechanisms implicated in ascriptive inequality. If, as Cancio et al. (1996) speculated, the declining enforcement of EEO laws widened the racial pay gap, we need to investigate how this occurred. Finally, demonstrated disparities beg the question of mechanisms. Smith's (2001, 2002) report that African-American workers are less likely than Whites to have authority or control over financial resources at work directs us to look for operative mechanisms.

Case studies of firms offer a third source for identifying mechanisms for study. Fernandez's (2001) detailed account of how technological change at a food-processing company increased race and sex wage inequality is a case in point. Mechanisms apparently contributing to these increases included skill upgrading concomitant with computerizing the production process, whose effects fell particularly heavily on the firm's Black workers. Dampening the ascriptive effect of technological change were a no-layoff policy during retooling, a wage guarantee for workers in retooled jobs, and substantial retraining. Of course, case studies do not permit conclusions about causal mechanisms unless they also consider events that did *not* occur (e.g., the firm declining to use upgrading as an opportunity to bust the union or to move to a right-to-work state, or failing to actively recruit minority and female candidates for the new high-tech jobs). In addition, they typically lack the covariation needed for conclusions about causal mechanisms. Nonetheless, case studies are excellent sources for identifying possible causal mechanisms (Cockburn, 1991; Cohn, 1985; Milkman, 1987; Pierce, 1998). Studies of organizations' attempts to reduce ascriptive inequality (e.g., Sturm, 2001) are especially likely to be useful.

Discrimination lawsuits provide a fourth source of possible mechanisms for systematic analysis. Because plaintiffs must assert exactly *how* employers have disadvantaged them, legal documents provide detailed accounts of employment practices from both sides. Nelson and Bridges's (1999) analyses of four discrimination cases illustrate how litigation can reveal possible causal mechanisms in ascriptive inequality. They found, for example, that by benchmarking predominantly male and predominantly female jobs to jobs in the private sector, public employers exacerbated private-sector pay disparities. They discovered too that unionization contributed to the earnings disparity between the sexes because men's jobs were more likely to be unionized, and male-dominated locals were more influential than female-dominated locals in the state's pay-setting bureaucracy. Law review articles also outline mechanisms (e.g., Oppenheimer, 1993; Schultz, 1998; Schultz and Petterson, 1992), and published lawsuits provide considerable detail as to mechanisms (e.g., *Wards Cove v. Atonio,* U.S. Supreme Court 493 U.S. 802; 110 S. Ct. 38 [1989]).

4. CONCLUSIONS

Insofar as data exist, sociologists have thoroughly documented sex and race disparities in work outcomes.[20] And there our achievements end. Although researchers try to explain observed inequality, theories about actors' motives guide the search for explanation, and it is all but impossible to know actors' motives. The product of this approach is not explanation, but a never-ending and unprofitable debate over the role of unobserved motives. Although the most satisfying explanations address both why and how, as Whorf (1956) put it, "The WHY of understanding may remain for a long time mysterious but the HOW ... of understanding ... is discoverable" (p. 239, capitalization in original). Hedström and Swedberg (1998, p. 10) concur that causal explanation must address *how* a relationship came about. If we are serious about explaining variation in inequality, our theories and analytic models must include indicators of causal mechanisms.

Two disciplinary practices reinforce our preoccupation with motive-based theories: the balkanization of research on ascriptive stratification and our reliance on individual-level data. The balkanization of research reflects the popular notion that different types of ascriptive inequality have different causes. This parochialism conceals their uniqueness as well as their fundamental similarities. All forms of ascriptive stratification involve long-standing relations of inequality within stable hierarchies that are similarly ordered across spheres. Only by breaking out of this parochialism can we find general explanations for ascriptive inequality *and* discover whether and how they must be modified for particular ascriptive characteristics. Certainly, the mechanisms that affect levels of ascriptive inequality are not unique to specific ascriptive divisions. The formalization of Home Depot's application and hiring procedures following a sex discrimination lawsuit benefited men of color in addition to all women (Sturm, 2001). Although interdisciplinary collaboration is in vogue, scholars interested in ascriptive inequality must begin with intradisciplinary dialogue and collaboration. For this to happen, the desire to develop better explanations will not suffice; we need mechanisms that foster intradisciplinary dialogue.

The second obstacle to identifing the mechanisms that cause ascriptive inequality is that most of the readily available data come from surveys of individuals. Data for individuals can address only the equality across groups of individual-level inputs and outcomes. As a result, the only explanations for which most individual-level data are suited are group-linked "deficiencies" (which are relevant because of employers' hypothesized motives) or the unobserved motives of unobserved actors. In analyses based on standard data sets, explanations involving unobserved motives are necessarily speculative because the data do not include allocators (and even if they did, their motives are all but impossible to know). Group-difference explanations are unsatisfying,

[20] Disparities across some racial categories, across ethnic groups, and by sexual orientation, disability, age, and religion are less well documented.

both because they rest on implicit assumptions about employers' unmeasured motives and because they fail to indicate *how* group differences on individual-level independent variables give rise to group differences in outcomes. And both approaches ignore our discipline's unique strength: the analysis of the operation of social structures. To explain variation in levels of inequality across ascriptively defined groups, across contexts, and over time, we must analyze data for organizational and individual allocators that include allocation mechanisms.

Intellectually, the solution is simple: concentrate on allocation mechanisms. In explaining social stratification, identifying mechanisms is particularly important because—as the methods for distributing social goods—they are the engines of equality and inequality. As a practical matter, reorienting our search for explanations will require a major shift in the kinds of data in which our discipline invests. A large share of public funding for sociology goes to surveying individuals. As a result, the burden of collecting data that include mechanisms has fallen on individual researchers.

Publicly available data on employers would permit a broad shift to the study of mechanisms. Much of the mechanism-based explanatory research on ascriptive inequality has come from just two data sets: the National Organizations Study (NOS) and the Multi-City Study of Urban Inequality (MCSUI). Although the researchers who collected these data made them available to the research community, the dissemination of such data can take years. Collecting data such as the NOS and MCSUI for public use will be expensive, but our continuing investment in surveying individuals is also costly in terms of the return in new knowledge. With respect to ascriptive inequality, increasingly sophisticated analyses of the same individual-level data usually tell us what we already know: that significant disparities exist. And they fail to reveal what we do not know: the mechanisms that cause ascriptive inequality to vary in intensity across groups and settings.

In the absence of public data sets that include indicators of mechanisms, our primary recourse is the systematic observation of how specific mechanisms in particular settings affect levels of ascriptive inequality. As we accumulate empirical knowledge, we can generalize to more abstract mechanisms whose explanatory power extends beyond the settings we have studied. My discussion of organizational-level mechanisms illustrates how we can theoretically aggregate specific mechanisms into more general ones. For example, organizations use many mechanisms to ensure that allocators know or are ignorant of the ascriptive characteristics of those they are evaluating; each mechanism entails attaching or eliminating ascriptive identifiers. For example, by investigating which organizations do one, the other, or neither; whether there are conditions under which the effect of attaching or eliminating ascriptive information is the opposite of those summarized above and similar questions, we can build general theory.

We stand to gain not only better research and better theory; we stand to gain the opportunity to meaningfully contribute to social policy. Stratification scholarship is not simply a matter of academic interest. It can be consequential for the kinds of jobs people have, the education they can afford for their children, whether they have health insurance, and whether young people in poor neighborhoods have any basis to hope for a better future. We have done a stellar job of documenting the disparities across ascriptively defined groups. Increasingly researchers mention the policy implications of their findings. For example, in the debate discussed above, Cancio et al. (1996) concluded from their analyses that we need better enforcement of anti-discrimination laws, and Farkas and Vicknair (1996) called for policies to upgrade minorities' cognitive skills. Both of these recommendations have merit, but neither of the analyses on which the recommendations were based provides persuasive support for the recommended policy. If our analyses cannot convince other sociologists, how can we hope to convince policy-setters? And analyses that do not address the causal mechanisms are not convincing.

By pursuing the mechanisms responsible for varying levels of inequality, our scholarship can contribute to ameliorating these disparities. The division of labor in the social sciences especially qualifies sociologists to address policies related to ascriptive inequality. In pursuing motive-based explanations and analyzing individual-level data, we have abdicated that role. Indeed, that abdication inevitably follows from estimating models without mechanisms, because such models provide no guidance for developing social policies for a more just society. Pursuing research that takes seriously how to reduce ascriptive inequality will advance scientific knowledge—and more important, it will produce scholarship that addresses the social inequality that drew many of us to sociology in the first place.

CHAPTER 5

Understanding the Sources of Ethnic and Racial Wage Gaps and Their Implications for Policy[1]

Pedro Carneiro, James J. Heckman and Dimitriy V. Masterov

ABSTRACT

Previous studies show that controlling for ability measured in the teenage years eliminates young adult wage gaps for all groups except Black males, for whom the gap is reduced by approximately three-fourths. This suggests that disparity in skills, rather than the differential treatment of such skills in the market, produces racial and ethnic wage differentials. However, minority children and their parents may have pessimistic expectations about receiving fair rewards for their skills in the labor market and so they may invest less in skill formation. Poor schools may also depress cognitive achievement, even in the absence of any discrimination.

We find that the evidence on expectations is mixed. Although all groups are quite optimistic about the future schooling outcomes of their children, minority parents and children have more pessimistic expectations about child schooling relative to White children and their parents when the children are young. At later ages, expectations are more uniform across racial and ethnic groups. Gaps in ability across racial and ethnic groups also open up before the start of formal schooling, and the different trajectories of Hispanic and Black students indicate that differences in schooling cannot be the source of cognitive disparities. Finally, test scores depend on schooling attained at the time of the test. Adjusting for differences in schooling attainment at the age the test is taken reduces the power of measured ability to shrink wage gaps for Blacks, but not for Hispanics.

We also document the presence of disparities in noncognitive traits across racial and ethnic groups. These characteristics have been shown elsewhere to be important for explaining the labor market outcomes of adults. This evidence points to the importance of early (preschool) family factors and environments in explaining both cognitive and noncognitive ability differentials by ethnicity and race.

[1] This research was supported by a grant from the American Bar Foundation and NIH R01-HD043411. Carneiro was supported by Fundação Ciência e Tecnologia and Fundação Calouste Gulbenkian. We thank Derek Neal for helpful comments and Maria Isabel Larenas, Maria Victoria Rodriguez and Xing Zhong for excellent research assistance.

L. B. Nielsen and R. L. Nelson (eds.), Handbook of Employment Discrimination Research, 99–136.

INTRODUCTION

Despite 40 years of civil rights and affirmative action policy, substantial gaps remain in the market wages of African-American males and females compared to White males and females. There are sizable wage gaps for Hispanics as well.[1] Columns I of table 1 report the mean hourly log wage gaps for a cohort of Black and Hispanic males and females. These gaps are for a cohort of young persons age 26–28 in 1990 from the National Longitudinal Survey of Youth of 1979, or NLSY79. They are followed for 10 years until they reach age 36–38 in 2000. These gaps are not adjusted for differences in schooling, ability, or other potential sources of racial and ethnic wage differentials.

Table 1 shows that, on average, Black males earn 25% lower wages than White males in 1990. Hispanic males earn 17.4% lower wages in the same year. Moreover, the gaps widen for males as the cohort ages. The results for women reveal smaller gaps for Black women and virtually no gap at all for Hispanic women.[2] The gaps for women show no clear trend with age. Altonji and Blank (1999) report similar patterns using data from the Current Population Survey (CPS).

These gaps are consistent with the claims of pervasive labor market discrimination against many minorities. However, there is another equally plausible explanation. Minorities may bring less skill and ability to the market. Although there may be discrimination or disparity in the development of these valuable skills, the skills may be rewarded equally across all demographic groups in the labor market.

These two interpretations of market wage gaps have profoundly different policy implications. If persons of identical skill are treated differently on the basis of race or ethnicity, a more vigorous enforcement of civil rights and affirmative action in the marketplace would appear to be warranted. If the gaps are due to unmeasured abilities and skills that people bring to the labor market, then a redirection of policy towards fostering skills should be emphasized as opposed to a policy of ferreting out discrimination in the workplace.

An important paper by Neal and Johnson (1996) sheds light on the relative empirical importance of market discrimination and skill disparity in accounting for wage gaps by race. Controlling for a measure of scholastic ability measured in the middle teenage years, they substantially reduce but do not fully eliminate wage gaps for Black males in 1990–1991. They more than eliminate the gaps for Black females. Columns II of table 1 show our version of the Neal–Johnson study,[3] expanded to cover additional

[1] The literature on African-American economic progress over the 20th century is surveyed in Heckman and Todd (2001).

[2] However, the magnitudes (but not the direction) of the female gaps are less reliably determined, at least for Black women. Neal (2004) shows that racial wage gaps for Black women are underestimated by these types of regressions since they do not control for selective labor force participation. This same line of reasoning is likely to hold for Hispanic women.

[3] We use a sample very similar to the one used in their study. It includes individuals born only in 1962–1964. This exclusion is designed to alleviate the effects of differential schooling at the test date on test performance and to ensure that the AFQT test is taken before the individuals enter the labor market (i.e., so that it is a premarket factor).

Table 1. Change in the Black–White log wage gap induced by controlling for age-corrected AFQT in 1990–2000

Year	1990		1991		1992		1993		1994		1996		1998		2000	
	I	II	I	II	I	II	I	II	I	II	I	II	I	II	I	II
A. NLSY Men Born After 1961																
Black	−0.250	−0.060	−0.251	−0.082	−0.302	−0.113	−0.282	−0.104	−0.286	−0.093	−0.373	−0.149	−0.333	−0.069	−0.325	−0.089
	(0.028)	(0.030)	(0.028)	(0.030)	(0.029)	(0.030)	(0.028)	(0.030)	(0.031)	(0.033)	(0.032)	(0.034)	(0.034)	(0.035)	(0.035)	(0.035)
Hispanic	−0.174	−0.035	−0.113	0.020	−0.146	−0.014	−0.159	−0.027	−0.143	0.005	−0.186	−0.031	−0.195	−0.006	−0.215	−0.053
	(0.032)	(0.032)	(0.032)	(0.033)	(0.033)	(0.032)	(0.032)	(0.032)	(0.036)	(0.036)	(0.038)	(0.038)	(0.040)	(0.038)	(0.040)	(0.038)
Age	–	0.050	–	0.030	–	0.038	–	0.030	–	0.023	–	0.020	–	0.014	–	0.008
	–	(0.014)	–	(0.014)	–	(0.014)	–	(0.014)	–	(0.016)	–	(0.016)	–	(0.017)	–	(0.017)
AFQT	–	0.183	–	0.161	–	0.179	–	0.172	–	0.188	–	0.216	–	0.254	–	0.241
	–	(0.013)	–	(0.013)	–	(0.013)	–	(0.013)	–	(0.014)	–	(0.015)	–	(0.015)	–	(0.015)
$AFQT^2$	–	−0.022	–	−0.007	–	−0.001	–	0.002	–	0.014	–	0.021	–	0.032	–	0.023
	–	(0.011)	–	(0.011)	–	(0.011)	–	(0.011)	–	(0.012)	–	(0.013)	–	(0.013)	–	(0.013)
Intercept	2.375	0.957	2.372	1.463	2.404	1.202	2.423	1.431	2.458	1.652	2.533	1.756	2.589	1.960	2.629	2.224
	(0.017)	(0.385)	(0.017)	(0.406)	(0.017)	(0.422)	(0.017)	(0.432)	(0.018)	(0.488)	(0.019)	(0.540)	(0.020)	(0.594)	(0.020)	(0.621)
N	1538	1505	1553	1514	1536	1503	1542	1504	1522	1485	1554	1519	1494	1462	1438	1404

Year	1990		1991		1992		1993		1994		1996		1998		2000	
	I	II	I	II	I	II	I	II	I	II	I	II	I	II	I	II
B. NLSY Women Born After 1961																
Black	−0.172	0.041	−0.200	0.030	−0.201	0.010	−0.167	0.093	−0.148	0.099	−0.147	0.132	−0.201	0.071	−0.200	0.069
	(0.031)	(0.033)	(0.032)	(0.035)	(0.031)	(0.033)	(0.035)	(0.037)	(0.035)	(0.037)	(0.035)	(0.036)	(0.034)	(0.036)	(0.036)	(0.038)
Hispanic	−0.003	0.154	−0.017	0.153	−0.059	0.114	0.009	0.198	−0.018	0.170	−0.006	0.193	−0.069	0.151	−0.064	0.149
	(0.035)	(0.035)	(0.037)	(0.038)	(0.036)	(0.035)	(0.039)	(0.039)	(0.040)	(0.040)	(0.041)	(0.039)	(0.039)	(0.039)	(0.041)	(0.041)
Age	–	0.010	–	0.038	–	0.016	–	0.016	–	0.008	–	−0.009	–	0.013	–	−0.018
	–	(0.015)	–	(0.017)	–	(0.016)	–	(0.017)	–	(0.018)	–	(0.018)	–	(0.017)	–	(0.018)
AFQT	–	0.217	–	0.234	–	0.229	–	0.271	–	0.267	–	0.283	–	0.274	–	0.273
	–	(0.016)	–	(0.018)	–	(0.017)	–	(0.018)	–	(0.019)	–	(0.018)	–	(0.018)	–	(0.018)
$AFQT^2$	–	0.005	–	0.000	–	−0.001	–	−0.012	–	−0.024	–	0.005	–	0.000	–	−0.008
	–	(0.014)	–	(0.014)	–	(0.014)	–	(0.015)	–	(0.016)	–	(0.015)	–	(0.015)	–	(0.015)
Intercept	2.141	1.750	2.175	0.982	2.193	1.615	2.174	1.558	2.218	1.858	2.246	2.412	2.311	1.724	2.339	2.867
	(0.019)	(0.420)	(0.020)	(0.467)	(0.019)	(0.458)	(0.021)	(0.520)	(0.022)	(0.555)	(0.022)	(0.582)	(0.021)	(0.603)	(0.022)	(0.663)
N	1356	1325	1335	1299	1317	1278	1319	1281	1318	1288	1381	1344	1370	1329	1316	1276

Age-corrected AFQT is the standardized residual from the regression of the AFQT score on age at the time of the test dummy variables. AFQT is a subset of 4 out of 10 ASVAB tests used by the military for enlistment screening and job assignment. It is the summed score from the word knowledge, paragraph comprehension, mathematics knowledge, and arithmetic reasoning ASVAB tests. All wages are in 1993 dollars. The coefficients on the AFQT variables represent the effect of a one standard deviation increase in the score on the log hourly wage. Since the wage is measured in log points, the gaps for Blacks and Hispanics correspond approximately to percentage point differences relative to the White mean; that is, the Black–White gap of −0.25 in 1990 corresponds to 25% lower wages for Blacks in that year.

years. For Black males, controlling for an early measure of ability cuts the wage gap in 1990 by 76%. For Hispanic males, controlling for ability essentially eliminates it. For women the results are even more striking. Wage gaps are actually reversed, and controlling for ability leads to *higher* wages for minority females.

Following the procedure of Neal and Johnson, these adjustments do not control for racial and economic differences in schooling, occupational choice, or work experience. Neal and Johnson argue that racial and ethnic differences in these factors may reflect responses to labor market discrimination and should not be controlled for in estimating the full effect of race on wages since this may spuriously reduce estimated wage gaps by introducing a proxy for discrimination into the control variables. They further argue that ability measured in the teenage years is a "premarket" factor, meaning that it is not affected by expectations or actual experiences of discrimination in the labor market. This chapter questions this claim. There is considerable arbitrariness in proclaiming what is or is not a "premarket" factor, and such determinations matter greatly for the size of the estimated adjusted wage gaps. When adjustments for schooling attainment at the date of the test are made, the adjusted wage gaps *rise.*

Gaps in measured ability by ethnicity and race are indeed substantial. Figures 1A and B plot the ability distribution as measured by age-corrected AFQT[4] for men and women, respectively. These differences are large. As noted by Herrnstein and Murray (1994), ability gaps are a major factor in accounting for a variety of racial and ethnic disparities in socioeconomic outcomes. Cameron and Heckman (2001) show that controlling for ability, Blacks and Hispanics are more likely to enter college than are Whites at a time when wage premia for education are rising considerably.[5]

The evidence in columns II of table 1 suggests that the major source of minority–majority differences in wages is the disparity in characteristics that minorities bring to the market rather than discrimination in the workplace. At first glance, the evidence in the table suggests that there is no racial or ethnic disparity in market payments for comparable levels of skill for all groups but Black males.

Though the facts displayed in table 1 and figures 1A and B are provocative, they are controversial for a number of reasons. The major points of contention are as follows:

1. The gaps in ability evident in figures 1A and B may stem from lowered academic effort in anticipation of future discrimination in the labor market. If skills are not rewarded fairly, the incentive to acquire them is diminished for those subject to prejudicial treatment. Discrimination in the labor market might not only sap the

[4] Age-corrected AFQT is the standardized residual from the regression of the AFQT score on dummy variables for age at the time of the test. AFQT is a subset of 4 out of 10 ASVAB tests used by the military for enlistment screening and job assignment. It is the summed score from the word knowledge, paragraph comprehension, mathematics knowledge, and arithmetic reasoning ASVAB tests.

[5] Urzua (2003) shows that this effect arises from greater minority enrollment in 2-year colleges. Controlling for ability, Whites are more likely to attend and graduate from 4-year colleges. Using the Current Population Survey, Black and Sufi (2002) find that equating the family backgrounds of Blacks and Whites eliminates the Black–White gap in schooling only at the bottom of the family background distribution. Furthermore, the gaps are eliminated in the 1980s, but not in the 1990s.

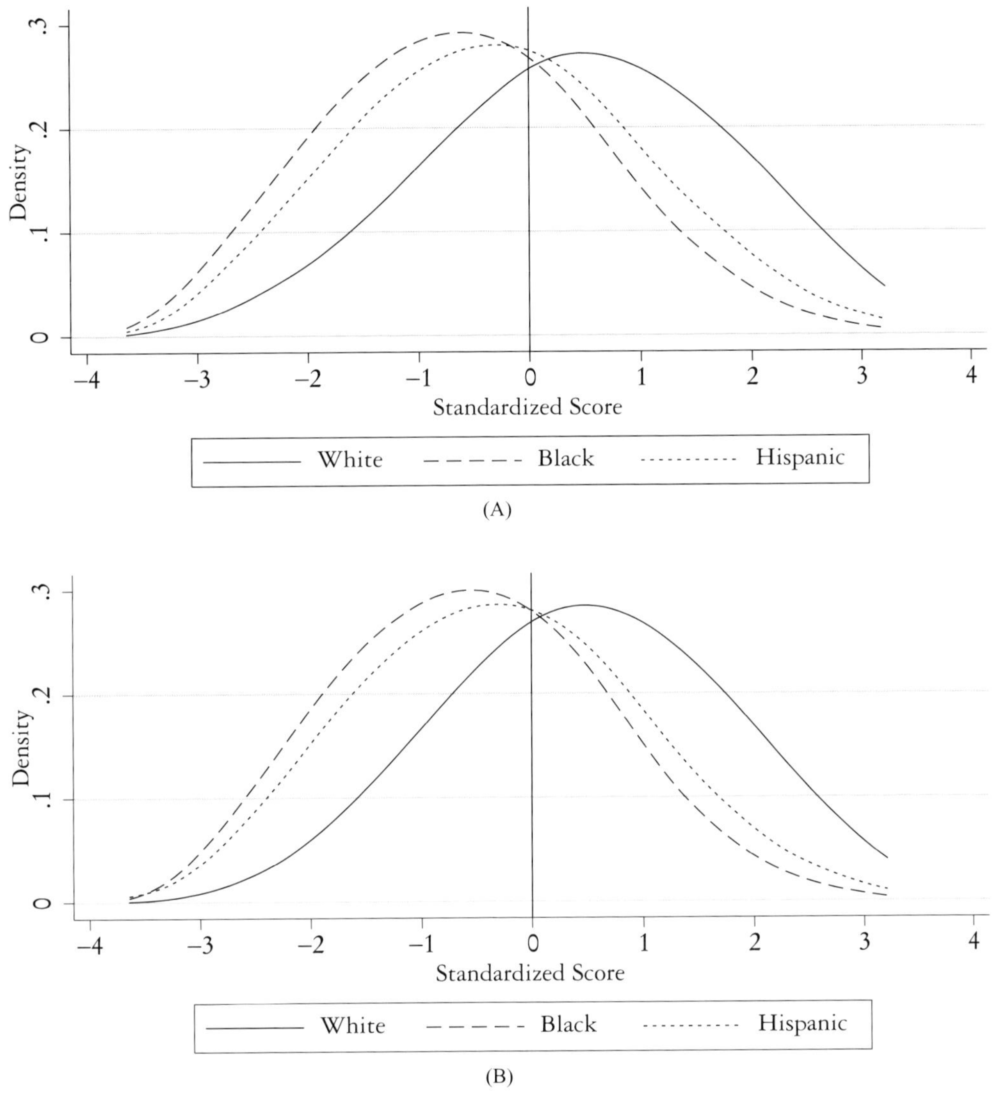

Figure 1. (A) Density of Age-Corrected AFQT NLSY79 Males Born after 1961; (B) Density of Age-Corrected AFQT NLSY79 Females Born after 1961 (Age-corrected AFQT is the standardized residual from the regression of the AFQT score on dummy variables for age at the time of the test. AFQT is a subset of 4 out of 10 ASVAB tests used by the military for enlistment screening and job assignment. It is the summed score from the word knowledge, paragraph comprehension, mathematics knowledge, and arithmetic reasoning ASVAB tests.)

incentives of children and young adults to acquire skills and abilities, but it may also influence the efforts they exert in raising their own offspring. This means that measured ability may not be a true premarket factor. Neal and Johnson (1996) mention this qualification in their original paper and their critics have subsequently reiterated it.

2. The gaps in ability may also be a consequence of adverse environments, and thus the appropriate policy for eliminating ability gaps is not apparent from table 1. Should policies focus on early ages through enriched Head Start programs or on improving schooling quality and reducing school dropout and repetition rates that plague minority children at later ages?

This chapter answers these and other questions. We show that:

(a) Ability gaps open up early, often by age one or two, and as a result minorities enter school with substantially lower measured ability than Whites. The Black–White ability gap widens as the children get older and obtain more schooling, but the contribution of formal education to the widening of the gap is small when compared to the size of the initial gap. There is a much smaller widening of the Hispanic–White gap with schooling.

Our evidence and that of Heckman, Larenas and Urzua (2004) suggest that school-based policies are unlikely to have substantial effects on eliminating minority ability gaps. Factors that operate early in the lifecycle of the child are likely to have the greatest impact on ability. The early emergence of ability gaps indicates that child expectations can play only a limited role in accounting for ability gaps since very young children are unlikely to have formed expectations about labor market discrimination and to take decisions based on those expectations. However, parental expectations of future discrimination may still play a role in shaping child outcomes.

(b) The early emergence of measured ability differentials casts doubt on the empirical importance of the "stereotype threat" (see Steele and Aronson, 1998) as a major factor contributing to Black–White test score differentials. The literature on this topic finds that Black college students at selective colleges perform worse on tests when they are told that the outcomes will be used in some way to measure Black–White ability differences, i.e., that the test may be used to confirm stereotypes about Black–White ability differentials. However, the children in our data are tested at a young age and are unlikely to be aware of stereotypes about minority inferiority or be affected by the stereotype threat which has only been established for students at elite colleges. In addition, large gaps in tests are also evident for Hispanics, a group for whom the stereotype threat has not been documented. We also show that increments in ability are equally rewarded in the labor market across all demographic groups, casting further doubt on the empirical importance of the stereotype threat which would in general predict different results for different true ability levels due to the mismeasurement of true ability.

(c) We find that differences in levels of schooling at the date tests are taken play a sizable role in accounting for measured ability differentials. Adjusting for the schooling attainment of minorities at the time that they take tests provides a potential qualification to the Neal and Johnson finding. Part of the ability gap demonstrated by Neal and Johnson is due to differential schooling attainment. An extra year of schooling has a greater impact on test scores for Whites and Hispanics than for Blacks. Adjusting the test score for schooling disparity at the date of the test raises the estimated wage gap and leaves more room for an interpretation of wage gaps as arising from labor market discrimination.

This finding does not necessarily overturn the conclusion of the Neal–Johnson analysis. At issue is the source of the gap in schooling attainment at the date of the test. Our analysis reveals that the amount of the wage gap that is explained by discrepancies in scholastic ability depends on the age and grade completed at the date of measurement of ability. Tests adjusted for schooling explain less of the Black–White wage gap compared to the unadjusted tests. The Neal–Johnson "premarket" factors are a composite of ability and schooling, and are likely to reflect both the lifecycle experiences and the expectations of the child. To the extent that they reflect expectations of discrimination as embodied in schooling that affects test scores, test scores are contaminated by market discrimination and are not truly premarket factors. An open question is how much of the gap in schooling is due to expectations about discrimination. For Black males, premarket factors account for half of the Black–White wage gap. We argue that our adjustment is overly conservative because much of the gap in schooling and ability opens up at an early age, before expectations of labor market discrimination or stereotype threat can be plausible explanations. The adjustments for the effect of schooling on test scores have much weaker effects for other demographic groups.

(d) The evidence from data on parent and child expectations tells a mixed story. If the rewards to schooling are lower for minorities, the return to schooling is lower and minority expectations of schooling attainment should be lower. Minority child and parent expectations measured when the children are 16 and 17 about the children's schooling prospects are as optimistic as White expectations, although actual schooling outcomes of Whites and minorities are dramatically different. Differential expectations at these ages cannot explain the gaps in ability evident in figures 1A and B.

For children of ages 14 and below, parent and child expectations about schooling are much lower for Blacks than for Whites, though only slightly lower for Hispanics than for Whites. All groups are still rather optimistic in light of later schooling attendance and performance. At these ages, differences in expectations across groups may lead to differential investments in skill formation. While lower expectations may be a consequence of perceived labor market discrimination, they may also reflect child and parent perceptions of the lower endowments possessed by minorities.

The fact that reported expectations are so inaccurate casts some doubt on the usefulness of expectations elicited by questionnaires for testing the actual expectations governing behavior. This is compounded by ambiguity of the source of the relatively pessimistic expectations.

(e) A focus on cognitive skill gaps, while traditional (see, e.g., Jencks and Phillips, 1998), misses important noncognitive components of social and economic success. We show that noncognitive (i.e., behavioral) gaps also open up early. Previous work shows that they play an important role in accounting for market wages. Policies that focus solely on improving cognitive skills miss an important and promising determinant of socioeconomic success and disparity that can be affected by policy (Carneiro and Heckman, 2003).

Section 1 presents evidence on the evolution of test score gaps over the lifecycle of the child. Section 2 discusses evidence on the quantitative unimportance of the stereotype threat. Section 3 presents our evidence on how adjusting for schooling at the date of the test affects the Neal–Johnson analysis, and how schooling affects test scores differentially for minorities. Section 4 discusses our evidence on child and parent expectations. Section 5 presents evidence on noncognitive skills that parallels the analysis of Section 1. Section 6 concludes.

1. MINORITY–WHITE DIFFERENCES IN EARLY TEST SCORES AND EARLY ENVIRONMENTS

The evidence presented in the Introduction suggests that a large fraction of the minority–White disparity in labor market outcomes that is frequently attributed to discrimination may be due instead to minority–White disparities in skill endowments. These skill endowments may be innate or acquired during the lifetime of an individual. In this section, we summarize evidence from the literature and present original empirical work that demonstrates that minority–White cognitive skill gaps emerge early and persist through childhood and the adolescent years.

Jencks and Phillips (1998) and Duncan and Brooks-Gunn (1997), among others, document that the Black–White test score gap is large for 3- and 4-year-old children. Using the Children of the NLSY79 (CNLSY) survey, a variety of studies show that even after controlling for many variables like individual, family and neighborhood characteristics, the Black–White test score gap is still sizable.[6] These studies also document that there are large Black–White differences in family environments. Ferguson

[6] In a similar study based on the Early Childhood Longitudinal Survey (ECLS), Fryer and Levitt (2004) eliminate the Black–White test score gap in math and reading for children at the time they are entering kindergarten, although not in subsequent years. However, the raw test score gaps at ages 3 and 4 are much

(2002a) summarizes this literature and presents evidence that Black children come from much poorer and less educated families than White children, and they are also more likely to grow up in single parent households. Studies summarized in Ferguson (2002b) find that the achievement gap is high even for Blacks and Whites attending high quality suburban schools.[7] The common finding across these studies is that the Black–White gap in test scores is large and that it persists even after one controls for family background variables. Children of different racial and ethnic groups grow up in strikingly different environments. Even after accounting for these environmental factors in a correlational sense, substantial test score gaps remain. Furthermore, these gaps tend to widen with age and schooling: Black children show lower measured ability growth with schooling or age than White children.

In this chapter, we present some evidence from CNLSY.[8] These are children born to women from the NLSY 1979 survey. We have also examined the Early Childhood Longitudinal Survey (ECLS) analyzed by Ferguson (2002a) and Fryer and Levitt (2004) and also the Children of the Panel Study of Income Dynamics (CPSID) and have found similar patterns. We broaden previous analyses to include Hispanic–White differentials. Figures 2A and B show the average percentile PIAT Math[9] scores for males and females in different age groups by race. Racial and ethnic gaps are found as early as ages 5 and 6 (the earliest ages at which we can measure math scores in CNLSY data).[10] On average, Black 5- and 6-year-old boys are almost 18 percentile points below White 5- and 6-year old boys (i.e., if the average White is at the 50th percentile of the test score distribution, the average Black is at the 32nd percentile of this distribution). The gap is a bit smaller—16%—but still substantial for Hispanics. The finding is similar for Black and Hispanic women who exhibit gaps of about 14% relative to Whites. These findings are duplicated for many other test scores and in other data sets, and are not altered if we use median test scores instead of means. Furthermore, as shown in figures 3A and B, even when we use a test taken at earlier ages, racial gaps in test scores can be found at ages 1 and 2, though not always for women.[11] In general, we find that the test score gaps emerge early and persist through adulthood.

smaller in ECLS than in CNLSY and other data sets that have been used to study this issue, and so their results are anomalous in the context of the larger literature.

[7] This is commonly referred to as the "Shaker Heights study," although it analyzed many other similar neighborhoods.

[8] For descriptions of CNLSY and NLSY79, see BLS (2001).

[9] The PIAT Math is the abbreviation for Peabody Individual Achievement Test in Mathematics. This test measures the child's attainment in mathematics as taught in mainstream education. It consists of 84 multiple choice questions of increasing difficulty, beginning with recognizing numerals and progressing to geometry and trigonometry.

[10] Instead of using raw scores or standardized scores we choose to use ranks, or percentiles, since test score scales have no intrinsic meaning. Our results are not sensitive to this procedure.

[11] Parts of the Body Test attempts to measure the young child's receptive vocabulary knowledge of orally presented words as a means of estimating intellectual development. The interviewer names each of ten body parts and asks the child to point to that part of the body.

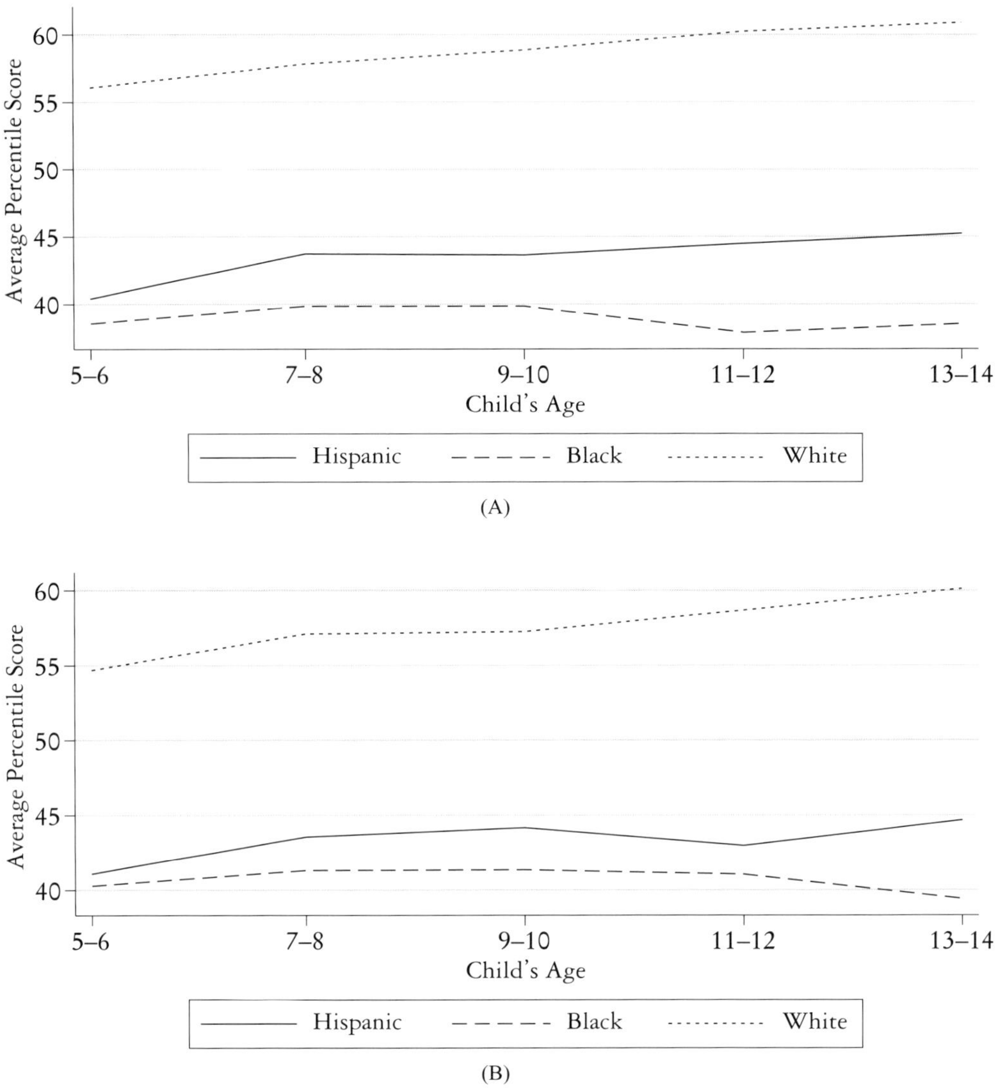

Figure 2. (A) Percentile PIAT Math Score by Race and Age Group Children of NLSY79 Males; (B) Percentile PIAT Math Score by Race and Age Group Children of NLSY79 Females (This test measures the child's attainment in mathematics as taught in mainstream education. It consists of 84 multiple-choice questions of increasing difficulty, beginning with recognizing numerals and progressing to geometry and trigonometry. The percentile score was calculated separately for each sex at each age.)

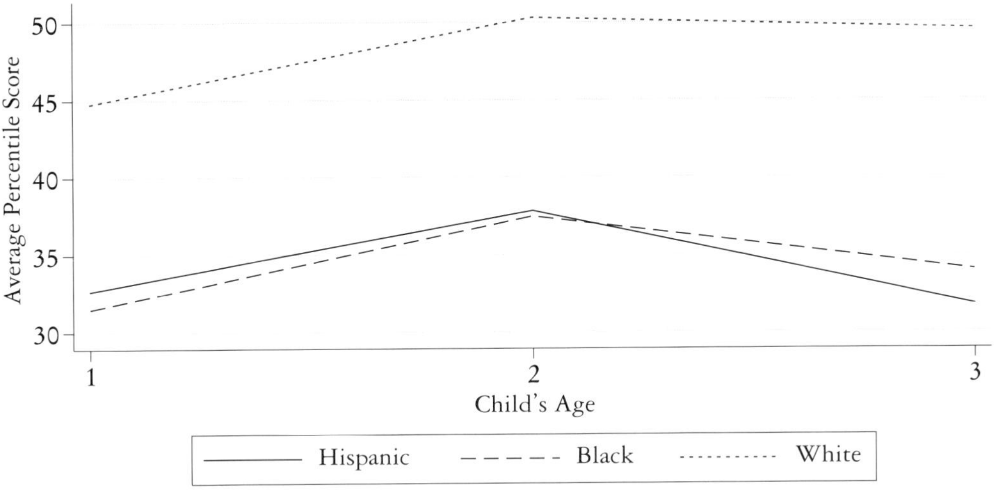

(A)

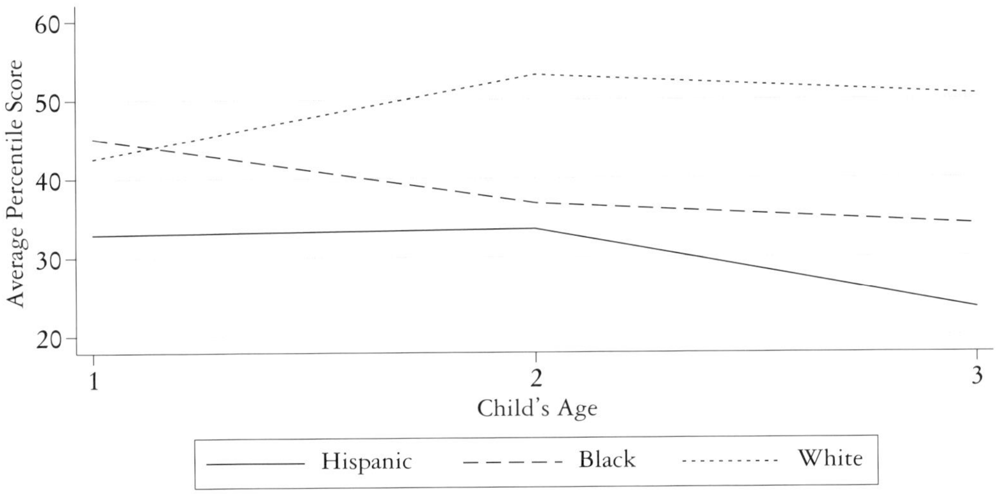

(B)

Figure 3. (A) Average Percentile Parts of the Body Score by Race and Age Children of NLSY79 Males; (B) Average Percentile Parts of the Body Score by Race and Age Children of NLSY79 Females (This test attempts to measure the young child's receptive vocabulary knowledge of orally presented words as a means of estimating intellectual development. The interviewer names each of 10 body parts and asks the child to point to that part of the body. The score is computed by summing the number of correct responses. The percentile score was calculated separately for each sex at each age.)

For simplicity, we will focus on means and medians in this chapter. However, figures 1A and B and 4A and B illustrate that there is considerable overlap in the distribution of test scores across groups in recent generations. Many Black and Hispanic children at ages 5 and 6 score higher on a math test score than the average White child. Statements that we make about medians or means do *not* apply to all persons in the distributions.

Figures 2A and B also show that the Black–White percentile PIAT Math score gap widens with age. By ages 13–14, the average Black is ranked more than 22 percentiles below the average White. In fact, it is well documented that these gaps persist until adulthood and beyond. At 13–14 Hispanic boys are almost 16 points below the average White. For Black and Hispanic girls, the gap widens to 21% and 16%, respectively.

In summary, when Blacks and Hispanics enter the labor market, on average they have a much poorer set of skills than Whites. Thus, it is not surprising that their average labor market outcomes are so much worse. Furthermore, these skill gaps emerge very early in the lifecycle, persist, and if anything, widen for some groups. Initial conditions (i.e., early test scores) are very important since skill begets skill (Heckman, 2000).

Even after controlling for numerous environmental and family background factors, the racial and ethnic test score gaps remain for many of these tests at ages 3 and 4, and for virtually all the tests at later ages. Figures 5A and B adjust the tests for measures of family background, such as family long-term or "permanent" income and mother's education, the mother's cognitive ability (as measured by age-corrected AFQT), and a measure of home environment called the home score.[12] The adjusted Black–White gap in percentile PIAT Math scores at ages 5–6 is almost 8 percentile points, and at ages 13–14 is close to 11 percentile points for boys. Hispanic–White differentials are reduced more by such adjustments, falling to 7 points at ages 5–6 and to 4 points at ages 13–14 for boys. For other tests, differentials frequently become positive or statistically insignificant. For girls, the gaps in PIAT Math are reduced to about 5 percentile points at ages 5–6 by the same adjustment, though the Hispanic gap falls to 4 percentile points while the Black gap rises to 6 percentile points by age 13–14. Web Appendix tables A.1A and A.1B report that even after controlling for different measures of home environments and child stimulation, the Black–White test score gap persists even though it drops considerably.[13] Measured home and family environments play an important role in the formation of these skills, although they are not the whole

[12] The home score is the primary measure of the quality of a child's home environment included in CNLSY. It is composed of various measures of age-specific cognitive and emotional stimulation based on dichotomized and summed responses from the mother's self-report and interviewer observation. Some items included in the home score are number of books, magazines, toys and musical recordings, how often mother reads to child, frequency of family activities (eating, outings), methods of discipline and parenting, learning at home, television watching habits and parental expectations for the child (chores, time use), home cleanliness and safety and types of mother–child interactions.

[13] Results for other tests and other samples can be found in the web appendix, available at http://jenni.uchicago.edu/ABF. Even though for some test scores early Black–White test score gaps can be eliminated once we control for a large number of characteristics, it is harder to eliminate them at later ages. In the analysis presented here the most important variable in reducing the test score gap is mother's cognitive ability, as measured by the AFQT.

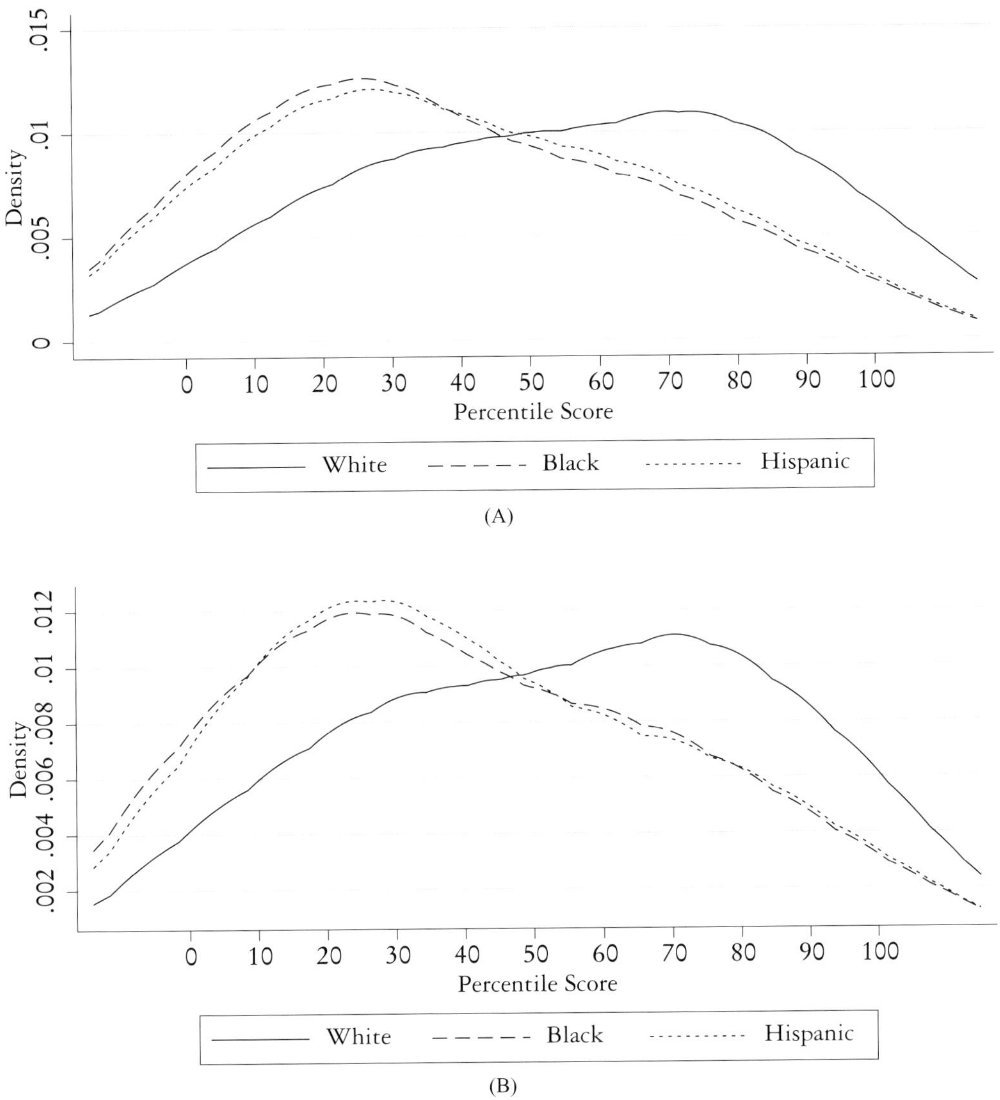

Figure 4. (A) Density of Percentile PIAT Math Scores at Ages 5–6 CNLSY 79 Males; (B) Density of Percentile PIAT Math Scores at Ages 5–6 CNLSY 79 Females (This test measures the child's attainment in mathematics as taught in mainstream education. It consists of 84 multiple-choice questions of increasing difficulty, beginning with recognizing numerals and progressing to geometry and trigonometry. The percentile score was calculated separately for each sex at each age.)

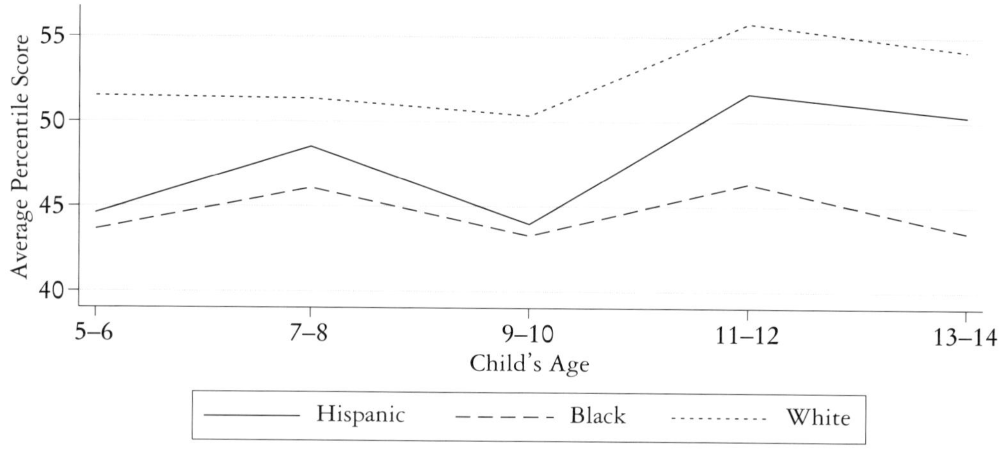

(A)

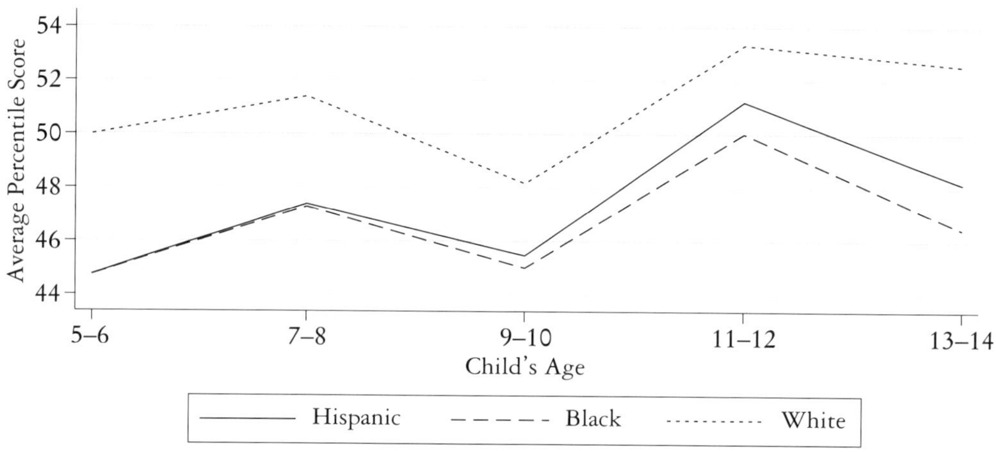

(B)

Figure 5. (A) Adjusted Percentile PIAT Math Score by Race and Age Group Children of NLSY79 Males; (B) Adjusted Percentile PIAT Math Score by Race and Age Group Children of NLSY79 Females (Adjusted by permanent family income, mother's education and age-corrected AFQT, and home score. Adjusted indicates that we equalized the family background characteristics across all race groups by setting them at the mean to purge the effect of family environment disparities. Permanent income is constructed by taking the average of annual family income discounted to child's age 0 using a 10% discount rate. Age-corrected AFQT is the standardized residual from the regression of the AFQT score on age at the time of the test dummy variables. Home score is an index of quality of the child's home environment.)

story.[14] For females, both raw and adjusted test score gaps are smaller than for males, but the overall story is the same.[15]

The evidence for Hispanics is different.[16] Early test scores for Blacks and Hispanics are similar, although Hispanics often perform slightly better. Figure 2A shows that for the PIAT Math score the Hispanic–Black gap is about 2 percentile points.[17] This is much smaller than either the Black–White or the Hispanic–White gap. For the PIAT Math test, the Black–White gap widens dramatically, especially at later ages, but the Hispanic–White gap does not change substantially with age. For other tests, even when there is some widening of the Hispanic–White gap with age, it tends to be smaller than the widening in the Black–White gap in test scores. In particular, when we look at the AFQT scores displayed in figures 1A and B, and which are measured using individuals at ages 16–23, Hispanics clearly have higher scores than Blacks. In contrast, figures 4A and B show a strong similarity between the math scores of Blacks and Hispanics at ages 5 and 6, although there are other tests where, even at these early ages, Hispanics perform significantly better than Blacks. When we control for the effects of home and family environments on test scores, the Hispanic–White test score gap either decreases or is constant over time while the Black–White test score tends to widen with age.

Racial ability gaps open up very early. Home and family environments at early ages, and even the mother's behavior during pregnancy, are likely to play crucial roles in the child's development, and Black children grow up in significantly more disadvantaged environments than White children. Figure 6 shows the distributions of long-term or "permanent" family income for Blacks, Whites and Hispanics. Minority children are much more likely to grow up in low-income families than are White children. Figure 7 shows the distribution of maternal education across racial and ethnic groups. Even though the overlap in the distributions is large, White children have more educated mothers than do minority children. The distribution of maternal AFQT scores, shown in figure 8, is again very different for minority and White children. Maternal AFQT is a major predictor of children's test scores.[18] Figure 9 documents that White mothers are much more likely to read to their children at young ages than are minority mothers, and we obtain similar results at young ages.[19] Using this reading variable and other variables in CNLSY such as the number of books, magazines, toys and musical recordings, family activities (eating, outings), methods of discipline and

[14] However, the home score includes variables such as the number of books, which are clearly choice variables and likely to cause problems in this regression. The variables with the largest effect on the minority–White test score gap are maternal AFQT and raw home score.

[15] See the web appendix.

[16] We already saw that wage gaps are completely eliminated for Hispanics when we control for AFQT, while they persist for Blacks.

[17] The test score is measured in percentile ranks. The Black–White gap is slightly below 18, while the Hispanic–White gap is slightly below 16. This means that the Black–Hispanic gap should be around 2.

[18] For example, the correlation between percentile PIAT Math score and age-corrected maternal AFQT is 0.4.

[19] See the results for all ages in http://jenni.uchicago.edu/ABF.

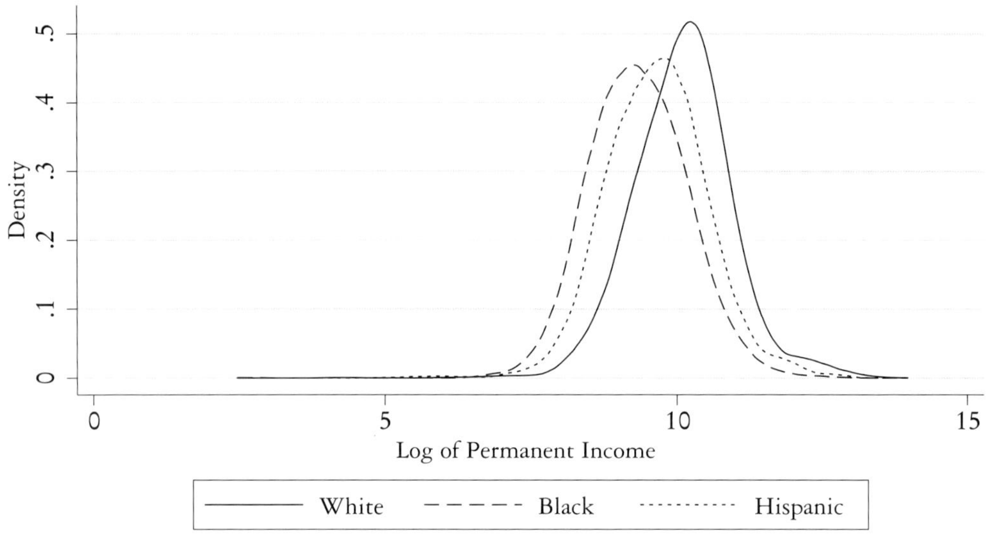

Figure 6. Density of Log Permanent Income CNLSY 79 Males and Females (Permanent income is constructed by taking the average of all nonmissing values of annual family income at ages 0–18 and discounted to child's age 0 using a 10% discount rate.)

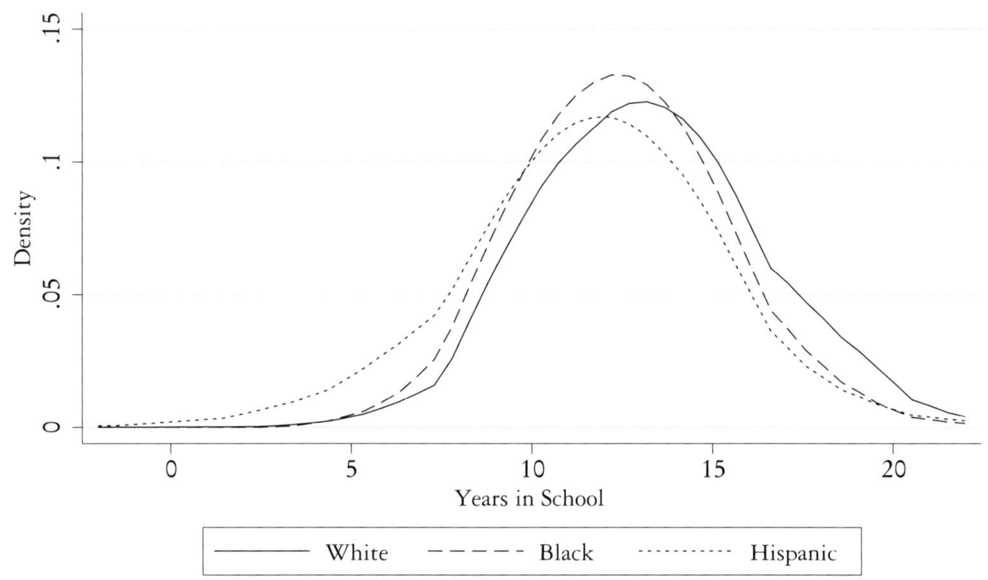

Figure 7. Density of Mother's Highest Completed Years of Schooling by Race CNLSY79 Males and Females

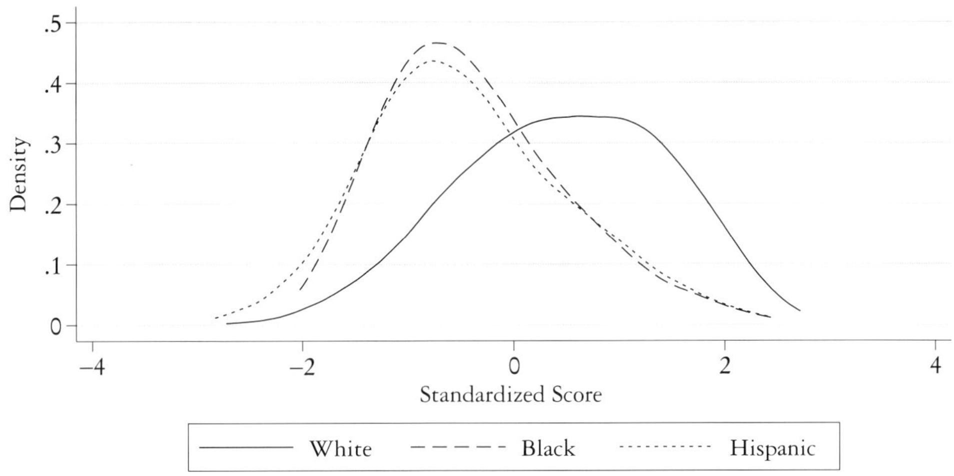

Figure 8. Density of Mother's Schooling-Corrected AFQT by Race CNLSY79 Males and Females (Schooling-corrected AFQT is the standardized residual from the regression of the AFQT score on age at the time of the test dummy variables and final level of schooling completed during lifetime. AFQT is a subset of 4 out of 10 ASVAB tests used by the military for enlistment screening and job assignment. It is the summed score from the word knowledge, paragraph comprehension, mathematics knowledge, and arithmetic reasoning ASVAB tests.)

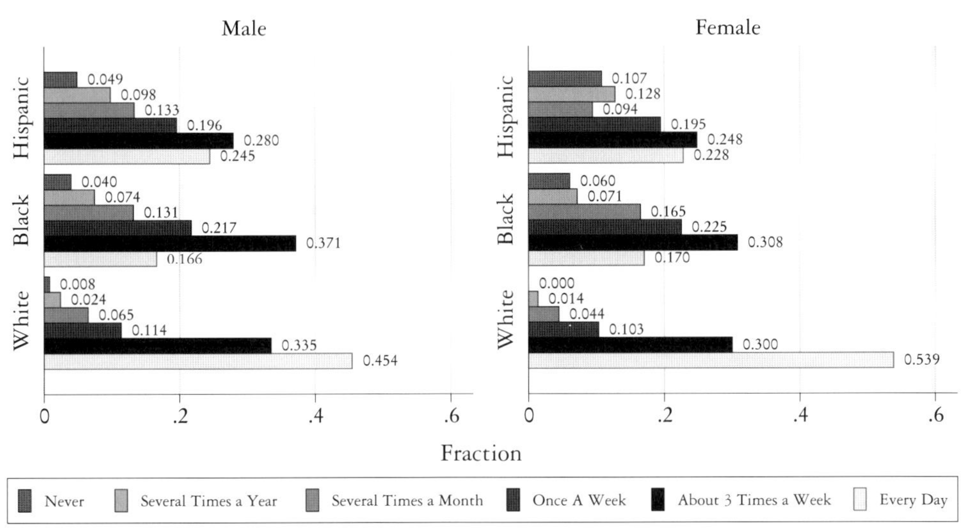

Figure 9. How Often Mother Reads to Child at Age 2 by Race and Sex CNLSY79 (The height of the bar is produced by dividing the number of people who report falling in a particular reading frequency cell by the total number of people in their race-sex group.)

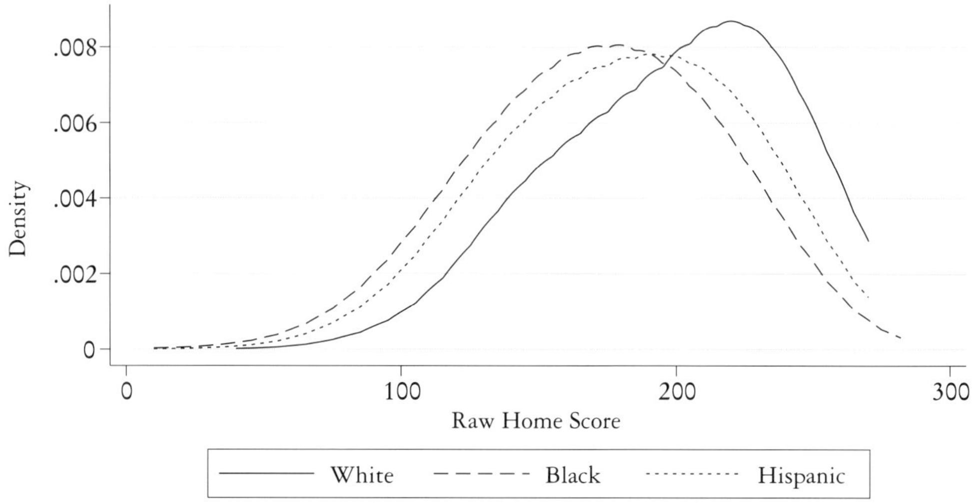

Figure 10. Density of Home Score by Race CNLSY79 Males and Females (Home score is an index of the quality of a child's home environment included in CNLSY79. It consists of various measures of age-specific cognitive and emotional stimulation based on dichotomized and summed responses from mother's self-report and interviewer observations.)

parenting, learning at home, TV watching habits, parental expectations for the child (chores, time use), and home cleanliness and safety, we can construct an index of cognitive and emotional stimulation—the home score. Figure 10 shows that this index is always higher for Whites than for minorities.[20] Figure 11 shows that Blacks are the most likely to grow up in broken homes. Hispanics are less likely than Blacks to grow up in a broken home, although they are much more likely to do so than are Whites. The research surveyed in Carneiro and Heckman (2003) suggests that enhanced cognitive stimulation at early ages is likely to produce lasting gains in achievement test scores in children from disadvantaged environments, although long lasting effects of such interventions on IQ are not found.

2. STEREOTYPE THREAT

The fact that racial and ethnic test score gaps open up early casts doubt on the empirical importance of the stereotype threat. It is now fashionable in some circles to attribute gaps in Black test scores to racial consciousness on the part of Black test takers stemming from the way test scores are used in public discourse to describe minorities (see Steele and Aronson, 1998). The empirical importance of the stereotype threat has

[20] In the web appendix, we document that both cognitive and emotional stimulation indexes are always higher for Whites than for Blacks at all ages.

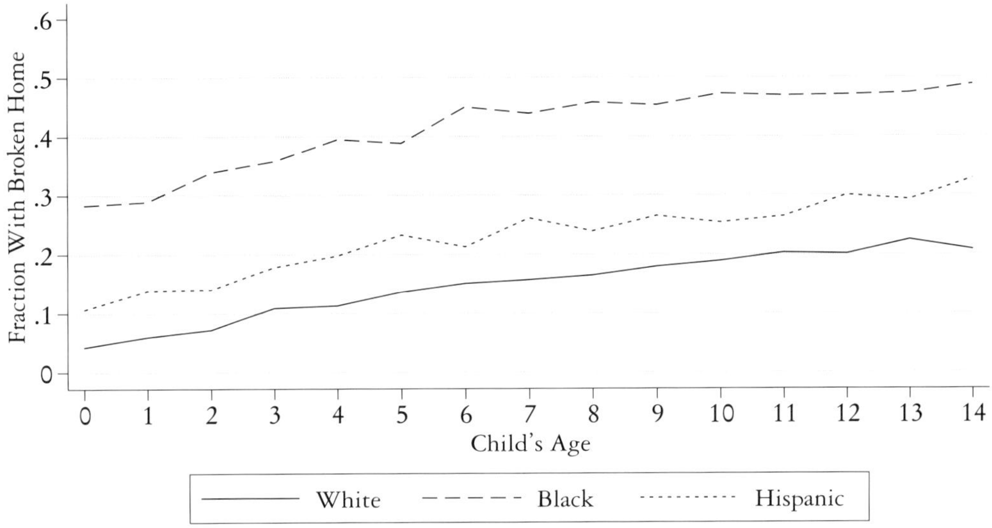

Figure 11. Fraction of Children Who Live in a Broken Home by Age and Race CNLSY79 Males and Females (Note: We define a child living in a broken home as a child who does not live in a household with two biological parents or in a household with the mother and her common law partner.)

been greatly overstated in the popular literature (see Sackett, Hardison, and Cullen, 2004). No serious empirical scholar assigns any quantitative importance to stereotype threat effects.

Stereotype threats could not have been important when Blacks took the first IQ tests at the beginning of the 20th century which documented the racial differentials that gave rise to the stereotype. Yet racial IQ gaps are comparable across time.[21] Young children, like the ones studied in this chapter, are unlikely to have the heightened racial consciousness about tests and their social significance of the sort claimed by Steele and Aronson (1998) in college students at a few elite universities. Moreover, sizable gaps are found for young Hispanic males—a group for which the "stereotype" threat remains to be investigated.

The stereotype threat literature claims that Black test scores underestimate true ability. If so, in general, Black test scores should receive a different incremental payment to ability in wage equations because they are mismeasured. Carneiro, Heckman,

[21] Murray (1999) reviews the evidence on the evolution of the Black–White IQ gap. In the 1920s—a time when such tests were much more unreliable and Black educational attainment much lower—the mean Black–White difference was 0.86 standard deviations. The largest Black–White difference appears in the 1960s, with a mean Black–White difference of 1.28 standard deviations. The difference ranges from a low of 0.82 standard deviations in the 1930s to 1.12 standard deviations in the 1970s. However, none of the samples prior to 1960 are nationally representative, and the samples were often chosen so as to effectively bias the Black mean upward.

and Masterov (2005) test and reject this hypothesis for both Blacks and Hispanics, singly and jointly. There is no evidence of differential incremental rewards to ability for Blacks or for Hispanics. Like Sackett et al. (2004), we find no evidence that the stereotype threat is an empirically important phenomenon.

One objection to this evidence is that Blacks face stereotype threat in the workplace and in the classroom and underperform everywhere. This version of the stereotype threat hypothesis is irrefutably true. It is a belief system and not a scientific hypothesis.

3. THE DIFFERENTIAL EFFECT OF SCHOOLING ON TEST SCORES

The previous section shows that cognitive test scores are correlated with home and family environments. Test score gaps increase with age and schooling. The research of Hansen, Heckman and Mullen (2004) and Heckman et al. (2004) shows that the AFQT test scores used by Neal and Johnson are affected by schooling attainment of individuals at the time they take the test. Therefore, one reason for the divergence of Black and White test scores over time may be differential schooling attainments. Figure 12 shows the schooling completed at the test date for the six demographic groups used in the Neal and Johnson sample. Blacks have (slightly) less completed schooling at test date than Whites, but substantially more than Hispanics.

Heckman et al. (2004) and Carneiro et al. (2005) use versions of a method developed in Hansen et al. (2004). This method isolates the causal effect of schooling attained

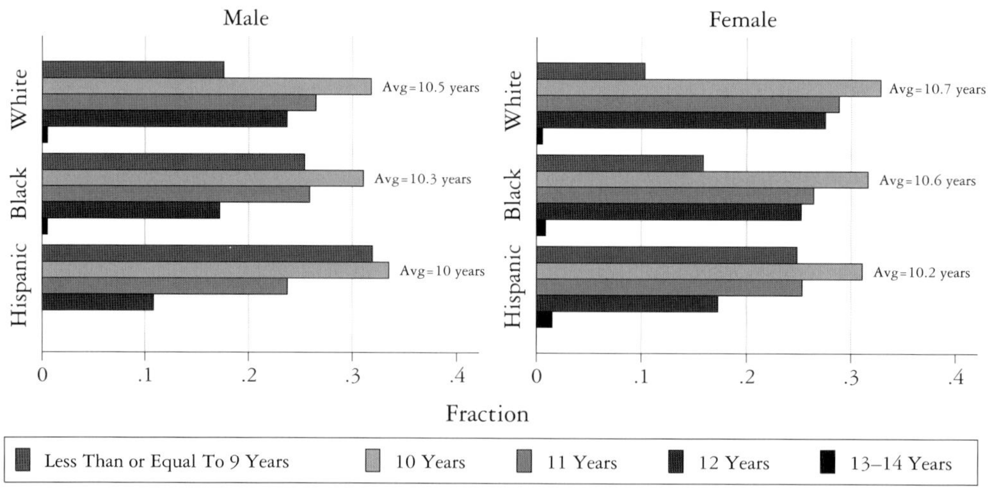

Figure 12. Highest Category of Schooling Completed at Test Date by Race, Sex, and Age NLSY79 Men and Women Born after 1961 (The height of the bar is produced by dividing the number of people who report falling in a particular education cell by the total number of people in their race-sex group.)

at the test date on test scores controlling for unobserved factors that lead to selective differences in schooling attainment. They establish that the effect of schooling on test scores is much larger for Whites and Hispanics than it is for Blacks over most ranges of schooling. As a result, even though Hispanics have fewer years of completed schooling at the time they take the AFQT test than do Blacks (see figure 12), on average Hispanics score better on the AFQT than do Blacks.

There are different explanations for their findings. Carneiro and Heckman (2003) suggest that one important feature of the learning process may be complementarity and self productivity between initial endowments of human capital and subsequent learning.[22] Higher levels of human capital raise the productivity of learning.[23] If minorities and Whites start school with very different initial conditions (as documented in the previous section), their learning paths can diverge dramatically over time. A related explanation may be that Blacks and non-Blacks learn at different rates because Blacks attend lower quality schools than Whites.[24]

Currie and Thomas (2000) show that test score gains of participants in the Head Start program tend to fade completely for Blacks but not for Whites. Their paper suggests that one reason may be that Blacks attend worse schools than Whites, and therefore Blacks are not able to maintain initial test score gains. Both early advantages and disadvantages as well as school quality are likely to be important factors in the human capital accumulation process. Therefore, differential initial conditions and differential school quality may also be important determinants of the adult Black–White skill gap.

In light of the greater growth in test scores of Hispanics that is parallel to that of Whites, these explanations are not entirely compelling. Hispanics start from similar initial disadvantages in family environments and face school and neighborhood environments similar to those faced by Blacks.[25] They also have early levels of test scores similar to those found in the Black population. Heckman et al. (2004) present a formal analysis of the effect of schooling quality on test scores, showing that schooling inputs explain little of the differential growth in test scores among Blacks, Whites and Hispanics.

What are the consequences of correcting for different levels of schooling at the test date? To answer this question, we reanalyze Neal and Johnson's (1996) study using AFQT scores corrected for the race- or ethnicity-specific effect of schooling while equalizing the years of schooling attained at the date of the test across all racial/ethnic groups. The results of this adjustment are given in table 2. This adjustment is equivalent

[22] For example, see the Ben-Porath (1967) model. See Carneiro, Cunha, and Heckman (2004).

[23] See the evidence in the paper by Heckman, Lochner and Taber (1998).

[24] Cunha et al. (2005) show that complementarity implies that early human capital increases the productivity of later investments in human capital, and also that early investments that are not followed up by later investments in human capital are not productive.

[25] The evidence for CNLSY is presented at http://jenni.uchicago.edu/ABF.

Table 2. Change in the Black–White log wage gap induced by controlling for schooling-corrected AFQT for 1990–2000

	1990		1991		1992		1993		1994		1996		1998		2000	
Year	I	II	I	II	I	II	I	II	I	II	I	II	I	II	I	II
A. NLSY Men Born After 1961																
Black	−0.250	−0.133	−0.251	−0.149	−0.302	−0.180	−0.282	−0.171	−0.286	−0.165	−0.373	−0.230	−0.333	−0.160	−0.325	−0.172
	(0.028)	(0.029)	(0.028)	(0.029)	(0.029)	(0.029)	(0.028)	(0.029)	(0.031)	(0.031)	(0.032)	(0.032)	(0.034)	(0.034)	(0.035)	(0.033)
Hispanic	−0.174	−0.070	−0.113	−0.013	−0.146	−0.044	−0.159	−0.058	−0.143	−0.029	−0.186	−0.067	−0.195	−0.047	−0.215	−0.088
	(0.032)	(0.032)	(0.032)	(0.032)	(0.033)	(0.032)	(0.032)	(0.032)	(0.036)	(0.036)	(0.038)	(0.038)	(0.040)	(0.038)	(0.040)	(0.038)
Age	–	0.065	–	0.043	–	0.055	–	0.045	–	0.040	–	0.039	–	0.036	–	0.029
	–	(0.014)	–	(0.015)	–	(0.015)	–	(0.015)	–	(0.016)	–	(0.017)	–	(0.017)	–	(0.017)
AFQT	–	0.153	–	0.131	–	0.155	–	0.144	–	0.159	–	0.184	–	0.221	–	0.211
	–	(0.013)	–	(0.013)	–	(0.013)	–	(0.013)	–	(0.014)	–	(0.015)	–	(0.015)	–	(0.015)
$AFQT^2$	–	0.001	–	0.009	–	0.015	–	0.017	–	0.028	–	0.031	–	0.040	–	0.036
	–	(0.010)	–	(0.010)	–	(0.010)	–	(0.010)	–	(0.011)	–	(0.012)	–	(0.012)	–	(0.012)
Constant	2.375	0.540	2.372	1.085	2.404	0.732	2.423	0.982	2.458	1.119	2.533	1.140	2.589	1.172	2.629	1.425
	(0.017)	(0.392)	(0.017)	(0.412)	(0.017)	(0.426)	(0.017)	(0.437)	(0.018)	(0.493)	(0.019)	(0.547)	(0.020)	(0.603)	(0.020)	(0.628)
N	1538	1505	1553	1514	1536	1503	1542	1504	1522	1485	1554	1519	1494	1462	1438	1404
	1990		1991		1992		1993		1994		1996		1998		2000	
Year	I	II	I	II	I	II	I	II	I	II	I	II	I	II	I	II
B. NLSY Women Born After 1961																
Black	−0.172	−0.045	−0.200	−0.066	−0.201	−0.083	−0.167	−0.020	−0.148	−0.014	−0.147	0.025	−0.201	−0.043	−0.200	−0.041
	(0.031)	(0.031)	(0.032)	(0.033)	(0.031)	(0.031)	(0.035)	(0.035)	(0.035)	(0.035)	(0.035)	(0.034)	(0.034)	(0.034)	(0.036)	(0.035)
Hispanic	−0.003	0.116	−0.017	0.107	−0.059	0.069	0.009	0.145	−0.018	0.119	−0.006	0.149	−0.069	0.098	−0.064	0.096
	(0.035)	(0.035)	(0.037)	(0.037)	(0.036)	(0.035)	(0.039)	(0.039)	(0.040)	(0.040)	(0.041)	(0.039)	(0.039)	(0.038)	(0.041)	(0.040)
Age	–	0.015	–	0.042	–	0.021	–	0.024	–	0.015	–	−0.003	–	0.019	–	−0.010
	–	(0.016)	–	(0.017)	–	(0.016)	–	(0.018)	–	(0.018)	–	(0.018)	–	(0.017)	–	(0.018)
AFQT	–	0.188	–	0.197	–	0.187	–	0.221	–	0.221	–	0.245	–	0.228	–	0.235
	–	(0.016)	–	(0.017)	–	(0.016)	–	(0.018)	–	(0.018)	–	(0.018)	–	(0.017)	–	(0.018)
$AFQT^2$	–	0.010	–	0.009	–	0.010	–	0.006	–	−0.008	–	0.022	–	0.017	–	0.005
	–	(0.013)	–	(0.014)	–	(0.013)	–	(0.015)	–	(0.015)	–	(0.015)	–	(0.015)	–	(0.015)
Constant	2.141	1.633	2.175	0.893	2.193	1.488	2.174	1.337	2.218	1.662	2.246	2.228	2.311	1.550	2.339	2.608
	(0.019)	(0.424)	(0.020)	(0.472)	(0.019)	(0.465)	(0.021)	(0.530)	(0.022)	(0.565)	(0.022)	(0.588)	(0.021)	(0.612)	(0.022)	(0.671)
N	1356	1325	1335	1299	1317	1278	1319	1281	1318	1287	1381	1343	1370	1328	1316	1276

Schooling-corrected AFQT is the standardized residual from the regression of the AFQT score on age at the time of the test dummy variables and final level of schooling completed during lifetime. AFQT is a subset of 4 out of 10 ASVAB tests used by the military for enlistment screening and job assignment. It is the summed score from the word knowledge, paragraph comprehension, mathematics knowledge, and arithmetic reasoning ASVAB tests. All wages are in 1993 dollars.

to replacing each individual's AFQT score by the score we would measure if he or she would have stopped his or her formal education after eighth grade.[26] In other words, we use "eighth grade" AFQT scores for everyone. Since the effect of schooling on test scores is higher for Whites than for Blacks, and Whites have more schooling than Blacks at the date of the test, this adjustment reduces the test scores of Whites much more than it does for Blacks. Although the Black–White male wage gap is still cut in half when we use this new measure of skill, the effect of AFQT on reducing the wage gap is weaker than in the original Neal and Johnson (1996) study. The adjustment has little effect on the Hispanic–White wage gap but a wage gap for Black women emerges when using the schooling-adjusted measure.

This finding does not necessarily invalidate the Neal–Johnson study. It shows that schooling can partially reduce the ability gap. It raises the larger question of what a "premarket" factor is. Neal and Johnson do not condition on schooling in explaining Black–White wage gaps, arguing that schooling is affected by expectations of adverse market opportunities facing minorities and conditioning on such a contaminated variable would spuriously reduce the estimated wage gap. We present direct evidence on this claim below.

Their reasoning is not entirely coherent. If expectations of discrimination affect schooling, the very logic of their "premarket" argument suggests that they should control for the impact of schooling on test scores when using test scores to measure for premarket factors. As we have seen, when this is done, the wage gap (conditional on ability adjusted by schooling) widens substantially for Blacks. There is still little evidence of discrimination for Hispanic females, but the evidence for Hispanic males comes close to demonstrating discrimination for that group.

Implicitly, Neal and Johnson assume that schooling at the time the test is taken is not affected by expectations of discrimination in the market, while later schooling is. This distinction is arbitrary. A deeper investigation of the expectation formation process and feedback between experience and performance is required. One practical conclusion with important implications for the interpretation of the evidence is that the magnitude of the wage gap that can be eliminated by performing a Neal–Johnson analysis depends on the age at which the test is measured. The earlier the test is measured, the smaller the test score gap, and the larger the fraction of the wage gap that is unexplained. Figures 13A–D show how adjusting measured ability for schooling attained at the time of the test at different levels of attained schooling affects the adjusted wage gap for Black males. In this figure, the log wage gap corresponding to grade of AFQT correction equal to 11 is the log wage gap we obtain when using "eleventh grade" test scores, i.e., scores adjusted to the eleventh grade level. The later the grade at which we adjust the test score, the lower the estimated gap. This is so because an ability gap opens up at later schooling levels, and hence adjustment reduces the gap.

[26] However, the score is affected by attendance in kindergarten, eight further years of schooling, and any school quality differentials in those years.

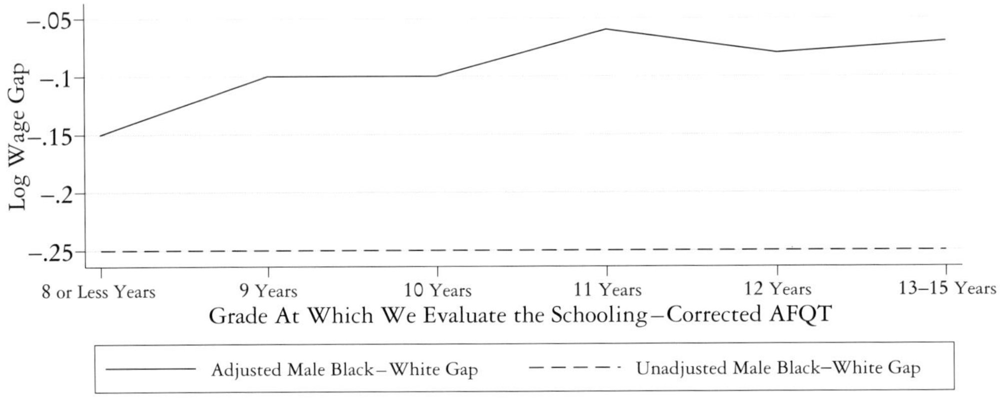

(A)

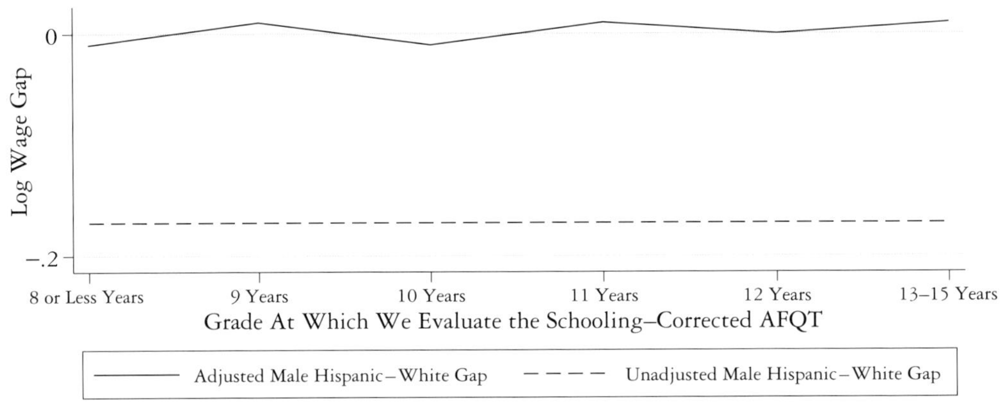

(B)

Figure 13. (A) Residual Black–White Log Wage Gap in 1991 by Grade at which We Evaluate the Schooling-Corrected AFQT NLSY79 Males; (B) Residual Hispanic–White Log Wage Gap in 1991 by Grade at which We Evaluate the Schooling-Corrected AFQT NLSY79 Males.

Finally, we show that adjusting for "expectations-contaminated" completed schooling does not operate in the fashion conjectured by Neal and Johnson. Table 3 shows that when we adjust wage differences for completed schooling as well as schooling-adjusted AFQT, wage gaps *widen*. This runs contrary to the simple intuition that schooling embodies expectations of market discrimination, so that conditioning on it will eliminate wage gaps.[27]

[27] The simple intuition, however, can easily be shown to be wrong so the evidence in these tables is not decisive on the presence of discrimination in the labor market. The basic idea is that if both schooling and the test score are correlated with an unmeasured discrimination component in the error term, the bias for the race dummy may be either positive or negative depending on the strength of the correlation among the contaminated variables and their correlation with the error term. See the Appendix in Carneiro et al. (2005).

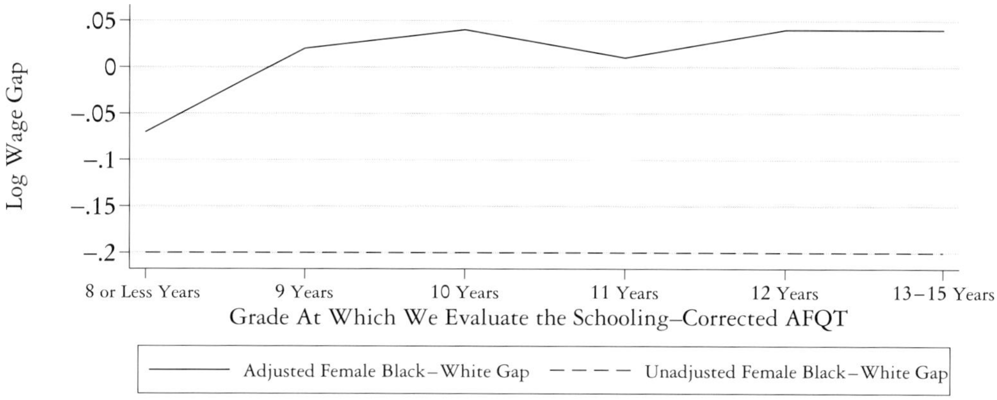

(C)

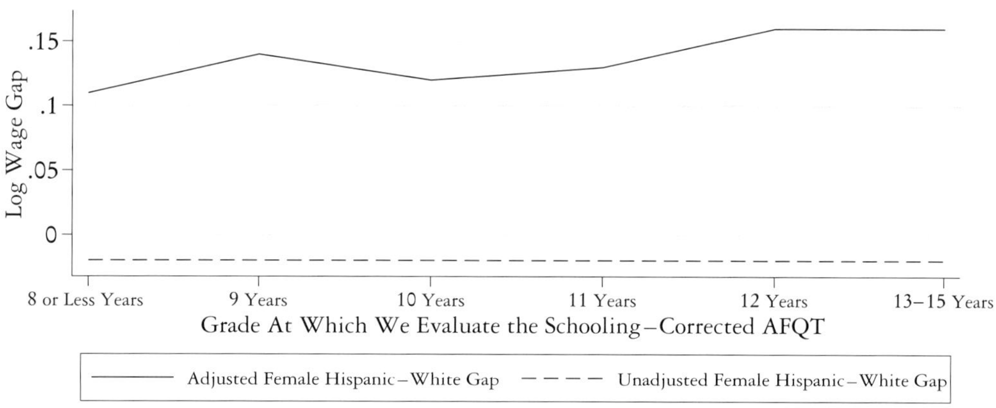

(D)

Figure 13. (*Continued*) (C) Residual Black–White Log Wage Gap in 1991 by Grade at which We Evaluate the Schooling-Corrected AFQT NLSY79 Females; (D) Residual Hispanic–White Log Wage Gap in 1991 by Grade at which We Evaluate the Schooling-Corrected AFQT NLSY79 Females (Note: We have omitted the results for the 16-or-more category because the low number of minorities in that cell makes the correction of the test scores to that schooling level much less reliable than the correction to the other schooling levels. The unadjusted line refers to the Black–White or Hispanic–White log wage gap we observe if we do not control for AFQT scores (column I in table 1). Therefore, it is a horizontal line since it does not depend on the grade to which we are correcting the test score. The adjusted line refers to the Black–White log wage gap we observe after we adjust for the AFQT scores corrected to different grades.)

Table 3. Change in the Black–White log wage gap induced by controlling for schooling-corrected AFQT and highest grade completed in 1990–2000

	1990		1991		1992		1993		1994		1996		1998		2000	
Year	I	II	I	II	I	II	I	II	I	II	I	II	I	II	I	II
								A. NLSY Men Born After 1961								
Black	−0.250	−0.144	−0.251	−0.158	−0.302	−0.189	−0.282	−0.182	−0.286	−0.175	−0.373	−0.241	−0.333	−0.175	−0.325	−0.194
	(0.028)	(0.028)	(0.028)	(0.028)	(0.029)	(0.028)	(0.028)	(0.028)	(0.031)	(0.031)	(0.032)	(0.031)	(0.034)	(0.032)	(0.035)	(0.032)
Hispanic	−0.174	−0.056	−0.113	0.005	−0.146	−0.032	−0.159	−0.044	−0.143	−0.018	−0.186	−0.056	−0.195	−0.040	−0.215	−0.070
	(0.032)	(0.032)	(0.032)	(0.032)	(0.033)	(0.032)	(0.032)	(0.032)	(0.036)	(0.035)	(0.038)	(0.036)	(0.040)	(0.037)	(0.040)	(0.037)
Age	–	0.062	–	0.041	–	0.052	–	0.042	–	0.036	–	0.033	–	0.031	–	0.024
	–	(0.014)	–	(0.014)	–	(0.014)	–	(0.014)	–	(0.016)	–	(0.016)	–	(0.017)	–	(0.016)
AFQT	–	0.096	–	0.079	–	0.097	–	0.082	–	0.098	–	0.093	–	0.130	–	0.119
	–	(0.015)	–	(0.015)	–	(0.015)	–	(0.015)	–	(0.016)	–	(0.017)	–	(0.017)	–	(0.017)
$AFQT^2$	–	−0.015	–	−0.005	–	−0.001	–	−0.001	–	0.010	–	0.005	–	0.013	–	0.008
	–	(0.010)	–	(0.010)	–	(0.010)	–	(0.010)	–	(0.011)	–	(0.012)	–	(0.012)	–	(0.012)
HGC	–	0.044	–	0.040	–	0.043	–	0.047	–	0.046	–	0.065	–	0.066	–	0.066
	–	(0.006)	–	(0.006)	–	(0.006)	–	(0.006)	–	(0.006)	–	(0.006)	–	(0.007)	–	(0.006)
Constant	2.375	0.113	2.372	0.668	2.404	0.281	2.423	0.501	2.458	0.679	2.533	0.540	2.589	0.549	2.629	0.802
	(0.017)	(0.390)	(0.017)	(0.410)	(0.017)	(0.422)	(0.017)	(0.431)	(0.018)	(0.488)	(0.019)	(0.531)	(0.020)	(0.586)	(0.020)	(0.608)
N	1538	1504	1553	1513	1536	1503	1542	1504	1522	1485	1554	1519	1494	1462	1438	1404

Table 3. Continued

Year	1990 I	1990 II	1991 I	1991 II	1992 I	1992 II	1993 I	1993 II	1994 I	1994 II	1996 I	1996 II	1998 I	1998 II	2000 I	2000 II
B. NLSY Women Born After 1961																
Black	−0.172	−0.081	−0.200	−0.101	−0.201	−0.131	−0.167	−0.073	−0.148	−0.069	−0.147	−0.035	−0.201	−0.088	−0.200	−0.086
	(0.031)	(0.030)	(0.032)	(0.032)	(0.031)	(0.030)	(0.035)	(0.033)	(0.035)	(0.034)	(0.035)	(0.033)	(0.034)	(0.032)	(0.036)	(0.034)
Hispanic	−0.003	0.120	−0.017	0.111	−0.059	0.073	0.009	0.139	−0.018	0.118	−0.006	0.137	−0.069	0.091	−0.064	0.096
	(0.035)	(0.033)	(0.037)	(0.036)	(0.036)	(0.033)	(0.039)	(0.037)	(0.040)	(0.038)	(0.041)	(0.037)	(0.039)	(0.036)	(0.041)	(0.038)
Age	–	0.013	–	0.036	–	0.013	–	0.014	–	0.006	–	−0.009	–	0.013	–	−0.017
	–	(0.015)	–	(0.016)	–	(0.015)	–	(0.017)	–	(0.017)	–	(0.017)	–	(0.017)	–	(0.017)
AFQT	–	0.106	–	0.113	–	0.094	–	0.121	–	0.111	–	0.130	–	0.119	–	0.127
	–	(0.017)	–	(0.019)	–	(0.017)	–	(0.019)	–	(0.020)	–	(0.019)	–	(0.019)	–	(0.020)
$AFQT^2$	–	−0.001	–	−0.002	–	−0.007	–	−0.009	–	−0.026	–	0.003	–	0.004	–	−0.007
	–	(0.013)	–	(0.014)	–	(0.013)	–	(0.014)	–	(0.015)	–	(0.014)	–	(0.014)	–	(0.014)
HGC	–	0.063	–	0.064	–	0.075	–	0.075	–	0.081	–	0.081	–	0.076	–	0.073
	–	(0.006)	–	(0.006)	–	(0.006)	–	(0.007)	–	(0.007)	–	(0.006)	–	(0.006)	–	(0.006)
Constant	2.141	0.913	2.175	0.270	2.193	0.784	2.174	0.720	2.218	0.932	2.246	1.397	2.311	0.802	2.339	1.928
	(0.019)	(0.413)	(0.020)	(0.460)	(0.019)	(0.443)	(0.021)	(0.508)	(0.022)	(0.538)	(0.022)	(0.558)	(0.021)	(0.583)	(0.022)	(0.643)
N	1356	1325	1335	1299	1317	1278	1319	1318	1286	1381	1343	1370	1328	1316	1276	

Schooling-corrected AFQT is the standardized residual from the regression of the AFQT score on age at the time of the test dummy variables and final level of schooling completed during lifetime. AFQT is a subset of 4 out of 10 ASVAB tests used by the military for enlistment screening and job assignment. It is the summed score from the word knowledge, paragraph comprehension, mathematics knowledge, and arithmetic reasoning ASVAB tests. All wages are in 1993 dollars. HGC is the highest observed level of schooling completed during the individual's lifetime.

Carneiro et al. (2005) and Bornholz and Heckman (2005) discuss the issue of what variables to include in wage equations to measure wage gaps. Dropping conceptually justified productivity variables because they might be contaminated is not an appropriate procedure. A better procedure is to remove the effect of contamination. Alternative conditioning variables define different wage gaps, all of which are valid once the effect of discrimination is removed from them.

Ours is a worst-case analysis for the Neal–Johnson study. If we assign all racial and ethnic schooling differences to expectations of discrimination in the labor market, their results for Blacks are less sharp. Yet the evidence presented in Section 1 about the early emergence of ability differentials is reinforced by the early emergence of differential grade repetition gaps by minorities documented by Cameron and Heckman (2001). Most of the schooling gap at the date of the test emerges in the early years at ages when child expectations about future discrimination are unlikely to be operative. One can of course always argue that these early schooling and ability gaps are due to parental expectations of poor labor markets for minority children. We next examine data on parental expectations.

4. THE ROLE OF EXPECTATIONS

The argument that minority children perform worse on tests because they expect to be less well rewarded in the labor market than Whites for the same test score or schooling level is implausible because expectations of labor market rewards are unlikely to affect the behavior of children as early as ages 3 or 4 when test score gaps are substantial across different ethnic and racial groups. The argument that minorities invest less in skills because both minority children and minority parents have low expectations about their performance in school and in the labor market receives mixed empirical backing.

Data on expectations are hard to find, and when they are available they are often difficult to interpret. For example, in the NLSY97, Black 17- and 18-year-olds report that the probability of dying next year is 22% while for Whites it is 16%. Both numbers are absurdly high. Minorities usually report higher expectations than Whites of committing a crime, being incarcerated and being dead next year, and these adverse expectations may reduce their investment in human capital. Expectations reported by parents and children for the child adolescent years for a variety of outcomes are given in table 4. Some estimates are plausible, while many others are not.

Schooling expectations measured in the late teenage years are very similar for minorities and Whites. They are slightly lower for Hispanics. Table 5 reports the mean expected probability of being enrolled in school next year, for Black, White and Hispanic 17- and 18-year-old males. Among those individuals enrolled in 1997, on average Whites expect to be enrolled next year with 95.7% probability. Blacks expect that they will be enrolled next year with a 93.6% probability. Hispanics expect to be

Table 4. Juvenile and parental expectations about future youth behavior at age 16–17 by race and sex, NLSY97 round 1

Behavior	Blacks	Hispanics	Whites	Males	Females
	A. Juvenile Expectations about Behavior at Age 17–18				
Enrolled in School	91.75	88.35	93.72	91.67	92.55
	(22.79)	(26.33)	(21.31)	(23.32)	(22.30)
Work for Pay over 20 Hours per Week and Be Enrolled	62.77	60.00	59.11	60.84	58.86
	(32.44)	(31.02)	(33.43)	(32.00)	(33.65)
Work for Pay over 20 Hours per Week and Not Be Enrolled	77.01	76.39	83.11	80.09	79.78
	(31.44)	(30.18)	(27.58)	(28.88)	(29.95)
Pregnant	7.99	7.78	4.68	0.00	6.32
	(20.43)	(17.64)	(12.99)	0.00	(16.53)
Impregnate Someone	13.52	12.33	6.27	9.46	0.00
	(21.75)	(20.65)	(14.77)	(18.39)	0.00
Seriously Drunk at Least Once	11.64	20.37	24.12	21.55	18.00
	(23.77)	(29.78)	(33.81)	(32.06)	(29.44)
Victim of Violent Crime	16.16	16.11	13.36	15.40	13.97
	(22.99)	(21.92)	(18.89)	(21.44)	(20.04)
Arrested	12.14	11.43	8.74	13.73	6.65
	(20.55)	(19.49)	(16.08)	(20.69)	(14.33)
Dead from Any Cause	22.53	19.02	16.56	17.55	19.75
	(25.35)	(23.00)	(20.36)	(21.92)	(23.03)
	B. Juvenile Expectations about Behavior at Age 20				
Receive a High School Diploma	92.99	88.92	95.44	92.33	94.57
	(19.45)	(23.64)	(15.57)	(19.63)	(17.58)
Serve Time in Jail or Prison	5.03	7.53	4.54	7.18	3.40
	(13.00)	(16.35)	(11.76)	(15.20)	(10.41)
Mother or Father a Baby	21.20	21.00	14.86	19.22	16.28
	(29.34)	(27.69)	(23.14)	(25.63)	(26.30)
Dead from Any Cause	22.27	21.48	19.01	19.60	21.08
	(24.73)	(23.60)	(20.72)	(22.20)	(22.75)
	C. Juvenile Expectations about Behavior at Age 30				
Earn a 4-Year College Degree	74.22	66.93	73.75	68.75	76.90
	(31.44)	(31.59)	(31.50)	(32.02)	(30.37)
Work for Pay over 20 Hours per Week	90.48	89.72	94.39	92.81	91.85
	(20.05)	(19.23)	(13.71)	(16.05)	(17.93)
	D. Parental Expectations about Youth Behavior at Age 17–18				
Enrolled in School	90.68	89.39	94.03	90.80	93.64
	(23.70)	(25.08)	(20.07)	(23.80)	(20.48)
Work for Pay over 20 Hours per Week and Be Enrolled	51.42	50.52	42.65	47.14	45.09
	(34.84)	(37.10)	(38.16)	(37.05)	(37.54)

(Continued)

Table 4. (*Continued*)

Behavior	Blacks	Hispanics	Whites	Males	Females
	E. Parental Expectations about Youth Behavior at Age 20				
Receive a High School Diploma	91.51	91.94	96.19	93.12	95.13
	(21.14)	(19.97)	(15.10)	(19.43)	(16.31)
Serve Time in Jail or Prison	4.77	3.87	2.62	4.84	2.06
	(14.35)	(12.99)	(9.39)	(13.93)	(8.76)
Mother or Father a Baby	17.55	19.32	12.58	15.54	14.94
	(28.84)	(27.81)	(21.55)	(24.66)	(25.68)
	F. Parental Expectations about Youth Behavior at Age 30				
Earn a 4-Year College Degree	68.29	67.15	69.85	65.68	72.77
	(33.44)	(32.35)	(32.29)	(34.03)	(30.63)
Work for Pay over 20 Hours per Week	93.22	92.89	94.95	95.87	92.18
	(16.17)	(17.82)	(13.30)	(12.93)	(16.96)

In round 1 of NLSY97, respondents who were born in 1980 or 1981 and their parents were surveyed on their beliefs about the respondents' future. Asked to assess the probability that a given event or behavior would occur by certain age, they were instructed to use a scale from 0 (impossible) to 100 (certain). The numbers in the table represent the average estimated probability of the event within that group. Standard deviations are displayed in parentheses below the means.

enrolled with a 91.5% probability. If expectations about the labor market are adverse for minorities, they should translate into adverse expectations for the child's education. Yet these data do not reveal this. Moreover, all groups substantially overestimate actual enrollment probabilities. The difference in expectations between Blacks and Whites is very small, and is less than half the difference in actual (realized)

Table 5. Juvenile expectations* about school enrollment in 1998, NLSY97 males

	Black		Hispanic		White	
	Expected	Actual	Expected	Actual	Expected	Actual
All Individuals	0.912	0.734	0.881	0.717	0.934	0.790
	(0.232)	(0.442)	(0.265)	(0.451)	(0.219)	(0.407)
Individuals Enrolled in 1997	0.936	0.764	0.915	0.758	0.957	0.819
	(0.188)	(0.425)	(0.217)	(0.429)	(0.173)	(0.385)

*In NLSY97 round 1, respondents who were born in 1980 or 1981 were surveyed on their beliefs about the future. Asked to assess the probability that certain events would occur in a specified time period, the respondents were instructed to use a scale from 0 (impossible) to 100 (certain). In the expected columns, we report the percentage of each race group that expects to be enrolled in the next year. In the actual columns, we report the percentage of each race group that is actually enrolled in that year. Expectations were measured at age 17–18.

Table 6. Parental expectations* about youth school enrollment in 1998, NLSY79 males

	Black		Hispanic		White	
	Expected	Actual	Expected	Actual	Expected	Actual
All Individuals	0.885	0.734	0.880	0.717	0.930	0.790
	(0.255)	(0.442)	(0.259)	(0.451)	(0.217)	(0.407)
Individuals Enrolled in 1997	0.909	0.764	0.911	0.758	0.954	0.819
	(0.221)	(0.425)	(0.220)	(0.429)	(0.169)	(0.385)

*In round 1, parents of NLSY97 respondents who were born in 1980 or 1981 were surveyed on their beliefs about their children's future. Asked to assess the probability that certain events would occur in a specified time period, the respondents were instructed to use a scale from 0 (impossible) to 100 (certain). In the expected columns, we report the percentage of each race group that expects to its children to be enrolled in the next year. In the actual columns, we report the percentage of each race group that is actually enrolled in that year. Expectations were measured at age 17–18.

enrollment probabilities (81.9% for Whites versus 76.4% for Blacks). The gap is wider for Hispanics. Table 6 reports parental schooling expectations for White, Black and Hispanic males for the same individuals used to compute the numbers in Table 5. It shows that, conditional on being enrolled in 1997 (the year the expectation question is asked), Black parents expect their sons to be enrolled next year with a 90.9% probability, while for Whites this expectation is 95.4%. For Hispanics this number is lower (88.5%) but still substantial. Parents overestimate enrollment probabilities for their sons, but Black parents have lower expectations than White parents. For females the racial and ethnic differences in parental expectations are smaller than those for males.[28]

For expectations measured at earlier ages, the story is dramatically different. Figures 14A and B show that, for the CNLSY, both Black and Hispanic children and their parents have more pessimistic expectations about child schooling than White children, and more pessimistic expectations may lead to lower investments in skills, less effort in schooling and lower ability. These patterns are also found in the CPSID and ECLS. It is curious that for CNLSY teenagers expectations seem to converge at later ages (see figure 14C).

If the more pessimistic expectations of minorities are a result of market discrimination, then lower investments in children that translate into lower levels of ability and skill at later ages are a result of market discrimination. Ability would not be a premarket factor. However, lower expectations for minorities may not be a result of discrimination but just a rational response to the fact that minorities do not do as well in school as Whites. This may be due to environmental factors unrelated to expectations of discrimination in the labor market. Whether this phenomenon itself

[28] See the web appendix.

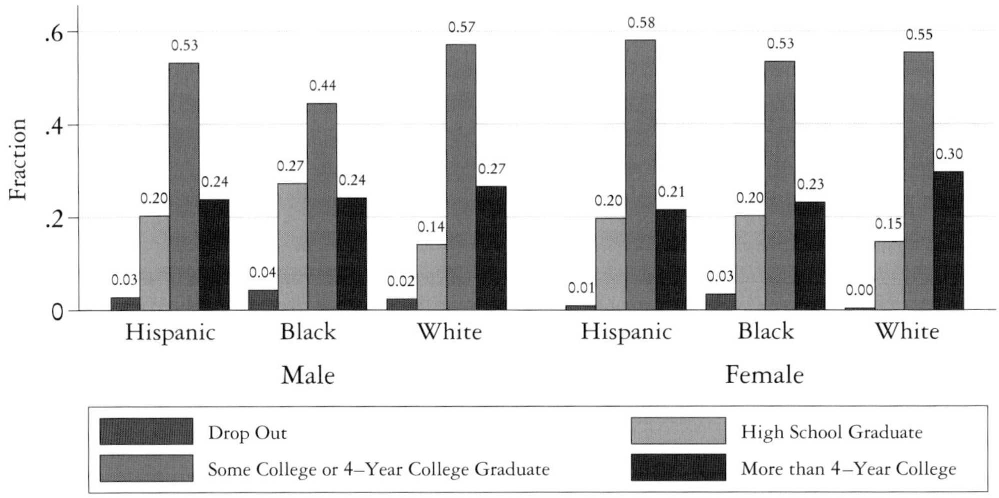

(A)

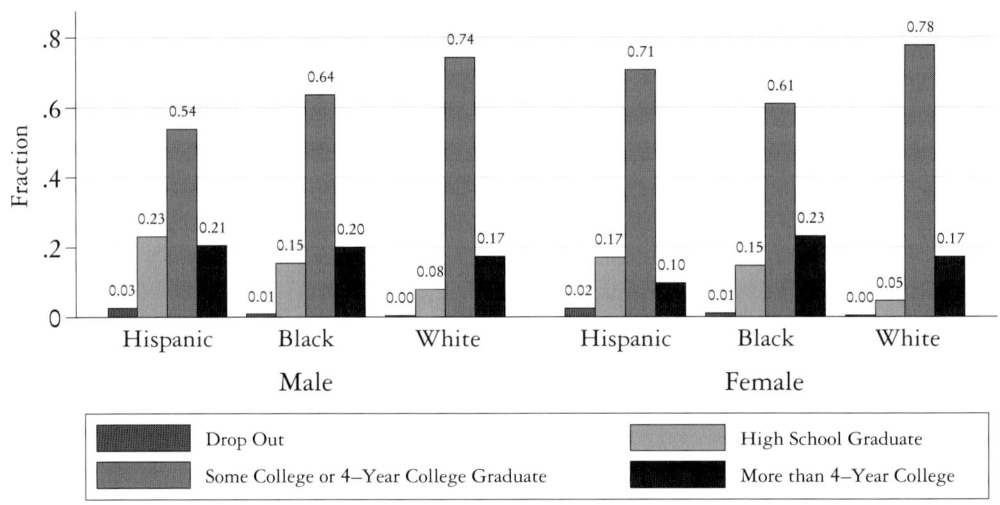

(B)

Figure 14. (A) Child's Own Expected Educational Level at Age 10 by Race and Sex Children of NLSY79; (B) Mother's Expected Educational Level for the Child at Age 6 by Race and Sex Children of NLSY79.

is a result of discrimination is an open question. Expectation formation models are very complex and often lead to multiple equilibria, and are, therefore, difficult to test empirically. However, the evidence reported here does not provide much support for the claim that the ability measure used by Neal and Johnson is substantially biased by expectations.

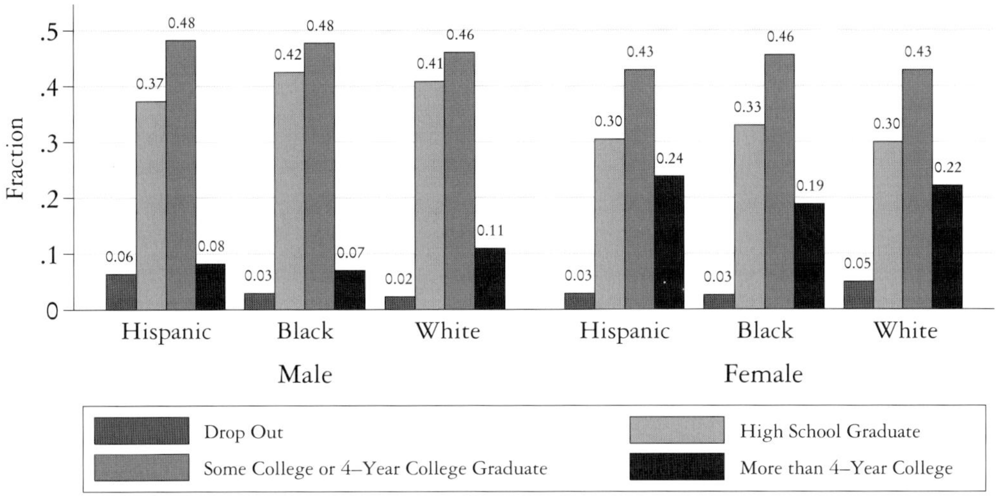

(C)

Figure 14. (*Continued*) (C) Young Adult's Own Expected Educational Level at Age 17 by Race and Sex (The height of the bar is produced by dividing the number of people who report falling in a particular educational cell by the total number of people in their race-sex group.)

5. THE EVIDENCE ON NONCOGNITIVE SKILLS

Controlling for scholastic ability in accounting for minority–majority wage gaps captures only part of the endowment differences between groups but receives most of the emphasis in the literature on Black–White gaps (see Jencks and Phillips, 1998). An emerging body of evidence, summarized in Bowles, Gintis, and Osborne (2001) and Carneiro and Heckman (2003), documents that noncognitive skills—motivation, self control, time preference, social skills—are important in explaining socioeconomic success and differentials in socioeconomic success.

Some of the best evidence for the importance of noncognitive skills in the labor market is from the GED (General Education Development) program. This program examines high school dropouts to certify that they are equivalent to high school graduates. In its own terms, the GED program is successful. Heckman and Rubinstein (2001) show that GED recipients and ordinary high school graduates who do not go on to college have the same distribution of AFQT scores (the same test that is graphed in figures 1A and B). They are psychometrically equated. Yet GED recipients earn the wages of high school dropouts with the same number of years of completed schooling. They are more likely to quit their jobs, engage in fighting or petty crime, or to be discharged from the military, than are high school graduates who do not go on to college or high school dropouts who do not get the GED (see Heckman and Rubinstein, 2001). Intelligence alone is not sufficient for socioeconomic success. Minority–White gaps in noncognitive skills open up early and widen over the lifecycle.

The CNLSY has lifecycle measures of noncognitive skills. Mothers are asked age-specific questions about the anti-social behavior of their children such as aggressiveness or violent behavior, cheating or lying, disobedience, peer conflicts and social withdrawal. The answers to these questions are grouped in different indices.[29] Figures 15A and B show that there are important racial and ethnic gaps in anti-social behavior index that emerge in early childhood. By ages 5 and 6, the average Black is roughly 10 percentile points above the average White in the distribution of this score (the higher the score, the worse the behavior).[30] The results shown in Figures 16A and B—where we adjust the gaps by permanent family income, mother's education and age-corrected AFQT and home score—also show large reductions.[31]

In Section 1, we documented that minority and White children face sharp differences in family and home environments while growing up. The evidence presented in this section shows that these early environmental differences can account (in a correlational sense) for most of the minority–White gap in noncognitive skills, as measured in the CNLSY.

Carneiro and Heckman (2003) document that noncognitive skills are more malleable than cognitive skills and are more easily shaped by interventions. More motivated children achieve more and have higher measured achievement test scores than less motivated children of the same ability. Carneiro and Heckman report that noncognitive skill gaps can be eliminated by equalization of family and home environments, while IQ gaps cannot. The largest effects of interventions in childhood and adolescence are on noncognitive skills which promote learning and integration into the larger society. Improvements in these skills produce better labor market outcomes, and less engagement in criminal activities and other risky behavior. Promotion of noncognitive skill is an avenue for policy that warrants much greater attention.

6. SUMMARY AND CONCLUSION

This chapter discusses the sources of wage gaps between minorities and Whites. For all minorities but Black males, adjusting for the ability that minorities bring to the market eliminates wage gaps. The major source of economic disparity by race and ethnicity in the current U.S. labor market is in endowments, not in payments to endowments.

[29] The children's mothers were asked 28 age-specific questions about frequency, range and type of specific behavior problems that children age 4 and over may have exhibited in the previous 3 months. Factor analysis was used to determine six clusters of questions. The responses for each cluster were then dichotomized and summed. The Antisocial Behavior index we use in this chapter consists of measures of cheating and telling lies, bullying and cruelty to others, not feeling sorry for misbehaving, breaking things deliberately (if age is less than 12), disobedience at school (if age is greater than 5), and trouble getting along with teachers (if age is greater than 5).

[30] In the web appendix http://jenni.uchicago.edu/ABF, we show that these differences are statistically strong. Once we control for family and home environments, gaps in most behavioral indices disappear.

[31] See Appendix tables A.2A and A.2B for the effect of adjusting for other environmental characteristics on the anti-social behavior score.

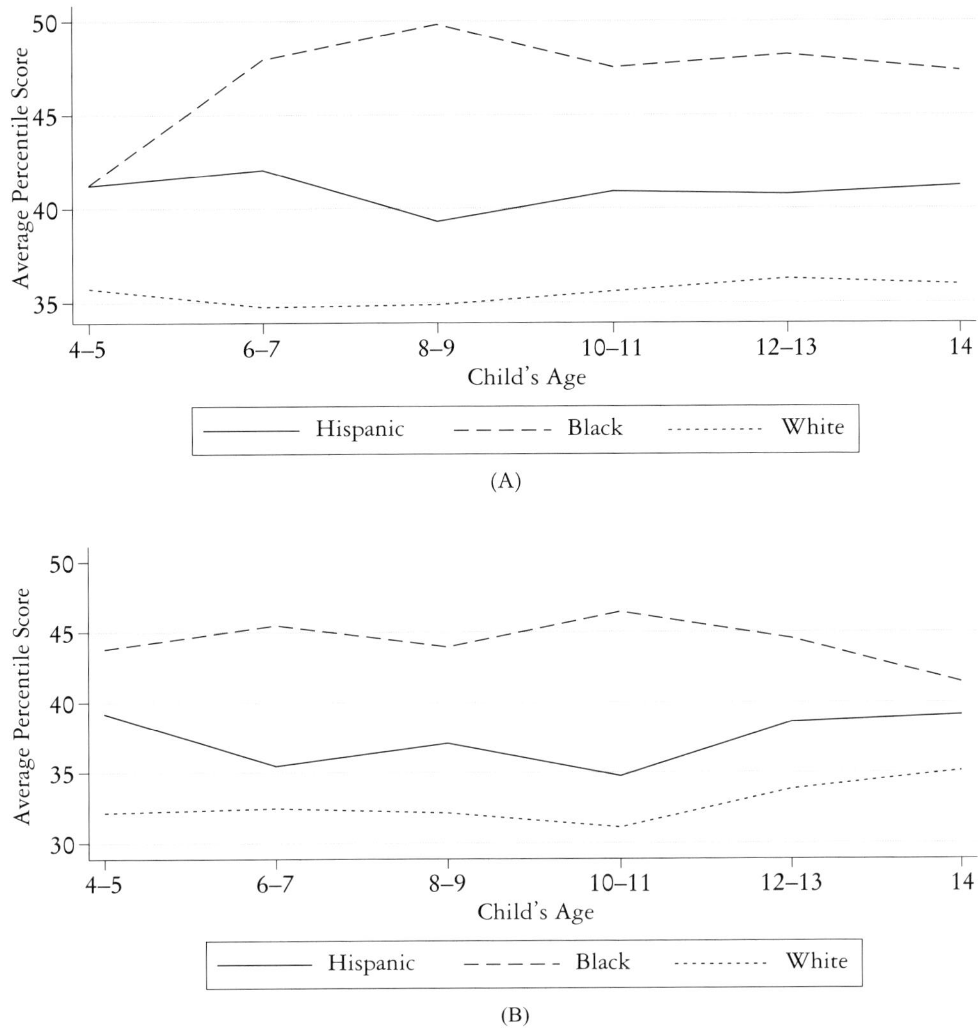

Figure 15. (A) Percentile Anti-Social Behavior Score by Race and Age Group Children of NLSY79 Males; (B) Percentile Anti-Social Behavior Score by Race and Age Group Children of NLSY79 Females (Mothers were asked 28 age-specific questions about frequency, range and type of specific behavior problems that children age 4 and over may have exhibited in the previous 3 months. Factor analysis was used to determine six clusters of questions. This test is one such cluster. The responses for each cluster were dichotomized and summed to produce a raw score. The percentile score was then calculated separately for each sex at each age from the raw score a higher percentile score indicates a higher incidence of problems.)

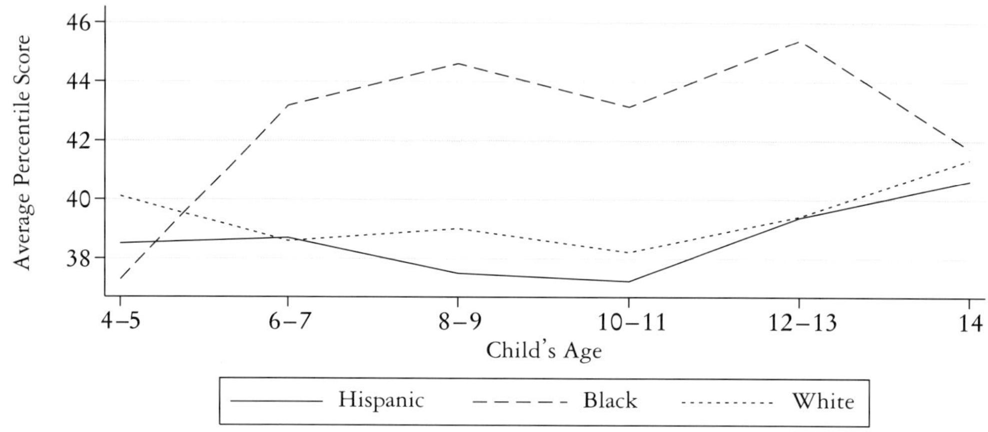

(A)

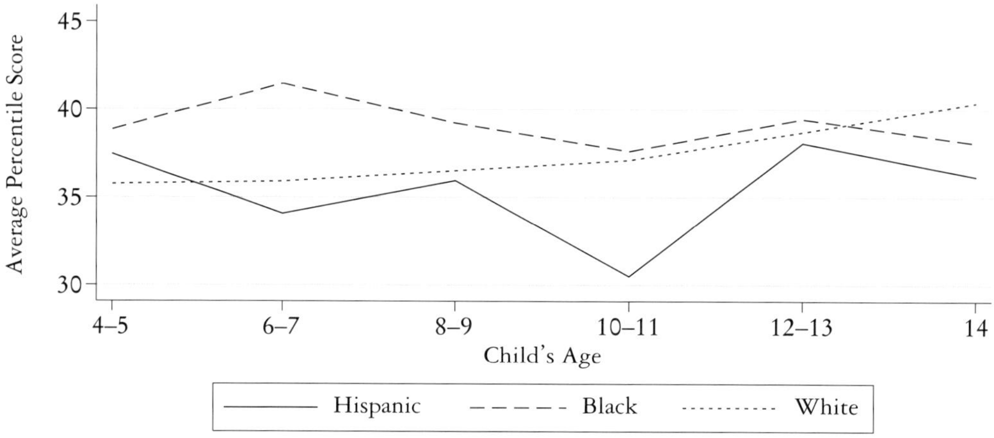

(B)

Figure 16. (A) Adjusted Percentile Anti-Social Behavior Score by Race and Age Group Children of NLSY79 Males. (B) Adjusted Percentile Anti-Social Behavior Score by Race and Age Group Children of NLSY79 Females (Adjusted by permanent family income, mother's education and age-corrected AFQT, and home score. Adjusted indicates that we equalized the family background characteristics across all race groups by setting them at the mean to purge the effect of family environment disparities. Permanent income is constructed by taking the average of annual family income discounted to child's age 0 using a 10% discount rate. Age-corrected AFQT is the standardized residual from the regression of the raw AFQT score on age at the time of the test dummy variables. Home score is an index of quality of the child's home environment.)

This evidence suggests that strengthened civil rights and affirmative action policies targeted at the labor market are unlikely to have much effect on racial and ethnic wage gaps, except possibly for those specifically targeted toward Black males. Policies that foster endowments have much greater promise. On the other hand, this chapter does not provide any empirical evidence on whether or not the existing edifice of civil rights and affirmative action legislation should be abolished. All of our evidence on wages is for an environment where affirmative action laws and regulations are in place.

Minority deficits in cognitive and noncognitive skills emerge early and widen. Unequal schooling, neighborhoods and peers may account for this differential growth in skills, but the main story in the data is not about growth rates but rather about the size of early deficits. Hispanic children start with cognitive and noncognitive deficits similar to those of Black children. They also grow up in similar disadvantaged environments, and are likely to attend schools of similar quality. Hispanics have substantially less schooling than for Blacks. Nevertheless, the ability growth by years of schooling is much higher for Hispanics than Blacks. By the time they reach adulthood, Hispanics have significantly higher test scores than Blacks. Conditional on test scores, there is no Hispanic–White wage gap. Our analysis of the Hispanic data illuminates the traditional study of Black–White differences and casts doubt on many conventional explanations of these differences since they do not apply to Hispanics who also suffer from many of the same disadvantages. The failure of the Hispanic–White gap to widen with schooling or age casts doubt on poor schools and bad neighborhoods as the reasons for the slow growth rate in Black test scores, since Hispanics experience the same kinds of poor schools and bad neighborhoods experienced by Blacks. Deficits in noncognitive skills can be explained (in a statistical sense) by adverse early environments; deficits in cognitive skills are less easily eliminated by the same factors. Heckman et al. (2004) present additional supporting evidence on these points.

Neal and Johnson document that endowments acquired before people enter the market explain most of the minority–majority wage gap. They use an ability test taken in the teenage years as a measure of endowment unaffected by discrimination. In this chapter, we note that the distinction between "premarket" factors unaffected by expectations of market discrimination and "market" factors so affected is an arbitrary one. Occupational choice is likely affected by discrimination. The proper treatment of schooling is less clear-cut. Neal and Johnson purposely omit schooling in adjusting for racial and ethnic wage gaps, arguing that schooling choices are potentially contaminated by expectations of labor market discrimination. Yet they do not adjust their measure of ability by the schooling attained at the date of the test, which would be the appropriate correction if their argument were correct. Hansen et al. (2004) and Heckman et al. (2004) show that the Neal–Johnson measure of ability is affected by schooling.

Adjusting wage gaps by both completed schooling and the schooling-adjusted test widens wage gaps for all groups. This effect is especially strong for Blacks. At issue is how much of the difference in schooling at the date of the test is due to expectations of labor market discrimination and how much is due to adverse early environments.

While this chapter does not settle this question definitively, test score gaps emerge early and are more plausibly linked to adverse early environments. The lion's share of the ability gaps at the date of the test emerge very early, before children can have clear expectations about their labor market prospects.

The analysis of Sackett et al. (2004) and the emergence of test score gaps in young children cast serious doubt on the importance of "stereotype threats" in accounting for poorer Black test scores. It is implausible that young minority test takers have the social consciousness assumed in the stereotype literature. If the stereotype threat is important, measured minority ability should receive different incremental payments. In a companion paper, Carneiro et al. (2005) find no evidence for such an effect.

Gaps in test scores of the magnitude found in recent studies were found in the earliest tests developed at the beginning of the 20th century, before the results of testing were disseminated and a stereotype threat could have been "in the air." The recent emphasis on the stereotype threat as a basis for Black–White test scores ignores the evidence that tests are predictive of schooling attainment and market wages. It diverts attention away from the emergence of important skill gaps at early ages, which should be a target of public policy.

Effective social policy designed to eliminate racial and ethnic inequality for most minorities should focus on eliminating skill gaps, not on discrimination in the workplace of the early 21st century. Interventions targeted at adults are much less effective and do not compensate for early deficits. Early interventions aimed at young children hold much greater promise than strengthened legal activism in the workplace.[32]

[32] See Carneiro and Heckman (2003) and Cunha, Heckman, Lochner and Masterov (2005) for the evidence on early interventions and later remedial interventions.

CHAPTER 6

Discrimination in Consummated Car Purchases

Ian Ayres[1]

ABSTRACT

Recent studies have examined the question of whether there is racial discrimination in car sales by analyzing newly available data about actual, consummated purchases of cars. This article reviews this research and compares it to my previous findings based on audit studies, in which Black and White testers were sent to car dealerships to negotiate, but not consummate sales. The studies using consummated purchase data contain strikingly similar results to those of the audit studies, and together they provide compelling evidence that Blacks pay substantially more for cars than Whites. The existence of this price differential is consistent with claims of racial discrimination and effectively rebuts claims that the audit studies are flawed because they do not reflect bargaining tactics that minorities could use in traditional, face-to-face car sales that would nullify the impact of discrimination. The new data also reveal that there is a much smaller price differential when Internet referral services are used, which is also consistent with claims of racial discrimination since the race of the buyer is harder to discern over the Internet.

INTRODUCTION

Two noted scholars have questioned whether audit tests of disparate treatment can provide compelling evidence of the economic injury borne by Blacks who in equilibrium might find a variety of ways mitigate its impact. For example, in critiquing my previous audit studies of new car sales, Epstein (1994), has argued that:

> [I]n open markets customers are free to select not only their bargaining strategies but also the dealerships they visit. If blacks or women know that they are apt to get a good deal from some small fraction of the market, then they can avoid other, less receptive dealerships and their unattractive offers. How much of the differential found by Ayres would thus have disappeared is hard to say. In addition it may be possible for a buyer to reduce the differentials even further by bringing along a friend, by eliciting a rival offer from another dealer over the telephone.... These tactics are of course also open to white males, but given the lower bids that they are able to elicit, they are likely to yield better returns when adopted by others who anticipate that they will be offered higher prices. (pp. 52–53)

[1] This chapter updates Chapter 4 of Ayres (2001).

L. B. Nielsen and R. L. Nelson (eds.), Handbook of Employment Discrimination Research, 137–148.

Epstein is somewhat agnostic (it is "hard to say") about the extent to which consumers might be able to avoid the effects of discrimination by patronizing dealerships that they know to be non-discriminating, but Heckman (1998) makes a more far-reaching claim:

> [Audit evidence of disparate racial treatment] is entirely consistent with little or no market discrimination at the margin. *Purposive sorting within markets eliminates the worst forms of discrimination.* There may be evil lurking in the hearts of firms that is never manifest in consummated market transactions. (p. 103)[2]

Without benefit of any empiricism, Heckman argues a theoretical possibility as an established fact. In essence, Heckman and Epstein are arguing that victim self-help could produce an equilibrium in which it would be "as if" discrimination did not exist. Blacks would receive (almost) the same prices as Whites.[3]

However, the audit tests themselves provide powerful evidence that African-Americans cannot protect themselves from the effects of discrimination by merely searching for and shifting their consumption to non-discriminating dealers (Ayres, 2001, pp. 70–71). An important finding of the audit regressions concerns the perva-

[2] The importance of these kinds of general equilibrium concerns has long been recognized in the labor market context. See, e.g., Siegelman (1999), Flinn and Heckman (1983), and Duleep and Zalokar (1991). Yinger (1997) formalizes the intuition that discrimination by sellers reduces the benefits of additional searches by buyers, causing them to accept higher prices or lower quality than they otherwise would. Yinger applies this methodology to the housing market, and finds that the costs of discrimination are roughly $4000 per minority household per search.

[3] Epstein (1994) has also criticized the audit approach for the small proportion of observations in which dealers attempted to accept a tester offer:

> [I]n [Ayres's] sample there were apparent contracts (i.e., a verbal agreement on the price that was not binding) in only 25 percent of the cases with white males, and in 15 percent of the cases with the remainder of his sample. The market would be in a state of perpetual turmoil if huge percentages of potential buyers were unable to buy cars at all. A technique of testing that leaves so many incomplete transactions cannot be an accurate replica of a functioning market. (p. 34)

This criticism ignores the structure of the audit. The testers were instructed to bargain until the dealership refused to negotiate further or attempted to accept one of their offers. The test focused on the lowest offer the dealer was willing to make—before refusing to negotiate further or in accepting the tester's predetermined offer. We could have had 100% of the observations end in a non-binding verbal agreement (which would have satisfied Epstein's definition) if we had merely instructed the testers to accept the dealer's last and lowest offer at the point the salesperson refused to bargain further.

And, in Chapter 3 of Ayres (2001), Peter Siegelman and I investigated whether our findings of race and gender discrimination might be linked to the fact that the dealerships' final offers were sometimes refusals to bargain further and sometimes acceptances of tester offers. We found that sessions ending in attempted acceptances had an approximately $400 lower final profit than those that ended in a refusal to bargain (and this result was statistically significant). The size of this acceptance effect, however, was the same for all testers. But the fact that sellers are more likely to accept offers from White males actually biases our estimates *against* finding discrimination because acceptances provide only an upper bound for sellers' reservation prices. That is, in those cases where dealers attempted to accept an offer from a White male tester, the dealers might have been willing to make an even lower offer, which would have increased our measure of discrimination.

siveness of discrimination across dealerships. The regressions suggest that Black consumers could not protect themselves by patronizing minority, and/or women-owned dealerships or by striving to bargain with minority and/or women salespeople. As Goldberg (1996) concluded:

> [The audit] experiment offers some direct evidence on the issue [of whether purposive sorting by testers mitigated the effect of dealership disparate treatment]: testers in the controlled experiment visit various dealerships in the Chicago area, some of which are located in poorer areas or in black neighborhoods, yet there is no evidence of any difference in the treatment minorities receive in such locations. (p. 643)

In short, our testing of over 400 dealerships in Chicagoland found pervasive prejudice. There were no statistically significant "safe harbor" dealerships where our testers could confidently go and uniformly bargain for a deal as good as White testers received.[4]

Still the audit does not exclude the possibility that minority purchasers might have been able to get a better deal at the same dealership if they had employed a different bargaining strategy. It is important to emphasize that forcing these minorities to use a different type of negotiation might itself represent an important type of race discrimination. This is especially true if the alternative path to a good deal was significantly more onerous. If Whites need only bargain for four hours to negotiate a low markup, but Blacks need to negotiate for eight hours, then a finding that Blacks in equilibrium paid the same for cars would not mean that Blacks were not injured by the dealerships' disparate treatment. However, it might as a theoretical matter be possible that the dealership does not require more onerous bargaining but merely different bargaining by Blacks and Whites: Whites may be penalized if they speak in a Black voice and vice versa. This "separate but equal" possibility would still be a form of disparate racial treatment, but the harms from discrimination would be more contestable.[5]

Accordingly, it is useful to test whether Blacks pay more in actual consummated transactions. Actual sales of course are not controlled tests, and while multivariate regressions might control for a handful of purchaser characteristics, it is, as a practical matter, impossible to econometrically control after the fact for the myriad of different ways that purchasers might bargain. Therefore, an analysis of consummated transactions does not provide independent evidence of disparate treatment. A finding that Blacks pay more than Whites does not—by itself—indicate that dealerships engage in race-based bargaining. Dealerships might bargain uniformly with all potential customers—conceding at a uniform rate against all potential purchasers—with White customers on average holding out for better deals than Black customers. Instead, a finding of disparate transaction prices would be at a minimum evidence that the dealerships' decisions to haggle (as opposed to the no-haggle policies of Saturn and others) have a disparate impact on Black purchasers. But when combined with the preceding

[4] A possible exception to this might be so-called no-haggle dealerships that will be discussed below.

[5] The social meaning of separate but equal regimes still can work substantial injury on traditionally subordinated people. See Rubenfeld (1998).

evidence of disparate treatment in dealership offers, a finding that Black purchasers pay more on average than White purchasers suggests that neither (1) purposive sorting, nor (2) alternative (and possibly more onerous) bargaining, nor (3) choosing not to purchase eliminates the effects of racially disparate dealership offers.

This chapter extends the meta-analysis first done in Ayres (2001) to compare seven different datasets of consummated and audit transactions:

(1) The Chicago "Pilot" Audit (Ayres, 1991): An audit analysis of six testers (three White males, one Black female, one Black male, one White female) at approximately 90 Chicagoland dealerships.
(2) Chicago Full Audit (Ayres, 2001): An audit analysis of 38 testers (18 White males, 7 White females, 5 Black males, and 8 Black females) at 242 Chicagoland dealerships.
(3) National Consumer Expenditure Survey (CES) Consummated Sales (Goldberg, 1996): A consummated sales analysis of national CES data (67 minority observations, 1,212 White observations).
(4) Atlanta Consummated Sales (Ayres, 2001): A consummated sales analysis of litigation-generated data from a single dealership (over 800 observations, approximately half were Black purchasers).[6]
(5) J.D. Powers 2000 National Consummated Sales (Harless and Hoffer, 2002): A consummated sales analysis of national J.D. Powers data (4,030 observations).
(6) National Consummated Sales—Traditional Bargaining (Scott Morton, Zettelmeyer, and Silva-Risso, 2003): A consummated sales analysis of national J.D. Powers-like data of traditional dealership sales (671,468 observations).
(7) National Consummated Sales—Autobytel Purchases (Scott Morton et al.): A consummated sales analysis of national J.D. Powers-like data of Autobytel referred sales. (Over 20,000 observations of which approximately 7,300 were African-American purchasers.)

This chapter's thesis is that the consummated transaction datasets are consistent with audit study findings that dealerships offer higher prices to Black consumers. Both the CES and Atlanta data on actual purchases show that Whites pay lower average prices than minorities (for CES data) and, more specifically, Blacks (for Atlanta data). Moreover, the sizes of the differentials are broadly similar. While the racial price differences are not statistically significant in Goldberg's (1996) analysis of the CES data, Ayres (2001) showed that this insignificance was a function of the noisiness of the data. In the less noisy audit and Atlanta purchases data, we observe similar coefficients and smaller standard errors—which allow us to identify the racial differentials as statistically significant. The newer data from the market research firms continue to confirm the absence of a gender effect and the general presence of a statistically significant race effect.

The first part of this chapter analyzes the datasets examined in recent articles by Harless and Hoffer (2002); Scott Morton et al. (2003); and Scott Morton, Zettelmeyer,

[6] An extended discussion of the first four datasets is included in Ayres (2001).

and Silva-Risso (2002). These articles exploit newly available market research data from J.D. Powers & Associates and an unnamed research firm in the automotive industry, which can provide the direct evidence on vehicle profits. The second part includes a meta-analysis of the seven datasets.

1. THREE NEW TRANSACTION STUDIES USING DEALER MARKET RESEARCH DATA

In the last two years, two new published articles (Harless and Hoffer, 2002; Scott Morton et al., 2003), and one unpublished study (Scott Morton et al., 2002) have exploited transaction data from J.D. Powers & Associates and an unnamed research firm in the automotive industry. These data include crucial information about vehicle profits for thousands of dealerships instead of just the single Atlanta dealership analyzed in Ayres (2001).[7] While this type of data has presumably been available to manufacturers for years, the recent academic access makes this a particularly exciting time to conduct automobile pricing studies—especially because the negotiation equilibrium may dramatically change with the resurgence of no-haggle dealerships on the one hand and the rise of Internet sales, referral services and research on the other.

1.1. The Harless and Hoffer Study

The first published study based on the new J.D. Powers data was by Harless and Hoffer (2002). Harless and Hoffer analyzed 4,030 purchases made from more than 2,300 dealerships (part of the Powers Information Network) in February 2000. The authors admirably emphasize a number of weaknesses with their data:

> First, the database does not include the race of the buyer. Hence, omitted variable bias is possible. If black males pay more than black females (as suggested in Ayres and Siegelman) then our model will not be as likely to detect a difference in profit between men and women. Second, to protect the privacy of dealers and customers, the database reports information in "cells" containing at least three transactions. Our dataset contains information on 4,030 transactions, but these 4,030 transactions are grouped in 414 cells with the cells containing from three to 74 transactions. Hence, our results are subject to the problem of ecological correlation (the possibility of drawing incorrect conclusions about individual outcomes from aggregated data), but the extent of this problem should be slight since the number of transactions per cell (median = 7) is quite small. Third, the J.D. Powers database reports dealer information only for the approximately 2,300 dealers who have been recruited to be included in the system. We cannot claim that this represents a random sample of dealers. While acknowledging that the sample of dealers is not random, it is noteworthy that vehicle manufacturers find the information sufficiently valuable to pay tens of thousands of dollars a month for access to the database. (Harless and Hoffer, 2002, pp. 271–272)

[7] The datasets themselves may be less biased because the source was not involved in ongoing litigation. The data also include a wealth of information on other sources of profit (trade-in and finance) that are ripe for further analysis.

To my mind the even bigger concern with the study is that the researchers could not observe the gender of who bargained for the car. Gender inferences were based on a probabilistic inference about the name of the titled purchaser:

> Buyers are classified as female or male as determined by a PIN proprietary probabilistic name program. If there are two or more buyers, the sex of the first recorded purchaser is used; we assume in such cases that the first name listed indicates the person who took the lead in negotiations. Misclassification would bias our results against finding differences between male and female buyers. Increasing our confidence in the accuracy of classification of sex by name, however, is that in 20 percent of all transactions the name could not be unambiguously assigned to a sex (and these cases are excluded from our sample). (Harless and Hoffer, 2002, p. 274)

Thus, if a man bargained but a woman was the titled owner, the data would report the transaction as being "female." Given these data limitations, it should not be surprising that Harless and Hoffer did not find a statistically significant gender disparity. The study found that women paid an average of $29 (or 1.9% higher mean gross profit) more for new cars than men, but the disparity was insignificant ($p = 0.47$) (2002, pp. 275–276, tab. 2, col. 2). Still, the finding of a small and statistically insignificant gender disparity conforms with the results of both the previous audit and purchase studies.

1.2. The Scott Morton, Zettelmeyer and Silva-Risso Study (2003)

Scott Morton et al. (2003) exploited an even larger dataset from an unnamed market research firm (which I would bet is also J.D. Powers). They analyzed 671,468 transactions at 3,562 dealerships concerning purchases made between January 1, 1999 and February 28, 2000. Unlike the Harless and Hoffer (2002) study, Scott Morton et al. observed individual transactions. But like Harless and Hoffer, Scott Morton et al. did not observe the gender or race of the bargainers. Like Harless and Hoffer, they inferred the gender of the titled purchaser by making probabilistic inferences about the purchaser's first name. They made inferences about the purchaser's race by exploiting census data about the racial composition of the "block group" (on average 1,100 people) where the purchaser resided. So this initial Scott Morton et al. study suffers from the same problems as Harless and Hoffer concerning gender identification. But the racial inference is not likely to be as problematic, if we believe that is less likely for cross-racial bargaining to occur (e.g., for a White to bargain on behalf of Black purchaser) than cross-gender bargaining. However, there can still be selection bias (for example, if Whites in a Black neighborhood are more likely to purchase a car).

With these limitations, Scott Morton et al. (2003) find that Black purchasers are expected to pay $456 more than White purchasers,[8] and this result is statistically

[8] Literally a purchaser from an all black block group is predicted to pay $456 more than a purchaser from an all white block group.

significant (p. 83, tab. 5, col. 1). Hispanic purchasers fared even worse—paying an estimated (and statistically significant) $523 more than Whites, while Asian purchasers fared the best, paying $218 less then Whites (again statistically significant). In contrast, female purchasers are predicted to pay just $48 more than male purchasers (statistically significant).[9]

The Scott Morton et al. (2003) study is also important because it is the first and only analysis of whether Internet referral services tend to reduce the racial disparities now repeatedly found in traditional negotiations. Specifically, they tested whether purchasers who used Autobytel, the largest Internet referral service at the time, received systematically different deals. In particular, they tested whether there were fewer racial disparities because the service may have negotiated better terms with the dealership and because the dealership may have had a weaker racial signal than in face-to-face transactions.[10]

Their results are striking. They found that Autobytel users paid approximately $273 less (1.2%) than non-Autobytel users (Scott Morton et al., 2003, p. 86, tab. 6, col. 1). Moreover, they found a marked decline in racial disparities: Black users were estimated to pay only $68 more than White users (compared to the $456 differential found in traditional sales); female users were estimated to pay $21 more than male users (compared to the $48 differential found in traditional sales); and Hispanic users were estimated to pay $285 *less* than Anglo users (compared to the $523 differential found in traditional sales) (Scott Morton et al., 2003, p. 86, tab. 6, col. 1).

Scott Morton, Zettelmeyer, and Silva-Risso have already followed up their excellent study (2003) with an unpublished second study (2002) which pairs the same type of vehicle profit information used in their first study (but limited to California sales in April and May of 2002) with responses from a survey that they mailed to 5,200 consumers—eliciting information about how informed the bargainer was and how he or she bargained (Scott Morton et al., 2002). The resulting dataset (after accounting for non-responses and incomplete surveys) had 1,507 observations.

The survey allows the authors to identify the gender and race of the real bargainers much more accurately than before. We learn for example that women purchasers were more likely to bring a man along to bargain than vice versa (69% of women versus 48% of men). While the paper estimates racial price results, they are generally insignificant because (as the authors emphasize) there are so few minorities in their final sample (for example, only 3.4% of the purchasers self-identified as African-American). But, even with much better gender information, the paper finds gender disparities identical

[9] These disparities should be interpreted as evidence of disparate racial and gender impacts. When the authors control for a variety of non-racial and non-gender characteristics concerning the transaction, the racial disparities decrease. For example, the differential for black purchasers drops to $342. However, the gender disparity remains $48 (Scott Morton et al., 2003, p. 76, tab. 2, col. 1).

[10] The race of a purchaser in an Autobytel transaction might still be inferred from the purchaser's name and address and, at times, from telephone conversations. Also Autobytel may not be able to protect purchasers from racial disparities in negotiating the price of a trade-in that must be done on a face-to-face basis.

to Scott Morton et al. (2003)—to wit, that women paid about a half a percent more than men in traditional bargains.

2. META-ANALYSIS OF THE SEVEN STUDIES

There now exist six different datasets to help assess whether Blacks are discriminated against in car purchasing. It is useful to take stock of the overall message of these data. While it is essential to undertake the micro-analysis of these data, it is also useful to step back and assess the broad contours of discrimination. Table 1 attempts just this task by summarizing the bottom line race/gender pricing differences. Of course, because the datasets come from such disparate sources, important caveats are in order. In interpreting this table, the reader should keep in mind the following:

(1) The transactions differ: the audit testers solicited offers, but did not purchase cars; the Goldberg (1996), Atlanta (Ayres, 2001), Harless and Hoffer (2002) and Scott Morton et al. (2003) datasets include consummated transactions.
(2) The price measures differ: the audit studies numbers are based on the profits implicit in the dealers' final offers; Goldberg's study is based on imputed differences in discounts from the sticker price; the Atlanta study is based on differences in total profit (including financing but excluding trade-in profit); and the Harless and Hoffer and Scott Morton et al. studies are based on just vehicle profits.
(3) The controls differ: the audit testers used a uniform bargaining strategy and were controlled on a host of verbal and non-verbal dimensions while the completed transaction data has no *ex ante* control, and we lack basic information about how purchasers bargained, which makes it impossible to control *ex post* with regressions.
(4) The racial groups differ: the audit, Atlanta, and Scott Morton et al. studies are tests of Black/White disparities (with the Scott Morton et al. study also examining disparities for Hispanics and Asians), while the Goldberg study is a test of "minority"/"non-minority" disparities, and the Harless and Hoffer data contain no racial information.
(5) The geographic areas differ: the audit data come from Chicago; the Goldberg, Harless and Hoffer, and Scott Morton et al. studies are based on a nationwide sample; and the Atlanta data are of course from Atlanta.
(6) The time periods differ: the pilot audit study was completed in 1989; the full audit study was completed in 1990; the Goldberg data covered transactions completed in 1983–1987; the Atlanta data covered transactions completed in 1990–1995; the Harless and Hoffer data covered February 2000; and the Scott Morton et al. study covered 1999 and the first 2 months of 2000.

Still, with all these caveats in mind, a global comparison of the race/gender differentials reveals striking similarities. The differentials for both Black males and Black females (i.e., the amount by which their profits exceeded the profits of White males)

Table 1. Meta-analysis of estimated dollar price premium over White males in four studies of markups on new cars, by demographic group

Demographic group	White females	Black females	Black males	Adjusted R-squared
Chicago "Pilot" Audit (Ayres, 1991)	$220 (129) [21]	$1,013*** (124) [23]	$283*** (136) [18]	0.37
Chicago Full Audit (Ayres, 2001)	216* (116) [53]	465*** (103) [60]	1,133*** (122) [40]	0.33
National CES Consummated Sales (Goldberg, 1996)	129 (117) [244]	426 (525) [28]	274 (263) [39]	0.14
Atlanta Consummated Sales (Ayres, 2001)	−11 (97) [164]	865*** (92) [224]	611*** (96) [178]	0.36
J.D. Powers Feb. 2000 Sales (Harless and Hoffer, 2002)	29 (38.9) [2,015]†			0.76
Scott Morton et al. (2003)	47.9*** (3.2) [241,729]	503.7*** (12.1) [14,383]	445.8*** (11.6) [38,514]	0.97
Weighted Average	47.8*** (3.7) [244,226]	509.7*** (14.7) [14,718]	457*** (12.4) [38,789]	
Scott Morton et al. (2003) (Autobytel purchases)	20.5 (13.6) [6,800]	88.9 (66.4) [204]‡	68.4 (65.0) [306]‡	0.98

Row 1, Ayres (1991).
Row 2, Ayres (2001), Chapter 2, Table 2.1, Col. 2.
Row 3, Goldberg (1996), Table 2, Col. 1 and Table 5. Goldberg tested for differences between "Minority" and "Non-Minority" purchasers.
Row 4, Ayres (2001), Table 4, Col. 6.
Row 5, Harless and Hoffer (2002), Table 2, Col. 1.
Row 6, Scott Morton et al. (2003), Table 5, Col. 1.
Row 8, Scott Morton et al. (2003), Table 6, Col. 2.
Standard errors in parentheses. Number of observations in brackets.
* Significantly different from zero at the 10% level.
** Significantly different from zero at the 5% level.
*** Significantly different from zero at the 1% level.
† Number of female transactions assumed to be half of total sample size (omitted in article).
‡ Cell size within Autobytel transactions assumed proportional to cell size over the full dataset.

are uniformly positive and substantial (ranging from $274 to $1,133, not including the Autobytel dataset). Moreover, of the five datasets addressing race in the traditional car sales market (i.e., excluding Harless and Hoffer, 2002 and Scott Morton et al., 2003, Autobytel data), four contain Black-male and Black-female differentials that are highly significant. Also in four of these same five datasets, Black women are estimated to pay more then Black men. And for heuristic purposes, if we combine the observations from these five different sources, we find that on average Black men pay (or are finally asked to pay) \$457 more than White men, and that Black women are asked to pay \$510 more than White men. These weighted average differentials, when compared to the combined standard deviation, are also statistically significant.[11] Thus, while the differentials uncovered by Goldberg (1996) in the CES data continue to be statistically insignificant, the high standard deviation applied to her small number of observations (28 out of a total of more than 14,000 minority-female observations) is not sufficient to render the global analysis statistically insignificant.

Indeed, several things are striking when comparing the Goldberg (1996) differentials with the differentials from the other datasets. Goldberg's standard errors for minority males and minority females are more than twice (and sometimes three and four times) the size of the comparable differentials, and her R-squared is less than half all of the other regressions. These are strong indications of the noisiness of her data. But the sizes of the differentials themselves are not so far from some of the other datasets. Goldberg's minority-female differential of \$426 is similar to the \$465 Black-female differential from the full audit study. And Goldberg's minority-male differential of \$274 is similar to the Black-male differential estimated in the pilot audit.

Still it must be admitted that the sizes of the differentials—while robustly positive—do vary. Two of the Black-minority-male differentials are near \$300 and two others are more than twice this amount (\$611 and \$1,133). Three of the Black-minority-female differentials are in the \$450–\$500 range, but the other two are roughly twice this amount (\$865 and \$1,013). These higher differentials are not only statistically distinct from Goldberg's estimates (Goldberg, 1996), but also a joint test rejects the null hypothesis of equal means. Still, given the important differences in the ways these data were produced and analyzed, I believe the similarities of the table far outweigh the dissimilarities.

The global analysis shows that on net Blacks pay substantially more than Whites in both audit testing and consummated transactions. Once we appreciate the noisiness of Goldberg's data (Goldberg, 1996), her analysis does not contradict, but adds marginal confirmation to this result. Counter to the conjectures of Heckman (1998) and Epstein (1994), additional search and/or alternative bargaining strategies seen in traditional negotiations do not eliminate or even significantly mitigate the amounts of discrimination discovered in the initial audits. Customers often do not have sufficient information to take such self-help measures, and, given the recalcitrance that dealerships across

[11] The combined standard deviation was computed to be:

$$\frac{\sum_{i=1} s_i^2(n_i - 1)}{\sum_{i=1} n_i - 4},$$

where s_i = the standard deviation of the ith dataset and n_i = the number of observations of the ith dataset.

the board showed in the audit testing, it is not clear that effective self-help measures currently exist.

However there is some evidence that Internet referrals may ultimately help confirm the Heckman/Epstein conjecture. The last row of Table 1 reports the analogous differentials found in the Scott Morton et al. (2003) Autobytel data. The racial and gender disparities are markedly lower and not statistically significant (even though there was a substantial sample size and R-squared). Moreover, Scott Morton et al. (2002) found that women and minorities were more likely to use the Autobytel service. Together this suggests that the emerging practice of researching and shopping via the Internet (where race and gender characteristics may be less knowable by sellers) may prove to reduce the persistent racial disparities found in traditional auto sales. However, while the penetration of Internet sales has been phenomenal, it still represents a small proportion of the overall market and hence provides only a limited (but rapidly growing) confirmation of the Heckman/Epstein conjecture.

This evidence of racial disparities in consummated vehicle pricing is also consistent with similar analyses of racial disparities in finance profits. Both the Ayres (2001) analysis of the Atlanta dataset and the more recent litigation-generated analysis of major automotive lenders suggest that Black borrowers are much more likely to have their interest rate marked up above their risk-adjusted rate of interest. A class action suit against General Motor's credit division, General Motors Acceptance Corp. (GMAC), has uncovered that financing profits for (African-American) borrowers are systematically higher than for White borrowers (*Coleman v. General Motors Acceptance Corp.*, 2000).[12] The basic facts of the suit can be easily summarized (albeit in a slightly stylized fashion). When a GM dealer approaches GMAC about financing a particular purchaser and passes on core information about the financial risk of lending to such a car buyer, GMAC responds by telling the dealership the minimum amount of interest rate (the risk-adjusted market rate) that the dealer can charge. But GMAC also allows the dealership to negotiate a higher and more profitable interest rate up to some maximum amount. The dealer and GMAC split the profits on any excess interest that the dealer can negotiate.

A report of plaintiffs' expert Marc Cohen shows that, controlling for a host of other variables, the excess profit on loans to Black consumers is \$377 higher than for White consumers. These are not quite as high as the racial differentials in financial profits uncovered in the Atlanta dataset (which range from \$453 to \$637), but are nonetheless highly significant.

The plaintiffs in this litigation are using the Equal Credit Opportunity Act (ECOA),[13] which allows plaintiffs to bring racial disparate impact suits in lending. In this case, the plaintiff class alleged that the financing company's decision to allow dealerships to negotiate had an unjustified disparate impact on African-American

[12] I have been retained as a plaintiff's expert in this case as well as a number of other cases challenging the disparate racial impacts of dealership markups.

[13] See also 12 C.F.R. §202.1; Interagency Policy Statement, 1994 WL 128417.

borrowers. This statute has provided a new weapon to attack not just racial disparities in excess interest charged—but also to attack racial disparities in the underlying purchase price of the car (the principal of the loan).

3. CONCLUSION

In closing, it is appropriate to comment on the catch-22 created by the Epstein/Heckman critique. Discrimination tests are often plagued by difficulties of creating "similarly situated" comparisons. Heckman (1998), for example, has criticized some audits for not adequately controlling for unobserved variables—factors other than race or gender but correlated with these traits that might offer non-discriminatory explanation for the audit results. Defendants in discrimination suits *always* claim that their behavior was not predicated on the plaintiff's race or sex but on some other characteristic.

The catch-22 (or what Margaret Radin (1990) calls a "double bind") comes however when researchers produce an effective test where Blacks and Whites (men and women) *do* behave the same. Then comes Heckman (1998) claiming that the result is uninteresting because it does not prove that Blacks (and/or women) might not have protected themselves by behaving differently than White men. Thus, as a researcher you are damned if you do and damned if you do not. If you do not adequately assure uniform tester behavior, you will be criticized for not proving disparate treatment. If you do adequately assure uniform tester behavior, you will be criticized for not proving that trivial self-help could have mitigated the harms of the seller's disparate treatment. By combining an analysis of both audit testing and consummated transactions, I hope to have at least partially responded to both of these criticisms. While it is still true that controlled testers who undertook slightly more aggressive search or bargaining strategies might have been able to mitigate the types of discrimination found, the empiricism put forward presents a strong prima facie case for the propositions that (1) a broad array of new car dealerships discriminate on the basis of race and (2) consumer self-help does not simply solve the problem.

CHAPTER 7

Racial Equality Without Equal Employment Opportunity? Lessons from a Labor Market for Professional Athletes

William Bridges

ABSTRACT

One rationale for Equal Employment Opportunity legislation and its enforcement is that market forces alone are insufficient to counteract discriminatory effects in labor markets. Whether highly competitive markets diminish the extent of invidious outcomes for minorities is a question that deserves rigorous empirical scrutiny. This chapter uses data from a professional labor market, that for major league baseball players, to examine the competition-equality hypothesis. While this market is relatively small, it contains both cross-sectional and longitudinal variation in the degree of effective market competition. The findings show that minorities are in a better position relative to whites when labor market competition is more intense. However, this outcome is itself a contingent one: It only operates for a subset of players who are in 'non-central' positions, i.e. position players. Finally, the existence of high levels of competition in the baseball labor market is itself a phenomenon that is enacted and sustained within a web of rules, agreements, and negotiations.

INTRODUCTION

The proposition that racial and other minorities might benefit from participating in labor markets that are *more* competitive is generally embraced by economists and disparaged by sociologists (Sowell, 1981; Baron and Newman, 1990). In particular, in sociology, split labor market theory sees both minority and majority workers losing out to capital in competitive situations, and studies of internal labor markets typically view minorities, once on the inside, as benefiting, relative to outsiders, from the sheltering effects of promotion ladders, restricted ports of entry, and grievance procedures (Bonacich, 1976). This issue is also present in recent debates about whether invidious labor market discrimination is eroded by market competition (see England, 1992, p. 62–68 for a useful summary). The widespread persistence of gender and racial pay gaps is frequently cited as evidence against the proposition that discrimination in competitive markets will be self-extinguishing (e.g., England, 1992, p. 118). However, the

L. B. Nielsen and R. L. Nelson (eds.), Handbook of Employment Discrimination Research, 149–167.

continuation of unexplained racial and gender disparities reflects two possible failings as implied by these questions: (1) is the competitive theorem itself deficient in some way? For example, is discrimination based on altruism in favor of a group less vulnerable to competitive pressures than discrimination based on animus against a group? (Goldberg, 1982; England, 1992); (2) to what extent do labor market transactions take place in the context of a fully competitive market situation? That is, even if competition "works" in the sense imagined in the theory, if many transactions take place outside the realm of competitive markets, invidious differences will continue to survive.

The answers to these questions are relevant to our understanding of the role and possible scope of anti-discrimination legislation and policies, regardless of whether these policies are of the "equal employment" variety or of the "affirmative action" variety. It would be useful not only to know whether more competitive markets are *ever* associated with diminished discrimination, but also to know the circumstances or contexts which enable this association to exist. In short, is equality possible outside the realm of EEO? If so, what other conditions must be true for this to occur?

This chapter uses data from one labor market, that for major league baseball players, at different points in time and at different points in players' careers to explore the relationship between degree of labor market competition and the relative economic standing of minority workers. The benefit of close examination of this professional labor market is that there is clear and observable exogenously induced variation in the degree of competition that exists for the services of different groups of players and at different historical times (see below). By looking within this industry, therefore, one is able to hold constant a variety of other influences, for example, EEOC enforcement activity (low or non-existent),[1] unionization (extensive), and to isolate the influence of the competition principle itself.

In addition, there are two other advantages to using this market as a test case: (1) it has been the subject of numerous studies, largely done by economists, which have identified key performance variables at the individual level (see Scully, 1974; Hanssen, 1998; Hanssen and Anderson, 1999; Pascal and Rapping, 1972; Cymrot, 1985; Kahn, 1992, Eide and Irani, 1995); (2) the market contains both cross-sectional and intertemporal variability in labor market arrangements. Beginning with the 1976 season, the "reserve clause" under which teams held absolute ownership rights to players was replaced by a negotiated system allowing some competitive bargaining. Under recent arrangements, individual players during the first 3 years in the major leagues have almost no access to competitive offers, during their third through their fifth years have access to salary arbitration provisions, and after that have the opportunity to seek competitive salary offers from other teams in one of the two major leagues. This pattern permits meaningful cross-sectional comparisons.

[1] Major league baseball teams do technically meet the criteria for coverage under Title VII of the EEO law; they employ more than 15 people for at least 20 weeks a year. Because the legal basis of the baseball "anti-trust exemption" are court rulings that far predate the passage of relevant civil rights laws, teams are not excused from liability on that grounds either. However, there appear to have been no cases in which players or coaches in MLB have pursued EEOC formal EEOC claims.

In theory, variation over time in baseball's labor market arrangements might also be used to look at how different market regimes or institutional arrangements affect the relative salaries of white and minority athletes. The most straightforward comparison would be to examine the performance-adjusted pay of majority and minority group players in the period before the 1976 system change and in the period following it. This approach is severely hindered by the absence of complete or even statistically representative player earnings data prior to the mid-1980's.[2] However, since 1976 there have been temporal variations in the manner in which the negotiated system of compensation has been implemented and the degree to which its provisions have been enforced. For example, it is widely acknowledged that at the end of the 1985, 1986, and 1987 seasons, baseball owners colluded to limit the size of the offers that they would be willing to make to "free agent" players. After an investigation, these anti-competitive activities were confirmed resulting in a 1988 ruling that restored free agency and imposed a 280 million dollar fine on the owners. A strong interpretation of the theory that market competition promotes racial equality would suggest that during this period of less than vigorous competition, minority players failed to reap the full benefits available under non-collusive regimes.

At the same time, the unusual nature of the professional baseball industry must also be taken into account, particularly in assessing how readily these results might generalize to other employment contexts. Professional sports, and baseball in particular, exist in an environment that is unique in several aspects. At the most general level, as a sector of the entertainment industry, sports may harbor inequalities of outcome, particularly by race, that are associated as much with the stereotyping of roles as they are with disparities in overall economic well-being. Second, the existence of vigorous competition for the services of some workers (players) does not reflect a naturally occurring state of affairs, but was instead only implemented as a result of organizational and political contention between owners and players. In other words, while the competition that exists may be more or less "perfect," it is no sense "pure" and is enacted and sustained within a web of rules, agreements, and negotiations.

1. HYPOTHESES

There are two major sets of hypotheses that will be examined in this chapter. First, I expect that the difference in salary between African-American and White players, after adjusting for measured performance, will be less when comparisons are made among players with more than 6 years of tenure than when comparisons are made among those in years three to five of their careers which in turn will be less than those observed among players with less than 3 years of experience. Second, I expect that the differences in relative racial outcomes due to player market status (i.e., years of service categories)

[2] Existing data for the pre-1976 period are used by several authors including Scully (1974), Pascal and Rapping (1972), and Medoff (1975).

will be dampened or non-existent during the non-competitive, "collusion" period, i.e., the competitive benefit will diminish as competition itself diminishes.

A test of the first hypothesis was carried out by Cymrot using data for position players (i.e., non-pitchers) for the period 1978–1980. He found differences in the predicted direction: a larger intercept and a greater return to players for the market size of the team, for Whites rather than Blacks, *but only among those ineligible for free agency.* Although Cymrot's study provides clear evidence in favor of the lessening discrimination hypothesis, this chapter augments his efforts in several useful ways. First, more recent and more complete data are available. Second, his analysis can be refined to enable more subtle tests of the non-market discrimination prediction. Third, as just mentioned, different temporal periods involve more and less unfettered competitive behavior on the part of employers, and this variability should also be reflected in the pattern of outcomes.[3]

Our analyses are also reported separately for pitchers and for position players (all non-pitchers). There are several reasons for proceeding in this way. First, and least important, is that it mirrors the practice used in several prior studies. Second, measures of performance are radically different for the two kinds of position, although the actual analytic methods employed here (see below) are not affected by this difference. Third, and more compelling, is that since 1950s the incorporation of Black players onto major league rosters has proceeded much further and faster for non-pitching positions than for pitchers.

The differential inclusion of minority athletes into some positions rather than others has been observed in a variety of different sports and studied under the rubric of the "stacking hypothesis" (see Washington and Karen, 2001, p. 192; Margolis and Piliavin, 1999; Jiobu, 1988, 525; Eide and Irani, 1995). Although this hypothesis is subject to varying interpretations, the basic notion seems to be the idea that there are "central" and "non-central" positions and that minorities are under-represented in central positions. The defining characteristic of central positions is that these roles exert more control over the flow of play and emphasize both intellectual and physical contributions in contrast to non-central positions which emphasize "physical" skills. In baseball, the two central positions are those of pitcher and catcher.

Less crucial to, but consistent with, the "stacking" hypotheses is the idea that the positive, although perhaps more physical, traits associated with non-central positions can be used by the media and by the sports industry generally to fashion a

[3] One might also expect significant team-to-team variability in the size of the discrimination coefficient faced by African-American players. This prediction rests on the assumption that such discrimination results from the animus of individual owners against African-American players, but that this animus is not uniform. (Baseball lore provides some evidence in favor of heterogeneous owner preferences. American league teams were much slower to integrate than National league teams; Owner Marge Schott of Cincinnati was precluded from participating in baseball decisions as a result of having made racist comments; former owner P. K. Wrigley of the Chicago Cubs was widely viewed as "unwilling" to pay high salaries to minority players.) In sum, market theory predicts not only a lowering in the level of discrimination against minorities, but also a decrease in its variability as discriminatory owners are disciplined by competitive forces.

particular stereotypical image of star Black athletes in each sport. In baseball, one such stereotyped role available to players of African descent is that of "Black slugger." If so, it might be necessary to further qualify the hypotheses we have offered. That is, the benefits of market competition to minority players may only be available to the extent that they conform to the role which is promoted for them. Thus, our expectation, at least with regard to African-American players, is that the salary increment associated with being in a labor market situation with more competition will be most readily apparent for position players than for pitchers.

1.1. Data

A major advantage of studying professional sports, in general, and baseball, in particular, is the wealth of performance data that have been amassed in books, magazines, encyclopedia, and, now, electronic media. This chapter derives variables related to on-field performance and work histories (i.e., number of teams played for, years of service, etc.) from an on-line database compiled by Sean Lahman and distributed electronically through the website http://baseball1.com/statistics/. This source consists of several large files devoted to pitching statistics, hitting statistics, team statistics, and player demographic information, e.g., place of birth, "debut year" in MLB, and so on.[4]

1.2. Independent Variables

Two different performance measures "Performance I" and "Performance II" are tabulated separately for each of the three groups of players: position players, starting pitchers, and relief pitchers. As in earlier work (Scully, 1974; Cymrot, 1985; Hanssen and Andersen, 1999), I characterize the contributions of position players entirely through their offensive outputs. For them, "Performance I" is the *offensive average* developed by Bennett and Flueck (1983) and also used by Cymrot (1985) and Hanssen and Andersen (1999). It is calculated by adding together three offensive outputs: total bases,[5] walks, and stolen bases and dividing this sum by the number of official at-bats plus walks. In the subsequent analysis, the offensive average is calculated for each position player as the cumulative measure of that statistic at the start of each season. The second measure for position players (Performance II) is the more familiar batting average, and it is calculated solely on each player's performance in the immediately preceding year. To allow more direct comparability between players at all positions, these statistics are converted into standardized scores within each of the eight field positions. For example, at the beginning of the1989 season, Carleton Fisk, a "star" catcher for the Chicago White Sox and future Hall-of-Fame inductee, had

[4] These files do not include any player racial identifications.

[5] Total bases is the sum of singles, doubles, triples, and homeruns where each type of hit is weighted by the value of the base reached, for example, triple is weighted three. This measure is also in the denominator of the more familiar "slugging average."

a standardized Performance I measure (lifetime offensive average) of +1.14; Bruce Benedict, then catching for the Atlanta Braves, had a standardized score of −0.256.

As mentioned above, starting and relief pitchers were each assigned position-specific measures on the two performance variables. For starting pitchers, Performance I was defined as *career* wins at the beginning of the relevant season, and for relievers Performance I was calculated as *career* saves. For both the types of pitchers, Performance II was defined as $-1 \times$ the previous season's Earned Run Average, a commonly used measure of effectiveness at that position. As with position players, these variables were standardized separately for starters and relievers. Additionally, for both position players and pitchers, proxy measures were used for rookies (first-year players) whose potential performance was indexed by the relevant statistics at the end of the season. As one final measure of player contribution (perhaps linked more to the box office appeal of the team than to its effectiveness at winning), I used the number of all-star appearances (selections). This variable was not standardized by position and was entered into all models in raw score form.

Players were classified into four racial-ethnic categories: White, African-American, Afro-Latino, and other Latino. These classifications were made on the basis of three sources: a baseball "preview" article published in the Spring of 1993 by Ebony magazine that profiled each African-American player in the major leagues; information on place of birth that was contained in the aforementioned baseball statistics database; and visual inspection photographs contained in a complete set of Topps 1989 baseball trading cards.[6] The largest uncertainties in these classifications are the designation of Latinos as either of African or other origin. For example, the current hitting star Sammy Sosa, who debuted in 1989, was classified into the Afro-Latino category, although other players were more difficult to place.

In the subsequent models, only one team-level variable proved useful in predicting salaries, the aggregate income of the population living in the metropolitan area hosting each team. This measure was calculated from 1990 U.S. and 1991 Canadian census data.

1.3. Salaries

The on-line archives of the *USA Today* newspaper contain team-reported salaries for almost every major league baseball player for the 1987, 1989, and 1990 seasons. The salaries for 1989 were those reported in early April prior to the beginning of the season and include only the team-paid base contract value exclusive of any performance bonuses or endorsement revenues. For 1990, the salary figures were reported in October, with total earnings and performance bonuses reported separately. For that year, in order to maintain maximal comparability with the first year, I subtracted out the performance bonuses to obtain pre-season, base contract amounts. (The 1990 figures

[6] This method was also used by Jiobu (1988), in his study of racial differences in the lengths of players' careers.

also did not include income from product endorsements.) In 1989, the negotiated minimum salary for players in MLB was $68,000, a value that increased to $100,000 in 1990. Following conventional practice, the dependent variable in the subsequent analysis is the natural log of each player's salary.

1.4. Sample

The basic set of observations for these analyses was made up of players who were on a major league roster during the 1987, 1989, and 1990 seasons. The sample was further restricted to those individuals who had appeared in at least 30 games in one of these years to provide greater stability in measurement for the key variables. In the subsequent analysis, the 1987 observations were treated as one time period (the collusion years), and the 1989–1990 data were pooled to represent the non-collusion years. The latter analysis group does include observations for some players who appeared in both 1989 and 1990 seasons. Altogether, the pooled set of observations (once missing values are removed) includes 91 players who played in 1989 but not in 1990, 161 who played in 1990 but not in 1989, and 478 who played in both the years. The latter contributes a total of 956 observations to the data set.[7]

2. RESULTS

Tables 1 and 2 display the results of predicting the log of player's salary separately for three groups of position players (i.e., non-pitchers): those with less than 3 years of experience who are not generally eligible for arbitration or free agency, those with 3–5 years of experience who are entitled to arbitration but not to free agency, and those with 6 or more years of major league experience who are eligible for individual bargaining, i.e., free agency. Table 1 presents the pooled data from the more competitive 1989–1990 seasons, and table 2 reports a similar analysis for the last season of the collusion era, 1987. As expected in table 1, players who compare well to others at their positions are generally rewarded for their performance on the field. For the primary performance measure, the offensive average, these amounts range from an enhancement of 0.044 in log earnings up to a 0.452 log earnings advantage for a one standard-deviation change in within-position performance score. As would be expected from prior research, from basic theory, and from the assertions of players' advocates, the smallest pay-for-performance linkages are found in the early years of players' careers when they are unable to avail themselves of an institutional (i.e., arbitration) or market mechanism for achieving these returns. A fact that is not consistent with these interpretations,

[7] These latter observations are not statistically independent because they represent the same individual at two different time points. As explained *infra*, this problem is corrected by using a robust estimation procedure in the subsequent analysis.

Table 1. Predictors of log salary for major league baseball position players, pooled 1989–1990 sample (by labor market status, robust standard error estimates)

	Captives (0–2 years major league experience)			Arbitration eligible (3–5 years major league experience)			Free agency eligible (≥6 years major league experience)		
Variable	Estimate	t Value	Pr > $\|t\|$	Estimate	t Value	Pr > $\|t\|$	Estimate	t Value	Pr > $\|t\|$
Intercept	11.718	261.140	0.000	12.481	188.35	<0.0001	13.236	281.56	<0.0001
Performance I*	0.044	2.780	0.006	0.380	5.750	0.000	0.452	7.180	0.000
Performance II*	0.000	0.020	0.987	0.054	0.950	0.345	0.107	1.620	0.107
All-Star Appearances	0.261	3.010	0.003	0.358	6.270	0.000	0.059	3.470	0.001
African-American†	−0.006	−0.130	0.898	0.132	1.270	0.206	0.194	2.640	0.009
Afro-Latino	0.128	1.000	0.315	0.303	1.650	0.100	0.125	1.180	0.239
Other Latino‡	0.021	0.490	0.622	0.243	1.620	0.105	0.099	0.480	0.631
First-Year Player	−0.219	−6.360	0.000	–					
Year = 1989	−0.297	−6.830	0.000	−0.278	−4.460	0.000	−0.099	−2.180	0.030
Aggregate Metro Income	0.003	0.230	0.820	−0.040	−0.920	0.358	0.037	1.190	0.236
No. of Obs. (R^2)	168	0.33		228	0.51		352	0.438	

*See text for definitions of performance variables.
†Tests of differences across groups: Arbitration Eligible vs. "Captives," $F = 1.53$, $p = 0.22$; Free Agent vs. "Captives," $F = 5.45$, $p = 0.020$.
‡Tests of differences across groups: Arbitration Eligible vs. "Captives," $F = 1.97$, $p = 0.161$; Free Agent vs. "Captives," $F = 0.14$, $p = 0.711$.

Table 2. Predictors of log salary for major league baseball position players, 1987 sample (by labor market status)

Variable	Captives (0–2 years major league experience)			Arbitration eligible (3–5 years major league experience)			Free agency eligible (≥6 years major league experience)		
	Estimate	t Value	Pr > |t|	Estimate	t Value	Pr > |t|	Estimate	t Value	Pr > |t|
Intercept	11.324	218.450	<0.0001	12.200	157.690	<0.0001	12.828	174.170	<0.0001
Performance I*	0.057	1.520	0.132	0.327	3.820	0.000	0.358	3.640	0.000
Performance II*	−0.012	−0.330	0.744	0.216	2.390	0.019	0.327	4.520	<0.0001
All-Star Appearances	0.084	2.060	0.043	0.206	4.420	<0.0001	0.076	3.730	0.000
African-American†	0.095	1.190	0.235	−0.055	−0.420	0.676	0.178	1.590	0.113
Afro-Latino	−0.018	−0.120	0.905	0.095	0.470	0.642	0.212	0.740	0.459
Other Latino‡	0.031	0.270	0.788	−0.070	−0.230	0.816	−0.110	−0.490	0.628
First-Year Player	−0.303	−3.810	0.000	–			–		
Aggregate Metro Income	0.047	1.360	0.177	0.074	1.290	0.202	−0.062	−1.170	0.244
No. of Obs. (R^2)	101	0.221		98	0.475		184	0.354	

*See text for definitions of performance variables.

†Tests of differences across groups: Arbitration Eligible vs. "Captives," $F = 0.59$ ns; Free Agent vs. "Captives," $F = 0.24$ ns.

‡Tests of differences across groups: Arbitration Eligible vs. "Captives," $F = 0.07$ ns; Free Agent vs. "Captives," $F = 0.25$ ns.

however, is that there is a large bonus for all-star appearances for so-called "captive" players. Those in the earliest stages of their careers reap a 0.261 gain in log salary each time they appear on an all-star roster; veteran players only about 0.06 for such an appearance. Because all-star appearances are necessarily very limited for early career players, this result is probably based on the experiences of very few individuals. (For example, for the 1989 portion of the sample among all "early career" players, 16 of 386 individuals had a total of 17 all-star appearances; among "veteran" players, 163 of 316 players made a total of 487 career appearances on all-star rosters.) For most players, then, cashing in on above average performance is tied to escaping from labor market captivity into a more powerful labor market position.

However, this study's primary concern is the effect that market (free agency) and quasi-market (arbitration eligibility) forces have on the earnings of players of different races. As expected, the coefficient for African-American players is negative for those in their early careers; however, this coefficient is not statistically significant and is substantively small. (The comparison group on which race coefficients are based is White players.) What is especially interesting is that the coefficient for being an African-American player becomes positive and statistically significant for the players with the best market access. Statistical tests of the difference in the African-American coefficients between "free agent" and "captive" subpopulations show a significant difference in the race effect in the expected direction. These coefficients can be translated into predicted log salaries for different racial ethnic groups in these different labor market statuses, and those predictions are graphed in figure 1. Although all groups

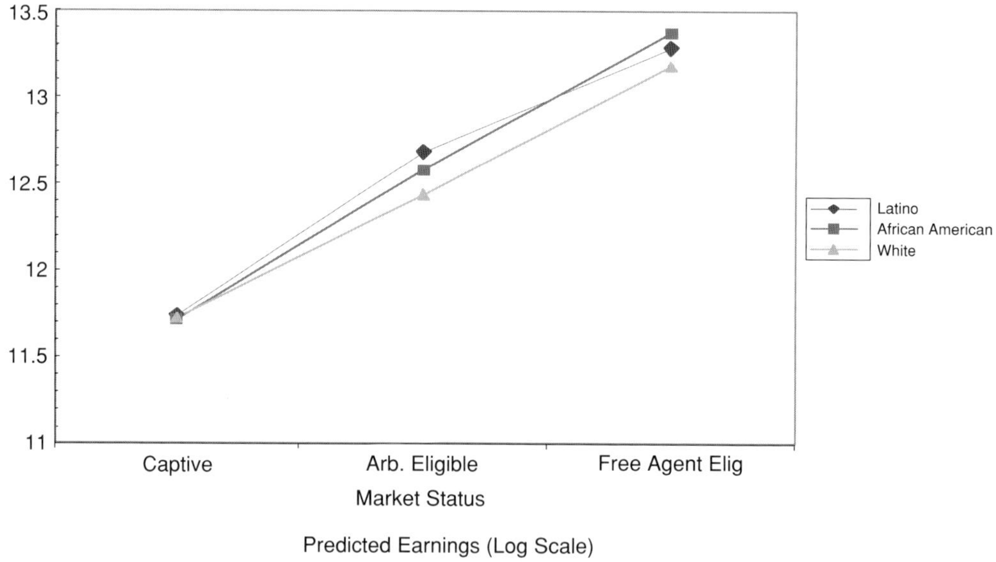

Figure 1. Predicted Earnings by Race/Ethnicity and Market Status, Position Players, 1989–1990.

of players clearly benefit from some form of market influence on their salaries, the benefits are noticeably larger for Black players than they are for Whites. This pattern confirms what was predicted by the market access hypothesis.

One question which these results raise is whether the salary advantage shown for Black ballplayers is in fact real. A part of this positive salary differential among the "veteran" players is explained by the superior performance of African-American players. Before performance and position variables are introduced, the salary coefficient is even larger: 0.279 rather than 0.193. It is possible that the inclusion of some additional performance or contribution measures might shrink this positive coefficient even more. One possibility is that including a more direct measure of "superstar" status than all-star appearances would have the desired effect. This is plausible, but a large portion of the variance in salary is already being explained by this model, and it is likely that most important factors have already been taken into account.

In table 2, results for an identical model are shown when estimated for the 1987 sample of position players. In comparing these coefficients to those for the later time period, one notices several findings of interest. First, average earnings tended to be much lower in 1987. For White, average performing, non-rookie position players with no all-star appearances, predicted earnings in 1987 and 1990 are shown in figure 2. Interestingly, the between-period gains seem to benefit players in all market statuses, not just those with the strongest market positions. Second, as predicted by our hypothesis, there is no longer an effect on salary of the interaction between being Black and one's

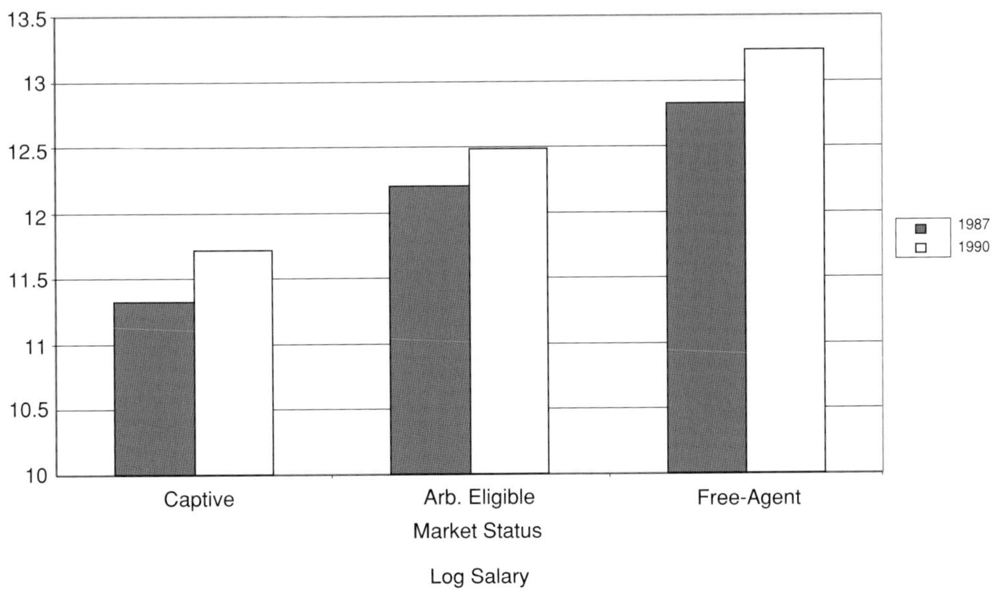

Figure 2. Comparison of Earnings for Position Players: 1987 and 1990.

market status. None of the coefficients for this variable are statistically significant, and the difference between them is similarly lacking in statistical significance.

Tables 3 and 4 report parallel results when the same models are applied to pitchers. Starting with table 3 and the performance measures, one sees that five of the nine possible "productivity" indicators are positive and statistically significant in the equation for pitchers in 1989–1990. Relief pitchers earn substantially less than starting pitchers regardless of labor market status. Pitchers who are free agents, and to some extent those who are eligible for arbitration, have higher salaries if they play for teams that are in more lucrative markets, that is, in those metropolitan areas with higher aggregate personal income. The effects of the racial identification variables are quite different than for position players, however. Consistent with the "positional stereotyping" hypothesis, Black players do no better relative to Whites if they are in the free agency years than if they are in their first 3 years of service. Interestingly, the situation is much more favorable for Latino pitchers who do reap benefits, again relative to Whites, if they are in a more open, competitive market situation. This suggests that the salary advantage shown for Black position players in table 1 does not generalize to all playing roles in which they might be used—it appears to be contingent on participating in a stereotyped modality.

Again, a useful point of comparison is provided by the salary coefficients in table 4 which are estimated for pitchers in the "collusion" year of 1987. Here, only two of nine possible performance indicators are statistically significant. More importantly, the pattern of race coefficients diverges from that shown for pitchers in the 1989–1990 seasons. For both Black and Latino pitchers, there are no significant differences among players in different market situations. (There is, however, a tendency for early career Latino pitchers to out earn their White counterparts.) On balance then, the overall pattern of results is not consistent with the unconditional market hypothesis, but it is in line with the qualified competition hypothesis. Minority workers (players) benefit from negotiated arrangements (e.g., free agent status) and owner practices (not colluding) that create more open-market competition. However, these benefits are contingent on being in positions which are consistent with, or at least not inconsistent with, stereotypical expectations.

3. DISCUSSION

Before returning to the main theme of this chapter, the efficacy of more competitive markets in promoting the interests of minority workers, I will offer some comments on the fact that almost all of the significant race/ethnic coefficients in the chapter are positive and not negative. That is markets, when they "work" for Black or Latino players, work by allowing them to earn higher salaries than comparable White players, not equal salaries. To begin, we put this finding into the context of other studies of this particular labor market and sport. In a longitudinal study of all-star votes cast by baseball fans, Hanssen and Andersen (1999) discover a long-term declining trend in

Table 3. Predictors of log salary for major league baseball pitchers, pooled 1989–1990 sample (by labor market status, robust standard error estimates)

Variable	Captives (0–2 years major league experience)			Arbitration eligible (3–5 years major league experience)			Free agency eligible (≥6 years major league experience)		
	Estimate	t Value	Pr > |t|	Estimate	t Value	Pr > |t|	Estimate	t Value	Pr > |t|
Intercept	12.833	316.78	<0.0001	13.224	214.07	<0.0001	13.545	298.14	<0.0001
Performance I*	1.264	5.640	0.000	0.821	5.340	0.000	0.113	2.140	0.033
Performance II*	0.015	1.360	0.176	0.130	1.760	0.079	0.287	4.280	0.000
All-Star Appearances	0.072	1.010	0.312	0.101	1.280	0.202	0.093	3.080	0.002
African-American†	−0.110	−1.910	0.057	0.208	1.130	0.259	−0.045	−0.310	0.755
Afro-Latino	−0.097	−1.220	0.224	−0.594	−5.990	0.000	0.121	1.310	0.193
Other Latino‡	−0.064	−1.110	0.269	0.406	1.210	0.228	0.278	2.310	0.022
Relief Pitcher	−0.479	−6.120	0.000	−0.531	−4.870	0.000	−0.510	−6.680	0.000
First-Year player	−0.190	−6.800	0.000	–			–		
Year = 1989	−0.314	−7.450	0.000	−0.235	−2.720	0.007	−0.056	−0.770	0.444
Aggregate Metro Income	0.038	1.310	0.191	0.064	1.810	0.072	0.059	2.050	0.041
No. of Obs. (R^2)	125	0.658		132	0.530		207	0.440	

*See text for definitions of performance variables.
†Tests of differences across groups: Arbitration Eligible vs. "Captives," $F = 2.72$, $p = 0.100$; Free Agent vs. "Captives," $F = 0.18$, $p = 0.675$.
‡Tests of differences across groups: Arbitration Eligible vs. "Captives," $F = 2.31$, $p = 0.129$; Free Agent vs. "Captives," $F = 6.55$, $p = 0.011$.

Table 4. Predictors of log salary for major league baseball pitchers, 1987 sample (by labor market status)

Variable	Captives (0–2 years major league experience)			Arbitration eligible (3–5 years major league experience)			Free agency eligible (≥6 years major league experience)		
	Estimate	t Value	Pr > |t|	Estimate	t Value	Pr > |t|	Estimate	t Value	Pr > |t|
Intercept	12.270	100.000	<0.0001	13.332	62.690	<0.0001	13.271	119.230	<0.0001
Performance I*	1.021	7.280	<0.0001	1.349	4.400	<0.0001	0.097	1.320	0.190
Performance II*	0.035	1.080	0.283	0.011	0.110	0.914	0.151	1.830	0.071
All-Star Appearances	−0.027	−0.490	0.627	0.010	0.110	0.916	0.087	1.840	0.070
African-American†	0.062	0.340	0.736	0.276	1.110	0.272	0.330	1.030	0.306
Afro-Latino	–			0.039	0.120	0.903	−0.387	−0.610	0.545
Other Latino‡	0.288	2.460	0.017	0.105	0.280	0.783	−0.231	−0.610	0.546
Relief Pitcher	−0.443	−5.410	<0.0001	−0.789	−4.860	<0.0001	−0.432	−3.150	0.002
First-Year player	−0.288	−4.260	<0.0001	–			–		
Aggregate Metro Income	0.017	0.490	0.623	0.093	1.550	0.128	0.035	0.500	0.616
No. of Obs. (R^2)	76	0.620		64	0.479		87	.242	

*See text for definitions of performance variables.

†Tests of differences across groups: Arbitration Eligible vs. "Captives," $F = 0.25$ ns; Free Agent vs. "Captives," $F = 0.37$ ns. ‡Tests of differences across groups: Arbitration Eligible vs. "Captives," $F = 0.18$ ns, $p = 0.01$; Free Agent vs. "Captives," $F = 1.87$ ns.

preference for White baseball players, with some evidence of a recent reversal such that African-American players are now likely to out poll their White contemporaries (after controlling for on-field performance). Their findings are worth quoting:

> In sum, there is evidence consistent with a fundamental shift in attitudes over the past 26 years. First today's fans discriminate less with respect to the average African-American player than did fans of the past. Second, yesterday's favorite players, all else equal, were white, and today's are black.

Among the studies surveyed by Kahn (1992), there are several that find a salary advantage in favor of Black players including studies by Pascal and Rapping (1972) (negative coefficient for White pitchers), Hill and Spellman (1984) (negative coefficient for White pitchers), and Christiano (1986) (negative coefficient for White position players). However, there are an equal number of studies cited that show no significant difference in salaries for players of different races. Finally, a few studies have found evidence of anti-African-American sentiment in the market for baseball trading cards (e.g., Nardinelli and Simon, 1999). While this outcome appears to contradict the results for actual salaries and for all-star voting, two qualifications need to be entered. First, as Hanssen and Anderson (1990) point out, the results of the trading card studies mostly pertain to a sample of players who were active in the 1960s and 1970s whose renown may have been somewhat suppressed by the prejudice of their contemporaries. Second, all-star voting (directly) and player salaries (indirectly) depend on the attitudes of a different population of fans than studies of baseball card prices. In the former case, what matters are the beliefs of those individuals who attend baseball contests in person (which at the time is the only place that ballots could be cast); in the latter, the beliefs in question are those that are held by a much more diffuse and amorphous audience, some of whom view investment in cards as an alternative to investment in other memorabilia, or perhaps even the stock market.

For now, the evidence is against those who would argue that the world of professional baseball is one marked by pervasive overt discrimination against all non-White players. However, the evidence also suggests that the gains and advantages of non-White players are linked to their ability to harness market forces to pull their careers ahead. Nevertheless, several questions should be addressed about the present analysis.

First, earlier studies (e.g., Scully, 1974) found evidence that over the course of players' careers, a pattern emerged in which African-American players had higher levels of performance relative to Whites, as their tenure in the major leagues increased. This has been interpreted as evidence of discrimination in "promotion," or at least survival, such that the performance requirements for continued employment are higher for Black players than for Whites. If true, this might mean that the salary advantage for veteran players that is found here could be explained by higher levels of "unmeasured" performance for African-American players in later career stages. However, evidence for the underlying premise is lacking in this case. Figure 3 shows that, if anything, it is White players who have higher relative performance in the later years of their careers. The overall impression left by this examination is that comparisons among more experienced players reveal diminished rather than exaggerated performance differences by race. Although race differences in year-to-year survival in the big leagues needs to be investigated directly, these results are at least superficially inconsistent with the "discrimination-in-survival" thesis.

Returning to the chapter's main theme may paradoxically help to explain the "favored" position which minorities in the most competitive markets find themselves. As I have emphasized in the analysis, the positive coefficients for minority players are doubly contingent. They depend not only on the player's market status (being eligible for free agency in a period when the owners are not colluding), but also on their role on the field of play. The widely acknowledged role of mass communication media on sports in general (see Washington and Karen, 2001) almost certainly has an impact on the perception and interpretation of the relative contribution of White and minority players. If, during the era under study in this chapter, owners, league officials, broadcasters, and sportswriters shared a common interest in promoting Black players as powerful sluggers, it would suggest that competition for their services would produce

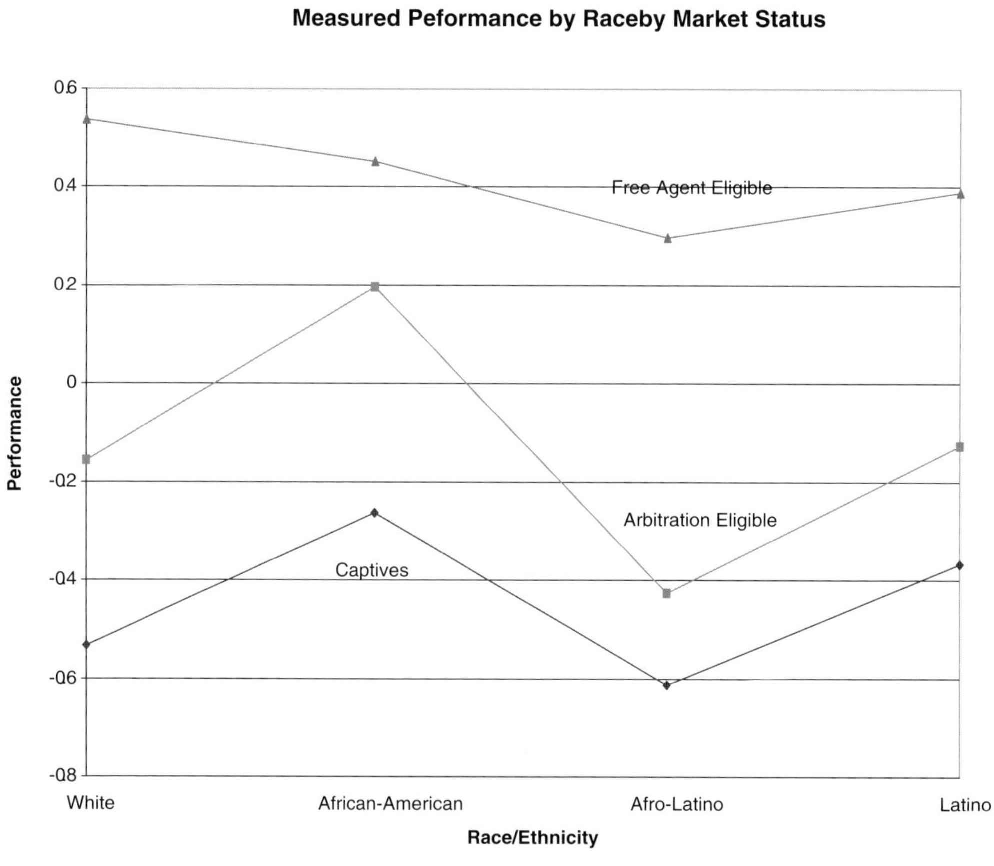

Figure 3.

an economic motive for paying them more than comparable White players. This interpretation is also consistent with the findings of Eide and Irani (1995) who discover increasing segregation of Black and White players during the 1980s, as Black players became increasingly under-represented as pitchers and increasingly over-represented as outfielders. Commenting on the consequences of this pattern they write:

> Another implication of persistent position segregation is the perpetuation of stereotypes of the kinds of positions that black players can play. Such stereotypes result in a lack of role models for young athletes, which in turn may lead young athletes to choose positions other than those in which they are most talented to the detriment of both the athlete and the game. (1995, p. 187)

Stereotypes are hardly rare in the marketing of popular entertainment, as the recent plethora of "reality" television programs makes clear, and it is at least plausible that deliberate channeling of players, driven in part by marketing considerations, had an effect on baseball salaries in the late 1980s. It is worth remembering that baseball slang refers to the top level in the sport not only as the "majors" or the "bigs," but also as the "show."

The other inquiry which motivated this analysis was whether EEOC enforcement is a *necessary* condition for minority success. These results provide a clear counterexample. However, it is one that is easily over-interpreted, and one that may not generalize even to all other sports. In professional basketball, for example, a series of studies indicates that after controlling for performance, African-American players might be at a salary *disadvantage* (see Kahn, 1992; Koch and Vanderhill, 1988). In baseball, the lack of White salary advantage is rooted in a context of strong player unions and high levels of potential political intrusion. For example, when recurring labor conflict in the industry results in work stoppages, lockouts, or even threats of these tactics, calls for Congress to revisit baseball's anti-trust exemption arise almost immediately. In short, the lesson of baseball for using the market to bring about racial and ethnic equality in salaries is as at least as much an argument for wholesale unionization and political activism in the labor market as it is an argument for diminishing the role of Equal Opportunity legislation.

CHAPTER 8

Employment Discrimination Based on Sexual Orientation: Dimensions of Difference

Kathleen E. Hull

ABSTRACT

This chapter addresses employment discrimination based on sexual orientation by examining three main subjects: the experience and impacts of discrimination for gay and lesbian workers, public attitudes about gays and lesbians generally and gays and employment specifically, and collective contests over implementing anti-discrimination laws and policies to protect gay and lesbian workers. A large percentage of gay and lesbian workers fear employment discrimination or believe they have experienced it. There is some evidence of a wage penalty for being gay, at least for males. Public attitudes toward gays and lesbians have softened in recent decades but they still remain an unpopular minority. Most Americans believe homosexuality is morally wrong, and many view it as a chosen behavior. Despite these views, there is relatively high public support for gay and lesbian employment rights. In collective contests over public anti-discrimination measures, the gay rights movement faces off against a powerful countermovement with roots in the Christian Right. Gay and lesbian activists have had growing success in the private sector, convincing employers to adopt anti-discrimination policies and to extend spousal benefits to same-sex domestic partners. The chapter concludes with reflections on the differences between sexual orientation discrimination and other forms of employment discrimination, which point to the need to disaggregate the various forms of discrimination and identify the distinct causes and consequences of each type.

INTRODUCTION

This chapter provides an overview of existing social scientific knowledge about employment discrimination against gay men and lesbians, with particular focus on three areas: the nature of the experience of sexual orientation (SO) discrimination from the perspective of its victims (including the material impacts of such discrimination); the evolving context of public attitudes toward gays and lesbians generally and toward employment protections based on sexual orientation specifically, in which battles over this form of employment discrimination play out; and, the history of collective

L. B. Nielsen and R. L. Nelson (eds.), Handbook of Employment Discrimination Research, 167–189.

action aimed at securing or blocking employment protections based on sexual orientation.[1]

Although gay rights activists and supporters frequently invoke analogies to race and gender discrimination to justify their efforts to extend employment protections to gays and lesbians, I will instead highlight crucial differences between employment discrimination based on sexual orientation versus other social statuses, pointing out the ways in which SO discrimination in fact differs from race or gender discrimination, in terms of the actual employment experiences of the victimized class, the public opinion context, and the critical dimensions of collective contests over employment rights. Attention to differences among the various forms of employment discrimination can lead to a broader, more comprehensive understanding of employment discrimination as a social phenomenon and can raise important questions about the appropriate legal and social responses to such discrimination in its various manifestations.

1. SEXUAL ORIENTATION EMPLOYMENT DISCRIMINATION: EXPERIENCE AND IMPACTS

Employment discrimination based on sexual orientation takes many forms, and its victims may be targeted based on their real or perceived sexual orientation. Specific manifestations of SO discrimination include unequal treatment in hiring, firing and promotion decisions, harassment, and unfair compensation practices. Recently, there has been a move toward framing the failure to extend "family" benefits (such as health insurance and survivor benefits in retirement plans) to the domestic partners of gay and lesbian employees as a form of SO discrimination. Informal discrimination occurs when workers are excluded from mentoring relationships and job-relevant social networks because of their sexual orientation. Some gay and lesbian workers, attempting to pass as heterosexual to avoid SO discrimination, may also engage in defensive practices to avoid the threat of disclosure of their orientation, for example, by avoiding social interactions that might otherwise increase job satisfaction and advancement. The social isolation that results from such behaviors may also increase absenteeism and turnover, and the energy expended on passing strategies may reduce productivity. In other words, in negotiating a potentially hostile workplace, some gays

[1] The focus of this chapter is sexual orientation discrimination, which includes discrimination against gays, lesbians, bisexuals, and heterosexuals. The vast majority of the research cited here focuses on gays and lesbians and omits any explicit treatment of bisexuals as an object of discrimination or of public opinion. Although discrimination against transgender people is sometimes discussed in the context of sexual orientation discrimination, it is best considered a distinct form of discrimination (based on gender identity, not sexual orientation). Very few laws addressing sexual orientation discrimination cover discrimination based on gender identity. Most social science research on sexual orientation discrimination focuses on the experiences of gays and lesbians. There is, however, a growing legal literature specifically addressing the question of gender identity discrimination and the possibility of legal protections for transgender people. For important recent works, see Cain, 1998; Currah and Minter, 2000; Feldblum, 2000; Flynn, 2001; Minter, 2000.

and lesbians take actions that may impede their own work performance. Badgett (1995) argues that the negative impacts of such behaviors constitute a form of indirect SO discrimination.

Gauging the prevalence of SO discrimination in the workplace is difficult. Claims data from states with comprehensive anti-discrimination laws provide some information on reported incidents. In 2001, there were a total of 925 SO employment discrimination cases in 12 states with comprehensive anti-discrimination laws, ranging from a low of six cases in both Rhode Island and Vermont to a high of 596 cases in California. These cases generally represent only a small percentage of all employment discrimination cases in a state (usually less than 5%), and there is no clear upward or downward trend in the volume of SO discrimination cases in these states over time (U.S. General Accounting Office, 2002). The General Accounting Office reports that "relatively few formal complaints of employment discrimination on the basis of sexual orientation have been filed, either in absolute numbers or as a percentage of all employment discrimination claims in the state" (U.S. General Accounting Office, 2002, p. 2). However, Rubenstein (2001) compared claims rates for SO discrimination to rates for gender and race discrimination and concluded that the SO rates were generally comparable to the race and gender rates, challenging the idea that SO claims are lower than should be expected in states with comprehensive anti-discrimination laws.

Although claims rates for SO discrimination may be comparable to rates for gender or race discrimination after adjusting for population, these rates may still be "low" compared to the real or perceived prevalence of SO discrimination in the workplace. Indeed, comparing perceptions of race discrimination to complaint rates suggests a huge gap between the number of workers who experience employment discrimination and the number who file a claim; Nielsen and Nelson (this volume) estimate that less than 1% of African-Americans who believe they encountered discrimination in a given year proceed to file a claim with the EEOC.

Various surveys of gay and lesbian workers conducted in the late 1980s and early 1990s found lifetime rates of employment discrimination ranging from 16% to 44% (Badgett, Donnelly, and Kibbe, 1992). Up to 19% of respondents reported being fired or asked to resign because of their sexual orientation, and up to 33% reported being denied a promotion. In several surveys, large majorities (up to 82%) reported fearing discrimination in the workplace or concealing their sexual orientation at work to avoid discrimination. A 1993 survey of gays and lesbians in Philadelphia found that 14% of gay men and 13% of lesbians believed they had experienced employment discrimination in the last year; lifetime rates were 30% for males and 27% for females (Badgett, 1997). In a 2000 *Newsweek* poll, 38% of gay and lesbian respondents said they "personally see or experience discrimination against gay people" in the workplace, but 53% also said their coworkers were more tolerant toward gays and lesbians than a few years ago.[2]

[2] The *Newsweek* poll results are from a telephone survey of 603 gays and lesbians, conducted March 8, 2000. The results were accessed on 3/2/03 at the Polling the Nations web site: http://www.orspub.com/.

Perceptions of SO discrimination at work appear to vary with work conditions and may impact workers' satisfaction and commitment. A recent study identified some of the factors that influence gay and lesbian workers' perceptions of discrimination (Ragins and Cornwell, 2001). Gay-friendly policies and practices—such as written anti-discrimination policies, domestic partner benefits, and inclusion of same-sex partners in company events—reduce perceived discrimination. Protective legislation and the presence of gay coworkers also lower workers' perceptions of discrimination. The study also found that workers who perceive discrimination are less likely to disclose their sexual orientation at work, less satisfied with their jobs, less committed to their work, and more likely to plan to look for other work. Another recent study concluded that "gay/lesbian workers are more likely to be 'out,' report less job discrimination, more favorable coworker reactions, and more fair treatment from their boss or supervisor when their organizations have written non-discrimination policies, actively show support for gay/lesbian activities, and offer diversity training that specifically includes gay/lesbian issues" (Griffith and Hebl, 2002, p. 1196).

Several studies examining the daily work experiences of gays and lesbians share the recurring theme of the closet. Regardless of their particular work setting, virtually all gay and lesbian workers must confront a series of difficult and potentially consequential decisions: whether to be "out" at work, how and to whom to disclose one's orientation, or how to conceal (or at least create uncertainty about) one's sexual identity.

In an interview-based study of 70 gay male professionals, Woods (1993) identified three main strategies for managing gay identity in the workplace. The *counterfeiting* strategy involves active attempts to pass as straight at work. Specific tactics include inventing a heterosexual sex life (possibly even an imaginary heterosexual partner) and conforming to the dominant gender norms for one's biological sex. Workers who pursue the counterfeiting strategy often attempt to maintain rigid boundaries between their work and personal life, to minimize the risk of any disconfirming evidence about their identity coming to light. The costs of counterfeiting include performance anxiety, ethical dilemmas, psychic disequilibrium, and lack of social validation for one's real identity. The second identity management strategy is *avoidance*. Workers who adopt this strategy reveal as little as possible about themselves at work, try to appear asexual, and deploy verbal and situational dodges to avoid potentially revealing conversations or social settings. Avoiders often try to control the direction of conversations with coworkers, resulting in the development of non-reciprocal work relationships. The price of the avoidance strategy is social ambiguity (not being sure who knows what) and social isolation, with potentially harmful career effects. The third strategy is *integration*, or coming out at work. Woods found that integrators try to actively manage their (stigmatized) identity in various ways. Some try to minimize their visibility in the work setting. Others try to normalize their identity by establishing common ground with straight coworkers. In hostile work settings, integrators may choose to politicize their marginality. The integration strategy can impose costs, exposing workers to discrimination and stigmatization. Integrators may feel a particular pressure to compensate for their devalued identity through stellar performance and an intense work ethic. But the positive effects of the integration strategy include a sense of relief, reduction of stress, and enhanced self-image.

The costs and benefits attached to different identity management strategies are likely to vary greatly across occupations and work settings. While openness may be a rewarding strategy in some professional settings, the public record contains numerous horror stories from other work settings. Ernest Dillon told his story to a Congressional subcommittee holding hearings on the need for federal protection against SO discrimination (Subcommittee, 1994, pp. 8–9). Dillon had worked for the U.S. Post Office in Detroit for about 4 years when a coworker began to verbally harass him about his sexual orientation. When Dillon reported the harassment to his supervisors he was told nothing could be done. The harasser eventually moved on to physical assault, attacking him in the men's room and inflicting serious injuries. Dillon missed 3 weeks of work and his attacker was fired, but when he returned to work other coworkers began to verbally harass him. After 3 years of continuing abuse, Dillon eventually left his job. Several years later, he resumed working for the Post Office at a different location.

Another witness recounted the story of Angela Romero, a Denver police officer who was reassigned from school-based work to street patrol after a coworker saw her buying a book in a lesbian bookstore (Subcommittee, 1994, pp. 39–41). Romero came out at work and spent 4 years fighting to be returned to her school-based position. During her years on street patrol, fellow officers routinely made anti-gay remarks in front of her and failed to respond to her calls for backup. Complaints to her superiors only led to further harassment, with unmarked police cars placed in front of her home and the homes of friends she visited while off duty. This sort of powerful anecdotal evidence suggests that the benefits of disclosing one's sexual orientation do not generalize across all work environments.

Particular occupations, including some professions, may be particularly hostile to out gay and lesbian workers. In a review of several studies of SO discrimination in the legal profession, Durkin (1998) concluded that many legal workplaces are not hospitable to openly gay attorneys, even in jurisdictions with legal prohibitions on SO discrimination. The hostility to gay and lesbian attorneys appears highest in private law firms, where they often face pressures to remain closeted to coworkers and clients and may face serious disadvantage in promotion to partnership. A study of gay and lesbian sociologists in academia (Taylor and Raeburn, 1995) suggests that, in some professional settings, it is not simply being out that produces disadvantage, but activities that call attention to one's sexual orientation. The study found that among sociologists who tried to promote gay and lesbian interests in academia, more than two-thirds believed their "activism" had negatively influenced their careers. By contrast, only about one-third of the sociologists who were out but did not engage in such activism believed their orientation had hurt their careers.

The issue of disclosure is especially vexing for gays and lesbians who work with children. Because of the stereotype of gays as child molesters, the gay educator is "homophobic society's archetypal villain" (Eisenmenger, 2002, p. 236). While the situation has probably improved in recent years, many gay and lesbian teachers still agonize over how to manage their sexual identity at work. A small study of lesbian physical education teachers found that teachers are sometimes torn between a desire to provide support and positive role models to gay or questioning students and a need to protect their own professional future (Woods and Harbeck, 1991).

Relatively little research has measured the concrete impacts of SO discrimination on gay and lesbian workers. Several studies examine wage impacts, and generally find a wage penalty for gay men but not lesbians. Studies using data from the General Social Survey find that gay men earn 11–28% less than comparable heterosexual men (Badgett, 1995; Badgett, 2001; Berg and Lien, 2002), but these analyses either find no wage differences between lesbians and comparable heterosexual women (Badgett, 1995; Badgett, 2001) or find a wage advantage of 13–47% for lesbians (Berg and Lien, 2002). Data from the U.S. Census now permit comparisons of partnered gays and lesbians to married or cohabiting heterosexuals.[3] One analysis of 1990 census data found that men residing with male partners earned significantly less than married men, whereas women living with female partners earned more than married women, although the female difference was not significant when the analysis was limited to full-time full-year workers (Klawitter and Flatt, 1998). A second study using the same data found a 16% wage penalty for same-sex male cohabitors compared to married men, but only a 2% penalty compared to unmarried males cohabiting with female partners (Allegretto and Arthur, 2001).

Why do the income studies consistently find a wage penalty for gay men but not lesbians? A number of possible explanations have been suggested. Lesbians may be less likely than gay men to come out, reducing their exposure to direct discrimination (Badgett, 1996). Employers may perceive lesbians and gay men quite differently, valuing lesbians' seeming lack of family responsibilities and feeling less threatened or offended by the presence of lesbian workers than gay workers (Badgett, 2001). The lack of a wage penalty for lesbians compared to heterosexual women may reflect stronger labor force attachment among lesbians, with fewer gaps in their work history and less part-time employment (Badgett, 1995). This stronger labor force attachment might be attributable to differences in family structure, including differences in child-rearing responsibilities[4] and in the ability to combine one's income with that of a male wage-earner. The wages of gay men but not lesbians may be affected by employers'

[3] In 1990, the U.S. Census began collecting data on "unmarried partners" residing in households. The wage studies cited here compare people with same-sex unmarried partners to those with opposite-sex spouses or cohabiting partners. Income studies based on the census data must be interpreted with great caution, for two reasons. First, only gays and lesbians currently living with a same-sex partner can be included in these analyses, since they are the only respondents who can be identified as gay or lesbian. This omits large segments of the gay and lesbian population from the income analysis, including people currently unpartnered and people who do not live with their partners. Second, many same-sex cohabiting couples are probably unwilling to self-identify as such on the census. Black, Gates, Sanders, Taylor (2000) estimate that only about one-third of same-sex cohabitors self-identified on the 1990 census.

[4] Data allowing direct comparison of the family responsibilities of lesbians and heterosexual women are not easily available, but there is some evidence to suggest that lesbians are somewhat less likely to have child-rearing responsibilities than heterosexual women. Specifically, data from the 2000 U.S. Census

concerns about hiring workers with HIV/AIDS (Badgett, 2001). Lesbians may self-select into lower-paying occupations in which they perceive the threat of discrimination to be lower, producing an indirect wage penalty that disappears when occupation categories are controlled (Badgett, 1995). Unfortunately, the datasets used in the wage analyses do not contain measures that allow testing of these competing explanations.

Wage differences between gays and straights may partly reflect discriminatory hiring decisions by employers, but very little research directly tests the prevalence of hiring discrimination. An audit study of the legal profession in Ontario, Canada, found that non-gay-identified applicants were almost twice as likely as gay-identified applicants to be offered a job interview (Adam, 1981). A more recent audit study compared the outcomes when gay-identified and non-gay-identified confederates visited retail stores to inquire about job opportunities. The gay-identified applicants did not experience significant formal discrimination in terms of being allowed to apply for a job or being called for an interview, but there were significant differences in their interactions with store personnel compared to the non-gay-identified applicants. Specifically, "employers were more verbally negative, spent less amount of time, and used fewer words when interacting with the stigmatized applicants than with the non-stigmatized applicants" (Hebl, Foster, Mannix, and Dovidio, 2002, p. 822).

Little evidence exists on whether lesbians and gay men are disproportionately represented in certain occupations or occupation categories, either as a result of indirect discrimination (self-selection into fields perceived as less hostile to gays) or direct discrimination (lower acceptance of gays by employers in some fields). Citing early studies that suggest gay men were concentrated in traditionally female occupations such as nursing, retail sales, and service work, Levine (1979, p. 161) proposed the concept of "job tracking" and suggested it often results in gays working in jobs beneath their level of skills and education. Badgett and King (1997) compared the occupational distributions of gays and lesbians to average levels of tolerance for gays among workers in various occupational categories and found that the occupational distributions of lesbians and gays do appear to differ from those of heterosexuals. Gay men are overrepresented in more tolerant occupational categories, including professional/technical and clerical/sales jobs, whereas lesbians were overrepresented in the less tolerant occupational categories of craft-operative and service jobs. The usefulness of this analysis is limited by the small size of the gay and lesbian sample and the broadness of the occupational categories.

There is a growing body of research on the stressful impact of minority status for gays and lesbians, but most of this research does not focus on employment specifically. Some research does establish a link between experiences of discrimination and mental and emotional problems (see DiPlacido, 1998 for a review). The stress experienced

indicate that 46% of households headed by a married couple include children under age 18, compared to 43% of households headed by unmarried opposite-sex partners and 34% of households headed by same-sex female partners (Simmons and O'Connell, 2003; Table 4). These data only include lesbians who reside with their partners, however, so they may not be representative of lesbians overall.

by gay and lesbian workers may have internal as well as external sources: many gays and lesbians have internalized society's negative messages about their identity, and the self-concealment and emotional inhibition that accompany some identity management strategies can have harmful effects (DiPlacido, 1998).

The preceding review suggests some important overlaps in gay men and lesbians' experience with employment discrimination and the experiences of other groups, including women and racial minorities. Like other minority groups, gays and lesbians often perceive the workplace as unwelcoming, with many reporting personal experience with discrimination on the job. And like women and some racial minorities, gays and lesbians appear to pay a real price for their devalued status in the work world. Gay men, if not lesbians, suffer a wage penalty based on their minority status. It is possible that a wage penalty applies to lesbians as well, but existing datasets do not have sufficiently detailed measures to control for potentially important differences between lesbian and heterosexual female workers, especially differences in labor force attachment. The continuities between SO employment discrimination and other forms of employment discrimination should not be ignored.

However, unlike most women and racial minorities, gays and lesbians have the option of trying to pass in the work world. On its face, this would appear to confer an advantage, giving gays and lesbians the opportunity to avoid the costs of direct discrimination. But the existing research on the everyday work lives of gay men and lesbians suggests that this seeming advantage is instead a double-edged sword. Non-disclosure probably takes a psychological toll on many gay and lesbian workers, resulting in feelings of guilt, anxiety, and isolation. Practices in support of a passing strategy may contribute to indirect discrimination as well. When workers strive to maintain rigid boundaries between their work and personal lives, when they isolate themselves from social interactions and develop non-reciprocal relationships with coworkers, they may cut themselves off from relationships and information that would facilitate their career advancement.

When workplaces encourage or require gays and lesbians to pass as straight in order to receive equal treatment, the effect is what Yoshino (2002, p. 781) calls "coerced assimilation." Passing falls in the middle of a continuum of assimilation strategies sketched by Yoshino. At one extreme is conversion—literally sacrificing one's identity completely in order to fit in. Passing appears to be a somewhat less onerous assimilation strategy, requiring only concealment rather than complete abandonment of the disfavored identity. But demands to pass are not necessarily less burdensome than demands to convert. (Yoshino uses the military's shift from outright exclusion of gays to the "don't ask, don't tell" policy to make this point convincingly.) At the other end of the assimilation continuum are covering demands, in which workers are expected to behave in a way that allows others to ignore their difference. Like passing demands, covering demands can strike at the core of identity when they affect behaviors that in a sense constitute the disfavored identity.[5] So, even gays who choose

[5] Yoshino (2002) argues that covering demands represent a point of commonality across race, gender, and sexual orientation discrimination. Just as gays may feel pressure to downplay their sexual identity in

to come out at work may feel pressured to make their orientation invisible to others. As Taylor and Raeburn's (1995) study of the sociology profession suggests, failure to cover may impose career costs on those who abandon the passing strategy.

All gay and lesbian workers face decisions about how to manage their sexual identity in the workplace. The costs and benefits of various identity management strategies probably vary across occupations and across individual workplaces, but the high percentage of gay and lesbian workers who believe they have encountered job discrimination in their lifetime, and the higher percentage who fear such discrimination or conceal their identity to avoid it, suggest there are no easy answers to the identity management question. These choices are further complicated by the fact that gays and lesbians face stigma based not merely on difference but on moral condemnation of their sexuality, often based on assumptions about the origins and mutability of sexual orientation.

2. PUBLIC ATTITUDES: GAYS AND LESBIANS AND THEIR RIGHTS

The issue of SO employment discrimination in the United States must be placed in the broader context of evolving public attitudes toward sexual minorities and their rights. Gays and lesbians have achieved unparalleled cultural visibility in recent years (Walters, 2001), and poll data indicate growing support for gay rights. Yet gays and lesbians remain an unpopular minority, subject to moral disapproval and viewed as less deserving of acceptance and protection than other minority groups.

Moral disapproval of homosexuality declined in recent decades but remains the majority view. Throughout the 1970s and 1980s, more than two-thirds of respondents in the General Social Survey said same-sex sexual relations are always wrong, and fewer than one in five said they are not wrong at all (Yang, 1997). There was a notable shift in the 1990s, however. Between 1990 and 2001, the percentage responding "always wrong" declined from 73% to 54%, and the percentage responding "not wrong at all" increased from 12% to 26%.[6] Still, a majority of respondents continues to believe homosexuality is always wrong.

Public opinion divides fairly evenly on whether homosexual behavior should be illegal. Support for outlawing homosexual behavior was highest in the mid-1980s, regularly exceeding 50%, but waned somewhat in the 1990s (Yang, 1997). By May 2003, a CNN/USA Today/Gallup poll found 60% support for legalizing homosexual

the workplace and to avoid behaviors that might call attention to it, women and racial minorities also feel pressure to cover in some situations. Women, for example, may feel pressure to conceal or minimize their responsibilities as a mother. Blacks may feel pressure to avoid language or grooming choices that are distinctively black. Yoshino suggests that victims of all kinds of covering demands should make common cause to challenge the assimilationist bias that informs the current approach to antidiscrimination law. He argues that discrimination should be reconceived as the harm of coerced assimilation, which is manifested in demands for conversion, passing, and covering.

[6] The 2001 GSS data were obtained from the Polling the Nations web site, accessed 3/2/03, http://www.orspub.com.

behavior, but support dipped to 48% in the wake of the U.S. Supreme Court's 2003 decision in *Lawrence v. Texas*, which overturned the remaining state anti-sodomy laws (von Sternberg, 2003).

Despite declining moral condemnation of homosexuality and growing support for legalizing homosexual behavior, gays and lesbians remain one of the least popular social groups in the United States. The National Election Studies (NES) survey asks people to rate various kinds of people from 0 to 100 on a "feeling thermometer," with zero representing the coldest possible feeling, 50 a neutral feeling, and 100 the warmest possible feeling. "Since their inclusion in the NES's feeling thermometer battery in 1984, gay men and lesbians have consistently been the most despised and least-liked social group," Yang notes (2001, p. 5). In the 2000 survey, the average rating for gays and lesbians was 47.5, compared to 67.5 for Blacks, 54.5 for feminists, and 51.9 for people on welfare (Yang, 2001).

Many polls gauge beliefs about the origins and mutability of homosexuality. The proportion that believes homosexuality is something people are born with seems to be increasing over time, although opinions are still divided and responses appear sensitive to question wording (Yang, 1997). In a 2001 Gallup poll, 40% said homosexuality is something people are born with and 39% said it is caused by upbringing or environment. When the possibility of choice or preference is introduced in questions about the causes of homosexuality, a plurality of respondents gravitate to a choice-based explanation, and poll questions that leave aside the issue of causes and simply ask whether being gay is a choice produce evenly divided responses. Echoing the findings of earlier polls, a 2000 Harris poll found that 46% believe SO can be changed "through will power, therapy or religious conviction" and 44% believe it cannot be changed.[7]

Despite ambivalence about the morality, mutability, and origins of homosexuality, a majority of Americans supports the idea of equal job opportunities for gays and lesbians. This majority support dates back to the 1970s and has increased steadily over time. The proportion supporting equal job opportunities rose from 56% in a 1977 Gallup poll (Yang, 1997) to 85% in 2001.[8] Support for specific legal protection for gay and lesbian workers is somewhat lower but follows the same upward trend. For example, only 47% of NES respondents supported "laws to protect homosexuals from job discrimination" in 1988, but support had increased to 64% by the year 2000 (Yang, 2001). Support for gay rights is generally lower when polls ask questions about incorporating protections for gays and lesbians into existing civil rights laws (Yang, 1997), and a large minority of Americans mistakenly believe there is already a federal law prohibiting SO job discrimination (Human Rights Campaign Foundation, 2001, p. 9).

In summary, gays and lesbians remain an unpopular minority despite recent trends toward greater acceptance and growing support for their rights. Most Americans judge

[7] The data from the 2001 Gallup poll and the 2000 Harris poll were obtained from the Polling the Nations web site, accessed 3/2/03, http://www.orspub.com.

[8] The 2001 Gallup data were obtained from the Polling the Nations web site, accessed 3/2/03, http://www.orspub.com.

homosexual relations to be wrong, and affect toward gays is more negative than positive. Furthermore, the very nature of gay and lesbian identity is disputed. A large proportion of people believes that being gay is a choice or a preference, and this belief figures prominently in public contests over gay rights (as will be seen in the next section). There are high levels of support for some gay and lesbian employment rights, but the support is sensitive to question wording: People express greater support for the idea of equal job opportunities in the abstract than for laws to secure non-discrimination in employment, and support weakens when questions are framed to suggest adding gays to existing civil rights laws covering women and other minority groups. While this may partly reflect negative attitudes toward civil rights laws generally, it also suggests possible resentment toward placing gays and lesbians in the same category as women, racial minorities, and other disadvantaged groups.

Gays and lesbians share with women and racial minorities a devalued identity as workers. But the basis for their devaluation is quite different. Women and racial minorities are stigmatized because they are different from the idealized White male worker, and possibly because they are assumed to be less capable than the idealized worker. Gay men and lesbians, however, face stigma and discrimination not only on the basis of difference and presumed inferiority, but also on the basis of moral judgments about their worth as human beings. The behavior that constitutes their identity is judged as morally wrong. Whereas women and racial minorities may sometimes have the ability to overcome discrimination by proving that they are not inferior workers, no amount of good performance is likely to change a fundamentally moral evaluation of gay and lesbian workers as people. The stigma of SO difference is often compounded by the fact that many people believe homosexuality is a choice and a behavior rather than an ascribed characteristic like race or gender. Opponents of gay rights have built on moral opposition to homosexual behavior and uncertainty about the role of choice in constituting gay identity to separate gays and lesbians from other disadvantaged groups that have already been included in anti-discrimination laws. By framing homosexuality as both a sin and a choice, gay rights opponents have reinforced the notion that gays and lesbians do not deserve a spot next to women, Blacks, and others under the existing anti-discrimination umbrella.

3. COLLECTIVE CONTESTS: LEGAL AND POLICY REMEDIES

Collective efforts to protect workers from SO employment discrimination take many forms. Perhaps the most visible efforts are attempts to pass anti-discrimination laws at the local, state and national level. But collective action has been important at the level of individual employers as well, usually with a focus on convincing employers to add SO non-discrimination to their existing anti-discrimination policies and to treat the domestic partners of gay and lesbian employees (and sometimes other unmarried employees) as equivalent to spouses under employee benefits programs. Some workplace activists have also sought formal recognition for gay and lesbian employee groups and company endorsement of the federal Employment Non-Discrimination Act (ENDA), which would outlaw SO employment discrimination nationwide.

Collective action on employment issues dates back to the pre-Stonewall era of gay and lesbian politics. The 1950s saw a Cold War panic over the "homosexual menace" in federal employment. Witch hunts led by anti-communist politicians depicted homosexuals as emotionally unstable, morally weak, enslaved by their sexual appetites, and hence a high risk for blackmail attempts and a threat to national security (D'Emilio, 1983). After President Eisenhower passed an executive order in 1953 establishing "sexual perversion" as sufficient and necessary grounds for disbarment from federal employment, dismissals of known or suspected homosexuals escalated. The military likewise intensified its efforts to purge homosexuals from its ranks at the peak of Cold-War hysteria in the 1950s. These actions had ripple effects beyond the federal civil service and the military, leading to the adoption of similar policies at the state and municipal level, tighter licensing standards for some occupations (to explicitly exclude gays), and implementation of anti-gay employment policies by private firms with government contracts. D'Emilio estimates that at one point, more than 20% of the U.S. labor force was subject to loyalty–security investigations meant to weed out both communists and homosexuals (1983, p. 46).

Gay political action on employment began in the early 1960s, when the Washington Mattachine Society (a chapter of the national homophile organization) broke with the accommodationist stance that characterized most Mattachine chapters and undertook an aggressive campaign to challenge the federal anti-gay policies. Under the leadership of activist Frank Kameny, the Washington Mattachine Society joined forces with a reluctant ACLU and scored an important early legal victory in a federal appeals court in 1965 in *Scott v. Macy*, which overturned the Civil Service Commission's refusal to hire an applicant on the basis of evidence of homosexual conduct (D'Emilio, 1983, pp. 154–156).

But gay rights activism on employment discrimination did not gather steam until after the Stonewall riots of 1969 and the birth of the modern gay liberation movement. Many of the early efforts were concentrated at the local level. In 1972, East Lansing, Michigan, became the first jurisdiction to outlaw SO discrimination in employment. The East Lansing law initially covered only city employees, but was expanded a year later to cover private employment, reflecting an incremental approach that was common among the early adopters of SO anti-discrimination laws (Button, Rienzo, and Wald, 1997, pp. 65–66). During the 1970s, efforts to pass SO anti-discrimination laws met with the most success in college and university towns and in larger cities with sizable gay and lesbian populations or large numbers of government employees. The first successful repeal of an SO anti-discrimination law was the repeal by referendum of an ordinance in Boulder, Colorado, in 1974 (Hardisty and Gluckman, 1997). But the successful campaign led by celebrity Anita Bryant 3 years later to repeal a Dade County, Florida, ordinance was much more visible and is credited with giving momentum to the emerging anti-gay rights movement.

Anti-discrimination ordinances continued to proliferate during the 1980s, despite the generally conservative political climate and the growth of an organized countermovement. The 1990s saw an upsurge in local anti-discrimination ordinances, and by this time the kinds of communities adopting SO protections were more diverse (Button et al., 1997). The first comprehensive state law passed in Wisconsin in 1982, but the period of greatest activity for states was the late 1980s and early 1990s, with eight more states passing SO anti-discrimination laws between 1989 and 1995 (U.S. General Accounting Office, 2002).

Efforts to establish SO anti-discrimination protection at the federal level date back to several failed attempts by Congress to add sexual orientation to the 1964 Civil Rights Act in the 1970s (Button et al., 1997, p. 26). The current incarnation of these efforts, the ENDA, was first introduced in Congress in 1994, and came within one vote of passage in the Senate in 1996. It has not been brought up for a vote since, and its prospects appear dim in the current political climate, despite the fact that the bill contains many provisions intended to make it more palatable to wavering politicians. The bill would prohibit public and private employers from using sexual orientation as the basis for employment actions including hiring, firing, promotion, and compensation. It does not prohibit discrimination based on gender identity. It provides for the same procedures as, but more limited remedies than, Title VII and the Americans with Disabilities Act. Employers with fewer than 15 employees, religious organizations (including religiously controlled educational institutions), and the armed services would be exempt from its provisions. It explicitly bars the use of quotas or preferential treatment based on sexual orientation, disparate impact claims, affirmative action, and federal collection of statistics on sexual orientation. While comprehensive federal protection appears unlikely in the short term, an executive order banning SO discrimination against non-military federal employees was signed by President Clinton in 1998 and remains in force.

Meanwhile, activism at the level of individual employers has produced steady increases in the number of employers with anti-discrimination policies that include sexual orientation. AT&T is believed to be the first employer to adopt such a policy, back in 1975 (Human Rights Campaign Foundation, 2000). The number of employers with such policies has risen dramatically in recent years. A total of 1,352 private, college, and university employers had such policies in 1999, and the number climbed to 2,253 employers by the end of 2003, a 67% increase in just 4 years (Human Rights Campaign Foundation, 2004, p. 28). The number of employers offering domestic partner benefits to gay and lesbian employees also rose sharply in recent years, partly in response to collective efforts targeting individual employers but mainly in response to equal benefits ordinances that require companies contracting with some cities to provide these benefits. Over 7,000 employers now offer domestic partner benefits, a more than 10-fold increase since 1996 (Human Rights Campaign Foundation, 2004, p. 20).

The successes of the gay rights movement generally outnumber the successes of its opponents in recent decades. An analysis of pro- and anti-gay policy efforts from 1974 to 1994 identified 309 pro-gay successes during this period, compared to only 68 anti-gay successes, and the success gap between pro-gay and anti-gay forces widened over time (Werum and Winders, 2001). Pro-gay successes outnumbered anti-gay successes in every category of policy effort except ballot initiatives (so-called direct democracy efforts). Pro-gay forces had only one successful referendum during this period, compared to 27 for anti-gay forces. The majority of gay rights successes took the form of local ordinances, whereas gay rights opponents were most successful with ballot initiatives.

The terms of the conflict over gay rights issues appear to shift when the scope of the conflict is expanded from routine political channels (legislative and executive actions) to the broader domain of direct democracy. An analysis of SO non-discrimination policies and anti-gay ballot initiatives found that gay rights protections enacted through legislative or executive channels fit an interest group model of politics: the strength of the gay rights movement is an important factor in the passage of such policies. Voting patterns in anti-gay ballot initiatives are more consistent with a morality politics model, reflecting the influence of religious groups and political partisanship (Haider-Markel and Meier, 1996).

A different analysis of adoption of gay rights ordinances or policies revealed that adoption was more likely in jurisdictions with larger populations and with a larger proportion of non-family households, consistent with the view that diverse urban settings are more hospitable to such policies (Wald, Button, and Rienzo, 1996). Gay-oriented services (including gay bars and other gay-related organizations) and openly gay political candidates were also positive predictors of policy adoption, suggesting the importance of resource mobilization to gay political success.

3.1. The Emergence of a Powerful Countermovement

The organization and discourses of the countermovement opposing gay rights have drawn a fair amount of scholarly attention recently, with good reason. In many parts of the country, it is impossible for gay rights supporters to advocate anti-discrimination policies without encountering impassioned and well-organized resistance. More than one quarter of the communities included in a survey of jurisdictions with gay rights policies reported that the anti-discrimination policy had faced one or more repeal efforts (Button et al., 1997). This figure understates the prevalence of repeal efforts, since only communities that fought off repeal are included in the sample.

The organized movement against gay rights is largely a religious movement. In her excellent study of gay rights opponents, Herman asserts that "it is the CR [Christian Right] that has instigated and led the public anti-gay agenda in the United States" (1997, p. 5). Button et al.'s survey revealed that conflict over anti-discrimination policies is generally higher in communities with large concentrations of religious traditionalists. Also, about two-thirds of the groups opposing anti-discrimination policies had religious connections; 53% were church or religious groups and 13% were organizations connected to the Christian Right (Button et al., 1997, pp. 174–176).

The dominance of conservative religious forces in the anti-gay rights movement has been evident in much of the movement's rhetoric. Two related themes are apparent in the movement's characterization of homosexuality: "First, homosexual practice is an incontrovertible sin. Biblical inerrancy demands this conclusion; any other is not truly Christian. Second, homosexuality is a chosen behavior, and not an immutable genetic or psychological trait" (Herman, 1997, p. 65). The gay man is the primary symbol for homosexuality in this world view, and gay male sexuality is routinely represented through tropes of disease and seduction, and as an expression of anarchic, pagan hypermasculinity. In the discourses of the Christian Right, gay sexual practices "not only lead to the acquisition of devastating illness... but are filthy, disgusting, and unnatural at their core" (Herman, 1997, p. 76).

But several scholars have observed an important shift in the rhetoric of the anti-gay movement over time (Button et al., 1997; Goldberg-Hiller, this volume; Hardisty and Gluckman, 1997; Herman, 1997; Schachter, 1994). Specifically, the movement has attempted to downplay the religious underpinnings of its anti-gay position and reframe its opposition in the language of rights. Button et al. identify three principles that now seem to guide the opponents of gay rights: avoiding "God talk," appearing tolerant, and making strategic use of rights talk (1997, p. 194). Although the older discourses of sin, disease, seduction, and anarchy can still be found in some anti-gay rights rhetoric, the discourse of the "rights pragmatists" has become dominant in the anti-gay rights movement. These rights pragmatists "have developed powerful, secularized arguments to construct lesbians and gay men as undeserving of rights" (Herman, 1997, p. 112). The newer discourse, in Herman's view, is more effective because it meets the rights claims of gay activists on their own turf and is more legally useful than discourses of disease and immorality. The new discourse also gets around the problem that the older discourses were increasingly perceived by people outside the Christian Right as hateful, extremist, and religiously motivated.

The newer discourse depicts gays and lesbians as a tiny but very wealthy and politically powerful group, therefore undeserving of "special rights." The anti-gay rights movement routinely deploys income data from unrepresentative marketing surveys (e.g., surveys of readers of glossy gay magazines) to "prove" that gays and lesbians are wealthier on average than other Americans. By depicting gays as a small, politically powerful minority, this discourse arguably "draws from and plays to pre-existing anti-semitic ideologies" (Herman, 1997, p. 125). Undeserving gays are contrasted with deserving, truly disadvantaged minorities, a move partly intended to foment anti-gay sentiment among African-Americans. In what Schacter (1994) calls the "discourse of equivalents," gays and lesbians are judged undeserving of civil rights protection because they are not sufficiently similar to other protected groups. Two main themes inform the discourse of equivalents. First, the lived experience of gays and lesbians is not sufficiently similar to the experiences of other protected groups to warrant civil rights protection. Gays are not really targets of discrimination. Second, the nature of gay and lesbian identity is not sufficiently similar to the identities of other protected groups to warrant protection. Gayness is an objectionable chosen behavior, not an immutable characteristic, so it does not deserve legal protection from discrimination (Schacter, 1994, p. 291).

These newer discourses—the rhetoric of special rights and the discourse of equivalents—have laid the groundwork for the success of the anti-gay rights movement at the ballot box. As noted earlier, direct democracy initiatives have been the most successful policy tool of gay rights opponents. Gamble (1997) catalogued all the civil rights-related direct democracy initiatives appearing on state and local ballots between 1959 and 1993. Almost 60% of the initiatives related to gay rights; almost all of these (88%) intended to restrict or repeal gay rights, and their pass rate was 79%. "Gay men and lesbians have seen their civil rights put to a vote more often than any other group," Gamble concluded (1997, p. 257). The rhetoric of special rights and the discourse of equivalents likely provide cover to voters who fear or dislike gays but do not want to think of themselves as intolerant or opposed to civil rights.

The anti-gay countermovement pushed the rhetoric of special rights and the tactic of direct democracy to their logical extreme in the case of Colorado's Amendment 2. A group called Colorado for Family Values, which drew its leadership from several prominent Christian Right organizations (including the Traditional Values Coalition, Focus on the Family, and the Promise Keepers), succeeded in placing an anti-gay rights initiative on the statewide ballot in 1992. The initiative's backers relied heavily on the "no special rights" message in building support for passage, although older rhetorics of disease and immorality crept into the initiative campaign in its final stages (Herman, 1997, p. 147). The initiative, which amended the Colorado constitution to repeal all existing local gay rights laws and prohibit the passage of any such laws at the state or local level in the future, passed with 53.4% of the vote. The amendment never took effect, however, as it faced immediate court challenges, culminating in a U.S. Supreme Court ruling in 1996. In *Romer v. Evans*, the Supreme Court ruled the amendment unconstitutional, finding that its scope was too broad to fulfill a legitimate state interest. The majority opinion specifically refuted the special rights rhetoric of the anti-gay forces, noting that there was "nothing special" in the protections voided by the amendment and asserting that the measure instead imposed a "special disability" on lesbians and gays (Herman, 1997, p. 158). Thus, *Romer v. Evans* began to circumscribe the reach and legal effectiveness of the anti-gay countermovement's preferred rhetoric and electoral tactics.

3.2. Debate Within Gay and Lesbian Movements

The push to secure legal protection against SO employment discrimination has not only faced a motivated and effective countermovement; it has also encountered skeptics within the ranks of gay and lesbian communities and movements. This skepticism comes from two distinct and decidedly non-overlapping sources: the neoconservative wing of the gay rights movement, and the perspective of queer/liberationist theory and activism.

The neoconservative critique of anti-discrimination law has been most forcefully articulated by gay author and activist Andrew Sullivan in his book *Virtually Normal* (1995, pp. 148–168). Sullivan argues against SO anti-discrimination laws on several grounds. The oppression that attends being gay is not directly comparable to the experiences of other minority groups, partly because gays and lesbians have the option to conceal their minority identity and partly because of differences in the nature and history of different forms of oppression. (Ironically, this argument closely parallels the anti-gay movement's discourse of equivalents.) The law is not a proper or effective tool for addressing the kinds of harms that gays and lesbians experience. The reactions evoked by homosexuality are so deep and so entwined with religious convictions that the "calm voice of liberal legalism" is not an effective response (p. 158). SO anti-discrimination laws are little used and provoke hostility among people who disagree with them or resent having their liberties curtailed by them. They involve the state in imposing a certain morality on all citizens, a fundamentally illiberal endeavor. The gay rights movement should focus on correcting government discrimination against gays and lesbians (such as the denial of marriage rights and the ban on military service) instead of attacking discrimination by private citizens. And, anti-discrimination laws cast gays as victims and "perpetuate a passivity among the minority culture that may make it more, rather than less, resistant to majority oppression" (p. 164).

The concerns of queer/liberationist theorists and activists are quite different. From their perspective, SO anti-discrimination laws are problematic for two main reasons. First, such laws reify the construction of gays and lesbians as a discrete, well-defined minority group. This runs counter to the queer ethos, which prefers to engage in a "deconstructionist politic" that seeks to break down rigid identity categories (which are viewed as a technology of social control and oppression) and blur group boundaries (Gamson, 1995, p. 391). Rubenstein (1998) illustrates these sorts of concerns in his reflections on studies of anti-gay bias in the legal profession. After making several specific recommendations for action based on the findings of these studies, Rubenstein observes:

> ... it is, finally, interesting to consider whether society would be better were there no recognizable sexual orientation categories. Many of the identity-based recommendations that have issued from these reports seem necessary to the short term goal of ensuring protection for lesbian, gay, and bisexual attorneys. But would it make more sense, in the long run, if benefit plans did not turn on the nature of one's sexual relationship or if it could not be assumed that there were certain luncheon speakers who would be of particular interest to gay employees? These identity-based efforts strive to change the conditions under which we all live. Yet the constant questioning of strategies and tactics—particularly at these sites of confrontation—may prove valuable, even if alternative approaches are ultimately rejected. (1998, p. 402)

Although Rubenstein does not go so far as to reject the usefulness of anti-discrimination protections, his line of thinking draws attention to the costs associated with deploying fixed identity categories in an effort to protect gay and lesbian workers.

McCreery (1999) also highlights the costs of playing identity politics in the realm of employment discrimination law in his critique of the proposed ENDA. ENDA would protect self-identified gay and lesbian people but would leave unprotected workers who engage in a range of "deviant" sexual practices. ENDA "would continue to privilege some sexual practices and habits while stigmatizing others," according to McCreery (1999, p. 40). Under ENDA, someone could still be fired for appearing in a pornographic film or for having sex in a public park, as long as the employment consequences of such actions were applied without regard to sexual orientation. Thus, narrow legal efforts like ENDA separate gays and lesbians from other "queers."

Second, the queer/liberationist perspective sees anti-discrimination laws as fundamentally assimilationist in their goals, seeking to allow gays and lesbians to integrate more smoothly into existing power structures rather than posing a deeper challenge to the world as it is. Vaid (1995), one of the most eloquent critics of the "mainstreaming" strategy of the gay rights movement, remarks:

> Rather than asking how gay and lesbian people can integrate themselves into the dominant culture, what if, instead, we affirm that our mission is explicitly to assimilate the dominant culture to us? To phrase the question that way suggests at once a pragmatic and transformational mission for our movement . . . Defining our movement's goal as the assimilation of our heterosexual families, employers, neighbors, and institutions to the normalcy of gay and lesbian people, we clarify the educational work we need to do. Immediately, what we must do extends beyond the law, into the principal sites of daily life: family, work, community, even faith. (p. 206)

This second critique is not so much an argument *against* anti-discrimination laws as a questioning of priorities. When the gay rights movement expends resources pursuing a narrow legal rights strategy, it makes an implicit choice not to devote those resources to broader goals, such as challenging cultural beliefs about the inferiority of certain sexual identities and practices or building coalitions with other disadvantaged groups (Rimmerman, 2002).

Despite these critiques of anti-discrimination law from within gay and lesbian movements, employment protection appears to be a high priority in the minds of average gays and lesbians. In a 2000 *Newsweek* poll, 92% of gay and lesbian respondents rated "equal rights for gays and lesbians in terms of job opportunities" very important. By comparison, 84% gave a very important rating to equal housing rights, 65% to serving openly in the military, and 46% to legally sanctioned gay marriages.[9]

In the realm of collective action, several features distinguish SO employment discrimination from other forms of discrimination. The fact that gays and lesbians are a small and relatively unpopular minority has implications for the collective contests over legal protections. The record of the past several decades suggests that gay rights advocates achieve the most success when the scope of conflict is limited to routine

[9] The 2000 *Newsweek* poll data were obtained from the Polling the Nations web site, accessed 3/2/03, http://www.orspub.com.

channels. Working through the legislative and executive branches of government has brought many victories; appeals to individual employers constitute an effective but more limited approach. When the scope of conflict expands to include the electorate at large, success becomes much more difficult. Gay rights advocates continue to confront a highly aggressive and motivated countermovement, one that has been able to adapt its rhetorical strategies to evolving political conditions and exploit public ambivalence about homosexuality in general and the need for SO anti-discrimination protections in particular. The rhetoric of special rights and the mechanisms of direct democracy have been the countermovement's most effective tools in recent years, resulting in many important victories (as well as a few high-profile defeats, such as Colorado's Amendment 2). And, the various elements of the gay rights movement, which is really not a single unified movement (see Epstein, 1999), do not share complete consensus on the desirability or priority of legal employment protections, although poll data suggest that average gays and lesbians view employment rights as highly important.

3.3. Dimensions of Difference

Today, a patchwork of public and private sector policies protects some but not all U.S. workers from employment discrimination based on sexual orientation. On the public side, 16 states and the District of Columbia now outlaw this form of discrimination in both public and private employment). A total of 285 cities, counties, and quasi-governmental organizations also prohibit SO discrimination, including 152 with laws covering both public and private employment (Human Rights Campaign Foundation, 2004, p. 30). Currently, 39% of the U.S. population live in states with comprehensive laws (covering public and private employment), and an additional 9% live in local jurisdictions with comprehensive laws, meaning that approximately 48% of the population now live in jurisdictions with comprehensive legal protection from SO discrimination in employment.[10] Repeated attempts to provide nationwide coverage by passing a federal SO non-discrimination law have failed.

On the private side, over 1,800 employers now have anti-discrimination policies that cover sexual orientation, including nearly three quarters of the Fortune 500 companies. When other types of employers—including colleges and universities, state and local governments, federal agencies, and congressional offices—are added to the count, the total number of employers with policies reaches 2,563. The policies are most common among larger employers. In addition, 7,334 employers of all types currently offer

[10] Population coverage was computed using 2000 census data, accessed at http://factfinder.census.gov. The percentage of *workers* covered by SO antidiscrimination laws may be somewhat larger or smaller than the percentage of the U.S. population residing in these jurisdictions, since people can live and work in different jurisdictions. It seems likely that the percentage of people working in covered jurisdictions is somewhat higher than the percentage living in those jurisdictions, since many of the local jurisdictions with coverage are larger cities and counties that probably draw workers from outlying residential areas that lack coverage.

health insurance benefits to the domestic partners of their gay and lesbian workers, and one state (California) and nine cities and counties have passed "equal benefits ordinances" that require employers with city or county contracts to provide domestic partner benefits (Human Rights Campaign Foundation, 2004).

This chapter has reviewed the existing state of knowledge about SO employment discrimination in three areas: the employment experiences of gays and lesbians, gay-related public attitudes (including attitudes about employment discrimination), and collective contests over policies to protect gays and lesbians from employment discrimination. The current state of partial protection, with only about half the U.S. population protected by comprehensive state or local anti-discrimination laws, can best be understood in the context of information about the experiences of gay and lesbian workers, public attitudes toward these workers and their rights, and collective struggles over anti-discrimination policies. Many sexual minorities choose not to come out at work, or attempt to minimize attention to their stigmatized identity in the workplace. Fears of coming out and the consequences of discrimination likely deter many gay and lesbian workers from pursuing workplace protections either through laws or employer policies. Such fears are not unfounded in a social climate characterized by increasing support for gay rights but continuing moral disapproval of gay behavior and negative affect toward gays as a social group. Such mixed attitudes have provided a foothold for both the gay rights movement and its powerful and well-organized countermovement.

I have tried to clarify some of the important ways that employment discrimination based on sexual orientation differs from other kinds of employment discrimination. While gays and lesbians share with other minorities the experience of devaluation and difference at work, their work lives are distinctively characterized by their ability to pass, and the identity management choices they face as a result. A review of public opinion data reveals two distinctive features of the minority status of gays and lesbians. Moral condemnation of homosexuality is substantial (although decreasing over time), and many view the identity as a mutable choice or behavior rather than an ascribed characteristic. Although Americans express strong support for gay employment rights in the abstract, this support is somewhat shallow: many are not sure the law should be used to ensure these rights, and even more are uncomfortable with placing gays and lesbians next to racial and gender minorities in the existing anti-discrimination laws. Views about the morality and mutability of homosexuality likely make analogies to race and gender problematic for some. The gay rights movement has scored an impressive number of victories in a relatively short time period in the area of employment rights, but the existence of an energized and savvy countermovement has stymied progress at the national level, in sharp contrast to the successes of advocates for the employment rights of women, racial minorities, and the disabled. More broadly, the differences between SO discrimination and other forms of employment discrimination call attention to the importance of social context in understanding various manifestations of workplace discrimination and the legal responses to discriminatory practices. The "social system" view of employment discrimination advocated by Nielsen and

Nelson (this volume) necessitates careful examination and analysis of the various factors that both contribute to the practice of discrimination and shape the legal and social responses to discrimination. As this chapter has shown, such factors are not identical across the different kinds of discrimination. The motivations to discriminate vary across the targeted social groups, as do the ground-level employment experiences of groups affected by discrimination and the contours of the political battles over the need for legal protections for various groups.

CHAPTER 9

Occupational Mobility Among African-Americans: Assimilation or Resegregation

Sharon M. Collins

ABSTRACT

Economic mobility among African Americans and the persistence of inequality both seem to be best explained by nonracial factors such as educational attainment on the one hand and, on the other, the erosion of race-linked bias in the culture and structure of employment. This chapter calls into question these interpretations by illustrating recialized patterns of job allocation. Put another way, it illustrates divisions of labor that are sensitive to race. Here I suggest that discrimination and opportunity can occur in the same historical instance. The post industrial and post civil rights U.S. labor market requires research to look beneath occupational categories to fully uncover what roles that race now plays.

INTRODUCTION

This chapter details evidence of a racialized division of labor among Black professionals and business people. Drawing on aggregate data but also in large part on two sets of interviews I conducted with Black executives in Chicago—the first set conducted in 1986, and the second set conducted in 1992—I illustrate that Black businesses and careers were tracked into niches in labor markets created to address the needs of Black people. Such niches can be seen in sectors, institutions, and occupations. In the public sector, for instance, the U.S. Department of Housing and Urban Development (HUD) is a prime example of a racialized institution responsible for enforcing the Fair Housing Act of 1968 which makes housing discrimination illegal. The Fair Housing Act became law 3 days after the assassination of Martin Luther King Jr., when cities erupted in racial violence, including the Nation's capital. HUD also enforces the Housing and Community Development Act of 1974 intended to revitalize the inner city and creating affordable housing. In the private sector, racialized niches emerge in subsets of personnel and public relations functions such as affirmative action, community relations, urban affairs, departments and managers, all of which were created with the onset of race riots, Black boycotts, and anti-bias employment regulations. The

L. B. Nielsen and R. L. Nelson (eds.), Handbook of Employment Discrimination Research, 189–200.

comparison category, "mainstream" labor market domains, in contrast lacks these race-based functional connotations.

First, I broadly outline some parameters of occupational inequality as it pertains to white-collar workers, in general, and then more specifically to Black managers and executives employed in Chicago corporations. Next, I show that Black professionals and administrators in the public sector and Black entrepreneurs are found in niches that are responsible for managing Blacks, for administering policies oriented to Blacks, and for delivering services and products to Black people. Finally, I present data published in an earlier analysis of the top strata of Black executives in Chicago corporations (Collins, 1997). In the perspective of this chapter, Black skills remain "functionally segregated" in labor markets and, as I will attempt to make clear in the case of Black executives, this segregation has consequences for individual careers and aggregate development.

I

The link between race and inequality in labor markets is well established and remains strong in spite of an array of government regulations and changing norms. We see this in a myriad of ways and especially when viewing how higher-paying and prestigious jobs are allocated in work organizations, which is the subject of this chapter. We know that Black managers and professionals are disproportionately concentrated in the public sector and this fact remains consistent both in the pre- and post-civil rights labor market. Therefore, the key to this disparity is found in private sector employment. Table 1 shows EEO-1 data on the participation rates of African-American workers in detailed occupations between the years 1966 and 1999 to illustrate.

In bold across the top are the percents of Blacks in the private sector in a given year. All else being equal, the percents in the corresponding columns should be about the

Table 1. Participation rates of workers in private sector, 1966–1999

Selected occupations	1966	1974	1978	1990	1992	1998	1999
All Occupations	8.2	11.0	11	13	12	13.7	14.0
Officials and Managers	0.9	2.9	3.7	5	5.3	5.9	6.2
Professionals	1.3	3.1	4	5.2	5.5	6.4	6.6
Technicians	4.1	7.3	8.2	10	10	11.0	11
Sales Workers	2.4	5.5	6.8	11	10	13.6	14
Office/Clerical	3.5	9	10	14	13	16.1	17
Skilled Craft	3.6	6.9	8	9.2	9.1	9.6	9.8
Operatives	11	15.7	16	17	17	17.1	17
Laborers	21	20.4	19	20	19	19.7	20
Service Workers	23	24	22	25	23	25	25

Source: EEO-1 data

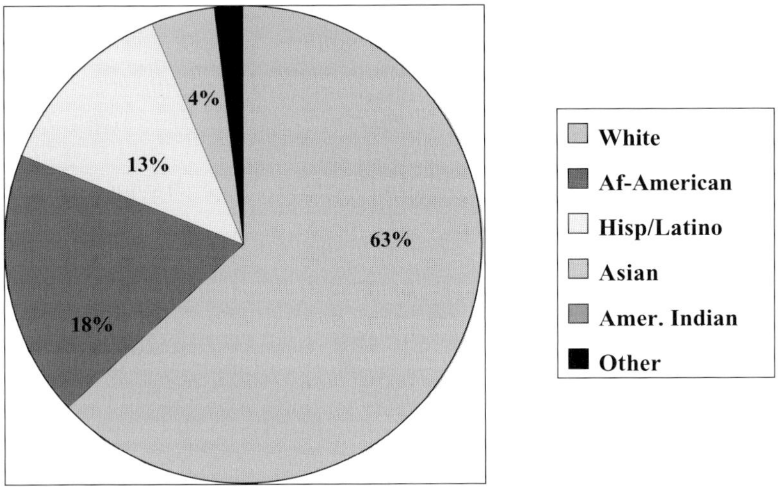

Figure 1. Percent Distribution of Chicago-Based Employees, by Race.

same as those at the top of the table. The table area that is in bold highlights the years in which African-Americans were under-represented in a field. Areas that are not in bold highlight jobs where Blacks are represented at or above the percent expected.

We see, first, that Black participation in the private sector increased over this span of 30 years: from 8.2% to 14% of private sector workers. We also see clear gains were made in every occupation where Blacks were under-represented in 1966, about when modern civil rights laws were first enacted. For example, African-Americans went from 3.6% to 9.8% of all skilled craft workers, from just less than 1% to 6.2% of all officials and managers and from 1% to over 6% of all professionals in the private sector. Social scientists wrote in the 1970s about unprecedented gains made by African-Americans in the post-1960 labor market and this figure is a good illustration of the degree of change they wrote about (see, for example, Freeman, 1976). Note here that the most striking rate of change coincides with the strengthening of federal anti-bias legislation and policies between 1966 and 1974, and that change drops markedly as the corporate response to federal regulations becomes routinized in corporate departments and functions. At the same time, we see that Black workers started and remain heavily over-represented in largely unskilled jobs. If we attribute change over time, at least in part, to the institutionalization of affirmative action and EEOC legislation, the figure shows that mandates were most effective in equalizing the playing field for those who occupy jobs on the lower rung of the white-collar hierarchy, office and clerical workers and sales workers. Conversely, we see that African-Americans remain *well* under-represented in the higher-paying and prestigious jobs, particularly in management, although progress has occurred (figure 1).

The next figures use Chicago area data to underline this idea of under-representation in high status positions in the corporate sector. Figure 2 summarizes the racial make-up

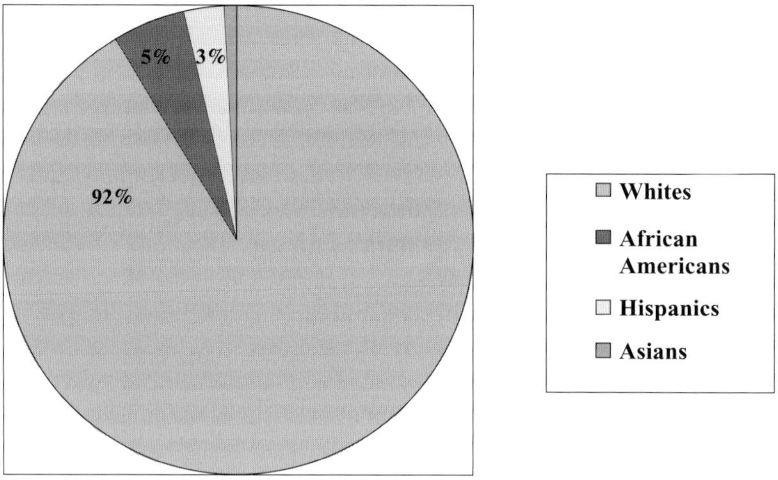

Figure 2. Percent distribution of corporate Officers, by Race.

of employees of 55 Chicago employers surveyed in 2001. The survey included the top 51 most profitable firms, an additional nine firms that are among the area's top employers (excluding government and education) and the top five employers among professional service firms, banks and insurance brokers. Crain's *Chicago Business* lists all of these companies. The overall workforce in responding companies is 18% African-American, 13% non-White Hispanic, 4% Asian, and 2% "other." At this aggregate level, the racial composition looks fairly representative of the pool of Chicago workers which is about 25% Black, 17% non-White Hispanic, and 4% Asian. However, a somewhat different picture of racial diversity emerges when we move further up into the hierarchy of powerful jobs in these companies.

Figure 3 shows that of the 670 corporate officers employed in these companies only 5% are African-American and 3% are Hispanic. Corporate officers in this study are defined as those officers with day-to-day responsibility for corporate operations and the power to legally bind their companies. They represent their companies on major decisions and are "ipso facto 'insiders' for certain financial and SEC purposes" (Catalyst, 1998, p. 6).

In sum, then, these data tell us that after more than 40 years of social and political pressure to diversify corporate manpower and management teams, the net result is more Black workers and even managers. At the same time, the further one goes up the status hierarchy in corporate management the greater the racial disparity (also see Korn and Ferry, 1986; Korn and Ferry, 1990; Theodore and Taylor, 1991).[1]

Core explanations of workplace inequality focus on the effects of the quality of Black labor on the one hand (Smith and Welch, 1983; Smith and Welch, 1986; Smith,

[1] In 2003, the obvious anomalies are the four African-Americans who are CEOs of industry's most powerful companies, AOL, Merrill Lynch, American Express, and Fannie Mae.

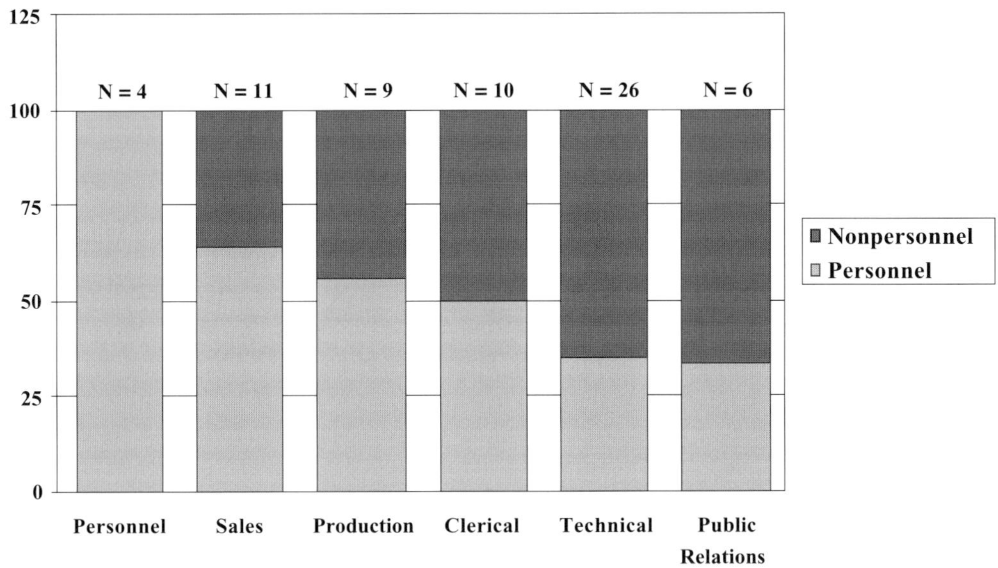

Figure 3. Percent of respondents who had at least one job in personnel by type of first job.

1984; Thernstrom et al., 1997), versus structural effects and employment discrimination on the other (Bendick, 1994; Collins, 1997a; Collins, 1997b; Fix, 1993; Fosu, 1993; Horton, 1995; Davis, 1995; Kirschenman and Neckerman, 1991). Put another way, the conversation is organized around the degree to which the attribute of race, per se, explains differences in allocation. For example, human capital theory in economic literature and status attainment theory in sociology argue that job allocation is a color-blind function of supply-side characteristics. In this scenario, Black workers are not found in top jobs because of productive deficits such as lower levels of education, lesser skills, and individual preferences. Conversely, the alternate viewpoint contends that structure and prejudice limit Black labor market attainments. This alternative viewpoint attributes people's progress to the characteristics of jobs and social barriers such that Blacks, like women, either are excluded from jobs or fill niches that are in decline or that do not lead to advancement (Kanter, 1977; Reskin and Roos, 1990).

Human capital theories of disparate qualifications and structural discrimination theories of disparate treatment are viewpoints argued as if they are oppositional insights into labor market inequality. In contrast, my research on the intersection of race and labor markets suggests that structure and human capital are not mutually exclusive but interactive explanatory schemes. One process I call attention to is how the managerial division of labor mediates the development of human capital. In the specific case of Black executives, a close look at the workplace shows that people start with a reservoir of expertise that becomes racialized, and hence marginalized and downgraded, through everyday work experiences.

Table 2. Percent distribution of black and white professionals, administrators and officials in city agencies: 1978 and 1990

City agency	1978 Black	White	1990 Black	White
Public Welfare	15	3	22	3
Corrections	3	1	3	1
Hospitals	22	11	14	9
Health	7	4	7	3
Housing	5	3	5	3
Community Development	4	4	3	3
Sanitation and Sewage	3	3	3	3
Financial Administration	14	18	16	15
Police	4	12	4	18
Streets and Highways	2	5	1	3
Natural Resources	8	6	5	5
Utility and Transportation	3	8	8	8
Fire	3	17	3	13
Other	6	4	4	3
Not Included	*	*	3	19
Total**	99	99	100	100

U.S. Equal Employ Opportunity Commission (1980); EEO-3 data: 1990.
*Not reported, or less than 0.5%.
**Totals do not add up to 100% due to rounding of non-reported figures.

II

Table 2 shows Equal Employment Opportunity (EEO) data on city employment for 1978 and 1990 and is used to illustrate the concept of racialized employment in public sector institutions. If we apply my analytic strategy whereby "racialized" means oriented to Blacks and "mainstream" lacks racial connotations, we see in these data evidence of functional segregation on the institutional level. By virtue of their lower positions in the income distribution, Blacks tend to be over-represented in populations utilizing public services such as public housing, health and hospital care, corrections, and city transportation systems. Looking at the percent distribution of Whites and Blacks in 1978, we see the percent of Black professionals is five times greater than the percent of White professionals, administrators and officials employed in public welfare. The Black percent is two times greater than the White percent in hospitals, and one-and-a-half times greater in housing and health. This is consistent with the idea of functional segregation. Black employment is concentrated in a Black-oriented system of services.

The 1990 survey of cities shows some changes in the employment distribution but we still can see a clear pattern of Black employment disproportionately concentrated in city functions used by Blacks by virtue of their socioeconomic position. There is an exception to this racialized employment pattern in 1990, found in financial administration, where the Black percent is greater than Whites' (16% versus 15%). But even here race-conscious influences may be underpinning of the difference. The increase in the percent of Blacks in financial administration may be due to the influx of Black mayors. As in the case of Chicago's Harold Washington, who was elected in 1980, Black mayors would appoint their own financial officers, probably Blacks whom they could trust. In the 1990 survey, Blacks are even more concentrated in public welfare functions. The Black percent is over seven times greater than the White percent of professionals, administrators and officials employed in public welfare.

Similar patterns of functional segregation can be found in a group of elite Black professional service firms in Chicago. Black businesses listed in the Chicago United Compendium of Professional Services (1980) are used as examples of the first wave of non-traditional Black firms specializing in professional services. Chicago United was established when a group of White and African-American business leaders who rarely, if ever, consorted with each other came together in the aftermath of the 1968 riots on Chicago's West Side. Black firms selected for listing in this compendium were publicly acknowledged successes and represented at the time a new and expanded Black business base. Professional service firms in accounting, engineering, and management consulting, law and advertising specialties were rare phenomena in the Black business community before the mid-1960s; rarer still were business opportunities with White clients. Rather, Black entrepreneurship was concentrated in segregated retail mom and pop ventures or in segregated personal services, such as Chicago-based Johnson (hair care) Products and in Black publishing (i.e., Chicago-based Johnson and Sengstacke Publications).

Businesses in this compendium are used to illustrate further a different intersection of Black business functions and market demands. Because these were the first Black entrepreneurs in Chicago to provide "cross-over" professional services to White, not just Black, clients one could expect that they represented the greatest potential to become integrated in the mainstream consumer market. The compendium lists Black firms in advertising (three firms), architecture and engineering (five firms), management consultation (six firms), certified public accounting (three firms), law (four firms), and personal services (seven firms). All except two firms listed were established between 1965 and 1979. Most, therefore, represent Blacks who were able to capitalize on race-related market incentives such as business set-aside programs, to establish a business base. The two exceptions to this pattern were firms in advertising (established in 1950) and accounting (established in 1939).

Table 3 shows the sector distribution of these firms' clients and whether or not they operated in racialized (R) or mainstream (M) functions. The type of function was categorized for each sector in which the firm was involved. If a sector involved both types of functions, the firms show up in both functional categories (R and M). All firms doing business with other Black firms were automatically classified under R functions, along with their other sector involvement.

Table 3. Black professional service firms by client sector and racialized and mainstream business functions

	Business Function*	
Client Sector	Racialized	Mainstream
Public	A E M M M M C C L L L	E E E C P
White Private	A A A M M M M L L P P P P	E E C C C L P P
Black Private	M C C C L L L L P P P A	
	Total racialized = 36	Total mainstream = 13

*The racialized category is the function directed at Black consumer/manpower needs; the mainstream category is the function directed at a general, that is non-racially differentiated, client/market.
A = advertising (3), C = certified public accounting (3), E = engineering and architecture (5), L = law (4), M = management consulting (5), and P = personnel services (6).

The most successful Black entrepreneurs in Chicago in the 1980s show up in racialized functions more often than not, even when discounting their dependence on the Black consumer market. This table is a business summary that shows that for these hypothetically assimilated firms one of the strongest footholds outside Black consumer markets is in "Black specialties" offered to White institutions. For example, Black law firms negotiated on behalf of their White corporate client when affirmative action or federal contract compliance was at issue. Black personnel service and management consulting firms were almost exclusively involved in Black manpower development, executive searches, and diversity interventions for White corporations and government agencies. Roles were race-specified even among those firms that dealt with White corporate structures in mainstream functions. Engineering firms with business in the White sector entered into these relationships as sub-contractors, based on the corporate need to hire minority firms to compete for federal contracts. Although these functions show up in the M category it can be debated whether or not they belong there.

In 1996, this pattern is more diversified, but only partially. Twenty-one of the original 26 Black entrepreneurs still owned thriving professional service firms. These 21 people joined in 1992 with other Black owners to form an association called the Alliance of Business Leaders and Entrepreneurs (ABLE). In this second category of owners are suppliers and retail manufacturers, and firms in construction, real estate, money management and television production. To be a member, a firm must be nominated by an ABLE member, have been in business at least for 3 years, and generate sales of at least $1 million annually.

Yet, the owners of professional service firms continue to occupy racialized and increasingly competitive niches as intermediaries between White structures and Black customers and clients. Burrell Communications, for instance, remains relegated to niche marketing although it is the largest Black owned advertising agency in the country. Moreover, Black advertising firms such as Burrell face increased competition generated by White firms now aggressively seeking business in ethnic markets. Having been convinced of the potential of the African-American consumer market, White companies now turn to their White agencies to help them deliver. Forty-nine percent of Burrell is now owned by Publicis, a French marking company, and one might wonder if the largest Black advertising firm will be "Black-owned" much longer.

Some members of this group are successful by any measure. They seem to be evidence that business set-aside programs do work toward more balanced business development. Or, they may be anomalies. For example, business set-asides in the private sector helped to create ABLE member John Rogers, the president of Ariel Capital, who built a billion dollar investment portfolio. Individuals like these operate at higher levels than those previous to set-asides and certainly at a much higher level than most other Black businesses.

Moving now to salaried Blacks employed in the White private sector, we continue to see evidence of functional segregation. Both small survey and census data show that Black managers and professionals disproportionately are found in personnel and public relations specialties (Heidrick and Struggles, 1979; Bureau of Labor Statistics, 2000). Hypothetically, these are corporate positions typically responsible for affirmative action plans and for mediating race-conscious labor and community relations. My study of Black executive careers directly tests this hypothesis.

III

Interviews with Chicago's top ranking Black executives in 1986 and again in the early 1990s suggest that they disproportionately are tracked into "racialized" roles in organizations. By "top" executives I mean corporate managers with a job title of Director or above (i.e., Vice President, Executive Vice President, President and Chief Officer). In 1986, I located these executives by first identifying Chicago-based *Fortune* 500 companies and then using informants knowledgeable of the Chicago business world to identify people in these companies who met my study's criteria.

The people I interviewed are in the first cohort of Blacks to break into non-traditional domains in the business world during the late 1960s and 1970s. They were hired into management and the business-related professions in White corporations. For a more detailed explanation of my analysis and research methods, as well as the degree to which I located the entire spectrum of high-ranking managers in corporate Chicago (see Collins, 1997). These data are used to exemplify the effects of racialized labor markets using the case of the Black executive careers. Over two-thirds of the 76 people I interviewed moved in and stayed in, or moved through a racialized job.

Figure 3 summarizes this movement by showing how respondents shifted from various areas of a company into personnel jobs. On the horizontal axis are the categories of the first private sector job held by each manager I interviewed. Above each stack is the number of managers whose first job was in that category. On the vertical axis is the percent of people in each job category who had at least one job in personnel during their career. For example, 100% of the 14 people whose first job was in personnel obviously had at least one personnel job. We can see that—for this group at least—all

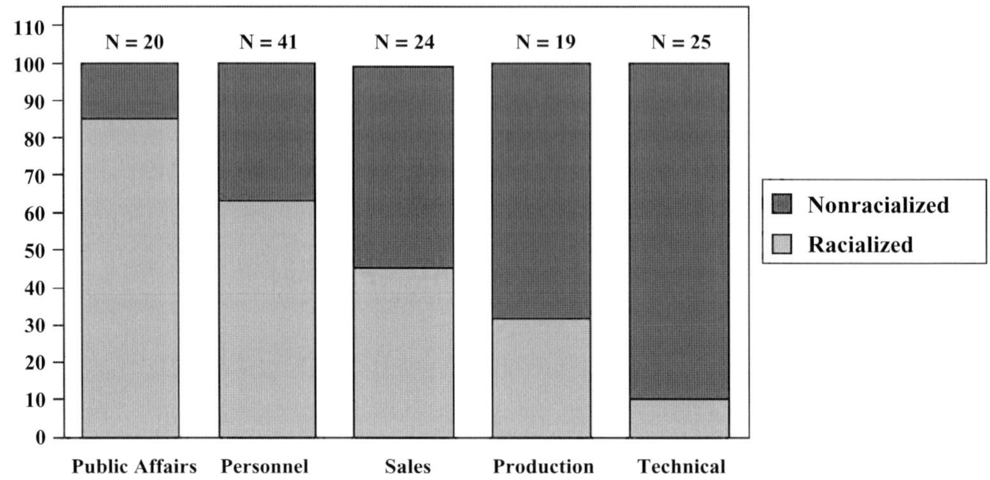

Figure 4. Managers in Racialized Functions, by Field.

routes led to jobs in corporate personnel departments. Sixty-four percent of 11 people who started in sales, 56% of 9 people who started in production, 50% of the 10 who started in clerical/administrative jobs, and 35% of the 26 who started in technical jobs had at least one job in personnel during their careers.

This figure reflects what executive surveys and census data consistently tells us. Salaried Blacks employed in the White private sector disproportionately show up in the staff areas of corporations, particularly in personnel. But the figure adds movement. It shows us companies drew heavily on Blacks from other areas to fill personnel jobs. Hypothetically, then, this is a racialized arena.

I extend the analysis to test this hypothesis by asking what proportion of respondents' experience in selected fields was racialized. Figure 4 records the number of people who ever had a job in one of the following five areas: public affairs, personnel, sales, production, or technical. It then shows the proportion of people who had a racialized job while in that area. We can see that racialized functions cut across fields but are most prevalent in public affairs and personnel fields. This is an organizational basis of discrimination in which inequality remains but is obscured by occupational titles. One manager summarized the environment when he commented:

> It was during the 1970s and there weren't very many people around that could do anything for minorities. All the companies were really scrambling. All you saw was minorities functioning in that . . . and it doesn't take much brain power to figure out that that's where most of us were going to end up.

In sum, Black community and regulatory pressures opened up a previously closed employment system. At the same time, it failed to level the playing field and led to racial steering of a different ilk: a previous system of total exclusion became one of racialized inclusion into the structure of management.

IV

I turn now to the implications of this mechanism of integration. Interviewing these very same executives in the early 1990s, I found that almost all of them indicated they hit what is popularly known as "the glass ceiling." The reasons are various and complex, but in part it was due to the fields they occupy.

Racialized jobs are not the feeders to the top jobs in companies. They are "support" jobs with no responsibility for profits or loss and, as such, are not typically part of the route to upward mobility into senior positions. White managers, in contrast, move into senior executive jobs through positions that contribute to the "bottom line," such sales, operations, and finance (Korn and Ferry, 1990). More interesting, however, is that while it is true support jobs have a more limited chain of career opportunity—the chain of opportunity becomes shorter still when such jobs are linked to racial purposes (Collins, 1997b).

The relatively lower career ceilings associated with these jobs result from the fact that they consist of administrative tasks extracted from a broader set of mainstream job functions. Directors of personnel, for example, are exposed to distinct functional components such as employee relations, employment, compensation and benefits, and labor relations. Directors of affirmative action, in contrast, are narrowly defined and have no such exposure. What we have then is a set of high paying and apparently high status managerial jobs filled by people who require little or no investment on the part of a company because they are not inaugurated by cross-functional training.

Human capital is devalued further still because success in performing these jobs builds on soft skills, such as interpersonal skills, and external (i.e., community) relationships. This competes with and undermines the development of hard skills such as administrative/decision-making and building internal (i.e., corporate) networks. The cumulative effect is that job holders can neither move up in the company beyond their current position in real terms, nor can they move over into a line position, nor can they move into mainstream personnel where they might expand their horizon. In short, the racialized job holder is trapped by their limited value to the corporate mainstream.

In conclusion, what I have shown here is an effect of race on mechanisms of allocation within organization that is less apparent, but not less real. The result is the reproduction of status subordination within companies. The observations derived from my study have various implications. The first concerns how inequality is manufactured. My study suggests a process of deskilling highly educated Blacks through the absence of certain on-the-job experiences. A second implication is that Black careers are constructed in a context of social closure among Whites attempting to defend their existing advantages. Put simply, White executives neither mentored nor nurtured their competition. Thus, the peculiar evolution of careers that I point to means that Black gains did not—and could not—blossom into meaningful numbers of executives in corporate Chicago in powerful decision-making roles in the year 2001.

I would urge that we look beneath occupational categories to understand how modern discrimination operates. While current theory contributes much to the knowledge of how and why the racial composition of organizations is constrained, as a general rule it fails to show how race-based constraints get manufactured within settings. In particular, the responsibilities and assignment accorded Black managers in the post-entry period are a crucial but neglected element for understanding how inequality is maintained. Contrary to essentially non-racial explanations of Blacks' status in the economy we see that as Blacks move up occupational ladders race interacts with the institutional roles they fill. These racialized roles in turn generate deficiencies in experience and in skill. The job functions and responsibilities of the managers in my study make this point.

SECTION III

Changing Boundaries: Historical and Social Development of Anti-Discrimination Law

CHAPTER 10

Discrimination and Diplomacy: Recovering the Fuller National Stake in 1960s Civil Rights Reform

Mary L. Dudziak

ABSTRACT

The conventional understanding of the history behind the passage of the Civil Rights Act of 1964 leaves out an important issue: the role of foreign relations. Legal scholarship on the basis for federal legislative power to regulate civil rights often focuses on the question of whether the Commerce Power was an appropriate basis for civil rights legislation. Congress turned to the Commerce Power because its earlier attempt to regulate race discrimination by private actors under the enabling clauses of the Thirteenth and Fourteenth Amendments was struck down by the Supreme Court. Concerned about that precedent, in the 1960s the Kennedy Administration and members of Congress saw the Commerce Clause as a promising source of congressional regulatory power. Evidence about the impact of race discrimination on interstate commerce was brought before the Senate Commerce Committee, and legislators debated whether the bill was really about commerce, or really about a moral issue, before passing the bill. This story leaves out an important issue, for a key Kennedy Administration witness before the Committee was Secretary of State Dean Rusk whose focus was neither commerce nor morality, but foreign affairs. The nation had a crucial stake in civil rights reform, Rusk argued, because race discrimination hampered U.S. relations with other nations during the crucial period of the Cold War. There was widespread international media coverage of brutal resistance to the civil rights movement, undermining U.S. prestige around the world, with hampered U.S. Cold War leadership. Rusk urged Congress to pass the civil rights bill to safeguard the nation's standing in the world, and he suggested that foreign relations concerns supported a broad reading of Congressional power. In essence, national security required a recalibration of federalism. This history can inform contemporary debates about the scope of Congressional power. In recent years, Congress' regulatory power under the civil rights enabling clauses has been constricted, and Congress' Commerce Power remains uncertain. Recovering the fuller national stake underlying the Civil Rights Act of 1964 can help us with the question of the proper scope of national authority over civil rights today.

L. B. Nielsen and R. L. Nelson (eds.), Handbook of Employment Discrimination Research, 203–218.

INTRODUCTION

What was at stake when Congress debated the Civil Rights Act of 1964? What reasons were given for federal government support for this extension of federal power? The standard account of this history centers on the need for federal action on the issue of civil rights, concerns about the scope of Congress' constitutional power under the 14th Amendment enabling clause, the turn to the commerce power as an alternative, and the evidence of the impact of segregation and discrimination on interstate commerce.[1] There is much to be said for the standard account, but it is only part of the story.

What of the broader history of civil rights? The story of American civil rights reform has sometimes been seen as a fairly simple narrative of an active grassroots movement, with charismatic leadership, pressing the case for racial justice, and the government responding. Historians have complicated this story in a number of ways, giving us a richer view of the grassroots, illuminating the politics within the movement, highlighting the role of women and of religion, and reexamining the role of massive resistance.[2] Scholars have also focused on the question of what, from the federal government's perspective, was at stake in 1960s civil rights reform. Reexamining civil rights history as an aspect of Cold War history, taking seriously the ubiquitous use of foreign policy arguments in civil rights debates, finding in State Department archives copious documentation of the negative impact of race discrimination on U.S. foreign relations, we see an extensive record of the relationship between civil rights and foreign relations. There is a Cold War history, an international history, underlying U.S. civil rights reform.[3]

[1] There is a rich literature on the Civil Rights Act of 1964. See, e.g., Nick Kotz, *Lyndon Baines Johnson, Martin Luther King Jr., and the Laws that Changed America* (Houghton Mifflin Co, 2005); Hugh Davis Graham, *The Civil Rights Era: Origins and Development of National Policy, 1960–1972* (Oxford University Press, 1990); Robert D. Loevy, ed., *The Civil Rights Act of 1964: The Passage of the Law that Ended Racial Segregation* (State University of New York Press, 1997); Robert D. Loevy, *To End All Segregation: The Politics of the Passage of the Civil Rights Act of 1964* (University Press of America, 1990); Daniel B. Rodriguez and Barry R. Weingast, "The Positive Political Theory of Legislative History: New Perspectives on the 1964 Civil Rights Act and its Interpretation," 151 *University of Pennsylvania Law Review* 1417 (2003).

[2] See, e.g., Charles Payne, *I've Got the Light of Freedom: The Organizing Tradition and the Mississippi Struggle* (University of California Press, 1995); John Dittmer, *Local People: The Struggle for Civil Rights in Mississippi* (University of Illinois, 1994); Glenda Gillmore, *Gender and Jim Crow: Women and the Politics of White Supremacy in North Carolina, 1896–1920* (University of North Carolina, 1996); Michael J. Klarman, *From Jim Crow to Civil Rights: The Supreme Court and the Struggle for Racial Equality* (Oxford University Press, 2004); David L. Chappel, *A Stone of Hope: Prophetic Religion and the Death of Jim Crow* (University of North Carolina Press, 2003).

[3] See Mary L. Dudziak, *Cold War Civil Rights: Race and the Image of American Democracy* (Princeton University Press, 2000); Thomas Borstelman, *The Cold War and the Color Line* (Harvard University Press, 2001); Philip Klinkner with Rogers Smith, *The Unsteady March* (University of Chicago Press, 1999). On race and U.S. foreign relations generally, see Brenda Gayle Plummer, *Rising Wind: Black Americans and U.S. Foreign Affairs, 1935–1960* (University of North Carolina Press, 1996); Penny Von Eschen, *Race Against Empire: Black Americans and Anticolonialism, 1937–1957* (Cornell University

Before the international turn in civil rights historiography, the role of foreign relations in Cold War-era civil rights reform had dropped out of the dominant narrative.[4] Meanwhile, the understanding of civil rights history within legal scholarship was constructed within that dominant narrative. Now that civil rights history has reopened the question of the role of international affairs in federal government support for civil rights reform, it is time to ask what the lessons of this history are for our understanding of civil rights law. At a time when the scope of Congressional power under both the commerce power and Section 5 of the 14th Amendment is in question, it is important to revisit the issue of the breadth of the national stake in 1960s civil rights reform.[5]

This chapter will examine the arguments about foreign affairs in the debate over the Civil Rights Act of 1964.[6] It will argue that *one* of the reasons President Kennedy supported a civil rights bill in 1963, and Congress passed one in 1964, was that race

Press, 1997); Gerald Home, *Black and Red: W.E.B. Dubois and the Afro-American Response to the Cold War, 1944–1963* (State University of New York Press, 1986); Michael Krenn, *Black Diplomacy: African Americans and the State Department, 1945–1969* (M. E. Sharpe, 1999); Carol Anderson, *Eyes Off the Prize: The United Nations and the African American Struggle for Human Rights, 1944–1955* (Cambridge University Press, 2003).

[4] There were some scholars who continued to raise this issue, but the argument remained marginalized and largely forgotten. See Locksley G. E. Edmundson, "Africa and the African Diaspora: The Years Ahead," in *Africa in World Affairs: The Next Thirty Years*, Ali A. Mazrui and Hasu H. Patel, eds. (The Third Press, 1973); Derrick A. Bell, Jr., "*Brown v. Board of Education* and the Interest-Convergence Dilemma," 93 *Harvard Law Review* 518 (January 1980). The new scholarship in this area became possible once previously classified State Department records became available at the National Archives. Such records are generally made available 30 years after they were produced.

[5] On the Supreme Court's current approach to the scope of Congressional power, see, e.g., Robert C. Post and Reva B. Siegel, "Equal Protection by Law: Federal Antidiscrimination Legislation After *Morrison* and *Kimel*, 110 *Yale L. J.* 441 (December 2000); Vicki C. Jackson, "Federalism and the Court: Congress as the Audience?" 54 *Annals* 145 (March 2001). Robert C. Post and Reva B. Siegel, "Protecting the Constitution from the People: Juricentric Restrictions on Section Five Power," 78 *Indiana Law Journal* 1 (2001); Kevin S. Schwartz, "Applying Section 5: *Tennessee v. Lane* and Judicial Conditions on the Congessional Enforcement Power," 114 *Yale Law Journal* 1133 (2005).

[6] The record of congressional debate over what would become the Civil Rights Act of 1964 is voluminous. For the purpose of this chapter, I will focus on hearings before the Senate Commerce Committee. That committee took up the question of whether the civil rights bill came within Congress's Commerce Power. It focused in particular on the issue of protection against discrimination in public accommodations, the area where legislation was thought to raise the most difficult constitutional questions. Protection against discrimination in public accommodations had been the focus of the 1875 Civil Rights Act, which the Supreme Court ruled exceeded Congress' power under Section 5 of the 14th Amendment and Section 2 of the 13th Amendment in the *Civil Rights Cases*, "with 'one stroke of the pen,'" 109 U.S. 3 (1883). It was because of the ruling in the *Civil Rights Cases* that Congress turned to the Commerce Power as an alternative source of authority for passage of civil rights legislation. In *Heart of Atlanta Motel v. United States*, 379 U.S. 241 (1964) and *Katzenbach v. McClung*, 379 U.S. 294 (1964), the Supreme Court held that the public accommodations provisions of the Civil Rights Act were within Congress' power under the Commerce Clause. Congressional power to enact laws prohibiting employment discrimination is also based in part on the Commerce Power. The foreign affairs concerns expressed in the 1963 Commerce Committee hearings extended to all forms of race discrimination, including discrimination in employment.

discrimination harmed the image of the United States in the world, which harmed U.S. foreign relations. In the context of the Cold War, perceived as a battle for the hearts and minds of the people of the world, the U.S. international image was thought to have great repercussions for U.S. national security. The chapter does *not* argue that Congress drew upon foreign affairs powers in passing the Civil Rights Act. Instead, it suggests that Cold War foreign affairs and national security were part of the calculus when Congress weighed the importance of the national interests at stake in civil rights reform, and that assessment of the national interest must be kept in mind when examining the impact of civil rights reform on federalism. The chapter will also suggest that the impact of foreign affairs and national security on federalism and the scope of federal power was not a new issue in the 1960s. Concerns about international affairs underlay the virtual elimination of federalism as a limit on the commerce power during World War II. Perhaps, it is easier to make the point now than it would have been before September 11, 2001, that when the Supreme Court strips the national government of power, those limitations can affect broad U.S. interests, including national security.

*****

President John F. Kennedy was slow to support civil rights reform, concerned that focusing on civil rights legislation would undercut his initiatives in foreign affairs and economic policy. The new president had only so much political capital, and he was reluctant to spend it on a difficult issue that was sure to cost him Southern votes in a 1964 reelection campaign. Although he courted the African-American vote during the 1960 presidential campaign, the President took so long to fulfill his campaign promise to end discrimination in federal housing programs "with 'one stroke of the pen,'" through an executive order, that civil rights supporters sent thousands of pens to the White House as a reminder. Kennedy was angered by the civil rights movement, as Freedom Riders rode buses through the South into Klan violence right before the President met with Soviet leader Nikita Khrushchev in 1961. "Get your friends off those buses!" he urged civil rights advisor Harris Wofford, concerned that the protests were "embarrassing him and the country on the eve of the meeting" with Khrushchev. However, Kennedy's advisors argued that the President must take up civil rights if he wanted to make progress on the areas closer to his heart, foreign affairs, and economic policy, because the three issues were interdependent. Civil rights, they argued, was "the third leg of the stool." By the end of his first year in office, progress on desegregation was listed in an internal draft of "Major Foreign Policy Measures Taken by the Kennedy Administration."[7]

[7] Dudziak, *Cold War Civil Rights*, 155–163; Aaronson/Wilkins, Confidential Memorandum, February 6, 1961, Papers of Theodore C. Sorensen, Subject Files, 1961–1964, Box 3, John F. Kennedy Library, Boston, Massachusetts; Battle to Dutton, September 19, 1961, Folder: Foreign Policy, 4/1/61–10/8/63, Papers of Theodore C. Sorensen, Subject Files, 1961–1964, Box 34, JFK Library, Boston; Richard Reeves, *President Kennedy: Profile of Power* (Simon and Schuster, 1994), 123; Harris Wofford, *Of Kennedys and Kings: Making Sense of the Sixties:* (Farrar, Straus, and Giroux, 1980), 125.

The impact of civil rights on foreign relations came to a dramatic head in the spring of 1963. The civil rights movement targeted Birmingham, Alabama, holding civil rights marches to protest pervasive race discrimination in employment, voting, and other areas. By early May 1963, Police Commissioner Bull Connor had filled the jails with civil rights protesters. Since the jails were full, he needed a different strategy to dissuade movement activity. And so, on May 3, the day of the children's campaign in Birmingham, thousands of peaceful young people marched in Birmingham in support of civil rights, and were met with police dogs and high power fire hoses that flattened demonstrators against storefronts, knocked them to the ground, and rolled at least one child down the street. News coverage, including photographs and televised images, was broadcast throughout the nation and the world. A reaction against Birmingham's brutality toward peaceful protesters helped generate greater political pressure within the United States for civil rights reform. The events were front-page news around the world, generating widespread international reaction, damaging the U.S. image around the world.[8] Just days after these horrific events, in Addis Ababa, Ethiopia, African heads of state gathered for the first meeting of what would become the Organization of African Unity. Birmingham was taken up on the opening day of the meeting, and African sentiment about Birmingham was so strong that when the delegates passed a compromise resolution on American race relations that did not call for a "break" in U.S.–African relations, but only suggested that a break might occur if episodes like Birmingham continued, the U.S. Ambassador to Ethiopia telegraphed his relief to the Secretary of State, indicating that under the circumstances, the resolution was the best they could have hoped for.[9]

The domestic and international pressure resulting from Birmingham ultimately led President Kennedy to throw his weight behind civil rights reform. As Burke Marshall, Assistant Attorney General for civil rights, later put it, Birmingham "was a matter of national and international concern. . . . [T]he pictures of police dogs and fire hoses going throughout the country stirred the feelings of every Negro in the country, most whites in the country, and I suppose particularly colored persons throughout the world. And all of that emotion was directed at President Kennedy. 'Why didn't he do something?' " The President sent Marshall to Birmingham to try to broker an agreement

[8] Taylor Branch, *Parting the Waters: America in the King Years, 1954–1963* (Simon & Schuster, 1988), 758–765; David Garrow, *Bearing the Cross: Martin Luther King, Jr., and the Southern Christian Leadership Conference* (William Morrow, 1986), 267–268; Diane McWhorter, *Carray Me Home: Birmingham, Alabama: The Climactic Battle of the Civil Rights Revolution* (Simon & Schuster, 2001); U.S. Information Agency, "Reaction to Racial Tension in Birmingham, Alabama," May 13, 1963, R-85-63 (A), RG 306, National Archives; Wilson to J. F. Kennedy, May 14, 1963, Folder: USIA (Classified) 1/63–11/63, Box 133, Papers of Pierre Salinger, Background Briefing Material, Kennedy Library; Richard Lentz, "Snarls Echoing 'Round the World: The 1963 Birmingham Civil Rights Campaign on the World Stage," *17 American Journalism* 69 (2000).

[9] Mary L. Dudziak, "Birmingham, Addis Ababa and the Image of America: International Influence on U.S. Civil Rights Politics in the Kennedy Administration," in Brenda Gayle Plummer, ed., *Window on Freedom: Race, Civil Rights, and Foreign Affairs, 1945–1988* (University of North Carolina Press, 2003), p. 181.

with local leaders, but Birmingham had become an international crisis, and it required a response that would have a global, as well as a local, impact. Then, after Alabama Governor George Wallace placed segregation again on the front pages of newspapers around the world, blocking a federal court order to desegregate the University of Alabama with his call for "Segregation now! Segregation tomorrow! Segregation forever!" President Kennedy put civil rights firmly on his agenda. On June 11, 1963, he delivered an impassioned address before a worldwide television audience. The President insisted that "this Nation ... will not be fully free until all its citizens are free." He challenged his audience: "We preach freedom around the world, and we mean it, and we cherish our freedom here at home, but are we to say to the world, and much more importantly, to each other that this is a land of the free except for the Negroes; that we have no second-class citizens except Negroes; that we have no class or caste system, no ghettoes, no master race except with respect to Negroes?" The President announced an ambitious civil rights agenda, that would include a strong new civil rights bill. The impact of the speech at home was important. It was also a salve to the U.S. image abroad. Distributed to all American diplomatic posts with directions from the Secretary of State regarding how to best use it, the speech accomplished a "quick turnaround in attitudes" in Ethiopia, and with the exception of the Soviet bloc, it had a similar impact around the world.[10]

While it might seem surprising to later generations to think of foreign policy as one of the issues in play during discussion of the 1964 Civil Rights Act, at the time the Act was debated the relationship between civil rights and foreign affairs was widely understood. An August 1963 Harris Poll reported that 78% of white Americans surveyed thought that race discrimination in the United States harmed the nation abroad. Twenty-three percent of respondents volunteered that the primary reason discrimination harmed the United States abroad was that it gave the communists a valuable propaganda weapon. The second major reason was that it generally gave the country a bad name. As a Kingsport, Tennessee lawyer put it, "The pictures of dogs attacking colored people in Birmingham have been sent abroad and you know what kind of opinion that gives them about us." Congress did not need to rely on a general understanding of this issue, however. When the Senate Commerce Committee held hearings on the Act, they were presented with data. Secretary of State Dean Rusk testified before the Committee, and Chairman Warren Magnuson received

[10] Burke Marshall, Oral History Interview, May 29, 1964, pp. 98–99, Kennedy Library; Reeves, *President Kennedy,* 514–522; John F. Kennedy, "Radio and Television Report to the American People on Civil Rights," June 11, 1963, *Public Papers of the Presidents: John F. Kennedy, 1963* (U.S. Government Printing Office, 1964), 468; Korry to J. F. Kennedy, June 28, 1963, Folder: Africa, General 7/63, Box 3, National Security Files—Countries—Africa, Kennedy Library; "Soviet Media Coverage of Current US Racial Crisis," June 14, 1963, Folder: Civil Rights, 6/11/63, National Security Files, Subjects, Box 295, Kennedy Library; USIA to J. F. Kennedy, June 14, 1963, Folder: Civil Rights, 6/11/63–6/14/63, National Security Files, Box 295, Kennedy Library, Carl M. Brauer, *John F. Kennedy and the Second Reconstruction* (Columbia University Press, 1979).

correspondence on the issue from the Director of the U.S. Information Agency and the General Counsel of the Department of Defense.[11]

Secretary Rusk was well acquainted with the impact of civil rights on foreign relations before his July 1963 appearance before the Senate committee. He would write in his memoir that "racism and discrimination . . . had a major impact on my life as secretary of state." So much did this issue affect him, that an entire chapter of Rusk's memoir is devoted to it. He explained, "Stories of racial discrimination in the United States and discriminatory treatment accorded diplomats from the many newly independent countries of the old colonial empires began to undermine our relations with these countries." Civil rights were so commonly associated with foreign relations during these years that Rusk and others felt the need to stress that civil rights reform was motivated by other objectives as well. Rusk's task was to inform the committee of the foreign policy implications of the public accommodations bill. He stressed, however, that "it is not my view that we should resolve these problems here at home merely in order too [sic] look good abroad. The primany [sic] reason why we must attack the problems of discrimination is rooted in our basic commitments as a nation and a people." Discrimination must be overcome "because it is incompatible with the great ideals to which our democratic society is dedicated." Of course, such selfless devotion to principle would have strategic advantages. According to Rusk, "If the realities at home are all they should be, we shan't have to worry about our image abroad."[12]

Rusk thought that "As matters stand . . . racial discrimination here at home has important effects on our foreign relations." The United States was, of course, not the only nation where discrimination was a problem, however "the United States is widely regarded as the home of democracy and the leader of the struggle for freedom, for human rights, for human dignity," Rusk explained. "We are expected to be the model. . . . So our failure to live up to our proclaimed ideals are [sic] noted—and magnified and distorted." The foreign relations impact of discrimination had become especially acute due to "one of the epochal developments of our time": decolonization. The liberation of colonized people occurred in the context of a broader Cold War struggle with the Soviet Union. While Rusk was hopeful, he warned that "in waging this world struggle we are seriously handicapped by racial or religious discrimination in the United States. Our failure to live up to the pledges of our Declaration of Independence and our Constitution embarrasses our friends and heartens our enemies."[13]

[11] *Washington Post*, August 26, 1963, p. 1, attached to Sanjuan to R. Kennedy, August 26, 1963, Folder: Sanjuan, Pedro: 8/1963, 10/1963, Box 51, Personal Papers of Robert F. Kennedy, Attorney General's Papers, General Correspondence, Kennedy Library; Statement of Dean Rusk, July 10, 1963. A Bill to Eliminate Discrimination in Public Accommodations Affecting Interstate Commerce: Hearing on S. 1732 Before the Senate Committee on Commerce, 88th Cong., Part 1, p. 281 (hereinafer "Hearings").

[12] Dean Rusk, *As I Saw It* (W. W. Norton, 1990), 581; Statement of Dean Rusk, July 10, 1963, Hearings Part 1, p. 281.

[13] Id., 281–82.

Race in America was a powerful weapon for the nation's adversaries. According to Rusk, "In their efforts to enhance their influence among the nonwhite peoples and to alienate them from us, the Communists clearly regard racial discrimination in the United States as one of their most valuable assets." Soviet propaganda on race in America focused on four themes:

1. Racism is inevitable in the American capitalist system.
2. Inaction by the U.S. Government is tantamount to support of what they call the racists.
3. Recent events have exposed the hypocrisy of U.S. claims to ideological leadership of the so-called free world.
4. The U.S. policy toward Negroes is clearly indicative of its attitude towards peoples of color throughout the world.[14]

The impact of Soviet exploitation of American race discrimination was not as damaging as it might have been due to four factors:

> The first is that nonwhite students have encountered race prejudice in Soviet bloc countries. The second is the loyalty of nonwhite Americans to the United States and its institutions.... The third reason... is that we have made progress in removing discriminatory laws and practices, have advanced toward full equality. And the fourth reason is that the power of the Federal Government—especially its executive and judicial branches—has been exerted to secure the rights of racial minorities."[15]

As an example of the importance of federal support for civil rights, Rusk pointed to the resolution at Addis Ababa. He told the Senators: "The recent meeting of African heads of state... condemned racial discrimination 'especially in the United States,' then approved the role of U.S. Federal authorities in attempting to combat it." As Rusk saw it, having embarked on a course of civil rights progress, the nation could not back down. "If progress should stop, if Congress should not approve legislation designed to remove remaining discriminatory practices, questions would inevitably arise in many parts of the world as to the real convictions of the American people. In that event, hostile propaganda might be expected to hurt us more than it has hurt us until now."[16]

The Secretary elaborated on a special problem that had plagued the Department of State, a problem the Civil Rights Act would help to redress: discrimination against non-white foreign diplomats and visitors. He stressed, "We cannot expect the friendship and respect of nonwhite nations if we humiliate their representatives by denying them, say, service in a highway restaurant or city cafe." Diplomats from around the world came to New York, the seat of the United Nations, and to Washington, D.C., and countless foreign visitors traveled to the country. Within the previous two years, "scores of incidents of racial discrimination" against foreign diplomats had been reported to the department. The Secretary detailed several examples. "One African Ambassador was en route here from New York. His first experience, even before he had a chance to present his credentials to the President, was that of being ejected

[14] Id., 282.
[15] Id., 282–283.
[16] Id., 283.

from a roadside restaurant." In another incident, "The Ambassador of one of the larger African countries was taking a trip involving a reservation at a large hotel. When the manager of the hotel realized that the Ambassador was not white he decided to cancel the reservation. It took several top level officials the better part of a day to persuade the management of that hotel to accept the Ambassador in order to avoid an international incident." Because of experiences like this, "The nonwhite diplomat often prefers to keep within the confines of the District of Columbia," since public accommodations in other parts of the nation "are potential places of trouble." African Ambassadors reported that they had received advice to wear robes when they went out to make it clear that they were diplomats to avoid discrimination.[17]

Rusk believed that the public accommodations provisions of the civil rights bill would "go a long way toward removing some of the most acute problems we have experienced in this area." But the Secretary stressed that he did not seek to protect rights for diplomats only—rights that were not also to be accorded to non-white Americans. "One should not need a diplomatic passport in order to enjoy ordinary civil and human rights." The State Department's interests required that discrimination against Americans be redressed.[18]

Rusk stressed that "The present racial crisis divides and weakens, and challenges the Nation both at home and in the world struggle in which we are engaged. I deeply hope that the issues involved can be approached on the basis of genuine bipartisanship, just as are the broad objectives of this country's foreign policy." The Secretary urged, "I want to reiterate most emphatically that in the fateful struggle in which we are engaged to make the world safe for freedom, the United States cannot fulfill its historic role unless it fulfills its commitments to its own people."[19]

Rusk's testimony was enthusiastically received by many members of the committee. Senator Pastore of Rhode Island congratulated Rusk, and said that "for the life of me, I can't see how any man in his right mind can dispute anything you have said here this morning." Senator Cotton of New Hampshire was also enthusiastic. Cotton focused on the issue of the great level of familiarity citizens of other nations had with the United States. Rusk agreed that the United States was under "the kleig lights of widest publicity.... It is partly because of our power; it is partly because of our general position in the world... but I think it is also because we have committed ourselves historically to some ideas which I consider to be still the most explosive political ideas in history—these notions of freedom."[20]

For the most part, Rusk wished to leave questions of constitutionality to the Justice Department, but when pressed by Senator Cotton on whether foreign audiences

[17] Id., 283–287. See George Collins, "Everybody Eats But Americans: 'His Highness is a mite hungry': August 1961," *Reporting Civil Rights: Part One, American Journalism 1941–1963* (The Library of America 2003), p. 607 (reprint of Baltimore *Afro-American* story about reporters who dressed up as Africans from a fictional African nation in an attempt to gain service in Maryland restaurants).

[18] Hearings, Part 1, p. 287.

[19] Id., 287–288.

[20] Id., 288.

would understand the complexities of the possible limits of Congress' power to regulate interstate commerce, Rusk responded that he was aware of the constitutional questions, and that "I do think it is relevant to bear in mind, in connection with the constitutional issues, that this does affect the power of the United States to conduct our foreign relations adequately abroad." The State Department was charged with protecting Americans abroad, regardless of race, and "against a background of, shall I say, disability in our own country on some of these same issues, our voice abroad, in seeking to protect American citizens abroad, is somewhat muted and uncertain. And I think this affects the elements of reciprocity under the conduct of our foreign relations as well as the broader issues in what might be called the propaganda and political field." The Secretary emphasized that "I think the foreign relations aspect of this at least has some bearing on the broad constitutional issue, although I would not say that was directly at issue here."[21]

While his point may have been inartfully made, the argument Secretary Rusk brought before the committee was that foreign policy, a matter clearly within the purview of federal power, was at stake in civil rights reform. The federal government's foreign policy imperatives provided support for a broad reading of Congressional power under the Commere Power, the specific tool lawmakers relied on. While foreign affairs might not have a bearing on understandings of "interstate commerce," it certainly affected the question of whether the national interests at state were so weighty that federalism concerns should not, in this context, act as a break on federal power.

Senator Strom Thurmond of South Carolina would subject the Secretary to a vociferous line of questioning.[22] Noting the use of American racial problems in Communist propaganda, Thurmond asked, "Mr. Secretary, by coming before Congress and testifying in this nature, aren't you lending at least tacit support to and approval of this Communist lie?" Rusk responded that he was simply advising the committee on the relationship between American racial problems and foreign relations. "I consider that relationship very grave, and I would certainly hope that no committee of Congress would ever take the view that a Secretary of State can't come before it without having it said he is supporting a Communist line."[23] Senator Thurmond wondered whether the Secretary thought that "Congress should be urged to act on some particular measure, because of the threat of Communist propaganda if we don't." In a widely reported exchange, the Senator asked the Secretary what he thought of civil rights demonstrations, and whether Congress should pass legislation because of them. At this point, as the *New York Times* reported it, Rusk "dropped his normal diplomatic

[21] Id., 290.

[22] For example, after Rusk indicated that he supported all the antidiscrimination provisions that would be covered in the Civil Rights Act, not just public accommodations, Thurmond suggested that since the legislation would permit the President to withhold public funds from institutions that discriminated, perhaps the same principle should be applied to foreign aid, withholding funds from nations that practiced discrimination. He went on to press the Secretary on whether newly independent African countries discriminated against whites. Id., 299–300.

[23] Id., 310.

manner of speaking." He responded: "If I were denied what our Negro citizens are denied, I would demonstrate."[24]

In light of Secretary Rusk's support for civil rights, a reader might wonder whether the foreign relations argument was constructed for the purpose of supporting a civil rights agenda, rather than being a motivating factor in its own right. Such an argument does not hold up against the long and extensive record of the impact of civil rights on foreign relations since World War II, the extensive diplomatic efforts to manage the problem, including the devotion of countless hours by State Department and U.S. Information Agency staff over the years. Presidents, Secretaries of State, and diplomats initially tried to address this problem with U.S. information programming, but came to understand that the only meaningful way to undo the harm of U.S. racism to the U.S. image overseas was to make visible progress on civil rights reform.[25]

In the Commerce Committee, Rusk's testimony was reinforced by others. Edward R. Murrow, Director of the U.S. Information Agency, wrote to Chairman Magnuson, endorsing the civil rights bill. The USIA was "in favor of the enactment of the proposed legislation," he wrote. The bill would aid the agency's mission. "In the everyday task of portraying the American scene to foreign audiences, the Agency has had the difficult task of counteracting the detrimental effects of civil rights violations," he wrote:

> We cannot make good news out of bad practice. Nor can we cover up the fact that we have important unfinished business in this country. What we have done and will continue to do, however, is to place our problems and difficulties in proper and truthful perspective, indicating the continuing progress we are making. Our Agency's real success in this area ultimately depends upon what we do domestically. For this reason the enactment of the proposed legislation would be a concrete act by the Government to redress existing inequities.

As Murrow saw it, "as the barriers to equal rights and opportunities for all in our Nation are broken down, the fact that the United States is a multiracial society will prove one of our greatest assets in the contest of ideologies." Lest civil rights reform be seen as an instrumental value, pursued to enhance U.S. foreign relations, rather than for its own value, Murrow stressed that the bill should not "be enacted solely because it would enhance the U.S. image abroad though it would clearly have that effect. We should attack the problem of segregation because it is right that we do so. To do otherwise, whatever the oversea [sic] reaction might be, would violate the very essence of what our country stands for."[26]

The Department of Defense also weighed in on the bill, arguing that proscribing discrimination in public accommodations would aid the military. Since 1948, equality in the military had been U.S. policy. Much progress had been made, however, when integrated troops were stationed in parts of the nation that practiced segregation, conflicts

[24] Id., 311, 315; *New York Times*, July 11, 1963, p. 16.

[25] This argument is more fully developed, and the historical record is fully documented, in Dudziak, *Cold War Civil Rights*. See also Borstelmann, *Cold War and Color Line*.

[26] Murrow to Magnuson, July 24, 1963, Hearings, Part 1, pp. 16–17.

arose. Off-base discrimination was a continuing concern. John T. McNaughton, General Counsel of the Department of Defense, wrote to Chairman Magnuson that

> Off-base discrimination against minority groups within the Armed Forces generates a serious morale problem for the military. In consideration of the purpose and the mission of the military establishment, it is neither feasible, expedient, nor justifiable to assign personnel to duty stations on the basis of race, color, or national origin. Consequently, servicemen belonging to minority groups have been forced to accept a set of standards, and have been denied privileges enjoyed by other military personnel in those areas where local custom supports discriminatory practices.[27]

The public accommodations bill would ease this problem for the military. "Military personnel, like other members of the American public, must rely upon the availability of public accommodations when traveling to new duty stations, when living in a civilian community adjacent to their duty station, or when on temporary duty in connection with military maneuvers." Military personnel moved every 3–4 years, and it was "a matter of military necessity" that they move "when and where ordered." When minority personnel encountered discrimination upon relocating, it was "an unnecessary and unjustifiable burden. The morale and discipline problems caused by such inequities can only have an adverse effect on military operations." For these reasons, the public accommodations bill was "a needed supplement to [the Department of Defense's] own existing policies."[28]

Senators shared these concerns. In a statement in support of the bill, Senator Philip A. Hart of Michigan illustrated the need for the bill, by referring to what he called commonplace occurrences: "The American soldier traveling from his home to an oversea [sic] assignment refused a cup of coffee at a lunch counter. . . . A diplomat from Ghana turned away when seeking night lodgings."[29]

That the world looked to the Civil Rights Bill as a crucial sign of progress on the American dilemma was powerfully illustrated in the international reaction to President Kennedy's assassination in November 1963. Amid the worldwide shock and despair, the U.S. Information Agency surveyed international opinion. While many nations focused on the prospects for Soviet–American relations and for peace, in Africa the focal concern was "the fate of the civil rights movement." In Lyndon Johnson's address to the nation, he urged that "[N]o memorial oration or eulogy could more eloquently honor President Kennedy's memory than the earliest possible passage of the civil rights bill for which he fought so long. . . . There could be no greater source of strength to this Nation both at home and abroad." The USIA reported that, due to their concerns

27 McNaughton to Magnuson, July 10, 1963, Hearings, Part 1, pp. 9–10.

28 Id., 10. Recently, national defense-related arguments resurfaced in a case involving affirmative action. Twenty-nine retired military leaders filed an *Amicus Curia* brief arguing that affirmative action served military necessity by ensuring racially diverse officers needed for today's racially diverse military. Justice Sandra Day O'Connor drew upon this brief in her majority opinion upholding the University of Michigan Law School's affirmative action program. Brief for Julius W. Becton, Jr. et al. as *Amici Curiae, Grutter v. Bollinger*, 539 U.S. 306 (2003), *Grutter*, 539 U.S. at 331.

29 Statement of Hon. Philip A. Hart, July 3, 1963, Hearings, Part 1, p. 180.

about civil rights, Johnson's address was met with "relief and gratification" in Africa, in spite of continuing concern that the assassination might have been prompted by Kennedy's civil rights stance. In South Asia, the "media were especially pleased to learn that President Johnson was determined to carry through President Kennedy's civil rights program." In later weeks, the Western European press "widely applauded" Johnson's support for the Civil Rights Bill, and in the far East, some felt that "President Kennedy's death would create an atmosphere conducive to public and Congressional progress" on civil rights.[30]

The international press followed the Civil Rights Bill as it made its way through Congress. When a Senate filibuster was ended by a cloture vote in June 1964, the vote was applauded by the *Philippines Herald*, the *Manila Times*, and other papers worldwide. As the bill neared a final vote in the House of Representatives later that month, USIA Director Carl Rowan wrote to the President, "[a]ll continents hail the imminent passage of the civil rights bill." In Tegucigalpa, the paper *El Nacional* wondered whether the United States appreciated "the dignity it has won in the eyes of the whole world." When the Act passed, the USIA reported that news commentators from around the world viewed the passage as the most important step forward in the American Negro's struggle for equality since the Emancipation Proclamation; as a "victory" that will "shape the future of the United States"; as a "turning point" in American history; as enhancing the international influence of the United States, reinforcing the moral authority of the United States and its dedication to freedom and social justice.[31]

Passage of the Civil Rights Act was widely used by the U.S. Information Agency and the Voice of America. U.S. diplomatic posts reported back to the State Department on the beneficial effect of these developments on U.S. relations with other nations. In Nigeria, for example, the foreign minister said that he thought the act's passage "would enhance [the] close association presently existing between Nigeria and [the] U.S." While civil rights in the United States had been a topic of concern at the first meeting of the Organization of African Unity, when African leaders gathered for the

[30] U.S. Information Agency, "Foreign Reaction to the Presidential Succession," December 6, 1963, pp. i–ii, 18, Folder: United States Information Agency Vol. 1 [3 of 3], National Security File, Agency File, Box 73, Lyndon Baines Johnson Library, Austin, Texas; Lyndon B. Johnson, "Address Before a Joint Session of the Congress," November 27, 1963, *Public Papers of the Presidents of the United States: Lyndon B. Johnson, 1963–1964* (U.S. Government Printing Office, 1965), 1:8–9; United States Information Agency, "Worldwide Reaction to the First Month of the Johnson Administration," December 24, 1963, p. 15, Folder: United States Information Agency Vol. I [3 of 3], National Security File, Agency File, Box 73, Johnson Library; Dudziak, *Cold War Civil Rights*, 200–207. President Johnson invoked the memory of Kennedy, yet hoped to use a legislative victory in part to make his own mark on the presidency.

[31] Rowan to Johnson, June 22, 1964, Folder: United States Information Agency Vol. 2 [2 of 2], National Security File, Agency File, Box 73, Johnson Library; Rowan to Johnson, June 23, 1964, Folder: United States Information Agency Vol. 2 [2 of 2], National Security File, Agency File, Box 73, Johnson Library United States Information Agency, "Foreign Reaction to Senate Passage of Civil Rights Bill," June 29, 1964, Folder: FG 296 U.S. Information Agency 5/22/64–6/30/64, White House Central Files, Subject File, Federal Government, Box 314, Johnson Library; Dudziak, *Cold War Civil Rights*, 209–211.

second meeting in July 1964, the USIA reported that passage of the Civil Rights Act was a "major theme" at the meeting. Guinea President Sekou Toure called it "a great victory." Meanwhile Malcolm X, who had attended the meeting in the hope of encouraging African leaders to bring U.S. human rights abuses against African-Americans before the United Nations, found that he had trouble gaining a hearing.[32]

The Civil Rights Act of 1964 was an important achievement in U.S. efforts to overcome the damage that American race discrimination had done to the image of the nation around the world. In the context of the Cold War, perceived to be a battle between the forces of good and evil in the world, this civil rights advance was seen—by the President, by the Secretary of State, by members of Congress, by the American public—as an achievement as well for U.S. foreign relations. Surely, we would like to think that overcoming the barriers of racism in American communities would be a sufficient reason for enough of the nation to support the Civil Rights Act of 1964 to carry the bill through Congress. Yet, as much as we might wish to believe that this moral victory was borne on the wings of justice alone, as much as historical memory has for years collapsed the story into a narrative of moral progress, the record of American civil rights reform presents a more complicated story. Morality was not all that was at stake in the Civil Rights Act. A civil rights bill was essential for U.S. foreign relations.

That the national stake in civil rights reform included foreign affairs should be seen, as Secretary Rusk suggested, as relevant to the scope of Congress' power. When Congress drew upon the commerce power to support civil rights reform, its assessment of the national interests at stake, and so its assessment of the need for broad national power, included concerns about U.S. foreign affairs and national security. This was not the first time that the scope of Congress' commerce power was affected by national security concerns. Indeed, the basis for the mid-20th century expansion of Congress' power lay, in part, in concerns about federal authority over a wartime economy. *Wickard v. Filburn*,[33] the case that for all practical purposes decimated federalism as a limit on Congress' commerce power, at least for a few decades, is often remembered as a New Deal-era case. Instead, this 1942 case about wheat farmers was decided in a wartime atmosphere, as the United States and Britain negotiated about U.S. wheat shipments to England. The farmer in the case, Roscoe Filburn, had exceeded his wheat quota with wheat consumed on his farm when he was confused about his obligations under the

[32] Rowan to Johnson, June 30, 1964, Folder: United States Information Agency Vol. 2 [2 of 2], National Security File, Agency File, Box 73, Johnson Library; Lagos to Department of State, July 10, 1964, RG 59, Central Foreign Policy Files, 1964–1966, SOC 14-1 US, National Archives; United States Information Agency, "African Reactions to Recent U.S. Civil Rights Developments," July 21, 1964, Folder: FG 296, 7/1/64–9/30/64, White House Central File, Federal Government, Johnson Library; Malcolm X to African Heads of State, July 1964, and Malcolm X interviewed by Milton Henry, in *Malcolm X Speaks: Selected Speeches and Statements,* George Brietman ed. (Pathfinder Press, 1965), 76; Peter Goldman, *The Death and Life of Malcolm X*, 2nd ed. (University of Illinois Press, 1979), 217–218; Dudziak, *Cold War Civil Rights*, 211–214, 221–223.

[33] 317 U.S. 111 (1942).

statute. His confusion stemmed from a speech given by the Secretary of Agriculture: "Wheat Farmers and the Battle for Democracy," which stressed the importance of stability in wheat production at a time when the United States needed to send wheat to England to help them fight the Nazis.[34] While national security was not drawn on explicitly by the Court as it struggled with this case, the wartime context was part of the record before the Court, and the case was decided during an era when members of the Court had committed themselves to the war effort, so much so that the imprint of the war extends through their jurisprudence.[35] This example helps us to see the way national interests and national security have affected American federalism in the development of mid-20th century commerce power jurisprudence.[36]

It should not be surprising that the "American Century" was the occasion for the expansion of U.S. power at home as well as internationally. And so Congressional power was extended to address national interests relating to the U.S. role in the world. Once a world leader, the U.S. federal government required greater control over matters affecting its global power and its international prestige. The expansion of federal power, and the consequent recalibration of federalism, gave the nation tools that world leadership required. In recent years, coinciding, perhaps coincidentally, with the end of the Cold War, the Supreme Court reconsidered the scope of federal legislative power. Congress's authority under Section 5 of the Fourteenth Amendment was constricted, and federalism re-emerged as a meaningful limit to the Commerce Power.[37] More recently, what seemed at one time to be an impending Rehnquist Court federalism revolution may have stalled. Faced with a federalism-based challenge to federal drug laws in a medical marijuana case, *Gonzales v. Raich*,[38] the Court appeared to reconsider the trajectory of its federalism caselaw. The Court upheld federal power to regulate marijuana even as applied to home grown marijuana used pursuant to a doctor's recommendation, which seemed far from the channels of interstate commerce. "The federalism boomlet has fizzled," concluded Michael S. Greve of the American

[34] Mary L. Dudziak, "'Wheat Farmers and the Battle for Democracy': Another Look at *Wickard v. Filburn* (unpublished paper)".

[35] See, e.g., "The Supreme Court and World War II," 1996. *Journal of Supreme Court History*, vol. 1 (1996); Daniel R. Ernst and Victor Jew, eds., Total *War and the Law: The American Home Front in World War II* (Praeger Publishers, 2002).

[36] Mary L. Dudziak, "Law in the Shadow of War," in Michael Grossberg and Christopher Tomlins, eds., *The Cambridge History of American Law* (Cambridge University Press, forthcoming). See also Michael Sherry, *In the Shadow of War: The United States Since the 1930s* (Yale University Press, 1997); Ira Katznelson and Martin Shefter, eds., *Shaped by War and Trade: International Influences on American Political Development* (Princeton University Press, 2002).

[37] See *United States v. Lopez*, 514 U.S. 549 (1995); *United States v. Morrison*, 529 U.S. 598 (2000); *Board of Trustees v. Garrett*, 531 U.S. 356 (2001). See also Robert C. Post and Reva B. Siegel, "Equal Protection by Law: Federal Antidiscrimination Legislation After *Morrison* and *Kimel*," 110 *Yale L. J.* 441 (2000); Vicki C. Jackson, "Federalism and the Court: Congress as the Audience?" 574 *Annals* 145 (2001); "Symposium: Shifting the Balance of Power? The Supreme Court, Federalism and State Sovereign Immunity," 53 *Stanford L. Rev.* 1115 (2001).

[38] 125 S. Ct. 2195 (2005).

Enterprise Institute, keeping the door open to broad federal regulatory power. For Mark Tushnet, however, *Raich* was "an easy case, a case at the heart of national regulatory authority," and hence the ruling "does not necessarily mean a retreat" from the Court's rulings limiting federal legislative power.[39] With the Court's trajectory uncertain, it is important to revisit the broader context underlying the Court's expansion of federal legislative power from the late 1930s through the 1960s, an era marked by concern over American world leadership and the impact of international affairs on American national security. During these years, the Court allowed Congress the powers it needed to address domestic questions that intersected with national security. A new century begun amidst new concerns about global affairs and domestic security would be an odd time for the Supreme Court to take Congressional power back to an era before world wars and global leadership had enmeshed "domestic" American affairs in those of the world.

[39] Linda Greenhouse, "The Rehnquist Court and its Imperiled States' Rights Legacy," *New York Times*, Late Ed., sec. 4, page 3, col. 1 (June 12, 2005).

CHAPTER 11

Sowing the Dragon's Teeth:[1] Materialization in Lesbian and Gay Anti-discrimination Rights

Jonathan Goldberg-Hiller

ABSTRACT

This chapter accounts for some of the political dynamics constituting the limits to public support for gay and lesbian anti-discrimination rights. Public ambivalence about these rights is revealed to "materialize" the legal subject at the same time that it constitutes the political body in ways that prevent the easy resolution of (sometimes imputed) rights demands. This materialization is explored within several tropes common to this public concern: the language of special rights, the suspicion of elites and the jurisprudence of wealth, and the rationality of the neoliberal marketplace.

INTRODUCTION

> "I oppose affirmative action. I think it divides us rather than joins us. I would oppose any effort to add sexual orientation as a protected class under the Federal affirmative action programs. That being said, I unequivocally oppose discrimination."
>
> Representative Thomas Bliley[2]

> "I am against discrimination. My support for the Defense of Marriage Act does not lessen in any way my commitment to fighting for fair treatment for gays and lesbians in the workplace."
>
> Senator Barbara Mikulski[3]

Public commitments such as these opposing discrimination against lesbians and gays are ironically entangled with the slow and painful development of

[1] The colorful phrase was spoken by Senator Robert Byrd in opposition to "the potential cost involved here" of failing to curtail the effects of same-sex marriage. Congressional Record (Senate, Wednesday, February 9, 1994 [Legislative day of Tuesday, January 25, 1994] 103rd Congress 2nd Session) 140 *Cong Rec* S 1250.

[2] Representative Thomas Bliley Congressional Record (Wednesday, August 5, 1998, 105th Congress, 2nd Session) 144 *Cong Rec* H 7250.

[3] Senator Barbara Mikulski, Congressional Record (Senate, Tuesday, September 10, 1996, 104th Congress 2nd Session) 142 *Cong Rec* S10115.

L. B. Nielsen and R. L. Nelson (eds.), Handbook of Employment Discrimination Research, 219–237.

anti-discrimination policy and jurisprudence. Local citizen action groups and the political referenda they often champion promise to "take back" Maryland or Vermont, "the schools," and "the culture" from "homosexuals," "liberals," and courts advocating rights advances, drawing the line at domestic partnership, same-sex marriage, and sometimes even taunting in the schools and employment nondiscrimination. At the national level, recent mobilizations behind the Defense of Marriage Act targeting same-sex marriage litigation, the Riggs Amendment opposing San Francisco's domestic partnership contract requirement, and the annual struggles against the proposed employment nondiscrimination act (ENDA), among others, have rhetorically valorized the national commitment to civil rights while proclaiming protections for lesbians and gays to be excessive, unnecessary, invasive, and unwarranted. To many opponents, rights protections for lesbians and gays go beyond defensible ideas of equal protection, forcing a choice "between civil and uncivil rights."[4]

The political fault-line running through these rights debates signals a changing legal culture. The implicit values of equality and nondiscrimination against which lesbian and gay identities and demands are assessed have displaced medicalized pathologies and dogmatic moralism, opening up the very possibility of rights claims. Parallel to these discursive changes, a growing social acceptance of gay and lesbian political demands has emerged. Strong public support for employment anti-discrimination protection is regularly voiced in opinion polls. Many employers have instituted benefits for same-sex partners, and unions increasingly bargain for these advances (Hunt, 1999; Santora, 2001). Cultural acknowledgement of gays and lesbians has become commonplace. Despite this growing liberalization—indeed, in its very enunciation—the public discourse of anti-discrimination frequently declares the limits to the acceptable. For nearly every voice supporting the propriety of nondiscrimination in employment, there is another raised against same-sex marriage,[5] and referenda on other civil rights issues—particularly regarding gays and lesbians—remains common, volatile, and limiting (Gamble, 1997; Wolfe, 1998, 77 pp. ff.). Public opposition to a broader rights agenda is articulated within this ambivalent sentiment: although discrimination is opposed and the democratic values of anti-discrimination extolled, some rights demands are seen as a hyper-extension of the law and a mockery of its authority.

This chapter seeks to account for some of the political dynamics constituting these limits to public support for gay and lesbian rights. I argue that discourse about gay and lesbian anti-discrimination rights works to "materialize" the legal subject at the same time that it constitutes the political body in ways that make it difficult to resolve these (often imputed) rights demands. This irresolution leaves no room for

[4] Testimony of the Hawai'i Catholic Conference against same-sex marriage, before the Hawai'i Senate Committee on the Judiciary, Honolulu, 22 February, 1996. Letter in possession of the author and in collected papers, University of Hawai'i.

[5] For example, the Harris Poll, 13 June 2001 finds 2 to 1 support for employment nondiscrimination that includes sexual orientation, from 61–20% to 58–29% depending on the specific questions asked. Referenda in Hawai'i and Alaska in 1998 showed 69% of voters opposed to same-sex marriage, a figure only slightly moderated in national polls since then.

preexisting natural political or social claims on which to base rights appeals, generating the contradictory commitments expressed in the epigraphs above.

I draw many of my ideas of materialization from Butler (1993) who has argued that bodies do not matter prior to their signification in language, but rather are articulated in "a process of materialization that stabilizes over time" (p. 9), a "performative" practice that "produces as an effect of its own procedure the very body that it nevertheless and simultaneously claims to discover as that which *precedes* its own action" (p. 30). The ontological certainty of bodies that seems to matter in some accounts of the appropriate legal subject for anti-discrimination law (e.g., are gays "made that way" and so deserving of protection or is this a "lifestyle choice" whose regulation escapes equal protection law?) is refigured in my materialist accounting as an epistemological investigation into what linguistic, rhetorical, and philosophical ideas constitute a subjectivity intelligible and sufficient for attention, denigration, protection, and assimilation. Lesbians and gays and their rights claims thus become a node at which multiple discourses about discrimination, identity and the community at large are worked and reworked until they appear natural, coherent, and politically assimilable, but never permanent. The continuing novelty of rights claims forms the ground around which such nodes gain their importance for the political understanding of discrimination law.

1. SUBJECTIVITY AND DISCRIMINATION

Recent debates over the extension of civil rights protection to new groups have been framed around a persistent asymmetry. Proponents of civil rights recognition have asked for rights as a hallmark of citizenship while claiming present laws to be inadequate; their opponents have argued that citizenship is not at stake, that new rights are redundant if not excessive, and consequently, the identities sought to be protected are artificial or misrepresented (Burlein, 2002; Cooper, 1998; Goldberg-Hiller, 2002; Goldberg-Hiller and Milner, 2003; Patton, 1995). "Post-civil-rights era" (Schacter, 1997) discourse has thus been marked both by challenges to the tactics and rhetoric of recognition as well as the boundaries of political bodies in which citizenship ought now inhere.

Mechanisms for establishing social identity and the related uncertain legal status of the gay and lesbian legal subject have engaged this discursive divide. *Romer v. Evans* (1996) implicitly overruled the denial of rights to privacy by which gays and lesbians were subjected in *Bowers v. Hardwick* (1986, formally repudiated in 2003). That earlier case cited the authority of a sovereign majority's historical, ethical, biblical, and natural "entitlement to hostility"[6] to homosexuality. Nonetheless, by finding that Colorado's discrimination against lesbians and gays merely fell short of a legal standard

[6] Justice Scalia's dissent in *Romer* upholding the *Bowers* standard used this very phrase. The various arguments in *Bowers v. Hardwick* for democratic antipathy to homosexuality outlined in the text can be found in the opinions of J. White and C.J. Burger.

of rationality, gays and lesbians have at most acquired from the *Romer* standard what one commentator has called "thin gay rights" (Massaro, 1996). Shed of criminal suspicion yet lacking suspect class standing, gays are left without clear legal identities, suspected of "deceptive" analogy to "authentic" civil rights subjects and burdened by the uncertain mapping of legal to social and political space.

This problematic cartography is further exacerbated by what Eskridge (2002, pp. 2266–2267) has recently called "the paradox of the tiers." Judicial scrutiny of acts against "discrete and insular minorities"[7] is stratified on the basis of three layered concerns: a rational relevance to public policy, the history of prejudice against the group, and the capacity of the political process to regulate these issues. It is this third problem of regulation that has emerged as a central paradox in the 20th century.

> During the period when a minority is truly marginalized politically because society accepts its defining trait as a malignant variation, its members would most benefit from a judicial corrective pluralism—but this is the period when the Court is least likely to respond to their political need. (2002, p. 2267)

Eskridge's paradox highlights the importance of legal culture for understanding anti-discrimination law but it misses, I think, the complex interactions between court and public that make legal culture even more ironic than he appreciates. In the case of civil rights for gays and lesbians, courts have increasingly played a vanguard role in the development of policy (e.g., despite its unavailability, same-sex marriage was in part created—legally and politically—by the Hawai'i Supreme Court). As a consequence, opposition to courts and law has become an integral aspect of cultural debates over social marginalization as well as "political need."

Social agency contributes to this political dynamic. The ethos of "coming out" (Blasius, 1992; Stychin, 1995, 143 pp. ff.) disrupts the settled contours of suburban and urban life, family and workplace, church and organization thereby challenging or "queering" the dominant social codes of nation, history, space, culture, and property (Berlant, 1997; Bravmann, 1997; Davies, 1999). As Patton (1997) has made clear, the queer strategy of boundary subversion is an infectious one. It has been mimicked, in particular, by some right-wing opponents of gay activism interested in supplanting "queer space" with "God's space" in an effort to reimagine the boundaries of community in distinctly religious terms.

Against deified boundaries, coming out is an act of personal courage with a risk of exposure; it is not the acknowledgment of a legal identity, but neither does it avoid

[7] This well-worn terminology is from Justice Stone who wondered in United States *v*. Carolene Products "whether prejudice against discrete and insular minorities may be a special condition, which tends seriously to curtail the operation of those political processes ordinarily to be relied upon to protect minorities, and which may call for a correspondingly more searching judicial inquiry" (304 U.S. 144, 152 [1938]). The determination of discrete and insular minorities has occupied scholars [e.g., Ely (1980)], the Court, and public opponents of civil rights since.

law. In a brilliant and important essay, Yoshino (2002) has recently argued that the norm of assimilation legally and culturally regulates coming out. Following the sociology of stigma first developed by Erving Goffman, Yoshino identifies three forms of assimilation: conversion in which gay identity is altered totally; passing in which identity is hidden and against which coming out asserts itself; and, finally, covering in which identity is acknowledged and even legitimated, but limits to its expression, place, time, and meaning are regulated in order to make it simple for others to "disattend [a] known stigmatized trait" (2002, p. 837). Law, in this account, plays a part in the regulation of identity (e.g., criminalizing sodomy, policing disclosure in the military), but it is an ancillary role. Stigma is modulated culturally and politically through silence, religious norms, political practices, and strategies of self-understanding.

Yoshino believes that covering "regimes" are becoming more common, and that gays and lesbians today face many more demands to limit behavioral expression rather than deny a "true" identity. Nonetheless, he insists that "one should not dismiss enforced covering as a trivial burden" (2002, p. 781). Regimes of assimilation do not simply terminate; while covering struggles may be more prominent than they once were, passing continues to be an important regulatory concern. Anti-discrimination jurisprudence, for example, continues to treat race, sex, age, and national origin as protected categories in some situations because it is difficult to pass on these social indicators. And as legal regimes move away from demands for conversion social problems can be magnified: "don't ask, don't tell" is not necessarily a better policy for uniformed gays; in some ways, it is worse because it burdens speech, self-disclosure, and other symbols of social identity while leaving animus in place (Halley, 1999; Yoshino, 2002, p. 833).

Yoshino's perspective raises important issues about the materialization of gay identity, and its political and legal consequences. Covering is problematic for Yoshino because of the type of burden it creates for the formation of the self. Rather than authenticate the truth claims underlying social identity propounded both by conversion and passing regimes—particularly, the idea that individuals exist *as* black or gay or female—covering regimes operate on the assumption that identities are best regulated symbolically. Because "acts of coming out can be sufficiently performative that one cannot burden acts of self-identification without simultaneously burdening the underlying status" (Yoshino, 2002, p. 833), requirements to cover nudge aside questions of ontology, in this case, the questions of essential identity that a "passing" jurisprudence demands. It is for this reason that analogies both found and confound anti-discrimination jurisprudence with questions such as whether same-sex marriage is like mixed-race marriage (Koppelman, 1988; Koppelman, 1994; Koppelman, 2001; Stein, 2001; Sunstein, 1994) and whether same-sex sexual taunting is like sexual harassment of women (Greenberg, 2002; Schwartz, 2002). I turn to a broader discussion of the main idiomatic organization of this discourse in the next section of the chapter.

2. SPECIAL RIGHTS AND THE MATERIALIZED SUBJECT

Opposition to the analogies that have yoked gay and lesbian nondiscrimination discourse to civil rights discourses have frequently targeted the ontological status of the gay and lesbian subject. Gays and lesbians have been depicted in socially inappropriate terms of disease and immorality in the United States, but by the 1990s this rhetoric stalled as it was increasingly alienating likely allies (Herman, 1997). While personal vilification of gays and lesbians continues in public discourse, the idiom of special rights is growing more common (Gerstmann, 1999, 99 pp. ff.; Goldberg, 1994; Keen and Goldberg, 1998). Special rights discourse has emerged as an important mechanism for regulating access to courts (thereby engaging Eskridge's "paradox of the tiers") and bolstering social demands for covering.

As Neal Milner and I (Goldberg-Hiller and Milner, 2003) have recently argued, special rights arguments are used to delegitimate some rights claims and the institutions, resources, identities, authorities and other meanings that undergird them, while calling upon another set of institutions, resources, identities, authorities, and meanings that are upheld as contrasting supports for "equal rights" or its equivalent. The tension between special rights and equal rights invokes a set of power dynamics with broad political and social consequences. "Most Americans believe that every human being has basic rights, and the American people stand for fairness, not for special breaks or special interests [for gays]."[8] As this public comment by Rep. Tom Delay's makes clear, to those who use the special rights idiom falls a double task: demonstrating that some subjects or their demands are unfit for inclusion or assimilation while showing that an "equal rights" space—citizenship more generally—is not in question.

Materialization reinforces both sides of this political equation by providing a normative metric against which fitness can be judged. Public discourse about gay and lesbian rights is not limited to issues of materialization, and other discourses provide arguments against civil rights and for an alternative equal rights space.[9] Nonetheless, materialization may organize other themes and so provide an important background against which to understand both the idiom of special rights, and the arguments against the authority of courts. In the discussion that follows, I choose two organizing themes that run through discourses of materialization. In the first, I examine issues of wealth and class used to materialize lesbians and gays as "special." I next turn to the ways in

[8] Congressional Record (House, August 5, 1998, 105th Congress, 2nd Session) 144 *Cong Rec* H7257.

[9] Numerous issues have been identified that infuse anti-gay rights sentiment. Hull (2001) has argued that tolerance and acceptance provide alternatives to a rights discourse in her study of Hawai'i's same-sex marriage case. Creed, Scully, and Austin (2002) identify four primary frames in the debates on ENDA: (1) Civil Rights, not special rights; (2) basic employment fairness/level playing field; (3) simple remedy; and (4)enlightened companies' competitive advantage. I argue in this chapter that many aspects of these frames are more highly integrated than they are presented in Creed et al.'s work (e.g., "basic employment fairness" (2) has much to do with "competitive advantage" (4)). Nonetheless, this supports the argument that economic issues are important aspects of these civil rights debates.

which society is materialized into a "body politic" regulated by "equal rights" norms through the articulation of economic processes and by the abjection of the gay and lesbian legal subject.

3. GAYS, JEWS AND OTHER ELITES

While the materialization of sexual "minorities" may find a more potent legal limit in the exclusion of transgendered individuals from anti-discrimination protection (Currah and Minter, 2000; Flynn, 2001), wealth comparisons provide an insidious and pervasive rhetorical wash that highlights the excess underlying special rights claims. From disputes over same-sex marriage, domestic partnership, and employment discrimination, gays, and less frequently lesbians, are often portrayed as rich, privileged, and socially aloof. Gays are "a special interest lobby—not a disadvantaged group that needs to be protected from bias and hatred,"[10] "a powerful, well-funded lobby, an interest group that believes that non-job-related behavior should be the deciding factor in hiring or promotion policies in our Government."[11]

> The true test of discrimination is economic hardship and lack of cultural opportunity the direct result of the lack of equal access to social and cultural institutions. In fact, [gays] more aptly represent the privileged strata of society with a higher than average level of education, 59.6% vs. 18% are college graduates, 49% vs. 15.9% holding professional or managerial positions with an average income of $55,430 versus $12,166 for African-Americans and $32,144 for the rest of the population.... They are not merely asking for their civil rights instead what they are really seeking are special privileges for their sexual preference.[12]

The language of gay wealth and intimations of its illegitimate deployment has its genealogy in anti-Semitic narratives that exercised post-War Christian-right movements (see Burlein, 2002, 39 pp. ff; Herman, 1997, esp. 125 pp. ff.). This cultural legacy certainly seems stronger than empirical evidence that casts doubt on claims about the exceptional material wealth of gays and lesbians (Allegretto and Arthur, 2001; Berg and Lien, 2002; Hutchinson, 2000, pp. 1373–1374). The ascription of wealth and power to gays, as it once was to Jews, materializes the gay body as privileged and, in light of discourses of moral approbation, duplicitous as an explanation for their economic reward. This materialization helps legitimate sentiments that gays and lesbians are motivated by questionable ends and undeserving of political or legal reward. As Senator Louch Faircloth illustrated in affirming the Defense of Marriage

[10] Written testimony of Carol Arnold, House Judiciary Committee Hearings on Same-sex Marriage, 20 October, 1993, Honolulu.

[11] Representative Joseph Pitts, Congressional Record (House, Wednesday, August 5, 1998, 105th Congress, 2nd Session) 144 *Cong Rec* H 7258.

[12] Written testimony of the Christian Coalition, House Judiciary Committee Hearings on same-sex marriage, 22 October 1993, Honolulu.

Act, same-sex love is handily replaced by economic motivations to castigate rights claims.

> Marriage most certainly should not be just another means of securing government benefits. Yet this is one of the arguments that proponents of same-sex marriage use to justify this unprecedented social experiment. They claim that laws restricting marriage to persons of the opposite sex are discriminatory in part because, after all, same-sex partners are not entitled to health and other benefits extended to dependent spouses. I can think of few worse reasons for getting married.[13]

I return to this theme of misplaced rationality below. What I wish to note here is that the construction of lesbians and gays as an economic lobby plays somewhat eerily against democratic theory. The market and the public have always engaged a delicate dance in American democracy (Lindblom, 1977; Lindblom, 2001). Madison saw economic interest as the primary cause of faction and Theodore Roosevelt decried the "malefactors of great wealth." Despite this unease, languages of class rarely have been able to draw a coherent bead on systemic mechanisms of inequality (Reinarman, 1987; Vanneman and Cannon, 1987). In the contemporary context of massive and growing social inequality, it has been more politically useful, as Phillips (2002, p. xiii) has recently argued, to indiscriminately "attack privileges, malefactors, elites, and corruption." When these targets include gay and lesbian rights-seekers, courts and judges that have occasionally been their institutional allies are easily swept along in the rising tide of opprobrium, isolating civil rights from democratic process. As Senator Don Nickles cogently expressed this in debate over DOMA, "the [legal] strategy of those who are advocating same-sex unions is profoundly undemocratic."[14]

The rhetorical barrier between democracy and courts energized by images of illicit gay wealth creates an ambivalence in the assessment of gay power. On the one hand, gays are seen to have undue influence over courts and judges who are sometimes depicted in public hearings as institutionally tyrannical.[15] This power often leaks beyond the formal confines of law into political influence; famously, Justice Scalia's dissent in *Romer v. Evans* excoriated "the efforts of a politically powerful minority to revise [sexual] mores through use of the laws."[16] On the other hand, while politics

[13] Congressional Record (Senate; 104th Congress 2nd Session), Tuesday, September 10, 1996, 142 *Cong Rec* S10117. Similarly, in the Hawai'i same-sex marriage case, eight Hawai'i legislators argued in an amicus brief to that state's Court, "If the State of Hawai'i permits same-sex couples to marry, marriage will be reduced to an entity formed by persons wishing to exploit its tax advantages and other benefits." Post-trial brief, *Baehr v. Miike*, 1996, filed by Representatives Abinsay, Kahikina, Kanoho, Meyer, Stegmaier, Swain, Cachola, Ward, p. 9.

[14] Senator Nickles, Congressional Record (Senate, Tuesday, September 10, 1996; 104th Congress 2nd Session) 142 *Cong Rec S*10103.

[15] Consider the pleas of Representative Terrance Tom of Hawai'i to limit judges such as those in Hawai'i who approved same-sex marriage raised in his testimony before the Senate Committee debating DOMA. "No single individual, no matter how wise or learned in the law, should be invested with the power to overturn fundamental social policies against the will of the people." Congressional Record (Senate, 104th Congress 2nd Session), Tuesday, May 15, 1996, Subcommittee on the Constitution.

[16] 517 U.S. 620 at 636 (1996).

provides "a demonstration of [gay] power, not powerlessness,"[17] gays are merely "loud" and the "vast majority of Americans reject their extremism"[18] and would do so given the opportunity to adequately mobilize. In this alternative view, gay power is a threat to deliberative democratic bodies who must—and can—organize in order to oppose antagonistic civil rights.

A democracy shorn of courts and civil rights demands new forms of governance in which law plays a less central role (Foucault, 1991; Rose, 1987; Rose, 1996; Rose and Miller, 1992). Cooper calls this type of organization of power "governance at a distance" because it relies upon "guiding the actions of subjects through the production of expertise and normative inculcation so that they govern themselves" (1998, p. 12), a contrast with more historical forms of direct governance "in which the parties to the relationship are clearly visible" (p. 13). Anti-discrimination law primarily seeks to remedy social marginalization with direct governance, strengthening visible relationships through "recognition" by courts and legislative bodies.

Governance at a distance, as anti-gay rights discourse often advocates, has two consequences for democratic theory. The first is a reconfiguration of sovereignty no longer based around a central notion of universal law.[19] Civil rights are not eliminated in this account, but reemerge in an inverted fashion through the depiction of a victimized and innocent majority requiring protection from inappropriate gay economic and political power and its judicial consorts. "I am getting tired of hearing about how homosexuals are so oppressed. In reality, it is the other way around."[20] "It almost seems that we're [straights are] being harassed."[21] As a conservative litigation strategist opposed to same-sex marriage frames the problem, gays, lesbians, and courts have taken unfair advantage of public decency.

> Same-sex marriage advocates have thus far been successful in their quest for the higher ground, while marriage advocates have apparently conceded much of the fight due to the unpleasantness of the subject matter. Same-sex advocates have . . . ma[d]e resistance to a radical homosexual agenda tantamount to bigotry. Gay marriage may seem wrong, but in the new scale of things there seems something harsh or tacky about the people who would argue about the matter in public. And so the political matrix: The judges advance the interests of gay rights at every turn, and those who resist them are labeled as the fanatics. (Schowengerdt, 2001/2002, p. 489)

[17] The words are those of Judge H. Jeffrey Bayless in *Evans v. Romer* (Denver District Court, unofficial transcript), December 14, 1993. Judge Bayless ruled in that opinion that Amendment 2 to the Colorado Constitution was unconstitutional.

[18] Testimony of Deborah Whyman, Michigan State Representative, Congressional Record (Senate, 104th Congress 2nd Session), Tuesday, May 15, 1996, Subcommittee on the Constitution.

[19] Consider this dicta from *Boddie v. Connecticut* (401 US 371 [1971]) (J. Harlan) "American society, of course, bottoms its systematic definition of individual rights and duties, as well as its machinery for dispute settlement, not on custom or the will of strategically placed individuals, but on the common-law model. It is to courts, or other quasi-judicial official bodies, that we ultimately look for the implementation of a regularized, orderly process of dispute settlement" (p. 375).

[20] Letter of Vanessa Birang, to the Editor, Honolulu *Star Bulletin*, Wednesday, January 4, 2001. Responding to Board of Education policy change to protect gay and lesbian students from harassment.

[21] Jeff Rezents, O‘ahu at large candidate for Board of Education, quoted in Honolulu *Star Bulletin*, 2 November, 2000.

In some cases, public innocence is reinforced through rhetoric that likens unwelcome demands for civil rights to rape:

> I believe that a small minority of homosexual marriage advocates are trying to force their values down the throats of the people of Hawai'i. I do not think that they're evil. I think they have an agenda.... And anyone who disagrees with them is labeled a homophobe, or is labeled a gay basher.[22]

By rhetorically reversing the public into a victimized minority, the identities and rights demands of lesbians and gays are obscured. The failure of courts to protect "real" victims of gay rights abuse permits the sovereign community to be reimagined without direct governance. Yet, pushing rights away paradoxically tends to recenter law through new ideas about political sovereignty: Congress, state legislatures, but especially churches, families, and voters now become the guardians of the people's rights.

The accusation that gays and lesbians terrorize the majority through a straitjacket of hate speech—the transmogrification of "homophobe" and "gay basher" into the equivalent of verbal assault—sets the ground for accusations of gay and lesbian deception. Advertisements in Hawai'i that opposed same-sex marriage during the campaign for an amendment to derail the marriage case made this clear by opposing "common sense" to "civil rights." One read, "Why are the same-sex marriage people playing 'Hide and Seek' with the issue? They hide behind civil rights while the people of Hawai'i seek only the truth—the real, common-sense issue that asks if we should preserve marriage between one man and one woman." Another, reproduced as figure 1, states "In most political campaigns, it's considered a bad thing to mention the opposition. But in this case the opposition is the bad thing. They're trying to deceive you." These accusations implicate the republican virtue of transparency in which citizens should seem to be in their public manifestations as they live in private (Berlant, 1997). In this discourse, civil rights reinforce duplicity while common sense substantiates the norms of democratic reason.

In a covering regime, management of speech and silence is an essential means of regulating the materialization of the subject. Yoshino (2002, p. 865) has suggested that some proscriptive demands to cover offensive acts or speech might be so "constitutive" of identity that they burden as much as demands to convert. Yoshino identifies sodomy as one, and same-sex marriage conjures for many uncomfortable public acknowledgement of a better-left-private sexual relationship. Interestingly, nearly all the briefs by conservative groups submitted in *Lawrence v. Texas* (2003) advocated the explicit destruction of *Bowers* in order to restore privacy rights. The abandonment of *Bowers* by conservatives—and now the Supreme Court—does not necessarily contravene other rhetoric opposing lesbian and gay rights. It signals, instead, the movement from the direct governance of courts to the local authority of emergent anti-gay rights majorities and governance at a distance.

Rather than the direct governance framework of 14th amendment law, gay rights are repositioned through these developments onto the terrain of 1st Amendment

[22] Mike Gabbard, President, Alliance for Traditional Marriage, speaking at a public forum on same-sex marriage, 20 October, 1998, Honolulu, Hawai'i. Transcript by the author.

Figure 1. Advertisement supporting a constitutional amendment to derail the Hawai'i same-sex marriage case. *Source:* Honolulu Advertiser, 30 September, 1998, p. A11.

free speech and religious free exercise.[23] Same-sex marriage, employment anti-discrimination protections, and gay-inclusive school programs can be—and are—opposed as "promoting homosexuality." "It has been clear from the beginning," testified one witness opposed to a school anti-harassment policy in Honolulu, "that homosexual activists intend to utilize the harassment policy as a vehicle to relentlessly promote homosexuality under the guise of diversity training, sexual awareness, and other strategies."[24] "No promo homo" efforts to limit anti-discrimination law are depicted to restore equal speech rights; discrimination becomes little more than the effects of unfair speech opportunities due to gays' material advantages, a "sneak-attack on society by encoding this aberrant behavior in legal form before society itself has decided it should be legal" as Senator Robert Byrd has called it.[25] The substitution of an equal right to debate for an equal right to protection redraws a level playing field and justifies affirmative action for straights (e.g., the promotion of "traditional"

[23] Even Vermont's Civil Union legislation has an opt-out clause for the state clerks responsible for recording these unions designed to preserve their rights to conscience. As the Vermont Supreme Court recognized, "the civil union law itself provides the means of avoiding any potential free exercise burden on town clerks, by expressly providing that "an assistant town clerk may perform the duties of a town clerk under this chapter." 18 V.S.A. @ 5161(b). Thus, the law itself offers an 'accommodation' for town clerks with religious reservations about issuing a civil union license." *Brady v Dean*, 790 A.2d 428, 434–435 (2001).

[24] Written testimony of Jim Titcomb, attachment to the minutes of the Hawai'i State Board of Education, 24 January 2002.

[25] Senator Byrd, Congressional Record (Senate, Tuesday, September 10, 1966; 104th Congress 2nd Session) 142 *Cong Rec S*10110.

marriage which is now under consideration in amendments to reauthorize the 1996 welfare reform law, Temporary Assistance to Needy Families[26]) under the rhetoric of appropriate self-defense and norms of fair play.

The viability of an "equal right" playing field on which gays and lesbians must prove their case is itself dependent on chains of analogies that are fundamentally disrupted by the association of gays with material wealth and power (Eskridge, 2002; Richards, 1999). For example, the analogies of contemporary struggles for same-sex marriage to the *Loving* (1967) opinion ending proscriptions against cross-race marriage has been a critical aspect of legal (e.g., *Baehr v. Lewin*), popular and scholarly debate (Koppelman, 1988; Koppelman, 2001; Stein, 2001). In addition, same-sex harassment doctrine depends on the understanding that discrimination against gays is a consequence of sex discrimination. Hutchinson (2000, pp. 1372–1375; 2001, p. 297) has noted that special rights discourse racializes gay privilege in three ways: through the explicit comparison of gays and lesbians and "people of color;" through the uncritical reliance on evidence of White lesbians and gays as exemplars of all; and by disaggregating racial subjugation from heterosexism. These mechanisms can be seen at work in figure 1, though with a particular island flavor. The juxtaposed images of one dark-skinned heterosexual couple wearing lei and one white skinned gay couple in mainland formal attire align sovereign boundaries with ethnic relations as a post-colonial reminder that same-sex marriage is likely the next assault on local dignity and values. The two White men exude wealth, their tuxedos radiate neocolonial authority; they are relatively too powerful, rich, and successful to need civil rights protection or to legitimately demand it as outsiders from an island community proud of local ways. Race, in this context, denies the possibility of covering; as race is considered immutable, it signifies at a naturalized, ontological level that gays and lesbians cannot reach nor easily illuminate with recourse to speech and debate.

The effects of this racialization impugn more than the civil rights analogy marriage advocates were advancing. They also transform local cultural contexts, limiting the ways in which "common sense" can be effectively deployed. In Hawai'i, for example, it is common sense for many local families to openly embrace their gay relatives and acknowledge their membership in the 'ohana [extended family]. Nonetheless, as one Native Hawaiian lesbian activist explained to me, the campaign against same-sex marriage alienated these forms of familial self-understanding.

> Gay is constructed as white, and the campaign looked so white. I think the idea [that] gay equals male, equals white, equals middle class . . . is a problem for a lot of our families here. This is the thing that keeps repeating over and over again in my work with gay men of color: our families think that we are white. You know, you can't think you are a lesbian and not be white. So you are either a betrayal to your race or you are an oreo or you are doing something weird. But you are not what we know to be our daughter.[27]

[26] See debates over *H.R. 4737*, the Personal Responsibility, Work, and Family Promotion Act, 2002; *Caring for Children Act of 2002, Promotion and Support of Responsible Fatherhood and Healthy Marriage Act of 2002.*

[27] Author's interview with Val Kanuha, 10 November, 1999.

The grounds on which the misrecognition of one's daughter is enabled fuses whiteness with this equation to maleness, to middle class, to outsider, to threat.

Certainly, wealth has long been a discursively uncomfortable attribute in public discourse; think, for instance, of President Bush II's charges of "class warfare" against those who have dared to point out the lopsided class benefits of proposed tax cuts. Likewise, the Supreme Court has only infrequently addressed the meaning of wealth for anti-discrimination law, but when it has, it has voiced ambivalence: on the one hand, proclaiming that "wealth, like race, creed, or color [should not be] germane to one's ability to participate intelligently in the electoral process"[28] while, on the other, resuscitating Anatole France's famous ironic quip[29] to acknowledge "a State need not equalize economic conditions.... Those are contingencies of life which are hardly within the power, let alone the duty, of a State to correct or cushion."[30] Discrimination against the poor, like discrimination against gays and lesbians, must only pass a rationality test to be constitutionally acceptable. The power that wealth asserts above and beyond the individualism of one man, one vote, is rarely a matter for equal protection nor is it constitutionally remarkable. The cocoon of silence swaddling the issues of wealth and economic inequality is broken most pointedly by materialized bodies that become metonyms of inappropriate citizenship and displacement for inchoate anger and anxiety over limited economic and social achievement.

4. MATERIALIZATION AND THE BODY POLITIC

Gay and lesbian bodies are caricatured as illegitimately and inappropriately raced, gendered, and wealthy, and so undeserving of civil rights. In implicating the place of courts and the limits of legal discourse, claims of the excesses of rights construct the gay legal subject at the same time as they transform the body politic. Foucault, in his narrative of modernity, has characterized the eclipse of liberal ideas of inherent rights as a rise of the *social*: discourses comprising what he has termed a governmentality inclusive of, but extending beyond, the boundaries of legality and sovereignty (Barry, Osborne, and Rose, 1996; Foucault, Burchell, Gordon, and Miller, 1991). Within the social discourses of governmentality, ideals of autonomy, rationality, and the like are frequently evaluated not as ends in themselves, but as specific values promoting identifiable social interests. It is for this reason that the association of civil rights discourse with citizenship and inclusion in the sovereign community is never far removed from the specific social rationales for inclusion.

Boyd (1996, 1999) has argued that the Canadian legal acceptance of the equal status of same-sex spouses finally achieved in 1999 followed just this Foucaultian

[28] *Harper v. Virginia* at 383 U.S. 663, 668 (1966).

[29] "The law, in its majestic equality, forbids the rich as well as the poor to sleep under bridges, to beg in the streets, and to steal bread." See *Griffin v. Illinois* 351 US 12, 23 (1956), J. Frankfurter, Concurring.

[30] *Ibid.* See also *San Antonio Indep. Sch. Dist. v. Rodriguez, 411 U.S. 1 (1973)* [wealth is an unwieldy mode of equal protection analysis].

strategic path. Rather than resonating as a claim for political equality or the rights to equal employment benefits, spousal benefits in Canada were "privatized" within the family by powerful materialist discourses. Same-sex spousal recognition was legitimated by its function of "alleviating the burden on the public purse to provide for dependent spouses," a "pressing and substantial" objective.[31] In the context of globalized neoliberalism in which social rights are increasingly depicted as competitive disadvantage, the economics of the public purse become all the more compelling, explaining, in part, contemporary reticence to imagine the equalization of economic opportunity or outcome. As Ertman (2001) points out, privatization and the implicit norms of a business model already infuse many aspects of family law in the United States.[32]

Rather than legitimating the status of same-sex spouses in this country, however, this economic frame further agitates opposition to such issues as same-sex marriage through fears of runaway costs and their consequences. As Senator Phil Gramm illustrated in the debates over DOMA:

> when compared to the power of the family as the foundation of our civilization and our culture, dollars and cents—in this context—are not terribly important. But, as a secondary issue, they are important, and let me explain where. A failure to pass this bill . . . will create . . . a whole group of new beneficiaries—no one knows what the number would be—tens of thousands, hundreds of thousands, potentially more—who will be beneficiaries of newly created survivor benefits under Social Security, Federal retirement plans, and military retirement plans. . . . It will impose through teacher retirement plans, State retirement plans, State medical plans, and even railroad retirement plans—a whole new set of benefits and expenses which have not been planned or budgeted for under current law.[33]

This slippery slope parallels and amplifies claims about gays' lack of reason, the impossibility of their sexual "continence," and the perversity of the powerful and economically advantaged asking for rights, all of which signal a violation of republican restraint incumbent upon proper citizens.

The state of Hawai'i put the economic cost of same-sex civil rights in the frame of another common budgeting idiom, a zero-sum accounting: "every dollar spent on a same-sex couple, or a cohabiting couple, of necessity strips a dollar from the State's ability to assist married couples."[34] Vermont likewise saw terrible consequences from the secondary effects of same-sex marriage that would diminish rights for others. Citing the likelihood that increased surrogacy contracts from same-sex couples desiring children would have an "obvious" impact "on the resources of the court system from

[31] *M. v. H.*, 171 D.L.R. (4th) 577 (1999), Cory, J., at para. 106. The phrase "public purse" used in this very manner appears more than a dozen times throughout the opinions.

[32] "Family law doctrine increasingly favors private ordering in matters such as entry into marriage, contractual ordering of marriage, nonmarital relationships, divorce, adoption, the use of reproductive technologies, and the privatization of domestic relations dispute resolution."

[33] Senator Phil Graham, Congressional Record (Senate, Tuesday, September 10, 1996; 104th Congress, 2nd Session) 142 *Cong Rec S*10106.

[34] State's legal brief, *Baehr v. Miike*, 1996, p. 34.

increased litigation," it concluded that "the Legislature could rationally decide to avoid these issues and costs by denying marriage to same-sex couples."[35] The civil union statute that has replaced marriage does entail costs, but by avoiding any federal status, it has fewer federal tax implications.

Tropes of economic scarcity and the political inability to contain fiscal demands have painted a boundary line against same-sex marriage in the United States. Economic arguments also affect other rights arguments, though ambivalently. One the one hand, corporations have increasingly come to view cultural prescriptions to cover and domestic partnership benefits designed to equalize benefit packages through the lens of good business practice; ignoring these changes can act "as a roadblock to retention, productivity, and a good public image that could enhance business."[36] Sentiments such as these go a long way to explaining why many corporations have complied with local and state-wide domestic partnership legislation.

On the other hand, when harassment and domestic partnership are identified as contributions to the bottom line, they become more resistant to being seen as "rights" which discursively remain costly and inefficient. In Hawai'i, for example, six large corporations fought the state's pioneering domestic partnership law in 1997, arguing successfully that the requirement to pay health care costs for registered same-sex partners was estopped by ERISA and other federal statutes.[37] Months later, three of the successful plaintiffs granted the same benefits to their employees, one explaining that "It's not a political issue; it's a business decision."[38] The 9th Circuit found the same to be true of those airlines challenging San Francisco's Equal Benefits Ordinance[39] that requires firms holding contracts with the city to pledge nondiscrimination in the securing of benefits. Many airlines had begun to extend domestic partnership benefits at the time they were appealing, a fact the court took to indicate that the economic burden of rights was inconsequential though not argumentatively irrelevant.[40] Politically, these

[35] State of Vermont Defendant's Brief, *Baker v. Vermont*, 1998.

[36] *Restaurant Business*, January 15, 2000, p. 32.

[37] Employee Retirement Income Security Act of 1974, (ERISA) 29. U.S.C.S. §1144. This has been a common and successful argument against domestic partnership legislation, especially where there has been no will political will for state's to request an exemption that is legal under the law. See the discussion of the Hawai'i case in Goldberg-Hiller (2002, ch 4), and Griffen (2001), Sherman (2001), and Turner (2002).

[38] "A Quiet Revolution," Honolulu *Star Bulletin,* 8 May, 1998, p. A1.

[39] Section 12B.2(b) of the Administrative Code of San Francisco. That code reads, in part, No contracting agency of the City, or any department thereof, acting for or on behalf of the City and County, shall execute or amend any contract or property contract with any contractor that discriminates in the provision of bereavement leave, family medical leave, health benefits, membership or membership discounts, moving expenses, pension and retirement benefits or travel benefits as well as any [other] benefits ... between employees with domestic partners and employees with spouses, and/or between the domestic partners and spouses of such employees, where the domestic partnership has been registered with a governmental entity pursuant to state or local law authorizing such registration ...

[40] *ATA v. San Francisco* 266 F.3d 1064, 1074 (2001). The court wrote, "Hypothetically, there might be some contract term the City could demand whose costs would be so high that it would compel the Airlines

arguments had more weight in the congressional challenge to the Ordinance that passed the House in 1998.[41] Rep. Frank Riggs who initiated the challenge saw it as an "unwarranted intrusion into the private sector" that would jeopardize contracts, disrupt funding for the homeless, and trip the avalanche that would bury the moral barriers against same-sex marriage.[42]

As Boyd's argument about Canada makes clear, marketplace analogies can also be turned toward the legitimation of some rights. Rep. Patrick Kennedy during the Riggs Amendment debates, for instance, argued, "[T]he marketplace dictates that [domestic partnership benefits] be provided. Do my colleagues know why? In order to get the best people.... The City of San Francisco should be no different from these private corporations."[43] The burden of having to make rights arguments compatible with market logic, however, is an encumbrance unlike that imposed historically on other rights claimants where the certainty of inalienable rights dissolve in the volatile whims of Wall Street.

If arguments against domestic partnership show the slide from equal protection under the purview of courts to a market-enforced economic protection, they also review a subtle shift toward indirect governance in the movement from 14th amendment jurisprudence to 1st amendment and privacy law. Rep. Riggs at times justified his legislation against the San Francisco ordinance as protection for groups like the Salvation Army who would be forced to comply with laws at odds with their "long-standing philosophical understanding,"[44] depicting them as victims of religious discrimination. Churches and religious agencies should be free, in this account, to provide social goods without legal interference. Privacy and free speech law have also been argued against the perennial debates over the never-successful ENDA. As Senator Don Nickles has argued,

> How is an employer to defend himself or herself [from claims arising under ENDA]?.... They have to show they have employed homosexuals and bisexuals. How do they show that? They have to ask questions.... They are going to have to ask people....: "What is your sexual orientation? Are you homosexual, are you bisexual, are you heterosexual," in order to defend themselves.[45]

to change their prices, routes or services.... Cf. *Travelers Ins., 514 U.S. at 655* (stating in dictum that there may be a point at which costs from a state law are so exorbitant that it could rise to the level of a substantive mandate). The nondiscrimination provisions at issue here, however, do not approach that level."

[41] The Riggs Amendment passed the House of Representatives 214–212 on July 29, 1998. It was not taken up by the Senate.

[42] Congressional Record (House, Wednesday, July 29, 1998, 105th Congress, 2nd Session) 144 *Cong Rec* H6582.

[43] Congressional Record, 1998 July, H6581–H6584.

[44] Rep. Riggs' spokesman, Beau Phillips, quoted in the San Francisco *Chronicle* 31 July, 1998, p A21.

[45] Congressional Record (Senate, 104th Congress 2nd Session, Monday, September 9, 1996) 142 *Cong Rec*S10066.

This demand for speech is not just another form of government victimization of others at the hands of gay activists; it is also unnecessary oversight of ennobled intentions, an intrusion of direct governance when distance will satisfy.

The intrusion of equal protection jurisprudence into a homeostasis of self-regulating enlightened practices explains away the need for anti-discrimination protection. The reliance upon the myriad social forms of governance at a distance nonetheless provides a reliable, fractal coherence around which the body politic can be imagined. Foucault calls this a form of *counter-memory*, "a transformation of history into a totally different form of time," "a parody" that takes identity as real and power as a fiction (Foucault, 1977, 160 pp. ff.). The temporality of this counter-memory is perhaps most easily revealed in the conservative commitment to "traditional" marriage that compresses the historical variability of legal relations (e.g., coverture, divorce), the widely assorted human motivations of spouses, and the vast diversity of sexual expression inside and outside heterosexual marriage into a singular norm that signifies a majoritarian identity even where the referent itself has dwindled to a numerical minority (Nicholson, 1997; Shapiro, 2001; Stacey, 1996). The rhetorical power of "traditional marriage" has been particularly ironic in Hawai'i where the historical acceptance of same-sex relationships is 1,500 years older than the proscriptions of Western law (Kame 'eleihiwa, 1992; Merry, 2000; Morris, 1996). This counter-memory extends beyond issues of marriage as it more generally reinforces a zero-sum articulation of a rights economy in which anti-discrimination law is now commonly attacked. That is because the invocation of tradition is rhetorically singular and its disparagement is invoked with every acknowledgment of exception. As Bauman (1996, p. 50) suggests, "the insecurity of speakers is the true subject matter of the discourse whose ostensible topic is the security of tradition." Insecurity is reinforced by the dissonance of the discourse of equality emblazoned on the decaying welfare state for it "re-casts the 'being for others', that cornerstone of all morality, as a matter of accounts and calculation, of value for money, of gains and costs, of luxury one can or cannot permit" (Ibid., p. 56).

5. CONCLUSION

Discourses arrayed against extending anti-discrimination machinery to lesbians and gays envision the site of law not in a courthouse nor in a legislature, but rather in a new center of popular authority. This sovereign is a point of enunciation for "equal rights" affirmed through discourse governing the bodies, aims, and places of lesbians and gays who metaphorize the "special rights" excesses of anti-discrimination law. While the laws of anti-discrimination are complex and overlapping, the materialization of lesbians and gays gives their detractors a coherence as it simultaneously provides a concern that energizes the limits of anti-discrimination protections, materializing bodies as the limits of the law.

CHAPTER 12

Rights or Quotas? The ADA as a Model for Disability Rights

Katharina Heyer

ABSTRACT

The 1990 Americans with Disabilities Act is considered a model of a new civil rights approach to disability discrimination. In contrast to traditional approaches to disability policy that respond to disability difference with separate welfare institutions, the ADA mandates equal opportunities, integration, and reasonable accommodations. This chapter analyzes the impact of the ADA as a model for two countries deeply embedded in the welfare approach: Germany and Japan. It illustrates the ways that the ADA has inspired German and Japanese disability activists to mobilize for the passage of similar antidiscrimination legislation and to reform existing disability policy. When it comes to disability employment policy, however, German and Japanese activists and policy makers tend to reject the ADA's equal opportunity mandate in favor of strengthening the disability employment quota. The chapter analyzes the resilience of the disability employment quota in light of cultural, constitutional, and labor marked differences. The chapter suggests that the injection of American–style disability rights discourse into two countries with positive employment rights poses important questions about the transformation of the rights model in different sociopolitical settings, and the ways this transformation may reflect alternative approaches to defining disability, discrimination, and employment rights.

INTRODUCTION: THE ADA ON THE ROAD

When Congress passed the Americans with Disabilities Act (ADA), the world's first comprehensive disability anti-discrimination legislation, disability activists around the globe celebrated a victory along with their American colleagues. Since its inception in 1990, the ADA has become a model of rights-based disability policy, recognizing people with disabilities as a minority group with a history of oppression. In contrast to traditional policy approaches to disability, which focus on institutionalization, compensation, and rehabilitation, the ADA interprets disability discrimination as a civil rights issue and mandates equal opportunities and reasonable accommodations for disability difference. As such, the ADA civil rights model has influenced disability law and activism in numerous countries across the globe. It has inspired similar anti-discrimination legislation in English-language common law countries and has

L. B. Nielsen and R. L. Nelson (eds.), Handbook of Employment Discrimination Research, 237–259.

been incorporated into United Nations and European Union Directives on disability discrimination.

This chapter examines the role of the ADA as an international model of disability rights. It looks at the ways that American legal and political approaches to remedy disability discrimination have become an increasingly popular model, commonly termed a rights model, that stands in direct contrast to a more traditional social welfare model. The chapter follows the movement of the U.S.-based disability rights model to two countries that are deeply embedded in the welfare model: Japan and Germany. It asks what happens when the ADA travels to countries with radically different approaches to disability policy, equal treatment, and the role of the state as a provider of welfare rights.

I chose Germany and Japan as my case studies for their prominence in the traditional welfare approach to disability politics. Both countries are considered leaders in Europe and Asia regarding their political commitment to maintaining an extensive but segregated disability welfare state, symbolized most prominently by disability employment quotas. For the purposes of this volume's emphasis on employment discrimination, these two countries provide a perfect scenario to examine the tensions between the rights model, which in the employment arena mandates equal employment opportunity, and the welfare model, which responds to employment discrimination by mandating quotas.

The passage of the ADA as the world's first comprehensive disability anti-discrimination law as well as the political mobilizing of the American disability rights movement have had a tremendous impact on countries across the globe. German and Japanese activists traveled in large groups to the United States to learn about disability activism from their American peers. For the first time, the rights model was considered a policy alternative. The German movement successfully mobilized around the passage of constitutional and civil equality mandates, whereas their Japanese counterparts worked toward laying the groundwork for initial legal reforms and increased rights consciousness. In both cases, however, the movement toward a rights model did not include the abolishment of the disability employment quota.

This is the central question I seek to address in this chapter: why does the road to disability rights in Japan and Germany not lead to the rejection of the traditional employment quota when in all other areas of disability activism such as independent living, equal access, and even education the rights model has almost universally replaced the welfare model? I will attempt to explain the resilience of the employment quota in light of cultural as well as constitutional and labor market differences.

This inquiry focuses on a familiar and well-theorized tension between two different approaches to non-discrimination and equal treatment (rights or quotas? equal rights or special needs? equal treatment or different treatment?), but it locates this tension in a comparative, non-American setting that disrupts common assumptions about the meaning of equality and difference and their implication for state policy. I argue that the injection of American-style disability rights discourse into two countries with positive employment rights poses important questions about the transformation of the rights model in different sociopolitical settings, and the ways this transformation may reflect alternative approaches to defining disability, discrimination, and employment rights.

I begin my analysis with an overview of different theoretical models for legislating disability rights: a social welfare model prominent in most civil law countries and originating in Western Europe, and a civil rights model prominent in most common law countries and originating in the United States. I introduce the German and Japanese employment quota systems as examples of the social welfare model in practice, and then examine the impact of international influences on German and Japanese disability activism: the United Nations Decade for the Disabled and the passage of the ADA. The rights model in Japan and Germany inspired a new generation of disability activists and initiated policy reforms. In both cases, however, the "paradigm shift" toward a rights model did not include the abolishment of the disability employment quota. I seek to explain the resilience of the employment quota by investigating the ways that the disability rights model has been shaped by the particular American experience. While the ADA has inspired disability movements worldwide to interpret disability discrimination as a civil rights issue, we need to keep in mind that approaches to legislating equality for people with disabilities are deeply embedded in social and political norms and assumptions about the meanings of disability and discrimination. As it travels to Germany and Japan, the disability rights model will see itself transformed to meet specific cultural and movement generating needs. I suggest that this journey of disability rights on the road offers important insights into the multiple and culturally specific working of rights in the formation of social movements and in their negotiations of stigmatized identities.

1. MODELS OF DISABILITY POLICY: SOCIAL WELFARE AND CIVIL RIGHTS MODELS

The social welfare model is based on a medicalized model of disability, which focuses on individualized cures, treatment, and rehabilitation for what are considered ailments and abnormalities, at the expense of seeing people with disabilities as a political group with a history of discrimination (Oliver, 1996). In its historic incarnation, the welfare model has marked people with disabilities as flawed, if not cursed individuals, with ailments that are to be feared and pitied, who cannot be expected or allowed to fulfill social obligations such as working and parenting. In its modern form, the welfare model has turned away from notions of stigma and shame, replacing them with pity, charity, and a sense of social responsibility for helping the weak and dependant.

Translated into policy, the social welfare model follows a difference or separate treatment doctrine, providing for the different needs of people with disabilities in segregated settings, such as special schools, sheltered workshops, or assisted living centers. These social institutions are created as a separate and parallel track that provides income and services for people with disabilities, apart from the welfare institutions that serve the non-disabled. The assumption here is that rather than making mainstream institutions accessible, the needs for people with disabilities are better served in separate facilities that can be constructed to meet very specialized needs.

This parallel track has proven the established policy choice in most industrialized countries—until the rise of the more recent rights model—primarily because it does not threaten existing institutions (Waddington, 1994). It permits welfare states to continue ignoring disability needs as equal to those of other welfare needs, knowing that these will be served in separate institutions. The exclusion of people with disabilities is not seen as discriminatory, but as a natural outcome of their medical limitations. In fact, many non-disabled policy makers see the welfare model as generous and desirable, and as a sign of welfare progress. They are especially proud of the employment quota as a sign of progressive labor policy. On the whole, most European welfare states have established generous social security and rehabilitation provisions that allow people with disabilities to live comfortable, albeit separate lives.

The civil rights model evolved as a critique of the social welfare model. Its principle aim is to replace the medical model's focus on the disabled individual with a focus on disabling environments and social structures. Thus, social exclusion is not to be seen as an inevitable consequence of disability. Rather, it is a result of discriminatory attitudes and a history of exclusion from institutions that have failed to adapt to the needs of people with disabilities in the same ways that they routinely adapt to the needs of the majority. The difference is that majority needs are being met as a matter of good social policy, whereas disability needs are stigmatized as "special needs" and therefore debatable. Rather than maintaining a parallel track, then, disability policy under a rights model should focus on ways to make social environments accessible and reform social institutions to include people with disabilities (Scotch, 2001). The assumption is that once the non-disabled majority gains increasing contact with their disabled peers, be it through integrated schools, neighborhoods, or the workplace, discriminatory attitudes and fears of the unknown "other" will disappear, prejudices will abate, and the necessity for legal intervention decreases.

Remedying the effects of a discriminatory society is not an act of charity or social benevolence from an enlightened majority, but a form of civil rights enforcement similar to that of other minority groups. People with disabilities have the right to a "level playing field" and to be treated as equals. In policy terms, then, the rights model replaces segregation with integration, and parallel tracks with equal opportunity and anti-discrimination mandates. Consequently, it opposes employment quotas as yet another stigmatized form of special treatment. The primary enforcement tool is the law. Accordingly, people with disabilities are transformed from passive patients and welfare recipients to people with civil rights that are enforceable by law (Silvers, 1998).

The mere description of these two approaches to disability makes evident the tension between them. They exist in binary oppositions of exclusion versus inclusion, welfare versus rights, disability versus ability, quotas versus EEO, and, most generally, difference versus equality. Yet, it is important to note that as much as the rights model grew both politically and theoretically out of a dissatisfaction with the welfare model, few disability policies are clear-cut representatives of one model.

2. THE RIGHTS MODEL IN PRACTICE: THE AMERICANS WITH DISABILITIES ACT

The ADA of 1990 is commonly seen as the origin of the disability rights model: it is the world's first, comprehensive anti-discrimination statute that defines disability as a civil rights issue and mandates equal opportunities, integration, and accommodations for difference. It has encouraged the development of civil rights discourse in international forums and countries everywhere. A host of countries have followed suit and adopted similar legislation: Australia (1992), New Zealand (1993), Great Britain (1995), Israel (1998), India (1998), and South Africa (1999).

The ADA begins with a view of people with disabilities as a "discrete and insular minority" with a history of discrimination. It defines a person with a disability as someone who has a "physical or mental impairment" that substantially limits one or more of the major life activities . . . has a record of such an impairment, or is being regarded as having such an impairment.[1] Its central mandate is to eliminate that discrimination, which it sees as a "serious and pervasive social problem."[2] By doing so, the ADA clearly orients itself along existing civil rights legislation, extending the kinds of protections Congress had already offered to women and minorities. Section 504 of the 1973 Amendment to the Rehabilitation Act had already provided groundwork for such protection by its non-discrimination mandate for all institutions receiving federal funds, covering areas such as education, employment, and housing. The ADA was meant to expand this mandate to the private sector. As such, the Act (Title I) prohibits employers from discriminating against qualified individuals who "with or without reasonable accommodations" can perform the essential functions of the job.[3] Similar anti-discrimination mandates cover public services and accommodations offered by public (Title II) and private entities (Title III). They require the provision of goods and services in "the most integrated setting appropriate to the needs of the individual" and the opportunity to participate in mainstream activities even if separate activities are also available.[4]

The ADA is based on a premise that discriminatory attitudes and lack of opportunities are the central problems for people with disabilities in the workplace. It also provides that the failure to offer reasonable accommodations to the known physical or mental disabilities of a worker is a form of discrimination, unless the employer can prove that this would constitute an "undue burden." Its main enforcement tool is the

[1] 42 U.S.C. § 12102 (2).
[2] 42 U.S.C. § 12101 (a) (2).
[3] 42 U.S.C. § 12112 (a).
[4] 42 U.S.C. § 12182.

civil suit. The ADA plaintiffs must demonstrate that they are qualified for the job, with or without reasonable accommodations, and that they qualified as disabled under the law.

3. THE WELFARE MODEL IN PRACTICE: EUROPEAN EMPLOYMENT QUOTAS

The disability quota system has its origins in the welfare legislation for the disabled veterans of the First World War (Waddington, 1994). It was deemed a matter of social obligation to provide for those who had given their limbs to the country with pensions and rehabilitation benefits and to allow them to compete with non-disabled non-veterans through the use of employment quotas.[5] Germany was the first country to implement a mandatory quota system in 1919, and other European countries soon followed.[6] By the end of WWII, the voluntary system had proven so ineffective and the unemployment rate of disabled veterans remained so high that the employment quota was adopted by most Western European countries. It was also extended to cover civilians, and by the 1960s it became anchored in an extensive network of disability welfare legislation. While disabled veterans were still privileged, this second period of disability law focused less on the causes of impairment, but on means of rehabilitation. The focus, then, was on the establishment of special education systems, medical and vocational rehabilitation, and institutionalized care. For the first time, people with disabilities became rights-holders, at least in terms of welfare rights, but at the high price of exclusion.

The European quota system is based on the assumption that without some kind of legislative intervention, people with disabilities would not become part of the labor force. The system furthermore assumes that employers will not hire large numbers of disabled workers unless they are required to do so, and similarly, that workers with disabilities are not able to compete for jobs with their non-disabled peers and win them on their merits. Such assumptions focusing on inability and dependency are viewed as disabling and patronizing by many European disability activists (Degener, 2000). Many advocacy groups thus oppose quotas for the stigmatization they embody.

4. DISABILITY EMPLOYMENT QUOTAS IN JAPAN AND GERMANY

Japan and Germany's dedication to the disability employment quota has its origin in historical processes that emphasize special needs over equal rights. Both countries cemented their commitment to positive employment rights in the immediate postwar

[5] In an interesting parallel, the return of disabled WWI veterans also led to the first federal rehabilitation legislation in the United States (the 1918 Smith-Sears Act), which never included employment quotas.
[6] Austria followed in 1920, Italy and Poland in 1921, and France in 1923.

period as part of their basic constitutional welfare state guarantees, and as a way to integrate injured war veterans into the growing labor market. This is because both countries have historically followed a special treatment doctrine in the creation of disability policy, providing for disability needs in segregated settings. In Germany, this has led to the establishment of one of the most comprehensive and extensive rehabilitation systems in the postwar period, rivaled only by those in Scandinavian countries. The German welfare system offers educational, vocational, and residential services providing cradle-to-grave care for people with disabilities. Likewise, Japan is considered a leader in rehabilitation programs in the Asia region and provides a great deal of development assistance in this field to other Asian nations.

German and Japanese disability policy is unique in their continuous commitment to the employment quota as a way of addressing a common problem: the extreme unemployment rates of disabled workers. Both countries have steadily increased the burden to employers and taxpayers in their effort to integrate disabled workers into the open labor market.[7] Currently, the Japanese employment quota lies at 1.8% (for private enterprises of 16 employees or more) and 2.1% (for government bodies). Employers who do not fulfill the quota are levied a monthly fine, which then funds a sophisticated network of rehabilitation facilities and grants to employers who do meet the quota. At present, however, the actual employment rate for people with disabilities still lies below the legal requirement (1.47% in 1997 with the quota still at 1.6%), which means that half of all enterprises do not reach the quota. Very large companies have developed a way to comply with the quota by establishing special "barrier-free" subsidiary companies (*tokurei kogaisha*); these hire primarily people with disabilities who then count for the parent company's employment quota. The Japanese government promotes the *tokurei kogaisha* system as the preferred means to boost the employment of people with disabilities, rather than as a *de facto* re-segregation into separate workplaces (Heyer, 2000).

Despite the quota system, then, which was designed to integrate people with disabilities into regular companies, the Japanese workplace remains segregated. Sheltered workshops are the main source of employment for Japanese people with disabilities. The majority of these are private community workshops, which exist as extralegal facilities outside of the sheltered workshops run by the Ministry of Health and Welfare.

Like Japan, the German employment quota has not significantly led to the integration of disabled workers into the common labor market. The current quota lies at 5% for every workplace of 25 or more employees, and levies for non-compliance are comparatively high, which, similar to Japan, has funded Germany's extensive vocational rehabilitation system. The German vocational rehabilitation remains highly segregated and continues to isolate people with severe, learning, or developmental disabilities into sheltered workshops rather than integrating them into the workforce. Politically, the quota system has been attacked as too weak by unions and disability

[7] For a detailed discussion of German and Japanese disability policy and employment quotas, see Heyer (1998) and (2003).

groups, and as destructive to business by the conservative party and employer organizations.[8] In turn, unions and disability activists have declared the levy as too low to be able to stimulate employment. They argue that as long as it is cheaper for employers to pay the levy than to hire a worker with a disability (who then not only qualifies for additional paid vacations but also enjoys special protections from dismissal), the quota will remain a *de facto* disability tax for employers, rather than an incentive to hire disabled workers.

Despite these weaknesses and points of political contention, employment quotas are alive and well in Japan and Germany. They remain a vital part of each countries' disability employment policy. Their resilience is especially important in light of the vast international influence on German and Japanese disability law and activism. This international trend clearly goes away from the welfare model, which embodies the employment quota, and toward the civil rights model, as symbolized internationally by the ADA.

5. INTERNATIONAL INFLUENCES ON GERMAN AND JAPANESE DISABILITY ACTIVISM

The passage of the ADA sent shockwaves through disability movements throughout the globe, and German and Japanese activists were not immune to its promise. Before this paradigm shift brought about by the American example, disability organizations in both countries were dominated by what I have termed "first generation" disability organizations (Heyer, 2000; Heyer, 2002). These were large, single issue disability organizations that consisted primarily of national associations of physical and psychiatric therapists, social workers, and parents organizations that were founded directly after the war and responded to the very real medical needs of their patients and clients. Both countries' large network of physical and occupational rehabilitation centers were founded and operated by these groups. They successfully organized themselves around the assertion of special needs, which resulted in welfare policies based on well-developed but still segregated facilities.

In the course of the 1960s and 1970s, disabled members became increasingly dissatisfied with what they perceived as patronizing attitudes of non-disabled leadership and as a continuous focus on the "parallel track." Inspired by other protest movements at the time—most notably the student movement in Germany and the *Buraku* anti-discrimination protests in Japan—people with disabilities began to form their own, "second generation" organizations, often beginning as simple social clubs to foster consciousness raising and to make connections to non-disabled groups. In Germany, for example, these social clubs initiated the protests against inaccessible

[8] In 1981, the Federal Constitutional Court ruled the quota to be permissible, arguing that the compensatory levy was a special contribution that was supposed to stimulate employers to law-abiding behavior and to provide compensation between employers.

public accommodations when disabled members pointed to the fact that there were few meeting spaces with accessible restrooms, or that they couldn't even get to the meetings because there was no accessible public transportation (Heiden, 1996). In Japan, parents groups developed critiques of stigmatized identities from the *Buraku* Liberation League's aggressive social critiques and human rights demands. Activists in the student movement became important allies as well, providing personal assistance to the first generation of activists struggling to leave the institutions to live on their own.

In comparison to the development of disability activism in the United States, however, disability activism in Japan and Germany did not follow naturally from other identity-based social movements and did not have a well-established civil rights frame as a cultural repertoire to apply to their political activism. Lacking a similar civil rights tradition, German and Japanese second generation activism was sparked by two major international events: the 1981 United Nations Year of the Disabled and the 1990 ADA.

The passage of the ADA pointed to a shift in thinking about disability policy away from welfare and medicine and toward independent living and equal rights, which became international doctrine through the workings of the United Nations. In 1981, the United Nations declared the International Year of Disabled Persons to mark the beginning of the International Decade of Disabled Persons (1983–1992), both under the motto of "full participation and equality." This motto emphasized the importance of equal rights, social integration, independent living, and government responsibility to combat discrimination against people with disabilities (Degener, 1995). At the end of this decade, the UN Economic and Social Commission on Asian and the Pacific decided that more work needed to be done in that area and declared 1993–2003 the UN Decade of Disabled Persons in Asia. This might explain why the UN equality and integration mandate had a much more profound impact on disability activism throughout Asia than it did in the Western world. It gave birth to a new generation of disability activism that is moving away from a welfare-based model and frames itself in the context of rights, equal access, and disability pride.

6. THE GERMAN AND JAPANESE LOVE AFFAIR WITH THE ADA

Besides the international attention on disability issues, activists in Germany and Japan had been following the activities of their American colleagues very closely, watching the protests surrounding implementation of section 504 of the 1973 Rehabilitation Act, which had mandated full accommodation for all facilities using public funds and, of course, the struggle for the ADA. Many German and Japanese disability groups traveled to the United States to learn about the movement there and returned full of enthusiasm and optimism about what might be possible with a shift from charity and dependence to equal rights and self-determination. It is safe to say that the majority of the German and Japanese leadership has made at least one trip to the United States, most commonly to Berkeley, the origin of the American Independent Living movement, and to Oregon, the origin of the People First movement of people with developmental disabilities.

German and Japanese activists are not unique in their enchantment with the promises of the ADA and the political activism of the U.S. disability rights movement. Disability activists across the globe tend to be very international in outlook and follow developments in other countries very closely. In fact, there is a tendency in international circles to construct hierarchies of disability policies, in which the ADA commonly reigns on top, closely followed by Scandinavian "normalization" policy. Japanese activists, for example, would repeatedly invoke this hierarchy during interviews, claiming that, "we in Japan are twenty years behind the Europeans in disability politics, and thirty years behind the United States." They see the ADA as a powerful vision of social change, a testament to a social movement's ability to affect policy, and an enviable alternative to the Japanese disability policy's emphasis on special needs and segregation.

7. THE ADA IN GERMANY: CONSTITUTIONAL AND CIVIL ANTI-DISCRIMINATION MANDATES

German activists are similarly inspired by the ADA's promises of equal treatment but tend to hold a more critical view of American social policy in general. There is a broad agreement that the liberal U.S. economic policy results in little to no state intervention concerning the well-being of its citizens, which translates into poor medical care, joblessness, and poverty. Nonetheless, the promise of an American anti-discrimination law was seductive: people with disabilities would no longer need to ask or beg for services: they have been transformed into rights-holders, self-confidently demanding that existing anti-discrimination laws are respected and complied with (Hermes, 1998). The confidence and sense of entitlement afforded to a rights-holder, according to both German and Japanese activists, has also affected the attitudes of the non-disabled population. They are convinced that non-disabled Americans tend to hold less disabling stereotypes than their German and Japanese counterparts because chances are that they went to school with disabled children, or have disabled colleagues at their workplaces. The American self-confidence is also evident in language. English-language terminology such as "peer counseling," "anti-discrimination," "empowerment," and "independent living" have found their way into movement circles in both countries, where they are used to mark their adoption of this new and progressive approach to disability rights.

It has become obvious, then, that most profound and powerful impact of the ADA internationally has been its politicizing effect on disability movements. German and Japanese activists speak of a "paradigm shift" in which they have come to embrace the theoretical ideals of the social model and the political promises of the rights model of disability. They feel liberated from the dictates of the welfare model, which has forced them to negotiate (however successfully in policy terms) their identities as lacking, helpless, and thus needing of state support. The resulting welfare and rehabilitation measures may take care of their special needs, but keep them separated from the mainstream. They now see the rights model as an enticing alternative, offering new opportunities to negotiate as equal citizens, entitled to complete integration and equal opportunities.

In Germany, this paradigm shift led to the passage of a constitutional equal rights amendment in 1994[9] and a civil anti-discrimination law in 2002 (Heyer, 2002). The ADA and the political activism of the American disability rights movement played a vital part in generating the political mobilizing that led to these reforms. They fueled German activists with the language and convictions that saw people with disabilities as equal citizens and political subjects, rather than as objects of welfare. The 2002 Federal Equalizing Law for People with Disabilities (*Bundesgleichstellungsgesetz für Behinderte*) focuses on barrier-free access to public goods and services. It comes as part of a three-part reform package along with legal reforms in social welfare and rehabilitation legislation, and employment law of, which reformed but not abolished the employment quota. It is significant that the German version of the rights model, heavily inspired by the ADA, nonetheless incorporates German legal and cultural norms emphasizing social solidarity and state support for special needs. Especially in the field of employment discrimination the law combines what are seen as legal opposites: equal employment opportunity guarantees and employment quotas.

8. THE ADA IN JAPAN: INITIATING LEGAL REFORMS AND RIGHTS CONSCIOUSNESS

The Japanese response to the ADA was similar to the German. Like in Germany, the passage of the ADA inspired a new generation of activists to adopt a new paradigm that de-emphasized welfare needs and began to embrace equal rights. Unlike their German counterparts, however, Japanese disability activists did not achieve passage of disability anti-discrimination legislation. The mobilization of legal resources is still in its infancy in Japanese disability activism. Nonetheless, the new generation disability organizations are increasingly using the language of rights in framing their interpretations of disability discrimination. This comes against a cultural and historical background that eschews the role of law as a tool of social change. Notions of equality and rights are seen as Western constructs alien to Japanese values of harmony and social hierarchy (Kawashima, 1963). These cultural explanations are being challenged by studies of social movements using the law for social reforms, which the Japanese legal literature terms "new rights movements." Born in the student protests of the 1960s, these new rights movements are new in the sense that they seek rights not mentioned in the Constitution—such as rights regarding the environment, taxpayers,

[9] Adding the sentence, *niemand darf wegen seiner Behinderung benachteiligt werden*, "nobody shall be discriminated against because of disability" to Article 3 (3) of the post unification German Constitution.

patients, AIDS, and most recently, disability rights. They are also new in the way that these rights are being pursued: they were generated by citizens' movements, rather than by individuals, they rely on the law as a significant tool for social change, and they use the media to influence public opinion and generate sympathy for their claims (Upham, 1987; Feldman, 2000).

As a new rights movement in Japan, disability activism is taking the first steps toward legal mobilization. The result has been a successful movement to remove restrictive licensing and certification requirements, which activists see as the first step toward a more comprehensive anti-discrimination law. Japanese law contains a large number of disqualifying clauses (*kekkaku jôkô*) which restrict, or even prohibit, people with disabilities from obtaining licenses or certifications, from being engaged in certain professions, and from using certain facilities and receiving services. Activists collected examples from other countries regarding the absence of such restrictive clauses, which they see as human rights violations and barriers to employment. They argued that qualification for licenses or certifications should be based on a person's ability to perform the tasks rather than on assumptions regarding limitations imposed by their physical or mental disability. This lobbying and shaming by using foreign examples was partially successful: a 1999 revision of *kekkaku jôkô* resulted in the abolishment of 6 of the 63 laws officially recognized by the Japanese government as discriminatory. The Health and Welfare Ministry acknowledged that some disabilities do not necessarily inhibit performance, and recommended that only those be barred from licenses whose disabilities prevented them from performing the necessary tasks.

Once Japanese law has been purged from these discriminatory clauses, activists argue that it will be ready for more comprehensive reforms cumulating in Japan's own disability anti-discrimination law, a JDA, "Japanese with Disabilities Act," closely modeled after the American example (Sekigawa, 1998). To promote the passage of such a law, Japanese disability groups are increasingly paying attention to the idea of rights consciousness, and promoting it as an import from the successful American movement. They argue that any form of anti-discrimination legislation will only be liberating for the movement if people with disabilities truly understand that they have rights and are willing to act upon them. Like in Germany, the proponents of this new rights consciousness have all traveled to the United States, particularly to Berkeley, CA, which is considered the Mecca of disability rights and activism. Like their German counterparts, their goal is to politicize the Japanese disability movement by increasing the role of rights and rights consciousness. People with disabilities should not only be aware of the rights they currently have, but also feel empowered by using them, making rights the main tool toward leading self-determined lives. Unlike their German or American counterparts, however, disability rights consciousness in Japan is challenged by deeply embedded cultural norms surrounding interdependence, care-giving, and selfishness. Talks about self-determination will usually end up with the question of, "how do we assert our rights without being seen as selfish?"

This question is likely to become a central issue in the Japanese disability movement's quest to emphasize rights consciousness and orient itself along a rights model.

How can rights become instruments for personal empowerment without the risk of alienation and separation from the community? How can rights be set to work in a historical and cultural setting that has emphasized difference and separate worlds, rather than equality and integration? Japanese cultural norms surrounding care-giving and gratitude pose a fundamental conflict between notions of rights and selfishness.

It light of these attitudes, second generation Japanese disability activism tends to shift away from radical political change or using the consciousness raising techniques they learned at Berkeley, such as occupying buildings and chaining themselves to trains. Instead, they advocate a gentler approach toward a "new, livable society" (*seikatsu shiyasui shakai*). They argue that changing attitudes surrounding social norms and disability will benefit not only people with disabilities themselves, but also the rest of society. Framing arguments for disability rights in terms of general social benefits—everybody will benefit from curb cuts, elevators at train stations, flexible work hours, and informed consent laws—will allow the movement to appear less self-centered and separate from the community.

9. THE RESILIENCE OF THE EMPLOYMENT QUOTA: THREE EXPLANATIONS

As I have shown in my two case studies, the road to disability rights does not necessarily lead to the rejection of certain aspects of the "outmoded" welfare model, most significantly, the employment quota. Japan and Germany instituted what are considered the most sophisticated employment quota systems in Asia and Europe today. Both countries recognized state responsibility for the employment of disabled workers. This might be testimony to a larger social welfare role of the state, as outlined in both countries' postwar constitutions.

At the same time, however, the policy effect of these employment quotas is an increasingly segregated labor market. Companies have accepted the employment quota as a *de facto* disability tax and fund the expanding rehabilitation system with their levy payments. They accept the underlying assumptions of the quota system that disabled workers are less valuable and less productive, and that, if such workers are to be integrated in the open labor market, employers need to be obliged to hire them, and sometimes even financially compensated for doing so. Employers tend not to view the quota as part of their social responsibility and prefer, instead, to buy themselves out of their obligation and continue to employ a largely non-disabled workforce. As Waddington (1996, p. 71) concludes, "the history of the European quota systems amply demonstrates that an employment system which is based on the idea that the protected group of workers are inferior cannot achieve permanent and significant success, since employers will attempt to evade their obligations to employ such workers."

Why do German and Japanese disability activists keep strengthening their commitment to employment quotas? Neither Germany nor Japan has accomplished its disability employment goals. In fact, a recent study for the European Commission analyzed employment policies for disabled persons in eighteen industrialized countries and found no examples where quota systems achieved their targets. Acknowledging the arguments that quota systems produce resources from levies or fines which can be used to support other employment development measures, and that in some cases sufficient disabled people may not be available to enable employers to meet their quotas, the study concluded that, "it is clearly the case that in most countries the tide is swinging away from quotas—either for their abandonment altogether (as in the UK), or for other measures (active employment support for individuals and/or stronger anti-discrimination laws) to be given higher profile and greater force."[10]

10. CULTURAL SIGNIFICANCE OF WORK

If the employment quota is an inferior method of increasing employment rates of disabled workers, then, it must hold other important functions for the German and Japanese disability movements. Its resilience as a movement goal speaks to the different cultural and political setting in which the German and Japanese rights discourse is emerging. The Japanese case is especially illustrative of the political as well as mobilizing functions of the employment quota. Disability activism in employment policies (unlike that in integrated education or independent living, for example) does not focus on American-style equal employment rights, but rather on the expansion and upgrading of the separate employment system already in place. The Japanese government's steadfast commitment to the quota and the growing number of sheltered workshops as well as *tokurei kogaisha* (the subsidiary companies formed to avoid paying levies for falling under the employment quota) also illustrate that the Japanese workplace remains segregated. The current trend to form *tokurei kogaisha* is testimony to the construction of more segregated workplaces with increasingly sophisticated workplace equipment. The drawback is that these institutions are still considered rehabilitation establishments rather than workplaces. Accordingly, they are under the bureaucratic control of the Health and Welfare Ministry and do not fall under the minimum wage or labor laws. Disability activists thus does not focus on equal access to the regular workplace, but on raising the employment quota and strengthening its enforcement as well as expanding the network of sheltered workshops.

More so than their German counterparts, who have launched criticisms of the disability quota as an outmoded form of social policy and as incompatible with equal employment guarantees (Degener, 2000), Japanese disability activists argue that the path toward an anti-discrimination law and increased rights consciousness must be able to integrate concerns for community and connection. In the policy setting, a move away from the welfare and rehabilitation model becomes problematic when the

[10] European Commission, "Benchmarking employment policies for people with disabilities." (2000: 207).

right to equal treatment does not include a guarantee to protect and accommodate difference. We cannot and should not assume that full integration is always going to be the best alternative in Japan, especially in a setting that has historically placed all its resources into separate facilities. Abandoning the quota system in favor of a law that forbids employers to discriminate in the first place would equally deprive activists of an important measure to get what they term, "a foot in the door." How else will we be able to combat disabling workplace stereotypes, they ask. The employment quota may rest on disabling assumptions, but it allows us to show our abilities and become part of the working world.

These deliberations are especially important when considering the cultural significance of labor force participation in Japan. Japanese people with disabilities have long fought not only the stigma and shame associated with their identities, but also the infantilizing assumptions that accompany it. A person with a disability is traditionally not expected to leave the parental home to marry or engage in gainful employment, two of the most important life stages in the Japanese path toward adulthood. Both employment and marriage, traditionally occurring in this order, mark a person for adulthood in Japan (Edwards, 1989; Rohlen, 1974). In fact, large Japanese companies typically engage in initiation ceremonies for their new recruits that resemble a coming of age ritual.[11] The literature on the Japanese employment system continuously stresses the importance of workplace identification and joining a company to become part of a group. Thus, it is the not the occupation (*shokugyo*) that counts, but the place of work (*shokuba*) (Cole, 1971, p. 67). Membership in a company, be it as regular employee or as one in a *tokurei kogaisha*, affords an important sense of social inclusion and mainstream identity. Employees of *tokurei kogaisha* typically work in workshops adjacent to regular employees and proudly sport the company's logo on their uniforms. As long as segregated employment remains the only path to enter this crucial part of the Japanese social identity, disability activists will be hesitant to challenge it in favor of anti-discrimination legislation that might take years to change social attitudes.

Japanese employment policy thus remains firmly lodged in a welfare- and separate treatment-based approach that does not easily accommodate disability rights. The Japanese disability rights movement faces the difficult challenge of translating rights-based principles into difference-based social policy and legislation so that they are both culturally appropriate and politically useful. Notions of equality and rights consciousness are still considered to be concepts foreign to Japanese civic culture, and as a strategizing tool, the difference-based welfare model used by traditional disability organizations has clearly been more successful than calls for equal rights and anti-discrimination legislation. When it comes to disability rights in employment, then, both German and Japanese disability activists chose to maintain the protections

[11] This is the case for both male and female employees. The adulthood rules for women do not necessarily include employment, however, just marriage and children. Both are typically denied to women with disabilities, especially those with developmental disabilities.

afforded by a paternalistic state to acknowledge the importance of work as a form of social participation.[12]

11. CONSTITUTIONAL MANDATES

This brings me to my second explanation. Employment rates for disabled workers are shamefully low in all industrialized countries, and the United States rate is only slightly higher that that of Japan and Germany. Empirically, then, it is difficult to compare the actual success rates of quota or rights models. The important distinction to point out, however, is the role of the state in managing the employment needs and rights of disabled workers. Here, we see the background for the German and Japanese comfort with the quota system: in both countries, the state is constitutionally mandated to guarantee positive labor and welfare rights. These rights have provided the basis for both countries' tremendous postwar economic miracles and they have cemented the state's role as both a provider and enforcer of equal employment rights.

In Japan, disability activists have anchored their demands in the Japanese Constitution's guarantee for individual dignity (Art. 13), equality of race, religion, social status, and gender (Art. 14), the right to a healthy and cultured life, including the state's duty to ensure a minimum standard of living (Art. 25), and the right (and duty) to work (Art. 27). Similarly, German activists have invoked the constitutional mandate of the "social welfare state principle" (*Sozialstaatsprinzip*) outlining the state's responsibility to ensure the basic social welfare of its citizens. This principle has been applied in the case of women in state and federal gender equalizing laws, and most recently was translated into an expansion of Germany's ERA during the 1994 Constitutional revision. Article 3 (2) was amended to include the phrase, "the state promotes the factual realization of equal rights of women and men and works toward the abolition of existing disadvantages." The terminology in the German version of the ADA deliberately chose the term, *Gleichstellung*, "making equal" or "equalizing," rather than just "equality," to signify the law's reach beyond mere anti-discrimination mandates, and to mark the state's active role in not only declaring equal treatment principles but also in ensuring that this equal treatment actually occurs. For example, Article 1§2 addresses the special situation of women with disabilities. It builds on existing federal equal rights legislation for women that recognizes the unequal situation of women and men and allows for affirmative action policies to achieve gender equality. The disability law thus enables the enactment of "special measures to promote the equalization of women with disabilities."

[12] German disability policy emphasizes that, "work is more than earning your daily bread. Working gives people with disabilities the opportunity to contribute their capabilities to the good of society. It also affords them a sense of personal fulfillment and the strengthening of their desire to live through the constant challenge of their capabilities." *4. Bericht der Bundesregierung zur Lage der Behinderten* (1997).

12. THE CIVIL RIGHTS MODEL AS AN AMERICAN TRANSPLANT

Finally, I seek to explain the resilience of the employment quota by investigating the ways that the disability rights model has been shaped by the particular American experience. The promises of the disability rights model in the American context lies in its use of the civil rights movement's "frame" of equal treatment and opportunities. The social movement literature on framing (Snow, 1992; Hunt, 1994) spells out some of the interpretive and political uses of frames, which it defines as an "interpretive schemata that simplifies and condenses the 'world out there' by selectively punctuating and encoding objects, situations, events, experiences, and sequences of actions within one's present or past environments" (Snow and Benford, 1992, p. 137). For social movement actors, frames "focus attention on a particular situation considered problematic, make attributions regarding who or what is to blame, and articulate an alternative set of arrangements including what the movement actors need to do in order to affect the desired change" (Hunt, 1994, p. 190). A frame thus allows activists to explain what is wrong with the world from their particular point of view, and how they propose to fix it.

The civil rights movement of the 1960s is commonly considered the originator of the civil rights "master frame" in that it has allowed for numerous oppressed groups to tap into it and elaborate their grievances in group-specific ways. Its emphasis on equal rights and opportunities resonated with fundamental American values and thus lent itself to extensive elaboration, especially for other identity-based movements. One characteristic of this master frame is that in the construction of diagnostic and prognostic frames, the question of blame is always externalized in that injustice and differential treatment are attributed to discriminatory social structures and prejudice, rather than to the victim's imperfections or inherent characteristics (Snow and Benford, 1992, p. 139).

The American civil rights movement origin of the equality master frame firmly locates its diagnostic and prognostic frames in the legal realm. While usefulness of such an association has been widely discussed in the law and society literature, the political realities of movement activism in the United States have made the use of the equality frame and its accompanying identification with the minority group model a political necessity. In the American context, then, groups marked as "different" in comparison to what Martha Minow (1990) calls "an unstated norm" have used the law, under the premises of the equality master frame, to gain access to the mainstream institutions of citizenship. In that sense, the U.S. disability rights movement faced a well-paved political terrain that offered a powerful frame to shape their movement and their political and legal responses to the discrimination they faced.

Claiming a civil rights heritage by making the connection between disability rights and other identity-based social movements has been perhaps the most powerful strategy for the U.S. disability rights movement. It has given the movement a degree of political legitimacy and organizing power that established it a model movement in the international hierarchy of disability rights. It is this success that drew Japanese and

German activists to travel to the United States and inject the idea of American-style rights consciousness into their respective movements. The generation of a disability identity to be considered as yet another minority group that can claim rights as a form of protection from an oppressive majority has not come without costs, however. Disability identity categories, and specifically the question, "who counts as disabled?" have been paramount in limiting the reach of disability anti-discrimination law in the U.S. court system.

13. PROBLEMATIZING DISABILITY IDENTITY: THE ADA IN THE COURTS

The ADA passed with a great bipartisan majority in the United States Congress and was signed by the United States Congress an enthusiastic President Bush.[13] It is widely considered a comprehensive anti-discrimination statute, firmly grounded in the 1964 Civil Rights Act's guarantee for equal treatment. Given the broad political consensus that produced the ADA, and the inclusion of most social institutions under its non-discrimination mandate, it is surprising to see how narrowly it has been interpreted in the courts. Rather than focusing on institutional practices that discriminate on the basis of disability, the courts have focused on questions of eligibility: whether or not plaintiffs are truly disabled and thus qualify to sue under the ADA.

Why this narrow interpretation? The ADA does not specify any impairment that is *per se* a disability under the law, as does Japanese law, for example. Instead, it defines it as a physical or mental impairment that substantially limits a major life activity. As a result, every claim of disability under the ADA is adjudicated on a case-by-case basis in which plaintiffs must prove that they have, in fact, an impairment (or are regarded as having one) that limits a major life activity. Thus, in a cluster of three prominent ADA cases in June of 1999 the Supreme Court has ruled that disabilities mitigated by glasses or heart medication (*Sutton v. United Airlines*,[14] *Albertsons, Inc. v. Kirkingburg*[15] and *Murphy v. United Parcel Service*[16]) do not qualify an individual to sue under the ADA. This precedent—that disability must be determined taking into account corrective measures to ameliorate an impairment—will exclude a large amount of workers from the ADA's employment protections. Plaintiffs must now prove their disability on the basis of their *corrected* impairments, even though employers had denied them jobs on the basis of their *uncorrected* impairment. Thus, the myopic airline pilots in *Sutton* were denied their jobs on the basis of their uncorrected vision, but disqualified as disabled (and thus from the protections of the ADA) by the fact that they could, after all, function perfectly with 20/20 vision once they wore their glasses.

[13] President Bush likened the passage of the ADA to the destruction of the Berlin Wall by declaring, "let the shameful wall of exclusion finally come down." (Shapiro, 1993).

[14] 527 U.S. 471 (1999).

[15] 527 U.S. 555 (1999).

[16] 527 U.S. 516 (1999).

The Supreme Court is effectively allowing employers to have it both ways: they can refuse to hire somebody for being too disabled and not qualified for the job, or not accommodate somebody's needs because they are not disabled enough to qualify for protection.

The Supreme Court's most recent ADA employment decision (*Toyota v. Williams*)[17] limits the disability category even further. The Court ruled unanimously that a woman with carpal tunnel syndrome did not qualify as disabled because she did not demonstrate that the limitation of her ability to perform manual tasks was "central to daily life," and not only to life at the workplace. Thus, because the plaintiff could still fix her own breakfast and brush her teeth, she did not qualify as disabled under the ADA. This decision confirms the trend to further narrow of the definition of a disability and focus almost exclusively on the plaintiff's identity—now made even more subjective by tests of what activities are centrally important to a person's life—rather than employers' discriminatory behavior.

The contradictions embodied in the treatment of the ADA in the courts give rise to another irony. In claiming disability discrimination, plaintiffs are asserting their fundamental equality with the able-bodied. They are applying a civil rights frame by claiming that they are just as qualified to perform a certain job and that they deserve an equal chance of competing for this job, or continuing to perform it. At the same time, however, the law demands that they emphasize their difference—their disability—for which they are being discriminated against in the first place. The law thus simultaneously forces an identity of disability that suggests inferiority, while pretending to hold plaintiffs to the same professional standard as any other worker. These ironies resulting from the restrictive category of disability in anti-discrimination law are a product of American individualism, argues legal scholar Paula Berg (1999). They reinforce the exalted status of the "overcomer" in American culture, "the individual, who through sheer determination, triumphs over daunting obstacles to achieve self-sufficiency and fulfill the social obligation to work." (Berg, 1999, p. 31) Indeed, Berg suggests that by legitimizing only those with the most severe impairments this narrow category creates, "inspirational role models—paragons of personal autonomy who serve as reminders that any and all impediments to work and self-sufficiency can and must be overcome, even (and perhaps especially) in this era of dwindling social services." (Berg, 1999, p. 31)

While the roots of disability anti-discrimination law clearly lie in American individualism in some of the ways that Berg describes, I suggest that this emphasis is exactly what makes the ADA so attractive to the German and Japanese disability movements. Germans and Japanese disability activists are still working to achieve the status of a self-sufficient individual, of competent worker, and perhaps even that of the "overcomer." American rugged individualism—and the promise of equal treatment it engenders—is a luxury for those confined to a group identity marked by the very loss of what lies at the center of our notion of citizenship: the ability and obligation to

[17] 534 U.S. 184 (2002).

work. Defined as a member of a disabled class, and marked by associations with the rehabilitation and welfare systems that keep them comfortable but out of the workplace, I suggest that German and Japanese disability rights activists look toward the ADA to provide a notion of citizenship that will grant them a truly equal status with other workers. Rather than adopt the ADA's inherent mobilization around a minority group model, then, German and Japanese activists move toward the expansion of the category of citizenship that will accommodate their important need—and right—to work.

14. CONCLUSIONS: THE ADA'S JOURNEY TO JAPAN AND GERMANY

This chapter has been an exploration into the different ways of legislating disability rights, tracing the movement from welfare-based to rights-based legislation. As the inaugural document of the rights approach, the ADA has set important standards of equality and non-discrimination and inspired movements around the globe to enact similar legislation. Using the traditional rhetoric of civil rights with its emphasis of formal equality, the American disability rights model has provided a compelling example for the framing of disability rights that is politically powerful but may not apply for other countries lacking such a civil rights tradition. It recognizes that classic notions of equality as sameness do not result in justice for people with disabilities by insisting that reasonable accommodation is not a form of affirmative action but simply part of a non-discrimination mandate.

The question remains how much longer it will remain the international model for disability rights, especially in Europe. While it continues to inspire movements there, it has also received its share of criticism, especially in British academic circles that have produced the bulk of theoretical work on the social model of disability. There is a growing concern over the ideal of independence and individual rights that has been promoted by the neo-liberal states anxious to reduce the loads on national welfare budgets (French, 1993). How can disability rights lead to more independence and self-determination without eradicating their basis in social justice? In other words, how can disability law guarantee the right to equal opportunity while maintaining protections for disability difference, especially when these differences increasingly call for social expenditures?

The international trend is to combine anti-discrimination mandates with more extensive social welfare guarantees. In its 2002 Madrid Declaration to welcome the 2003 European Year of People with Disabilities, the European Congress spelled out its formula for a successful disability politics: "non-discrimination plus positive action results in social inclusion."[18] There is an increasing awareness that anti-discrimination alone cannot respond to the employment needs of disabled workers, and that the ADA model is lacking in social solidarity. At the same time, however, the commitment to

[18] http://www.madriddeclaration.org/en/dec/dec.htm.

positive action tends to discourage the use of employment quotas. Germany is unique in its insistence to combine equal treatment and special treatment models. I will be interesting to see how Germany will continue to merge the two models.

The journey of disability rights, originating in the United States and transplanted on German and Japanese soil offers an important case study of the workings of notions of rights and remedies in different sociopolitical settings. How does the transformation of disability rights reflect alternative approaches to defining disability, discrimination, and the mobilization of the law as a tool for social change? German and Japanese activists invoke the symbolic power of the law, as a symbol of enlightened disability politics and the political successes of the movements that use it. Yet, the actual reform of German and Japanese disability law is fundamentally different from the ADA. In both of my case studies, there is a recognition that the rights model is entering very different political and institutional territory. In Germany the individualized rights model collides with labor and welfare traditions that offer more comprehensive or positive rights against the state. In Japan, it encounters communitarian critiques of rights that challenge the individualizing effect of rights talk and focus on the importance of community integration. As disability rights travel to Germany and Japan and set foot on foreign soil, they become re-thought and reinterpreted in ways that may offer more comprehensive interpretations of the equality guarantee.

SECTION IV

Mobilizing Law: Rights Consciousness, Claiming Behaviour, and the Dynamics of Litigation

CHAPTER 13

The Evolution of Employment Discrimination Law in the 1990s: A Preliminary Empirical Investigation*

John J. Donohue III and Peter Siegelman

ABSTRACT

Two major pieces of employment discrimination legislation were passed in the early 1990s: the 1991 Civil Rights Act and Americans with Disabilities Act. Using some simple regression models, we examine the effects of this legislation on the volume, content, and outcomes of employment discrimination cases filed in federal courts. We find, first, that the volume of discrimination cases nearly doubled between 1992 and 1997, in contrast to a 10% decline during the previous 8 years, and despite a sharply falling unemployment rate that—in the past—would have substantially reduced the amount of litigation. We also observe a significant shift in the composition of suits filed, with race and age discrimination cases declining substantially as a share of the total and sex and disability discrimination cases increasing. We tie these developments, as well as changes in the relationship between plaintiff win rates and the business cycle, to changes in the law that diminish the importance of back-pay damages. We conclude by tentatively suggesting how the meaning of and protection afforded by employment discrimination law have changed over the past 35 years.

INTRODUCTION

At least in the national discourse, these seem to be relatively quiet times for employment discrimination law. While specialists in the field recognize that there are always cutting-edge developments in particular areas—the law governing disabled workers is one current example—the field as a whole is not subject to the same kind of extended national scrutiny and debate as it was when Congress was considering the 1990 and 1991 Civil Rights Acts (CRA), or during the Clarence Thomas hearings.

* This work was completed while Donohue was at Stanford Law School and Siegelman was at Fordham Law School. We benefitted from helpful comments by seminar participants at UConn. Law School, Fordham Law School, the American Bar Foundation, and conference participants at the American Law and Economics Association. Thanks to Katie Bilodeau and Jinhui Pan for excellent research assistance.

L. B. Nielsen and R. L. Nelson (eds.), Handbook of Employment Discrimination Research, 261–285.

Despite this lack of attention, however, we suggest that employment discrimination law has undergone some dramatic yet largely unrecognized changes since the start of the last decade, changes that are substantial enough to amount to a revolution, albeit a quiet one. For one thing, the number of employment discrimination suits filed in federal district courts doubled between 1992 and 1997 (litigation volume reached a peak of more than 20,000 suits per year in 1995 and then fell by some 21% by 1997). During the previous 8 years, in contrast, the volume of litigation had actually declined by some 10%.

Moreover, the explosive rise in the volume of litigation during the 1990s occurred against a backdrop of unparalleled economic prosperity and falling unemployment rates. This is significant because—as we demonstrated in a series of articles in the early 1990s—there has traditionally been a strong negative relationship between the volume of employment discrimination suits and prosperity the labor market (Donohue and Siegleman, 1991; Siegelman and Donohue, 1991; Donohue and Siegelman, 1993; Siegelman and Donohue, 1995). Indeed, as we show below, what was once a robust relationship between the volume of employment discrimination litigation and the unemployment rate has completely broken down during the last 10 years. This suggests that more than a mere quantitative change has occurred: we do not just have a *lot* more suits being filed than 10 years ago; we seem to have an entirely different relationship between the volume of litigation and the rest of the economy.

Figure 1 provides compelling graphical evidence of this structural change. In the top half, it plots the number of employment discrimination suits filed in federal district courts during each calendar quarter from 1969 through 1997 (the circles), along with the predicted number of suits based on a simple model that utilizes only the lagged unemployment rate and a time trend as explanatory variables (the solid line). As can be seen, the model fits the actual data remarkably well during the period before the third quarter of 1991. At that point, however, the model appears to break down completely: while the sample regression model (estimated prior to 1992) would have predicted that the volume of litigation should have declined modestly as the unemployment rate fell (see bottom panel, which plots the de-trended unemployment rate), the actual number of suits skyrocketed over the next 5 years—more than doubling during this period, despite a steady downward trend in the unemployment rate.

In addition to changes in the *number* of suits filed, it would be helpful to identify changes in the *composition* of litigation since 1991. Unfortunately, the case-filing data do not allow a direct identification of the type (race, sex) or basis (hiring, firing, harassment) being alleged. Information on charges of discrimination filed with the EEOC can be used as a rough supplement to the data on filed cases, however, and these data reveal a pattern that is roughly consistent with the importance of the 1991 CRA as a source of the increased caseload.

Together, these structural changes cry out for an explanation. It would indeed be surprising if the underlying acts of discrimination rose 2.5-fold between 1992 and 1996. Has something about the evolution of the law during this period made it more attractive for plaintiffs to bring certain kinds of suits that they would formerly not

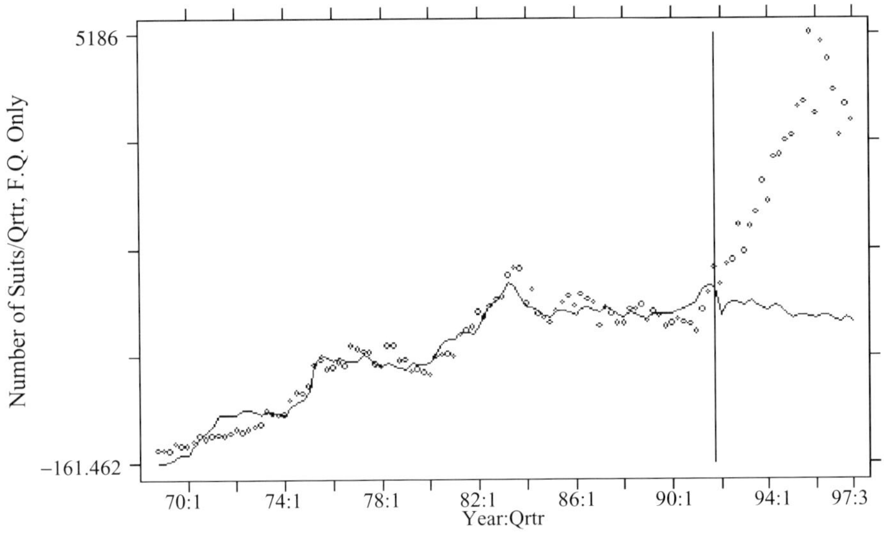

Actual, Fitted & Forecast Volume of Litigation

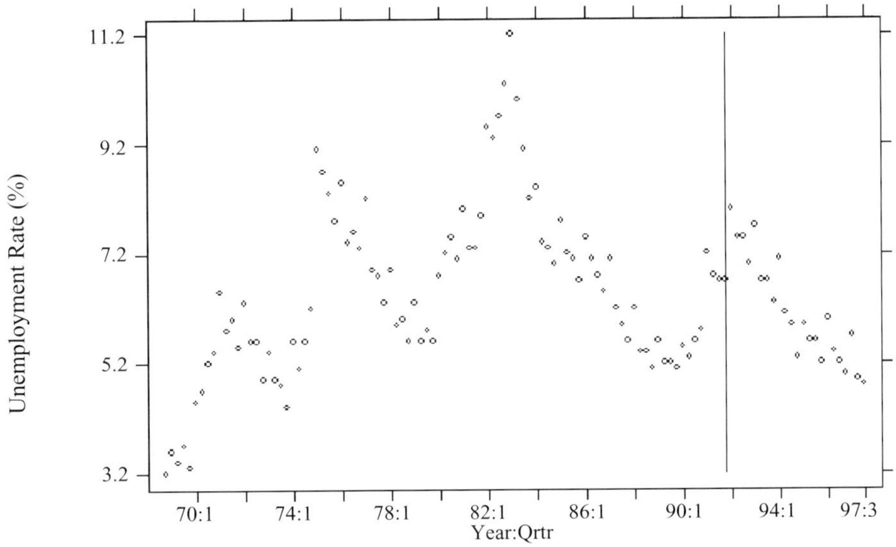

Changes in the Unemployment Rate Over Time

Figure 1. Actual, fitted, and forecast volume of litigation and changes in the unemployment rate over time.

have chosen to file? Has it been the expansion of possible causes of action that has generated the increased caseload? Or perhaps an extra-legal story involving increased mobilization of potential plaintiffs lies behind the rise in litigation. In addition, the kinds of structural changes we document below raise significant questions about who

Table 1. Effects of an increase in the unemployment rate on volume and outcomes of employment discrimination litigation, 1970–1989

	Cases/Quarter	Settlement Rate	Win Rate
At Unemployment Rate = 6.04%	1,367	61.3%	20.9%
For the Additional Cases Generated by Rise in Unemployment Rate to 8.66% (2 Std. Dev. Increase)	515	84.6%	16.4%
At Unemployment Rate = 8.66%	1,882	67.7%	20.3%
Percentage Change	+37.7	+10.4	−0.97

Source: Siegelman and Donohue (1995).

employment discrimination law actually protects, from what kinds of discrimination, and how well.

In the rest of this chapter, we attempt a preliminary assessment of the state of employment discrimination law in the 1990s, focusing not on the evolution of doctrine, but on the evolution of the law "in action"—on how people now use the law that is available to them. Section I begins by briefly sketching in the rules of employment discrimination law before 1990, stressing in particular the rules for calculating damages in discrimination suits. Our earlier work demonstrated that damages have traditionally played a vital role not only in determining the *number* of suits filed, but also the rate at which suits go to trial and the rate of plaintiff victories. Congress substantially changed the rules for calculating damages during the early 1990s, at least for some classes of suits, and a new basis for liability—disability discrimination—was added to the body of employment discrimination law. After describing these changes, we go on to evaluate their effects in Section II. We look at three different kinds of evidence: changes in the composition of the federal employment discrimination caseload after 1992; changes in the relationship between the business cycle (unemployment rate) and the volume and outcomes of employment discrimination litigation; and changes in the size distribution of awards to prevailing plaintiffs (table 1). Almost all of this evidence is consistent with our argument about the importance of the 1991 CRA and the ADA, but there are qualifications and uncertainties that are unresolvable with the existing data. In the final section, we offer some speculations about the future of employment discrimination law.

1. STRUCTURAL CHANGES IN THE 1990s

1.1. The Importance of Back Pay Before 1991

In a series of papers written in the late 1980s, we developed what then appeared to be a coherent economic account of the forces driving several aspects of employment discrimination litigation. This section briefly summarizes the theoretical and empirical insights that emerged from these papers, as they applied to the world of employment discrimination litigation before the passage of the 1991 CRA and the Americans With Disabilities Act.

Briefly put, the key to understanding a plaintiff's behavior in deciding whether or not to bring an employment discrimination claim in the first place—and, once the claim is filed whether or not to settle—is the way that damages are calculated.

Before 1992, damages in employment discrimination suits were largely limited to back pay. The basic pre-CRA of 1991 rule was that "Title VII provides only equitable remedies; damages other than back pay are not recoverable" (Cox, 1987, pp. 5–17; *DeGrace v. Rumsfeld, Harrington v. Vandalia-Butler Bd. of Educ, Pearson v. W. Elec. Co.*). Reinstatement, promotion, and changes in employment practices had also been available as remedies, but our data suggest that plaintiffs ask for and secure them through settlement or judgment *far* less frequently than they receive monetary settlements or awards (Donohue and Siegleman, 1991).

The Age Discrimination in Employment Act (ADEA) offers a limited version of punitive damages: conditional on a proof of willful violation of the statute, double recovery of actual damages is available (Cox, 1987, pp. 23–14; *Fortino v. Quasar Co.*). Punitive and compensatory damages as such, however, were not available under the ADEA (Cox, 1987, pp. 23–16). Suits under the Reconstruction Era Civil Rights Act, §1981, do allow for punitive damages in addition to back pay, but cover only discrimination on the basis of race.

Consider someone who lost her job because of a discriminatory firing and was then unemployed for 12 weeks. Assume that she was initially making $500 per week and that her new job pays the same salary as her old one. Her back-pay damages simply are the difference between what she would have earned but for discrimination (12 weeks at $500/week = $6,000) and her actual earnings (in this case, zero) for the period during which she was unemployed. Hence, she will be entitled to $6,000 in back pay.[1]

Several important facts about employment discrimination litigation followed from this observation. First, back-pay awards under the pre-1991 CRA were usually small and were positively related to a plaintiff's wage. A prevailing plaintiff who had been earning $5 per hour could expect to receive only $10,000 in back-pay damages if she were unemployed for a year after losing her job (as a result of discrimination). Even a very highly paid employee could not expect to earn much more than $150,000 under similar circumstances.

Second, as our examples just indicated, the size of her back-pay award depends on the length of time that the plaintiff was unemployed. Since the duration of

[1] This is the simplest possible case, a stylized example designed to illustrate the basic forces at work. Further wrinkles include what happens when the plaintiff takes a new job at a wage lower than her previous one; whether unemployment compensation is deductible from back-pay awards (courts were divided on this issue during the period before 1991); whether awards are subject to federal income tax (again a circuit split, plus changes in the tax code); how to calculate the period over which back-pay accumulates (see *Ford Motor Co. v. EEOC*, holding that a rejected offer of (re)employment from the original employer, without retroactive seniority, is sufficient to toll the accumulation of back pay), and so on.

unemployment spells tends to be longer in recessions—when the unemployment rate is high—and shorter during periods of economic prosperity, it follows that average awards were more generous in slumps than during booms. This, in turn, suggests that plaintiffs should have been more willing to bring employment discrimination cases during recessions: the rewards for doing so were larger than when the economy was robust, while the costs were presumably the same.

Furthermore, if plaintiffs brought cases during recessions that they would not otherwise have brought, these recession-induced cases should have had a lower probability of plaintiff victory than those brought during booms. Suppose that the risk-neutral plaintiff knows she will receive a back-pay award of $10,000 if she prevails. Given costs of $1,000, she will only bring suit if the probability of victory is greater than 10%. However, if the award size increases to $20,000, the plaintiff only requires a probability of victory of 0.05. By raising damages conditional on victory, a recession induces some low-probability plaintiffs—who would not otherwise have found it worthwhile to file suit—to come forward and do so. Hence, the average win rate should fall during recessions, as the mix of cases shifts to include those with lower win rates.

Our back-pay-driven model yielded at least three empirically testable predictions:

1. the size of awards to prevailing plaintiffs should be larger for cases filed when the unemployment rate is high than for those filed when it is low;
2. the number of suits filed should rise during recessions and fall when the unemployment rate is low;
3. the plaintiff win rate in tried cases should fall during recessions and rise when the economy is prosperous.

Using data obtained from the Administrative Office of the US Courts (AO) and supplemented by our own data collection, we were able to confirm all three of these predictions and to reject various other alternative explanations for our findings, as summarized in table 2.

1.2. Changes in the Early 1990s

1.2.1. The 1991 Civil Rights Act

Spurred in part by a number of Supreme Court decisions restricting the scope of federal employment discrimination law, as well as by complaints of inequitable treatment of sex discrimination claims, Congress passed the 1991 CRA.[2] The legislation modified

[2] *Ward's Cove Packing v. Atonio* (broadening business necessity defense in disparate impact claims), *Patterson v. McLean Credit Union* (restricting coverage of post-contractual discrimination under §1981), *Price Waterhouse v. Hopkins* (restricting plaintiff's recovery in "mixed-motive" disparate treatment cases), *Martin v. Wilks* (requiring joinder of adversely affected "outsiders" such as White employees in civil rights actions), *Lorance v. ATT Technologies* (requiring challenges to seniority system be filed within statutory 300-day period starting from the adoption of the seniority rules, not from when the rules had an effect on plaintiffs). Since the mid-1970s, most *race* discrimination plaintiffs have had a choice of federal statutes

Table 2. Back-Pay damages as the link to the business cycle. A summary of previous findings

Damages	One percentage point ↑ in unemployment rate → ↑ damages to prevailing plaintiffs by \$2,000–\$3,000. Flanagan (1987) found identical effects using better-quality data on back-pay damages under NLRA
Volume of Suits	Counter-cyclical (↑ during recessions). Each 1% ↑ in unemployment rate ↑ number of suits filed by about 150 per quarter after lag of 3–6 months. Plaintiffs bring more suits when damages are higher
Plaintiff Win Rate	Increases for cases filed during booms, falls during recessions. Plaintiffs willing to bring lower-probability suits when awards, *conditional on winning,* are higher
Settlement Rate	Increases for cases filed in slumps, falls during booms. Weaker cases brought during slumps tend disproportionately to settle, as predicted by, e.g., the Priest/Klein (1984) model
Composition of Suits	Did *not* change over the business cycle, either by basis of discrimination (race, sex, etc.) or by type of discrimination (hiring, firing, etc.)
Suits Against US Government	Increased during recessions (counter-cyclical), as did suits against pvt. defendants. However, US government doesnot lay people off in recessions; so, we are not observing a layoff effect
Lags	Lag between changes in unemployment and suit filing too short to be explained by layoffs. It takes at least 6 months to get through the EEOC; so, if upturn in unemployment rate causes increase in filings with a lag of, e.g., 3 months, it cannot be true that the effect is due to increased number of firings
Discrimination	May rise during recessions, but suggests plaintiff win rates should also increase at such times, rather than falling

many aspects of federal employment discrimination law, but the most important aspects are summarized in table 3 and discussed briefly here.

The most significant changes wrought by the 1991 CRA were designed to provide greater equity for sex and other non-race discrimination plaintiffs, who were considered to be at a disadvantage because they were not able to utilize §1981. Thus, for so-called "ineligible cases," the 1991 CRA expanded the realm of potential damages beyond back pay to include compensatory damages (e.g., for psychological distress, therapy expenses, and medical bills) and punitive damages in cases of intentional

under which they could challenge discriminatory practices. Such practices are forbidden under Title VII of the 1964 CRA, but most are also prohibited under §1981 of the 1866 CRA, which bars discrimination on the basis of race (but not sex) in the "making and enforcement of contracts." (The Supreme Court held that the statute covered employment contracts in *Johnson v. Railway Express Agency.*) Section 1981 offers plaintiffs several important advantages over Title VII: fewer procedural hurdles (no requirement of a right to sue letter from the EEOC, looser statutes of limitations), the right to a jury trial, and expansive remedies beyond back pay (including compensatory and punitive damages). It does not, however, cover sex discrimination, nor does it recognize cases of race discrimination based on disparate impact theories. The 1991 CRA, which modified all these areas of law, became effective when it was signed by President Bush, on November 21, 1991.

Table 3. Summary of changes under 1991 CRA

For Title VII, cases *not* eligible under §1981 (including sex discrimination complaints, especially harassment, and retaliation).	Allowed compensatory damages (e.g., for emotional distress). Allowed punitive damages (capped by firm size). Also allowed jury trials and added non-back-pay damages
Overturned *Patterson v. McLean Credit Union,* 491 U.S. 164 (1989)	§1981 *does* cover post-contract formation discrimination, including firing.
Misc. other provisions	Extended Title VII to Congressional employees; Overturned *Wards Cove Packing Co. v. Antonio,* 490 U.S. 642 (1989) (tightened standard for business necessity in disparate impact cases); Overturned *Price-Waterhouse v. Hopkins,* 490 U.S. 228 (1989) (allowed damages in some "mixed-motives cases"); Overturned *Lorance v. AT&T Technologies,* 490 U.S. 900 (1989) (lengthened filing period for challenges to discriminatory seniority systems); allowed for recovery of expert witness fees by prevailing plaintiffs; overturned *Martin v. Wilks*, 490 U.S 755 (1989) (expanded possibilities for challenging civil rights consent decrees)

discrimination (limited, however, by the size of the defendant firm).[3] This had the effect of turning disparate treatment employment discrimination cases into suits at law, rather than equitable actions (back pay had been considered an equitable, rather than a legal, remedy). As a result, the 7th Amendment's right to a jury trial in civil cases meant that Congress was forced to confer the right to jury trials while it expanded damages. "Forced" may be the wrong verb, since the right to a jury trial was generally viewed with enthusiasm by plaintiff advocacy and Civil Rights groups, as we discuss below.[4]

Together, these changes meant that non-race discrimination plaintiffs were eligible for substantially higher awards than previously. Moreover, what was once the only monetary remedy—back pay—became just one part of a much larger array of potential

[3] "Ineligible" refers to those Title VII plaintiffs who could not *also* bring a §1981 claim of racial discrimination. See §102 of the 1991 CRA, 42 U.S.C. §1981a (2002). These include plaintiffs claiming intentional discrimination on the basis of sex, religion, or national origin, by far the majority of which comprise sex discrimination claims. See table 3.

[4] Many of the other provisions in the 1991 CRA were largely symbolic or of minimal importance to the overall volume and composition of the employment discrimination caseload. These include extending Title VII protection to Congressional employees, changing the interpretation of the statute of limitations for challenges to intentionally discriminatory seniority systems, and changing the definition of "business necessity" in disparate impact cases. Because of the preponderance of firing cases in the federal employment discrimination caseload, §101 of the Act (overturning the Supreme Court's holding in *Patterson v. McLean Credit Union* that §1981s anti-discrimination prohibition did not cover "post-contract formation" discrimination such as discrimination in firing) might be of greater importance than the other provisions discussed above.

damages that non-race discrimination plaintiffs were allowed to collect for the first time. Since there is unlikely to be a strong link between the size of non-back-pay awards (e.g., for emotional distress) and the business cycle, we might expect to see that the volume and win rate in employment discrimination cases would be less sensitive to the state of the economy after the 1991 Act.

1.2.2. The Americans with Disabilities Act

The 1991 CRA was not the only important piece of employment discrimination passed by Congress in the early 1990s. Passed a year earlier than the CRA, the Americans with Disabilities Act's employment provisions became effective, 6 months after the 1991 CRA went into effect. A far-ranging piece of legislation, the ADA extended beyond employment to testing, architectural design, and many other areas of life. We focus on the employment provisions in Title I, whose effective date for firms with more than 25 employees was July 26, 1992. Those with 15–25 employees were given an additional 2 years before the act was extended to cover them.

The ADA created two distinct causes of action for covered employees: first, it gave workers the right to be free of discrimination because of their disability, just as Title VII gave them the right to be free of discrimination because of their race or sex. Remedies were essentially the same as those under the post-1991 CRA Title VII.[5]

In addition, however, the ADA created an affirmative duty for employers to make "reasonable accommodations" to the needs of "qualified" employees with disabilities, defined as someone who has the "requisite skill, experience and education requirements of the employment position, and who, with or without reasonable accommodation, can perform essential functions of such position." §101(8). Hence, under the ADA, qualified disabled employees can require employers to make buildings more accessible (e.g., installing ramps instead of stairs), to modify work schedules (e.g., allowing part-time work), to install special equipment (e.g., specialized computer screens with larger type), to grant them more time to complete examinations or other performance evaluations, and so on.[6]

[5] The question of exactly what constitutes a disability under the ADA is complex and still subject to significant uncertainty. The statute speaks of persons with an "impairment" that "substantially limits" a major life activity, but the precise meaning of these phrases is still far from clear, even after a number of Supreme Court decisions. See *Sutton v. United Air Lines; Murphy v. United Parcel Service; and Albertson's, Inc. v. Kirkingburg.*

[6] The right to require reasonable accommodation by one's *current employer* is unique to the ADA and is likely to be especially valuable for disabled employees, whose current employer may be their *final* employer in many cases. "Most disabilities occur among older adults who have little opportunity to change occupations or acquire new job skills. The late onset of disability implies that an employer had an opportunity to observe the worker's productivity prior to his becoming disabled and is better informed than other employers regarding his likely productivity as a disabled worker. Thus the pre-injury employer may be the only potential employer of a disabled worker. In many cases, the ability of a disabled worker to work is determined by whether or not his pre-injury employer is willing to provide accommodations for his functional limitations" (Burkhauser, 1990). In our earlier work, we found that before 1991, only 10% of employment discrimination plaintiffs were suing their current employer. We expect that this fraction rose after passage of the ADA, although we currently lack data on this question.

In sum, both the ADA and the 1991 CRA gave plaintiffs' expanded opportunities to seek remedies beyond back pay. For plaintiffs with disabilities, the reasonable accommodations requirement meant that they could, for the first time, force their employers to alter working conditions in a way that would allow them to keep their jobs. The 1991 CRA granted some plaintiffs the right to compensatory and punitive damages that were previously unavailable to them.

Cutting in the other direction, we note that the Supreme Court held in 1992 that payments received in settlement of a back-pay claim under Title VII were not excludable from the recipient's gross income under §104(a)(2) of the Internal Revenue Code, which allows for exclusion of "damages received on account of personal injuries." (*United States v. Burke*). This, of course, reduced the after-tax amount of Title VII damages, at least in those circuits that did not already follow this rule. It thus cuts in the opposite direction from the other changes discussed above that increased the size of expected awards to plaintiffs.

The net consequences of these developments are spelled out more fully and tested against the existing evidence, below.

1.3. Data and Sample Partition Issues

Below, we present data from the Administrative Office of the U.S. Courts (AO), which records all "Employment Civil Rights" cases filed in federal district courts. The AO began tracking employment discrimination cases filed after January 1969. Our previous dataset ended in June 1989, but the data now extend through September 1997. (We constructed a quarterly time series by simply counting the number of cases filed in each 3-month period starting on January 1, 1969. Outcome variables—how a case was decided—only became available for cases closing after 1978 and, of course, are not available for cases that were still pending as of September 1997. There is reason to believe that such cases might differ systematically from those that had already closed. For example, most cases filed in 1995 had closed by 1998; those that had not might be unusually complex, unusually large, or otherwise atypical. In order to dampen the effect of this duration dependence, we eliminated all cases filed after 1996:3, 1 year before the data ended, in our analysis of win rates.)

In what follows, we use the number of "Federal Question" employment discrimination suits filed per calendar quarter as the measure of the employment discrimination caseload. (This measure excludes all suits in which the federal government is either the plaintiff or the defendant. We omitted federal-plaintiff suits because of a concern that government-litigated cases are likely to be different from garden-variety employment discrimination suits. Presumably, the former have larger stakes, involve more complicated legal and factual issues and more time-consuming preparation, and focus on different subjects. We omitted cases in which the federal government was a defendant because our previous research revealed that many of these are due process cases, with different procedures and remedies from those available to Title VII, ADA, or §1981 plaintiffs.) Since the dataset and its limitations have already been described at considerable length in our previous papers, we do not repeat that material here.

Our method for assessing the effects of the civil right legislation of the early 1990s on the volume of suits filed or other aspects of litigation is quite simple. If these laws did have a significant effect on the volume of litigation (or its relationship to the business cycle or to the passage of time), then we would expect to see a break or turning point in the time series at roughly the time that the legislation went into effect. Our strategy, then, is to divide the period from 1969 to 1997 into two parts—one before and one after the new laws went into effect—and look for differences.

Since the laws did not go into effect at the same time, however, we have to decide the appropriate point at which to partition the sample. The effective date of the 1991 CRA was November 21, 1991. The ADA went into effect in two phases: firms with 25 or more employees were covered as of July 26, 1992 while those with 15–24 employees were covered as of July 26, 1994. The second round added about 9% of the labor force that was employed at firms with 15–24 employees to the covered population (Statistical Abstract of the United States, 1997, tables 621, 844, and 847). We chose January 1, 1992, largely for convenience. This is the earliest possible reasonable date to divide the sample and hence maximizes the number of observations in the second part of the sample, which is still substantially shorter than the first. It turns out that the results that follow are not sensitive to the choice of a later partition date, as figure 1 suggests graphically.

2. PREDICTING THE EFFECTS OF THE NEW LAWS: WHAT SHOULD WE LOOK FOR AND HOW SHOULD WE LOOK?

This section presents several different pieces of evidence on the effects of the early 1990s legislation. We examine a proxy for changes in the composition of the federal employment discrimination caseload after 1992, changes in the relationship between unemployment rates and the volume and outcomes of litigation, and changes in the size distribution of awards to prevailing plaintiffs. Almost all of this evidence is consistent with our argument about the importance of the 1991 CRA and the ADA, but there are qualifications and uncertainties that are unresolvable with the existing data.

2.1. Caseload Composition: A Shift in Favor of "New" Areas of Law

The simplest test for the effects of the new legislation would be to look at the growth in litigation by the type of discrimination alleged. For example, if much of the increase in litigation came from Age Discrimination cases, whose rules were not altered by the new laws, it would be difficult to attribute the observed growth to the statutes. In contrast, if we saw tremendous growth in claims alleging disability or sex discrimination, we would have a stronger case that the legislation of the early 1990s was responsible.

Indeed, sincedisability discrimination claims were essentially not cognizable before 1992, *any* increase in disability claims must be due to the ADA, at least as a "but-for" cause.

Unfortunately, however, the AO data do not permit one to disaggregate "Employment Civil Rights" cases by the type of discrimination (age, sex, disability, race, etc.) being alleged. Hence, no direct test along these lines is possible. Instead, we have to rely on charges of discrimination filed with the EEOC. Except for cases raising only a §1981 or Equal Pay Act claim, all employment discrimination cases that wind up in federal district court must first have been processed through the EEOC.[7] Unlike the Administrative Office of the US Courts, the EEOC does keep track of the type of discrimination alleged by the charging party, and these data thus provide a window on the composition of filed cases, even though historically only 10% of EEOC charges have gone on to generate a federal district court filing. (These data are naturally subject to sample selection problems, since the process by which a charge becomes a filed case is assuredly not random; hence, the picture derived from aggregate charge data at the EEOC may not accurately reflect the selected subset of claims that then go on to become filed cases in federal district courts. Although our earlier work did not find any evidence of such selection, the ability to test for these problems is limited.)

Table 4 examines charges of discrimination with the EEOC for a number of different categories of employment discrimination claims. While we have noted that the overall caseload has risen despite the steadily dropping unemployment rate of the 1990s, table 4 reveals that race and age discrimination charges filed with the EEOC actually experienced a *decline* in over the period from 1991 to 1996. Since the legislation offered little or no encouragement to these kinds of claims, these results are more in keeping with our earlier work that would have suggested that the booming economy would lead to a decline in the absolute numbers of cases. Conversely, sex discrimination charges grew by 31.2%, again consistent with the positive incentives created by the 1991 CRA. Finally, disability discrimination charges, which became legally cognizable for the first time in the 1990s, grew from a small number to 18,000 in 1996—a figure higher than the number of age discrimination cases and about 75% of the number of sex discrimination cases.

In conclusion, the large growth in federal district court filings of employment discrimination cases is substantially higher than the growth in discrimination complaints filed with the EEOC. Race and age discrimination charges filed with the EEOC were

[7] "All claims filed pursuant to Title VII of the CRA of 1964 must be processed initially by the EEOC, as is also true for claims filed under the Age Discrimination in Employment Act and the Americans With Disabilities Act. See 42 U.S.C. §2000e-5 (1988); 29 U.S.C. §626(d) (1994) (Age Discrimination in Employment Act); 42 U.S.C. §12117(a) (1988 & Supp. V 1993) (Americans with Disabilities Act). The only exceptions are for claims filed pursuant to 42 U.S.C. §1981 (1988 & Supp. V 1993), which applies to race and national origin discrimination, and under the Equal Pay Act, 29 U.S.C. §206(d) (1988).... Most §1981 claims filed in federal court include a Title VII allegation, which means that the underlying claim was processed by the EEOC. As a result, ~85% of employment discrimination cases are initially processed by the EEOC." (Selmi, 1996).

Table 4. Numbers of charges filed with EEOC, by type of discrimination, selected EEOC fiscal years*

				% Change	
	FY 1992	FY 1996	FY 1999	1992–1999	1992–1996
Race Claims	29,548	26,287	28,819	−11.0	−2.5
% of Total	40.9	33.7	37.2		
Age Claims	19,573	15,719	14,141	−19.7	−27.8
% of Total	27.1	20.2	18.3		
Sex Claims	21,796	23,813	23,907	9.3	9.7
% of Total	30.1	30.6	30.9		
Retaliation Claims					
All Statutes	11,096	16,080	19,694	44.9	77.5
% of Total	15.3	20.6	25.4		
Title VII	10,499	14,412	17,883	37.3	70.3
% of Total	14.5	18.5	23.1		
Disability Claims	1,048	18,046	17,007	1621.9	1522.8
% of Total	1.4	23.2	22.0		
Other Claims	10,116	9,220	9,963	−8.9	−1.5
% of Total	14.0	11.8	12.9		
Total *Charges*	72,302	77,900	77,444	7.7	7.1
Total Claims†	103,676	123,577	131,414	19.2	26.8
Claims/Charge	1.43	1.58	1.70	10.5	18.9

* Since charges can claim more than one type of discrimination (e.g., race and sex), Total Charges is the number of filed charges, not the total number of claims of discrimination.

† Total Claims is the actual column sum.

declining modestly in the early 1990s while sex discrimination and disability charges with the EEOC were growing briskly. Still, the increase in the total number of federal court cases and federal court trials was far greater than the increase in the EEOC filings. The desire to get before a jury for the first time and to collect compensatory and punitive damages might explain the greater federal litigation concerning sex discrimination complaints, since these options only became available with the CRA of 1991. However, this option was always available in race cases (because of section 1981) and age cases.

2.2. Weakened Business Cycle Sensitivity

2.2.1. The Volume of Litigation

As suggested earlier, both the ADA and the 1991 CRA reduced the importance of back-pay damages, albeit in different ways. The CRA expanded monetary remedies for a class of cases (predominantly allegations of sex discrimination) that had previously been eligible to collect only back-pay damages. After 1991, sex discrimination plaintiffs could get punitive and compensatory damages and could take their cases to a jury, rather than a generally less-sympathetic judge. The ADA's "reasonable accommodations" requirement meant that disabled plaintiffs could force employers to change the organization of the workplace to make it more conducive to their continued employment. This, too, reduced the importance of back-pay damages in a plaintiff's assessment of the remedies available under employment discrimination laws.

By increasing the possible benefits available to plaintiffs, both statutes should increase the volume of litigation, at least in the short run, simply because some plaintiffs who would not have found it desirable to sue under the old rules would look at the enhanced damages under the new regime and conclude that litigation was worthwhile. Of course, the ADA also created a whole new cause of action that was not cognizable before its passage, and this alone should lead to an expansion of litigation.

Moreover, both statutes should attenuate the relationship between the business cycle and the volume and outcomes of employment discrimination litigation. As back pay becomes less important in the total package of damages available to plaintiffs, the link between plaintiffs' decisions and the unemployment rate should grow correspondingly weaker. When back pay was all a plaintiff could get, business cycle-induced changes in the amount of back pay should have mattered much more than they do under today's rules.[8] In short, we would expect both statutes to generate more litigation and to diminish the importance of business cycle effects on the number of suits filed.

Tables 5 and 6 test these predictions by presenting some summary statistics and regression results for a simple model in which the volume of suits filed in quarter t depends on the number of quarters that have elapsed since January 1, 1969 (as well as its square) and on the unemployment rate in quarters $t - 1$ and $t - 2$. This was our standard model developed for the 1969–1989 data, and as evidenced by figure 1, it fits the data for that period extremely well.

Table 6 takes a somewhat different approach from figure 1. Rather than using the pre-1991 model to *forecast* the volume of suits in the post-1991 period, we estimated a different equation for each period and then compare them. There are some telling differences in the relationships for the two periods. Most importantly, while there is strong evidence of a business cycle effect before 1992, the effect seems to vanish after that date.

Before 1992, a 1 percentage point increase in the unemployment generated about 145 additional employment discrimination suits two quarters later. Both the one- and two-quarter lagged values of the unemployment rate coefficient were positive and

[8] Somewhat more formally, suppose that under the pre-1991 rules, damages were a function of the unemployment rate and other random factors, so that $D_0 = D(U, \epsilon_0)$, where U is the unemployment rate and ϵ_0 is other factors uncorrelated with the business cycle. By the rules for calculating backpay, $dD_0/dU > 0$, so that higher unemployment rates lead to higher damages. After the 1991 CRA, $D_1 = D(U, \epsilon_1)$, where $\sigma_1^2 > \sigma_0^2$ is the variance of ϵ, the non-back-pay component of damages. Since the variance of ϵ has increased due to the legislation, post-1991 damages, D_1, will depend less on changes in the unemployment rate than pre-1991 damages did: random variation in non-back-pay damages will attenuate the measured effect of unemployment on damages after 1991, even though the *direct* effect of an increase in U will not have changed.

Table 5. Summary statistics for partitioned sample (before and after effective date of 1991 CRA)

	1969:1–1991:4			1992:1–1997:3		
Variable	Mean	Std. Dev.	Min, Max	Mean	Std. Dev.	Min, Max
Number of Suits	1,182	647	0, 2270	3,644	909	2,054, 5,186
Time	46	27	0, 92	104	6.8	93, 115
De-trended Unemployment Rate, −1*	0.0	1.12	−2.0, 3.6	0.0	0.4	−1.0, 0.8
De-trended Unemployment Rate, −2*	0.0	1.11	−2.0, 3.6	0.0	0.5	−0.8, 0.9
N		92			22	

*De-trended Unemployment Rate is the residual from a regression of the lagged unemployment rate on Time and Time^2 with correction for AR(1) errors. Separate regressions were used for the two sample halves. The number following the minus means a lag of one or two quarters—i.e., the unemployment rate in the quarter previous to the one in which the number of suits filed is being measured.

statistically significant during the first part of the sample. In contrast, there is no discernible relationship between unemployment and the volume of litigation during the period after 1991. During this period, a 1 percentage point increase in the unemployment rate was associated with 30 fewer suits per quarter (two quarters later). Moreover, the net measurement obscures the fact that one of the estimated unemployment coefficients is positive while the other is negative, and neither is statistically significant in the post-1991 data. In other words, there is essentially no business cycle relationship apparent for the period after 1991.

Table 6. Regression of number of employment discrimination suits per quarter on time and de-trended unemployment rates,* first and second halves of sample

	1969:1–1991:4		1992:1–1997:3	
Variable	Coeff.	T-Stat.	Coeff.	T-Stat.
Time†	46.56	9.76	269.1	5.34
Time^2	−0.27	−5.43	−6.96	−3.16
De-trended Unemployment Rate, −1‡	94.85	5.75	173.21	1.08
De-trended Unemployment Rate, −2‡	49.63	3.01	−203.88	−1.33
Constant	−180.18	−1.90	1833.35	7.63
		Summary Statistics		
Adjusted R^2	0.77		076	
Durbin–Watson	1.90		1.97	
ρ	0.70		0.24	
N	92		22	

*Regressions estimated using Prais–Winston correction for AR(1) errors.

† Time and Time^2 are reset to zero for the second period regression.

‡ De-trended Unemployment Rate is the residual from a regression of the lagged unemployment rate on Time and Time^2. Separate de-trending regressions were used for the two sample halves.

Although a simple visual inspection of the table reveals the different business cycle relationships across the two periods, there are also several formal ways to test whether the unemployment (and other) coefficients in the pre- and post-1992 periods are statistically significantly different from each other. All of these tests demonstrate conclusively that the relationship between unemployment rates and the volume of suits filed is indeed different across the two periods.

Unfortunately, however, there is a technical problem with interpreting these results as evidence in support of our story about the effects of the legislative interventions in the early 1990s. Because unemployment followed an almost steady downward path between 1991 and 1997, the regression has a hard time accurately assigning responsibility for the rising number of suits during this period to either the time trend or the unemployment rate—the two factors are statistically almost indistinguishable, a classic multicollinearity problem.[9] Put another way, the observed increase in the correlation between unemployment rates and the time trend for the post-1992 data will *by itself* tend to produce large standard errors and statistically insignificant unemployment coefficient estimates for this period. This is precisely the same result we would predict on the basis of our story about the legislative interventions of the early 1990s. If business cycle effects on the volume of suits necessarily *appear* weaker after 1992, *regardless of whether they actually are*, then it is hard to use this evidence in support of our explanation about the effects of the CRA and ADA.

2.2.2. Litigation Outcomes—Settlement and Win Rates Over the Business Cycle

2.2.2.1. Why should the business cycle influence the win rate?

The back-pay mechanism linking the *volume* of litigation with the business cycle is simple: assuming that the costs of litigation are relatively invariant, an increase in plaintiffs' damages makes them more likely to pursue litigation, and higher unemployment rates cause longer durations of unemployment and larger awards to prevailing plaintiffs. The link between unemployment rates and the *outcomes* of litigation follows almost directly from this observation. When plaintiffs expect to receive higher damages *if they win*, they are willing to bring cases that have a lower probability of winning. For example, suppose that a lawsuit costs $2,000 to bring, and the plaintiff will recover

[9] To solve the problem of multicollinearity, we de-trended the unemployment rate by regressing it against a time trend and keeping the residuals from this regression. This guarantees that there will be no correlation between the de-trended unemployment rate and time. Having done this, however, the problem is that for the period after 1992, there is very little variation left in the unemployment rate once the trend has been subtracted out. The bottom half of figure 1 demonstrates this visually: post-1992 unemployment rates follow a downward trend very closely. Alternatively, consider table 5, which compares the standard deviation of de-trended unemployment rates in the two sample periods: the second period standard deviation is one-third the size of the first. The "insufficient variance" problem was absent before 1992, since the economy experienced several complete business cycles during the first 92 quarters of our dataset. There were thus periods of rising and falling unemployment, and there was plenty of variation "left" in de-trended unemployment rates before 1992 after the time trend had been netted out. While clearly undesirable from the perspective of national welfare, a significant recession is needed to be able to differentiate between the effects of unemployment and the mere passage of time after 1992.

$20,000 in damages if she prevails. Then if she is risk-neutral, she will want to bring any suit whose chance of success is greater than 10%, since any such suit will have a positive net expected value. Now suppose that because of a recession, the plaintiff's damages, if she prevails, rise from $20,000 to $30,000. The plaintiff now requires only a 6.66% chance of success in order to make filing suit economically worthwhile. The additional cases brought forth by a rise in the unemployment rate should, therefore, have lower plaintiff win rates, and the average win rate for all cases filed during recessions should thus be lower than for cases filed when the unemployment rate is low. This link between the business cycle and the plaintiff win rate is not merely hypothetical. In earlier work, we demonstrated that, at least for the period before 1989, an increase in the unemployment rate did in fact call-forth cases with lower plaintiff win rates (Siegelman and Donohue, 1995). As summarized in table 1, we found that an increase in unemployment from one standard deviation below to one standard deviation above its mean generated a fall in the plaintiff win rate of about 1% (0.6 percentage points). The marginal cases brought forth by the increase in the unemployment rate had a win rate that was about 21% (4.5 percentage points) lower than the average for the baseline cases.

The connection between the business cycle and the *adjudication* rate—the rate at which filed cases go to trial rather than settling—is somewhat more complex and less intuitive.[10] Again, however, our earlier work demonstrated that in the period before 1989, the rate at which filed cases settle, rather than going to trial, did indeed increase during recessions, exactly as predicted by at least some models of settlement and litigation.

In sum, there is strong evidence that the business cycle influenced the outcomes of employment discrimination for cases filed before 1989. As we discussed earlier, the legislation of the early 1990s diluted the importance of back pay, and we would, therefore, predict that the effect of business cycles on litigation outcomes should be weaker after 1992 than it was before.

2.2.2.2. Empirical evidence

Table 7 provides some evidence on what happened to the business cycle effects on outcomes of employment discrimination in the 1990s. In the period before 1992, a 1 percentage point increase in the unemployment rate raised the settlement rate by about 4% and lowered the plaintiff win rate by about one-tenth of that amount, with both magnitudes statistically significant. After 1991, however, the business cycle relationships essentially vanish. Neither the win rate nor the settlement rate appears to be influenced by the unemployment rate at all: both coefficients change sign (a recession

[10] The Priest/Klein model of the selection of disputes for litigation (Priest and Klein, 1984) predicts that settlement rates will increase when (a) employer/defendants have higher stakes in litigation than do employee/plaintiffs and (b) the amount of damages increases. The first claim is arguably true of employment discrimination cases, since plaintiff win rates are so low. The second claim is true whenever a recession induces longer unemployment spells and greater back-pay damages (Siegelman and Donohue, 1995).

Table 7. Effect of a 1 percentage point increase in the de-trended unemployment rate, before and after 1992*

Effect on:	1977:2–1991:4	1992:1–1996:3
Settlement Rate†	+3.9%	−5.4%
Win Rate‡	−0.36%	+1.8%
N	58	18

*All estimates based on grouped logistic regressions with separate time trends for each period. See footnote ‡ of table 6.

† Both pre-1992 estimates statistically significant at 5%.

‡ Neither post-1992 estimates statistically significant at 10%.

now appears to *raise* the plaintiff win rate!), but neither effect is statistically significant at even modest levels.

This evidence is entirely consistent with our theory. Unfortunately, however, the same problems discussed earlier with respect to the volume of litigation are present here as well. The sharply lower variance in de-trended unemployment rates during the post-1992 period means that the regression has lower power to detect any business cycle effects that do exist. Moreover, the shortened sample after 1992 exacerbates these problems. Hence, we might expect to see weaker business cycle effects *regardless* of the effect of the early 1990s legislation, merely as a result of reduced statistical precision in the estimates.

2.3. Award Sizes

The Administrative Office data contain a measure of the amount of damages awarded to prevailing plaintiffs; so, some of our predictions about the effects of the early 1990s legislation on award sizes can be tested directly.[11]

Our analysis of the early 1990s legislation leads us to predict that smaller awards should fall as a proportion of the total while larger awards should increase. The logic here is simple. Smaller awards are mostly back pay. However, the import of both the CRA and the ADA is that more plaintiffs are eligible for awards beyond back pay; so, we would expect the fraction of all awards that are "small" to be declining. Larger

[11] The award size data are somewhat problematic, however. Our earlier research revealed that the data are subject to frequent miscoding, especially for larger awards (The problem seems to be that clerks entered the award size directly when it was supposed to be entered in thousands of dollars. Thus, an award of $2,000 should be coded as 2, but if it is instead entered as $2000, it will be read as $2,000,000 (Donohue and Siegelman, 1993, note 104). Since few plaintiffs will earn more than $10 million (except perhaps for some of the largest class actions), it probably makes sense to look only at those cases with awards of <9999 rather than including all awards, as in the next row. This conclusion is strengthened by the fact that there were no cases with awards of 9999 in the post-1992 period, presumably because coding errors decreased over time.

awards will tend to include punitive and compensatory damages, and their share of all awards should increase under the new laws.

One might argue that the number of small award cases should fall absolutely, not just as a proportion of the total. After all, the economy has been increasingly healthy in the post-1992 period, and the declining unemployment rate should generate smaller back-pay awards to prevailing plaintiffs. However, there are two reasons to be cautious here. First, despite the steady improvement in unemployment since 1992, the average post-1992 unemployment rate was only 0.5 percentage points lower than the average for the previous period. Moreover, non-random settlement may mean that smaller-award cases are not equally likely to settle.

Table 8 presents several aspects of the award size distribution that allow us to test our predictions against the available data. As predicted, small awards (e.g., those under $25,000 in constant dollars) fall as a proportion of all awards during the post-1992 period. Awards under $25,000 comprised almost half (48.2%) of all awards to prevailing plaintiffs before 1992 while these small awards were only 39.9% of all awards in the subsequent period. Table 8 also reveals that overall, more prevailing plaintiffs were getting larger awards: the larger the top award size, the more rapid the *growth rate* in average award size (in the last column). For example, the average award

Table 8. Average real awards in $1000s, by award size* (for cases filed before and after effective date of 1991 CRA)

	58 Quarters from 1977:2 to 1991:4			18 Quarters from 1992:1– to 1996:3			
All awards less than:	*N*	Mean award	% of all awards	*N*	Mean award	% of all awards	% Change in avg. award
$25,000	2,507	8.9	48.2%	756	9.1	39.9%	2.2
$50,000	3,216	14.9	61.9%	1,020	15.9	53.9%	6.7
$100,000	3,773	23.1	72.6%	1,276	26.7	67.4%	15.6
$200,000	4,162	34.1	80.1%	1,494	43.7	78.9%	28.2
$500,000	4,420	50.3	85.1%	1,665	69.6	87.9%	38.4
$9.999 Million†	5,153	528.6	99.2%	1,894	594	100.0%	12.4
All Awards(incl. 9,999)	5,196	615.1	100.0%	1,894	594	100.0%	−3.4
Median for Awards<$1 Million	4,602	20.8		1,713	32.7		57.2
	N	Rate		*N*	Rate		% Change in rate
Total Plaintiff Wins	7,095	20.5%		2,206	13.1%		−36.2%
Adjudicated Cases	34,562	30.6%		16,886	23.7%		−22.6%
Total Cases	112,845			71,213‡			—
Cases/Quarter	1,946			3,956			103
Unemployment Rate	58	6.9%		18	6.4%		−7.2

* Awards are not on a per plaintiff basis.

† "9,999" may have been used to indicate missing values or "not-applicable."

‡ Includes 6,458 open cases not included in award size tabulations above.

among those plaintiffs receiving less than $25,000 grew by only 2.2% in real terms, whereas the average award for those plaintiffs receiving less than $500,000 rose by more than 38%. (Awards between $1 million and $9.998 million are more likely to be multiple-plaintiff cases. Since we have no way of controlling for the number of plaintiffs in any given case, or to track changes in the number of plaintiffs per case over time, it is safest to focus on awards of less than $1 million.) Although it was still surprisingly small, the median award among awards less than $1 million also rose substantially after 1992: half of all awards before 1992 were smaller than $20,800 while the post-'92 median was $32,700, an increase of more than 57%.

2.4. California Filings

In many states, employment discrimination plaintiffs have a choice of filing a claim in state court under a state anti-discrimination statute or in federal court under Title VII. For some time, California employment discrimination law has offered plaintiffs expanded remedies (beyond backpay), coverage for disability discrimination, and the right to a jury trial. Even after the passage of the 1991 CRA, plaintiffs in California could have litigated the same causes of action and obtained the same or better damages and remedies by suing under state law.[12] Hence, if the 1991 CRA were driving the growth in litigation, we might expect to see little or no increase in federal district court filings in California, Since the legislation provided California plaintiffs with nothing more than they could have already obtained in state court.

Figure 2 plots the growth of federal district court filings in California and in the rest of the country. Contrary to our predictions, federal district court filings in California track those in the rest of the country very closely, even though the 1991 CRA did not provide any additional advantages for California plaintiffs. This may suggest that the allure of federal court is substantial for California plaintiffs, even though on many dimensions, state employment discrimination law is more favorable than federal law.

3. WHAT DOES IT ALL MEAN?

So, there are a lot more suits than there used to be, awards to prevailing plaintiffs are up, at least in the larger size categories, and the business cycle no longer seems to have much of an effect on any aspect of employment discrimination litigation. So what? Are these more than just a set of technical findings or economist's *curiosa*? Here, we attempt some partial and tentative answers.

Like any other social phenomenon, Title VII was a product of its time. It was largely designed to address a particular problem—the inability of African-Americans

[12] Indeed, informal conversations with several California lawyers who represent defendants in employment discrimination suits have strongly suggested that plaintiffs should always prefer to file in state court rather than federal court.

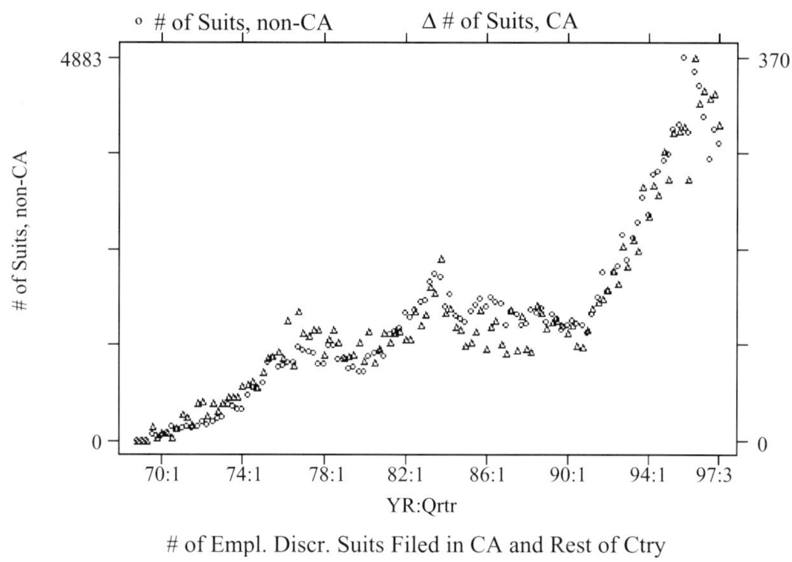

Figure 2. Number of employment discrimination suits filed in CA and rest of the country.

to break into many jobs in many regions of the country because many employers simply refused to hire (or even to consider) them. That Title VII also addressed discrimination in firing and promotion, and discrimination on the basis of national origin, religion, and (especially) sex is largely a result of political maneuvering and luck. The legislative history of the employment provisions of the 1964 CRA makes it very clear that, in the minds of both its supporters and opponents, the chief "problem" against which it was directed was exclusion on the basis of race at the hiring stage. Other types of discrimination (e.g., on the basis of sex) were either not taken seriously or, in the case of firing, were not a serious problem because there were essentially no blacks in jobs other than at the lowest echelons of the employment structure.

While the evidence we present in this chapter is limited in scope, it seems almost axiomatic that the civil right legislation of the 1990s is a product of its time–*our* time–no less than its predecessor was. In this section, we succumb to the temptation to go beyond what the evidence clearly demonstrates and speculate about the meaning of employment discrimination law at the start of the new millennium. What, then, might our new employment discrimination law(s) say about us?

3.1. The Decline of Back Pay, and the Increasing Role of Juries in Deciding Cases and Setting Damages

In fashioning remedies for victims of employment discrimination, the drafters of Title VII faced a serious concern. The 7th Amendment gives either party the right to a jury trial in a civil case. Civil right supporters were thus worried that defendants would elect a jury and—given the substantial opposition to civil rights (especially among Southern whites) and the under-representation of blacks on jury panels—would be able to escape any liability for their discriminatory behavior. The compromise that was reached was to limit damages to back pay: since this was considered equitable rather than legal relief, the 7th Amendment would not come into play, preventing defendants from requesting a jury trial. Greater certainty of punishment was explicitly traded-off against lower monetary awards.

The text of the 1991 CRA and the behavior of the employment discrimination caseload in the 1990s suggest that the problem of racist white juries refusing to sanction discriminatory employers no longer seems to be a serious concern. In fact, it is often employment discrimination *plaintiffs* who want a jury trial today, and Civil Rights groups, such as NAACP, were strong supporters of the 1991 CRA. Admittedly, many of the reasons had nothing to do with jury trials. It seems clear, however, that if the NAACP thought plaintiffs would be seriously disadvantaged by jury trials, they would have made this an issue. All these suggest that the anti-discrimination principle is more widely accepted than it used to be (a proposition for which there is abundant evidence from other sources) and that even Civil Rights groups recognize this fact.

3.2. The Decline of "Pure" Wage Discrimination and the Rise of New Damages

Thirty-five years ago, the paradigmatic case of employment discrimination was an employer's outright refusal to hire someone because of his or her race. Title VII recognized a simple remedy for this problem—the victim of discrimination was entitled to receive back-pay damages equal to the difference between what she would have earned in the job she did not get, less the amount she actually earned (or could reasonably have earned) over the relevant time period. In a world where many firms—perhaps a majority—discriminated, a worker who was turned down by one firm would often have found it difficult to land an alternative job, since other employers were engaging in the same discriminatory practices as the firm that rejected her in the first instance.

Other things equal, therefore, the more pervasive is discrimination, the larger back-pay damages will be, since victims of discrimination will have a more difficult time mitigating damages on their own *via* the market when discrimination is widespread. Conversely, as the share of discriminators among all employers declines, the monetary cost to those job applicants who *do* experience discrimination should fall: when an applicant who is rejected by firm 1 because of her race can walk across the street to firm 2 and be hired immediately, firm 1's behavior imposes essentially no *monetary* cost on the applicant.

In Becker's (1956) animus-based theory of discrimination, the amount of economic discrimination (measured as the wage difference between equally productive Black and White workers) is set by the tastes of the least discriminatory employer. If there are any employers who do not have a discriminatory premium, then there will be zero economic discrimination in the long run, since in equilibrium, all black workers will be able to work for these employers with no wage penalty at all. Becker's model predicts perfect segregation, but no loss in wages to black workers, and since it assumes away any dignitary harms to blacks, all the costs of discrimination are borne by the discriminators in equilibrium.

Becker's key conclusion—that in the long run discrimination is costless—rests on a crucial assumption that there are no dignitary or psychological harms (or search costs) borne by its victims. Rather than assuming them away, it seems more plausible to imagine that such costs will likely be felt even in a segregated Beckerian equilibrium when a victim of discrimination suffers no loss in *earnings*. Consider the case of discrimination by taxicab drivers, for example. A recent study in Washington DC study revealed that Blacks had to wait about 5.7 minutes to get a taxi to stop for them while it took Whites 4.5 minutes. (The study is unpublished, but the results are presented and critiqued in Siegelman (1999).) If we make the mistake of treating this as a purely monetary harm, then we might value the 72 seconds of lost time at $12.50 per hour, roughly the average wage. In that case, the monetary "cost" is a modest $0.25. However, the *psychological* harms are quite likely to be substantially greater than this. The problem is not that certain persons cannot get a cab at all or have to wait for hours to get one. Rather, the harms seem to be much more connected to the loss of dignity that occurs when one is passed-over by a cab driver solely because of one's race.[13]

As the distinguished sociologist Patterson (1997) suggests, dignitary harms can increase—even as the amount of racism falls and the rate of integration rises—for two reasons. First, as Blacks encounter Whites more frequently, their possible exposure to discriminatory behavior will rise, even as the proportion of interactions that are discriminatory goes down. Second, members of traditionally disadvantaged groups now have an expectation of better treatment than they would have had 40 years ago. When these higher expectations are not met, persons affected by discrimination may experience psychological costs that would not have been felt at a time when discrimination was simply "the way things were."

Returning to the employment context, if—as seems reasonable—the costs of discrimination are increasingly lost *utility* and dignitary harms, rather than lost income or earnings (Neal and Johnson, 1998), we might need to start to thinking differently about what employment discrimination law should and actually does protect. Instead of compensating persons for lost earnings, we might want to broaden the scope of legally cognizable harms to include damages that are not recognized under the simple back-pay model of Title VII. A modest movement in this direction already seems to be under way.

[13] In the wake of a celebrated incident involving Danny Glover, the problems of race-based refusal of service by New York taxicabs attracted considerable attention in the press. The comments of many who were interviewed comport with the notion that dignitary harms, rather than financial losses, were especially on victims' minds. Chen (1999) quotes black residents the effect that "being bypassed hurt them to the core."

3.3. The Declining Relative Significance of Race Discrimination?

Race discrimination claims have apparently fallen—at least as a share of EEOC complaints—and now constitute a plurality of such claims by a small and shrinking margin. Many other kinds of discrimination now compete for the attention of the media, for the sympathies of the voter, and for the government's scarce enforcement budget.

What should we make of this? On the one hand, it is a tribute to the power of the traditional civil rights model that it has been so widely adopted by other groups (women, the disabled, gays and lesbians, the elderly). It is difficult to be against civil rights for everyone. However, the widespread adoption of civil rights rhetoric and civil rights remedies could come at a serious cost if it causes us to lose sight of the uniquely perfidious history of discrimination against African-Americans.

CHAPTER 14

Perceiving and Claiming Discrimination

Brenda Major and Cheryl R. Kaiser

ABSTRACT

This chapter reviews social psychological theory and research examining the extent and conditions under which people perceive themselves as victims of discrimination and/or publicly claim that they have been discriminated against. Evidence indicates that perceptions of discrimination directed against the self vary widely, and depend on characteristics of the person, the situation, and the social structure. People who do perceive themselves as victims of discrimination are often reluctant to make this claim publicly. This reluctance occurs in part because individuals who claim they are victims of discrimination are viewed negatively by others even when the claim is well justified. Discussion highlights the complexity involved in detecting prejudice and the social costs associated with claiming discrimination.

1. PERCEIVING AND CLAIMING DISCRIMINATION

Imagine that Jane has been working at a firm for 10 years. Her boss is retiring, and she wants his job. She has an excellent performance record, and has been a loyal and reliable employee. She believes she deserves the promotion. Instead of choosing Jane as his replacement, however, her boss chooses a coworker who not only is younger than Jane, but who also has worked for the firm fewer years than she. When Jane demands to know why she was passed over, her boss tells her that Joe (her coworker) has more leadership potential than she and that he thinks the clients will respond better to him than to her. Jane wonders: Does Joe really have more leadership ability than I do? Is something the matter with me, or have I been a victim of sex (or age, or race) discrimination?

This example illustrates the predicament experienced by potential targets of discrimination. Considered in isolation, actions usually have a number of possible causes. Although the selection of Joe over Jane may in fact be due to discrimination, a number of other explanations are also possible. Objective standards by which to determine definitively whether discrimination has or has not occurred are usually lacking. Consequently, judgments of personal discrimination are uncertain, subjective, susceptible

L. B. Nielsen and R. L. Nelson (eds.), Handbook of Employment Discrimination Research, 285–301.

to human error, and prone to dispute. Furthermore, making a mistake can be costly. Failing to see when one has been a victim of discrimination can result in getting less than one deserves. However, seeing discrimination that does not exist engenders suspicion and hostility. The target's predicament is made worse by the fact that whether judgments of discrimination are accurate or inaccurate, publicly *claiming* that one has been a victim of discrimination can be interpersonally costly.

In this chapter, we consider how people resolve predicaments like this. We first address theory and research on whether people accurately *perceive* when they are victims of discrimination and consider personal and situational factors that affect these perceptions. We next consider when people will publicly *claim* that they are victims of discrimination, and examine the social consequences of such claims. In this chapter, we focus on perceptions and claims of *personal* rather than *group* discrimination. In addition, we focus primarily on the responses of individuals who possess an attribute that makes them chronically vulnerable to discrimination, such as women, ethnic minorities, gays and lesbians, and the physically disabled.

We regard a judgment of personal discrimination as having two essential components: (1) a judgment that treatment was unjust, and (2) a judgment that treatment was based on social identity/group membership (Major, Quinton, and McCoy, 2002). According to our definition, individuals who are negatively treated can believe that their treatment was based on aspects of their personal identity and was just (e.g., "I did not get the job because I am not the most qualified,") or was based on their personal identity and was unjust (e.g., "I did not get the job because I am not well-connected."). Neither of these is a judgment of discrimination because both lack the judgment that social category was responsible for one's treatment. Individuals can also recognize that their social identity was responsible for their negative treatment but not see this as unjust. For example, a woman might think that she did not get a particular job because she is a woman, but also believes that women are not as capable of performing that job as men. We regard this as a perception of justifiable differential treatment, rather than a perception of discrimination.

2. JUDGMENTS OF PERSONAL DISCRIMINATION

How accurate are people's judgments that they have, or have not, been a victim of discrimination? When they err, are their judgment errors more likely to be "misses"—failing to see discrimination that objectively exists, or "false alarms"—seeing more discrimination than actually exists? Two different perspectives on these issues exist in the literature.

2.1. Minimization of Personal Discrimination

According to one view, members of disadvantaged groups typically miss, underestimate, or deny the extent to which they are personally targets of prejudice. This view is reflected in the writings of many psychologists, political scientists, sociologists, and philosophers, who observe that social systems of inequality persist in large part because members of low status groups fail to recognize the illegitimacy of the status system and of their own disadvantaged position within it (e.g., Crosby, 1984; Jost, 1995; Major, 1994; Sidanius and Pratto, 1999). That is, they fall prey to "false consciousness" (Marx and Engels, 1846/1970). Consistent with this view, women and ethnic minorities often have difficulty recalling times when they were targets of prejudice (Stangor, Swim, Sechrist, Decoster, VanAllen, and Ottenbreit, 2003), typically report that they personally experience less prejudice than they perceive the average member of their group to experience (Crosby, 1984; Taylor, Wright, and Porter, 1994), and avoid labeling negative treatment that they have received as discrimination, even when the treatment objectively qualifies as such (Magley, Hulin, Fitzgerald, and DeNardo, 1999; Vorauer and Kumhyr, 2001).

Why might people fail to recognize when they are victims of discrimination? Several motivational factors may contribute to the underestimation of personal discrimination. First, people are strongly motivated to believe that their outcomes are under their personal control and often perceive themselves as having more control over events than they actually have (Langer, 1975; Taylor and Brown, 1988). Second, people are motivated to perceive the world as a just place where people get what they deserve (Lerner and Miller, 1978). Third, people are motivated to justify and maintain their worldview and the existing status system (Jost and Banaji, 1994; Pyszczynski, Greenberg, and Solomon, 1997). The judgment that one has been a victim of discrimination requires acknowledging that one's outcomes are under the control of bigoted and capricious others and threatens the need to view the world and the existing status system as just. Consequently, even when existing status hierarchies and distributions are disadvantageous to themselves or their group, people may nonetheless be motivated to perceive them as fair (e.g., Jost and Banaji, 1994; Kleugel and Smith, 1986; Major, 1994; Sidanius and Pratto, 1999).

Cognitive factors also contribute to why people may not recognize when they are victims of discrimination or might underestimate its extent. Whenever two individuals differ on multiple attributes that are relevant to outcomes, such as seniority, performance, etc., there may be several possible explanations for their differential outcomes. Take, for example, the scenario with which we began this chapter. Jane has more seniority, but according to her boss, her coworker Joe has more leadership potential than she does. Perhaps this justifies her boss's choice of him rather than her for the job. This attributional ambiguity makes it difficult to detect discrimination on a case-by-case basis. As was shown in an experiment, discrimination on the basis of group membership usually becomes apparent only when data are aggregated across a number of individuals, thereby making the link to group membership more salient (Crosby, Clayton, Alksnis, and Hemker, 1986). Detecting discrimination is made even more difficult by the fact that overt expressions of prejudice and discrimination are not only considered socially inappropriate in many circumstances, but are often legally sanctioned (Devine, 1989). Hence, discrimination frequently is masked or disguised.

Social comparison biases also work against detecting discrimination. Perceptions of personal discrimination require comparing one's own inputs and outcomes with the inputs and outcomes of others. In general, people tend to compare their own situations with other people like themselves, such as other ingroup members. Thus, people who belong to disadvantaged groups are likely to compare with others who are similarly disadvantaged. As a result, they may be unaware of the extent to which they and others like them are unfairly treated (Major, 1994). In sum, there are both motivational and cognitive reasons why people are likely to miss, underestimate, or deny the extent to which they are targets of discrimination.

2.2. Vigilance for Personal Discrimination

A second view is that chronic targets of discrimination are *vigilant* to cues in their environment that signal that they may be targets of prejudice and discrimination, and may see discrimination when it does not objectively exist. For example, Allport (1954/1979, p. 144) observed that members of minority groups can become "on guard" to signs of prejudice in others and "hypersensitive" to even the smallest of cues indicating prejudice in order to defend their egos against anticipated or experienced rejection. Steele, Spencer, and Aronson (2002) observed that people who realize that they may be discriminated against in a particular setting may become vigilant to a wide range of cues in that setting that might indicate the presence of prejudice and negative stereotypes. Feldman-Barrett and Swim (1998) suggested that previous experience with prejudice or discrimination can set the stage for members of stigmatized groups to use a "zero miss" signal detection strategy, wherein even subtle injustice cues in the environment trigger vigilance for discrimination and increased perceptions of discrimination. Although experimental evidence consistent with the vigilance perspective is scarce, some does exist. For example, Cohen, Steele, and Ross (1999) found that African-American college students who received critical feedback on an essay were more likely to say that the evaluator was biased than were European-American students who received the same type of feedback, even though both groups had received identical critical comments and the essays had been corrected blind to race of essay. African-American students did not see the evaluator as more biased, however, when the critical comments were accompanied by comments indicating that the evaluator thought the essay writer was capable of meeting high standards. This study makes the important point that vigilance is sensitive to contextual cues: some cues made African-American students vigilant to bias that did not objectively exist, and other cues mitigated this vigilance.

Both motivational and cognitive factors may contribute to vigilance among chronic targets of prejudice. When the social environment is very hostile and life threatening, the costs of a "miss" may be greater than the cost of a "false alarm" (Feldman-Barrett and Swim, 1998). In such environments, vigilance may be highly adaptive (Feldman-Barrett and Swim, 1998; Grier and Cobbs, 1968; Vorauer and Ross, 1993). The motivation to protect self-esteem from threat (ego-defense) may also underlie vigilance to prejudice (Allport, 1954/1979). People engage in a wide variety of self-serving strategies to protect and enhance their personal (individual) and social (collective) self-esteem (Pyszczynski et al., 1997; Rosenberg and Simmons, 1972; Tajfel and Turner, 1986). Blaming negative outcomes on external causes, such as the prejudice of others, rather than on internal causes, such as one's own lack of ability, can help to protect self-esteem under some circumstances (Crocker and Major, 1989; Major, Kaiser and McCoy, 2003).

Furthermore, for groups that historically have been targets of discrimination, prejudice and discrimination are likely to be repeatedly primed and highly accessible cognitive constructs (Inman and Baron, 1996). As a result, the possibility of discrimination may be easily activated in ambiguous circumstances and bias perceptions of those circumstances. Members of disadvantaged groups (women), for example, are more likely to label negative actions committed by a high status perpetrator against a low status victim as discrimination than are members of privileged groups (men) who witness the same action (Rodin, Price, Bryson, and Sanchez, 1990). In sum, there are both motivational and cognitive reasons why chronic targets of discrimination may be vigilant for, and sometimes overestimate the extent to which they are targets of discrimination.

3. PREDICTING JUDGMENTS OF PERSONAL DISCRIMINATION

Which of these perspectives is correct? A growing body of experimental research indicates that either minimization/underestimation or vigilance/overestimation may occur, depending upon characteristics of the situation and on characteristics of the person. In the following section, we present a brief review of this research (see Major, McCoy, Kaiser, and Quinton, 2003; Major and O'Brien, 2005; Major et al., 2002; Stangor et al., 2003 for more extensive reviews).

3.1. Situational Cues

Judgments of discrimination are more likely in contexts in which cues alert targets to the possibility of injustice and make group membership salient as a possible cause of the injustice. Experiments that have manipulated situational cues and measured attributions to discrimination indicate that the more explicit or clear the cues are to discrimination (injustice + group membership) in a situation, the more likely people are to report that they have been a target of discrimination (e.g., Major, Quinton, and Schmader, 2003). For example, women in one study received a negative or positive evaluation from a male partner. Women were more likely to blame the evaluation on discrimination if it was negative than positive, and if they had learned that the evaluator held very traditional rather than liberal attitudes toward women's roles (Crocker, Voelkl, Testa, and Major, 1991). In another study, members of minority ethnic groups were more likely to attribute negative treatment from a White partner to discrimination if they had learned that their partner held anti-diversity rather than pro-diversity views (Operario and Fiske, 2001, study 2).

Other experiments indicate that alerting people to the possibility of discrimination increases their vigilance for seeing discrimination as a cause of negative outcomes. For example, in one set of studies, women were led to expect that their work would be evaluated by a panel of male judges. Some women were told that none of the judges discriminated against women, some were told that 50% of the judges discriminated, and some were told that 100% discriminated. Not surprisingly, women who were led to expect discriminatory judges were more likely to blame a subsequent poor evaluation on discrimination than women who did not expect discriminatory judges. More interesting was the finding that women led to expect that *half* of the judges discriminated were just as likely to blame poor feedback on discrimination as women who had been told that *all* of judges discriminated (Inman, 2001; Kaiser and Miller, 2001a). These studies indicate that leading people to expect discrimination affects their interpretations of feedback. There also is evidence that subtly priming thoughts of discrimination can have an effect on perceptions (Gomez and Trierweiler, 2001). In this study, White women and African-Americans were asked how frequently they were the targets of negative events at work (such as being treated with disrespect by others). More frequent negative treatment was reported if participants responded on a questionnaire labeled "Discrimination" than if they responded on a questionnaire labeled "Everyday Experiences."

Situational cues that make group membership salient as a possible cause of negative outcomes also increase the likelihood that individuals will see themselves as targets of discrimination. For example, people are more likely to report that they have been discriminated against when they are treated negatively by an outgroup member than by an ingroup member (Dion, 1975). They are also more likely to claim that they are targets of discrimination when they know that their group membership is known rather than unknown to an outgroup evaluator (Crocker et al., 1991; Dion and Earn, 1975). In sum, given the same potentially discriminatory event, the likelihood that an individual will judge him or herself to have been a target of discrimination varies as a function of cues in the situation. Whereas some situational cues increase the likelihood of perceiving discrimination (e.g., knowledge that an evaluator holds prejudicial or biased attitudes, forewarning of the possibility of discrimination), other cues diminish it (e.g., knowledge that an evaluator holds nonbiased attitudes; negative evaluations by a member of one's own group).

3.2. Individual Differences

People also differ in their chronic propensity to see (or not see) themselves as targets of discrimination. Individual differences in perceptions of discrimination are linked to people's tendencies to see themselves in terms of their group memberships, and to see the world as just and fair in which outcomes are deserved.

3.2.1. Group-Related Beliefs

People differ in the extent to which they identify themselves in terms of their group memberships. *Group identification* is typically conceptualized as how important the group is to self-definition and how strong feelings of attachment to the group are (Tajfel and Turner, 1986). Many studies have shown that among socially devalued groups, group identification is positively correlated with perceptions of personal, as well as group discrimination (e.g., Branscombe, Schmitt, and Harvey, 1999; Crosby, Pufall, Snyder, O'Connell, and Whalen, 1989; Dion, 1975; Gurin and Townsend, 1986; Major and Quinton, 2001; Operario and Fiske, 2001, study 1).

Differences in perceptions of discrimination between people who are high versus low in group identification are most pronounced in attributionally ambiguous situations (Major et al., 2003; Operario and Fiske, 2001). For example, in one study (Major et al., 2003) women who were high or low in gender identification received a negative evaluation from a male under conditions of clear prejudice cues, ambiguous prejudice cues, or no prejudice cues. Regardless of whether they were high or low in gender identification, women did not blame their poor evaluation on discrimination in the absence of cues to prejudice and were highly likely to do so in presence of blatant cues to prejudice. When prejudice cues were ambiguous, however, gender identification mattered. Women who were highly gender identified were significantly more likely than low gender-identified women to blame a negative evaluation on sex discrimination when cues to discrimination were ambiguous. Further, highly gender-identified women were just as likely to attribute negative feedback to sex discrimination in the ambiguous cue condition as they were in the blatant cue condition. In contrast, among low gender-identified women, attributions to sex discrimination were as low in the ambiguous condition as they were in the no cues condition (see figure 1). These findings suggest that in attributionally ambiguous circumstances, individuals who are highly identified

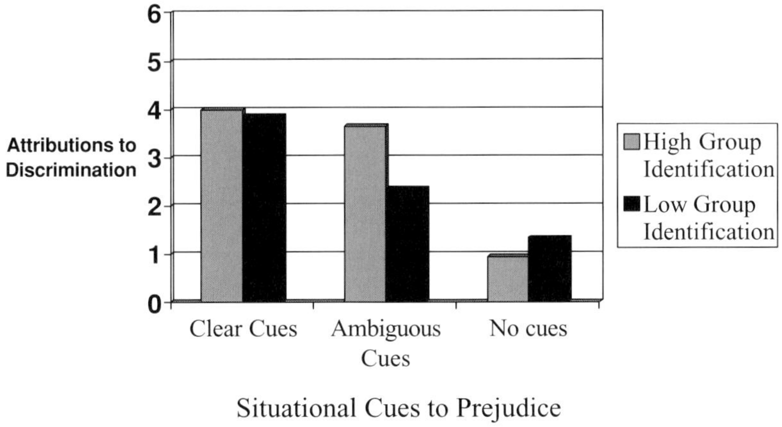

Figure 1. Attributions to discrimination as a function of clarity of prejudice cues and group identification (from Major et al., 2003).

with their groups are vigilant for discrimination, whereas individuals who are low in group identification minimize discrimination.

Group consciousness also is associated with more vigilance for discrimination. Group consciousness incorporates aspects of group identification as well as elements of perceived injustice directed against the group, and is sometimes referred to as "politicized group identification" (Gurin, Miller, and Gurin, 1980). Major and Quinton (2001) found significant positive correlations between feminist self-labeling (a measure of group consciousness among women) and perceptions of personal discrimination ($r = 0.29$) and discrimination against women ($r = 0.25$, $p < 0.001$) in a sample of 696 university women. Similarly, Swim, Hyers, Cohen, and Ferguson (2001) observed a positive correlation between feminist beliefs and the number of sexist events women reported experiencing over a 7-day period ($r = 0.39$, $p < 0.01$).

People also differ in the extent to which they are chronically sensitive to the possibility of being a target of negative stereotypes and discrimination because of their group membership. One measure of this is "stigma-consciousness" (Pinel, 1999). Women who score high on a female-specific "stigma consciousness scale" endorse statements such as: "When interacting with men I feel like they interpret all my behaviors in terms of the fact that I am a woman" Across a variety of stigmatized groups, including African-Americans, Latino(a)-Americans, Asian-Americans, and women, stigma consciousness is strongly and positively correlated with perceived personal and group discrimination and negatively correlated with distrust of others in general (Pinel, 1999). Furthermore, women who are high in stigma consciousness allocate more of their attention towards subliminally presented sexism-related words relative to women who are low in stigma consciousness (Kaiser, Vick, and Major, 2005).

A related construct is "race-based rejection sensitivity," which is defined as a personal dynamic whereby individuals anxiously expect, readily perceive, and intensely react to rejection that has a possibility of being due to race (Mendoza-Denton, Purdie, Downey, Davis, and Pietrzac, 2002). Race-based rejection sensitivity is assessed by asking people to read attributionally ambiguous scenarios (e.g., "Imagine that you have just finished shopping and you are leaving the store carrying several bags. It is closing time, and several people are filing out of the store at once. Suddenly, the alarm begins to sound, and a security guard comes over to investigate."), and to indicate, for each scenario, how concerned they are that a negative outcome would be due to their race and the likelihood that a negative outcome would be due to their race. In a longitudinal diary study, race-based rejection sensitivity assessed among African-American students before they entered a predominately White university predicted the frequency with which they reported a negative race-related experience (e.g., feeling excluded, insulted, or receiving poor service because of one's race) during their first 3 weeks at university (Mendoza-Denton et al., 2002). Race-based rejection sensitivity also predicted their tendency to feel less belonging at the university and greater negativity toward both peers and professors. Taken together, the above studies indicate that people's thoughts about and identification with their group influence their propensity to perceive discrimination, especially in ambiguous situations.

3.2.2. Justice-Related Beliefs
Individuals also differ in their beliefs about why status differences exist among groups in society. These beliefs influence their likelihood of seeing their own and others' outcomes as deserved or undeserved. Belief systems that justify hierarchical and unequal relationships among groups in society have been called "legitimizing ideologies" (Sidanius and Pratto, 1993). In the United States, examples of such beliefs include the belief in a just world (Lerner, 1980), personal control (Langer, 1975), a meritocratic society (Sidanius and Pratto, 1999), individual mobility (Tajfel and Turner, 1986), and the Protestant Work Ethic (PWE) (Mirels and Garrett, 1971). Each of these beliefs tends to center causality within the individual and hold people personally responsible for their outcomes. Consequently, they encourage the perception that an individual's outcomes are deserved. Because endorsement of these legitimizing ideologies lead the disadvantaged to blame themselves, rather than others, for poor outcomes, the more members of disadvantaged groups individuals endorse such beliefs, the less likely they should be to perceive themselves as victims of personal discrimination (Major, Gramzow, McCoy, Levin, Schmader, and Sidanius, 2002). Legitimizing ideologies are an important mechanism of social control and promote system stability (Sidanius and Pratto, 1993).

The belief in personal control reduces perceptions of discrimination, both against self and others. People who are believed to have control over their outcomes or to have controllable stigmas (e.g., the obese) are judged as more responsible and blameworthy than those whose outcomes or stigmas are perceived as less controllable (e.g., gender, ethnicity; Weiner, Perry, and Magnusson, 1988). People also see it as more justifiable to discriminate against people with controllable stigmas (Rodin et al., 1990); a belief shared even by those who are themselves stigmatized (Crandall, 1994). It is thus not surprising that people who believe they have been treated negatively on the basis of a controllable attribute (e.g., obesity) are relatively unlikely to say they are victims of discrimination. For example, compared to standard weight women who were rejected by a male partner, overweight women were significantly more likely to attribute their rejection to their weight, but were *not* more likely to attribute their rejection to their partner's concern with appearance or his personality (Crocker, Cornwell and Major, 1993). Crocker and Major (1994) argued that because weight is viewed as controllable, overweight women regarded their rejection on the basis of weight as justified differential treatment rather than discrimination. In general, we conjecture that to the extent that targets feel some control over the onset, maintenance, or elimination of their stigmatizing attribute, they are less likely to see themselves as victims of discrimination.

The belief in a just world (Lerner, 1980) also can lead targets to blame bad outcomes on themselves, rather than on discrimination (Olson and Hafer, 2001). Working women who endorse the belief in a just world, for example, report less discontent with the employment situation of working women than do those who endorse this belief less strongly (Hafer and Olson, 1993). The more undergraduate women endorse the belief in a just world, the less they perceive that they personally experience discrimination because of their gender, the less they perceive that women are discriminated against, and the less likely they are to interpret ambiguous negative events as being due to sexism (Major and Quinton, 2001). The belief that status systems are permeable and allow for individual mobility also is associated with reduced perceptions of personal discrimination among members of disadvantaged groups. For example, in a laboratory-based study Major et al. (2002) found that the more ethnic minority students endorsed the ideology of individual mobility, the less likely they were to say that an interpersonal rejection by a same-sex European-American student under ambiguous circumstances was due to discrimination. In contrast, among European-American students, endorsement of the ideology of individual mobility was associated with increased attributions to discrimination when an ethnic minority student rejected them. Major et al. (2002) observed a similar finding in a second study in which women and men were rejected by a member of the other sex. The more women endorsed the ideology of individual mobility, the less likely they were to say they were discriminated against. The reverse pattern was observed among men. Collectively, these studies demonstrate that individual differences in endorsement of justice-related beliefs are an important determinant of how potentially discriminatory situations are construed and explained.

4. CLAIMING DISCRIMINATION

Once individuals *perceive* themselves as victims of personal discrimination (either correctly or incorrectly), how likely are they to make that perception public by *claiming* or *reporting* it to others? Consider the situation of Jane, with whom we began this chapter. If she believes her boss discriminated against her when he chose Joe instead of her for the promotion, what should she do? Should she report it? If so, to whom? Her boss? Some other authority? A friend or coworker? We discuss the predicaments of reporting discrimination in the following section.

4.1. Confronting the Perpetrator or Reporting Discrimination to Authorities

Do people who believe they have been victims of discrimination attempt to remedy this situation by either directly confronting the perpetrator of discrimination, or by reporting discrimination to authorities? Research suggests that both responses are infrequent. People who perceive themselves to have been a target of discrimination are often quite reluctant to directly confront the perpetrator, even when discrimination is blatant (Kaiser and Miller, 2004; Shelton and Stewart, 2004; Swim and Hyers, 1999; Woodzicka and LaFrance, 2001). For example, in one study (Swim and Hyers, 1999) undergraduate women engaged in a small group discussion in which a male confederate voiced a series of scripted, blatantly sexist or nonsexist comments. The majority of women subjected to sexist comments (55%) did not verbally express their displeasure either to the confederate or to others in the group. Their silence did not mean, however, that they did not perceive discrimination. In private ratings made after the interaction, 75% of the women who failed to publicly acknowledge discrimination rated the confederate as sexist, and 91% had negative thoughts and feelings about him. Thus, despite recognizing and feeling angry about the sexist treatment, most of the women did not confront the perpetrator of the sexist act.

Another set of studies illustrated that women's expectations about how they would behave when targeted by sexual harassment are often discrepant with how they actually behave in real interactions with sexual harassers (Woodzicka and LaFrance, 2001). In the first study of this series, women imagined being interviewed by a man who posed several sexually harassing interview questions (e.g., Do you have a boyfriend? Do you think it is important for women to wear bras to work?). Most (68%) of the women in this study anticipated refusing to answer at least one of the interviewers' questions. Women also thought they would feel more anger than fear in response to the questions. In a second experiment, a new group of women were actually interviewed by a man who actually posed these harassing questions or control questions. Contrary to the results of study 1, when women were *actually* confronted with harassing questions, *not a single participant refused to answer the questions*. Moreover, emotionally, far more women reported fear than anger. In short, these data suggest that women are unable to predict their feelings and their behavior toward perpetrators when confronted with sexual harassment.

Reporting discrimination to authorities may be even rarer. Although we are unaware of any experiments examining the likelihood of reporting discrimination to authorities, several organizational field studies of reporting sexual harassment are relevant. This research indicates that formally reporting harassment to employment authorities is the least frequent response that women who have experienced sexual harassment make (Fitzgerald, Swan, and Fischer, 1995; Loy and Stewart, 1984). A variety of factors likely contribute to the low rates of filing formal sexual harassment-related charges. These are discussed later in the chapter.

4.2. Reporting Discrimination to Trusted Others

Although targets of prejudice appear reluctant to report prejudice to its perpetrators and to formal authorities, they are more willing to report this information to friends, family, ingroup members, and others from whom they might expect support or confirmation of their perception. Indeed 68% of sexual harassment victims discuss their harassment with coworkers and 60% discuss it with friends and family (Merit Systems Protection Bd, 1981).

Using group membership as a marker for social support, Stangor, Swim, Van Allen, and Sechrist (2002) examined whether women and African-Americans are more likely to report discrimination to members of their own group than to members of higher status outgroups. They hypothesized that members of low status groups must contend with impression management concerns in the presence of members of higher status groups (e.g., Fiske, Morling, and Stevens, 1996). Hence, they hypothesized that members of lower status groups are behaviorally constrained from expressing their opinions about discrimination in the presence of higher status individuals. To test their hypothesis, Stangor et al. (2002) conducted two experiments in which members of low status groups (women and African-Americans) received failing feedback on a test of creative thinking from an outgroup evaluator (men and European-Americans, respectively) who also expressed blatantly prejudiced attitudes. After receiving negative feedback, participants were asked the extent to which they thought their test grade was due to discrimination and to the quality of their test answers. One-third of the participants made these reports in complete anonymity, another third made them out loud in the presence of an ingroup member (another woman or African-American, respectively), and a final third made them out loud in the presence of an outgroup member (a man or a European-American, respectively). When women and African-Americans had to state the reasons for their treatment publicly in the presence of an outgroup member, they were less likely to say that their poor grade was due to discrimination than when they had to state the reasons in the presence of an ingroup member or when they were alone. Ratings in the private and ingroup reporting conditions did not differ from each other. This study suggests that while members of disadvantaged groups may be reluctant to report discrimination to people who are members of the same group as the perpetrator of discrimination, they are more willing to claim that they were discriminated against if they are in the company of their own group.

This willingness to report discrimination to ingroup members may have occurred because members of stigmatized groups perceive their own group as more trustworthy and supportive than outgroups. This suggests that contextual cues and settings that promote intergroup trust and harmony might also increase individuals' willingness to report discrimination. For example, organizations that promote diversity, recognize discrimination, and provide access to social support may create a safer environment for targets of prejudice to report experiences with discrimination.

4.3. The Costs of Claiming Discrimination

Why would people who believe that they are targets of discrimination be reluctant to report it? Evidence indicates that this reluctance stems from the belief that the costs of doing so will be too high. For example, women who are sexually harassed and who do not report it cite a number of reasons for not doing so, including anticipation of retaliation, fear of not being believed, and not wanting to harm the harasser (Fitzgerald et al., 1995). Women who participated in the study by Swim and Hyers (1999) reported that directly responding to sexist remarks (commenting on their inappropriateness) was more risky (in terms of perceived reactions of the perpetrator) than ignoring the remarks, and just as risky as physically aggressing against the perpetrator.

People who report discrimination to authorities or the perpetrator report they often are targets of retaliation (Bergman, Langhout, Palmieri, Cortina, and Fitzgerald, 2002; Crosby, 1993; Feagin and Sikes, 1994; Fitzgerald et al., 1995; Kaiser and Miller, 2001b; Kaiser and Miller, 2003; Kaiser and Miller, 2004; Latting, 1993). Experiments show that blaming outcomes on discrimination can damage perceptions of the blamer's

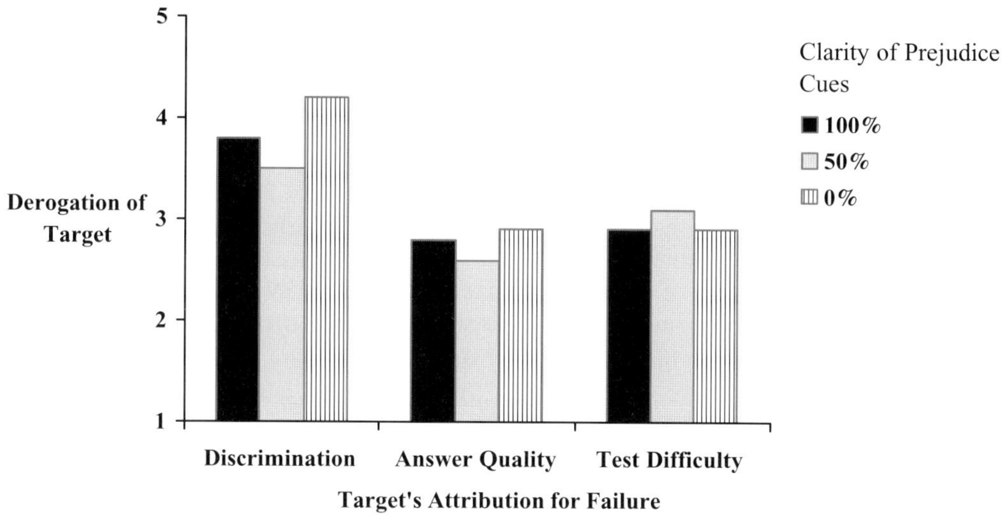

Figure 2. Derogation of an African-American target person as a function of target's attributions for failure and the clarity of cues to prejudice (from Kaiser and Miller, 2001b).

character, even if he or she has a very good reason for making this claim. For example, participants in one experiment (Kaiser and Miller, 2001b, study 2) read about an African-American target who had received a failing test grade and who attributed the grade either to discrimination, to his poor test answers, or to the difficulty of the test. Participants also learned that the test administrator had informed the target that either that there was no chance, a 50% chance, or a 100% chance that a racist European-American evaluator graded the target's test. All participants then rated the target. The target who blamed his failing grade on discrimination was derogated (seen as hypersensitive, irritating, a troublemaker) more than the target who attributed his failure to his test answers or to the difficulty of the test (see figure 2). Remarkably, this effect occurred regardless of the objective probability that a racist evaluator graded the target's test. In other words, the target who claimed discrimination experienced damage to his reputation *even when prejudice was clearly responsible for the event.* In a subsequent experiment, Kaiser and Miller (2003) assessed the boundaries of this effect by making the prejudice of the person responsible for making a hiring decision very obvious. White participants evaluated an African-American job applicant who attributed a job rejection to prejudice or other causes. The person responsible for rejecting the applicant made extremely blatant old-fashioned racist statements ("Black people are just not as smart as White people") or no such statements. Again, the applicant who blamed his rejection on discrimination was derogated more than the applicant who blamed his rejection on other causes. And again, this was true regardless of how bigoted the person responsible for the rejection was. Thus, these experiments indicate that people who claim discrimination as a cause of their poor outcomes will be derogated, even if they have an excellent basis for their claim.

There are undoubtedly individual differences in the tendency to derogate discrimination claimants. For example, discrimination claims may be particularly threatening to individuals who strongly endorse legitimizing ideologies, such as belief in a just world or the Protestant Work Ethic (PWE) (Jost and Burgess, 2000; Kaiser, Shatzki, and Bartholomew, 2004). Claims of discrimination challenge their belief that outcomes directly reflect inputs and efforts, that individuals should take personal responsibility for their successes and failures in life, and that people get what they deserve. When individuals experience a threat to their belief system, one way to deal with that threat is by derogating the source of the threat (Pyszczynski et al., 1997). Thus, the tendency to derogate people who claim they are victims of discrimination is likely to be more pronounced among those who endorse BJW or PWE ideologies.

In a test of this hypothesis, Kaiser et al. (2004) examined whether individuals who endorse the PWE are more likely than individuals who reject this belief to derogate discrimination claimants. Participants (all of whom had previously completed a PWE measure) read about an African-American target person who received negative academic feedback from a highly racist evaluator. Participants also learned that the target attributed the feedback either to discrimination, his academic performance, or the difficulty of the test. As in previous research, participants derogated the individual who attributed his failure to discrimination. However, this effect was moderated by participants' endorsement of the PWE. When the target attributed his failure to discrimination, endorsing the PWE was strongly positively correlated with derogation of the target person. PWE was not significantly related to derogation in the other attribution conditions. One implication of these findings is that claiming discrimination might be particularly costly in environments where beliefs advocating the payoff of hard work are salient. These beliefs about effort and rewards are likely to be highly prevalent in employment contexts. Thus, members of stigmatized groups may be particularly unwilling to report discrimination in their work environments.

5. CONCLUSIONS

This chapter addressed how members of disadvantaged groups navigate situations in which they are potential victims of discrimination. Because few objective standards exist for determining the presence of discrimination in isolated instances, assessments of the accuracy of discrimination judgments are difficult. Some perspectives suggest that chronic targets of prejudice tend to minimize or underestimate the extent to which they are personally victimized by discrimination. Other perspectives suggest that chronic targets of prejudice are vigilant for, and sometimes oversensitive to signs that they are being personally victimized by discrimination. In our view, both responses are possible, and which response occurs depends on characteristics of the person, the situation, and the social structure. Our discussion highlights the complexity involved in detecting prejudice and offers a number of suggestions for better understanding when individuals will or will not perceive themselves as targets of prejudice. We also reviewed evidence suggesting that even when people perceive themselves as victims of discrimination, they may be reluctant to make this claim publicly. One determining factor is the audience of the claim: individuals are more willing to report their experiences to ingroup members or close others than to challenge the perpetrators of discrimination or report it to formal authorities. Research indicates that people who claim they are victims of discrimination are negatively viewed even when their claim is well justified. Thus, targets' reluctance to report discrimination to those outside their inner circle may be an important strategy for protecting their reputation and their interpersonal relationships.

CHAPTER 15

Mobilizing Employment Rights in the Workplace

Catherine R. Albiston*

ABSTRACT

Employment rights are primarily enforced through a private right of action. This mode of enforcement makes understanding the process through which workers come to recognize and exercise their rights essential. This chapter analyzes that process in the context of the Family and Medical Leave Act. The analysis draws on interviews with workers who negotiated contested leaves without going to court, focusing on workers' experiences and their perceptions of what is fair, appropriate, and just. The chapter concludes by discussing some implications for social change through legal reforms.

INTRODUCTION

Until recently, the United States was virtually the only major industrialized country without a family leave policy. Employers could legally fire workers who needed time off to care for seriously ill children, spouses, or parents. Employers could also legally fire workers temporarily unable to work due to serious illnesses or injuries. And employers could legally fire women who needed time off for pregnancy, childbirth, or related medical conditions so long as they also denied time off to nonpregnant employees who were unable to work. Time off after the birth of a child remained a benefit provided at employers' discretion, a benefit primarily available to well-paid professional or management workers.

A recent new employment law, the Family and Medical Leave Act of 1993 ("FMLA"), now provides some workers with a legal right to unpaid, job-protected leave. The FMLA requires covered employers to provide 12 weeks of leave per year to certain workers who need time off for family or medical crises.[1] Workers may use

* This research was generously supported by the National Science Foundation, #SES-0001905, and the Sloan Foundation through the Center for Working Families, University of California, Berkeley. An earlier analysis of data from this study appears in *Law & Society Review*, Vol. 39, No. 1 (2005).

[1] 29 U.S.C. § 2612. Workers who have worked for their employers for less than 1 year are not eligible for FMLA leave. In addition, workers who work for companies with less than 50 employees are not covered by the FMLA. 29 U.S.C. § 2611.

L. B. Nielsen and R. L. Nelson (eds.), Handbook of Employment Discrimination Research, 301–325.

FMLA leave for childbirth or other temporary disabilities, and both men and women may take leave to care for a sick child, parent, or spouse, or a new child in their family.[2] The statute protects workers who use leave from retaliatory harassment, termination, and discrimination.[3] The law also requires employers to provide leave even if they do not allow time off for any other reason. In other words, the statute creates an entitlement because it does not allow employers discretion to deny leave to qualified workers.[4]

The FMLA may create new rights, but will those rights mean substantial change in the workplace? The answer depends, in part, on how law interacts with other systems of meaning that govern the workplace. For example, law can be displaced or transformed by alternative normative systems (Ellickson, 1991; Macaulay, 1963) or by organizational practices and goals (Edelman, Erlanger, and Lande, 1993; Heimer, 1999). Nevertheless, although other systems of meaning matter, actors may still draw upon law as a cultural resource to interpret their social experiences, and to influence the behavior of others. Often, law and other social institutions act in concert to give meaning to social life.

Law may be most likely to clash with other social institutions when new rights attempt to change longstanding social practices. Civil rights laws, in particular, often challenge social arrangements that evoke strong normative commitments (Engel and Munger, 1996; Krieger, 2000). In the civil rights context, rights provide one cultural frame for understanding social events, but other institutions provide competing frames. Accordingly, actors who "mobilize" rights engage not only with legal systems of meaning, but also with the established practices and expectations that rights were intended to change. Consequently, civil rights claims can become a location for negotiating contested meanings, perhaps in ways that bring about social change.

This chapter examines informal rights mobilization and how other systems of meaning can transform rights in the workplace. FMLA rights are particularly well-suited to this inquiry because they highlight how law and other social institutions interact with and challenge deeply held beliefs about what work and being a good worker mean. For example, the law erodes certain taken-for-granted expectations about work, such as unbroken attendance as the measure of a good worker and employer control over work schedules. It also challenges gendered ideologies about the division of labor in the family by requiring work to accommodate family needs on a gender-neutral basis. And by protecting the jobs of workers who are temporarily too sick to work, it undermines conceptions of "disability" and "work" as mutually exclusive categories. By attempting to restructure longstanding work practices, the FMLA reconceptualizes the relationships among work, gender, and disability, and creates an opportunity for social change.

Although the FMLA attempts to change work practices, the cultural systems of meaning and material conditions associated with work do not disappear overnight. Workers mobilize their rights to leave in workplaces where these institutionalized

[2] 29 U.S.C. § 2612.

[3] 29 U.S.C. § 2614, 2615.

[4] The statute does, however, allow employers to require medical certification of the need for leave, and to deny leave if the worker fails to provide this certification. 29 U.S.C. § 2613.

meanings and expectations are likely to persist. Although the law may construct leave-taking as legitimate, entrenched norms about work, gender, and disability may construct different meanings for the same behavior. Whether the FMLA can successfully reinterpret the meaning of leave depends on how these competing cultural schemas play out when workers mobilize these rights.

The following sections examine how these competing systems of meaning shape the process of rights mobilization in the workplace. The first section discusses rights mobilization and social change, and also examines institutionalized work practices and expectations that may influence mobilization of FMLA rights. The sections that follow draw on interviews with workers to analyze how social context and social institutions affect rights mobilization in the workplace. The chapter concludes by suggesting how social institutions can both shape and be shaped by civil rights laws that seek to bring about social change.

1. RIGHTS MOBILIZATION, INSTITUTIONS, AND SOCIAL CHANGE

Most studies of rights mobilization and social change focus on landmark litigation or collective action, rather than the micro-level process of informal workplace negotiations (Burstein, 1991; Burstein and Monaghan, 1986; Marshall, 1998; McCann, 1994; McCann, 1998; Rosenberg, 1991; Schultz, 1990). The earlier, more informal stages of mobilization also matter, however, because few people with potential civil rights claims take formal action. Instead, most grievants either negotiate their claims informally or simply lump it (Bumiller, 1988; Galanter, 1974; Miller and Sarat, 1981; Tucker, 1993). Accordingly, a complete understanding of mobilization requires attention to how actors mobilize law in informal as well as formal contexts.

Along with the recent interpretative turn in approaches to law and social change (McCann, 1994), researchers have begun to explore these informal processes in more detail (Bumiller, 1988; Engel and Munger, 1996; Morgan, 1999). Like interpretive studies of litigation as a mobilization strategy, these micro-level studies examine how rights work as cultural discourse or "schemas" in informal settings and everyday life (Bumiller, 1988; Ewick and Silbey, 1998). This cultural approach grows out of broader sociological theories about how cultural schemas constrain consciousness and shape action to conform to, and therefore reproduce, existing social structure (Berger and Luckman, 1967; Bourdieu, 1977; Sewell, 1992). From this perspective, law is one of many available frames through which actors make sense of the social world, and actors can invoke or "mobilize" law as a cultural resource to interpret events and to influence behavior (Lempert, 1976; Lempert, 1998; Scheingold, 1974; Swidler, 1986).

Viewing rights as symbolic resources suggests one potential mechanism of social change: mobilizing rights even in informal contexts can undermine taken-for-granted understandings of social organization and delegitimize conduct previously accepted as natural and normal (Engel and Munger, 1996; Sarat and Kearns, 1993; Williams, 1991). Of course, law may also constrain change by narrowly defining the claims that are possible, and by obscuring other avenues for action (McCann, 1994; McCann, 1998). In addition, legal rights compete with alternative ideologies that shape how actors understand their experiences (Swidler, 1986). Although workplace actors may encourage change by using rights to legitimate taking leave, they may also draw on existing discourses about work and family to undermine legal reforms. Accordingly, like formal legal contests, informal rights negotiations can be seen as an interpretive space for both reinforcing and potentially changing social structure.

The idea that law competes with other norms is not new; several studies demonstrate how competing normative systems can displace law in informal settings (Ellickson, 1991; Macaulay, 1963). Nevertheless, often these studies treat law and other norms as an either/or proposition: either social relationships are ordered according to law or there is "order without law." Less is known about the complex process through which law *interacts* with alternative normative systems (Jacob, 1992). Some scholars, however, have begun to connect those competing normative systems to broader social institutions that come into conflict with legal reforms (Edelman et al., 1993; Heimer, 1999; Nelson and Bridges, 1999). These "new institutionalists" focus on how institutionalized practices and meanings in non-legal settings can shape the meaning of legal rights in particular social contexts.

A new institutionalist approach is well-suited to study the FMLA because this law challenges deeply entrenched work practices and norms. Indeed, longstanding practices and expectations associated with work seem likely to affect how workers think about using their rights to leave. Two aspects of work are particularly salient here. The first of these is power in the employment relation. The second is how established norms and expectations about work reflect the historical relationships among work, gender, and disability.

It has long been recognized that the employment relation is one of unequal power. For example, the at will employment doctrine gives employers broad powers to fire at will, and employers rather than workers typically control work schedules. In general, employers have far more power than their workers over the everyday operation of the workplace. These modern workplace arrangements reflect an uneasy truce in an historical struggle over control of the production process and timing of work, a truce that the FMLA potentially disrupts (Edwards, 1979; Gordon, Edwards, and Reich, 1982; Jacoby, 1985; McEvoy, 1998; Montgomery, 1976; Montgomery, 1987; Thompson, 1967; Tomlins, 1993).

Unequal power in the workplace may affect rights mobilization in a number of ways. For example, employers who have more resources than their workers may be more likely to prevail in conflicts over rights. In addition, employers can prevent grievances from becoming public disputes by creating internal procedures to divert conflict away from formal legal forums (Edelman, Uggen, and Erlanger, 1999), and through their implicit power to demote or terminate workers. Power can also mean the ability to prevent workers from recognizing grievances at all. For example, employers may withhold information or use persuasion to make workplace practices seen natural and normal rather than problematic or unfair (Felstiner, Abel, and Sarat, 1981; Gramsci,

1971; Lukes, 1974). In addition, cultural ideologies associated with work may subtly shape how actors understand social experiences in ways that maintain existing power relations (Bourdieu, 1977; Foucault, 1979; Gramsci, 1971; Sewell, 1992).

A second salient aspect of the institution of work—the historical connections among gender, disability, and work—suggests how these cultural ideologies might play out in the context of leave rights. Indeed, with regard to the FMLA, seemingly neutral features of work, such as how attendance and time invested in work rather than productivity have come to define "good workers," become particularly important (Schor, 1992; Thompson, 1967). For example, recent research documents how workers who meet a normative standard of 40-hour work weeks, regular schedules, and uninterrupted year-round work are valued more, and how nonstandard workers sacrifice job security, pay, and benefits (Fried, 1998; Hochschild, 1997; Kalleberg, 1995; Schor, 1992; Williams, 2000).

The temporal requirements of work reflect existing relations of inequality, particularly those based on gender and disability. Feminist and disability scholars have long recognized that standard work schedules are implicitly gendered and able-bodied because they do not accommodate family responsibilities and disabilities that require temporary absences from work (Drimmer, 1993; Hochschild, 1997; MacKinnon, 1989; Okin, 1989; Oliver, 1990; Pateman, 1988; Williams, 1989; Williams, 2000). Nevertheless, normative work schedules have become so taken-for-granted that the barriers they create appear to arise from the personal circumstances of women or people with disabilities rather than from the structure of work itself (MacKinnon, 1989; Oliver, 1990). For example, caring for family is viewed as a "private" problem and accommodations to disabilities are labeled as "special treatment." In this way, the role that work's time standards play in recreating inequality becomes invisible.

Although these aspects of work seem natural and unchanging, work as a social institution is the product and embodiment of history. For example, modern conceptions of work reflect historical struggles to associate work with masculinity and citizenship (Fraser and Gordon, 1994; Kessler-Harris, 1982; Kessler-Harris, 2001). Work's structure reflects early 20th century assumptions that the normative worker is a male breadwinner with a stay-at-home wife (Folbre, 1991; Frank and Lipner, 1988; Fraser and Gordon, 1994; Glenn, 2002; Okin, 1989; Pateman, 1988). Modern work practices also reflect how individuals with disabilities were historically segregated and excluded from civic life (Finkelstein, 1980; Oliver, 1990; Stone, 1984). In addition, to avoid undermining incentives to work, some social welfare laws explicitly define "disability" to mean the inability to work (Stone, 1984). As a result, culturally, "work" and "disability" have acquired mutually exclusive and oppositional meanings that delegitimate workplace disability claims as "shirking" (Drimmer, 1993). Thus, much more is at stake than ad hoc work arrangements in the changes the FMLA attempts to make; these changes disrupt relations of power between employers and workers, as well as deeply entrenched understandings of work, gender, and disability.

The following sections examine how the social institution of work affects workers' mobilization of FMLA rights. They investigate how informal rights negotiations take place not only in the "shadow of the law" (Mnookin and Kornhauser, 1979), but also in the shadow of the institutionalized practices and meanings that constitute work. The analysis focuses on the following questions: How do workers who need leave but encounter resistance from their employer make sense of their situations? How do they understand conflict over leave and their choices about mobilizing their rights? How do social institutions and cultural systems of meaning shape the mobilization process? And perhaps the most significant question, what are the implications for social change through legal reform?

2. METHOD AND DATA

This project uses semi-structured telephone interviews of individuals who experienced conflict over leave but did not go to court to examine informal mobilization of workplace rights. Respondents were located through a state-wide telephone information line in California run by a nonprofit organization that gives informal legal assistance to workers. Attempts were made to contact the universe of individuals who called the information line with questions about family and medical leave during a one-year period. Twenty-four of the 35 individuals in this group agreed to be interviewed, yielding a response rate of almost 70 percent.[5] Despite the small number of respondents, this group was fairly diverse in terms of age, race, education, marital status, and income (see Appendix).

The interviews, which typically lasted about 45 minutes, were tape-recorded and transcribed. The data were then analyzed using NUD*IST, a qualitative analysis software program that allows the researcher to identify and code themes as they emerge from the transcripts. The analysis identified common themes in workers' experiences, including the factors they considered in deciding whether to mobilize their rights and the problems they experienced taking leave. Initial multiple readings of the transcripts followed by more systematic coding and analysis using NUD*IST allowed themes such as gender, "slackers," and the meaning of time to emerge. Although the small sample size here requires caution in drawing generalizations, an in-depth approach such as this has the potential to reveal considerable nuance and detail about the mobilization process.

As this study focuses on how workers who were aware of their leave rights negotiated their leaves in the workplace, the subjects are not and were not intended to be a random sample of the population of potential leave users. For this reason, I make no claims about how frequently problems with leave arise, or about the differences between workers who experience problems and those who do not. Instead, this study focuses on the experiences of workers who anticipated or experienced some difficulty in obtaining leave, and how those workers thought about mobilizing their rights.

[5] Four individuals could not be contacted after multiple attempts, four individuals refused to be interviewed, one number had been disconnected, and two numbers were incorrect.

Focusing on these problem cases is appropriate for a theory-generating project such as this because these circumstances are more likely to yield rich data about the process of mobilization.

The qualitative data from this study complement other ethnographic and quantitative studies of family and medical leave (Commission on Leave, 1996; Fried, 1998; Gerstel and McGonagle, 1999; Hochschild, 1997). For example, these data add to quantitative research about patterns of leave-taking in general (see, e.g., Gerstel and McGonagle, 1999) because they access cognitive processes that contribute to choices about leave and rights. Similarly, this project differs from recent ethnographic studies of leave-taking and corporate culture within a single organization (see, e.g., Fried, 1998; Hochschild, 1997), because it uses respondents as informants about diverse work settings to identify patterns that bridge multiple workers and workplaces. This approach helps identify common patterns *across* workplaces and *across* organizational boundaries that reveal how institutionalized practices and expectations regarding work can transform leave rights.

3. THE PROCESS OF RIGHTS MOBILIZATION IN THE WORKPLACE

Individual rights negotiations are to some extent idiosyncratic and variable. They depend on many factors, including the nature of the conflict, the social setting in which it takes place, and the characteristics of the parties. Nevertheless, common themes emerged from these data that suggest that larger social institutions systematically shape how workers think about and mobilize FMLA rights. The discussion below addresses two broad findings in particular: how rights mobilization remains embedded in relations of power, and how institutionalized norms and expectations associated with work, gender, and disability can transform the meaning of FMLA rights in the workplace.

4. POWER AND RIGHTS MOBILIZATION IN THE WORKPLACE

4.1. Knowledge as Power: Law as a Symbolic Resource in Leave Negotiations

Resources are one type of power in rights mobilization that can take many forms: time, money, energy, and legal expertise (Galanter, 1974; Morgan, 1999); emotional support from friends and family (Morgan, 1999); and even rights themselves as a symbolic resource that legitimates and reinforces the moral authority of claims (Lempert, 1998; Minow, 1987; Williams, 1991). Indeed, resources, broadly defined, shaped how respondents thought about mobilizing their rights to leave. For example, respondents said that unpaid leave drained their economic resources, and respondents who were sick often lacked the energy to pursue their rights. Also, mobilizing rights could drain time and energy that workers needed to care for their families. For example, this respondent describes how she decided to quit rather than assert her rights after her employer disciplined her for taking leave to care for her dying daughter:

> [I was] extremely angry when I had time to think about it. But the realization came, I'm getting nowhere with them and my daughter is failing right before my eyes. I wanted to make things as good as could be, knowing what was going to happen, her daughters knew what was happening and her husband knew what was happening and my two sons . . . I was ambivalent, I was angry, it was everything rolled into one what came to the forefront was my daughter and the family's needs. (1005)

This example illustrates how workers consider their relationships with others as well as their financial resources when deciding whether to mobilize rights (cf. Morgan, 1999). In general, respondents said these subjective concerns were at least as important as material resources in how they thought about their rights.

Workers also reported that even when they lacked material resources, they felt empowered by the symbolic meaning of a legal entitlement to leave. For example, respondents felt morally justified in pursuing claims to leave once they knew that their employer acted illegally. As one worker put it,

> [Information about FMLA rights] gave me a leg to stand on. And some kind of moral or ethical support knowing that this is what my rights were . . . (1003)

Respondents also described law as a pragmatic resource for confronting employers, even when they did not make a formal legal claim. For example, this worker used legal knowledge to negotiate successfully with her employer:

> [When my employer denied my leave request] I didn't say, "It's not legal," I said, "According to this state statute . . . " I put the statute number and stuff, so that they know that I know what I'm talking about . . . [A] lot of people will go, "Are you sure this is legal?" . . . and then they'll try and like moonshine their way around it. And rather than have people do that to me, I just got to where when stuff comes up, I'll learn the legal statute numbers and it's more effective for me that way. . . . [Information about my rights] gave me knowledge which gave me the power to act on what was going on. (1021)

Learning about their rights helped workers frame their experiences in both legal and moral terms, and gave them confidence to press for time off. Workers also drew on legal discourse to interpret leave as an entitlement, rather than a personal problem. Thus, even workers who lack financial resources for a court battle can still informally mobilize law to validate their claims to leave.

In an earlier study of rights mobilization, Bumiller (1988) found that some individuals chose not to pursue civil rights claims to avoid taking on a victim identity. Respondents in the research reported here did not express similar concerns. Of course, not all laws construct the same symbolic meaning. The FMLA frames leave as an entitlement rather than a protection based on status, which may avoid constructing claimants as "victims." Also, my respondents differ from the "unmobilized" subjects in Bumiller's study in that they took some steps toward mobilization. Nevertheless, even respondents who abandoned potential claims did not say they did so to avoid the victim label. Accordingly, it may be that whether actors see the law as empowering or disempowering varies with the substance of particular rights.

4.2. Information Control, Agents of Transformation, and Worker Solidarity

Another important theme that emerged from these interviews is that unequal power in the workplace can affect how workers think about rights mobilization. For example, employers can threaten termination to silence objections to unfair treatment.

> Um, when I was pregnant, my doctor put in writing that I could not, he didn't want me bending for long periods of time, or looking up for long periods of time because I have a tendency to get dizzy and get off balance when you're pregnant... So, everything that [my supervisor] wanted me to do was 4–6 inches from the floor. And there were other courtesy clerks there that could have done the job, but she wanted me to do it. She didn't care if my stomach is showing and everything. There were guys there that were courtesy clerks that could have did the job. And when I told her, "I don't think I'm supposed to be doing this." She'd tell me, "You don't like your job?" You know. And I felt that was pretty cruel, you know for her to treat me that way... So... [I did the work and] I ended up losing my baby... When I returned to work, she started right back up. She told me that she did everything while she was pregnant with no restrictions. That's what she told me.[6] (1017)

A threat may not be necessary if workers fear other penalties at work. For example, this respondent did not pursue her right to return the same or equivalent job after leave, even though her hours were cut in half when she returned to work:

> I just didn't want to make, cause he's a new manager and I hadn't worked with him. I didn't want to come back with an attitude and then him kind of be negative toward me. It hurt, but I thought well, I still have my job. It's going to be rough because, you know, 20 hours a week. (1018)

In addition respondents worried that being fired would not only deprive them of a job, but also harm their ability to find future employment. They justified voluntarily quitting rather than pursuing their rights and risking termination by pointing out that no one wants to hire a fired worker, particularly a "troublemaker" who sued a former employer.

Power can also operate in more subtle ways to shape how workers come to understand and even know about their workplace rights. Along these lines, one theme that emerged from these interviews is that information about rights matters, and that those who control that information have an advantage in workplace negotiations over leave. Information is critical to "naming," or saying to oneself that a particular experience has been injurious, and "blaming," or holding another responsible for the injury (Felstiner et al., 1981). Indeed, the FMLA recognizes the link between information

[6] This particular respondent's situation was covered by state law in California, rather than the FMLA. California law requires employers to accommodate pregnancy-related restrictions on the tasks a worker can perform by transferring her to a less strenuous or hazardous or position where that transfer can be reasonably accommodated. Cal. Gov. Code § 12945. This passage also suggests that the respondents' supervisor is applying certain norms about ideal workers. That dynamic is discussed in more detail below.

and enforcement by placing affirmative obligations on employers tell workers about their leave rights.[7]

One way to limit rights mobilization is to withhold or manipulate information that may allow rights holders to recognize a legal injury. In this way, employers can act as "agents of transformation" to shape the way in which workers understand their experiences (Felstiner et al., 1981). For example, when workers request leave, employers can stonewall by asserting that the statute does not apply unless the worker can prove otherwise.

> I mean the initial reaction . . . was just sheer, "We're not going to even use this law because we don't know what we can get away with. We don't know . . . if you qualify so until we do, you don't." That was my feeling that's how they treated that law . . . Their whole attitude is stalwart it or whatever the word is, block it the best you can. Make these folks fight for it . . . That's the reaction I got. (1002)

Employers can also simply remain silent and wait to see whether workers recognize that leave rights might apply.

> [T]he way [R's employer] is . . . if you don't do your homework they'll let you ride with what you know and if you don't know enough then you shorten yourself. So you had to go in there with as much knowledge as I had you know, to talk to them. (1010)

Another strategy is to provide information about rights to some workers but not to others. For example, one respondent reported that her employer told office workers about their leave rights, but not the maids in the hotel where she worked. Informal practices such as these give employers more control over who will take leave, and thus can transform a legal entitlement into a more discretionary benefit.

Employers can also act as agents of transformation through internal processes that shape how workers understand conflict over leave (Edelman et al., 1993; Felstiner et al., 1981). These processes can "drain the dispute of moral content and diffuse responsibility for problems" (Felstiner et al., 1981). For example, one respondent's concerns about being denied leave were diverted into the Employee Assistance Program (EAP), a counseling program paid for by the employer. The counselor then constructed her problem as a personal issue, rather than a legal violation.

> Well, the EAP person at work [was helpful] . . . He was very understanding and he felt that [my situation] was a rotten deal but, you know, "Hey, there's nothing anybody can do about it." (1006)

By framing this respondent's situation as just the way things are, a product of her personal circumstances, the counselor helped diffuse conflict about leave and deflect a potential legal claim.

Although employers shaped respondents' perceptions by controlling information about FMLA rights, respondents also talked with friends, family, and others to find information about the law and to discuss possible responses to conflict over leave.

[7] 29 C.F.R. §§ 825.301, 825.302.

These social interchanges with others influenced how respondents thought about mobilization.

> I felt like I was kind of in a situation that nobody had really been in, and so I didn't really know what to do. So people's opinions and their thoughts of what I should do made a big impact because I really had no idea of where to go from here. And I have some friends who were very supportive of this and said, "No, you have to go forward with this. You have to go through with it because they can't get away with this." (1015)

For these respondents, mobilization was not a solitary decision based on preexisting preferences, but instead a social process in which others' opinions about what they *should* do shaped their choices. In other words, respondents formed their preferences in part in response to norms and perceptions communicated by others.

Friends, family, and others can act as agents of transformation in several ways. First, they can encourage workers to mobilize their rights, sometimes by framing a particular experience as unacceptable or illegal.

> I talked to . . . the guy I was co-managing the store with and I talked to another manager [about my situation] . . . Both of them felt like I had been misled [by the company]. And that [it] had been done purposely.
>
> Interviewer: And did that influence what you did in your situation in any way?
>
> It made me want to talk to somebody in the law. (1008)

Exchanges with others can also warn workers about the risks of claiming rights, however.

> [Y]ou know I've heard horror stories about people taking time off when their baby was born and were getting a lot of flack from their bosses because they took the time . . . I heard, there was this one guy, he has a shift that is mid-shift, 12–8:30 and when he came back to work they changed it on him . . . They changed his shift to a graveyard shift, Monday through Friday when he came back . . . I worked graveyard for four years, I didn't want to go back to that. (1010)

This last example suggests how actions taken against only one worker can influence how many others think about mobilizing their rights. Stories of retaliation, passed through social networks in the workplace, can discourage workers from requesting leave even absent any explicit threat directed toward them.

On the other hand, social interactions about rights can also build solidarity among workers. By discussing problems with leave with others, workers may uncover a larger pattern of shared grievances. Also, as the following example illustrates, conversations about leave rights can help build informal networks for pooling knowledge about the law.

> Several of us were tempted to get together and get a suit going, but getting together with a lawyer is very difficult. And no one is really willing to commit to helping at all to start it. But all of us had had issues as far as FMLA, knew each other's issues . . . So . . . we would advise new employees a lot of the time if they had issues come up, they would come to us . . . As new people came in we would let them know, we've gone through quite a bit if you need

> any help with anything as far as your benefits, your health or whatever, just let us know . . . [W]e all kind of pooled our knowledge. We all had a much more expansive knowledge of what was going on. As far as influencing me, I didn't think that I could get FMLA [leave] for my condition and one of my coworkers said, "Yes you can." So it did directly affect the course I took. (1021)

In this way, negotiating individual rights can become a collective concern, and workers can gain greater leverage in negotiations over leave.

This last point contradicts the critique that rights undermine collective action by atomizing disputes and isolating grievances from their social context (McCann, 1986; Scheingold, 1974). This critique may place too much emphasis on how *formal* rights claims in court atomize grievances by narrowing disputes to legally relevant facts and individualized remedies. Also, this critique tends to assume that rights mobilization is a solitary, rather than social process. This assumption overlooks how the *informal* process of mobilizing rights—finding information about rights and caucusing with other workers about what is appropriate and legal—can help build connections and common interests among grievants. The social process of mobilization may also show workers how rights claims extend beyond their individual interests. Indeed, several respondents said they took steps to pursue their rights to prevent future workers from having a similar experience.

This insight is important because it suggests that individuals who mobilize their rights in informal settings can set in motion a framing process that may lead to eventual collective action (Snow, Rochford, Worden, and Benford, 1986). Just as rights litigation in courts can provide a public rallying point and publicity for a social movement (McCann, 1994), informal rights mobilization through workplace interactions can build solidarity among workers who share common grievances. It can also encourage workers to conceptualize their problems as part of a broader system of power and control. In other words, rights do not *inherently* create an ideological framework that *always* causes workers to view workplace problems as individual difficulties rather than collective concerns. Instead, even individual rights can be a mechanism for building awareness and solidarity among workers through informal social processes in the workplace.

5. RIGHTS MOBILIZATION IN THE SHADOW OF SOCIAL INSTITUTIONS

Perhaps the most subtle form of power is how the established practices and expectations that make up institutions shape social action to recreate the inequalities embodied in those institutions. Along these lines, the following sections discuss three themes that emerged from these interviews that illustrate how workers' negotiations over FMLA rights are embedded within the social institution of work. First, I examine how family wage ideology, or the assumption that the normative worker is a male breadwinner with a stay-at-home wife, can shape how workers and others think about the meaning of leave rights. Second, I document how a "slacker" narrative can undermine the FMLA in ways that subtly reinforce the constitutive relationship between disability and work. Finally, I look at how employers can reinterpret leave rights in terms of management objectives, weakening the normative power of the law in the workplace.

5.1. Family Wage Ideology

Respondents who took pregnancy or parental leave discovered that despite the law, family wage discourse framed the meaning of their leave. For example, women found that taking leave often changed perceptions of them at work because it seemed to signal that they were no longer committed to their job. For the most part, female respondents had no difficulty initially taking leave, but when they attempted to return, they encountered resistance and perceptions that they were less reliable and committed to their work.

The experience of a respondent who took pregnancy leave when she had twins illustrates this phenomenon. Even though this respondent worked for her employer for sixteen years before she needed leave, her employer assumed she would not return and cancelled her health insurance while she was in the hospital. In addition, her boss told coworkers that she did not need her job because her husband could support her.

> [T]hey were saying, "Well she doesn't need to get paid," my boss was saying. "She has money—her husband is a doctor." (1009)

Despite her years of service, her employer presumed that her husband was the breadwinner, and therefore she did not "need" her job. Her supervisor attempted to justify letting her go by mobilizing a cultural discourse that women (particularly mothers) are and should be economically dependent on their husbands.

Legal rights also frame her understanding of her situation, however. A friend who was a lawyer told her that she would have a strong legal claim if she tried to return and was fired, and she expressed outrage that her employer ignored her legal entitlement to leave. Nevertheless, she feared that no future employer would hire her if she was fired. She knew that her employer had fired other long-term employees who needed leave, and she decided to quit.

> [T]hose two got fired first and then I just said, you know, I don't want to get fired. I mean I have a good record and I would hate to have to go and start somewhere at, in your mid-thirties and then your employer that you've worked for 16 years fired you? That doesn't look good. And my husband said, "Is it really worth it all?" (1009)

When she left, however, to avoid a confrontation with her employer she told her supervisor she could not return to work because she lacked childcare.

This respondent's experience illustrates how legal and non-legal frames for interpreting leave can affect informal rights negotiations. To decide whether to mobilize her rights, this respondent must reconcile legal discourse with family wage ideology in a context already structured by power, gender, and taken-for-granted expectations about work. Her problems with leave arise in part because gendered assumptions about work and family give meaning to her use of leave, and obscure how her employer's power to fire her influences her decision. Although she interprets her experience as a violation of her rights, she avoids conflict by drawing on a gendered cultural discourse to give an acceptable reason to quit: lack of childcare. As a result, on the surface, her choice appears to be a voluntary "choice" to stay home and care for her children because her husband can support her; the roles of law and power in her decision remain invisible. In this way, gendered assumptions about women and work can be recreated, while legal entitlements to leave are undermined and obscured.

Male respondents who took family leave had somewhat different experiences. In fact, both male and female respondents reported informal workplace norms that men should not take all the parental leave legally available to them. For example, in one respondent's workplace, it was unthinkable that a new father would take more than a week or two of leave.

> [T]here was another guy who was having a baby and I think that they got more pressure to come back to work, okay, "It's okay for you to take a week off and maybe a week and a half off, but let's not go crazy here." And that wasn't, I don't think they would have been open for the FMLA for the men. At least the men I knew just took their vacation and didn't take, didn't use the FMLA when they could've. Because they were pressured to come back to work, like "Hey, *you* didn't have a baby."
>
> Interviewer: And there wasn't the same kind of pressure on women?
>
> No. (1020)

Whereas female respondents were expected to take leave to care for others, male respondents reported that their employers and coworkers were incredulous and even hostile when they decided to take family leave. Thus, the same family wage discourse constructed different meanings for respondents' leaves depending upon their gender.

These deeply entrenched expectations about work and gender also shaped workers' legal consciousness. For example, male respondents who took unpaid family leave struggled to reconcile leave rights with norms that men should prioritize work over family needs. Along these lines, one respondent who took leave to care for his terminally ill wife encountered criticism from coworkers for missing work, and also received a disciplinary letter from his employer telling him to keep his leave use to a minimum. When his coworkers, his employer, and even his wife questioned his time away from work, he drew on legal norms to legitimate his leave:

> I always made them understand that I'm under Family Leave . . . and that allows me the right [to take leave] . . . [M]y wife a lot of times, says "Babe, you can't miss this much work," this and that, and I'd say "Honey, you know, I'm not missing work to miss work. You're sick or whatever and if you need me, I'm here and that's what Family Leave is, that's why I'm under it, and that's why we fill out the Certification papers with your medical provider to protect me in these times of need." (1012)

At the same time, however, he believed he should not seek to advance at work while he might need family leave.

> [T]here has been plenty of opportunities for me to move up and stuff, but I didn't pursue them because... I'm not ready to give 100% responsibility. My responsibility deals with my wife and family at this time. And I've known how sick she is so I didn't pursue any of those advancements for that reason. It was that my priorities are with my family and not moving up at this time... [W]e are pretty middle class. I mean there is nothing we are deprived of. We probably have more things than what most people got, but that has never been a priority to me, like having more or whatever. You know, my priority is my family and that's how I'd like to keep it. (1012)

Even though he knew about his legal rights and took leave, this respondent understands leave and advancement at work to be an either/or choice—one cannot both pursue a career and also care for sick family members. When he justifies taking leave by arguing he passed up opportunities for advancement, he both accepts and reinforces the family wage norm that ideal workers should have no responsibility to care for others. At the same time, his statement that his family is "pretty middle class" despite his choice to put family first implicitly references cultural expectations about the male breadwinner role and justifies his choice against those norms. That his choice requires justification, however, reveals how these rights are embedded within other systems of meaning that construct men taking leave as illegitimate.

Female respondents also struggled with the double bind of expectations about being both a good worker and the family caretaker. Women, however, faced different contradictory norms about working women and "good mothers." One respondent's experience with maternity leave illustrates how these norms shaped her choices about mobilizing her rights. When she tried to return to work after her leave, she discovered that her employer had filled her position. She was angry, and when friends suggested that she contact a lawyer about pursuing her rights, she did. At the same time, she worried that she was to blame for her situation, and that she had violated norms about being a good worker by taking leave.

> I was speaking with a lawyer all that time, trying to get back my job and see if they would offer me anything else, but they just wanted to put me in housekeeping. They couldn't find anything for me. At least that's what they were saying. Other situations they were hiring for, other things like sales. And I was like, "Well I can learn sales, anything." A lot of my friends tell me that it's not my fault, that people are just like that. I felt like I was to blame. I even talked to my boss about it. I said, "Didn't I do a good job ?"... (1013)

Although her boss assured her that she had performed well, he also demoted her from human resources assistant to hotel housekeeper. She continued to work as a housekeeper for several months while her lawyer negotiated for her job.

While negotiating her rights, she also worried about failing to meet her obligations as a mother, saying "I just felt that no one else would take care of [my child] like a mother would." She was ambivalent about returning to work because she no longer had the job she loved, and she had to leave her child with another caretaker to work as a housekeeper for less pay.

> I felt bad in my own way and I was very sad. And I think a lot of it was because I knew my child was with this other person. I couldn't do anything about it. My job went to another woman and what was I going to do? All I could do is cry. (1013)

Although some of her friends thought she should continue to fight, others suggested a different solution:

> I have one friend, she was always telling me, "[Maria] if you feel this way why don't you just quit your job and just take care of your son?" Then my husband got a better job offer so that's when I said, I think I will do that. (1013)

Eventually, she gave up her negotiations with her employer and quit her job.

This respondent negotiated her rights within three overlapping and contradictory frames: legal entitlements to leave, institutionalized expectations about what it means to be a good worker, and deeply entrenched norms about what it means to be a good mother. The conflict among these frames made claiming her rights psychologically taxing. She hired a lawyer to fight for her job, but she also felt unsure of her claim to being a good worker after missing work for pregnancy leave. At the same time, she worried about not meeting an idealized norm of a mother's intense and personal care (Hays, 1996). Her legal consciousness reflects contradictory legal and cultural schemas about the meaning of leave.

Although this respondent decided to quit, it is simplistic to interpret her choice as the result of immutable gendered "preferences" without considering how cultural norms and structural conditions shaped her preferences. Perhaps she would have made a different choice if her employer had allowed her to return to her former position. Also, by suggesting that she should quit and care for her son, her friend frames her situation as a choice between work and motherhood, rather than as a legal violation. Norms about the mutually exclusive roles of mother and worker undermine her resolve to pursue her legal rights, and construct a culturally acceptable solution for resolving her stress. Her choice, channeled in part by the cultural conflict between being a good worker and a good mother, helps reinforce that cultural bind despite the protections of the law.

As these examples illustrate, workers who take family leave negotiate their rights within a web of meaning made up of not only law, but also deeply entrenched assumptions about work and gender. In addition, although workers may negotiate their rights within the same web of meaning, the interpretations that flow from those frames vary with gender. As the responses of employers, friends, and family suggest, culturally, women are expected to quit work to care for new children, whereas men are expected to make work their first priority. By framing social events in these terms, agents of transformation help define the meaning of leave, and sometimes identify a cultural path of least resistance for resolving conflict over leave. In this way, institutions can shape the direction rights negotiations may take: by providing a graceful explanation for the first respondent to quit, by defining a compromise through which the second respondent justifies his decision to take leave, and by suggesting to the third respondent that quitting to care for others is the solution to her dispute. Because they reinforce traditional gender roles, these paths of least resistance help recreate the gendered institution of work that the FMLA was meant to change.

5.2. Slackers and Workers

In contrast to the gendered norms that defined parental leave, different informal norms that leave-taking was "shirking" shaped the experiences of respondents who needed leave for their own serious health conditions. In their workplaces, despite legal entitlements to leave, "committed" workers were expected to come to work even when sick. Conversely, workers who were unwilling or unable to work while sick were perceived as less valuable.

> There seemed to be kind of, I forgot the proper way to word this, the company's attitude towards people working when they're ill and working to the point of causing illness, that was sort of a badge of courage. And I had seen other people in the company pretty much be discounted as valuable employees because they wouldn't or couldn't work when they were sick. And I think that's where my fear came from. (1008)

Even coworkers sometimes interpreted taking leave as shirking.

> Well some people consider that you're a slacker or whatever... because you're off. They don't consider sick at any point. They know I'm very energetic and hyper and all this stuff, but I should just retire or quit or whatever. I'm in the way... [S]ome people who are real company oriented or upward, yuppy types feel like you're not being a good employee if you're off. Even if you do the job efficiently. (1003)

Employers communicated this norm through concrete practices: by passing over leave takers for promotion, by transferring (or refusing to transfer) them, by cutting their hours, or by assigning them undesirable work or shifts. These responses mark those who take leave as poor workers, despite legal rights to leave.[8]

Everyday workplace practices can reinforce perceptions that taking leave for an illness is a form of shirking. For example, not replacing workers who take leave can encourage hostility toward leave takers.

> Like for instance the, well the FMLA they have to give you. But what they do is some departments and most of the departments actually, they won't replace you when you get sick, so it causes peer pressure and creates hostility.... [a]mongst your own co-workers.... "Well if this person didn't have so much family leave all the time," you know, that type of situation.... You call in and say, "I'm sick, I'm taking a family leave day." But the end result of that is that it creates hostility in the workplace. They're not supportive because the employer doesn't replace the person. (1006)

[8] Many of these practices are technically illegal. For example, the FMLA prohibits discrimination against workers who use leave rights, including using the taking of leave as a negative factor in employment actions such as hiring, promotions, or disciplinary actions. 29 C.F.R. § 825.220. These kinds of claims can be very difficult to prove, however.

By framing workload problems as a conflict among workers, rather than between workers and the employer, this particular workplace practice deflects blame for the extra workload away from the employer. Although the law has changed, this workplace continues to be structured around the always-ready always-present worker; the employer lacks any contingency plan or substitute staff to cover workers who are on leave.

The slacker discourse suggests how systems of meaning other than law can create resistance to rights and discourage workers from using leave. By drawing upon the cultural image of the "slacker," employers and co-workers reinterpret mandatory leave rights as a form of shirking. It is important to realize, however, that the slacker image is not a spontaneous local norm; its roots lie in the historical construction of "work" in opposition to "disability." The slacker image reflects assumptions that work and disability are mutually exclusive and therefore one cannot legitimately claim to be both a worker and disabled. In other words, the slacker label references deeply-held beliefs that being "really" disabled means not being able to work at all. Accordingly, leave takers find themselves straddling the cultural line between disability and work, and disrupting the mutually constitutive relationship between the two. The slacker discourse both reflects and polices this line by penalizing workers who claim a disability, however temporary that disability may be.

Workers can draw on law as a symbolic discourse, however, to reconstruct the meaning of taking leave, as this respondent discovered:

> [W]hat I've done because of this situation and because I've heard all these things, is I've been meeting with groups of employees and telling them that you don't need to go there. People are entitled to this [leave]. If it was you or your family member you would want this leave too. And you sure wouldn't want to come back to work and find out that your own coworkers are being ugly about it. And if they don't replace you, it's not the employees' fault. It actually has to do with the employer. And trying to appease people. I talk to them and explain to them what the rules are and explain to them that the person who is the sick person, is entitled to this time. And you're just making it worse by doing this to them.
>
> Interviewer: And how has this been received?
>
> "Actually pretty good. I've been trying to get them not to fuss with each other. . . ." (1006)

By referencing legal rights, this respondent undermines the slacker discourse. First, she explains "what the rules are": that leave is an entitlement, and therefore not subject to qualification or discussion. Second, she references legal norms of equal treatment by pointing out that all workers can benefit from the FMLA's protections. She also undercuts management's "slacker" interpretation by pointing out that management, not the absent worker, controls workload distribution. This counterdiscourse reveals how the slacker label obscures the employer's responsibility for the increased workload.

This example illustrates how workers can draw on law as a symbolic resource to challenge institutionalized practices and meanings in workplace negotiations over leave. In these micro interactions, legal discourse has the potential to disrupt existing social practices and show alternative ways of organizing work life. To the extent that larger social structures are created and recreated through micro-interactions such as these (Sewell, 1992), this may be one mechanism for bringing about social change.

5.3. Managerial Norms and Needs

FMLA rights also clash with another institutionalized work practice: employers' unilateral control over the schedule of work. Legal reforms can have difficulty penetrating institutionalized practices such as these that shape how managers respond to the law. For example, Edelman et al. (1993) show how organizational conflict managers reinterpret civil rights objectives in terms of managerial norms. Respondents reported a similar pattern in which employers used informal workplace practices to regain control over time off.

Some management strategies for taking back control reflected staffing concerns. For example, one respondent's employer told him about his rights to parental leave, but then asked him not to use them because the employer was short staffed. Another strategy was to limit informally the number of workers who took leave at any one time.

> [My supervisor] said well "So and so's on family leave and this one's on family leave and they haven't complained." Yeah they're not working it the same way with them. And then... she was telling me that they had family leave but that we couldn't discuss it. And then she says, "Oh someone else is applying for family leave, but we tried to keep [the number of people on leave] down to one a line."... And I'm saying "Hey, that's not what the law says."
>
> Interviewer: And what did she say when you said that?
>
> "Well, that's just what we try to do." (1003)

A second respondent's employer also seemed to manage leave requests in a way that minimized staffing concerns.

> [D]epending upon your job position you were treated differently.
>
> Interviewer: Oh really? And how was that, I mean which jobs were treated better and which were treated worse?
>
> Well, I was treated worse. And I was a hostess. And the server that had had the same experience, she was treated better because I think there was more room for her to be accommodated in the schedule because there's 30 servers but there's only three hosts.... They just... it's again, whatever's convenient for them. It's nor about the law with them. (1015)

Note that these employers did not completely ignore the law. They complied at least partially by telling workers about their rights, or by allowing some workers to take leave. Nevertheless, they implemented the law in a way that emphasized managerial norms about work schedules and staffing, rather than the entitlement to leave in the statute. In other words, these informal workplace practices did not produce "order without law," but instead subtly transformed leave rights in the workplace to be consistent with managerial needs.

Managerial practices could affect workers choices about leave in more subtle ways as well. For example, one respondent described how a management scheme that rewarded workers for meeting production targets undermined leave rights.

> [I]t was bad because we were self directed, there was a lot of talk about you know, how will [the new law] affect us, as far as covering production numbers and all that when people take and make use of this Act. . . . [T]hey diffuse everything because they get this self-directed, you're your own boss team oriented thing. . . . In order of importance its production, safety and whatever after that. Who knows. Production and safety is all we had to worry about. Fly like a bat out of hell, get it out the door, but don't hurt yourself. (1002)

As Burawoy notes, by setting workplace rules and production standards and then allowing workers to run the production process, employers can "manufacture" consent to production norms and rules:

> [J]ust as playing a game generates consent to its rules, so participating in the choices capitalism forces us to make also generates consent to its rules, its norms. It is by constituting our lives a series of games, a set of limited choices, that capitalist relations not only become objects of consent but are taken as given and immutable. We do not collectively decide what the rules of making out will be: rather, we are compelled to play the game, and we then proceed to defend the rules. (Burawoy 1979: 93)

By setting goals solely in terms of production and safety, and then rewarding self-directed workers for meeting those goals, employers can create "rules of the game" that undermine collective support for leave. In this workplace, workers enforce time standards against each other to ensure that they meet their production goals, and in the process reinforce and legitimate work practices that devalue leave. Other possible and desirable goals, such as balancing production needs against a worker's need for leave are not considered. Also, to the extent the workers buy into managerial norms, these norms can diffuse worker resistance by providing ready justifications for denying leave.

These data suggest that leave rights, which are statutory entitlements, can be reshaped and transformed by informal workplace norms. Reformulating rights in this way helps employers regain control over work schedules without appearing to refuse to comply with the law. Although these respondents recognized and resisted this transformation, other workers may simply accept employers' reinterpretation of their rights and not take leave.

6. CONCLUSION

Because law is an authoritative institution, legal rights seem to be an obvious solution to workplace conflict over family leave. This study cautions, however, that leave rights remain embedded within existing practices, deeply held beliefs, and taken-for-granted expectations about work, gender, and disability. As these data illustrate, these respondents negotiated their rights not only in the shadow of the law, but also in the shadow of other social institutions. This social context has important implications for civil rights laws, which are primarily enforced through an individual, private right of action that workers negotiate within these conflicting meanings.

Along these lines, one theme that emerges from this study is how the local practices and norms that influence mobilization can have roots in larger social structures. For example, workplace rights negotiations are embedded within unequal relations of power that are inherent in the employment relation. Formally, rights appear to be non-negotiable entitlements enforceable by law. In practice, however, legal conflict over leave rights may never arise because workers fear shift changes, bad relations with managers, or the stigma of termination if their employer retaliates. In addition, employers can shape how workers understand and respond to conflict over leave simply by exercising their control over the workplace to limit information about rights.

Power goes deeper than just the material relations of employment, however. It also resides in institutionalized norms about work and its implicit relation to gender and disability, By enacting the FMLA, Congress did not eradicate deeply-entrenched beliefs about work that shape perceptions that leave takers are shirkers, or that women do not need their jobs because they can be supported by their husbands. Also, cultural ideologies and material conditions can work together to resist rights. Material relations may determine, for example, which cultural frame is most likely to be deployed, as employers' strategies for controlling information suggest. Conversely, cultural meanings like the slacker narrative can obscure how employers exercise power over work rules, such as production goals or staffing levels. In the workplaces in this study, these factors combine to reinforce existing conceptions of work that disadvantage women and people with disabilities.

A second, related theme that emerges from this study is how social interactions help shape respondents' preferences and actions to reinforce these institutionalized norms. Often mobilization decisions are treated as rational choices based on preexisting preferences, but treating these larger social forces as atomized "preferences" obscures how institutions can shape agency. For example, family, friends, and coworkers can all act as agents of transformation by drawing on both legal and non-legal cultural discourses to interpret the meaning of leave. In this way, these actors help shape what workers believe to be appropriate and possible responses to their situations. Also, when agents of transformation articulate cultural schemas that conflict with legal entitlements, they can create uncertainty within the minds of workers about what they normatively *should do*. In short, preferences about mobilization do not seem to be preexisting and static; instead, they emerge from an interactive social process that is shaped by existing norms and social structure, sometimes in ways that can undermine civil rights goals.

Ironically, formal rights may obscure how institutions and power shape agency because rights appear to provide a legal remedy when employers resist leave. For example, when women quit their jobs without asserting their rights, it may confirm deeply held beliefs that most women prefer caring for children to work because those who preferred to work could have sued. But relying on objective behavior alone to interpret preferences overlooks how power and legal norms influenced these respondents. It also ignores how unequal power can help prevent legal disputes from arising in the first place, even where workers recognize their legal rights. For this reason, qualitative studies that reveal the subjective interplay of these factors are particularly important.

What are the implications of this study for rights and social change? Certainly, institutions can constrain social change by displacing law or transforming it to be consistent with existing practices and norms. Nevertheless, respondents' experiences indicate that rights can also function as a powerful cultural discourse. Workers can draw on rights as a symbolic resource to legitimate claims to leave and to gain leverage in negotiations with employers. And contrary to the critique that rights atomize disputes and undermine collective action, in some instances, rights can help build solidarity among workers. Thus, rights can still matter even when workers lack the resources to hire an attorney and pursue a formal legal claim.

Finally, it is important to remember that law is also a social institution that gives meaning to social events and structures social life. Although legal rights may not always be the dominant normative system, legal entitlements help make the contradictions in workers' circumstances more visible. They reveal cracks in the hegemonic institution of work, and allow workers to question the idea that penalties for leave are natural and normal. Certainly pervasive practices and expectations can constrain social change by resisting rights, but norms can also change in response to legal reforms. The FMLA provides an alternative discourse through which work can be restructured, reinterpreted, and reimagined, and in this way may bring about social change.

APPENDIX

ID	Gender	Ethnicity	Age range	Marital status	Education	Income	Leave reason[a]
1001	female	white	50–64	married	college grad	30K–50K	multiple-pg
1002	male	white	35–49	divorced	high school grad	<20K	own condition
1003	female	white	50–64	widowed	some college	30K–50K	own condition
1004	female	white	25–34	married	some college	50K–75K	multiple-pg
1005	female	white	65+	divorced	some college	50K–75K	sick child
1006	female	Hispanic	35–49	married	college grad	75K+	own condition
1007	female	white	50–64	married	college grad	75K+	own condition
1008	female	white	25–34	live w/partner	some college	30K–50K	own condition
1009	female	Hispanic	35–49	married	some college	75K+	multiple-pg
1010	male	Asian	25–34	married	some college	75K+	new child
1011	female	white	18–24	separated	some college	<20K	pregnancy
1012	male	Hispanic	35–49	married	high school grad	<20K	spouse
1013	female	Hispanic	25–34	married	some college	<20K	multiple-pg
1014	female	black	25–34	live w/partner	some college	50K–75K	multiple-pg
1015	female	white	18–24	married	some college	30K–50K	multiple-pg
1016	male	Hispanic	25–34	married	some college	75K+	new child
1017	female	black	25–34	widowed	some college	50K–75K	pregnancy
1018	female	white	35–49	separated	some college	50K–75K	sick child
1019	female	white	35–49	live w/partner	some college	30K–50K	own condition
1020	female	white	35–49	married	graduate school	75K+	multiple-pg
1021	female	other	25–34	live w/partner	some college	20K–30K	own condition
1022	male	white	25–34	married	graduate school	75K+	spouse
1023	female	Asian	25–34	married	some college	30K–50K	multiple-pg
1024	female	white	35–49	married	some college	50K–75K	multiple-pg

[a]"Multiple-pg" designates a leave taken for pregnancy and other reasons, such as recovering from a pregnancy-related illness after childbirth, or parental leave after childbirth.

CHAPTER 16

The Intersectionality of Lived Experience and Anti-discrimination Empirical Research

Tanya Katerí Hernández[1]

ABSTRACT

Working from the perspective of critical race theory, this chapter provides an empirical illustration of intersectionality theory in the context of employment discrimination complaints. Based on original research and other published data, I demonstrate that African-American women are more likely than their white female counterparts to file charges of sexual harassment at work. I then explore whether the difference is attributable to different levels in amount or severity of harrassment against black women. I conclude by calling for more intersectional research that can better address the lived experience of women who make harrassment claims, both women of color and other groups.

INTRODUCTION

Traditional legal theory and anti-discrimination law have rigidly viewed individuals in categorically simplistic terms such that a human being has either a gender or a race but rarely both. For instance, in order to prevail on a Civil Rights Act of 1964 Title VII statutory claim of discrimination, a plaintiff must demonstrate that he or she has a particular identity trait protected by the legislation (like race or gender) and that he or she has been targeted for discrimination based on that trait.[2] A number of scholars have detailed the ways in which the legal system's narrow focus on single categorical sources of discrimination have obscured the way multiple sources of discrimination

[1] Support for this research project was provided by the Rutgers University Law School-Newark Phillip Shuchman Empirical Research Fund.

[2] *See McDonnell Douglas Corp. v. Green* (1973) (explaining first requirement for plaintiff's prima facie case under Title VII's prohibition against race discrimination as showing "that he belongs to a racial minority"); *Int'l Bd. of Teamsters v. United States* (1977) ("The importance of McDonnell Douglas lies . . . in its recognition of the general principle that any Title VII plaintiff must carry the initial burden of offering evidence adequate to create an inference that an employment discrimination decision was based on a discriminatory criterion illegal under the Act.").

L. B. Nielsen and R. L. Nelson (eds.), Handbook of Employment Discrimination Research, 325–337.

can simultaneously and uniquely affect an individual living at the intersection of multiple categories.[3] Women of color have been particularly disadvantaged by the single category approach to discrimination inasmuch as the employment hostility they experience is often both about race and gender, but judges refuse to examine evidence of both under a claim for racial discrimination or a claim of gender discrimination.[4]

For example, the 8th circuit provides no claim for a Black woman whose employer systematically fires or fails to promote Black women but who hires and promotes White women and Black men. The 8th circuit affirmed this logic when it failed to critique the unitary analysis of the lower court decision in *DeGraffenreid v. General Motors*. The lower court adamantly refused to examine the ways in which discrimination against Black women can occur because of their status as women of color that is distinct from the sex discrimination White women experience and the race discrimination men of color experience, because it is a symbiosis of both sex discrimination and race discrimination. The court explicitly stated that "this lawsuit must be examined to see if it states a cause of action for race discrimination, sex discrimination, or alternatively either, but not a combination of both" (*DeGraffenreid*, 413 F. Supp. at 143). A few other courts have instead tried to accommodate the unique combination of discrimination claims of women of color by instead allowing the women to articulate their harms as a "sex-plus" claim (*Jefferies v. Harris Community Action Center*, 1980). But a number of commentators have observed that the sex-plus framework also misapprehends the intersectional nature of the discrimination against women of color (Scarborough, 1989, p. 1473). This is because sex-plus claims use sex as the main method of analysis and subordinate race to a secondary factor as if it were merely an aggravating element to a "traditional"/White female sex discrimination claim. Sex-plus claims are particularly ineffective for women of color when a jurisdiction follows the *Judge v. Marsh* holding of limiting sex-plus pleading to just one "plus" factor (*Judge v. Marsh*, 1986). The *Judge* limitation thereby hampers a judicial understanding of the ways in which discrimination is a holistic dynamic that cannot be compartmentalized neatly for women who can be simultaneously located at many sites of oppression like gender, race, national origin, age, sexuality, disability, etc.

Gay men and lesbians of color experience a similar judicial schism.[5] As legal scholar Suzanne Goldberg so accurately states "courts have often disregarded that multidimensionality [of a plaintiff's multiplicity of identity categories] and instead dissected the plaintiff, analyzing each protected trait separately rather than recognizing and responding to the discrimination based on all of the targeted traits as a synergistic whole" (Goldberg, 2003). In short, while civil rights legislation is flexible enough to encompass the complexity of overlapping forms of discrimination, the judiciary has

[3] See Crenshaw (1991, pp. 1242–1244); see also Harris (1990, p. 608) and Hernández-Truyol (1994, p. 429).

[4] See Scarborough (1989) and Scales-Trent (1989); see also Abrams (1994) and Iglesias (1993).

[5] See, e.g., *Williamson v. A.G. Edwards* (1989) (rejecting discrimination claim by Black gay man on grounds that the discrimination suffered related to plaintiff's sexual orientation rather than race).

been resistant to formulating a mechanism for adequately examining such complexity in its totality.

1. INTERSECTIONALITY THEORY IN LAW AND SOCIAL SCIENCE RESEARCH

In part, as a result of anti-discrimination law's singular focus on isolated categories as the cause of discrimination, empirical research about employment discrimination has usually followed the pattern of viewing the race of the respondent as relevant solely for questions of race discrimination or the gender of the respondent as relevant solely for questions of sex discrimination. Yet, just as individuals are simultaneously identified by a myriad of characteristics, their subordination in the workplace can also defy simplistic categorization. Intersectionality theory underscores the necessity of seeing the interactive reality of individuals as raced and gendered in ways that make their experiences not simply a sum total of characteristics like race and gender, but instead a unique reality with a unique form of subordination. "Intersectionality,' means the examination of race, sex, class, national origin, and sexual orientation, and how their combination plays out in various settings" (Delgado and Stefancic, 2001, p. 51).

The origins of intersectionality theory are rooted in the Black feminist analysis of how racism differentially forms the gender experiences of Black women (Hooks, 1981, p. 3; Hull et al., 1982; Lugones and Spelman, 1983; Spelman, 1988). In particular, Black feminists documented the ways in which stereotypes about Black women are distinct from those of White women and Black men (Jewell, 1993). Specifically, from slavery through the present, Black women have been depicted as sexually promiscuous women who are natural whores. Historically, they symbolized sexual savages and "the embodiment of female evil and sexual lust" (Collins, 1990), in contradistinction to the stereotypes of White women as inherently respectable and pure (Balos and Fellows, 1999). Legal scholar, Kimberlé Crenshaw was at the vanguard of incorporating Black feminist writings into her legal analysis for the construction of intersectionality theory. With the incites of Black feminism in mind, Crenshaw articulated the legal dilemma of women of color who are multiply burdened and have discrimination claims that cannot be understood as resulting from discrete sources of discrimination. This dynamic is aptly elucidated by Crenshaw's analogy to a traffic intersection.

> Discrimination, like traffic through an intersection, may flow in one direction, and it may flow in another. If an accident happens in an intersection, it can be caused by cars traveling from any number of directions and, sometimes, from all of them. (Crenshaw, 1989, p.149)

Thereafter, other legal scholars have continued to develop intersectionality theory to encompass the legal issues of all women of color. For example, Trina Grillo explicitly used the intersectionality theory to discuss the nature of multiracial identity within Black movements (Grillo, 1995) and Laura Padilla has similarly used the theory to situate women of color in the affirmative action dialogue (Padilla, 1997).

While legal scholars have begun to actively apply intersectionality approaches to their own research, intersectionality theory has largely been absent from the world of empirical research. In fact, sociologist Leslie McCall observes that in the discipline of Women's Studies, which was early to embrace the importance of intersectionality, a methodology for studying intersectionality has yet to be fully developed (McCall, 2001a). McCall notes that "there is much hostility to such complexity in the mainstream journals with their devotion to additive linear models and incremental improvements in already well-developed bodies of research. In the language of statistics, intersectionality usually requires the use of 'interaction effects'—or 'multilevel,' 'hierarchical,' 'ecological,' or 'contextual' modeling—all of which introduce more complexity in estimation and interpretation than is required by the additive linear model." (Id. at 19). McCall concludes that the failure to utilize complex intersectional research methods limits knowledge about the subject matter analyzed (Id. at 22).

The challenge then for those conducting empirical research interrogating the nature of employment discrimination is not only the challenge of accurately reflecting the unique experiences of individuals, but also the interlocking nature of various systems of oppression that those individuals experience. For instance, Kimberlé Crenshaw has noted the way in which those social scientists who actively research the position of women of color as both victims of racism and sexism, often still use a dichotomized theoretical framework which then undermines the precision of the analysis (Crenshaw, 1991, p. 1275). The classic example Crenshaw presents is that of Gary LaFree's study on rape (LaFree, 1989). Briefly, LaFree's focus on racial discrimination in rape as an issue of the differential punishments Black men receive for raping White women, in comparison to the punishment White men receive for raping White women, is seen as incomplete by Crenshaw. She states:

> In order to understand and treat the victimization of Black women as a consequence of racism and sexism, it is necessary to shift the analysis away from the differential access of men and more toward the differential protection of women. Throughout his analysis, LaFree fails to do so. His sexual stratification thesis—in particular its focus on the comparative power of male agents of rape—illustrates how the *marginalization of Black women in antiracist politics is replicated in social science research*. Indeed, the thesis leaves unproblematized the racist subordination of less valuable objects (Black women) to more valuable objects (White women), and it perpetuates the sexist treatment of women as property extensions of "their" men. (Crenshaw, 1991, emphasis added).

It is thus with due cause that Crenshaw critiques analyses such as La Free's as an incomplete social science assessment of the racial and gender-based discrimination of women of color. What was lacking was the application of intersectionality theory.

The particular value of applying intersectionality theory to empirical research is the aid that it can provide in the enforcement of anti-discrimination law. With the empirical documentation of the complex manifestation of intersectional discrimination, jurists and legislators may be persuaded to reevaluate their narrowly focused assumptions about how discrimination is manifested and instead consider how individuals experience discrimination from different complex positions. Accordingly, intersectional empirical research has the potential to provide legal actors with a more nuanced narrative of how discrimination occurs in real life, that may in turn influence the legal system to be more responsive to the realities of employment discrimination rather than continuing to focus on the simplicity of unitary categories. In short, empirical research is not only relevant to proving the elements of an anti-discrimination claim in court, but also in constructing how that claim can be understood. A concrete illustration for how the intersectional empirical research approach can potentially be of tremendous assistance to legal actors is in the context of the occurrence of racial disparity in the formal filing of the Title VII gender discrimination claim of sexual harassment.

2. INTERSECTIONALTIY IN OPERATION: THE SEXUAL HARASSMENT EXAMPLE

Despite the fact that early on some commentators, observed the salience of racism to the occurrence of sexual harassment, courts by and large view sexual harassment as a transgression without color (MacKinnon, 1979, p.53). Sexual harassers are presumed to be color blind in their selection of victims and sexual harassment is generally viewed as a civil rights violation in which issues of race are irrelevant. Yet, in the face of judicial incomprehension of intersectionality, a number of commentators have begun to elaborate the particularities of the racialized sexual harassment that women of color experience (Abrams, 1994; Arriola, 1990; Cho, 1997; Crenshaw, 1992; Dennis, 1996; Ontiveros, 1993). What all these commentators have noted is that because racism and sexism often blend together in the mind of the harasser, the manifestation of sexual harassment for women of color is an inseparable occurrence of both racism and sexism (Ontiveros, 1993, p. 819). For instance, most women of color accounts of sexual harassment indicate the use of racial epithets that accompany unwanted sexual touching and commentary in a manner that White women do not describe. In fact, the distinctiveness of the women of color experience of sexual harassment has motivated Sumi Cho and others to advocate for the development of a racialized sexual harassment cause of action that would be especially tailored for the unique sexual harassment experiences of women of color who are subject to a racially hostile form of sexual harassment, but often find their cases dismissed on summary judgment because of juridical discomfort with multiple-category causes of action (Cho, 1997). Furthermore, despite the fact that some courts have begun to theoretically acknowledge the intersectional position of women of color by allowing "race and sex" sex-plus claims that aggregate evidence of racial hostility with evidence of sexual hostility (*Hicks v. Gates Rubber Co.*), they often fail to discuss the distinctive nature of the discriminatory animus so that triers of fact cannot see the racial element in sex discrimination and the sexual element in the race discrimination (Abrams, 1994, pp. 2501–2502).[6]

[6] The judicial failure to meaningfully deploy intersectionality in the interpretation of a sexual harassment case is also very likely part of the larger judicial failure to apply a more broad-based understanding of what constitutes sexual harassment to begin with. See Beiner (2002) (detailing the ways in which judges have a much narrower understanding of what is sexual harassment in comparison to the general public).

Yet, the empirical research on the intersectional sexual harassment experiences of women of color is at a preliminary stage despite the fact that in 1994 the Labor Institute issued a report in which they noted that women of color were more vulnerable to sexual harassment because of their more precarious economic position and prevailing racial stereotypes (Szymanski and Pullman, 1994, p. 94–100). One survey of female faculty members in 1994 indicated that women of color were disproportionately targeted for sexual harassment despite making up a small percentage of the faculty (Brandenburg, 1997). The survey tallied the following rates of sexual harassment amongst the female faculty: African-Americans, 16.2%; Whites, 15.4%; Native-Americans, 14.6%; Latinos, 14%; and Asian-Americans, 13.7% (Id.: 46). In a more comprehensive inquiry into intersectional sexual harassment, the Center for Women in Government at the University of Albany examined EEOC sexual harassment statistics from 1992, and reported that Black women complainants accounted for 14.4% of sexual harassment charges, women of other races (not specified) accounted for 14.7% of sexual harassment charges and White women accounted for 61.9% (Women's Public Service, 1994). Although White women complainants accounted for the vast majority of EEOC sexual harassment charges, in racially comparative terms, White women were under-represented as complainants. White women accounted for only 61.9% of the sexual harassment charges in 1992, even though they made up 84.8% of all women employed in the civilian labor force in that same year (U.S. Bureau of Census, 1993). Furthermore, the data indicates an overrepresentation of women of color as complainants in comparison to their representation in the female labor force. Black women, at the time the studied statistics were gathered, made up only 11.5% of all women employed in the civilian labor force and yet they accounted for 14.4% of the sexual harassment charges. (Id.). Other women of color only made up 3.7% of women employed in the civilian labor force but accounted for 14.7% of the sexual harassment charges. (Id.). Particularly troubling is the fact that the 1992 EEOC data were not an aberration.

My own published analysis of EEOC sexual harassment charge statistics from 1992 to 1999, and Lexis-Nexis and Westlaw electronic reports of sexual harassment complaints from 1975 to 2000, indicates that the race-based disparity in filing charges is a longstanding pattern among women who formally filed complaints (Hernández, 2001). What immediately became apparent in the statistical analysis of sexual harassment charges in the United States was the overrepresentation of women of color and the under-representation of White women in the charging parties when compared with their demographic presence in the female labor force (Hernández, 2001: pp. 186–188). An analysis of the large-scale standard deviations in the comparison of observed values with expected values in the study of EEOC charge statistics led to the conclusion that although a number of factors could plausibly contribute to the racial disparity in sexual harassment charge statistics, the salience of race was inescapable. What is uncertain is the way in which race influences the sexual harassment context. Do the racially disparate statistics correlate with a racial disparity in the occurrence of sexual harassment? Or do the statistics instead correlate with the disparate influence of race in the formal reporting of sexual harassment? A review of the existing social science literature highlights the need for a self-conscious intersectional approach to empirical research.

3. SURVEY OF THE EXISTING SEXUAL HARASSMENT RESEARCH LITERATURE

Before 1992, the sexual harassment literature presented descriptive evidence indicating that women of color were disproportionately represented among the female population of early sexual harassment complainants. Legal scholars MacKinnon and Kimberlé Crenshaw theorized that the racialized nature of sexual harassment women of color experienced made it easier for them, and for Black women in particular, to conceptualize their victimization as sexual harassment, whereas White women might have experienced greater difficulty in articulating their experiences as something other than overly aggressive dating overtures (MacKinnon, 1979 and Crenshaw, 1992). Since then, political scientist Anna-Maria Marshall's study of all pivotal sexual harassment cases has begun to provide an empirical validation of the descriptive evidence (Marshall, 1998). Marshall has similarly theorized that Black women's "heightened consciousness around issues of race may have also made the law a more salient resource" in challenging their experiences of sexual harassment.

After 1992, it became harder to rely upon that conjecture as the sole explanation for the continuing racial disparities in female sexual harassment charge statistics for several reasons. In October 1991, the publicly aired testimony of Anita Hill during the Clarence Thomas Supreme Court confirmation hearing raised public awareness about the nature of sexual harassment. In addition, Congress enacted the Civil Rights Act of 1991, which allows sexual harassment plaintiffs in all states to recover compensatory and punitive damages. Thereafter, the EEOC published a layperson-friendly four-page pamphlet entitled *Questions and Answers About Sexual Harassment*, which started the public campaign to bring greater awareness of the nature of sexual harassment to the public at large and to the many employers who began instituting sexual harassment policies of their own (U.S. EEOC, 1992).

In short, since 1991, not only are all women in the United States better informed about the existence of a sexual harassment cause of action, but they are also better educated about the ways in which its manifestations give rise to a remedy at law. The view of sexual harassment as a legal claim is "now part of the national consciousness," according to legal scholar Vicki Schultz (Schultz, 1990). In fact, the number of EEOC sexual harassment charges increased approximately 112% from 1989 to 1993 (moving from 5,623 to 11,908 over the 4-year period), with 1992 being the year of the greatest single increase, when charges went up 53% (U.S. EEOC, 2001). Not only have the annual number of sexual harassment complaints filed with the EEOC more than doubled since 1989, but the EEOC also reports that sexual harassment is the fastest growing area of employment discrimination. Therefore, the racial disparity in sexual harassment charge statistics can no longer be correlated solely with the "benefit" women of color have in experiencing sexual harassment as a more "easily recognizable" racial hostility.

Empirical studies conducted by James Gruber and another by Richard Sorenson also dispute the premise that women of color are more prone to file sexual harassment charges than White women who experience the same victimization (Gruber and Bjorn, 1982; Sorenson, 1998). In fact, social scientists like Jann Adams and Audrey Murrell, who have discussed the role of race in sexual harassment observe that women of color may actually have a tendency to under-report instances of sexual harassment (Adams, 1997; Murrell, 1996). Kohlman's study of reports of sexual harassment in the General Social Surveys of 1994 and 1996 concludes that women of color are less likely to report sexual harassment than are White women (Kohlman, 2000). This is true despite Azy Barak's, Darlene DeFour's, and Audrey Murrell's empirical studies which suggest that women of color are disproportionately targeted as sexual harassment victims (Barak, 1997; DeFour, 1990; Murrell, 1996). In fact, Mary Giselle Mangione-Lambie's study suggests that White women tend to perceive incidents of sexual harassment as more serious than women of color do, and Lawrence Neuman's study suggests that White women have a broader range of behaviors that they classify as sexual harassment (Mangione-Lambie, 1994; Neuman, 1992). Some psychologists like Angela Hargrow theorize that because women of color are accustomed to racist and sexist behavior in the workplace, they may be less prone to immediately filing a sexual harassment complaint (Hargrow, 1996). Kathleen Rospenda's study found that sexual harassment victims are more likely to use internal coping methods when the harasser is outside of their racial or ethnic group—of particular salience to women of color who are primarily victimized in the workplace by White men according to the Merit Systems Protection Board study (Rospenda, 1998; Merit Systems Protection Board, 1981). Therefore, when a geographically diverse sample of Black working women was surveyed, the study found that Black women see Black male subordinates and supervisors as more harassing than White males with the same job status. Consequently, no support was found for the hypothesis that Black women were more likely to report a White harasser than a Black harasser. Similarly, Obermayer's recent hierarchical log-linear analysis of a sample of the data collected by the Department of Defense for their 1995 study of sexual harassment in the military, suggests that when women of color are subjected to unwanted crude sexual attention by someone of a different race they will respond with coping and avoidance strategies rather than reporting the behavior as they would otherwise do with harassers of the same race (Obermayer, 2001). Obermayer notes that reporting rates increase with harassers of the opposite race for incidents of sexual coercion, yet my own 2001 article notes that sexual coercion cases are the most infrequent of sexual harassment cases (Hernández, 2001). Furthermore, Karen Dugger's study concluded that while being employed empowers White women to challenge dominant gender role attitudes, it does not have the same effect for women of color and Black women in particular (Dugger, 1988).

In addition, the argument that the racial disparity in charge statistics is primarily the result of the lower socioeconomic status of women of color is undercut by examining the prevalence of sexual harassment across all occupational levels (Gruber, 1997), and Barbara Gutek's early empirical data indicating that women with fewer personal resources tend to respond in an indirect manner rather than filing formal complaints (Gutek, 1985). Furthermore, Azy Barak's study that measured sexual harassment across occupational groups still found that 16.6% of White women indicated they had been sexually harassed in comparison to 48.6% of Black women (Barak, 1997). This finding is consistent with the work of noted sociologist James Gruber, who asserts that occupational status does not greatly influence women's responses to sexual harassment (Gruber and Smith, 1995). Nor does the educational level of the victim appear to have a significant impact on victim selection according to Constance Thomasina Bails (Bails, 1994).

In contrast, Gruber and Smith state that the severity of harassment is a stronger predictor of a woman's willingness to report the incident (Gruber and Smith, 1995). An avenue to be explored is the premise that disproportionate filing of sexual harassment complaints by women of color may be a result of enduring more severe experiences of sexual harassment, which thereby compel formal resolution. Yet, further study is needed before being able to draw any definitive conclusions that could inform the reform of sexual harassment as a legal cause of action. But, whether the racially disproportionate filing statistics can be explained as a consequence of greater severity, or as a reflection of a higher rate of sexual harassment for women of color, or some other reason, what is clear is the need to more closely research the influence of race in the occurrence of sexual harassment.

4. THE ROLE FOR INTERSECTIONAL EMPIRICAL RESEARCH IN THE STUDY OF SEXUAL HARASSMENT

Given the dearth of sexual harassment studies that examine the salience of racial difference let alone principally focus upon race as a category of analysis, an empirical study that will directly explore many of the causal factors that may influence the racial disparity in sexual harassment filing statistics is needed. For instance, an intersectional study could be developed to investigate whether there is some correlation between rates of sexual harassment and race-based decision-making on the part of harassers as revealed by their reference to racialized sexual stereotypes during the victimization. What the data may suggest is that sexual harassers target White women as victims at disproportionately lower rates than women of color. Such a hypothesis is consistent with some of the few empirical studies to specifically focus on the influence of race on sexual harassment. Alternatively, harassers may disproportionately target women of color due to their more precarious economic position as primary wage earners for their families with greater fears of terminating their employment despite the harassment (Morgan, 1999).

In addition, the racial disparity in sexual harassment complaint filing rates could instead be attributed to an inclination to file official complaints that is racially influenced.

For instance, the interaction that women have with their human resources department that are by and large staffed by White women may vary by race. Specifically, White women's claims may be viewed as more credible and thus more likely to be resolved informally. While, in contrast, human resources may view the claims of women of color as more suspect thereby heightening the need for women of color to seek agency-based and judicial paths to justice. In addition to exploring the role of the human resources department in the racial disparity of filing rates, a study could also examine whether White women may generally have greater access to White male defenders in the workplace who can informally resolve the dispute that is not as readily accessible by women of color. For instance, in Celia Morris's interviews of women for the book "*Bearing Witness: Sexual Harassment and Beyond—Every Woman's Story*" published in 1994, several of the White women interviewed indicated that the sexual harassment they experienced on the job ended when a White male authority figure in the workplace informally discussed the matter with the harasser on their behalf (Morris, 1994). None of the women of color who were interviewed had such a defender in the workplace.

Another theory that could be explored is the premise that White women have greater access to the option of exit by terminating employment where the harasser is located and seeking employment elsewhere given the higher percentage of White women with managerial and professional jobs, higher salaries, and thus fewer barriers to obtaining other employment. A related theory that also surfaces in Celia Morris's collection of interviews is the notion that higher-ranking White women may be less inclined to file formal charges because of the professional prestige they stand to lose by doing so, while at the same time being able to make the internal complaint procedure more responsive to their concerns because of their power in the organization. While several White women indicated that they ultimately decided not to file a complaint because of their concern that it would bar their career advancement, none of the women of color interviewed discussed their claim in relation to their professional standing.

Thus, in the few sexual harassment narratives that present racial data in the women's own account of sexual harassment, there seem to be some racial patterns that merit empirical inquiry. And while a review of the existing sexual harassment social science literature leaves us with many more questions than answers with respect to the role of race in complaint filing rates, what is clear is the great potential that an intersectional empirical analysis of sexual harassment has in contributing to our understanding of sexual harassment as a form of gender discrimination let alone in our general understanding of multidimensional discrimination.

5. CONCLUSION

Anti-discrimination advocates need social science researchers in their efforts to make the law more responsive to the lives of real people. Because discrimination is such a complex social and psychological process, it is difficult for courts to grasp the particular permutations of intersectional acts of discrimination that do not fit neatly into just one category of analysis. The value of intersectional empirical research is the assistance it can provide in educating jurists about the true nature of discrimination. With the proliferation of intersectional empirical research endeavors, jurists will hopefully be persuaded to be more receptive to addressing the full complexity of the cases brought before them. "[O]nly a rich synthesis of information on gender, race, class, and local economic conditions enables us to interpret fully the causes of inequality, the consequences of inequality, and the remedies to inequality" (McCall, 2001b, p. 31). The context of sexual harassment is but one example of a discrimination cause of action that could provide relief to more plaintiffs, if intersectional empirical research were brought to bear on the complex realities of women of color and other multiply subordinated discrimination victims. In short, intersectionality is a theory that is not only useful in the context of framing a discrimination cause of action, but also in the framing of social science discrimination research. In both contexts, intersectionality theory attempts to better reflect the social realities of women of color and others.

CHAPTER 17

Law at Work: The Endogenous Construction of Civil Rights

Lauren B. Edelman

ABSTRACT

This chapter extends extant theory on organizational response to law by proposing a theory of law as *endogenous*—that is, as *generated within the social realm that it seeks to regulate*. As organizations respond to legal ideals by themselves becoming legalized, they shape social understandings of law and of the meaning of compliance. Courts, as actors within the same broad social environments—or organizational fields—as organizations, tend to incorporate ideas about law that have arisen and become institutionalized within these fields. Thus, as law becomes progressively institutionalized in organizational fields, it is simultaneously transformed by the very organizational institutions that it is designed to control.

INTRODUCTION

The realm of law is generally viewed as above and outside of the realm of organizations. Organizations may resist the force of law or they may embrace it, and they may tweak the meaning of law at the margins, but they are essentially the receivers rather than the producers of legal rules. Law, on the other hand, is generally viewed as determinative and coercive. In this typical vision of law and organizations, law is *exogenous* to organizations; that is, law is formed prior to and relatively autonomously from organizational actors, structures, and institutions.

In this essay, I propose an alternative model of law, which treats the legal and organizational realms as integrally intertwined and mutually constitutive. My model treats law as *endogenous*, that is, as taking shape *within* the social fields that it seeks to regulate. Legal endogeneity is made possible in the civil rights realm because law regulating employment tends to be broad and ambiguous. Legal ambiguity leaves organizations substantial latitude to construct the meaning of compliance (Edelman, 1992). Understandings of "compliance" with law, and ultimately of the meaning of law itself may be crystallized by the courts but those understandings derive in large part from institutionalized organizational patterns, structures, practices, rituals, and

L. B. Nielsen and R. L. Nelson (eds.), Handbook of Employment Discrimination Research, 337–352.

culture. This essay outlines the process by which organizations interpret, mediate, construct, and ultimately shape the meaning of civil rights law.

By understanding law as endogenous, it becomes possible to understand how and why laws regulating organizations often take unanticipated forms, and why judicial interpretations of those laws often fail to remedy inequality in the workplace. A theory of endogenous law also provides a framework for understanding how and why statutes that regulate organizations have limited impact, and how the courts legitimate and institutionalize forms of compliance that undermine the very legal rights they apparently enforce. Endogeneity theory is not, however, simply an explanation for the claims made by critical legal scholars regarding the incapacity of law to reform social institutions. Endogeneity theory also explains how law may produce significant social change in subtle, indirect, and unexpected ways by altering conceptions of what constitutes good management, organizational fairness, and employee rights.

1. THEORETICAL FRAMES

The idea of legal endogeneity draws both on neo-institutional organization theory, which emphasizes the cultural environments of organizations, and socio-legal scholarship, which emphasizes the cultural life of law. Neo-institutional organizational theory developed in the late 1970s. Whereas earlier organizational studies, following the writings of Weber (1947), generally emphasized the rational, purposive, and strategic nature of bureaucracy,[1] neo-institutional accounts highlight the role of taken-for-granted cultural rules, models, and myths in structuring organizations.

Seminal neo-institutional works by Meyer and Rowan (1977), DiMaggio and Powell (1983), and Meyer and Scott (1983) suggest that organizations exist within "*organizational fields*," which are defined as "organizations that, in the aggregate, constitute a recognized area of institutional life: key suppliers, resource and product consumers, regulatory agencies, and other organizations that produce similar services or products" (DiMaggio and Powell, 1983, p. 148). Organizations within those fields tend to incorporate institutionalized models not only because of rational analysis of their costs and benefits but also because certain actions, forms, or rituals come to be understood as proper and natural.

Because it emphasizes the cultural aspects of organizational life, neo-institutional theory provides a frame for theorizing the intersection of law and organizations. However, there is a curious paradox in the predominant conceptualization of law in neo-institutional theory. While neo-institutional theory understands *organizations* as complex institutions that, in addition to their formal structures and roles, are constituted by their cultural environments and social contexts, its conceptualization of *law* is far less institutional. Law is generally understood as a set of formal rules that are fairly stable

[1] Some of the classic works in this vein are Blau and Scott (1962); Stigler (1971); Pfeffer and Salancik (1978); Thompson (1967); see Scott (2003) for a thorough review of the "rational perspective."

and coercive; there is little attention to the cultural life of law or the way in which law is shaped through and by social actors, norms, rituals, and meaning-making (Suchman and Edelman, 1996). Further, neo-institutional organization theory (like most organization theory) theorizes law as a top–down phenomenon: law causes or sets the stage for organizational change but it is not itself the product of organizational life (e.g., Meyer and Rowan, 1977; DiMaggio and Powell, 1983; Fligstein, 1990).

In stark contrast to the simplistic, exogenous, and coercive vision of law that one finds in organization theory, the law and society tradition holds that law itself is a culturally and structurally embedded social institution. Although early law and society scholarship rarely considered the interplay of law and organizations (Selznick (1969) and Macaulay (1963) are notable exceptions), the law and society perspective was a natural fit with the more cultural conception of organizations developed in neo-institutional organization theory. Neo-institutional work on law and organizations combines organizational scholars' insights on the institutional nature of organizations with socio-legal scholars' insights on the institutional nature of law (Edelman, 1990; Edelman, 1992; Suchman and Edelman, 1996; Edelman and Suchman, 1997).

Building on DiMaggio and Powell's construct of organizational fields, I have argued in earlier work that organizations are highly responsive to their "legal environments" or the law-related aspects of organizational fields (Edelman, 1990; Edelman, 1992). Legal environments include formal law and its associated sanctions; informal practices and norms regarding the use, non-use, and circumvention of law; ideas about the meaning of law and compliance with law, and the broad set of principles, ideas, rituals, and norms that may evolve out of law (Edelman, 1990; Edelman, 1992; Edelman and Suchman, 1997; Cahill, 2001).

Because employment-related civil rights law is highly ambiguous, organizations turn to their legal environments for ideas about what it means to be in compliance with the law. Legal environments become the arena within which organizations collectively construct the meaning of compliance. Through organizational mimicry and the normative claims of professionals within organizations, certain forms of compliance become institutionalized, that is, they attain a mythical and taken-for-granted form of rationality and spread quickly among organizational populations (Edelman, 1992). The institutionalization of forms of compliance appears to be relatively independent of legal ideals, enabling organizations to comply with law symbolically but without much substantive change (Edelman and Petterson, 1999).

This essay extends extant theory on organizational response to law by proposing a theory of law as *endogenous*—that is, as *generated within the social realm that it seeks to regulate*. As organizations respond to legal ideals by themselves becoming legalized, they shape social understandings of law and of the meaning of compliance. Courts, as actors within the same broad social environments—or organizational fields—as organizations, tend to incorporate ideas about law that have arisen and become institutionalized within these fields. Thus, as law becomes progressively institutionalized in organizational fields, it is simultaneously transformed by the very organizational institutions that it is designed to control. As organizations become increasingly legalized, the law becomes managerialized.

2. THE ENDOGENEITY OF LAW

The central actors in the legalization of organizations and the managerialization of law are *compliance professionals*—that is, professionals both within and outside of organizations whose work involves managing the law and legal requirements. Compliance professionals within organizations include human resource professionals who handle legal requirements or design organizational policy in light of law; in-house counsel who handle compliance or legal issues either as a major or minor component of their work; compliance specialists such as affirmative action or safety officers; and general administrators whose roles include the administration of legal requirements. Compliance professionals outside of organizations include lawyers who advise organizations on legal issues or handle legal problems, and various management consultants who provide similar sorts of advice. Attorneys who represent either organizations or parties who have complaints against organizations also act as compliance professionals. In some cases, external compliance professionals work closely with organizations, as in the case of lawyers on retainer or regular management consultants; in other cases, compliance professionals have more fleeting interactions with organizations, as in the case of consultants who provide one-shot advice or who maintain web sites that offer advice.

Compliance professionals act as social filters through whom legal ideas must pass on their way to organizations and through whom organizational constructions of law must pass on their way back to the legal realm. In the process of making policy, advising clients, resolving problems, or seeking change, these compliance professionals have multiple opportunities to shape both organizations and law.

Figure 1 shows the circular path along which law travels through social space, creating (simultaneously) a legalization of organizations and a managerialization of law. For the purposes of this analysis, the circle begins with the broad and ambiguous civil rights legislation that regulates organizations (Edelman, 1992). This analysis focuses on the process by which enacted legislation is constructed through the actions of organizations, compliance professionals, and courts. It is important to recognize, however, that ambiguity of employment regulation is itself the product of organizational lobbying and the social construction of (previous) law.

This essay identifies six stages that contribute to the construction of statutory law: (1) the professional construction the legal environment; (2) the construction and diffusion of symbolic forms of compliance; (3) the construction of law within organizations; (4) the formation of legal consciousness; (5) the mobilization of law; and (6) judicial deference to organizational institutions. These stages give rise to several macro-level transformations in law. As the meaning of law evolves, there is an increasing legalization of organizations (as legal ideas become institutionalized within

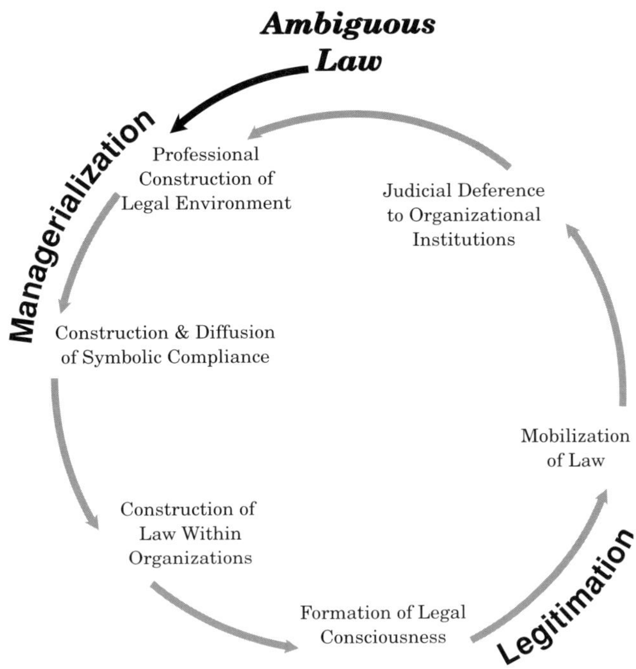

Figure 1. The Endogeneity of Law

organizational fields) but also an increasing managerialization of law (as managerial ideologies and traditional managerial prerogatives influence understandings of ambiguous legal rules). As organizational life gives rise to legal disputes and the mobilization of law, moreover, there is an increasing legitimation of managerialized understandings of law. In the remainder of this section, I discuss each of the stages of legal evolution.

2.1. The Professional Construction of the Legal Environment

Laws become relevant parts of organizational fields only when they are made known to organizational actors. Actors within organizations generally learn about the law not by reading statutes or cases or administrative regulations but rather through the compliance professionals in and around their organizations. Myriad professional journals, websites, workshops, and consultants provide filtered accounts of what the law is and how it is relevant to organizations. Informed by these sources, compliance professionals communicate to organizational administrators what laws are relevant, how they are relevant, and how much threat they pose.

Of course, different compliance professions are likely to present somewhat different visions of the legal environment, reflecting the logics of the fields within which they work. Persons within a given profession often have similar forms of education (and sometimes social background) and tend to be connected through professional networks; they interact at conferences, write for and read their professional journals, participate in on-line forums and workshops, and exchange views at work or in the context of professional transactions. Thus, certain ideas about law tend to become institutionalized within particular professions.

There is in fact a complex relation—to some extent a hierarchy—among the professions, which promotes a systematic transformation of legal information as it enters organizational fields. Lawyers often stand at the apex of this hierarchy by providing initial admonitions about changes in law or new threats posed by patterns of litigation. These lawyers write for web sites and professional journals; they lead workshops for other lawyers and for managers; they serve as consultants to more general lawyers and, especially, to in-house counsel for organizations. Slightly lower in the hierarchy are management consultants, who often work in tandem with lawyers and also help to diffuse "knowledge" about the threat of law and about what constitutes compliance. Compliance professionals who are regular employees (e.g., human resource personnel and other administrators) tend to learn about law from external lawyers and management consultants through workshops, journals, and websites. These lower level compliance professions are most likely to blur the boundaries of law and management, interpreting law in ways that make it consistent with their everyday managerial experience and treating law-related problems as a form of normal managerial problems.

When lawyers and management consultants present the legal environment to the business world, they also help to construct for the business world the extent to which law threatens traditional managerial prerogatives, the meaning of law for organizational policy, the likelihood of lawsuits and liability, and what actions or structures constitute reasonable means of compliance. Lawyers and management consultants often emphasize or even exaggerate the threatening aspects of legal environments, both because they see their role as "bulletproofing the workplace" (Bisom-Rapp, 1999) and because, by emphasizing the threat and offering a solution to that threat, they stand to gain a larger market for their services and to gain power and stature within organizational fields (Edelman, Abraham, and Erlanger, 1992).

From its initial exposure in organizational fields, the law becomes what its interpreters make it. Stories about large jury verdicts in favor of employees are told and retold, often without authority to back up the claims. In a study of organizational response to wrongful termination lawsuits based on breach of implied contract, for example, Edelman et al. (1992) found that exaggerated accounts of huge jury verdicts in favor of employees were repeatedly cited in personnel journals. Although wrongful termination is a common law doctrine that varied considerably by state, the management literature described cases almost exclusively from those states where courts were most sympathetic to employees (such as California and Michigan). Even there, exaggerations were rampant. Articles in management journals repeatedly cited the "half million" figure as a typical jury verdict, saying nothing about state variation and providing no authority to support this figure. Yet in a systematic survey of outcomes in implied contract wrongful discharge cases, Edelman et al. (1992) found that even in the two states most sympathetic to the implied contract action, the figures were far lower. In California, the median jury verdict in implied contract wrongful termination cases was $93,750 and a mean was $188,278; in Michigan, the median was $100,000 and the mean was $168,072.

Characterizations of the threat of wrongful discharge, moreover, varied both with the profession of the author and with the intended audience of the journal. Journal articles written by managers were significantly more likely to exaggerate the threat of wrongful discharge than were those written by lawyers, and journals aimed at managers were more likely to exaggerate the threat than journals aimed more at management academics. Although limited to the wrongful termination context, these findings suggest that characterizations of legal threats may become more extreme as they move out of legal fields and into organizational fields.

2.2. The Construction and Diffusion of Symbolic Forms of Compliance

Armed with a vision of law and legal threats provided by compliance professionals, actors within organizations seek rational solutions to those threats. But how to comply with law is often not obvious because anti-discrimination law tends to be broad, ambiguous, and procedurally oriented. Statutory proscriptions against employment decisions "based on" race or sex give employers very little guidance about what they may or should do. In a national survey of employers' responses to civil rights law from 1964 to 1989, Edelman (1992) shows that certain forms of compliance diffuse quickly throughout organizational fields. She argues that civil rights law interacts with public support for civil rights to produce a normative environment in which fair treatment of employees becomes increasingly valued and racial or gender disparities may be challenged as violations of that value. As this value becomes increasingly accepted—or institutionalized—organizations become more likely to incorporate structures that visibly demonstrate attention to that value. In some cases, especially early on, organizations strategically design structures that symbolize attention to legal values in order to gain legitimacy; in other cases, especially later in the institutionalization process, organizations may adopt these structures because they come to be seen as natural and proper and are even equated with "compliance."

Given the murkiness of both "the law" and "compliance," organizations turn to the organizational fields around them for models of how to comply. Especially in the mid-1960s, when there were few models for how to comply with civil rights law, public governance served as a ready source of legitimized models for private governance, and therefore as a source of solutions to laws that challenge organizational governance. In response to the ambiguous civil rights mandates of the 1960s and 1970s, employers created rules and policies that look like statutes, offices that look like administrative agencies, compliance officers who look like administrative officers or even police, and grievance procedures that look like courts (Edelman, 1992; Edelman, Uggen, Erlanger, 1999). These anti-discrimination rules, civil rights offices, grievance procedures, and other legal structures served as visible symbols of attention to law.

The forms of compliance adopted by these trend-setting organizations in turn served as ready models of legitimate compliance for other organizations. Networks of compliance professionals helped to diffuse these forms of compliance. As certain forms of compliance became increasingly prevalent, the rationality of those solutions became "mythical" or taken-for-granted, and organizations adopted those structures at increasing rates (Edelman, 1990; Edelman, 1992; Sutton, Dobbin, Meyer, and Scott, 1994). Edelman (1992) shows, for example, that the creation rates of discrimination grievance procedures were low for the first few years following the enactment of the 1964 Civil Rights Act, but then increased dramatically during the mid-1970s as the form became institutionalized. Similar patterns hold for EEO offices and rules (Edelman and Petterson, 1999) and for at-will clauses in employment contracts (Sutton et al., 1994). These diffusion patterns reflect a rationalization and institutionalization of symbolic structures. Over time, these structures came to be seen as evidence of compliance, even though nothing in the statutory language mandated that organizations create them.

2.3. The Construction of Law Within Organizations

Once in place, compliance structures tend to serve as vehicles for the making of legal meaning, often evolving independently of the intentions of organizational strategists. As compliance professionals confront the everyday problems of organizational life (such as hiring, job assignment, employee discipline, dispute handling; and federal, state, and local reporting requirements), they construct the meaning of law *within* organizations.[2]

As compliance professionals go about making sense of the law in the context of their daily activities, they do so not as autonomous individuals but rather as inhabitants of organizational fields. In most cases, managers and even lawyers in the arena of human relations learn about the law not through an independent reading and analysis of statutes and cases but rather through common networks, through professional journals and workshops, and through business schools. Because compliance professionals inhabit common organizational fields, the ideas that become institutionalized in those fields influence how compliance professionals interpret legal requirements, process legal paperwork, and attempt to resolve law-related problems.

[2] In some organizations, those who construct the meaning of law within organizations are the same people who construct the legal environment generally. In many other organizations, the environment is constructed by legal and management consultants outside the formal organizational structure, while the day-to-day construction of law is in the hands of the compliance professionals who are employees (predominantly human resource managers, other administrators, and in-house counsel). In some cases, the construction of the legal environment occurs simultaneously with the construction of law within organizations. More frequently, however, organizations respond to law initially by elaborating their formal structures to create symbols of compliance, leaving the details of legal meaning to be worked out in the day-to-day context of organizational life.

The meaning of law, therefore, is filtered through the lens of managerial norms and tempered by managerial concerns. This filtering process has a dual nature: on one hand, it eases the way for legal ideals to enter organizational terrain by rendering those ideals more consistent with the logic of organizational fields, thus producing a *legalization of organizations*. On the other hand, it means that legal ideals tend to become infused with traditional managerial ways of thinking, thus producing a *managerialization of law* (Edelman, Fuller, and Mara-Drita, 2001). As law becomes managerialized, the logic of efficiency and rationality will often trump the logic of rights and justice.

The managerialization of law, then, occurs as law is subtly framed by managerial logic. Law is framed by managerial logic through two processes: *the internalization of law*, in which organizations internalize elements of legislation, adjudication, and advocacy that are otherwise handled outside the boundaries of organizations; and the *rhetorical reconstruction of legal ideals*, which occurs as managerial rhetoric reframes the goals of law in ways that conform to managerial objectives.

2.3.1. The Internalization of Law

The internalization of law occurs as organizations create internal rules that mimic formal legislation, create internal dispute processing mechanisms that act as a substitute for formal litigation, and create in-house counsel who take over functions formerly handled by lawyers outside of organizations. Each of these types of internalization gives organizations greater control over the law and greater opportunities to influence the form and content of law (Edelman and Suchman, 1999).

Internal legislation involves the creation of internal rules designed to mimic formal legislation, for example, anti-discrimination or anti-harassment or safety policies. The symbolic value of these policies lies merely in their existence. But internal legislation does not ensure replication of public law or recognition of legal ideals. Rather, organizations have significant latitude in *how* they actualize the law in internal policies. In an effort to combine legal and managerial goals, managers are likely to build discretion into rules, to replace legal standards (such as disparate treatment) with managerial standards (such as consistency), or even to circumvent legal standards.

In some cases, moreover, internal legislation may even "legislate" away some or all of the thrust of legal ideals (Edelman and Suchman, 1999). For example, when courts began to articulate a theory under which terminated employees could sue employers for violation of an "implied contract," employers quickly began to revise their personnel policies and employment contracts to avoid legal risk by explicitly specifying that their employees worked "at will" and thus could be fired without reason (Edelman et al., 1992; Sutton et al., 1994).

Internal legislation, even when it mimics public law fairly closely, need not constrain organizational activities. Because it is generally the form rather than the substance of compliance that attains an institutionalized status, there is variation in how enthusiastically management, as well as the personnel who staff compliance structures, embraces legal ideals. In some cases, structures have both symbolic and substantive significance—their form signals attention to legal ideals and they operate to enhance the workplace status and conditions of legally protected employees. In other cases, however, the structures fit the law in form but lack substantive effect. Organizations may strategically seek to create compliance structures merely as symbolic gestures by "decoupling" those structures from core organizational activities (Edelman, 1992). Organizations may, for example, create affirmative action officer positions but give the officer little or no autonomy or authority (Chambliss, 1996) or create grievance procedures that are hard to access and known to provide little relief.

In an empirical study of the impact of four types of compliance structures from 1984 to 1989 in a national sample of organizations, Edelman and Petterson (1999) found that neither formal EEO offices nor affirmative action plans significantly improved the workforce representation of women or minorities. Affirmative action plans in fact had a statistically significant negative impact on the representation of women, a result consistent with Baron, Mittman, and Newman's (1991) finding that affirmative action plans had a negative impact on gender equity among California public employers. Edelman and Petterson did find, however, that organizations with EEO offices were significantly more likely to create affirmative action recruitment and training programs, and recruitment programs were in fact associated with an increase in minority representation. The late 1980s were, of course, not a time of active enthusiasm for civil rights; a similar study conducted during an earlier time period might have produced different results. Nonetheless, these results suggest that more basic compliance structures are more likely to be merely symbolic than more specific recruitment and training programs.

A second form of the legal internalization of law is internal adjudication, which is becoming increasingly common in organizations (Edelman et al., 1999). Internal adjudication facilitates the managerialization of law as internal complaint handlers make sense of the law on a case-by-case basis. While internal dispute resolution is far less formal than court adjudication and does not involve written decisions, it nevertheless helps to shape how legal rules are understood and experienced within organizations. As managers resolve disputes, they also shape understandings about what constitutes a problem, whether the problem is legal in nature, whether the problem can or should be resolved, whether and how legal standards might affect the resolution of the problem, and how the problem ought to be resolved.

In an empirical study of how managers within organizations handle discrimination complaints, for example, Edelman, Erlanger, and Lande (1993) find that complaint handlers tend to recast complaints of discrimination as typical managerial problems, such as poor management or interpersonal difficulties, and to resolve them in those terms. Poor management may be remedied by training or through pragmatic solutions such as transferring the employee; interpersonal difficulties are handled with therapeutic solutions, such as counseling, employee assistance programs, or mediation-like exchanges. While these remedies serve the organization's purpose in ensuring smooth employment relations and often resolve the employees' complaints, they tend to discourage attention to legal rights. In so doing, these remedies depoliticize and delegalize issues, potentially affecting not only the particular dispute but also both employee and employer reactions to future disputes (Edelman et al., 1993; Edelman and Cahill, 1998; Edelman and Suchman, 1999). Internal dispute resolution gives rise, then, to a "common law of the organization" that merges legal and managerial logics.

A third important form of legal internalization is the ascendance of the in-house counsel's office. In recent years, organizations have built increasingly large and sophisticated internal legal staffs (Chayes and Chayes, 1985; Rosen, 1989; Galanter and Rogers, 1991, pp. 22–25; Nelson, 1994; Nelson and Nielsen, 2000). In large firms, these lawyers not only handle complaints and litigation but also screen corporate documents for possible exposure to liability and manage the distribution of work to outside counsel. Although many firms still use outside lawyers, they tend to rely on in-house counsel to manage the outside law firms, deciding which issues will be handled in-house and which contracted out. In interactions with outside attorneys, in-house counsel draw strength not only from their co-equal claims to legal expertise, but also from their extensive discretion over the selection of outside law firms for future business (Chayes and Chayes, 1985, p. 292; Nelson, 1994, p. 355). The power to control out-bidding to private attorneys and to handle legal issues internally substantially expands the role and influence of staff attorneys.

As in-house counsel plays a greater role in organizations' legal business, they may not make organizations more compliant, but rather more skillfully evasive. Relative to private counsel, in-house counsel tend to identify more with the interests of the organizations they serve, to see law more as barrier than as norm, and to seek loopholes through those barriers. In-house counsel not only knows more about the constraints of law, but also knows more about which constraints are somewhat flexible. They can act more as strategic advisors to organizations than as cautionary enforcers (Rosen, 1989). The more deeply lawyers are embedded in the organization, the more likely they become to use their expertise to serve, rather than to question, prevailing managerial objectives.

2.3.2. The Rhetorical Reconstruction of Legal Ideals

Models of management—such as "t-groups," "quality circles," "corporate culture," "total quality management," and "business process reengineering" come and go like fashions, yet can have lasting effects on organizational structure and culture (Abrahamson, 1996). Generally designed as ways to enhance productivity by "manufacturing consent" (Burawoy, 1979), these managerial philosophies can subtly yet powerfully infuse legal constructs with managerial ideas (Edelman et al., 2001).

Edelman et al. (2001) study the managerialization of the construct of "diversity" during the 1980s and 1990s. Managerial rhetoric about diversity appears to stem from *Workforce 2000* (Johnston and Packer, 1987), a 1987 study by a private consulting firm that warned that by the year 2005, the workforce would become predominantly non-White and would require dramatically different management skills. Although the prediction was based on a faulty assumption (Friedman and DiTomaso, 1996), it became the rallying call for a new model of management centered on "valuing diversity," i.e., recognizing the varying backgrounds and viewpoints of a diverse workforce could be harnessed for productive purposes. The authors show that by the early 1990s, articles on "diversity" had largely replaced articles on "civil rights" or "affirmative action" in the management literature. But while managerial rhetoric on diversity appears to buttress EEO law and to draw on the same moral ideal, the shift from equal opportunity to diversity language is much more than a change in packaging. Through a content analysis of the professional management literature, the authors show that whereas accounts of diversity initially emphasized legally protected categories such as race, sex, and national origin, the focus gradually expanded to include a wide variety of extra-legal dimensions of diversity including cultural differences, geographical differences, lifestyle differences, and even differences in communication style, dress style, and taste in food. Further, managerial rhetoric about diversity tends to portray anti-discrimination law in a negative light, asserting that while law imposes inefficient rules on organizations, diversity management promotes creativity, harmony, and profit. Managerial rhetoric about diversity has produced a dramatic shift in how diversity is understood in management, largely disassociating the construct from its legal context and linking it instead to traditional managerial values and goals.

These examples illustrate but do not exhaust the ways in which law is managerialized once it enters organizational fields. The managerialization of law may hasten the legalization of organizations in that legal values recast in managerial terms may be more easily assimilated into organizational governance. However, the managerialization of law may also weaken, deemphasize, and depoliticize legal ideals by subsuming them within managerial goals.

2.4. The Formation of Legal Consciousness

The stages discussed so far—the professional construction of the legal environment, the creation and diffusion of symbolic forms of compliance, and the managerialization of law—all help to shape employees' *legal consciousness*, which may be understood as the cultural schemas that employees use to make sense of the law and of its relevance to their everyday lives (Ewick and Silbey, 1998; Nielsen, 2000; Kostiner, 2003). Employees' legal consciousness comprises how individuals within and around organizations view the ideals of law, the reach of law, the threat of law, and the fairness and legality of employers' law-related actions and structures (Fuller, Edelman, and Matusik, 2000).

Many factors help to shape employees' legal consciousness. At the individual level, legal consciousness is likely to vary with individual social characteristics such as age, gender, race, education, and individual experiences such as perceived rights violations and responses to those violations (Fuller et al., 2000). At the organizational level, legal consciousness is likely to be shaped by the compliance structures that employers create, by employers' actions, and by ideas about law that become institutionalized within an organization and throughout organizational fields. In particular, employees are likely to compare the perceived consistency or inconsistency between the symbols employers foster through compliance structures and employers' actions. Inconsistencies are likely to produce skepticism of employers and of legal rights (Fuller et al., 2000).

To the extent that symbolic forms of compliance and managerialized conceptions of law become institutionalized, employees' legal consciousness is likely to incorporate those institutionalized conceptions. While variation along individual characteristics may produce some differences in the schema that individuals use to understand the law, collective experiences and social networks among employees are likely to produce a core of institutionalized schema that are widely shared among employees (Quinn, 2000; Marshall, forthcoming).

Employees' legal consciousness, then, is in part the product of managerialized conceptions of law that become institutionalized in organizational fields, but it is also in part the producer of problems that travel back into legal fields. To the extent that the employees' legal consciousness reflects managerialized conceptions of law, events that might otherwise seem problematic may be viewed as normal, proper, and fair.

2.5. The Mobilization of Law

Research in the sociology of law suggests that the vast majority of individuals who believe that their rights have been violated take no formal action to redress those violations, especially when those violations occur in the employment context (Felstiner, Abel, and Sarat, 1981; Miller and Sarat, 1981; Bumiller, 1987; Bumiller, 1988; Quinn, 2000; Hoffmann, 2001, 2003; Albiston 2003; Marshall, 2003). Employees' legal consciousness can have a significant impact on what behaviors employees believe are problematic, the likelihood that employees will see those behaviors as constituting legal violations, and the likelihood that employees will mobilize their rights (Fuller et al., 2000; Hoffmann, 2001; Cahill, 2001).

As questions of interpretation arise in organizations, compliance professionals—both managers and lawyers—play an important role in framing the legal issues that travel back into the legal realm. Complaint handlers and other managers within organizations serve as gatekeepers who seek to resolve complaints internally to insulate organizations from exposure to legal liability (Edelman et al., 1993; Edelman et al., 1999; Chambliss, 1996). Beyond the boundaries of organizations, officials in state and federal fair employment agencies and employee's (generally plaintiffs) lawyers play an important role in shaping which complaints become formal legal complaints and how those complaints are framed. Employers' (generally defendants) lawyers further shape the form of complaints both through their settlement behavior and through their responses (in particular, through the affirmative defenses that they offer) (Albiston, 1999).

Both employees' and employers' lawyers, in different ways, help to reinforce and legitimate managerialized models of compliance. Employees' lawyers are less likely to pursue actions where employers meet the institutionalized ideals of compliance. Even where employees have good reason to avoid an internal grievance procedure, for example, plaintiffs' lawyers are less likely to pursue a case where employees failed to use those procedures. Employers' lawyers act as conduits of managerialized logic to the court by framing their law-related procedures and policies *as compliance* and by defending their actions in terms of legitimized rationales such as market rates and business necessity. To the extent that managerialized conceptions of law seep into the emergence and framing of disputes by employers, employees, and lawyers, those conceptions also shape both the logic and the lexicon of disputing in the legal realm.

2.6. Judicial Deference to Organizational Institutions

Whereas traditional top–down perspectives on law suggest that courts ought to serve as a corrective to organizational constructions of compliance that deviate from legal purposes, the idea of legal endogeneity suggests instead that courts tend to be influenced by compliance practices that become institutionalized in organizational fields.

Just as employers tend to take their cues from norms and practices in their legal environments, judges tend to take their cues from norms and practices that become institutionalized in organizations. Because organizational and legal fields overlap, institutionalized ideas about law and compliance flow unobtrusively into the judicial realm. Thus, courts often accept employers' symbolic indicia of compliance without recognizing the extent to which employers' legal structures fail to protect legal rights, and in some cases even thwart those rights. In this way, institutionalized—and managerialized—organizational practices tend to be (re)incorporated into judicial standards for EEO compliance. When courts incorporate ideas from the organizational realm into new case decisions, law becomes endogenous (Edelman et al., 1999).

The endogeneity of law is perhaps clearest with respect to employers' internal grievance procedures. The personnel profession promoted the legal value of grievance procedures during the 1970s and early 1980s even though there were no statutes mandating grievance procedures, and even though—at the time—courts tended to reject the idea that such procedures could constitute evidence of EEO compliance. Most EEO cases at that time were decided using a vicarious liability standard under which employers are held responsible for the wrongful acts of their employees regardless of whether they knew about the wrongdoing. Under that standard, neither a policy against discrimination nor a grievance procedure would help an employer escape liability. Personnel professionals claimed, nonetheless, that grievance procedures would be viewed by judges as evidence of fair treatment, and that employers therefore would be well-served by creating them (Edelman et al., 1999).

In the mid-1980s, courts began to do precisely what the personnel professionals had been suggesting. In 1986, the Supreme Court in *Meritor Savings Bank v. Vinson* (106 S. Ct. 2399) suggested that an effective grievance procedure might protect an employer from liability for sexual harassment.[3] Shortly thereafter, a federal circuit

[3] The Supreme Court in *Meritor Savings Bank v. Vinson* (106 S. Ct. 2399) adopted a direct liability theory in sexual harassment cases involving hostile environments. Though the Court held that the grievance procedure in question was inadequate to insulate the employer from liability (because it required the

court of appeals adopted a similar standard in race harassment cases (*Hunter v. Allis-Chalmers*, 797 F. 2d 1417 (1986)). And in 1998, the Supreme Court declared that an employee's failure to use an employer's internal grievance procedure might protect an employer from liability for harassment by its supervisory employees (*Faragher v. City of Boca Raton* 118 S. Ct. 1115; *Burlington Industries v. Ellerth* 524 U.S. 742). Most recently, in *Pennsylvania State Police v. Suders* (542 U.S. 129 2004), the Supreme Court extended the Faragher/Ellerth doctrine to constructive discharge cases, holding that employers may escape liability for constructive discharge by showing that they have in place an effective policy for reporting and resolving complaints and that the employee unreasonably failed to avail herself of that policy. When courts proclaimed that internal grievance procedures could help employers avoid liability, they reinforced the legitimacy and rationality of grievance procedures as a form of compliance with law (even though those grievance procedures may in fact do little to ensure equal employment opportunity).

A similar process can be seen in the evolution of judicial standards in wage discrimination cases. In wage discrimination cases, employers often offer a "market defense" for wage inequality, arguing that they cannot be held responsible for paying women less than men because such pay disparities represent market rates. Nelson and Bridges (1999) show that, over time, courts have accepted and legitimized employers' reasoning. Rather than looking into the many ways in which employers create and exacerbate pay inequities in their own markets, courts have accepted—and thereby legitimized—employers' market defense. In so doing, Nelson and Bridges (1999) argue that courts have "legaliz[ed] gender inequality."

Law regulating organizations is endogenous, then, because its meaning is formed in part through the actions of organizations and the models of organizational action that become institutionalized in organizational fields. Legal ambiguity encourages organizations to create internal legal structures designed to symbolize attention to law. Once in place, those structures engender struggles over the meaning of law as professionals and other officials seek to implement law within organizations. Because of their training, experience, and professional purview, organizational actors tend to construct law in ways that are consistent with traditional managerial prerogatives and goals. Over time, as these constructions of law become institutionalized, they subtly and gradually affect how other social actors—including judges—understand the meaning of law, and of rational compliance with law.

3. CONCLUSION

I have argued that scholarship on law and organizations should be more attentive to the endogeneity of law, or the process by which law is shaped by the social realms that

victim to complain directly to her alleged harasser), it noted that in a future case, a better grievance procedure might provide such insulation.

it seeks to regulate. In any given situation, law may appear exogenous to particular organizational actions or structures and organizations may be seen as either complying or resisting the force of law. But attention to the *process* of legal construction is likely to reveal that the legal environments of organizations—which lie at the intersection of organizational and legal fields—are a fertile ground of legal *and* of organizational construction. It is in these spaces that boundary-spanning professionals such as lawyers, managerial consultants, personnel officers, compliance officers, and others interpret and ultimately construct the meaning of law.

While I have provided an initial sketch of a theory of the endogeneity of law in the employment context, similar processes are almost certainly at work in other social arenas. Healthcare, antitrust, bankruptcy, the environment, and crime are among the arenas in which attention to the endogeneity of law is likely to prove fruitful. In these and other areas, law and society scholarship should seek to delineate the social fields in which understandings of law develop, the social actors that span the boundaries of social fields, and the processes of social interaction and institutionalization that generate both legal and social change.

Cross-national analyses of legal endogeneity are also important. Differences in the roles of courts and training of judges between civil and common law nations may affect the extent to which institutionalized organizational practices may seep into legal decision-making. And national culture is likely to interact with organizational culture and individual legal consciousness in ways that alter the extent and process of legal endogeneity (cf. Cahill, 2001).

The policy implications of legal endogeneity, moreover, are critical. To the extent that law is endogenous, or shaped within the organizational fields that it seeks to regulate, the social control *of* organizations is in a very real sense social control *by* organizations—not overtly, but rather through the influence of institutionalized models of governance.

CHAPTER 18

Discrimination against Caregivers? Gendered Family Responsibilities, Employer Practices, and Work Rewards

Erin L. Kelly

ABSTRACT

This chapter discusses economic inequalities between caregivers and other workers, the mechanisms that produce them, and the possibility of using anti-discrimination law to challenge them. I first examine the consequences of gendered family responsibilities, specifically motherhood, for occupational status and wages. Then I present common explanations for the economic consequences of caregiving, contrasting human capital theory with a structural perspective that investigates the organizational mechanisms—the concrete policies and practices and the unquestioned assumptions in workplaces—that help create these inequalities. I review the legal strategies proposed by feminist legal scholars and then draw on empirical studies of changes in organizational policies and practices in the wake of anti-discrimination law to discuss the likely effects of those strategies. I suggest that defining the economic marginalization of caregivers as discrimination would provide a new language and legitimacy for workers faced with work-family conflicts but the resulting organizational changes would not fully erase the inequalities documented here.

INTRODUCTION

There have been significant improvements in the economic status of employed women in the U.S. over the past 30 years. Women's employment has increased dramatically during this period, particularly among White women and mothers (Cohen and Bianchi, 1999) and the pay gap has narrowed such that women employed full-time, year-round earn 77.5% of what comparable men earn (Leonhardt, 2003; Blau and Kahn, 2000). But stubborn inequalities remain. I contend that we must examine and interrogate the experiences of caregivers, i.e. workers with extensive family responsibilities, in the workplace in order to understand gender inequality in the United States today.

This chapter discusses the extent of these inequalities between caregivers and other workers, the mechanisms that produce them, and the possibility of using anti-discrimination law to challenge them. I first examine the social science evidence on the consequences of gendered family responsibilities, specifically motherhood,

L. B. Nielsen and R. L. Nelson (eds.), Handbook of Employment Discrimination Research, 353–375.

for occupational status and wages. Unfortunately, there has been much less research on the effects of fatherhood or elder care responsibilities. Then, I present common explanations for the economic consequences of caregiving, contrasting human capital theory with a structural perspective that investigates the organizational mechanisms—the concrete policies and practices and the unquestioned assumptions in workplaces—that help create these inequalities. I examine the legal strategies proposed by feminist legal scholars and then discuss the likely effects of those strategies. I suggest that defining the economic marginalization of caregivers as discrimination would provide new cultural resources for workers faced with work–family conflicts, including a new language and sense of legitinacy, but the resulting organizational changes would not fully erase the inequalities documented here.

Caregivers may, of course, be male as well as female and some may ask what gender has to do with caregiving. I argue that the treatment of caregivers within organizations is directly related to gender inequality because family responsibilities are "gendered" in our culture. This means both that there are differences in the family responsibilities of women and men, on average, and that there are different cultural scripts and expectations for mothers and fathers.

Numerous studies show that women still spend significantly more time on housework and childcare than men do, and that this basic gender difference holds for couples at various stages of life and with various employment situations (e.g., Bianchi, Milkie, Sayer, and Robinson, 2000; Brines, 1994; Hochschild, 1989; South and Spitze, 1994). The gender differences in time spent on housework and childcare are less dramatic than in the past but, as of 1995, women still spent 1.8 hours for each hour of housework done by men and 1.8 hours for each hour of primary childcare performed by men (Bianchi et al., 2000, p. 208). If a workplace is hostile to workers with significant caregiving responsibilities, women are more likely to be affected than men.

In addition to these gender gaps in the time spent on housework and childcare, family responsibilities are gendered in the sense that acting in the expected ways reinforces individuals' gender identities while acting in non-normative ways requires women and men to account for their deviance (Berk, 1985; West and Zimmerman, 1987; cf. Acker, 1990). Although expectations for women's and men's behavior are less rigid and more varied than in the past, there are still cultural prescriptions for family roles that differ by gender. In American culture, mothers are expected have unlimited time, energy, and emotional capacity for caring for family members and coordinating family life (Hays, 1992; Williams, 2000). Some mothers also work for pay and they are known as "working mothers." In this phrase, the employment status of women modifies their core identity as mothers (Garey, 1999; Chamallas, 1986). The cultural expectations regarding fatherhood are less clear (Gerson, 1993; Coltrane, 1996; Townsend, 2002; Waller, 2002). Fathers are increasingly expected to care for family members by performing day-to-day chores and tending to the emotional lives of family members, but these tasks are often understood to be secondary to fathers' core task of providing income. The phrase "working fathers" is not used in everyday conversation because work is not a modifier for fathers; it is the core responsibility of all adult men, including fathers. Instead, we talk about "involved fathers" when

we want to specify those men who prioritize family caregiving as much as or more than paid work. These men may be praised by some, but they may also face questions about their commitment to work, their ambition, and their gender identity as "normal men" (Cooper, 2000; Gerson, 1993; Pleck, 1993; West and Zimmerman, 1987).

1. THE ECONOMIC CONSEQUENCES OF CAREGIVING

Employees are generally expected to work full-time, full-year, and over-time as needed over many years if they want to do well and move ahead in their careers. But many caregivers—particularly mothers—do not meet these expectations of long hours and continuous employment. Despite the fact that many more mothers of young children are employed than in the past, *most* mothers of young children are not working in the full-time and over-time jobs that produce high incomes and good opportunities for advancement. Cohen and Bianchi (1999) remind us that 71% of married mothers with children under six were employed at some point in 1997 but only 35% of these mothers (and 38% of single mothers with young children) worked full-time, year-round. Furthermore, only 7% of mothers with children under 18 years of age work 49 hours a week or more (Williams, 2000, p. 2). In contrast, 96% of fathers with children under six were employed in 1997 and the vast majority of those men worked full-time, year-round (U.S. Department of Labor, 1999).

These work patterns mean that the common economic indicators of gender equity, including the sex gap in wages, do not reflect the reality of most women's experiences. Reports that women earn 75–78% of what men earn, compare the wages of women working full-time, year-round to men working full-time, year-round. Approximately two-thirds of mothers of young children are excluded from this comparison; including the hourly wages of part-time or part-year workers would increase the reported sex gap significantly.

1.1. Glass Ceilings and Mommy Stations

The mismatch between organizational expectations and mothers' work patterns helps explain women's (particularly mothers') underrepresentation in the upper echelons of management and high-status professions. Women continue to be underrepresented in top management positions. In 2000, 12.5% of the corporate officers in Fortune 500 companies were women and only 7% of line officers were women (Catalyst, 2000a). Another study found that, "among those who have risen to within three levels of the CEO position, fewer than half (49%) of the women have children, compared with 84% of the men" (Crittendon, 2001, p. 35; Catalyst, 2000b). In public sector management, the patterns are similar. As of the early 1990s, women held only 10% of the top positions in the federal government and mothers fared worse than women without children and worse than men, even when their level of experience and education was similar (Crittendon, 2001, p. 41; U.S. Merit Systems Protection Board,1992).

Women are also less likely to achieve top positions within the high-status professions. Only 13% of the partners at the 1,160 largest law firms were women as of 1995 and only 7% of the equity partners (who share in the firm's profits) were women (Crittendon, 2001, p. 37). Small firms are not much better for women's achievement of partner status; only 13% of partners at all firms with two or more attorneys were female as of 1995 (Williams, 2000, p. 67). Women make up close to half the population of medical students and about a quarter of the doctors, but they are underrepresented in the prestigious positions in academic medicine. Only 10% of full professors in medical schools were women as of 1994 (Crittendon, 2001, p. 43; Conley, 1998). The studies of attorneys and doctors do not reveal what percentage of the high-status women are mothers (much less how other caregiving roles affect occupational position), but research on other professions, particularly college and university faculty, suggests that high-status women are often not mothers.

Using data that follows new Ph.D.s through the first 14 years of their careers, Mason and Goulden (2002) examine the family decisions and achievement of tenure among this cohort of faculty. In 1999, 29% of tenured professors in American colleges and universities were women, up from 18% in 1971 (National Science Foundation WebCASPAR, 2003). But Mason and Goulden (2002) show that a disproportionate number of tenured women faculty are not mothers. Among the cohort they study, 62% of tenured women in the humanities and social sciences and 50% of tenured women in the sciences do *not* have children in their household. The comparable figures for tenured men are 39% and 30%, respectively. They also find that mothers of "early babies," i.e. babies born within 5 years of the Ph.D., are less likely—about 20% less likely—than fathers of "early babies" to receive tenure.[1]

In the academic world, it is difficult to find a "mommy track" if this term is understood as a slower movement up the career system that is dominant in the field. Instead, there is a fairly unforgiving career track and what I call a "mommy station," where caregivers—as well as people who are less lucky, productive, or connected than others—are literally stuck in adjunct and lecturer positions with low wages, low status, no job security, and often no possibility for advancement. Because women are more likely to choose or end up in these part-time positions, "the segmentation of academic life into an over-worked core and a marginalized periphery tends to perpetuate gender inequality" (Jacobs, 2004).

Professionals and managers in other industries may be able to negotiate part-time work but they, too, often give up high-status assignments, important fringe benefits, and job security by becoming contractors rather than employees (Kalleberg et al., 1997). In short, professionals and managers across a variety of industries face the choice of very long hours—which conflict with ingrained and gendered expectations

[1] If a woman finished a B.A. at the age of 22, went straight to graduate school and moved fairly quickly graduate school, the 5 years after the Ph.D. would likely be ages 28–33. Women faculty with "early babies" are on the verge of being labeled "older mothers" by the rest of society and the medical profession, unless they had their children during or before graduate school.

of appropriate caregiving—or marginalization and economic insecurity as a part-timer (Williams, 2000).

1.2. The Motherhood Penalty in Wages

Mothers tend to earn less than men and less than women who do not have children. As noted above, mothers tend to work fewer hours and so we would expect and accept a difference in the annual earnings of mothers and other workers. But there is also a difference in the hourly wages of mothers as compared to women without children and to men. In 1991, young mothers' hourly wages were 81% of other young women's wages and 73% of young men's hourly wages (Waldfogel, 1998a; Table 5). This "family gap" has grown in recent years even as the sex gap in wages has fallen. As Waldfogel (1998a, p. 148) notes, "by 1991, the pay gap between mothers and non-mothers had become larger than the gap between women and men."

Mothers' lower wages reflect mothers' lower levels of experience on the job, which result from mothers' higher odds of exiting the labor force when they have young children and working fewer hours when employed. But mothers' lower wages cannot be entirely explained by these differences in experience; the residual wage gap raises the question of wage discrimination against mothers.

1.2.1. The Wage Consequences of Breaks and Part-time Work

Women who leave the labor force to care for children or other relatives obviously forego wages while out of the labor force, but they also earn less once they return to paid work. The wage penalties associated with a break in employment continue for many years, creating significant cumulative consequences for lifetime earnings. For example, Noonan (2002) estimates that a woman who was out of the labor force for one year would make 32% less in the first year after she returned to work than a comparable woman who was continuously employed. Furthermore, this woman would still be making 24% less than a comparable woman in the 10th year after her break (Noonan, 2002; calculated from Table 2). The wage penalties seem to continue beyond that time frame as well. Jacobsen and Levin (1995) report that, even 20 years after a return to paid work, women with interrupted work histories earn 5–7% less than women with continuous labor force attachment.

Because women who stay in the labor force when they have young children may avoid the wage penalties associated with breaks in employment, access to maternity leave is economically important to women. Longitudinal studies show that women who take only short breaks after a birth and then return to the same employer earn more than other mothers (Waldfogel, 1998b).[2] Additionally, access to decent maternity leave is associated with continuous labor force attachment (Estes and Glass, 1996; Liebowitz

[2] Some of the differences in the wage rates between leave-taking mothers and other mothers reflect selection bias, since more privileged women have access to family leaves in the first place (England, 1997). This was certainly true before the passage of the Family and Medical Leave Act of 1993 but the

and Klerman, 1995), a higher likelihood of keeping the same job (Glass and Riley, 1998), and quicker returns to full-time work (Hofferth, 1996).

However, taking maternity or family leave may have its own consequences. One study of managers and professionals who worked full-time and continuously from 1990 to 1995 in a large, multinational financial services organization found that taking a leave was associated with lower performance evaluations, lower odds of promotion, and slightly smaller salary increases (Judiesch and Lyness, 1999). This study did not identify any gender differences in the consequences of leave (perhaps because only two men in this sample of about 12,000 managers had taken a family leave!) but a Swedish study found that a one *year* leave cost male managers 5.2% of their expected earnings growth over 5 years and cost female managers only 1.7% of their expected earnings growth (Stafford and Sundstrom, 1996).[3] The authors note that men's use of family leave may be interpreted by managers and co-workers as a sign of relatively low commitment to work, even in a country where paternity leave is much more common than in the U.S. In contrast, women's use of family leave may have smaller consequences because it is expected and accepted as appropriate.

Shifting to part-time work allows caregivers to maintain employment while caring for family members. What are the consequences of this strategy? Part-time workers are paid less, per hour, than full-time workers; part-time workers are less likely to receive employee benefits; and part-time experience is rewarded lesser than full-time experience (Ferber and Waldfogel, 1998; Budig and England, 2001; Glass, 2004). However, part-time experience does improve women's wages, suggesting that part-time work yields better wages for women, in the long run, than time out of the labor force. Returns to part-time work are approximately half the size of returns to full-time work for women (Ferber and Waldfogel, 1998), although one study finds that part-time workers do better if they change employers (Glass, 2004). Glass (2004) hypothesizes that part-time workers find it hard to get a raise, perhaps because employers feel they are already doing a favor for these employees by allowing them to work part-time, and so part-timers must move to a new job to improve their wages.

Although most studies of the consequences of part-time work in the U.S. have examined women's wages, there is some evidence that part-time work has more dramatic consequences for men's wages. The differences between full-time workers' and part-time workers' hourly wages are greater for men than for women (Ferber and Waldfogel, 1998). Also, whereas part-time experience gets half the rewards of full-time experience among women, men's wages did not improve at all with part-time experience (Ferber and Waldfogel, 1998; Table 6). Employers apparently discount men's part-time work so thoroughly that they might as well be out of the labor force. These wage

passage of the federal law did not erase the disparities in women's access to leave because more privileged women are more likely to work for covered employers (Gerstel and McGonagle, 1999).

[3] These 1-year leaves had much smaller wage consequences for parents in Sweden than a 1-year break in employment does in the U.S. National policies that establish family leave, as well as other state supports for families, clearly affect the economic consequences of caregiving (Gornick and Meyers, 2003; Stier, Lewis-Epstein, and Brain, 2001; Stryker, Eliason, and Tranby, 2004).

penalties probably discourage some fathers and men with elder care responsibilities from seeking part-time work when they would like to do so.

1.2.2. Unexplained Wage Penalties for Mothers and Pay Gaps

Caregiving reduces the wages and occupational status of mothers through reduced experience, penalties for breaks in employment, penalties for taking leaves, and smaller returns for part-time experience, but there is also a wage penalty for motherhood even when one controls for these effects and for a variety of individual and job-level traits (Anderson et al., 2003; Avellar and Smock, 2003; Budig and England, 2001; Waldfogel, 1997). Budig and England (2001; Table 3) find that there is a penalty of 5% for having one child, 11% for having two children, and 15% for having three of more children. These penalties are net and fixed effects, which control for unobserved individual traits, marital status, and a host of human capital variables such as education, current enrollment in school, work experience, seniority, current hours, and previous breaks in employment. Waldfogel (1997) finds quite similar penalties, of 4% for one child and 12% for two or more children, while Anderson et al. (2003) find smaller penalties of 3% for one child and 5% for two or more children. These studies demonstrate that mothers' reduced experience and increased propensity to breaks in employment cannot fully explain the gap between mothers' wages and the wages of other women.

1.3. What are the Consequences of Caregiving for Men?

Compared to the literature on motherhood, there is much less evidence about the economic consequences of fatherhood. Several studies have found that fathers receive wage premiums of approximately the same size as mothers' wage penalties (e.g., Hersch and Stratton, 2000; Lundberg and Rose, 2000; Noonan, 2001). In addition, researchers consistently find that married men earn more—between 10% and 30% more—than unmarried men with similar educational levels, experience, and occupational location (Hersch and Stratton, 2000; Waldfogel, 1998a). We know that there is wide variation in the caregiving performed by fathers—with some devoting as much time to child care as mothers and some devoting very little time—but research has not yet identified the effects of fathers caregiving separately from the effects of fatherhood as a status.

The research that comes close to disentangling the effects of men's care work from the effects of family status examines how time spent on housework affects men's earnings. Hersch and Stratton (2000) found that men's housework time reduced their wages, although the size of this effect was small. Noonan (2001) examined the effects of "female-typed tasks"—like cooking, cleaning up dishes, laundry—that must be done on workdays or at unpredictable times and that may consequently tire out an employee more than tasks—like yard work or paying bills—that can be done at any time. Time spent on these time-sensitive tasks reduces time spent at work and also reduces men's and women's earnings (Noonan, 2001). However, these effects are found *in addition to* a wage penalty for mothers and a wage premium for fathers so differences in the type of housework performed by men and women cannot fully account for the wage gap between mothers and fathers. Neither of these studies was able to investigate the consequences of time spent in child-care activities specifically.

2. EXPLAINING THE ECONOMIC CONSEQUENCES OF CAREGIVING

The studies reviewed above demonstrate that caregivers (or at least mothers, who have received more attention from scholars) face real economic penalties. Is this a problem for our society? If so, what should be done about it? The answers to these questions depend on how one explains the existence of these penalties.

2.1. Human Capital Theory and Caregivers' Careers

Human capital theorists assert that differences in wages and occupational attainment reflect differences in "human capital" and productivity that arise because many women specialize in family work rather than market work (Becker, 1991). Human capital theory claims that, because of their family responsibilities and anticipated family responsibilities, women are more likely to leave the workforce at some point, work fewer hours when employed, invest less in education and training, expend less effort when working, and choose occupations or jobs that have lower penalties for intermittent work histories, greater possibilities for part-time work, smaller returns for training, and fewer demands or stressors on the job (Becker, 1991). The gender gap in experience and effort is believed to explain the gender gap between men's and women's wages. In turn, women's lower wages reinforce the rationality of women concentrating on family responsibilities rather than market work (Becker, 1991, pp. 38–39, 42). Human capital theory emphasizes individual, and couple, decisions about allocating time and effort. From this perspective, the economic penalties associated with caregiving are the expected consequences of specialization. These penalties are assumed to be offset, at the couple level, by the higher wages of the partner who specializes in market work.[4]

Although experience, education, and other "human capital" variables are important for understanding wage attainment and related topics, sociologists have challenged various parts of this theory. First, scholars have asked whether women today anticipate specializing in family work or whether women's orientations towards market work and family work are variable and responsive to their opportunities. Research suggests that many—perhaps most—young women do not have stable expectations about their adult lives (Gerson, 1985; Hakim, 2002). Rather than socialization or stable preferences, it is the economic opportunities available to young women in the workplace that lead some women towards market work, some towards family work, and others towards combining the two sets of responsibilities simultaneously (Gerson,

[4] The specialization strategy obviously works only for married couples and this model assumes that most individuals expect to get and stay married.

1985; see also Kanter, 1977; Schultz, 1990). Second, researchers have attempted to gauge whether women, particularly wives and mothers, put in less effort (per hour) in their market work. Bielby and Bielby (1988) find evidence that, instead, women report working harder than men in comparable work and family statuses. Mothers of young children do report expending less effort at work than other women, but their effort falls only to the level of men—not below it (Bielby and Bielby, 1988, p. 1048). Third, because sex segregation is a powerful force in the maintenance of gender inequalities at work, sociologists have tried to ascertain whether this segregation arises because mothers seek out less demanding, female-dominated jobs in order to conserve energy for family work, as human capital theory implies. In contrast to the predictions of human capital theory, women without children are just as likely as mothers to work in female-dominated occupations (Tomaskovic-Devey, 1993; Budig and England, 2001; cf. Okamoto and England, 1999). Scholars have also asked whether female-dominated jobs are less demanding and more accommodating of family responsibilities. Glass and Camarigg (1992) report that flexible schedules and the ease of doing the job are the characteristics most closely related to low levels of work–family conflict among parents. But they find that female-dominated jobs are no more likely to have flexible schedules or reported ease. Also, mothers are no more likely than women without children to be in jobs with these traits. These findings suggest that sex segregation is a separate, parallel process that works simultaneously but largely independently of the marginalization of caregivers.

2.2. A Structural Perspective: Gendered Organizations Theory

In contrast to the human capital model, which claims that gender differences in specialization create the sex gap in wages, a structural model argues that organizational practices and processes are at least partially responsible for the inequalities between women and men and between caregivers and unencumbered workers. This argument begins by claiming that organizations operate with old-fashioned, gendered policies, practices, and expectations and that these organizational structures encourage the economic marginalization of caregivers (e.g., Acker, 1990; Williams, 2000; Moen and Roehling, 2005). For example, Acker (1990) provocatively argues that the very category of a "job" reflects and perpetuates gendered divisions between employment and reproductive labor. The concept of jobs and hierarchies of jobs form the basis of organizational theorizing inside and outside of firms, and these theories implicitly assume an abstract worker who fills an abstract job and exists only to fill the job:

> The closest the disembodied worker doing the abstract job comes to a real worker is the male worker whose life centers on his full-time, life-long job, while his wife or another woman takes care of his personal needs and his children . . . The woman worker, assumed to have legitimate obligations other than those required by the job, did not fit with the abstract job . . . The concept 'a job' is thus implicitly a gendered concept, even though organizational logic presents it as gender neutral. 'A job' already contains the gender-based division of labor and the separation between the public and private sphere. (Acker, 1990, p. 149)

Organizations depend on and exploit the reproductive labor done by (female) caregivers while also excluding or marginalizing employees who do significant amounts of that work. Similarly, Williams (2000, p. 5) reviews employers' expectations that "serious" and "committed" and "promising" employees be willing to work long hours, with no breaks in employment or limits on working time, and travel or relocate as requested, and concludes that this "way of defining the ideal worker is not ungendered. It links the ability to be an ideal worker with the flow of family work and other privileges typically available only to men (see also Moen and Roehling, 2005)."

Scholars working with a structural perspective acknowledge that, faced with organizational policies, practices, and assumptions that are based on (privileged White) men's traditional life experiences, some caregivers "choose" to leave the labor force, shift to less rewarding part-time work, and limit their commitment to the organization. But this perspective views these decisions as strategic responses to organizational inflexibility, not unconstrained individual choices.

The structural perspective also suggests that wages and other work rewards do not simply reflect the even-handed assessment of a worker's performance and productivity. Performance and productivity emerge from an organizational context rather than simply reflecting the human capital investments and other traits of an individual worker (Kanter, 1977). An individual's performance or productivity depends on access to training and to good assignments that will allow the employee to develop and show off his or her skills. The implication is that caregivers will be more likely to perform at a high level in workplaces that recognize their skills and do not limit training opportunities and good work assignments to unencumbered, "ideal" workers.

2.3. Employers' Practices

What are the specific policies, practices, and assumptions that penalize caregivers and thereby "gender" organizations in pernicious ways? Many organizations expect employees to work long hours and to follow rigid career tracks. When caregivers do not meet the expectations of the organization, their wages, chances for promotion, and job security may suffer. These expectations obviously vary by occupation as well as by organization, but they affect a wide variety of workers in both low-status and high-status jobs.

Long hours are expected for managerial and professional positions in most organizations, but long hours and unpredictable hours are also part and parcel of many jobs that do not have an obvious "career track." Mandatory overtime increased for many hourly workers in the 1990s (Williams, 2000, p. 8). In some para-professional settings and service sector organizations, workers are expected to be available to clients, patients, or customers at any time—even if they are only employed part-time. For example, in retail organizations that are attractive because they are thought to offer "flexible hours," employees found that they were often pressured to "be available" for any shift that opened up. Workers who tried to maintain some control over their hours and weekly routine were not seen as "team players" and managers regularly penalized these workers by cutting their shifts and therefore their wages (Waxman and Lambert, 2002). Faced with pressures to work long or unpredictable hours, caregivers may withdraw from the labor force (Stone and Lovejoy, 2004), look for another employer, or limit their work hours and accept marginalization as a reasonable "trade-off".

Caregivers may also be disadvantaged by rigid career tracks of various types. The up-or-out tenure systems found in colleges and universities and the up-or-out partnership tracks in law firms, accounting firms, and management consulting firms are obvious examples of rigid career tracks. These high-stakes systems require intense investment in work during the early years of one's career. Because these years are also the normative time for childbearing and raising young children, parents—particularly mothers—often find it difficult to establish their careers in these professions (Hochschild, 1975; Jacobs, 2004). Rigid career tracks may also require relocation in order to get on a career track (as with faculty jobs and medical residencies) or to move along a career track (as with many management positions, including store and restaurant managers in the service sector). If organizations provide very limited family leaves to employees, they are also conveying the message that staying on the career track—and often continuation of employment—requires absolutely no deviation from the pattern of continuous, full-time employment. Leaves may be inadequate if they are very short, if they do not allow a phased return to full-time hours, or if they do not allow paid leave time to be used to care for family members.

Rigid career tracks may exclude caregivers from the beginning by discouraging caregivers from seeking these positions or they may push caregivers off track later, perhaps when a family member becomes seriously ill or when family responsibilities change. The consequences of leaving the career track are often marginalization in a part-time, no-advancement position within the organization or a break in employment, which has the long-term wage consequences reviewed above.

2.4. Changing Policies and Practices

Although scholars of gender and organizations continue to see policies, practices, and assumptions that limit caregivers' opportunities, many organizations have added "family–friendly" policies to address at least some of these problems. Recent surveys of medium and large organizations find that almost all of these employers now offer a variety of family leaves of various sorts and that a significant minority provide basic childcare benefits and allow flextime hours (Kelly, 2000; Galinsky and Bond, 1998). But do these family policies result in fewer or smaller penalties for caregivers?

The empirical evidence based on U.S. samples is still scant, but there are some hints that changing employers' policies and practices can improve caregivers' careers. At the individual level, we know that maternity leaves improve mothers' wages and occupational status by helping mothers remain in the labor force (Estes and Glass, 1996; Klerman and Liebowitz, 1995; Glass and Riley, 1998; Waldfogel, 1998b). At the organizational level, a recent study found smaller gaps between the wages of mothers and other women among employees of organizations described as "family–friendly" than among employees of less supportive organizations (Friedman and Greenhaus, 2000, p. 111).[5] Also, a case study of one large medical organization found no evidence that shifting to part-time work had negative effects on primary care physicians' careers (Briscoe, 2003). Perhaps this organization has avoided penalizing part-time work because (1) the actual work performed is the same for part-time and full-time employees, (2) there are multiple paths to advancement depending on specialty and interest in administration, and (3) highly regarded physicians have always cut back on their clinic hours in order to pursue research or teaching, so there is not a tight conceptual link between working part-time and gendered caregiving responsibilities (Briscoe, 2003).

But "family–friendly" policies may create their own problems. Workers in many organizations perceive that there will be negative career consequences if they use the officially available policies (Blair-Loy and Wharton, 2002; Fried, 1998; Hochschild, 1997). These fears (and the roadblocks created by managers in some organizations (Albiston, this volume)) help explain the relatively low utilization rates in many organizations. Recent studies confirm that these fears are well-founded, at least in some organizations. Glass (2004) followed a cohort of new mothers for several years and found that mothers who used the "family–friendly" arrangements had a slower rate of wage growth than mothers who did not (see also Judiesch and Lyness, 1999; Stafford and Sundstrom, 1996). These findings reveal an economic penalty for taking advantage of family policies and suggest that adding these policies may be only a first step in improving caregivers' careers.

2.5. Beyond Family–Friendly Policies

I argue that caregivers will benefit from family policies most if and when organizations integrate those policies with existing human resources practices, specifically their supervision of the work process and their performance evaluation systems. Yet my interviews in 41 organizations and others' research on the implementation of family policies suggests that most organizations have added family policies without re-examining the way work is done or the way workers are evaluated (Kelly and Kalev, 2003; Fried, 1998; Hochschild, 1997; Rudd, 2001).

Flextime, telecommuting, reduced-hours schedules, and decent family leaves are attractive because they allow workers to work in "non-standard" ways while continuing their employment. However, in many organizations these new options are understood as deviations from the standard system and as "accommodations" available to a favored few (Lee, MacDermid, and Buck, 2000; Kelly and Kalev, 2003). One human resources manager I interviewed worked 85% time, but felt it was important to seem available at any time and eager for any task; for her this meant hiding her part-time status from some colleagues. In response to my question "What about someone who's worked a

[5] These data are cross-sectional and have fairly crude measures, but this is among the best information we have for comparing the wage gap *across organizations* so far.

reduced schedule for a good long time? Do you think that has long-term penalties?" she replied: "Well, I must think about that because I don't personally advertise the fact that I work part-time." She went on to describe how she avoids the subject with co-workers, even when they are scheduling meetings:

> ... even if somebody would say, "Well, is that OK with you? I know you work part-time," I will react against that and I'll say "I'm available whenever the team [wants to meet]. I have a flexible schedule and I'm here to work on this project." I don't want them first of all to know [that I work part-time]. If they do know, I don't want them to use that as some kind of reasoning that maybe their schedules need to be adjusted because [someone] works part time, or "Do you even care about this project? You just work part-time. Does it really impact you?" or whatever.

This manager has worked part-time for 15 years and yet she understands her schedule as a deviation from the legitimate expectation that all employees will be available at any time and that their non-work schedules will not influence the team's work process in any way. She believes that other employees will equate her part-time schedule with a lack of interest or investment in projects and, earlier in the interview, she explicitly said she hid her part-time status in order to have a better chance of moving "up the ladder" or getting "more challenge in the assignments." This organization is known nationally for its family–friendly initiatives, but this manager's experiences suggest that the expectation that all employees are full-time, on-site workers is still influential within the organization.

What organizational changes would transform caregivers and other workers on non-standard schedules from deviant employees to normal workers? Re-examining and reforming performance evaluation systems might be a crucial step. Even when organizations have identical family policies, they may differ in how they fit these employees into the existing systems for measuring work performance, assigning work, and distributing rewards such as raises, promotions, and training opportunities. In many organizations, there is no formal guidance on how to incorporate "non-standard" workers into the "normal" system and so there may be extensive variation between supervisors in how they assess the contribution of employees who took a leave, worked part-time, or worked from home. How should the contributions of employees who work part-time be evaluated, in relation to the contributions of those working full-time and over-time? When there are concrete measures of productivity, such as sales or client contact hours, it seems logical to have a pro-rated target for part-time employees, but we do not know whether this measurement strategy is a common practice. When it is more difficult to measure productivity or performance directly, it will be more difficult to weigh the relative contributions of part-time workers or telecommuters who put in less "face time."

Revising performance evaluation systems is especially important now because performance evaluations increasingly determine pay and job security as well as advancement opportunities. Many organizations have moved to "merit pay" and "pay for performance" systems in the last 20 years, and perhaps a third of American organizations have done away with across-the-board or seniority-based pay increases altogether (Cappelli, 1999, p. 150). Performance evaluations increasingly affect job security too, because more companies are instituting forced ranking, where all employees in a group or team are numerically ordered from "best to worst" and the employees near the bottom of the list are "counseled out" or marked as targets of any future downsizing (*Time,* 2001; Gladwell, 2002). Forced rank systems (nicknamed "rank and yank" systems) are likely to be as susceptible to bias as other performance evaluation practices, particularly if the measures of productivity or performance are vague or subjective. It is easy to imagine that those who limit their travel, refuse to work much overtime, or shift to part-time schedules or telecommuting arrangements will not do well in these tough performance evaluation systems, particularly because few organizations explicitly tell supervising managers how to count the contributions of those who take advantage of these new work arrangements.

In addition to marginalizing those who use family policies or work part-time, performance evaluation systems often fail to question what counts as work in the first place and ignore important skills and behaviors traditionally associated with women. Although organizations increasingly emphasize teamwork and empowering workers, the actual work of keeping a team functioning is generally seen as "extra" work if, indeed, it is recognized as work at all. This work includes the emotional labor of reassuring peers and supervisors that they are doing well, encouraging discouraged team members, and winning cooperation from reluctant superiors, co-workers, or subordinates as well as the training, mentoring, and coordination work needed to empower other workers (Fletcher, 1999). This "relational practice" (to use Fletcher's term) or "capacity-building work" (in my terminology) is ignored and devalued partly because of its association with femininity. Instead, "individual" achievements carry the most weight in assessments of employees' performance and productivity even if those achievements require collaboration, support, and guidance from others whose contributions are soon forgotten or hidden (Ely and Meyerson, 2000; Fletcher, 1999; Rappoport et al., 2001). The devaluation of capacity-building work may affect women disproportionately, if they are more likely to devote time and energy to this work (Fletcher, 1999). The discounting of this work could conceivably affect caregivers disproportionately as well; these employees may have highly developed skills in negotiating, coordinating, and mentoring that are not recognized as valuable within the organization.

3. DISCRIMINATION AGAINST CAREGIVERS? POSSIBLE LEGAL CLAIMS

If we believe that the economic marginalization of caregivers is largely, or even partially, caused by organizational practices, policies, and assumptions and that many of these practices, policies, and assumptions are no longer rational responses to business needs (if, indeed, they ever were), then we should encourage organizations to change these practices, policies, and assumptions. Anti-discrimination law is one possible tool—although not the only tool (Gornick and Meyers, 2003; Rapoport et al., 2001) or necessarily a manageable tool (Edelman, this volume)—for inducing organizational change. Indeed, in response to the marginalization of caregivers, legal scholars in the U.S. have proposed either using existing sex discrimination law or creating new laws that require reasonable accommodation of caregivers in order to prompt organizational changes.[6]

3.1. Sex Discrimination Law and Caregivers

To make sex discrimination claims about practices that marginalize caregivers, advocates emphasize the disproportionate representation of women in the group of caregivers and/or argue that the marginalization of caregivers is gender discrimination even when it affects men because male caregivers are punished for enacting a traditionally feminine role (Williams, 2000; Williams and Segal, 2003). Claims of disparate treatment based on "sex-plus" family status have some potential for challenging the marginalization of caregivers. The famous *Phillips v. Martin-Marietta* case, in which the Supreme Court recognized the sex-plus disparate treatment theory of sex discrimination, involved an employer who refused to hire mothers (but not other women or fathers) for certain jobs because of worries about their child care arrangements. Disparate treatment cases require evidence of discriminatory intent, such as "smoking gun" comments by decision-makers. Because norms of polite conversation and perhaps the forms of discrimination have changed in recent decades, it is now rare to have this kind of evidence (Krieger, this volume). However, some decision-makers still make surprisingly blunt comments about working mothers (Williams and Segal, 2003; cf. Chamallas, 1999). For example, in *Santiago-Ramos v. Centennial P.R. Wireless Corp* (217 F.3d 46 (1st Cir. 2000)), a high-level, female manager was asked to comment on a company hiring profile that excluded mothers from certain positions. A vice-president in the organization told her the "profile was 'nothing against you,' but that he preferred unmarried, childless women because they would give 150% to the job" (217 F.3d 46 [1st Cir. 2000], p. 51; cited in Williams and Segal, 2003). Also, in *Moore vs. Alabama State University,* (980 F. Supp. 426; Williams and Segal, 2003), an admissions officer applied for but was not chosen for the vacant position of Admissions Director. When she was visibly pregnant, a university officer who played a central part in the hiring decision told her, "I was going to put you in charge of the office, but look at you now" (980 F. Supp. 426, p. 431; also cited in Williams and Segal, 2003).

[6] Advocates for caregivers in other nations are less likely to turn to anti-discrimination law as a vehicle for changing the workplace because they have much more extensive public policies and benefits for parents and other caregivers with which to work (see Gornick and Meyers (2003) for a thorough review of family policies in other industrialized nations).

An April 2004 decision by the Second U.S. Circuit Court of Appeals illustrates the potential of disparate treatment claims under the Equal Protection Clause of the 14th Amendment, in addition to claims made under Title VII of the Civil Rights Act of 1964. In *Elana Back v. Hastings-on-Hudson Union Free School District* (365 F.3d 107), the appellate court allowed a school psychologist who was denied tenure to proceed with her case against her former principal and the school district's former personnel director. Back alleged that, after she returned from maternity leave, her supervisors began to question her devotion to the job and her willingness to put in the long hours that they believed the position required. The supervisors allegedly suggested that she wait a few years to have another child, stated that her job was not appropriate for a mother because of its long hours, and questioned her devotion to the job over the long run because of her family commitments. The Appeals Court found that this case:

> asks whether stereotyping about the qualities of mothers is a form of gender discrimination, and whether this can be determined in the absence of evidence about how the employer in question treated fathers. We answer both questions in the affirmative.

Although the district court eventually ruled against Back, the Second Circuit Court's recognition of discriminatory stereotyping of mothers received significant attention in the press and among human resources managers (Crary, 2004; Kleinman, 2004; Vuocolo; 2004), as I discuss below.

Disparate treatment theory is limited, though, because successful plaintiffs are usually mothers who were willing, able, and eager to meet the job requirements—including working long hours, traveling, etc.—rather than caregivers who argued that expectations of long, unpredictable hours were unnecessary in the first place and discriminatory as well. Sex-plus disparate treatment cases may help female caregivers who actually function as "ideal workers"—like Elana Back who reportedly put in the expected hours and received excellent performance evaluations—but this theory has been less successful in making jobs more amenable to caregiving (Kessler, 2001) or improving the work conditions and rewards in part-time jobs (Chamallas, 1986).

Title VII's disparate impact theory, which holds employers accountable for facially neutral practices that disproportionately disadvantage workers in protected categories, may also be useful for (female) caregivers making discrimination claims. As Travis (2003, p. 341) notes:

> This model focuses on inequitable results, and does not require discriminatory intent. Accordingly, this model appears well-suited to address aspects of women's inequality that stem from basic, structural aspects of the workplace that help to create, retrench, or magnify women's work/family conflicts.

Disparate impact theory explicitly invites the examination and interrogation of employers' existing policies and practices and thereby creates the possibility for changing those policies and practices in ways that may benefit women and/or caregivers.

Disparate impact claims have had some success challenging restrictive leave policies that disproportionately affect women because they are more likely to need time off due to childbirth (e.g., *Abraham v. Graphic Arts International* [660 F.2d 811 [D.D.C. 1981]], *EEOC v. Warshawsky & Co.* [768 F. Supp. 647 [N.D. Ill. 1991]]). Disparate impact discrimination claims—or more accurately, the possibility of them and public claims that inadequate maternity leaves are discriminatory—prompted many employers to adopt new leave policies in the 1970s and early 1980s, even though the courts were divided in their acceptance of these arguments (Kelly and Dobbin, 1999). Similar arguments might be used to challenge restrictions on part-time work, working from home, or working rigid hours. There are active cases challenging the limited promotion opportunities for part-time workers and those using flexible work arrangements (Williams and Segal, 2003), but the potential of disparate impact theory for caregivers is not yet clear.

Applying disparate impact theory to caregivers may be challenging because many courts have a narrow conception of what constitutes "a particular employment practice" (Travis, 2003). Employers' institutionalized and entrenched practices do not feel like chosen "practices" but like "the way things are done." In other words, they are taken-for-granted and assumed to be rational and efficient responses to real demands on the organization. The rigid career track is one such institutionalized system that affects caregivers, who are disproportionately women. Organizations assume that workers who do not work full-time (and overtime), year-round, with no breaks in employment are legitimately excluded from certain jobs and from moving to higher positions within the organization. Employers and, often, the courts see this as "the way things are done" and not as optional ways of organizing work and work rewards (cf. Nelson and Bridges, 1999). While these institutionalized practices do not necessarily reflect conscious decisions by organizational actors, they are nonetheless actions that can be made conscious when employees or peer organizations present alternative possibilities. For example, requiring all incumbents of a certain job to work at least 40 hours per week is an action on the employer's part. It may not be a conscious action until and unless an employee requests a part-time schedule, but it is still an employment practice. After the employee makes a request or after the employer learns that peer organizations are allowing part-time schedules in comparable positions, the choice to continue that exclusionary practice is more obviously a choice and therefore it is more obvious that courts could scrutinize that practice using disparate impact theory.

An additional difficulty with disparate impact cases brought by marginalized caregivers is the need to establish that women, or mothers, are *disproportionately* disadvantaged by a given employment practice if there are no men, or women without children, who are similarly situated (Travis, 2003, pp. 345–349). The preponderance of sex-segregated jobs can make it difficult to find men in similar situations. Courts may ask: Are the employees who work a reduced-hours schedule or who work from home treated differently than full-time, on-site workers *doing the same job*? Plaintiffs may not be able to meet this requirement for showing disparate impact because the marginalization of non-standard workers occurs *through* the assignment of tasks and the definition of jobs (Williams, 2000). Many part-time workers are given slightly different work to do—often more routine and sometimes less challenging work. Yet, it is precisely the practice of assigning part-time employees, who are more likely to be women, different work and refusing to promote part-time employees that might be challenged using disparate impact arguments.

3.2. Reasonable Accommodation of Caregiving

Enacting a new anti-discrimination statute requiring reasonable accommodation of caregiving could also challenge the work practices that marginalize caregivers. This statute could be modeled on anti-discrimination laws that target people with disabilities or on the religious accommodation provisions in Title VII (Kessler, 2001; Travis, 2003). Employers would be required to "accommodate" caregivers' needs through flexible work arrangements or other revisions of current work practices unless those changes are shown to be unreasonable. As Travis (2003, p. 324) notes: "The accommodation concept is appealing because it explicitly recognizes that the workplace is mutable." Furthermore, this approach is gender neutral and so it is more easily applied to men, as well as to workers of either sex who are caring for seriously ill or disabled relatives, elderly parents, or other loved ones outside a narrowly defined family.

Australia now has legislation along these lines.[7] Both federal sex discrimination law and statutes in most Australian states prohibit discrimination on the basis of employees' family responsibilities or "carers' responsibilities" (Bourke, 2004). The New South Wales legislation, modeled on disability statutes, requires employers to make "reasonable accommodation" unless the caregiving employee is "unable to carry out the inherent (or essential) requirements of the job" or unless such changes would constitute "unjustifiable hardship" for the employer (Bourke, 2004, pp. 33–35). The law includes direct and indirect discrimination, which parallel the American concepts of disparate treatment and disparate impact discrimination. Recent Australian case law reveals "a general willingness to interpret carers' responsibilities legislation broadly and beneficially" (Bourke, 2004, p. 38). It has been surprisingly difficult for employers to defend themselves with claims that standard work practices are essential job requirements or business necessities. Tribunals and courts have required employers to allow part-time work and job-sharing in professional and management positions, to set up telecommuting arrangements, to reinstate an employee who was terminated after she refused to work overtime on short notice, and to experiment with flexible schedules when it was not clear whether or not a new schedule would be feasible in a given job (Bourke, 2004, pp. 39–58). In short, the presumption has been that new work arrangements should be allowed except in unusual situations.

[7] Australia, the country that has arguably gone the farthest in incorporating caregivers into anti-discrimination law, ranks with the U.S. as the only developed countries that do not provide paid leave to new parents. This suggests that advocates may focus on anti-discrimination law in the absence of more direct means of meeting caregivers' needs.

4. CONCLUSION: WOULD IT WORK?

Would these legal developments inspire organizations to change their policies, practices, and expectations? And would those organizational changes reduce or eliminate the economic marginalization of employed caregivers? My own assessment, based on studies of organizational responses to other anti-discrimination laws and current thinking about the impact of employers' anti-discrimination programs on employees' careers, is that legal changes would provide a new framework for understanding the experiences of caregivers, alter the negotiations between employees and employers, and prompt many organizations to add or elaborate their "family–friendly" policies. However, those policies, on their own, would not erase the economic and occupational penalties that caregivers face.

Legal claims that existing organizational practices, policies, and assumptions can constitute discriminate against caregivers would transform current understandings of caregivers' place in the workplace. My interviews and analyses of the popular and business press reveal that employers, commentators, and probably most employees conceptualize "work–family conflicts" as individual problems rather than a broader social and organizational problem (Kelly, 1999; Moen, 2003; Williams, 2000). The solutions offered include teaching employees to better "juggle" their work and family roles or providing minimal "accommodations" if and when these adjustments are convenient and attractive to managers. "Discrimination talk" can be a powerful tool for challenging these privatized understandings of the problem (Williams, 2000; Williams and Segal, 2003), even if relatively few cases are successful in the courts (Stryker, 1994; McCann, 1994). The cultural power of law is that it can de-legitimate previously unquestioned actions and assumptions and suggest new actions and identities (see Albiston, this volume). A working mother who feels scattered, stressed, and guilty about asking her employer to let her change her hours or work from home can be transformed (in theory, at least) into a caregiver who views her own situation as part of larger social changes in family life and the economy, expects reasonable accommodations at work, and labels her employer's intransigence as discrimination.

Recent history suggests that legal recognition of discrimination against caregivers would lead many organizations to add or improve their "family–friendly" policies, such as family leaves and flexible work arrangements. Previous expansions of anti-discrimination law prompted the widespread adoption of many common policies and practices, including formal job descriptions, formal performance evaluations, job ladders, equal opportunity statements, grievance procedures, diversity policies, sexual harassment training, as well as new staff positions (Dobbin, et al., 1993; Dobbin and Kelly, 2005; Dobbin and Sutton, 1998; Edelman, 1990; Edelman, 1992; Edelman et al., 1999). Because the Civil Rights Act of 1964 and other anti-discrimination statutes are quite ambiguous (Edelman, 1992), there is a collective, iterative process in which employers and their agents propose certain responses to the new (or newly reinterpreted) law and then courts and regulatory agencies comment on these practices and policies.

Those practices and policies that judges and regulators accept as signals of compliance diffuse widely, although managers often downplay their efficacy as legal signals and present these actions as rational responses to economic conditions.

These studies lead me to expect that new understandings of sex discrimination law or the passage of a law requiring reasonable accommodations for caregivers would spur the diffusion of new "family–friendly" policies and perhaps the elaboration of existing policies because employers would want to signal their attention to and compliance with the new legal environment with some organizational change. In fact, this process occurred in the 1970s when maternity leave was popularized after women's movement advocates, the Equal Employment Opportunity Commission, and some lower courts claimed that a failure to provide maternity leave constituted sex discrimination (Kelly and Dobbin, 1999). The Supreme Court did not accept this argument in the 1976 *General Electric v. Gilbert* case, but employers had already responded to the lower court decisions and to the media's framing of maternity leave as an equal opportunity issue (Kelly and Dobbin, 1999).

The early press coverage of *Back v. Hastings-on-Hudson Union Free School District* suggests that employers might make changes in organizational policies and practices in response to claims about discrimination against caregivers. Even though the Second Circuit Court of Appeals simply returned the case to the district court, the case has got attention in many newspapers (e.g., Crary, 2004; Kleiman, 2004; Vuocolo, 2004) and it may help employees and employers reframe "work-life issues" as a legal matter. The Associated Press story about the Back case introduces scholar Joan Williams' concept of "the maternal wall," as a parallel to the glass ceiling, and quotes Williams as saying that "discrimination against parents and other caregivers" is "a new battleground" (Crary, 2004). It is not clear what lessons human resources managers will see in this case, but previous studies suggest that the lessons applied by managers may not mirror the actual risk of liability or the meaningful changes in the legal doctrine (Edelman et al., 1993; Edelman et al., 1999). For example, none of the articles that I have located note that the Second Circuit Court agreed with the district court that the school district and school superintendent are not responsible for the alleged discrimination in this case although other school officials may be. Instead, the articles emphasize what organizations should do to avoid similar claims. The Associated Press article identifies five different responses that employers might take, including offering flexible work arrangements to more employees, expanding existing EEO policies to cover caregivers, and training supervisors that bias against caregivers is unacceptable (Crary, 2004). One human resources manager shared with me that she will now incorporate the facts of the Back case in her "coaching sessions" about how supervisors can avoid "inappropriate conversations around marital status, religion, and age."

Yet there are several reasons to believe that the organizational changes prompted by changes in discrimination law would not erase the inequalities between caregivers and other workers. First, when organizations respond to anti-discrimination law, they do not simply follow the instructions laid out in the law. Instead, they help construct the meaning of the law by developing policies and programs that they then present as signals of compliance. In this process, managers (or their attorneys and consultants) try to maintain managerial discretion as much as possible and thereby create non-threatening, if not quite empty, gestures of compliance (Edelman, 1992; Edelman, this volume; Edelman et al., 1993; Edelman et al., 1999; Kelly, 2003). Second, employers often do not have strong incentives to create meaningful changes. Research has not yet shown whether these policies are empty gestures or not, but courts often given employers the benefit of the doubt if they have the expected policies in place. Scholars find it difficult to study the effects of organizational policies on protected categories of workers (cf. Reskin and McBrier, 2000; Kalev et al., 2004) and employers either do not pursue these questions or do not share the results. Legal scholars suggest that employers avoid evaluating the effectiveness of their anti-discrimination policies because they fear such information could be used against them in court (Bisom-Rapp, 1999; Sturm, 2001, p. 461). Ironically, courts often accept employers' claims of compliance without significant analyses of actual data (Nelson and Bridges, 1999; Sturm, 2001). Third, there may be concerted resistance to the kinds of changes that would help caregivers. Previous changes related to anti-discrimination law having focused on the margins of organizational life—policies and procedures for hiring, firing, and the handling of disputes—rather than the work process itself or the system of allocating rewards. It seems likely that there would be greater resistance to changes in these domains of work. Indeed, researchers find significant resistance to changing the way work is done, as required by the Americans with Disabilities Act (Harlan and Robert, 1998; Travis, 2003), and to granting workers time off, as required by the Family and Medical Leave Act (Albiston, this volume).

Still, some scholars find hope in recent legal developments and in the changes occurring in some progressive organizations.[8] For example, Sturm (2001) argues that the old-fashioned, rule-based, court-centered regulatory system is not a good match for the "second generation discrimination" that arises from cognitive bias, institutionalized structures of decision-making, and unquestioned patterns of interaction rather than deliberate racism or sexism. But she sees a new system of enforcement emerging, which emphasizes "problem-solving" over "gestures of compliance" and attempts to help employers manage a complex workforce in addition to avoiding bias. In this system, compliance is understood as the "capacity to identify, prevent, and redress exclusion, bias, and abuse" (p. 463).

In this new system, each organization would develop or customize its policies and practices but the reforms would have several traits in common. According to Sturm (2001, p. 519), organizations' equal opportunity and diversity initiatives should be (1) problem-oriented (i.e., created to respond to an organizationally defined problem as well as to broad anti-discrimination concerns), (2) functionally integrated with

[8] Some organizational scholars are hopeful about "dual agenda" interventions that attempt to reduce gender inequalities while promoting organizational efficiency and effectiveness (Rappoport et al., 2001; Perlow, 1997; Ely and Meyerson, 2000). These studies make it clear, though, that such changes in organizational life require enormous investments of time and energy and change if often short-lived.

other systems in the organization, (3) data driven with many opportunities for the organization to evaluate its own progress towards its goals, and (4) accountable to external actors, such as the courts, as well as to internal constituencies affected by the practices. Managerial discretion would be maintained, in some form, but it would be limited by concrete procedures and by the possibility of being held accountable for inequitable outcomes as well as discriminatory motives (see also Reskin, 2003).

If anti-discrimination enforcement moved in these directions and if anti-discrimination law was expanded to include caregivers as a protected category of workers, we could very well see organizations that (1) recognize the marginalization of caregivers as an inefficient use of human resources as well as a potential source of legal liability, (2) seriously re-evaluate the way work is done and the way workers are evaluated in light of the needs and experiences of caregivers, (3) periodically evaluate the place of caregivers within the organization to be sure workers are not penalized for taking advantage of leaves, telecommuting, reduced hours schedules, and other new arrangements, and (4) know they must attend to all these tasks or face criticism and sanctions from their workers, the public, and the courts. If anti-discrimination law worked like that, we could very well see significant improvements in caregivers' careers. We are not there yet.

SECTION V

Social Psychology of Bias

CHAPTER 19

Aversive Racism: Bias without Intention

Samuel L. Gaertner; John F. Dovidio; Jason Nier; Gordon Hodson
and Melissa A. Houlette

ABSTRACT

This chapter examines one form of contemporary racism, "aversive racism." Aversive racism is characterized by a conflict between the denial of personal prejudice and unconscious negative feelings and beliefs, which may be rooted in normal psychological processes (such as social categorization). In the chapter, we review experimental evidence of the existence and operation of aversive racism in the behavior of Whites toward Blacks, with emphasis on studies of *unintentional* discrimination in selection and hiring. Then we explore approaches for combating aversive racism. Specifically, within the framework of the Common Ingroup Identity Model, we demonstrate how developing a sense of shared identity between members of different groups can redirect the forces of social categorization toward the reduction of racial biases. We conclude with a discussion of the social and legal implications of aversive racism and strategies for combating it.

INTRODUCTION

Racism is easy to recognize in its most blatant forms. The traditional form of racism in the United States has involved open and direct expression from anti-locution to public lynching and murder. In contemporary times, racism has produced racial segregation in neighborhoods and schools, and open discrimination in employment and educational opportunity (Jones, 1997). The Civil Rights Legislation of the 1960s defined racism not only as morally inappropriate but also as legally improper. Krieger (1995) notes that according to existing law, a person who initiates an employment discrimination suit "must prove not only that s(he) was treated differently, but that such treatment was caused by *purposeful* or *intentional* discrimination" (p. 1168). Research in social psychology over the past 25 years, however, reveals that even racially well-intentioned people are often racist, and they are often racist without intention or awareness. Given the abyss between the evidence about the occurrence of unintentional, nondeliberate bias and the legal standard that must be satisfied, many instances of disparate treatment on the basis of race, gender, or national origin are denied successful legal recourse.

L. B. Nielsen and R. L. Nelson (eds.), Handbook of Employment Discrimination Research, 377–395.

The purpose of the present chapter is to review some of our own work on aversive racism that reveals how subtle, unintended racial bias may operate and also to address our work on the Common Ingroup Identity Model that suggests how such biases may be reduced, if not eliminated. First, we consider the nature of aversive racism. Second, we offer experimental evidence of its existence and operation in the behavior of Whites toward Blacks. Third, we illustrate how the principles of the Common Ingroup Identity Model can be applied to combat aversive racism. We conclude by considering implications of aversive racism, its bases, and its consequences, for the legal system.

1. AVERSIVE RACISM AND CONTEMPORARY BIAS

Whereas overt expressions of prejudice have declined significantly over the past 35 years (Dovidio and Gaertner, 1998; Dovidio and Gaertner, 2000; Schuman, Steeh, Bobo, and Krysan, 1997), contemporary forms of prejudice continue to exist and affect the lives of people in subtle but significant ways (Dovidio and Gaertner, 2004; Gaertner and Dovidio, 1986). For these more subtler contemporary forms of prejudice, bias is expressed in indirect, often unintentional, ways. Nevertheless, the consequences of these prejudices (e.g., the restriction of economic opportunity) may be as significant for people of color and as pernicious as those of the traditional, overt form of discrimination (Dovidio and Gaertner, 1998; Gaertner and Dovidio, 1986; Sears, 1988). Aversive racism is hypothesized to be qualitatively different than the old-fashioned, blatant kind, and it is presumed to characterize the racial attitudes of most well-educated and liberal Whites in the United States (see also Kovel, 1970; Pettigrew and Meertens, 1995). It is more indirect and subtle than the traditional form of prejudice, but its consequences are no less destructive.

1.1. Aversive Racism, Duality, and Ambivalence

A critical aspect of the aversive racism framework is the conflict between the denial of personal prejudice and the underlying unconscious negative feelings and beliefs. Because of current cultural values, most Whites have strong convictions concerning fairness, justice, and racial equality. However, because of a range of normal cognitive, motivational, and socio-cultural processes that promote intergroup biases, most Whites also develop some negative feelings toward or beliefs about Blacks. The existence of these nearly unavoidable racial biases along with the simultaneous desire to be nonprejudiced represents a basic duality of attitudes and beliefs for aversive racists that can produce racial ambivalence (see also Katz and Hass, 1988; Katz, Wackenhut, and Hass, 1986). We recognize that all racists are not aversive or subtle, that old-fashioned racism still exists, that there are individual differences in aversive racism, and that some Whites may not be racist at all. Nevertheless, we propose that aversive racism generally characterizes the racial attitudes of a large proportion of Whites who express nonprejudiced views and who intentionally try to avoid discriminating against Blacks and other minorities.

1.2. Feelings and Beliefs

In contrast to traditional approaches that emphasize the *psychopathology* of prejudice (e.g., Adorno, Frenkel-Brunswik, Levinson, and Sanford, 1950; see Duckitt, 1992), the feelings and beliefs that underlie aversive racism are hypothesized to be rooted in *normal*, often adaptive, psychological processes (see Dovidio and Gaertner, 1998; Gaertner and Dovidio, 1986). These processes involve both individual factors (such as cognitive and motivational biases and socialization) and intergroup elements (such as realistic group conflict or biases associated with the mere categorization of people into ingroups and outgroups).

In addition, in contrast to the feelings of open hostility and clear dislike of Blacks, the feelings aversive racists experience are typically more diffuse, such as feelings of anxiety and uneasiness. There is also the possibility that subtle forms of bias—such as aversive racism, may be characterized by a significant component of pro-White (i.e., pro-ingroup) attitude that does not seem racist to the individual him/herself. Indeed, Brewer (1979) proposed that much of intergroup bias, particularly when interactants do not perceive themselves in direct conflict, is characterized by ingroup favoritism rather than outgroup derogation. To the extent that intergroup processes initiated by social categorization represent a foundation for aversive racism to develop, aversive racism may be characterized by similar effects. We do not intend to argue that all of racism can be attributed simply to ingroup–outgroup, we–they distinctions. Racism is also deeply embedded in a historical, social, political, and economic context that sculpts its characteristics. However, we do want to suggest that if aversive racism is rooted at least in part on social categorization, then strategies to eliminate aversive racism may be productively directed at this underlying process.

1.3. Subtle Bias

The aversive racism framework also helps to identify when discrimination against Blacks and other minority groups will or will not occur. Whereas old-fashioned racists exhibit a direct and overt pattern of discrimination, aversive racists' actions may appear more variable and inconsistent. Sometimes they discriminate (manifesting their negative feelings), and sometimes they do not (reflecting their egalitarian beliefs). Our research has provided a framework for understanding this pattern of discrimination.

Because aversive racists consciously recognize and endorse egalitarian values and because they truly aspire to be nonprejudiced, they will *not* discriminate in situations with strong social norms when discrimination would be obvious to others and to themselves. Specifically, we propose that when people are presented with a situation in which the normatively appropriate response is clear, in which right and wrong is clearly defined, aversive racists will not discriminate against Blacks. In these contexts, aversive racists will be especially motivated to avoid feelings, beliefs, and behaviors that could be associated with racist intent. Wrong-doing, which would directly threaten their nonprejudiced self-image, would be too costly. However, because aversive racists still possess feelings of uneasiness, these feelings will eventually be expressed, but they will be expressed in subtle, indirect, and rationalizable ways. For instance, discrimination will occur in situations in which normative structure is weak, when the guidelines for appropriate behavior are vague or when the basis for social judgment is ambiguous. In addition, discrimination will occur when an aversive racist can justify or rationalize a negative response on the basis of some factor other than race. Under these circumstances, aversive racists may engage in behaviors that ultimately harm Blacks but in ways that allow Whites to maintain their self-image as nonprejudiced and that insulate them from recognizing that their behavior is not color blind.

Generally, then, aversive racists may be identified by a constellation of characteristic responses to racial issues and interracial situations. First, aversive racists, in contrast to old-fashioned racists, endorse fair and just treatment of all groups. Second, despite their conscious good intentions, aversive racists unconsciously harbor feelings of uneasiness toward Blacks, and thus try to avoid interracial interaction. Third, when interracial interaction is unavoidable, aversive racists experience anxiety and discomfort, and consequently they try to disengage from the interaction as quickly as possible. Fourth, because part of the discomfort that aversive racists experience is due to a concern about acting inappropriately and appearing prejudiced, aversive racists strictly adhere to established rules and codes of behavior in interracial situations that they cannot avoid. Fifth and finally, their feelings will get expressed, but in subtle, unintentional, rationalizable ways that disadvantage minorities or unfairly benefit the majority group. Nevertheless, in terms of conscious intent, aversive racists intend not to discrimination against people of color—and they behave accordingly, when it is possible for them to monitor the appropriateness of their behavior.

The term "aversive" in this form of racism thus refers to two aspects of this bias. It reflects the nature of the emotions associated with Blacks, such as anxiety, that lead to avoidance and social awkwardness rather than to open antagonism. It also reflects the fact that, because of their conscious adherence to egalitarian principles, these Whites find any indication that they might be prejudiced to be aversive.

In general, then, the aversive racism framework considers the situation as a critical factor influencing the expression of racial bias by Whites toward Blacks. Although social influences can directly influence the level of bias that is expressed (Pettigrew, 1959), we emphasize the *moderating* role of situational factors on whether the unconscious negative aspects of aversive racists' attitudes are manifested in terms of racial discrimination. That is, whether the situation is one in which a negative act toward a Black person would be attributed to racial intent, by others or by the aversive racist himself or herself, determines whether bias will be expressed.

Consistent with the aversive racism perspective, other theories of contemporary racism also hypothesize that bias is currently expressed more subtly than in the past. One such approach is Symbolic Racism Theory (Sears, 1988; Sears, Henry, and Kosterman, 2000) or a closely related derivation called Modern Racism Theory (McConahay, 1986). According to Symbolic Racism Theory, negative feelings toward Blacks that Whites acquire early in life persist into adulthood but are expressed indirectly and symbolically, in terms of opposition to busing or resistance to affirmative action, rather than directly or overtly, as in support for segregation. McConahay (1986) further proposes that because modern racism involves the rejection of traditional racist beliefs and the displacement of anti-Black feelings onto more abstract social and political issues, modern racists, such as aversive racists, are relatively unaware of their racist feelings. However, whereas symbolic and modern racism are subtle forms of contemporary racism that seem to exist among political conservatives, aversive racism seems to be more strongly associated with liberals.

We have found consistent support for the aversive racism framework across a broad range of situations (see Dovidio and Gaertner, 2004; Gaertner and Dovidio, 1986). Our work mainly considers the influence of contemporary racial biases of Whites toward Blacks because of the central role that racial politics has played in the history of the United States. In addition, much of the research reported in this chapter focuses on the responses of White college students—well-educated and typically liberal people—who are presumed to represent a prime population for aversive racism. Nevertheless, we note that many of the findings and principles we discuss extend to biases exhibited by liberal noncollege populations (e.g., Gaertner, 1973) and to biases toward other groups (e.g., Hispanics; Dovidio, Gaertner, Anastasio, and Sanitioso, 1992). In the next sections, we describe examples of a series of different studies to illustrate the operation of aversive racism. The evidence we present in this section of the chapter comes from paradigms involving interventions to help people in need and employment or admission selection decisions.

1.4. Serendipity and Aversive Racism

We began our research on racism naively with a simple assumption: based on differences in their expressed racial attitudes (see Adorno et al., 1950), conservative Whites would behave in a more racially discriminatory way than would liberal Whites. However, we discovered, somewhat serendipitously, that racial discrimination was complex, and it occurs in subtle as well as overt ways.

In this initial study of contemporary racism and interracial helping (Gaertner, 1973), White participants residing in Brooklyn, New York, were selected for a field experiment on helping on the basis of their liberal or conservative orientations, as indicated by their political party affiliations (i.e., Liberal or Conservative parties in New York State) which were a matter of public record. Both the liberal and the conservative households received wrong-number telephone calls that quickly developed into requests for assistance. The callers, who were clearly identifiable from their dialects as being Black or White, explained that their car was disabled and that they were attempting to reach a service garage from a public phone along the parkway. The callers further claimed that they had no more change to make another call and asked the participant to help by calling the garage. If the participant agreed to help and called the number, ostensibly of the garage, a "helping" response was scored. If the participant refused to help or hung up after the caller explained that he or she had no more change, a "not helping" response was recorded. If the participant hung up before learning that the motorist had no more change, the response was recorded as a "premature hang-up."

The first finding from this study was direct and predicted. Conservatives showed a higher "helping" response to Whites than to Blacks (92% versus 65%), whereas liberals helped Whites somewhat, but not significantly, more than Blacks (85% versus 75%). By this measure, conservatives were more biased against Blacks than were liberals. Additional inspection of the data, however, revealed an unanticipated finding. Liberals "hung up prematurely" much more often on Blacks than they did on Whites (19% versus 3%), and especially often on a Black male motorist (28%). Conservatives did not discriminate in this way (8% versus 5%). From the perspective of Black callers, the consequence of a direct "not helping" response and of a "premature hang-up" was the same: they would be left without assistance. From the perspective of the participants, however, the consequences were different. Whereas a "not helping" response was a direct, intentional form of discrimination because it should have been clear to participants that their help was needed, a "premature hang-up" was a more indirect form because participants disengaged from the situation before they learned of the other person's dependence on them, and thus participants never overtly refused assistance. Indeed, to refuse help that is perceived to be needed clearly violates the social responsibility norm, whereas the appropriateness of hanging-up prematurely is unclear. Therefore, both conservative and liberal Whites discriminated against Blacks but in different ways.

1.5. Emergency Intervention

Another one of our early experiments (Gaertner and Dovidio, 1977) demonstrates how aversive racism can operate in fairly dramatic ways. The scenario for the experiment was inspired by an incident in the mid-1960s in which 38 people witnessed the stabbing of a woman, Kitty Genovese, without a single bystander intervening to help. What accounted for this behavior? Feelings of responsibility play a key role (see Darley and Latané, 1968). If a person witnesses an emergency knowing that he or she is the only bystander, that person bears all of the responsibility for helping. Consequently, the likelihood of helping is high. In contrast, if a person witnesses an emergency but believes that there are several other witnesses who might help, then the responsibility for helping is shared. Moreover, if the person believes that someone else will help or has already helped, the likelihood of that bystander taking action is significantly reduced.

We created a situation in the laboratory in which White participants witnessed a staged emergency involving a Black or White victim. We led some of our participants to believe that they would be the only witness to this emergency, while we led others to believe that there would be other White people who also witnessed the emergency. We predicted that, because aversive racists do not act in overtly bigoted ways, Whites would not discriminate when they were the only witness and the responsibility for helping was clearly focused on them. However, we anticipated that Whites would be much less helpful to Black than to White victims when they had a justifiable excuse not to get involved, such as the belief that one of the *other* witnesses would take responsibility for helping.

The results strongly reflected these predictions. When White participants believed that they were the only witness, they helped both White and Black victims very frequently (over 85% of the time) and equivalently. There was no evidence of blatant racism. In contrast, when they thought there were other witnesses and they could rationalize a decision not to help on the basis of some factor other than race, they helped Black victims only half as often as White victims (37.5% versus 75%). Thus, these results illustrate the operation of subtle biases in relatively dramatic, spontaneous, and life-threatening circumstances involving a failure to help, rather than an action intentionally aimed at doing harm. This research, therefore, shows that although the bias may be subtle and the people involved may be well-intentioned, its consequences may be severe.

1.6. Selection Decisions

Labor statistics continue to demonstrate fundamental disparities in the economic status of Blacks relative to Whites—a gap that has not only persisted but also, in some important aspects (e.g., family income), has widened in recent years (see Blank, 2001). Aversive racism may be one factor that contributes to disparities in the workplace. Subtle biases can influence both the access of Blacks to the workplace and their performance in it.

At the time of hiring, aversive racism can affect how qualifications are perceived and weighed in a manner that systematically disadvantages Black relative to White applicants. In particular, the aversive racism framework suggests that bias will not be expressed when a person is clearly qualified or unqualified for a position, because the appropriate decision is obvious. However, bias is expected when the appropriate decision is unclear, for example, because of ambiguous evidence about whether the candidate's qualifications meet the criteria for selection or when the candidate's file has conflicting evidence (e.g., some strong and some weak aspects).

In one study of hiring decisions (Dovidio and Gaertner, 2000), we presented college students with excerpts from an interview and asked them to evaluate candidates for a position in an ostensibly new program for peer counseling at their university. Specifically, White participants evaluated a Black or White candidate who had credentials that were systematically manipulated to represent very strong, moderate, or very weak qualifications for the position. These findings were supportive of the aversive racism framework. When the candidates' credentials clearly qualified them for the position (strong qualifications) or the credentials clearly were not appropriate (weak qualifications), there was no discrimination against the Black candidate. However, when candidates' qualifications for the position were less obvious and the appropriate decision was more ambiguous (moderate qualifications), White participants recommended the Black candidate significantly less often than the White candidate with exactly the same credentials. Moreover, when we compared the responses of participants in 1989 and 1999, whereas overt expressions of prejudice (measured by items on a self-report prejudice scale) declined over this 10-year period, the pattern of subtle discrimination in selection decisions remained essentially unchanged.

In subsequent research (Hodson, Dovidio, and Gaertner, 2002), participants were asked to help make admissions decisions for the university. Given the social climate on college campuses today, it is possible that even higher prejudice scoring students may be concerned about viewing themselves as prejudiced. Consequently, as we have observed among lower prejudiced participants in the past, these individuals may currently express their negative attitudes in subtle, indirect, and rationalizable ways—and, relative to the general population, these higher prejudiced scoring college students, may actually be low to moderate in prejudice and not view themselves as racially prejudiced. Indeed, among a comparable sample of higher prejudice scoring participants, only 15% regarded themselves as "prejudiced against Blacks."

Again, we found no anti-Black bias among our higher and lower prejudice scoring college participants when applicants had uniformly strong or uniformly weak college board scores and records of high school achievement. When applicants were strong on one dimension (e.g., on college board scores) and weak on the other (e.g., high school grades), however, Black applicants tended to be recommended less strongly than were White applicants among higher scoring prejudice participants. Moreover, these participants systematically changed how they weighed the criteria to justify their decisions as a function of race. For Black applicants, higher prejudice scoring college participants gave the weaker dimension (college board scores or grades) greater weight in their decisions, whereas for White applicants they assigned the stronger of the qualifications more weight. Taken together, these findings suggest that when given latitude for interpretation, higher prejudice White college participants (whom relative to the general population may be regarded as generally moderate to low prejudiced, see Schuman et al., 1997), give White candidates the "benefit of the doubt," a benefit they do not extend to Blacks.

The behavior of aversive racists is thus characterized by two types of inconsistencies. First, aversive racists exhibit an apparent contradiction between their expressed egalitarian attitudes and their biased (albeit subtle) behaviors. Second, sometimes (in clear situations) they act in an unbiased fashion, whereas at other times (in ambiguous situations) they are biased unintentionally against Blacks.

Overall, we have offered evidence across time, populations, and paradigms that illustrates how aversive racism—racism among people who are good and well-intentioned—can produce disparate outcomes between Blacks and Whites. As we noted earlier, although the bias of aversive racists may be subtle and unintentional, its consequences may ultimately be just as severe as old-fashioned racism. In the next section, we examine a strategy we propose that can combat this insidious type of bias.

2. COMBATING AVERSIVE RACISM

When we described our findings formally, in papers and presentations, and informally, a common question arose, "What can we do about subtle biases, particularly when we do not know for sure whether we have them?" Like a virus that has mutated, racism may have evolved into different forms that are more difficult not only to recognize but also to combat. Because of its pervasiveness, subtlety, and complexity, the traditional techniques for eliminating bias that emphasized the immorality of prejudice and illegality of discrimination are not effective for combating aversive racism. Aversive racists recognize that prejudice is bad, but they do not recognize that *they* are prejudiced.

One basic argument we have made in our research on aversive racism is that the negative feelings that develop toward other groups may be rooted, in part, in fundamental, normal psychological processes. One such process, identified in the classic work of Tajfel, Allport, and others, is the categorization of people into ingroups and outgroups—"we's" and "they's." People respond systematically more favorably to others whom they perceive to belong to their group than to different groups. Thus, if bias is linked to fundamental, normal psychological processes, then attempts to ameliorate bias should be directed not at eliminating the process but rather at redirecting the forces to produce more harmonious intergroup relations. By shifting the basis of categorization from race to an alternative dimension we can potentially alter who is a "we" and who is a "they," undermining a contributing force to aversive racism.

As these ideas were developing, we also began to consider the possibility that the discrimination we were observing in our studies of aversive racism may have reflected discrimination not only *against* Blacks but also discrimination *in favor of* Whites. That is, we began to view aversive racism as a problem that, in part, involved Whites having a more generous, helpful, and forgiving orientation toward Whites than toward Blacks. Even though this pro-White form of racism can be as pernicious as anti-Black bias, it does not assume an underlying motivation to be hurtful—either consciously or unconsciously. Rather, for aversive racists, part of the problem may be that there is no emotional connection to Blacks and other minorities and they do not regard them as part of their circle of inclusion for sharing and caring as readily as they accept Whites. Racially dissimilar others, then, do not ordinarily have the same capacity as fellow Whites to elicit empathic, prosocial reactions. But, what if Whites perceived Blacks and other minorities, even temporarily, as members of their own group—as ingroup members—rather than as members of different groups? Would behavior toward them become more favorable? And how specifically can intergroup contact be structured to reduce bias and conflict? In the next section, we focus on interventions that target social categorization and ingroup favoritism (see also Gaertner and Dovidio, 2000).

2.1. Redirecting Ingroup Bias

Social categorization, particularly in terms of ingroups ("we's") and outgroups ("they's") is a fundamental process that contributes to aversive racism (Gaertner et al., 1997). In general, the mere categorization of people into ingroups and outgroups has a profound influence on social perception, affect, cognition, and behavior. When others are distinguished by their ingroup or outgroup membership, people exaggerate differences between members of the groups (Abrams, 1985; Turner, 1985), spontaneously experience more positive feelings toward ingroup members (Otten and Moskowitz, 2000), remember more positive information about ingroup members (Howard and Rothbart, 1980), and behave more helpfully to ingroup members (Dovidio, Gaertner et al., 1997). Because race is a fundamental type of social categorization in the United States, race is associated with strong ingroup biases.

The process of social categorization, however, is not completely unalterable. Categories are hierarchically organized, with higher-level categories (e.g., nations) being more inclusive of lower-level ones (e.g., cities or towns). By modifying a perceiver's goals, motives, perceptions of past experiences, expectations, as well as factors within the perceptual field and the situational context more broadly, there is opportunity to alter the level of category inclusiveness that will be most influential in a given situation. This malleability of the level at which impressions are formed is important because of its implications for altering the way people think about members of ingroups and outgroups, and consequently about the ways Whites in general, and aversive racists in particular, respond to Blacks.

Because categorization is a basic process that is fundamental to intergroup bias, we have targeted this process as a way of addressing the effects of aversive racism. In the next section, we explore how the forces of categorization can be harnessed and redirected toward the reduction of racial biases. This approach is represented by the Common Ingroup Identity Model (Gaertner and Dovidio, 2000; Gaertner, Dovidio, Anastasio, Bachman, and Rust, 1993).

2.2. The Common Ingroup Identity Model

The Common Ingroup Identity Model is rooted in the social categorization perspective of intergroup behavior and recognizes the central role of social categorization in reducing as well as in creating intergroup bias (Tajfel and Turner, 1979). Specifically, if members of different groups are induced to conceive of themselves more as a single, superordinate group rather than as two separate groups, attitudes toward former outgroup members will become more positive through processes involving pro-ingroup bias. Thus, changing the basis of categorization from race to an alternative dimension can alter who is "we" and who is "they," undermining a contributing force to contemporary forms of racism, such as aversive racism. Formation of a common identity, however, does not necessarily require groups to forsake their ethnic or other subgroup identities. It is possible for members to conceive of themselves as holding a "dual identity" in which both subgroup and superordinate groups are salient simultaneously. Substantial evidence across a variety of settings in support of the Common Ingroup Identity Model has been found (Gaertner and Dovidio, 2000).

In one test of the Common Ingroup Identity hypothesis, we conducted an experiment that brought 2 three-person laboratory groups together under conditions designed to vary independently: (1) the members' perceptions of the aggregate as one group or two groups through manipulation of the contact situation and (2) the presence or absence of intergroup cooperative interaction (Gaertner, Mann, Dovidio, Murrell, and Pomare, 1990). The interventions designed to emphasize common group membership through structural changes in the contact situation (e.g., integrated versus segregated seating; a new group name for all six participants versus the original group names, the same or different colored t-shirts for both groups) and to encourage cooperative interaction (joint evaluation and reward versus independent outcomes) both reduced intergroup bias. Moreover, they did so through the same mechanism. Contextual features emphasizing common "groupness" and cooperation each increased one-group representations (and reduced separate-group representations), which in turn related to more favorable attitudes toward original outgroup members and lower levels of bias. Consistent with the Common Ingroup Identity Model, more inclusive, one-group representations *mediated* the relationship between the interventions and the reduction of bias.

In a series of studies with a different methodological approach, we utilized survey techniques under more naturalistic circumstances to examine the impact of common group identity across a variety different intergroup settings. These studies offer converging support for the hypothesis that the features specified by the Contact Hypothesis (Allport, 1954; Williams, 1947) reduce intergroup bias, in part, because they transform members' representations of the memberships from separate groups to a single, more inclusive group. Participants in these studies included students attending a multiethnic high school (Gaertner, Rust, Dovidio, Bachman, and Anastasio, 1996), banking executives who had experienced a corporate merger involving a wide variety of banks across the United States (Bachman, 1993), and college students from blended families whose households are composed of two formerly separate families trying to unite into one (Banker and Gaertner, 1998).

Consistent with the role of an inclusive group representation that is hypothesized in the Common Ingroup Identity Model, across all three studies (1) conditions of intergroup contact that were perceived as more favorable predicted lower levels of intergroup bias, (2) more favorable conditions of contact predicted more inclusive (one group) and less exclusive (different groups) representations; and (3) more inclusive representations mediated lower levels of intergroup bias and conflict (see Gaertner, Dovidio, Nier, Ward, and Banker, 1999). Recently, a longitudinal study of stepfamilies found evidence supportive of the direction of causality between the constructs proposed by our model across time (Banker, 2002). Thus, across a variety of intergroup settings and methodological approaches we have found reasonably strong and consistent support for the Common Ingroup Identity Model.

2.3. Reducing Racial Biases: Experimental Evidence

We have applied the general principles of the Common Ingroup Identity to reducing racial biases in laboratory and field settings. Two studies reported by Nier, Gaertner, Dovidio, Banker, and Ward (2001) illustrate the effectiveness of this approach for addressing Whites biases toward Blacks specifically. Another study (Houlette et al., 2004) explored a range of biases, including racial bias, among elementary school children.

In one study (Nier et al., Study 1), a laboratory experiment, White college students participated in a session with a Black or White confederate. These students were induced to perceive of themselves as separate individuals participating in the study at the same time or as members of the same laboratory team. The participants evaluated their Black partners significantly more favorably when they were teammates than when they were just individuals without common group connections. In contrast, the evaluations of the White partner were virtually equivalent in the team and individual conditions. Thus, inducing a common ingroup identity was particularly effective at producing positive responses toward Blacks.

The second study (Nier et al., Study 2), was a field experiment conducted at the University of Delaware football stadium prior to a game between the University of Delaware and Westchester State University. Black and White students approached fans from both universities just before the fans entered the stadium. These fans were asked if they would be willing to be interviewed about their food preferences. Our student interviewers wore either a University of Delaware or Westchester State University hat. By selecting White fans wearing clothing that identified their university affiliation, we systematically varied whether fans and our interviewers had a common or different university identities in a context in which we expected university identities to be particularly salient. We predicted that making a common identity salient would increase compliance with the interviewer's request, particularly when the interviewer was Black.

Supportive of predictions from the Common Ingroup Identity Model, White fans were significantly more cooperative with a Black interviewer when they shared a superordinate university identity than when they did not (60% versus 38%). For White interviewers, with whom they already shared racial group membership, the effect was much less pronounced (43% versus 40%). Thus, in field and laboratory settings, racial outgroup members were accorded especially positive reactions when they shared common ingroup identity with White participants relative to when the context did not emphasize their common group membership. These studies suggest the value of combating aversive racism at its roots, by strategically controlling the forces of ingroup favoritism that can produce the subtle racial biases associated with aversive racism (see Gaertner et al., 1997).

In a recent study (Houlette et al., 2003), we attempted to extended these principles and findings to a study of a range of biases (based on weight and sex, as well as race and ethnicity) with young children. Several years ago, we became aware of the Green Circle elementary school-based intervention program, which is now run by the National Conference of Community and Justice of Northern Delaware, that is practically and theoretically compatible with the Common Ingroup Identity Model. The guiding assumption of Green Circle is that helping children brings people from different groups conceptually into their own circle of caring and sharing fosters appreciation of their common humanity as well as respect for their differences.

In the program, a Green Circle facilitator, who visits each class for about 40 minutes per session four times over a 4-week period, shows children a small green circle on a felt board and told, "Whenever you see the green circle, you should think about your world of people; the people who you care about and the people who care about you." A stick figure is added to the circle and the students are told that the figure represents themselves. The facilitator explains that each person has "a big job of deciding who is going to be in your circle, how to treat people, and how big your circle will grow," and engages children in a variety of exercises designed to expand the circle. The facilitator points out that, "All of us belong to one family—the human family." Paralleling the Common Ingroup Identity Model, Green Circle assumes that an appreciation of common humanity will increase children's positive attitudes toward people who would otherwise remain outside of their circle of inclusion. This collaboration with the Green Circle staff provided an applied opportunity to test the general principles of the Common Ingroup Identity model and also offered the Green Circle program an evaluation of their intervention's effectiveness.

On the basis of the goals of the Green Circle program and the principles of the Common Ingroup Identity Model, we expected that children receiving the program would be more inclusive of others who are different than themselves in playing and sharing following the implementation of the program relative to pre-test levels and also relative to children in a control condition who did not yet receive the program. To evaluate attitudes toward children similar and different in sex, race, and weight, children were asked about their willingness to share with and play with (by selecting "feeling faces" ranging from frowns to smiles) each of eight different children depicted in specially commissioned, professional color-pencil drawings. These eight drawings systematically varied whether the child depicted was a boy or girl, Black or White, and average-weight or very much overweight. Each drawing was numbered and the participants were also asked to indicate with which child pictured would they *most* like to play.

Overall, our results revealed that first- and second-grade children in fairly well-integrated classrooms still have a general preference for playing and sharing with children who are racially the same as themselves over children who are racially different. We note, however, that children's racial preferences were not as large as their biases favoring same-sex and average-weight children. Nevertheless, the operation of categorical thinking coupled with significant racial preferences among first- and second-grade students forms a basis for even more crystallized racial biases to develop during adolescence and beyond into adulthood in the absence of intervention.

In terms of outcomes, although the Green Circle intervention did not influence children's sharing and feelings about playing with children of a different sex and race generally (using the "feeling faces" measure), it did lead them to be more inclusive in their *most preferred playmate*. Specifically, compared to children in the control condition who did not participate in Green Circle activities, those who were part of Green Circle showed significantly greater change in willingness to select other children who were different than themselves in race and in sex as a child that they "would most want to play with." These changes in the most preferred playmate involve a child's greater willingness to cross-group boundaries in making friends—a factor that is one of the most potent influences in producing more positive attitudes toward the outgroup as a whole (Pettigrew, 1998a). In addition, these intergroup friendships can have cascading effects by reducing bias among peers. Making people aware that their friends have friends from another group also reduces prejudice toward the group as a whole (Wright, Aron, McLaughlin-Volpe, and Ropp, 1997). Therefore, if Green Circle can change the cross-racial friendship patterns among just a few children, this could have escalating, positive consequences through both direct contact and through this extended contact effect.

Conceptually, the Green Circle findings illustrate how interpersonal and intergroup routes toward reducing intergroup biases can involve complementary processes that reciprocally facilitate one another. That is, changes in intergroup boundaries can facilitate the occurrence of positive interpersonal behaviors across group lines such as self-disclosure and helping in college students (Dovidio et al., 1997), and, as the Green Circle study illustrates, preferred playmates in children.

The experiments that we have reviewed in this section show that creating a common group identity can combat a range of overt expressions of racial bias. In the next section, we consider how creating a common ingroup identity can influence the basic motivational orientations and cognitive processes that form the basis for racial biases.

2.4. A Common Ingroup Identity and the Motivational Orientation of Aversive Racists

Within the aversive racism framework, we propose that the negative feelings, beliefs, and behaviors will often be expressed subtly and indirectly—in ways that are not readily attributable (by others or themselves) to racial bias and thus do not threaten an aversive racist's nonprejudiced self-image. From this perspective, a major motive of Whites in interracial situations is to *avoid wrong-doing*. Supportive of this view, we have found across a variety of different studies that Whites typically do not discriminate against Blacks in situations in which norms for appropriate behaviors are clearly defined. Thus, Whites can, at least under some circumstances, successfully suppress negative beliefs, feelings, and behavior toward Blacks when it is obvious that expressing such reactions reflects racial bias. That some people are motivated to avoid thinking, feeling, or behaving in a prejudicial way is a positive quality that can limit or lessen social conflict. Nonetheless, aversive racism may still have negative consequences given its unintentional and subtle nature.

Unfortunately, the motivation to avoid or suppress wrong-doing has two important potential costs for interracial interactions. First, this concern about avoiding wrong-doing may increase anxiety that can, in turn, motivate avoidance or premature withdrawal from the interaction. This avoidant reaction precludes the opportunity for meaningful, self-revealing exchanges between ingroup and outgroup members. Also, in view of recent work on stereotype suppression and rebound (e.g., Bodenhausen and Macrae, 1996), it is possible that once this self-imposed suppression is relaxed, negative beliefs, feelings, and behaviors would be even *more likely* to occur than if they were not suppressed initially.

In the search for strategies that could eliminate the indirect, rationalizable ways that aversive racists discriminate, we considered the importance of establishing positive interpersonal and intergroup motivations rather than simply suppressing negative motivations. The Common Ingroup Identity Model, because it focuses on redirecting the forces of ingroup favoritism, offers such promise. Specifically, the recognition of a common ingroup identity potentially changes the motivational orientation or intentions of aversive racists from trying to avoid wrong-doing to trying to *do what's right.*

Although this change is subtle, it can have fundamental benefits. For instance, it may relieve intergroup anxiety (see Stephan and Stephan, 1985) and reduce the likelihood of negative consequences of effortful attempts to avoid wrong-doing, such as the increased accessibility of negative thoughts, feelings, and behavior that occur when suppression is relaxed (Monteith, Sherman, and Devine, 1998; Wegner, 1994). Some preliminary evidence from our laboratory suggests the potential promise of a common ingroup identity to alter motivation in just such a positive way (Dovidio, Gaertner, and Kawakami, 1998; Gaertner and Dovidio, 2000).

In this experiment, White participants who were about to interact with a White or a Black confederate were either asked to try to avoid wrong-doing, instructed to try to behave correctly toward the other person, informed that they were part of the same team with their partner and competing against a team at a rival institution, or were given no instructions. The dependent measure of interest was the relative accessibility of negative thoughts, as assessed by changes in responses on a Stroop color-naming task after the interaction relative to responses on a baseline Stroop task administered before the interaction (see Lane and Wegner, 1995). A rebound effect would be reflected in greater accessibility (operationalized in terms of longer color-naming latencies) of negative relative to positive words on the post-test Stroop task.

We hypothesized that, because the primary motivation of aversive racists in interracial interaction is to avoid wrong-doing and thus to suppress negative thoughts and feelings, participants explicitly instructed to avoid wrong-doing and those given no instructions would show relatively strong accessibility of negative thoughts after interacting with a Black confederate. In contrast, we expected participants instructed to behave correctly and those in the "same team" condition (who were hypothesized to adopt a positive orientation on their own) would escape such a rebound effect.

The results, while preliminary, are very encouraging. When the confederate was White, the experimental conditions did not differ significantly in the accessibility of negative thoughts from one another or from baseline. When the confederate was

Black, however, the increased accessibility of negative relative to positive characteristics (from the pre-test to the post-test) in the avoid wrong-doing and no instructions conditions was significantly greater than in the do right and same team conditions, in which there was an increase in the accessibility of positive relative to negative thoughts. The pattern of these findings suggests that the development of a common ingroup identity can alter motivation in interracial situations from one of suppressing negative thoughts, feelings, and actions to one that is positive, more appetitive and prosocial—and in a way that does not ironically result in further increases in negative thoughts. These findings are particularly encouraging to us because they illustrate the effectiveness of the Common Ingroup Identity Model for addressing individual-level biases and particularly the underlying dynamics of aversive racism.

3. SUMMARY AND IMPLICATIONS

In this chapter, we have described the concept of aversive racism, considered the factors contributing to aversive racism, demonstrated empirically how it affects outcomes for Blacks, and explored how it can be combated. Despite apparent consistent improvements in expressed racial attitudes over time, aversive racism continues to exert a subtle but pervasive influence on the lives of Black Americans. This bias is expressed in indirect and rationalizable ways that restrict opportunities for Blacks while insulating aversive racists from ever having to confront their prejudices. It is an elusive phenomenon, and the situation plays a critical moderating role. When an interracial situation is one in which an action could be readily attributed to racial bias, aversive racists carefully monitor their interracial behaviors and *intentionally* do not discriminate. In fact, they may respond even more favorably to Blacks than to Whites as a way of affirming their nonprejudiced self-images. When the situation is ambiguous, when norms for appropriate behavior are not clear, when the circumstances permit a justification for negative behavior on the basis of some factor other than race, or when aversive racists are not conscious of their actions, however, their bias is expressed, often subtlety and *unintentionally*. Nevertheless, the fact that the motivation for aversive racists' biases may be unconscious and their discrimination may be unintentional and subtle should not exonerate them from responsibility for their actions.

The challenge of addressing aversive racism resides in its elusiveness. Because aversive racists are unaware of their unconscious negative attitudes and truly embrace their egalitarian self-image, they are motivated to deny the existence of these feelings and not to recognize or take responsibility for the adverse impact of their behavior on Blacks. Moreover, the subtle processes underlying discrimination motivated by aversive racism can be identified and isolated under the controlled conditions of the laboratory. However, at the societal and organizational levels, at which the controlled conditions of an experiment are rarely possible and multiple factors may shape decision-making simultaneously, these processes associated with aversive racism present a substantial challenge to the equitable treatment of members of disadvantaged groups. For example, Krieger (1995), in the *Stanford Law Review,* observed: "Herein lies the practical problem .... Validating subjective decision-making systems is neither empirically nor economically feasible, especially for jobs where intangible qualities, such as interpersonal skills, creativity, and ability to make sound judgments under conditions of uncertainty are critical" (p. 1232). Thus, the operation of aversive racism may go largely unnoticed and unaddressed in naturalistic settings.

In addition, to the extent that discrimination reflects ingroup favoritism (see also Gaertner et al., 1997), it is particularly difficult to address legally. Krieger (1998) adds, "Title VII is poorly equipped to control prejudice resulting from ingroup favoritism.... Ingroup favoritism manifests itself gradually in subtle ways. It is unlikely to trigger mobilization of civil rights remedies because instances of this form of discrimination tend to go unnoticed. If they are noticed, they will frequently seem genuinely trivial or be economically unfeasible to pursue.... For this reason as for others, we cannot expect existing equal opportunity tools adequately to prevent, identify, or redress this more modern form of discrimination" (pp. 1325–1326). As we have proposed, new techniques are needed to address contemporary forms of racism.

Developing interventions that not only control the expressions of aversive racism but also address the negative components of aversive racism has critical social implications. Aversive racism represents a latent form of bias whose expression is strongly moderated by social circumstances and norms. A change in conditions or norms can allow this bias operate more directly and openly. For instance, research on interracial aggression has demonstrated that under normal circumstances Whites are not more aggressive and harmful toward Blacks than toward Whites. Overt and unprovoked aggression toward Blacks would readily be perceived as racist behavior. However, when Whites are first antagonized by another person's aggressiveness, when they feel freed from prevailing norms through conditions that make them feel anonymous and deindividuated, or when norms change from censuring to supporting aggression, Whites exhibit more aggressiveness toward Blacks than toward Whites (Donnerstein and Donnerstein, 1973; Donnerstein, Donnerstein, Simon, and Ditrichs, 1972; Kawakami, Spears, and Dovidio, 2002; Rogers and Prentice-Dunn, 1981). Thus, if left unaddressed, aversive racism provides the seed for bias to emerge when conditions allow or encourage a more open expression of discrimination. We believe that addressing aversive racism at its roots is essential for moving toward a truly egalitarian society. Simply controlling the negative expressions of aversive racism today cannot, by itself, guarantee racial harmony or equality tomorrow.

CHAPTER 20

Applying Social Research on Stereotyping and Cognitive Bias to Employment Discrimination Litigation: The Case of Allegations of Systematic Gender Bias at Wal-Mart Stores

William T. Bielby

ABSTRACT

This chapter is an edited version of the expert report I submitted in 2003 on behalf of plaintiffs who were seeking class action status in a gender discrimination lawsuit against Wal-Mart Stores, Inc. To do the report, I was given access to thousands of pages of company documents relating to personnel policy and practices, extensive testimony from Wal-Mart managers and top executives, and statistical data on gender disparities compensation and promotion. Relying on social science research on stereotyping and cognitive bias, I explain how subjective and discretionary features of the Wal-Mart personnel system created systematic barriers to the career advancement of women.

1. QUALIFICATIONS, ASSIGNMENT, AND MATERIALS REVIEWED

I have been retained by Brad Seligman and Jocelyn Larkin of the Impact Fund and by the law firm of Cohen, Milstein, Hausfeld, and Toll, counsel for plaintiffs in *Betty Dukes et al. v. Wal-Mart Stores, Inc.* ("Wal-Mart"). I have been asked to review materials pertaining to personnel policies and practices of Wal-Mart and to address three issues. The first is whether key elements of the personnel system at Wal-Mart are uniform across the U.S. retail divisions. Second, I have been asked to determine whether uniform features of the Wal-Mart personnel system create barriers to women's career advancement in the company, especially with respect to promotion into management and compensation. The third issue I have been asked to address is the adequacy of Wal-Mart's policies and practices in the areas of affirmative action, equal employment opportunity (EEO), and diversity for identifying, monitoring, and eliminating potential discriminatory barriers faced by women employed by the company.

I have testified as an expert witness in both California Superior Court and Federal Court on cases involving workplace discrimination. I have served as an expert in several other cases involving issues of gender discrimination in large, multi-establishment

L. B. Nielsen and R. L. Nelson (eds.), Handbook of Employment Discrimination Research, 395–408.

national and regional retail firms, including class action cases involving Lucky Stores, Publix, Sherwin-Williams, and Home Depot.

I have reviewed the deposition testimony of Wal-Mart managers responsible for creating and implementing the company's personnel policies, as well as the testimony of managers who made decisions about compensation, hiring, promotion, job assignment, and related personnel matters. I have also reviewed the documents used as exhibits in the depositions of these individuals.

The documents I reviewed included organizational charts; correspondence, memos, reports, and presentations relating to personnel policy and practice, diversity, and EEO issues; and documents describing the culture and history of the company. In addition to documents that are deposition exhibits, I was also provided with the expert report of Dr. Marc Bendick and tables from the report of Dr. Richard Drogin.

In addition to the materials described earlier, I have also relied upon a large body of social research on organizational policy and practice and on workplace bias. Social research conducted across many decades has generated considerable knowledge about what generates and sustains workplace inequalities. The same research, either directly or by implication, points to the kinds of workplace policies and practices that are likely to minimize bias. The relevant research has applied multiple methodologies in a variety of contexts, including experiments in controlled laboratory settings; ethnographies and case studies in "real world" organizations both large and small, public and private, and in a range of industries; surveys done with representative samples of workers and employers; and historical studies based on archival materials from the United States and abroad. Thus, the scientific evidence about gender bias, stereotypes, and the structure and dynamics of gender inequality in organizations that I rely upon has substantial external validity and provides a sound basis for analyzing the policies and practices of Wal-Mart. My method is to look at distinctive features of the firm's policies and practices and to evaluate them against what social science research shows to be factors that create and sustain bias and those that minimize bias. In litigation contexts, this method of analysis is known as "social framework analysis."[1] In what follows, I describe the firm-wide policies and practices at Wal-Mart that create and sustain barriers to women's career success and the effectiveness of the firm's efforts to identify and eliminate those barriers and guarantee EEO.

2. PATTERNS OF GENDER SEGREGATION AT WAL-MART

At Wal-Mart in 2001, women outnumbered men by nearly two to one in the hourly ranks (65.2% female for Wal-Mart and Sam's combined) and men outnumbered women by almost two to one in salaried management positions (33.2% female). At Wal-Mart Stores (Wal-Mart/Supercenter/Neighborhood Markets) in 2001, women's representation among hourly supervisors (78.5% of Team Leaders) exceeded their representation

[1] See Monahan and Walker (1998).

among hourly salespersons (64.4% of Sales Associates). Sales Associate is the largest job classification in the company, employing over 200,000 individuals, and there is substantial segregation within that job category. For example, in 2001, women comprised over 90% of those employed as Sales Associates in men's wear, infant/toddlers, health and beauty aids, domestic goods, and ladies sportswear, and <25% of those employed as Sales Associates in hardware and in Supercenter food departments such as dairy products, meat, frozen food, and produce. Few men work in the front-end position of Cashier (the second largest job category, with over 150,000 employees), which was 89.5% female in 2001. Not every department is sex segregated; for example, the gender mix is relatively balanced among Sales Associates in automotive (43.6% female), electronics (47.2% female), and candy, tobacco, and cookies (55.4% female).

In store-level supervisory and salaried management positions, women's representation drops with each step up the job hierarchy. Although women outnumber men by nearly four to one among hourly supervisors, in 2001 they comprised only 45.1% of the Support Managers, the highest-level hourly supervisory position. Moving into salaried management, in 2001 they comprised only 37.6% of Assistant Managers, 21.9% of Co-Managers, and 15.5% of Store Managers. A similar pattern holds at Sam's Club, but at a somewhat lower level of segregation.

3. SUBJECTIVE AND DISCRETIONARY FEATURES OF THE WAL-MART PERSONNEL SYSTEM CONTRIBUTE TO GENDER BARRIERS IN PROMOTION AND COMPENSATION

3.1. Factors That Create and Minimize Workplace Gender Bias: Findings from Social Science Research

In this section of my report, I summarize the scientific literature upon which my opinions are based. In footnotes, I provide citations to sources in peer refereed journals, in important books and edited volumes in relevant fields of social science research, and, whenever possible, to review articles by leading experts who summarize the findings of social science research on gender bias in organizations, stereotypes, and related topics.

3.1.1. Sources of Workplace Gender Bias

Depending on the job, organizational setting, and work environment, there are many reasons why men and women can have different career trajectories. For example, jobs may have job-related skill and experience requirements that differ, on average, between men and women. Gender disparities arising from such factors would not be considered discriminatory, so long as the employer is not responsible for differences in men's and women's qualifications (e.g., by not providing equal access to training). Conversely, employers create gender barriers when they make decisions about individuals' suitability for jobs, training, and support or their compensation based on beliefs about a person's gender rather than on his or her actual qualifications. Employers also create gender barriers when they ignore (or encourage) an organizational climate that is hostile toward women and inhibits them from performing to their full potential. Sometimes, practices that appear to be gender-neutral have the effect of denying to women the same opportunities that are available to men. For example, using employee referrals as a recruitment mechanism is likely to reinforce a workforce's existing gender composition.[2]

One way that gender bias affects career outcomes is when stereotypes are allowed to affect personnel decisions. *Gender stereotypes* are beliefs about traits and behaviors that differ between men and women.[3] For example, men are believed to be competitive, aggressive, assertive, strong, and independent, whereas women are thought to be nurturing, cooperative, supportive, and understanding. Men are assumed to place a high priority on their careers, whereas women are assumed to be more strongly oriented toward family, even though research demonstrates that the commitments of men and women with similar job opportunities and family situations are virtually identical.[4]

These kinds of stereotypes are relevant to how men and women advance in careers with Wal-Mart. For example, if women are believed to be committed to and constrained by family circumstances, and men are not, women will not be given the same consideration as men for management positions that are believed to interfere with family obligations, especially if there is no reliable and systematic way to assess employees' interests in management positions.

When women perform successfully in male-dominated contexts, their accomplishments are more likely to be attributed to luck, help from others, or special circumstances rather than to their ability, whereas comparable performance by men is more likely to be attributed to their superior skills.[5] Moreover, stereotypical behaviors that are believed to be typical of men are often viewed as *inappropriate* for women. For example, it is less acceptable for a married woman with young children to place a high priority on her career than it is for a married man. Similarly, a woman who behaves in a competitive, assertive, and independent manner often elicits disapproval from those around her.[6]

Because of gender stereotypes, individuals tend to ascribe "masculine" traits to men and "feminine" traits to women, and individuals tend to assume that the prevalence of "masculine" traits among women and "feminine" traits among men is rare. A large body of research demonstrates that the tendency to invoke gender stereotypes in making judgments about people is spontaneous and automatic.[7] As a result, people are often unaware of how stereotypes affect their perceptions and behavior, and

[2] For a review of relevant research, see Marsden and Gorman (2001).

[3] Fiske (1998).

[4] For a review, see Bielby (1992) and Marsden, Kalleberg, and Cook (1993).

[5] For a review of relevant research, see Swim and Sanna (1996).

[6] Eagly and Karau (2002).

[7] See, for example, Banaji and Hardin (1996). For a review, see Bargh and Chartrand (1999).

individuals whose personal beliefs are relatively free of prejudice or bias are susceptible to stereotypes in the same ways as people who hold a personal animosity toward a social group.[8]

In the employment context, career barriers resulting from gender stereotypes and gender bias are likely to be consequential for women working in a traditionally male domains, such as the middle to upper managerial and professional ranks of large corporations, engineering divisions of firms, in the military, and in historically male-dominated industries such as skilled crafts and construction trades.[9] At Wal-Mart, women comprise a majority of employees overall and about two-thirds of those in hourly positions, but they comprise only about one-third of those in salaried management positions, and most higher level management positions have a low representation of women.

A large body of social science research demonstrates that stereotypes are especially likely to influence personnel decisions when they are based on informal, arbitrary, and subjective factors.[10] In such settings, stereotypes can bias assessments of a woman's qualifications, contributions, and advancement potential, because perceptions are shaped by stereotypical beliefs about women generally but not by the actual skills and accomplishments of the person as an individual.[11] In decision-making contexts characterized by arbitrary and subjective criteria and substantial decision-maker discretion, individuals tend to seek out and retain stereotyping-confirming information and ignore or minimize information that defies stereotypes.[12]

Social research establishes clearly that the historical representation of women in a job has a substantial impact on compensation and other job rewards, mobility prospects, and workplace culture.[13] In retailing, management has historically been viewed as "men's work," whereas women were viewed as appropriate for cashier and clerk positions. Wal-Mart's founder, Sam Walton, described the traditional view of men's and women's roles in the industry as follows:

> In the old days, retailers felt the same way about women that they did about college boys, only more so. In addition to thinking women weren't free to move, they didn't think women could handle anything but the clerk jobs because the managers usually did so much of the physical labor—unloading trucks and hauling merchandise out of the stockroom on a two-wheeler, mopping the floors and cleaning the windows if necessary.[14]

[8] Fiske (1998), Bodenhausen, Macrae, and Garst (1998).

[9] Bielby and Baron (1986), Deaux and Ullman (1983), Kanter (1977), Glick, Zion, and Nelson (1988).

[10] For a review, see American Psychological Association (1991). Also see Nieva and Gutek (1980), Krieger (1995), and Bielby (2000).

[11] For review articles on gender bias in evaluation, see Nieva and Gutek (1980) and Kalin and Hodgins (1984).

[12] This kind of biased information-processing has been examined and replicated in numerous experimental studies. See, for example, Banaji, Hardin, and Rothman (1993) and Hodgins (1995).

[13] England (1992), Reskin, McBrier, and Kmec (1999).

[14] Walton and Huey (1992). Mr. Walton continued: "Nowadays, the industry has waked up to the fact that women make great retailers. So, we at Wal-Mart, along with everybody else, have to do everything

Experimental studies on stereotyping show that male and female job applicants with identical personal traits are matched according to their gender to jobs that are considered predominantly male and predominantly female.[15] In addition, studies done in both experimental and natural settings demonstrate the impact of "sex role spillover," whereby gender-linked traits associated with male-dominated occupations can profoundly affect the working climate for women.[16]

A large body of research in industrial sociology, dating back to the 1950s, shows that individuals who find their opportunities for advancement blocked response by lowering their goals and aspirations and by lowering their commitment to their work compared to others with more promising career prospects.[17]

3.2. Discretionary and Subjective Procedures for Making Decisions That Affect Promotion and Compensation

3.2.1. Managers Have Substantial Discretion on Criteria Used to Make Promotion and Compensation Decisions

Written guidelines for promotion are not absent in the Wal-Mart Personnel System. However, the materials I have reviewed indicate that: (1) written guidelines provide only minimum criteria for advancement, and managers can and do add additional criteria at their own discretion; (2) managers are able to modify or disregard written guidelines at their own discretion; and (3) there is little monitoring or oversight regarding how managers exercise their discretion in making promotion decisions.

Deponents ranging from Store Managers to top operation executives testified that there are no written criteria for selecting hourly associates for promotion into management or for promotions into Co-Manager or Store Manager positions, beyond the minimum requirements. They also testified that managers who make those selections have discretion to devise their own criteria, with no monitoring or oversight over how those criteria are devised or applied.

Wal-Mart managers gave similar testimony about promotion to hourly supervisory positions such as Support Manager. Company guidelines specify minimum criteria based on discipline, tenure, and performance evaluations; however, there is no other written policy or guideline specifying the criteria to be used to select among candidates who meet the minimum criteria. Store Managers are allowed to consider other factors and apply other criteria, and it is left to their discretion to devise and apply them. For example, Store Manager Arturo Mireles testified that he was aware of no written criteria to be used in making decisions about promotion to Department Manager or Support Manager. His practice was to rely on a range of unwritten criteria, including

we possibly can to recruit and attract women." As I show below, one of the innovations supported by Mr. Walton to recruit women into management, the Resident Assistant Manager program, has been largely ignored in the years since his death.

[15] Glick et al. (1988).

[16] Gutek and Morasch (1982), Gutek (1985), Burgess and Borgida (1997).

[17] Markham, Harlan, and Hackett (1987), Bielby (1992).

subjective factors such as teamwork, ethics, integrity, ability to get along with others, and willingness to volunteer to come in to assist in the store or at another store outside of regular work hours. While factors like these might have common sense appeal and some might, in fact, be appropriate to consider in making promotion decisions, assessments will be biased unless they are assessed in a systematic and valid manner, with clear criteria and careful attention to the integrity of the decision-making process.[18]

The same kind of discretion is allowed in decisions about compensation for hourly employees. For example, in Division 1, each job is categorized into one of five job classifications, each with its own hourly starting rate. However, according to company policy, the Store Manager can pay up to two dollars per hour above the stated rate, based on his or her assessment of factors such as previous pay and experience. There is no company guideline and no training on when and how to adjust pay upwards, and while overall payroll is monitored, there is no monitoring of these individual adjustments. In fact, at the Store Manager's discretion, a new employee can be paid more than two dollars above the specified start rate, and in such instances, no exception report is generated.

Annual pay increases in Division 1 are tied to performance evaluation ratings, with a percentage increase guideline specified by the Home Office. A Store Manager can give a raise larger than the specified amount at his or her own discretion. In addition, employees can be given merit increases for "exceptional performance." The company guideline is that a merit increase of 4% or 5% can be given no more than once per year, and it cannot be granted within 90 days of an annual performance increase or raise due to a promotion. However, there is no guideline for assessing "exceptional performance" and no monitoring of the number of people who receive increases and how frequently they are given to any specific employee. Managers can and do give merit raises more than once per year.

3.2.2. Availability and Interest in Advancement Are Not Assessed Systematically for Promotion Into Management

Consistent and systematic job posting is an effective way to determine who is interested in and available for promotion to higher-level positions. An effective system also communicates clear and accurate information to employees about the training and experience required to become eligible for a job, about job conditions, and about how the job fits into a career path in the organization.[19] Wal-Mart People Division Vice President Harper agreed that the company benefits from posting, by allowing people to show interest in a position. He added: "I think anytime you get the right candidate into the right job, the success of that person would certainly reflect in the performance of their area of responsibility." He agreed that posting benefits employees by giving them "an opportunity for promotion or an opportunity for diversifying their career

[18] Gatewood and Field (1994), Heneman, Heneman, and Judge (1997).

[19] Heneman et al. (1997), Kleiman and Clark (1984), Levine (1994), Markham et al. (1987), Rudin and Boudreau (1996).

by being able to work in different parts of the store." Coleman Peterson, the Executive Vice President of the company's People Division, gave similar testimony: "Job posting ensures the company that it is able to attract and identify as many talented people as possible for jobs that are needed and for the individuals, it provides an opportunity to apply for positions in the company that can allow them to move forward in their careers." Mr. Peterson, who has been an advocate for the adoption of posting policies at the company, has also testified about their impact on workplace fairness. He testified that posting reduces litigation expenses because it affects "the fairness of how people get picked for jobs." According to Mr. Coleman: "People understand where the jobs are and they understand what it is you need to do to qualify for the jobs." The testimony of these two executives from the company's People Division is consistent with the professional literature on human resource policy. Unfortunately, Wal-Mart's posting systems do not meet the criteria of effective and fair policy and practice. Wal-Mart has separate posting systems for hourly and management positions, and each has identifiable deficiencies that make them vulnerable to bias.

Current company policy specifies that openings for hourly supervisory positions are to be posted within the store where the opening occurs. Online, computerized posting began in the late1990s; prior to that, there was paper posting of some positions. However, under current policy, Store Managers have the authority to choose not to post a position. There are no written guidelines regarding when to depart from the posting policy, and there is no monitoring or review of exceptions to posting of hourly positions. Store Managers also have authority to waive minimum requirements regarding time in current position and coachings, and there are no guidelines specifying when this is appropriate. In addition, there is no requirement to post openings that are filled by lateral moves; so, for example, a manager can choose not to post an open supervisory position and instead informally approach an existing supervisor and ask that person if he or she would like the position.

Prior to 1998, management positions in Division 1 were not posted. Since then, posting of Store Manager, District Manager, and some other positions has been done via the computerized Management Career Selection ("MCS") system, although an employee needs the approval of his or her District Manager before applying via the MCS system. Co-Manager, Assistant Store Manager, and Management Trainee positions are generally not posted. As with hourly promotions, the Regional Personnel Managers (RPMs) have discretion to depart from the policy on posting management positions, although there is no written policy on when it is appropriate. An exception report shows whether or not a position was posted and how long it took to fill a position, but no record is made of reasons for exceptions to the posting policy, and no statistical summary is complied regarding exceptions to the posting policy. At Sam's Club, management positions are not posted, and on-line posting of management trainee positions began just recently, in early January of 2003.

The company's practice of requiring relocation across stores in order to move into salaried management positions makes the promotion process especially vulnerable to gender stereotyping. While it may indeed be the case that, on average, more women than men face family constraints that limit their ability to relocate for a management position, stereotypes lead people to act on assumptions that overstate the extent to which that is true. The absence of a systematic mechanism for determining which employees are available for and interested in promotion from the hourly ranks into management is especially problematic in this context. In the absence of systematic, reliable, and timely information on the interests and availability of individual men and women, stereotypes about women's and men's family commitments and constraints will lead decision-makers to overlook or discount the availability of qualified women who want to advance into the salaried ranks. Similarly, District Managers who must give their approval before a salaried employee responds to a posting under the MCS system are likely to be influenced by stereotypes in the same way.

Lack of clarity in the relocation requirements associated with promotion to salaried management positions is likely to discourage some women from seeking promotions. Managers consistently testify that hourly employees usually move to a different store when they become management trainees and are promoted to Assistant Store Manager positions, and promotion to Co-Manager and Store Manager almost always involves relocation as well. Less consistent is testimony about whether an employee must be able and willing to relocate their place of residence in order to be considered for a management position. For example, some managers insist that geographic relocation is necessary to advance into salaried management, whereas other managers testify that ability and willingness to relocate one's place of residence are not absolute requirements for promotion, although moving from one store to another usually is required. It is likely that hourly department heads considering a career in salaried management or Assistant Managers considering higher-level salaried positions may well be receiving mixed messages about whether they are required to indicate a willingness to relocate to any area of Wal-Mart's operations in order to be given serious consideration for a promotion. An individual who is not able to make that commitment is likely to be discouraged by the apparent emphasis on relocation, even when a move to a new store within a district or region would be possible.

Wal-Mart's founder, Sam Walton, recognized that the emphasis on relocation could work to the disadvantage of talented women who are qualified for management positions and that the business case for the emphasis on relocation might be overstated. In his autobiography, he discussed the original management philosophy, which one had to be ready to relocate on a moment's notice to move into management, and his views of the shortcomings of that approach:

> Maybe that was necessary back in the old days, and maybe it was more rigid than it needed to be. Now, though, it's not really appropriate anymore for several reasons. First, as the company grows bigger, we need to find more ways to stay in touch with the communities where we operate, and one of the best ways to do that is by hiring locally, developing managers locally, and letting them have a career in their home community—if they perform. Second, the old way really put good, smart women at a disadvantage in our company because at the time they weren't as free to pick up and move as many men were. Now I've seen the light on the opportunities we missed out on with women.

To open more opportunities for women in management, Mr. Walton was a strong supporter of the Resident Assistant Manager program. In the late 1980s, Wal-Mart implemented and later formalized a policy creating the position of Resident Assistant Manager for individuals who were eligible to be Assistant Managers but not able to relocate. Resident Assistant Managers were eligible to move into a Co-Manager position without relocating. According to Executive Vice President of Operations Jim Haworth, the program was phased out, although some Assistant Managers have been "grandfathered" into the program, and it is being "tested" in some areas currently. This program, originally implemented in part to create more management opportunities for women, appears to have little effect anymore as a route to management for employees who have personal or family commitments that tie them to a specific community geographic region.

4. WAL-MART'S DIVERSITY EFFORTS ARE INADEQUATE FOR ELIMINATING BARRIERS TO WOMEN'S CAREER ADVANCEMENT

Organizational policies and practices that create barriers to career advancement for women and minorities, once in place, become institutionalized and rarely change in the absence of any substantial change in a firm's business, technical, or legal environment.[20] This is especially true of personnel practices and policies that are reinforced by the firm's culture.[21] However, gender bias in the workplace is by no means inevitable, and social science research shows what kinds of policies and practices effectively minimize bias.

Through deliberate efforts, the effects of stereotypes can be controlled.[22] Research studies show that the effects of stereotypes and outgroup bias on evaluative judgments such as those involved in recruitment, hiring, job assignment, promotion, and assessments of skills and qualifications can be minimized when decision-makers know that they will be held accountable for the criteria used to make decisions, for the accuracy of the information upon which the decisions are based and for the consequences their actions have for EEO.[23] However, as I described earlier, at Wal-Mart, personnel decisions regarding promotion and hourly compensation rely significantly on discretionary and subjective criteria, with little monitoring and oversight.

Formal written policies alone are not sufficient to minimize bias in personnel decisions. A written EEO policy that is simply reactive and lacks effective accountability is vulnerable to bias against women and minorities. Often, such a system constitutes what social scientists call symbolic compliance: an exercise in "going through the motions," with little substantive impact on creating a work environment that is free of bias.[24] True "EEO accountability" has three key elements: (1) monitoring and

[20] Stinchcombe (1965), Hannan and Freeman (1984), Baron (1991).

[21] Doeringer and Piore (1971).

[22] Devine (1989) and Fiske, Lin, and Neuberg (1999).

[23] Nelson, Acker, and Manis (1996), Eberhardt and Fiske (1996), and Konrad and Linnehan (1995).

[24] Edelman (1992) and Edelman, Patterson, Chambliss, and Erlanger (1991).

analysis of disparities in career trajectories; (2) systematic evaluation of managers on their contributions to the firms' goals regarding diversity and EEO; and (3) monitoring and analysis of employees' perceptions of discriminatory barriers and career opportunities.[25] In what follows, I assess the effectiveness of Wal-Mart's policies and practices on each of these dimensions.

4.1. Monitoring of Gender Disparities

Effective EEO policy includes the regular monitoring and analysis of patterns of segregation and differences by gender and race in pay and career advancement as a routine part of an organization's personnel system. Such monitoring is used to assess whether disparities are greater than what plausibly might be expected based on differences in job-related knowledge, skills, abilities, interests, availability, and other job-related factors that influence an employee's contributions to the organization.

Gender composition in Wal-Mart jobs is tracked in several reports. The Vice President of the People Division reviews the monthly People P & L report and a quarterly People Update reporting the gender composition of Wal-Mart's hourly workforce and salaried management. A quarterly Diversity Report Card compiles regional People P & L statistics in a single report.[26] However, statistics on gender composition are not analyzed to assess factors that could account for the disparity in women's representation among salaried management positions compared to the representation in the hourly workforce and in hourly department head positions. Managers testified consistently that they did not believe that women were less qualified than men for management positions in the company, and Wal-Mart has taken a similar position in its responses to plaintiffs' interrogatories. Yet, there have been no attempts to explain, for example, why it is that women in Division 1 represent more than three quarters of all hourly department heads but only 38% of Assistant Managers. Nor is there any regular monitoring of gender disparities in compensation among hourly or managerial employees. In addition, there have been no studies of whether women are less interested than men in management positions. In sum, Wal-Mart's policies and practices regarding EEO include no systematic assessment of disparities by gender in pay, promotion, and other career outcomes designed to identify possible discriminatory barriers and remedy them.

4.2. Evaluation of Managers on Contributions to Company EEO and Diversity Objectives

The second component of EEO accountability is explicit evaluation of managers and supervisors on their contributions to an organization's EEO objectives. Nearly all medium-to-large-scale organizations have a written anti-discrimination policy. Many have a written policy stating that implementing the objectives of the Affirmative

[25] Bielby (2000).

[26] Harper depo., pp. 273–280; Ruiz depo., p. 170.

Action Plan is the responsibility of every employee, a statement often repeated by top executives. However, such policies are merely symbolic unless they also delineate explicit duties and responsibilities relating to EEO in each manager's or supervisor's job description, which can then be related to specific evaluative dimensions in the performance reviews of those employees.

One way of evaluating managers' contributions is to establish numerical goals and assess managers on progress toward achieving those goals. At Wal-Mart, goals have been established for women's representation in management, and diversity has been added to the "people" dimension of managers' performance evaluation. However, the numerical goals themselves are not based on any assessment of women's representation among those qualified and available for salaried management positions and the rate at which women would be expected to move into those positions, absent any barriers to EEO. Instead, Wal-Mart's goals for women's representation are based on the principle that they should reflect the "community" (i.e., roughly 50%), without any regard to gender composition of the relevant applicant pools. In fact, the goals themselves are established in an ad hoc manner, without any guidelines. For example, in Division 1, since 2000, District Managers have devised their own goals, which are compiled and aggregated by RPMs into goals for each region, which are in turn compiled and aggregated by People Directors and forwarded to the People Division Vice President. District Managers, RPMs, and Regional Vice Presidents are not given any instruction on how to determine their goals other than to increase representation, and there is no written document describing the goal-setting process. Managers at the level of District Manager and higher are evaluated on progress toward those goals. A similar process has been used for setting goals at Sam's Club. Not surprisingly, Wal-Mart managers set modest goals that are slightly higher than the current representation.

In the absence of guidelines, managers who are aware that they are evaluated relative to diversity goals have an incentive to establish modest goals, and there is little incentive to work aggressively to meet them, because evidence of improvement, rather than meeting the goal, is viewed as satisfactory performance. Overall, contribution toward diversity goals is at best only weakly tied to the compensation of managers. For Store Managers and Co-Managers, performance evaluation is not a factor for either base salary or incentive pay; so, evaluation on contributions to diversity goals has no impact on their compensation. For others, diversity is one component of one dimension of the performance evaluation, and it is the overall aggregate score that is tied to managers' percentage raises. Of course, evaluation of diversity contributions has no effect at all on motivating managers' behavior if they are not aware that they are being evaluated, and there is deposition testimony suggesting that it is the case for some managers.

The materials I have reviewed show that there has been an increased emphasis on diversity issues by high-level human resources executives at Wal-Mart since the late 1990s, but that commitment has had little impact on actual personnel policy and practice, as it relates to compensation among hourly employees and promotion into field management. The company's diversity efforts have been weak in assessing and addressing vulnerabilities to bias created by discretionary and subjective aspects of the personnel system. The process for setting diversity goals and evaluating contributions to diversity objectives is not linked in any meaningful way to identifying and eliminating barriers to EEO.

Although Wal-Mart Stores Chief Executive Officer Thomas Coughlin has testified that responsibility for diversity is shared equally by all management employees, awareness of diversity goals is limited both among top operations executives and store-level managers. While operational aspects of Wal-Mart's business are run with centralized coordination and oversight, Mr. Coughlin rejects having the same kind of oversight and accountability in the area of diversity. In the absence of this kind of accountability, true integration of diversity policy into the personnel practices in the operating divisions and genuine commitment to diversity efforts by managers and executives who oversee and make decisions about pay and career advancement are unlikely to take place. In addition, other proactive efforts that have the potential to contribute to enhanced diversity in the management ranks, such as recent efforts to identify and develop highly qualified women and minority employees, are likely to have limited success.

4.3. Monitoring Employees' Perceptions of Discriminatory Barriers

The third component of EEO accountability is systematic analysis of feedback from employees about perceptions of barriers to and opportunities for career advancement. Systematic monitoring of trends in employees' perceptions of barriers to career advancement and of top management's commitment to EEO can be used to identify subtle forms of bias and related problems not immediately apparent from analyses of more objective workforce data.

Wal-Mart surveys its employees annually as part of its Grass Roots Survey program. The survey is designed to assess employees' perceptions on work-related issues. Results are tabulated by store, and the top three concerns are posted at each store. Store Managers are expected to meet with their employees to discuss those concerns and to develop specific action plans for addressing them. Responses to the survey are also used to compute an Unresolved People Index ("UPI," formerly called the Union Potential Index), which is used to identify stores at risk of union organizing activity. Stores scoring high on the index are targeted for intervention by company management and are subsequently re-surveyed to assess whether there is any improvement in employee morale following intervention.

The Grass Roots Survey, which has been conducted annually since 1994, would seem to be an efficient mechanism for assessing employees' perceptions about barriers to equal opportunity associated with gender. However, the survey has never been used to assess employees' perceptions on issues such as whether they have been treated unfairly due to gender (or race) or the firm's commitment to diversity. Nor have the results of Grass Roots Surveys ever been analyzed by gender or race in order to assess perceived discriminatory barriers. Indeed, according to the company's deponent on surveys, there have been no employee surveys of any kind addressing diversity issues or the treatment of women employees.

In sum, Wal-Mart has a range of diversity and equal opportunity policies and initiatives, many of them implemented in the past few years. Unfortunately, they have identifiable weaknesses that limit their effectiveness for identifying and eliminating discriminatory barriers. The process for setting goals is not linked to a systematic assessment of the policies and practices that influence the rate at which men and women advance through their careers at Wal-Mart. Evaluation of managers on contributions to the company's diversity and EEO objectives is too weak to have any significant effect, and the company fails to use the tools available to it to systematically assess employees' perceptions of discriminatory barriers related to gender. In contrast to the centralized coordination and control that characterizes the operations side of Wal-Mart's operations, its human resources practices regarding equal employment opportunities are too diffuse to establish meaningful oversight and accountability.

5. CONCLUSION

I have concluded that subjective and discretionary features of the company's personnel policy and practice make decisions about compensation and promotion vulnerable to gender bias. In addition, I have concluded that there are significant deficiencies in the way the company monitors its personnel policies and practices, establishes diversity goals, and evaluates managers' contributions to equal opportunity objectives. Personnel policy and practice at Wal-Mart as implemented in the field has features known to be vulnerable to gender bias. Discretionary and subjective elements of Wal-Mart's personnel system and inadequate oversight and ineffective anti-discrimination efforts contribute to disparities between men and women in their compensation and career trajectories at the company.

References

Abrahamson, E. 1996. Management fashion. *Academy of Management Review* 21(1):254–285.

Abraham, K. S. 2003. The lawlessness of arbitration. *Connecticut Insurance Law Journal* 9:355.

Abrams, D. 1985. Focus of attention in minimal intergroup discrimination. *British Journal of Social Psychology* 24:65–74.

Abrams, K. 1994. Title VII and the complex female plaintiff. *Michigan Law Review* 92:2479–2540.

Acker, J. 1990. Hierarchies, jobs, bodies: A theory of gendered organizations. *Gender and Society*. 4(2):139–158.

Adam, B. D. 1981. Stigma and employability: Discrimination by sex and sexual orientation in the Ontario legal profession. *Canadian Review of Sociology and Anthropology* 18:216–221.

Adams, J. H. 1997. Sexual harassment and black women: A historical perspective. In W. O'Donohue (Ed.), *Sexual Harassment: Theory, Research and Treatment* (pp. 213–224). Boston, MA: Allyn and Bacon.

Adorno, T. W., E. Frenkel-Brunswik, D. J. Levinson, and R. N. Sanford. 1950. *The Authoritarian Personality*. New York: Harper.

Albiston, C. 1999. The rule of law and the litigation process: The paradox of losing by winning. *Law and Society Review* 33(4):869.

Albiston, C. R. Bargaining in the shadow of social institutions: Competing discources and social change in workplace mobilization of civil rights. *Law and Society Review* 39(1):11–50.

———. 2000. Legal consciousness and the mobilization of civil rights: Negotiating family and medical leave rights in the workplace. In *Law and Society Association Annual Meeting*. Miami, FL.

———. 2001. The struggle to care: Negotiating family and medical leave in the workplace. In *Center for Working Families*, Vol. Working Paper No. 26. University of California, Berkeley.

Allegretto, S. A. and M. M. Arthur. 2001. An empirical analysis of homosexual/heterosexual male earnings differentials: Unmarried and unequal? *Industrial and Labor Relations Review* 54:631–646.

Allport, G. 1954. *The Nature of Prejudice*. New York: Anchor Doubleday.

Allport, G. 1954. *The Nature of Prejudice*. Reading, MA: Addison-Wesley.

———. 1954/1979. *The Nature of Prejudice*. New York: Doubleday Anchor.

Altemeyer, B. 1996. *The Authoritarian Specter*. Cambridge: Harvard University Press.

Altonji, J. and R. Blank. 1999. Gender and Race in the Labor Market in *Handbook of Labor Economics*, O. Ashenfelter and D. Card, eds., Vol. 3C, pp. 3143–3259. New York: Elsevier Science Press.

American Psychological Association. 1991. In the supreme court of the United States: Price Waterhouse v. Ann B. Hopkins: Amicus Curiae brief for The American Psychological Association. *American Psychologist* 46:1061–1070.

Anderson, D. J., M. Binder, and K. Krause. 2003. The motherhood wage penalty revisited: Experience, heterogeneity, work effort, and work-schedule flexibility. *Industrial and Labor Relations Review* 56(2):273–294.

AO. annual. 2002. Federal Court Cases: Integrated Data Base, 1970–2001 [Computer File]. 2nd ICPSR version. Vol. 2002: Washington, D.C.: Federal Judicial Center [producer]. Ann Arbor, MI: Interuniversity Consortium for Political and Social Research [distributor].

Arriola, E. R. 1990. What's the big deal? Women in the New York construction industry and sexual harassment law 1970–1985. *Columbia Human Rights Law Review* 22:21–71.

Ashenfelter Orley and D. Card. 1986. *Handbook of Labor Economics* (Vol. 3C). New York, NY: Elsevier Science Press.

Avellar, S. and P. J. Smock. 2003. Has the price of motherhood declined over time? A cross-cohort comparison of the motherhood wage penalty. *Journal of Marriage and Family* 65:597–607.

Ayres, I. 1991. Fair driving: Gender and race discrimination in retail car negotiations. *Harvard Law Review* 104:817–872.

———. 2001. *Pervasive Prejudice? Unconventional Evidence of Race and Gender Discrimination.* Chicago: University of Chicago Press.

Bachman, B. A. 1993. An intergroup model of organizational mergers. Unpublished PhD Dissertation, University of Delaware, Newark, DE.

Badgett, L., C. Donnelly, and J. Kibbe. 1992. *Pervasive Patterns of Discrimination Against Lesbians and Gay Men: Evidence from Surveys Across the United States*. Washington, D.C.: National Gay and Lesbian Task Force Policy Institute.

Badgett, M. V. L. 1995. The wage effects of sexual orientation discrimination. *Industrial and Labor Relations Review* 48:726–739.

———. 1996. Employment and sexual orientation: Disclosure and discrimination in the workplace. *Journal of Gay and Lesbian Social Services* 4:29–52.

———. 1997. Vulnerability in the workplace: Evidence of anti-gay discrimination. *ANGLES: Policy Journal of the Institute for Gay and Lesbian Strategic Studies* 2(1):1–4.

———. 2001. *Money, Myths, and Change: The Economic Lives of Lesbians and Gay Men*. Chicago: University of Chicago Press.

Badgett, M. V. L. and M. C. King. 1997. Lesbian and gay occupational strategies. In A. Gluckman and B. Reed (Eds.), *Homo Economics: Capitalism, Community, and Lesbian and Gay Life* (pp. 73–86). New York: Routledge.

Bails, C. T. 1994. Female reactions to sexual harassment in the workplace and the impact of race, at v. Unpublished PhD Dissertation (on file with author), Philadelphia, PA: Temple University Press.

Baldi, S. and D. B. McBrier. 1997. DO the determinants of promotion differ for blacks and whites? *Work and Occupations* 24:478–497.

Balos, B. and M. L. Fellows. 1999. A matter of prostitution: Becoming respectable. *New York University Law Review* 74:1220–1303.

Banaji, M. R. and C. D. Hardin. 1996. Automatic stereotyping. *Psychological Science* 7:136–141.

Banaji, M. R., C. Hardin, and A. J. Rothman. 1993. Implicit stereotyping in person judgment. *Journal of Personality and Social Psychology* 65:272–281.

Banker, B. S. 2002. Intergroup conflict and bias reduction in stepfamilies: A longitudinal examination of intergroup relations processes. Unpublished PhD Dissertation, University of Delaware, Newark, DE.

Banker, B. S. and S. L. Gaertner. 1998. Achieving stepfamily harmony: An intergroup-relations approach. *Journal of Family Psychology* 12:310–325.

Barak, A. 1997. Cross-cultural perspectives on sexual harassment. In W. O'Donohue (Ed.), *Sexual Harassment: Theory, Research and Treatment* (pp. 263–300). Boston, MA: Allyn and Bacon.

Bargh, J. A., M. Chen, and L. Burrows. 1996. Automaticity of social behavior: Direct effects of trait construct and stereotype activation on action. *Journal of Personality and Social Psychology* 71:230–244.

Bargh, J. A. 1999. The cognitive monster: The case against the controllability of automatic stereotype effects. In S. Chaiken and Y. Trope (Eds.), *Dual-Process Theories in Social Psychology* (pp. 361–382). New York: Guilford.

Bargh, J. A., P. Raymond, J. B. Pryor, and F. Strack. 1995. Attractiveness of the underling: An automatic power → sex association and its consequences for sexual harassment and aggression. *Journal of Personality and Social Psychology* 68:768–781.

Bargh, J. A. and T. L. Chartrand. 1999. The unbearable automaticity of being. *American Psychologist* 54:462–479.

Barnes, J. 2004. *Overruled? Pluralism, Court–Congress Relations, and Legislative Overrides in an Age of Statutes*. Stanford: Stanford University Press.

Baron, J. N. 1991. Organizational evidence of ascription in labor markets. In R. Cornwall and P. Wunnava (Eds.), *New Approaches to Economic and Social Analyses of Discrimination*. Westport, CT: Praeger.

Baron, J. N. and A. E. Newman. 1990. For what it's worth: Organizations, occupations, and the value of work done by women and non-whites. *American Sociological Review* 55:155–175.

Baron, J. N., B. S. Mittman, and A. E. Newman. 1991. Targets of opportunity: Organizational and environmental determinants of gender integration within the California civil service, 1979–1985. *American Journal of Sociology* 96:1362–1402.

Baron, J. N. and J. Pfeffer. 1994. The social psychology of organizations and inequality. *Social Psychology Quarterly* 57:190–209.

Barry, A., T. Osborne, and N. S. Rose. 1996. *Foucault and Political Reason: Liberalism, Neo-Liberalism and Rationalities of Government.* Chicago: University of Chicago Press.

Bauman, Z. 1996. Morality in the age of contingency. In S. L. Paul Heelas and Paul Morris (Eds.), *Detraditionalization: Critical Reflections on Authority and Identity* (pp. 49–58). Oxford: Blackwell.

Becker, G. 1956. *The Economics of Discrimination*. Chicago: University of Chicago Press.

———. 1971. *The Economics of Discrimination*. Chicago: University of Chicago Press.

Becker, G. S. 1991. *A Treatise on the Family*. Cambridge, MA: Harvard University Press.

Beggs, J. J., W. J. Villemez, and R. Arnold. 1997. Black population concentration and black-white inequality. *Social Forces* 76:65–91.

Beiner, T. M. 2002. Let the judges decide: The gap between what judges and reasonable people believe is sexually harassing. *Southern California Law Review* 75:791–846.

Bellinger, N. 2000. The ADA—A practitioner's guide in the aftermath of Sutton: Sutton v. United Air Lines. *Pace Law Review* 21:271.

Bendick and Egan, Washington D.C., http://bendickegan.com.

Bendick, M. Jr., C. Jackson, and V. Reinoso. 1994. Measuring employment discrimination through controlled experiments. *Review of Black Political Economy* 23:25–48.

Bennett, J. M. and R. A. Flueck. 1983. An evaluation of major league baseball performance models. *The American Statistician* 37:76–82.

Ben-Porath, Y. 1967. The production of human capital and the life cycle earnings. *Journal of Political Economy* 75(4, part 1):352–365.

Berg, N. and D. Lien. 2002. Measuring the effect of sexual orientation on income: Evidence of discrimination? *Contemporary Economic Policy* 20(4):394–414.

Berg, P. 1999. Ill/Legal: Interrogating the meaning and function of the category of disability in antidiscrimination law. *Yale Law and Policy Review* 18:1–51.

Berger, P. L. and T. Luckman. 1967. *The Social Construction of Reality*. New York: Anchor Books.

Berger, J., B. P. Cohen, and M. Zelditch. 1972. Status characteristics and social interaction. *American Sociological Review* 37:241–255.

Bergman, M. E., R. D. Langhourt, P. A. Palmier, L. M. Cortina, and L. F. Fitzgerald. 2002. The (un)reasonableness of reporting: Antecedents and consequences of reporting sexual harassment. *Journal of Applied Psychology* 87:230–242.

Berk, S. F. 1985. *The Gender Factory: The Apportionment of Work in American Households*. New York: Plenum Press.

Berlant, L. G. 1997. *The Queen of America Goes to Washington City: Essays on Sex and Citizenship* (Series Q). Durham, NC: Duke University Press.

Bernstein, L. 1996. Merchant law in a merchant court: Rethinking the code's search for immanent business norms. *University of Pennsylvania Law Review* 144:1765.

Bianchi, S. M., M. A. Milkie, L. C. Sayer, and J. P. Robinson. 2000. Is anyone doing the housework? Trends in the gender division of household labor. *Social Forces*. 79(1):191–228.

Bickenbach, J. E. 2000. *The ADA v. the Canadian Charter of Rights. Americans with Disabilities: Exploring Implications of the Law for Individuals and Institutions. L. P. a. A. S. Francis*. New York, Routledge.

Bielby, D. D. and W. T. Bielby. 1988. She works hard for the money: Household responsibilities and the allocation of work effort. *American Journal of Sociology* 93(5):1031–1059.

Bielby, D. D. 1992. Commitment to work and family. *Annual Review of Sociology* 18:281–302.

Bielby, W. T. 2000. Minimizing workplace gender and racial bias. *Contemporary Sociology* 29: 120–29.

Bielby, W. T. and J. N. Baron. 1986. Men and women at work: Sex segregation and statistical discrimination. *American Journal of Sociology* 91:759–799.

Bielby, W. T. and M. Bourgeois. 2002. Insuring Discrimination: Making a Market for Employment Practice Liability Insurance. In *American Sociological Association Annual Meeting*. Chicago, IL.

Bielby, W. T. and M. Bourgeois. 2002. Insuring discrimination: Making a Market for Employment Practice Liability Insurance, paper presented at the Annual Meetings of the American Sociological Association.

Bisom-Rapp, S. 1999. Bulletproofing the workplace: Symbol and substance in employment discrimination law practice. *Florida State University Law Review* 26(4):959–1038.

———. 1999. Discerning form substance: Understanding employer litigation prevention strategies. *Employment Rights and Employment Policy Journal*. 3:1–65.

———. 2001. An ounce of prevention is a poor substitute for a pound of cure: Confronting the developing jurisprudence of education and prevention in employment discrimination law. *Berkeley Journal of Employment and Labor Law* 22:1–47.

Black, H. C. 1979. *Law Dictionary.* St. Paul, MN: West Publishing.

Black, D., G. Gates, S. Sanders, and L. Taylor. 2000. Demographics of the gay and lesbian population in the United States: Evidence from available systematic data sources. *Demography* 37(2):139–154.

Black, S. E. and A. Sufi. 2002. Who Goes to College? Differential Enrollment by Race and Family Background, NBER Working Paper No. w9310.

Blair, I. V. and M. R. Banaji. 1996. Automatic and controlled processes in stereotype priming. *Journal of Personality and Social Psychology* 70:1142–1163.

Blair-Loy, M. and A. S. Wharton. 2002. Employees' use of work-family policies and the workplace social context. *Social Forces*. 80(3):813–845.

Blalock, H. M. 1956. Economic discrimination and negro increase. *American Sociological Review* 21:584–588.

———. 1991. *Understanding Social Inequality: Modelling Allocation Processes.* Newbury Park: Sage.

Blank, R. M. 2001. An overview of trends in social and economic well-being, by race. In N. J. Smelser, W. J. Wilson, and F. Mitchell (Eds.), *Racial Trends and Their Consequences* (Vol. 1, pp. 21–39). Washington, D.C.: National Academy Press.

Blasius, M. 1992. An ethos of lesbian and gay existence. *Political Theory* 20:642.

Blau, P. and W. Richard Scott. 1962. *Formal Organizations: A Comparative Approach.* San Francisco: Chandler.

Blau, P. M. 1977. *Inequality and Heterogeneity.* New York: Free Press.

Blau, F. D. and L. M. Kahn. 2000. *Gender differences in pay*. Working Paper 7732. National Bureau of Economic Research, available at http://www.nber.org/papers/w7732.

Blau, F. D., M. A. Ferber, and A. E. Winkler. 2001. *The Economics of Women, Men, and Work.* Upper Saddle River, NJ: Prentice Hall.

Bluestone, B. and M. H. Stevenson. 2000. *The Boston Renaissance: Race, Space, and Economic Change in an American Metropolis*. New York: Russell Sage.

Blumer, H. 1958. Race prejudice as a sense of group position. *Pacific Sociological Review* 1:3–7.

Blumrosen, A. W. 1993. *Modern Law.* Madison: University of Wisconsin.

BMA, L. M. 1994. Dritter Bericht der Bundesregierung über die Lage der Behinderten und die Entwicklung der Rehabilitation (The Federal Government's Third Report on the Situation of the Disabled and the Development of Rehabilitation), German Labor Ministry.

Bobo, L. 2000. Race and beliefs about affirmative action: Assessing the effects of interests, group threat, ideology, and racism. In D. O. Sears, J. Sidanius, and L. Bobo (Eds.), *Racialized Politics: The Debate About Racism in America* (pp. 137–164). Chicago: University of Chicago Press.

Bobo, L. and S. A. Suh. 2000. Surveying racial discrimination: Analyses from a multiethnic labor market. In M. L. Oliver, L. D. Bobo, J. H. Johnson, and A. Valenzuela (Eds.), *Prismatic Metropolis: Inequality in Los Angeles* pp. (523–560) New York: Russell Sage Foundation.

Bobo, L. D. 2001. Racial attitudes and relations at the close of the twentieth century. In N. J. Smelser, W. J. Wilson, and F. Mitchell (Eds.), *American Becoming* (pp. 264–301). Washington, D.C.: National Academy Press.

Bodenhausen, G. V. and C. N. Macrae. 1996. The self-regulation of intergroup perception: Mechanisms and consequences of stereotype suppression. In N. Macrae, C. Stangor, and M. Hewstone (Eds.), *Stereotypes and Stereotyping* (pp. 227–253). New York: Guilford.

Bodenhausen, G. V., C. N. Macrae, and J. Garst. 1998. Stereotypes in thought and deed: Social cognitive origins of intergroup discrimination. In C. Sedikides, J. Schopler, and C. A. Insko (Eds.), *Intergroup Cognition and Intergroup Behaviors* (pp. 311–335). Mahwah, NJ: Erlbaum.

Bodenhausen, G. V., C. N. Macrae, and J. Garst. 1998. Stereotypes in thought and deed. In C. Sedikides, J. Schopler, and C. A. Insko (Eds.), *Intergroup Cognition and Intergroup Behaviors* (pp. 311–335). Mahway, NJ: Erlbaum.

Bonacich, E. 1976. Advanced capitalism and black–white relations in the United States. *American Sociological Review* 41:34–51.

Bone, R. and E. David. 2002. Class certification and the substantive merits. *Duke Law Journal* 51:1251.

Bornholz, R. and J. J. Heckman. 2005. Measuring disparate impacts and extending disparate impact doctrine to organ transplantation. *Perspectives in Biology and Medicine* 48(1): S95–S128.

Bourdieu, P. 1977. *Outline of a Theory of Practice*. Cambridge: Cambridge University Press.

Bourke, J. 2004. Using the law to support work/life issues: The Australian experience. *Journal of Gender, Social Policy, and the Law* 12(1):19–68.

Bowles, S., H. Gintis, and M. Osborne. 2001. The determinants of earnings, a behavioral approach. *Journal of Economic Literature* 39:1137–1176.

Boyd, S. 1996. Case comment: Best friends or spouses? Privatization and the recognition of lesbian relationships in M. V. H. *Canadian Journal of Family Law* 13:321–341.

———. 1999. Family, law and sexuality: Feminist engagements. *Social and Legal Studies* 8(3):369–390.

Boyle, M. 2001. Performance reviews: Perilous curves ahead—grading employees via forced rankings is a valuable management tool. A slew of employees beg to differ. *Fortune*. 143(11):187.

Brandenburg, J. B. 1997. *Confronting Sexual Harassment: What Schools and Colleges Can Do*. New York: Columbia University Teachers College Press.

Branscombe, N. R., M. T. Schmitt, and R. D. Harvey. 1999. Perceiving pervasive discrimination among African Americans: Implications for group identification and well-being. *Journal of Personality and Social Psychology* 77:135–149.

Bravmann, S. 1997. *Queer Fictions of the Past: History, Culture, and Difference, Cambridge Cultural Social Studies*. Cambridge, U.K., New York, NY: Cambridge University Press.

Bravo, E. and E. Cassedy. 1992. *The 9to5 Guide to Combating Sexual Harassment: Candid Advice from 9to5, The National Association of Working Women*. New York, NY: Wiley.

Brest, P. 1976. Forward: In defense of the anti-discrimination principal. *Harvard Law Review* 90:1.

Brewer, M. B. 1979. Ingroup bias in the minimal intergroup situation: A cognitive-motivational analysis. *Psychological Bulletin* 86:307–324.

Brewer, M. B. and R. J. Brown. 1998. Intergroup relations. In D. T. Gilbert, S. T. Fiske, and G. Lindzey (Eds.), *Handbook of Social Psychology* (pp. 554–594). New York: McGraw-Hill.

Brewer, M. B. and R. J. Brown. 1998. Intergroup relations. In D. T. Gilbert, S. T. Fiske, and G. Lindzey (Eds.), *Handbook of Social Psychology* (pp. 554–594). New York: McGraw-Hill.

Brines, J. 1994. Economic dependency, gender, and the division of labor at home. *American Journal of Sociology*. 15:652–688.

Briscoe, F. 2003. Are Part-Time Doctors Stigmatized? Paper presented at the From 9- to-5 to 24/7: How Workplace Changes Impact Families, Work, and Communities Conference, Orlando, FL, February 2003.

Brown, R. J. 1995. *Prejudice.* Oxford: Blackwell.

Budig, M. J. and P. England. 2001. The wage penalty for motherhood. *American Sociological Review* 66:204–225.

Bumiller, K. 1987. Victims in the shadow of the law: A critique of the model of legal protection. *Signs* 12:421–434.

———. 1988. *The Civil Rights Society: The Social Construction of Victims.* Baltimore: Johns Hopkins University Press.

Burawoy, M. 1979. *Manufacturing Consent: Changes in the Labor Process Under Monopoly Capitalism.* Chicago: University of Chicago Press.

Bureau of Labor Statistics. 1988. *Current Population Survey: 1988 Annual Averages.* Washington, D. C.: The Bureau of Labor Statistics.

Bureau of Labor Statistics. 2001. *NLS Handbook 2001.* Washington, D.C.: U.S. Department of Labor.

Burgess, D. and E. Borgida. 1997. Sexual harassment: An experimental test of sex-role spillover theory. *Personality and Social Psychology Bulletin* 23:63–75.

Burke, T. 2003. How do rights work? The case of the Americans with disabilities Act. *Rights and Realities: Legal and Social Scientific Approaches to Employment Discrimination.* Stanford Law School.

Burke, T. F. 2002. *Lawyers, Lawsuits, and Legal Rights.* Berkeley: University of California Press.

Burkhauser, R. V. 1990. Morality on the cheap: The Americans with Disabilities Act. *Regulation* 13:52.

Burlein, A. 2002. *Lift High the Cross: Where White Supremacy and the Christian Right Converge.* Durham, NC: Duke University Press.

Burr, J. A., O. R. Galle, and M. A. Fossett. 1991. Racial occupational inequality in southern metropolitan areas, 1940–1980. *Social Forces* 69:831–850.

Burstein, P. 1989. Attacking sex discrimination in the labor market. *Social Forces* 67:641–665.

Burstein, P. and K. Monaghan. 1986. Equal employment opportunity and the mobilization of law. *Law and Society Review* 20:355–388.

Burstein, P. 1991. Legal mobilization as a social movement tactic: The struggle for equal employment opportunity. *American Journal of Sociology* 96:1201–1225.

Burstein, P. and M. E. Edwards. 1994. The impact of employment discrimination litigation on racial disparity in earnings. *Law and Society Review* 28:79–111.

Butler, J. 1993. *Bodies That Matter.* New York: Routledge.

Button, J. W., B. A. Rienzo, and K. D. Wald. 1997. *Private Lives, Public Conflicts: Battles Over Gay Rights in American Communities.* Washington, D.C.: CQ Press.

Bylsma, W. H. and B. Major. 1992. Two routes to eliminating gender differences in personal entitlement. *Psychology of Women Quarterly* 16:193–200.

Cahill, M. L. 2001. *The Social Construction of Sexual Harassment Law: The Role of the National, Organizational, and Individual Context.* Burlington, VT: Ashgate.

Cain, M. 1994. The symbol traders. In M. Cain and C. Harrington (Eds.), *Lawyers in a Postmodern World* (p. 15). Buckingham: Open University Press.

Cain, M. and A. Hunt. (Eds.). 1979. *Marx and Engels on Law.* New York: Academic Press.

Cain, P. A. 1998. Stories from the gender garden: Transsexuals and anti-discrimination law. *Denver University Law Review* 75:1321–1359.

Cameron, S. and J. J. Heckman. 2001. The dynamics of educational attainment for blacks, whites and hispanics. *Journal of Political Economy* 109(3):455–499.

Cancio, A. S., T. D. Evans, and D. J. Maume, Jr. 1996. Reconsidering the declining significance of race. *American Sociological Review* 61:541–556.

Carneiro, P. and J. J. Heckman. 2003. Human capital policy. J. Heckman and A. Krueger (Eds.), *Inequality in America: What Role for Human Capital Policy?* Cambridge, MA: MIT Press.

Carniero, P., J. J. Heckman, and D. V. Masterov. 2005. Labor market discrimination and racial differences in Premarket Factors. *Journal of Law and Economics*. 47(1):1–39.
Carroll, G. R. and M. T. Hannan. 2000. *The Demography of Corporations and Industries.* Princeton, NJ: Princeton University.
Cassirer, N. 1996. Race composition and earnings: Effects by race, region, and gender. *Social Science Research* 25:375–399.
Catalyst. 1998. *Some Workplace, Different Realities*? New York: Pricewaterhouse Coopers.
———. 2000b. *Women and the MBA: Gateway to Opportunity*. New York: Catalyst.
Census. 2000. Selected characteristics of people 15 years and over by total money income in 2000, work experience in 2000, race, hispanic origin, and sex. http://ferret.bls.census.gov/macro/032001/perinc/new01_018.htm.
Center for Cooperative Resolution/Office of the Ombudsman. 2001. *Annual Report*. Washington, D.C.: Center for Cooperative Resolution.
Chamallas, M. 1986. Women and part-time work: The case for pay equity and equal access. *North Carolina Law Review.* 64:709–774.
———. 1999. Mothers and disparate treatment: The ghost of Martin Marietta. *Villanova Law Review.* 44:337–354.
Chambliss, E. 1996. Title VII as a displacement of conflict. *Temple Political and Civil Rights Law Review* 6:1.
Charny, D. 1996. Illusions of a spontaneous order, "norms" in contractual relationships. *University of Pennsylvania Law Review* 144:1841–1852.
Charny, D. and G. G. Mitu 1998. Efficiency wages, tournaments, and discrimination: A theory of employment discrimination law for "high-level" jobs. *Harvard Civil Rights and Civil Law Review* 33:57.
Chayes, A. and A. H. Chayes. 1985. Corporate counsel and the elite law firm. *Stanford Law Review* 37:277–300.
Chen, D. W. 1999. Many riders see nuances in bias by Cabbies. *New York Times* B3.
Chen, M. and J. A. Bargh. 1997. Nonconscious behavioral confirmation process. *Journal of Experimental Social Psychology* 33:541–560.
Cho, S. K. 1997. Converging stereotypes in racialized sexual harassment: Where the model minority meets Suzie Wong. *1 Iowa Journal of Gender Race and Justice* 177–211:209.
Christiano, K. 1986. Salary discrimination in major league baseball: The effect of race. *Sociology of Sport Journal* 3:144–153.
Clayton, S. D. and F. J. Crosby. 1992. *Justice, Gender, and Affirmative Action. Ann* Arbor: University of Michigan.
Clermont, K. and T. Eisenberg. 2001. Appeal from jury or judge trial: Defendant's advantage. *American Law and Economics Review* Spring 2001, 3:125–164.
Cockburn, C. 1991. *In the Way of Women: Men's Resistance to Sex Inequality in Organizations.* Ithaca: Industrial Labor Relations Press.
Cohen, L. E., J. P. Broschak, and H. A. Haveman. 1998. And then there were more? The effects of organizational sex composition on hiring and promotion. *American Sociological Review* 63:711–727.
Cohen, P. N. 1998. Black concentration effects on black-white and gender inequality. *Social Forces* 77:207–229.
Cohen, G. L., C. M. Steele, and L. D. Ross. 1999. The mentor's dilemma: Providing critical feedback across the racial divide. *Personality and Social Psychology Bulletin* 25:1302–1318.
Cohen, J. L. 2002. *Regulating Intimacy: A New Legal Paradigm* (p. 143). Princeton: Princeton University Press.
Cohen, P. N. and M. L. Huffman. 2002. Race and Gender Devaluation across U.S. Labor Markets, presented at the Annual Meetings of the American Sociological Association, Chicago.
Cohen, P. N. and S. M. Bianchi. 1999. Marriage, children, and women's employment: What do we know? *Monthly Labor Review* 112(12):22–31.

Cohn, S. 1985. The *Process of Occupational Sex Typing.* Philadelphia: Temple University.

Cole, J. 1991. A theory of limited differences: Explaining the productivity puzzle in science, in women in the scientific community (Zuckerman, Cole, and 18 See Suchman and Edelman, Legal Rational Myths: The New Institutionalism and the Law and Society Tradition. 21 Law and Soc. Inquiry 903 (1996).

Cole, R. 1971. *Japanese Blue Collar*. Berkeley, LA: University of California Press.

Colker, R. 1999. The Americans with disabilities act: A windfall for defendants. *Harvard Civil Rights—Civil Liberties Law Review* 34:99–162.

Collins, R. 1975. *Conflict Sociology.* New York: Academic Press.

Collins, P. H. 1990. *Black Feminist Thought: Knowledge, Consciousness, and the Politics of Empowerment*. London: Routledge.

Collins, S. M. 1997a. *Black Corporate Executives: The Making and Breaking of a Black Middle Class.* Philadelphia: Temple University Press.

———. 1997b. Black mobility in white corporations: Up the ladder but out on a limb. *Social Problems* 44:55–67.

Coltrane, S. 1996. *Family Man: Fatherhood, Housework, and Gender Equity.* New York: Oxford University Press.

Commission on Leave. 1996. *A Workable Balance: Report to Congress on Family and Medical Leave Policies*. Washington D.C.: Commission on Family and Medical Leave.

Conley, D. 1999. *Being Black, Living in the Red: Race, Wealth, and Social Policy in America*. Berkeley, CA: University of California Press.

Conley, F. K. 1998. *Walking Out on the Boys.* New York: Farrar, Straus and Giroux.

Cooper, D. 1998. *Governing Out of Order: Space, Law, and the Politics of Belonging*. London, New York: Rivers Oram Press, Distributed in the USA by New York University Press.

Cooper, M. 2000. Being the "Go-To Guy": Fatherhood, masculinity, and the organization of work in the Silicon Valley. *Qualitative Sociology* 23:379–405.

Cordova, D. I. 1992. Cognitive limitations and affirmative action. *Social Justice. Research* 5:319–333.

Cox, P. N. 1987. *The Law of Employment Discrimination: Cases and Commentary*. Lupus Publications.

Crandall, C. S. 1994. Prejudice against fat people: Ideology and self-interest. *Journal of Personality and Social Psychology* 66:882–894.

Crary, D. 2004. Courts tell bosses: Don't assume working mothers aren't committed to their job. *Associated Press State and Local Wire*, July 20, 2004.

Creed, W. E., D. M. Scully, and J. Austin. 2002. Clothes make the person? The tailoring of legitimating accounts and the social construction of identity. *Organization Science* 13(5):475–496.

Crenshaw, K. 1989. Demarginalizing the intersection of race and sex: A black feminist critique of antidiscrimination doctrine, feminist theory and antiracist politics. *University of Chicago Legal Forum* 1989:139–167.

———. 1991. Mapping the margins: Intersectionality, identity politics, and violence against women of color. *Stanford Law Review* 43(1241–1299):1242–1244.

———. 1992. Race, gender, and sexual harassment. *Southern California Law Review* 65:1467–1475, 1470.

Crittendon, A. 2001. *The Price of Motherhood: Why the Most Important Job in the World is Still the Least Valued.* New York: Metropolitan Books.

Crocker, J., B. Cornwell, and B. Major. 1993. The stigma of overweight: Affective consequences of attributional ambiguity. *Journal of Personality and Social Psychology* 64:60–70.

Crocker, J. and B. Major. 1989. Social stigma and self-esteem: The self-protective properties of stigma. *Psychological Review* 96:608–630.

———. 1994. Reactions to stigma: The moderating role of justifications. In M. P. Zanna and J. M. Olson (Eds.), *The Psychology of Prejudice: The Ontario Symposium* (Vol. 7, pp. 289–314). Hillsdale, NJ: Erlbaum.

Crocker, J., K. Voelkl, M. Testa, and B. Major. 1991. Social stigma: The affective consequences of attributional ambiguity. *Journal of Personality and Social Psychology* 60:218–228.

Crosby, F. (1984). The denial of personal discrimination. *American Behavioral Scientist* 27:371–386.

Crosby, F., A. Pufall, R. C. Snyder, M. O'Connell, and P. Whalen. 1989. The denial of personal disadvantage among you, me, and all the other ostriches. In M. Crawford and M. Gentry (Eds.), *Gender's Thought: Psychological Perspectives* (pp. 79–99). New York: Springer-Verlag.

Crosby, F. J. 1993. Why complain? *Journal of Social Issues* 49:169–184.

Crosby, F., S. Bromley, and L. Saxe. 1980. Recent unobtrusive studies of Black and White discrimination and prejudice: A literature review. *Psychological Bulletin* 87:546–563.

Crosby, F., S. Clayton, O. Alksnis, and K. Hemker. 1986. Cognitive biases in the perception of discrimination: The importance of format. *Sex Roles* 14:637–646.

Cuddy, A. J. C., S. T. Fiske, and P. Glick. 2005. The BIAS map: Behaviors from intergroup affect and stereotypes under review, on file with author.

Cuddy, A. J. C., S. T. Fiske, V. S. V. Kwan, and P. Glick, et al. 2005. Is the stereotype content model culture bound? A cross-cultural comparison reveals systematic similarities and differences. *British Journal of Social Psychology*. In press.

Cunha, F., J. J. Heckman, L. Lochner and D. V. Masterov. 2005. In E. Hanushek and F. Welch (Eds.), *Handbook of the Economics of Education*. Amsterdam: North Holland, in press.

Currah, P. and S. Minter. 2000. Unprincipled exclusions: The struggle to achieve judicial and legislative equality for transgender people. *William and Mary Journal of Women and the Law* 7:37.

Curran, B. A. 1977. *The Legal Needs of the Public: The Final Report of a National Survey*. Chicago: American Bar Foundation.

Currie, J. and D. Thomas. 2000. School quality and the longer-term effects of Head Start. *Journal of Human Resources* 35(4):755–774.

Cymrot, D. 1985. Does competition lessen discrimination: Some evidence. *Journal of Human Resources* 20:605–612.

Danziger, S. H., R. Farley, and H. J. Holzer. 2000. *Detroit Divided*. New York: Russell Sage.

Darley, J. M. and B. Latané. 1968. Bystander intervention in emergencies: Diffusion of responsibility. *Journal of Personality and Social Psychology* 8:377–383.

Darley, J. M. and R. H. Fazio. 1980. Expectancy confirmation processes arising in the social interaction sequence. *American Psychologist* 35:867–881.

Davies, M. 1999. Queer property, queer persons: Self-ownership and beyond. *Social and Legal Studies* 8(3):327–352.

Davis, K. and W. E. Moore. 1945. The continuing debate on equality/some principle of stratification. *American Sociological Review* 10:242–249.

Deaux, K. 1995. How basic can you get? The evolution of research on gender stereotypes. *Journal of Social Issues* 51:11–20.

Deaux, K. and J. C. Ullman. 1983. *Women of Steel: Female Blue-Collar Workers in the Basic Steel Industry*. New York, NY: Praeger.

Deaux, K. and M. E. Kile. 1991. Gender stereotypes. In F. Denmark and M. Palud (Eds.), *Handbook on the Psychology of Women*. Westport, CT: Greenwood Press.

Deaux, K. and T. Emswiller. 1974. Explanations of successful performance on sex-linked tasks: What is skill for the male is luck for the female. *Journal of Personality and Social Psychology* 29:80–85.

DeFour, D. C. 1990. The interface of racism and sexism on college campuses. In M. A. Paludi (Ed.), *Ivory Power: Sexual Harassment on Campus* (pp. 45–47, 48–49). Albany, NY: SUNY Press.

Degener, T. 1995. Disabled persons and human rights: The legal framework. In T. Degener and Y. Koster-Dreese (eds.), *Human Rights and Disabled Persons* (pp. 9–39). The Netherlands: Kluwer.

Degener, T. 2000. *From Pity Law to Citoyen Law*. Chicago: Society for Disability Studies Conference.

Delgado, R., C. Dunn, P. Brown, H. Lee, and D. Hubbert. 1985. Fairness and formality: Minimizing the risk of prejudice in alternative dispute resolution. *Wisconsin Law Review* 1359.

Delgado, R. and J. Stefancic. 2001. *Critical Race Theory: An Introduction*. New York: NYU Press.

D'Emilio, J. 1983. *Sexual Politics, Sexual Communities: The Making of a Homosexual Minority in the United States*. Chicago: University of Chicago Press.

Dennis, A. L. 1996. Note, because I am black, because I am woman: Remedying the sexual harassment experience of black women. *Annual Survey of American Law Issue* 4:555–582.

DeParle, J. 1990. Talk of government being out to get Blacks falls on more attentive ears. *New York Times* B7.

Devine, P. G. 1989. Stereotypes and prejudice: Their automatic and controlled components. *Journal of Personality and Social Psychology* 56:5–18.

———. 2001. Implicit prejudice and stereotyping: How automatic are they? Introduction to the special section. *Journal of Personality and Social Psychology* 81:757–759.

Dijksterhuis, A. and J. A. Bargh. 2001. The perception-behavior expressway: Automatic effects of social perception on social behavior. In M. P. Zanna (Ed.), *Advances in Experimental Social Psychology* (Vol. 33, pp. 1–40). New York: Academic Press.

Dijksterhuis, A., R. Spears, and V. Lepinasse. 2001. Reflecting and deflecting stereotypes: Assimilation and contrast in impression formation and automatic behavior. *Journal of Experimental and Social Psychology* 37:286–299.

DiMaggio, P. J. 1991. Constructing an organizational field as a professional project: U.S. art museums, 1920–1940. In W. W. Powell and P. J. DiMaggio (Eds.), *The New Institutionalism in Organizational Analysis* (pp. 267–292). Chicago: University of Chicago Press.

DiMaggio, P. J. and W. W. Powell. 1983. The iron cage revisited: Institutional isomorphism and collective rationality in organizational fields. *American Sociological Review* 48:147–160.

Dion, K. L. 1975. Women's reactions to discrimination from members of the same or opposite sex. *Journal of Research in Personality* 9:294–306.

Dion, K. L. and B. M. Earn. 1975. The phenomenology of being a target of prejudice. *Journal of Personality and Social Psychology* 32:944–950.

DiPlacido, J. 1998. Minority stress among lesbians, gay men, and bisexuals: A consequence of heterosexism, homophobia, and stigmatization. In G. M. Herek (Ed.), *Stigma and Sexual Orientation: Understanding Prejudice Against Lesbians, Gay Men, and Bisexuals* (pp. 138–159). Thousand Oaks, CA: Sage.

Dixon, K. A., D. Storen, and C. E. Van Horn. 2002. A workplace divided: How Americans view discrimination and race on the job. Rutgers, The State University of New York, John J. Heldrich Center for Workplace Development.

Dobbin, F., J. R. Sutton, J. W. Meyer, and W. R. Scott. 1993. Equal opportunity law and the construction of the internal labor markets. *American Journal of Sociology* 99(2):396–427.

Dobbin, F. and J. R. Sutton. 1998. The strength of a weak state: The rights revolution and the rise of human resources management divisions. *American Journal of Sociology* 104(2):441–476.

Dobbin, F. and E. Kelly. 2005. A tale of two sectors: The spread of anti-harassment remedies among public and private employers. Manuscript submitted for publication.

Doeringer P. and M. Piore. 1971. *Internal Labor Markets and Manpower Analysis*. D. C. Heath.

Donnerstein, E. and M. Donnerstein. 1973. Variables in interracial aggression: Potential ingroup censure. *Journal of Personality and Social Psychology* 27:143–150.

Donnerstein, E., M. Donnerstein, S. Simon, and R. Ditrichs. 1972. Variables in interracial aggression: Anonymity, expected retaliation, and a riot. *Journal of Personality and Social Psychology* 22:236–245.

Donohue, J. J. and J. J. Heckman. 1991. Continuous Versus Episodic Change: The Impact of Civil Rights Policy on the Economic Status of Blacks. *Journal of Economic Literature* 29(4):1603–1643.

Donohue, J. J. and P. Siegelman. 1991. The changing nature of employment discrimination litigation. *Stanford Law Review* 43:983–1033.

———. 1993. Law and macroeconomics: Employment discrimination over the business cycle. *Southern California Law Review* 66:709.

———. 2002. The Evolution of Employment Discrimination Law in the 1990s: An Empirical Investigation (on file with author).
Dorf, M. C. and Charles F. Sabel. 1998. A constitution of democratic experimentalism. *Columbia Law Review* 98:267, 345.
Dovidio, J. F., N. Evans, and R. B. Tyler. 1986. Racial stereotypes: The contents of their cognitive representations. *Journal of Experimental Social Psychology* 22:22–37.
Dovidio, J. F., J. C. Brigham, B. T. Johnson, and S. L. Gaertner. 1996. Stereotyping, prejudice, and discrimination: Another look. In N. Macrae, C. Stangor, and M. Hewstone (Eds.), *Stereotypes and Stereotyping* (pp. 276–319). New York: Guilford.
Dovidio, J. F., K. Kawakami, and S. L. Gaertner. 2002. Implicit and explicit prejudice and interracial interaction. *Journal of Personality and Social Psychology* 82:62–68.
Dovidio, J. F. and S. L. Gaertner. (Eds.). 1986. *Prejudice, Discrimination, and Racism*. San Diego, CA: Academic Press.
Dovidio, J. F. and S. L. Gaertner. 1996. Affirmative action, unintentional racial biases, and intergroup relations. *Journal of Social Relations* 52:51–75.
———. 1998. On the nature of contemporary prejudice: The causes, consequences, and challenges of aversive racism. In J. Eberhardt and S. T. Fiske (Eds.), *Confronting Racism: The Problem and the Response* (pp. 3–32). Newbury Park, CA: Sage.
———. 2000. Aversive racism and selection decisions: 1989 and 1999. *Psychological Science* 11:319–323.
Dovidio, J. F. and S. L. Gaertner. 2004. Aversive racism. In M. P. Zanna (Ed.), *Advances in experimental social Psychology* (pp. 1–52). San Diego, CA: Academic Press.
Dovidio, J. F., S. L. Gaertner, A. Validzic, K. Matoka, B. Johnson, and S. Frazier. 1997. Extending the benefits of re-categorization: Evaluations, self-disclosure and helping. *Journal of Experimental Social Psychology* 33:401–420.
Dovidio, J. F., S. L. Gaertner, and K. Kawakami. 1998. *Multiple Attitudes and Contemporary Racial Bias*. Paper presented at the annual meeting of the Society for Experimental Social Psychology, Lexington, KY.
Dovidio, J. F., S. L. Gaertner, P. A. Anastasio, and R. Sanitioso. 1992. Cognitive and motivational bases of bias: The implications of aversive racism for attitudes toward Hispanics. In S. Knouse, P. Rosenfeld and A. Culbertson (Eds.), *Hispanics in the Workplace* (pp. 75–106). Newbury Park, CA: Sage.
Drimmer, J. C. 1993. Cripples, overcomers, and civil rights: Tracing the evolution of federal legislation and social policy for people with disabilities. *UCLA Law Review* 40:1341–1410.
Duckitt, J. 1992. *The Social Psychology of Prejudice*. New York: Praeger.
———. 2001. A dual-process cognitive-motivational theory of ideology and prejudice. In M. P. Zanna (Ed.), *Advances in Experimental Social Psychology* (Vol. 33, pp. 41–113). New York: Academic Press.
Dugger, K. 1988. Social location and gender-role attitudes: A comparison of Black and White women. *Gender and Society* 2:425–448.
Duleep, H. O. and N. Zalokar. 1991. The measurement of labor market discrimination when minorities respond to discrimination. In R. Cornwall and P. Wunnava (Eds.), *New Approaches to Economic and Social Analyses of Discrimination*. New York: Praeger Press.
Duncan, G. and J. Brooks-Gunn. 1997. *Consequences of Growing Up Poor*. New York: Russell Sage Foundation.
Durkheim, E. 1964. 1858–1917: *The Division of Labor in Society; Trans*. George Simpson. New York: Free Press.
Durkin, J. 1998. An examination of the first eleven studies of sexual orientation bias by the legal profession. *UCLA Women's Law Journal* 8:343–378.
Eagly, A. H. 1987. *Sex Differences in Social Behavior: A Social-Role Interpretation*. Mahwah, NJ: Erlbaum.

Eagly, E. A. and S. J. Karau. 2002. Role congruity theory of prejudice toward female leaders. *Psychological Review*. 109:573–598.

Eberhardt, J. L. and S. T. Fiske. 1996. Motivating individuals to change: What is a target to do? In C. N. Macrae, C. Stangor, and M. Hewstone (Eds.), *Stereotypes and Stereotyping* (pp. 369–415). New York, NY: Guilford Press.

Eberhardt, J. L. and S. T. Fiske. (Eds.). 1998. *Confronting Racism: The Problem and the Response.* Thousand Oaks, CA: Sage.

Edelman, L. B. 1990. Legal environments and organizational governance: The expansion of due process in the workplace. *American Journal of Sociology* 95(6):1401–1440.

———. 1992. Legal ambiguity and symbolic structures: Organizational mediation of civil rights law. *American Journal of Sociology* 97(6):1531–1576.

———. 1992. Legal ambiguity and symbolic structures. *American Journal of Sociology* 97:1531–1576.

Edelman, L. B., C. Uggen, and H. S. Erlanger. 1999. The endogeneity of legal regulation: Grievance procedures as rational myth. *American Journal of Sociology* 105:406–454.

Edelman, L. B., H. S. Erlanger, and J. Lande. 1993. Internal dispute resolution: The transformation of civil rights in the workplace. *Law and Society Review* 27(3):497–534.

Edelman, L. B. and M. Cahill. 1998. How law matters in disputing and dispute processing (Or, The Contingency of Legal Matter in Alternative Dispute Resolution). In B. Garth and A. Sarat (Eds.), *How Law Matters* (pp. 15–44). Chicago: Northwestern University Press.

Edelman, L. B. and M. C. Suchman. 1997. The legal environments of organizations. *Annual Review of Sociology* 23:479–515.

———. 1999. When the haves hold court: Speculations on the organizational internalization of law. *Law and Society Review* 33(4):941–991.

Edelman, L. B. and R. Stryker. 2005. A sociological approach to law and the economy. In R. Swedberg and N. Smelser (Eds.), *The Handbook of Economic Sociology* (2nd ed.). New York: Russell Sage Foundation, Princeton, NJ: Princeton University Press.

Edelman, L. B., S. Patterson, E. Chambliss, and H. S. Erlanger. 1991 Legal ambiguity and the politics of compliance: Affirmative action officers' dilemma. *Law and Policy* 13:73–97.

Edelman, L. B. and S. Petterson. 1999. Symbols and substance in organizational response to civil rights law. *Research in Social Stratification and Mobility* 17:107–135.

Edelman, L. B., S. E. Abraham, and H. S. Erlanger. 1992. Professional construction of law: The inflated threat of wrongful discharge doctrine. *Law and Society Review* 26(1):47–83.

Edelman, L. B., S. R. Fuller, and I. Mara-Drita. 2001. Diversity rhetoric and the managerialization of law. *American Journal of Sociology* 106(6):1589–1641.

Edwards, H. T. 1986. Alternative dispute resolution: Panacea or anathema? *Harvard Law Review* 99:668.

Edwards, R. 1979. *Contested Terrain: The Transformation of the Workplace in the Twentieth Century.* New York: Basic Books, Inc.

Edwards, W. 1989. *Modern Japan Through Its Weddings.* Stanford: Stanford University Press.

EEOC. 2003a. Charge statistics FY 1992 through FY 2002. www.eeoc.gov/stats/.

———. 2003b. Sexual harassment charges EEOC and FEPAs combined: FY 1992–FY 2002. http://www.eeoc.gov/stats/harass.html.

Eide, E. and D. Irani. 1996. Positional segregation in major league baseball: 1961–1990. In J. Fizel, E. Gustafson, and L. Hadley (Eds.), *Baseball Economics: Current Research* (pp. 179–190). Westport, CT: Praeger.

Eisenberg, T. 1989. Litigation models and trial outcomes in civil rights and prisoner cases. *Georgetown Law Journal* 77:1567.

Eisenmenger, M. 2002. Sexual orientation discrimination: Teachers as positive role models for tolerance. *Journal of Law and Education* 31:235–244.

Ellickson, R. 1991. *Order Without Law: How Neighbors Settle Disputes.* Cambridge: Harvard University Press.

Elliott, J. R. 2001. Referral hiring and ethnically homogeneous jobs. *Social Science Research* 30:401–425.

Elster, J. 1989. *Nuts and Bolts for the Social Sciences.* New York: Cambridge.

Ely, R. J. and D. E. Meyerson. 2000. Theories of gender in organizations: A new approach to organizational analysis and change. *Research in Organizational Behavior* 22:103–151.

Engel, D. M. and F. W. Munger. 1996. Rights, remembrance, and the reconciliation of difference. *Law and Society Review* 30:7–53.

England, P. 1992. *Comparable Worth: Theories and Evidence*. New York: Aldine de Gruyter.

———. 1994. Neoclassical economists' theories of discrimination. In P. Burstein *Equal Employment Opportunity* (pp. 59–69). New York: Aldine De Gruyter.

———. 1997. Commentary. In F. D. Blau and R. G. Ehrenberg (Eds.), *Gender and Family Issues in the Workplace* (p. 130). New York: Russell Sage.

Epstein, C. F., C. Seron, B. Oglensky, and R. Saute. 1998. *The Part-Time Paradox: Time Norms, Professional Lives, Family, and Gender.* New York: Routledge.

Epstein, R. A. 1994. Standing firm, on forbidden grounds. *San Diego Law Review* 31:1–56.

Epstein, S. 1999. Gay and lesbian movements in the United States: Dilemmas of identity, diversity, and political strategy. In B. D. Adam, J. W. Duyvendak, and A. Krouwel (Eds.), *The Global Emergence of Gay and Lesbian Politics: National Imprints of a Worldwide Movement* (pp. 30–90). Philadelphia: Temple University Press.

Equal Employment Opportunity Commission's Alternative Dispute Resolution Policy Statement. (1995). http://www.eeoc.gov/docs/adrstatement.html.

Ertman, M. 2001. Marriage as a trade: Bridging the private/private distinction. *Harvard Civil Rights—Civil Liberties Law Review* 36:79–132.

Eskridge, W. 2002. Some effects of identity-based social movements on constitutional law in the twentieth century. *Michigan Law Review* 100:2062.

Estes, S. B. and J. L. Glass. 1996. Job changes following childbirth: Are women trading compensation for family-responsive work conditions? *Work and Occupations* 23(4):405–436.

Estreicher, S. and M. C. Harper. 2000. *Cases and Materials on Employment Discrimination and Employment Law*. St. Paul, MN: West Group.

Ewick, P. and S. S. Silbey. 1998. *The Common Place of Law: Stories from Everyday Life*. Chicago: University of Chicago Press.

Farkas, G. and K. Vicknair. 1996. Appropriate tests of racial wage discrimination require controls for cognitive skill: Comment on Cancio, Evans, and Maume. *American Sociological Review* 61:557–560.

Feagin, J. R. 1991. The continuing significance of race: Antiblack discrimination in public places. *American Sociological Review* 56:101–116.

Feagin, J. R. and M. P. Sikes. 1994. *Living with Racism: The Black Middle-Class Experience*. Boston: Beacon Press.

Feeley, M. and R. Edward. 2002. Responsive law and the judicial process: Implications for the judicial function. In R. Kagan, M. Kriygier, and K. Winston (Eds.), *Legality and Community: On the Intellectual Legacy of Philip Selznick* (pp. 249, 262). Berkeley, CA: Berkeley Public Policy Press.

Fein, S. and S. J. Spencer. 1997. Prejudice as self-image maintenance: Affirming the self through derogating others. *Journal of Personality and Social Psychology* 73:31–44.

Feldblum, C. R. 2000. Gay people, trans people, women: Is it all about gender? *New York Law School Journal of Human Rights* 17:623–702.

Feldman-Barrett, L. and J. K. Swim. 1998. Appraisals of prejudice and discrimination. In J. K. Swim and C. Stangor (Eds.), *Prejudice: The Target's Perspective* (pp. 12–37). San Diego: Academic Press.

Feldman, E. 2000. *The Ritual of Rights in Japan: Law, Society, and Health Policy*. Cambridge, Cambridge University Press.

Felmlee, D. 1995. Causes and consequences of women's employment discontintuity, 1967–1973. *Work and Occupations* 22:167–187.

Felstiner, W. L. F., R. L. Abel, and A. Sarat. 1981. The emergence and transformation of disputes: Naming, blaming, claiming.... *Law and Society Review* 15:631–654.

Ferber, M. A. and J. Waldfogel. 1998. The long-term consequences of nontraditional employment. *Monthly Labor Review* 121(5):3–13.

Ferguson, R. 2002a. Why America's black–white school achievement gap persists. Unpublished Manuscript, Harvard University.

———. 2002b. What Doesn't Meet the Eye: Understanding and Addressing Racial Disparities in High Achieving Suburban Schools, Special Edition, *Policy Issues Report*. Naperville, IL: North Central Regional Educational Laboratory.

Fernandez, R. 2001. Skill-biased technological change and wage inequality. *American Journal of Sociology* 107:273–320.

Fernandez, R., E. J. Castilla, and P. Moore. 2000. Social capital at work. *American Journal of Sociology* 105:1288–1356.

Fernandez, R. and N. Weinberg. 1997. Sifting and sorting: Personal contacts and hiring in a retail bank. *American Sociological Review* 62:883–902.

Finkelstein, V. 1980. *Attitudes and Disabled People*. New York: World Rehabilitation Fund, Inc.

Fisher, A. 2002. Do I fire the bottom 10% just because Jack did?" *Fortune* 146(4):210.

Fiske, M. L. and S. L. Neuberg. 1999. The continuum model: Ten years later. In S. Chaiken and Y. Trope (Eds.), *Dual Process Theories in Social Psychology* (pp. 231–54). New York: Guilford Press.

Fiske, S., B. Morling, and L. E. Stevens. 1996. Controlling self and others: A theory of anxiety, mental control, and social control. *Personality and Social Psychology Bulletin* 70:491–512.

Fiske, S. T. 1989. Examining the role of intent: Toward understanding its role in stereotyping and prejudice. In J. Uleman and J. Bargh (Eds.), *Unintended Thought: The Limits of Awareness, Intention, and Control* (pp. 253–283). New York: Guilford.

———. 1993. Social cognition and social perception. In M. R. Rosenzweig and L. W. Porter (Eds.), *Annual Review of Psychology* (Vol. 44, pp. 155–194). Palo Alto, CA: Annual Reviews.

———. 1993a. Controlling other people: The impact of power on stereotyping. *American Psychologist* 48:621–628.

———. 1998. Stereotyping, prejudice, and discrimination. In D. T. Gilbert, S. T. Fiske, and G. Lindzey (Eds.), *Handbook of Social Psychology* (4th ed., Vol. 2, pp. 357–411). New York: Mc-Graw Hill.

———. 1998. Stereotyping, prejudice, and discrimination. In D.T. Gilbert, S.T. Fiske, and G. Lindzey (Eds.), *The Handbook of Social Psychology* (pp. 357–411). Boston: McGraw.

———. 2000. Interdependence reduces prejudice and stereotyping. In S. Oskamp (Ed.), *Reducing Prejudice and Discrimination* (pp. 115–135). Mahwah, NJ: Erlbaum.

———. 2000b. Stereotyping, prejudice, and discrimination at the seam between the centuries: Evolution, culture, mind and brain. *European Journal of Social Psychology* 30:299–322.

———. 2002. What we know now about bias and intergroup conflict, problem of the century. *Current Directions in Psychological Science* 11:123–128.

———. 2004. *Social Beings: A Core Motives Approach to Social Psychology. Chapter 11: Stereotyping, Prejudice, and Discrimination: Social Biases*. New York: Wiley.

Fiske, S. T., A. J. Cuddy, P. Glick, and J. Xu. 2002. A model of (often mixed) stereotype content: Competence and warmth respectively follow from perceived status and competition. *Journal of Personality and Social Psychology* 82:878–902.

Fiske, S. T., D. N. Bersoff, E. Borgida, K. Deaux, and M. E. Heilman. 1991. Social science research on trial: The use of sex stereotyping research in Price Waterhouse v. Hopkins. *American Psychologist* 46:1049–1060.

Fiske, S. T. and P. Glick. 1995. Ambivalence and stereotypes cause sexual harassment: A theory with implications for organizational change. In E. Borgida and S. T. Fiske (Eds.), Gender stereotyping, sexual harassment, and the law. *Journal of Social Issues* 51: 97–115.

Fiss, O. 1971. A theory of fair employment laws. *University of Chicago Law Review* 38:23.

———. 1976. *Groups and the Equal Protection Clause*. Philosophy and Public Affairs 5(2):107–177.

———. 1979a. The forms of justice. *Harvard Law Review* 93:1, 9, 30.

———. 1984. Against settlement. *Yale Law Journal* 93:1073.
Fitzgerald, L. F., S. Swan, and K. Fischer. 1995. Why didn't she just report him? The psychological and legal implications of women's responses to sexual harassment. *Journal of Social Issues* 51:117–138.
Fix, M. E. and R. J. Struyk. 1993. *Clear and Convincing Evidence*. Washington, D.C.: The Urban Institute.
Flack, M. 1999. Working the family in. Unpublished Doctoral Dissertation, Ohio State University, Columbus, OH.
Flanagan, R. 1987. *Labor Relations and the Litigation Explosion*. Washington, D.C.: Brookings Institution.
Fletcher, J. K. 1999. *Disappearing Acts: Gender, Power, and Relational Practice at Work*. Cambridge, MA: MIT Press.
Fligstein, N. 1985. The spread of the multidivisional form among large firms 1919–1979. *American Sociological Review* 50(3):77–91.
———. 1990. *The Transformation of Corporate Control*. Cambridge, MA: Harvard University Press.
Flinn, C. and J. J. Heckman. 1983. Are unemployment and out of the labor force behaviorally distinct states? *Journal of Labor Economics* 1:28–42.
Flynn, T. 2001. Transforming the debate: Why we need to include transgender rights in the struggles for sex and sexual orientation equality. *Columbia Law Review* 101:392.
Foddy, M. and M. Smithson. 1999. Can gender inequalities be eliminated? *Social Psychology Quarterly* 62:307–324.
Folbre, N. 1991. The unproductive housewife: Her evolution in nineteenth-century economic thought. *Signs* 16:463–484.
Fordham, E. W. 1951. *Notable Cross-Examinations*. London: Constable.
Foschi, M. and V. LaPointe. 2002. On conditional hypotheses and gender as a status characteristic. *Social Psychology Quarterly* 65:146–162.
Fossett, M. A. and K. J. Kiecolt. 1989. The relative size of minority populations and white racial attitudes. *Social Science Quarterly* 70:820–835.
Fosu, A. K. 1993. Do black and white women hold different jobs in the same occupation? A critical analysis of the clerical and service sectors. *The Review of the Black Political Economy* (Spring):67–81.
Foucault, M. 1977. *Language, Counter-Memory, Practice: Selected Essays and Interviews*. Ithaca: Cornell University Press.
———. 1979. *Discipline and Punish*. New York: Vintage Books.
———. 1991. Governmentality. In G. Burchell, C. Gordon, and P. Miller (Eds.), *The Foucault Effect: Studies in Governmentality*. Chicago: University of Chicago Press.
Foucault, M., G. Burchell, C. Gordon, and P. Miller. 1991. *The Foucault Effect: Studies in Governmentality*. Chicago: University of Chicago Press.
Frank, M. and R. Lipner. 1988. History of maternity leave in Europe and the United States. In E. F. Zigler and M. Frank (Eds.), *The Parental Leave Crisis: Toward a National Policy* (pp. 3–22). New Haven: Yale University Press.
Fraser, N. and L. Gordon. 1994. A genealogy of dependency: Tracing a keyword of the U.S. welfare state. *Signs* 19:309–336.
Freeman, R. 1977. *The Black Elite*. New York: McGraw Hill.
Freeman, A. 1998. Antidiscrimination law from 1954 to 1989: Uncertainty, contradiction, rationalization, denial. In D. Kairys (Ed.), *The Politics of Law: A Progressive Critique* (3rd ed., pp. 285–311). New York: Basic Books.
Freeman, A. D. 1982. Antidiscrimination law: A critical review. In D. Kairys (Ed.), *The Politics of Law*. New York: Patheon Books.
French, S. 1993. In John Swain (Ed.), *Disability, Impairment or Something In-between? Disabling Barriers-Enabling Environments* (pp. 17–25). London: Sage Publications.
Freshman, C. 2000. Whatever happened to anti-semitism? How social science theories identify discrimination and promote coalitions between "different" minorities. *Cornell Law Review* 85:313.

Fried, M. 1998. *Taking Time: Parental Leave Policy and Corporate Culture*. Philadelphia, PA: Temple University Press.

Friedman, J. J. and N. DiTomaso. 1996. Myths about diversity: What managers need to know about changes in the U.S. labor force. *California Management Review* 38(4):54–77.

Friedman, L. M. 1987. *Total Justice: What Americans Want from the Legal System and Why*. Boston: Beacon Press.

Friedman, S. D. and J. H. Greenhaus. 2000. *Work and Family–Allies or Enemies? What Happens When Business Professionals Confront Life Choices*. New York: Oxford University Press.

Fryer, R. and S. Levitt. 2004. Understanding the black–white test score gap in the first two years of school. *Review of Economics and Statistics* 86(2):447–464.

Fuller, S. R., L. B. Edelman, and S. F. Matusik. 2000. Legal readings: Employee interpretation and mobilization of law. *The Academy of Management Review* 25(1):200–216.

Gaertner, S. L. 1973. Helping behavior and racial discrimination among liberals and conservatives. *Journal of Personality and Social Psychology* 25:335–341.

Gaertner, S. L., J. A. Mann, J. F. Dovidio, A. J. Murrell, and M. Pomare. 1990. How does cooperation reduce intergroup bias? *Journal of Personality and Social Psychology* 59:692, 704.

Gaertner, S. L. and J. F. Dovidio. 1977. The subtlety of white racism, arousal, and helping behavior. *Journal of Personality and Social Psychology* 35:691–707.

———. 1986. The aversive form of racism. In J. F. Dovidio and S. L. Gaertner (Eds.), *Prejudice, Discrimination, and Racism* (pp. 61–89). Orlando, FL: Academic Press.

———. 2000. *Reducing Intergroup Bias: The Common Ingroup Identity Model*. Philadelphia, PA: The Psychology Press.

Gaertner, S. L., J. F. Dovidio, B. Banker, M. Rust, J. Nier, G. Mottola, and C. Ward. 1997. Does racism necessarily mean anti-blackness? Aversive racism and pro-whiteness. In M. Fine, L. Powell, L. Weis, and M. Wong (Eds.), *Off White* (pp. 167–178). London: Routledge.

Gaertner, S. L., J. F. Dovidio, J. Nier, C. Ward, and B. Banker. 1999. Across cultural divides: The value of a superordinate identity. In D. Prentice and D. Miller (Eds.), *Cultural divides: Understanding and overcoming group conflict* (pp. 173–212).

Gaertner, S. L., J. F. Dovidio, M. C. Rust, J. Nier, B. Banker, C. M. Ward, G. R. Mottola, and M. Houlette. 1999. Reducing intergroup bias: Elements of intergroup cooperation. *Journal of Personality and Social Psychology* 76:388–402.

Gaertner, S. L., J. F. Dovidio, P. A. Anastasio, B. A. Bachman, and M. C. Rust. 1993. The common ingroup identity model: Recategorization and the reduction of intergroup bias. In W. Stroebe and M. Hewstone (Eds.), *European Review of Social Psychology* (Vol. 4, pp. 1–26). New York: John Wiley and Sons.

Gaertner, S. L., M. C. Rust, J. F. Dovidio, B. A. Bachman, and P. A. Anastasio. 1996. The contact hypothesis: The role of a common ingroup identity on reducing intergroup bias among majority and minority group members. In J. L. Nye and A. M. Brower (Eds.), *What's Social About Social Cognition?* (pp. 230–360). Newbury Park, CA: Sage.

Galanter, M. 1974. Why the haves come out ahead: Speculations on the limits of legal change. *Law and Society Review* 9:95–160.

———. 1988. The quality of settlements. *Journal of Dispute Resolution* 55.

Galanter, M. and J. Rogers. 1991. *Transformation of American Business Disputing? Some Preliminary Observations*. Working Paper, Madison: Institute of Legal Studies.

Galanter, M. S. 1983. Reading the landscape of disputes: What we know and don't know (and think we know) about our allegedly contentious and litigious society. *UCLA Law Review* 31(4).

Gamble, B. 1997. Putting civil rights to a popular vote. *American Journal of Political Science* 41(1):245–269.

Gamson, J. 1995. Must identity movements self-destruct? A queer dilemma. *Social Problems* 42:390–405.

Gatewood, R. D. and H. S. Field. 1994. *Human Resource Selection* (3rd ed.). Dryden Press. Ft. Worth, TX: Harcourt Publishing.

Garey, A. I. 1999. *Weaving Work and Motherhood.* Philadelphia: Temple University Press.

Gerson, K. 1985. *Hard Choices: How Women Decide about Work, Career, and Motherhood.* Berkeley: University of California Press.

———. 1993. *No Man's Land: Men's Changing Commitments to Family and Work.* New York: Basic Books.

Gerstel, N. and K. McGonagle. 1999. Job leaves and the limits of the family and medical leave act: The effects of gender, race and family. *Work and Occupations* 26:510–534.

Gerstmann, E. 1999. *The Constitutional Underclass: Gays, Lesbians, and the Failure of Class-Based Equal Protection*. Chicago: University of Chicago Press.

Gilbert, D. T. and J. G. Hixon. 1991. The trouble of thinking: Activation and application of stereotypic beliefs. *Journal of Personality and Social Psychology* 60:509–517.

Gladwell, M. 2002. The talent myth. *New Yorker* July 22, 2002.

Glass, J. 2004. Blessing or curse? Family responsive policies and mother's wage growth over time. *Work and Occupations.* Forthcoming.

Glass, J. and L. Riley. 1998. Family responsive policies and employee retention following childbirth, *Social Forces* 76(4):1401–1435.

Glass, J. and V. Camerigg. 1992. Gender, parenthood, and job-family compatibility. *American Journal of Sociology* 98(1):131–151.

Glenn, E. N. 2002. *Unequal Freedom: How Race and Gender Shaped American Citizenship and Labor*. Cambridge, MA: Harvard University Press.

Glick, P., C. Zion, and C. Nelson. 1988. What mediates sex discrimination in hiring decisions? *Journal of Personality and Social Psychology* 55:178–186.

Glick, P. and S. T. Fiske. 1996. The ambivalent sexism inventory: Differentiating hostile and benevolent sexism. *Journal of Personality and Social Psychology* 70:491–512.

———. 2001a. Ambivalent sexism. In M. P. Zanna (Ed.), *Advances in Experimental Social Psychology* (Vol. 33, pp. 115–188). Thousand Oaks, CA: Academic Press.

———. 2001b. Ambivalent stereotypes as legitimizing ideologies: Differentiating paternalistic and envious prejudice. In J. T. Jost and B. Major (Eds.), *The Psychology of Legitimacy* (pp. 278–306). New York: Cambridge University Press.

Goldberg-Hiller, J. 2002. *The Limits to Union: Same-Sex Marriage and the Politics of Civil Rights*. Ann Arbor: University of Michigan Press.

Goldberg-Hiller, J. and N. Milner. 2003. Rights as excess: Understanding the politics of special rights. Forthcoming in *Law and Social Inquiry* 28(4):1075–1118.

Goldberg, M. S. 1982. Discrimination, nepotism, and long-run wage differentials. *The Quarterly Journal of Economics* 97:307–319.

Goldberg, P. K. 1996. Dealer price discrimination in new car purchases: Evidence from the consumer expenditure survey. *Journal of Political Economy* 104:622–654.

Goldberg, S. 1994. Gay rights through the looking glass: Politics, morality and the trial of Colorado's amendment. *Fordham Urban Law Journal* 2(XXI):1057.

Goldberg, S. B. 2005. On making anti-essentialist arguments in court. Forthcoming in *Oregon Law Review* 81:629–661.

Goldin, C. and C. Rouse. 2000. Orchestrating impartiality. *American Economic Review* 90:715–741.

Gomez, J. P. and S. J. Trierweiler. 2001. Does discrimination terminology create response bias in questionnaire studies of discrimination? *Personality and Social Psychology Bulletin* 27(5):630–638.

Gordon, D. M., R. Edwards, and M. Reich. 1982. *Segmented Work, Divided Workers: The Historical Transformation of Labor in the United States*. Cambridge: Cambridge University Press.

Gornick, J. C. and M. K. Meyers. 2003. *Families That Work: Policies for Reconciling Parenthood and Employment.* New York: Russell Sage.

Graham, H. D. 1990. *The Civil Rights Era*. New York: Oxford.

Gramsci, A. 1971. *Selections from the Prison Notebooks*. New York: International Publishers.

Greenberg, J. 2002. Title VII and gender nonconformity discrimination: Protection for transsexuals, intersexuals, gays and lesbians. *Thomas Jefferson Law Review* 24:149–159.

Green, D. P., D. Z. Strolovitch, and J. S. Wong. 1998. Defended neighborhoods, integration, and racially motivated crime. *American Journal of Sociology* 104:372–403.

Green, D. P., J. Glaser, and A. Rich. 1998. From lynching to gay bashing: The elusive connection between economic conditions and hate crime. *Journal of Personality and Social Psychology* 75:82–92.

Greenwald, A. G. and M. R. Banaji. 1995. Implicit social cognition. *Psychological Review* 102: 1–27.

Greenwald, A. G., D. E. McGhee, and J. L. K. Schwartz. 1998. Measuring individual differences in implicit cognition: The implicit association test. *Journal of Personality and Social Psychology Bulletin* 74:1464–1480.

Grier, W. H. and P. M. Cobbs. 1968. *Black Rage*. New York: Basic Books.

Griffen, E. 2001. Relations stop nowhere: ERISA preemption of San Francisco's domestic partner ordinance. *California Law Review* 89:459–505.

Griffith, K. H. and M. R. Hebl. 2002. The disclosure dilemma for gay men and lesbians: 'Coming out' at work. *Journal of Applied Psychology* 87:1191–1199.

Grillo, T. 1991. The mediation alternative: Process dangers for women. *The Yale Law Review* 100:6.

———. 1995. Anti-essentialism and intersectionality: Tools to dismantle the master's house. *Berkeley Women's Law Journal* 10:16–30.

Grodsky, E. and D. Pager. 2001. The structure of disadvantage: Individual and occupational determinants of the black–white wage gap. *American Sociological Review* 66:542–567.

Grodsky, E. and D. Pager. 2001. The structure of disadvantage. *American Sociological Review* 66:542–567.

Gruber, J. E. 1997. An epidemiology of sexual harassment: Evidence from North America and Europe. In W. O'Donohue (Ed.), *Sexual Harassment: Theory, Research, and Treatment* (pp. 84–98). Boston, MA: Allyn and Bacon.

Gruber, J. E. and L. Bjorn 1982. Blue-collar blues: The sexual harassment of women autoworkers. *Work and Occupations* 9:271–298.

Gruber, J. E. and M. D. Smith. 1995. Women's responses to sexual harassment: A multivariate analysis. *Basic and Applied Social Psychology* 17:543–562.

Gurin, P., A. H. Miller, and G. Gurin. 1980. Stratum identification and consciousness. *Social Psychology Quarterly* 43:30–47.

Gurin, P. and A. Townsend. 1986. Properties of gender identity and their implications for group consciousness. *British Journal of Social Psychology* 25:139–148.

Gutek, B. 1985. *Sex and The Workplace* (pp. 1–216). San Francisco, CA: Jossey-Bass.

Gutek, B. and B. Morasch. 1982. Sex ratios, sex-role spillover, and sexual harassment of women at work. *Journal of Social Issues* 38:55–74.

Gutek, B. and M. P. Koss. 1996. How women deal with sexual harassment and how organizations respond to reporting. In D. K. Shrier (Ed.), *Sexual Harassment in the Workplace and Academia: Psychiatric Issues* (pp. 39–57). Washington, D.C.: American Psychiatric Press.

Haagsma, R. 1998. Statistical discrimination in the labour market. *The Economist* 146:321–345.

Haberfeld, Y. 1992. Employment discrimination. *Academy of Management Journal* 35:161–180.

Hafer, C. L. and J. Olson. 1993. Beliefs in a just world, discontent, and assertive actions by working women. *Personality and Social Psychology Bulletin* 19:30–38.

Haider-Markel, D. P. and K. J. Meier. 1996. The politics of gay and lesbian rights: Expanding the scope of the conflict. *Journal of Politics* 58:332–349.

Hakim, C. 2002. Lifestyle preferences as determinants of women's differentiated labor market careers. *Work and Occupations* 29(4):428–459.

Halley, J. 1999. *Don't: A Reader's Guide to the Military's Anti-Gay Policy, Public Planet Books*. Durham, N.C.: Duke University Press.

Hannan M. T. and J. H. Freeman. 1984. Structural inertia and organizational change. *American Sociological Review* 43:143–164.

Hansen, K., J. J. Heckman, and K. Mullen. 2004. The effect of schooling and ability on achievement test scores. *Journal of Econometrics* 121:39–98.

Hanssen, A. 1998. The cost of discrimination: A study of major league baseball. *Southern Economic Journal* 64:603–627.

Hanssen, A. and T. Andersen. 1999. Has discrimination lessened over time? A test using baseball's all-star vote. *Economic Inquiry* 37:326–352.

Hardisty, J. and A. Gluckman. 1997. The hoax of 'special rights': The right wing's attack on gay men and lesbians. In A. Gluckman and B. Reed (Eds.), *Homo Economics: Capitalism, Community, and Lesbian and Gay Life* (pp. 209–222). New York: Routledge.

Hargrow, A. M. 1996. Speaking to our realities: From speculation to truth concerning African American women's experiences of sexual harassment 56. Unpublished PhD Dissertation (on file with author), Ohio State University.

Harlan, S. L. and P. M. Robert. 1998. The social construction of disability in organizations: Why employers resist reasonable accommodations. *Work and Occupations* 25(4):397–435.

Harless, D. W. and G. E. Hoffer. 2002. Do women pay more for new vehicles? Evidence from transaction price data. *American Economic Review* 92:270–279.

Harrell, S. P. 2000. A multidimensional conceptualization of racism-related stress: Implications for well-being of people of color. *American Journal of Orthopsychiatry* 70:42–57.

Harris, A. P. 1990. Race and essentialism in feminist legal theory. *Stanford Law Review* 42:581–616.

Hart, A. J., P. J. Whalen, L. M. Shin, S. C. McInerney, H. Fischer, and S. L. Rauch. 2000. Differential response in the human amygdala to racial outgroup vs ingroup face stimuli. *Neuroreport: For Rapid Communication of Neuroscience Research* 11:2351–2355.

Hays, S. 1996. *The Cultural Contradictions of Motherhood*. New Haven: Yale University Press.

Hebl, M. R., J. B. Foster, L. M. Mannix, and J. F. Dovidio. 2002. Formal and interpersonal discrimination: A field study of bias toward homosexual applicants. *Personality and Social Psychology Bulletin* 28:815–825.

Heckman, J. J. and B. S. Payner. 1989. Determining the impact of federal antidiscrimination policy on the economic status of blacks. *American Economic Review* 79:138–177.

Heckman, J. J. 2000. Policies to foster human capital. *Research in Economics* 54(1):3–56.

———. 1998. Detecting discrimination. *Journal of Economic Perspectives* 12:101–116.

Heckman, J. J., M. Larenas, and S. Urzua. 2004. Accounting for the Effect of Schooling and Abilities in the Analysis of Racial and Ethnic Disparities in Achievement Test Scores. Working paper, University of Chicago.

Heckman, J. J., L. Lochner, and C. Taber. 1998. Explaining rising wage inequality: Explorations with a dynamic general equilibrium model of labor earnings with heterogeneous agents. *Review of Economic Dynamics* 1(1):1–58.

Heckman, J. J. and P. Todd. 2001. Understanding the contribution of legislation, social activism, markets and choice to the economic progress of African Americans in the twentieth century. Unpublished manuscript, American Bar Foundation, Chicago, IL.

Heckman, J. J. and Y. Rubinstein. 2001. The importance of noncognitive skills: Lessons from the GED testing program. *American Economic Review* 91(2):145–149.

Hedström, P. and R. Swedberg. (Eds.). 1993. *Social Mechanisms.* Cambridge, NY: Cambridge University Press.

Heiden, H. -G. 1996. Niemand Darf Wegen Seiner Behinderung Benachteiligt Werden (Nobody Should Be Discriminated Against Because of Disability). Hamburg, rororo.

Heidrick and Struggles, Inc. 1979. *Profile of a Black Executive*. Chicago: Heidrick and Struggles.

Heimer, C. A. 1999. Competing institutions: Law, medicine, and family in neonatal intensive care. *Law and Society Review* 33:17–66.

Hebl, M. R., J. B. Foster, L. M. Mannix, and J. F. Dovidio. 2002. Formal and interpersonal discrimination. *Personality and Social Psychology Bulletin* 28:815–825.

Heneman, H. G. III, R. L. Heneman, and T. A. Judge 1997. *Staffing Organizations* (2nd ed.). Mendota House and Richard D. Irwin.

Herman, D. 1997. *The Antigay Agenda: Orthodox Vision and the Christian Right*. Chicago: University of Chicago Press.

Hermes, G. (Ed.). 1998. Traumland USA: Zwischen Antidiskriminierung und Sozialer Armut (Dreamland USA: Between Discrimination and Social Poverty). Kassel, Bifos.

Hernández, T. K. 2001. Sexual harassment and racial disparity: The mutual construction of gender and race. *Iowa Journal of Gender, Race and Justice* 4:183–224.

Hernandez-Truyol, B. E. 1994. Building bridges—Latinas and latinos at the crossroads: Realities, rhetoric, and replacement. *Columbia Human Rights Law Review* 25:369–430.

Hernes, G. 1998. Real virtuality. In P. Hedström and R. Swedberg (Eds.), *Social Mechanisms* (pp. 74–101). Cambridge: Cambridge University.

Herrnstein, R. and C. Murray. 1994. *The Bell Curve: Intelligence and Class Structure in American Life*. New York: Free Press.

Hersch, J. and L. S. Stratton. 2000. Household specialization and the male marriage premium. *Industrial and Labor Relations Review* 54:78–94.

Hewstone, M. 1990. The ultimate attribution error? A review of the literature on intergroup causal attribution. *European Journal of Social Psychology* 20:311–335.

Heyer, K. 2000. From welfare to rights—Japanese disability law. *Asia-Pacific Law and Policy Journal*, p. 6, available at www.hawaii.edu/aplpj.

———. 2002. The ADA on the road: Disability rights in Germany. *Law and Social Inquiry* 27:901.

Hill, J. R. and W. Spellman. 1984. Pay discrimination in baseball: Data from the seventies. *Industrial Relations* 23:103–112.

Hochschild, A. 1997. *The Time Bind: When Work Becomes Home and Home Becomes Work*. New York: Metropolitan Books.

Hochschild, A. R. 1975. The effects of transitions in marital status on men's performance inside the clockwork of male careers. In F. Howe (Ed.), *Women and the Power to Change*, (pp. 49–80). New York: McGraw-Hill.

———. 1989. *The Second Shift: Working Parents and the Revolution at Home.* New York: Viking.

———. 1997. *The Time Bind.* New York: Metropolitan.

Hodgins, H. S. 1995. Hypothesis confirmation: The joint effect of positive test strategy and acquiescence response set. *Journal of Personality and Social Psychology* 68:52–60.

Hodson, G., J. F. Dovidio, and S. L. Gaertner. 2002. Processes in racial discrimination: Differential weighting of conflicting information. *Personality and Social Psychology Bulletin* 28:460–471.

Hofferth, S. L. 1996. Effects of public and private policies on working after birth. *Work and Occupations* 23:378–404.

Hoffmann, E. A. 2001. Confrontations and compromise: Dispute resolution at a worker cooperative coal mine. *Law and Social Inquiry* 26:555–596.

Hoffmann, E. A. Dispute resolution in a worker cooperative: Formal procedures and procedural justice. *Law and Society Review* 39(1):51–82.

Holzer, H. H. 1996. *What Employers Want.* New York: Russell Sage.

Hooks, B. 1981. *Ain't I A Woman: Black Women and Feminism*. Boston: South End Press.

Horton, H. D. 1995. Population change and the employment status of college educated blacks. *Race and Ethnic Relations* 8:99–114.

Houlette, M., S. L. Gaertner, K. M. Johnson, B. S. Banker, B. M. Riek, and J. F. Dovidio. 2004. Developing a more inclusive social identity: An elementary school intervention. *Journal of Social Issues* 60(1):35–56.

Howard, J. M. and M. Rothbart. 1980. Social categorization for in-group and out-group behavior. *Journal of Personality and Social Psychology* 38:301–310.

Howard, P. K. 1994. *Death of Common Sense: How Law is Suffocating America*. New York: Random House.

———. 2001. *The Lost Art of Drawing the Line: How Fairness Went Too Far*. New York: Random House.

Huffman, M. L. and S. C. Velasco. 1997. When more is less. *Work and Occupations* 24:214–244.

Hull, G. T., P. B. Scott and B. Smith. (Eds.). 1982. *All The Women are White, All the Blacks are Men, But Some of Us are Brave: Black Women's Studies*. New York, NY: The Feminist Press at The City University of New York.

Hull, K. 2001. The political limits of the rights frame: The case of same-sex marriage in Hawaii. *Sociological Perspectives* 44(2):207–232.

Human Rights Campaign Foundation. 2000. *The State of the Workplace For Lesbian, Gay, Bisexual and Transgender Americans, 2000*. Washington, D.C.: Human Rights Campaign Foundation.

———. 2001. *The State of the Workplace for Lesbian, Gay, Bisexual and Transgender Americans, 2001*. Washington, D. C.: Human Rights Campaign Foundation.

———. 2004. *The State of the Workplace For Lesbian, Gay, Bisexual and Transgender Americans, 2003*. Washington, D.C.: Human Rights Campaign Foundation.

Hunt, G. 1999. *Laboring for Rights: Unions and Sexual Diversity Across Nations, Queer Politics, Queer Theories*. Philadelphia: Temple University Press.

Hunt, A., R. D. Benford, and D. Snow. 1994. Identity fields: Framing processes and the social construction of movement identities. In H. J. E. Laraña and J. R. Gusfield (Eds.), *New social movements From Idology to Identity* (p. 185). Philadelphia: Temple University Press.

Hutchinson, D. 2000. Gay rights for gay whites?: Race, sexual identity, and equal protection discourse. *Cornell Law Review* 85:1358.

———. 2001. Identity crisis: Intersectionality, multidimensionality, and the development of an adequate theory of subordination. *Michigan Journal of Race and Law* 6:285–317.

Iglesias, E. M. 1993. Structures of subordination: Women of color at the intersection of title VII and the NLRA. Not! *Harvard Civil Rights-Civil Liberties Law Review* 28:395–503.

Inman, M. L. 2001. Do you see what I see?: Similarities and differences in victims' and observers' perceptions of discrimination. *Social Cognition* 19:521–546.

Inman, M. L. and R. S. Baron. 1996. Influence of prototypes on perceptions of prejudice. *Journal of Personality and Social Psychology* 70:727–739.

Issachoroff, S. 1999. Governance and legitimacy in the law of class actions. *Supreme Court Review* 337:367.

Jacob, H. 1992. The elusive shadow of the law. *Law and Society Review* 36:565–590.

Jacobs, J. A. 1999. The sex segregation of occupations. In G. N. Powell (Ed.), *Handbook of Gender and Work* (pp. 125–141). California: Sage.

———. 2001. Evolving patterns of sex segregation. In I. Berg and A. L. Kallerberg (Eds.), *Sourcebook of Labor Markets: Evolving Structures and Processes*. New York: Plenum Publishers.

———. 2004. The faculty time divide. *Sociological Forum* 19:3–27.

Jacobsen, J. P. and L. M. Levin. 1995. Effects of intermittent labor force attachment on women's earnings. *Monthly Labor Review* September 14–19, 1995.

Jacoby, S. M. 1985. *Employing Bureaucracy: Managers, Unions and the Transformation of Work in American Industry, 1900–1945*. New York: Columbia University Press.

Jencks, C. and M. Phillips. 1998. *The Black–White Test Score Gap*. Washington, D.C.: The Brookings Institution.

Jencks, C. and M. Phillips. (Eds.). 1998. *The Black-White Test Score Gap*. Washington, D.C.: Brookings.

Jewell, K. S. 1993. *From Mammy to Miss America and Beyond: Cultural Images and the Shaping of U.S. Social Policy*. London: Routledge.

Jiobu, R. M. 1988. Racial inequality in a public arena: The case of professional baseball. *Social Forces* 67:524–534.

Johnston, W. B. and A. E. Packer. 1987. *Workforce 2000: Work and Workers for the 21st Century*. Indianapolis, IN: Hudson Institute.

Jones, J. M. 1997. *Prejudice and Racism* (2nd ed.). New York: McGraw-Hill.

Jost, J. T. 1995. Negative illusions: Conceptual clarification and psychological evidence concerning false consciousness. *Political Psychology* 16:397–424.

Jost, J. T. and B. Major. (Eds.). 2001. *The Psychology of Legitimacy*. New York: Cambridge University Press.

Jost, J. T. and D. Burgess. 2000. Attitudinal ambivalence and the conflict between group and system justification motives in low status groups. *Personality and Social Psychology Bulletin* 26:293–305.

Jost, J. T. and M. R. Banaji. 1994. The role of stereotyping in system-justification and the production of false consciousness. *British Journal of Social Psychology* 33:1–27.

Judiesch, M. K. and K. S. Lyness. 1990. Left behind? The impact of leaves of absence on managers' career success. *Academy of Management Journal* 42(6):641–651.

Kagan, R. A. 2001. *Adversarial Legalism: The American Way of Law*. Cambridge: Harvard University Press.

Kahn, L. M. 1992. Discrimination in baseball. In Paul M. Sommers (ed.), *Diamonds are Forever: The Business of Baseball* (pp. 163–88). Washington, D.C.: The Brookings Institution.

Kaiser, C. R. and C. T. Miller. 2001a. Reacting to impending discrimination: Compensation for prejudice and attributions to discrimination. *Personality and Social Psychology Bulletin* 27:1357–1367.

———. 2001b. Stop complaining! The social costs of making attributions to discrimination. *Personality and Social Psychology Bulletin* 27:254–263.

———. 2003. Derogating the victim: The interpersonal consequences of blaming events on discrimination. *Group Processes and Intergroup Relations* 6:227–237.

———. 2004. A stress and coping perspective on confronting sexism. *Psychology of Women Quarterly* 28:168–178.

Kaiser, C. R., P. Dyrenforth, and N. Hagiwara. 2005. An interpersonal analysis of attributions to discrimination: The dominant Ideology threat model of reactions to discrimination claimants. Manuscript submitted for publication under review, on file with author.

Kaiser, C. R., S. Shatzki, and M. Bartholomew. 2004. Meritocracy Beliefs Under Threat: Investigating the Interpersonal Consequences of Claiming Discrimination, paper presented at the fifth Annual Meeting of the Society for Personality and Social Psychology, Austin, TX.

Kaiser, C. R., S. B. Vick, and B. Major. 2005. Prejudice expectations moderate preconscious attention to social identity threatening cues. Manuscript submitted for publication under review, on file with author.

Kaiser, V. and Major. 2005.

Kalev, A., F. Dobbin, and E. Kelly. 2004. Two to tango: Affirmative action law, diversity management and women and African-Americans in management, 1971–1999. Manuscript submitted for publication.

Kalin, R. and D. C. Hodgins. 1984. Sex bias and occupational suitability. *Canadian Journal of Behavioral Science* 16:311–325.

Kalleberg, A., E. Rasell, N. Cassirer, B. F. Reskin, K. Hudson, D. Webster, E. Appelbaum, and R. M. Spalter-Roth. 1997. *Nonstandard Work, Substandard Jobs*. Washington, D.C.: Economic Policy Institute.

Kalleberg, A. L. 1995. Part-time work and workers in the United States: Correlates and policy issues. *Washington and Lee Law Review* 52:771–798.

Kalleberg, A. L. and B. F. Reskin. 1995. Gender differences in promotion in the United States and Norway. *Research in Social Stratification and Mobility* 14:237–264.

Kalleberg, A. L., D. Knoke, P. V. Marsden, and J. L. Spaeth. 1996. *Organizations in America*. Thousand Oaks: Sage.

Kame'eleihiwa, L. 1992. *Native land and foreign desires—Ko Hawai'i 'Aina a me na koi puumake a ka Po'e Haole*. Honolulu: Bishop Museum Press.

Kanter, R. M. 1977. *Men and Women of the Corporation*. New York: Basic Books.

Katz, I. and R. G. Hass. 1986. Racial ambivalence, value duality, and behavior. In J. F. Dovidio and S. L. Gaertner (Eds.), *Prejudice, Discrimination, and Racism* (pp. 35–59). Thousand Oaks, CA: Academic Press.

———. 1988. Racial ambivalence and value conflict: Correlational and priming studies of dual cognitive structures. *Journal of Personality and Social Psychology* 55:893–905.

Katz, I., J. Wackenhut, and R. G. Hass. 1986. Racial ambivalence, value duality, and behavior. In J. F. Dovidio and S. L. Gaertner (Eds.), *Prejudice, discrimination, and racism* (pp. 35–59). Orlando, FL: Academic Press.

Kawakami, K., R. Spears, and J. F. Dovidio. 2002. Disinhibition of stereotyping: Context, prejudice and target characteristics. *European Journal of Social Psychology* 32(4): 517–531.

Kawashima, T. 1963. *Dispute Resolution in Contemporary Japan. Law in Japan: The Legal Order in a Changing Society. A. T. v. Mehren* (pp. 41–72). Cambridge: Harvard University Press.

Keen, L. and S. Goldberg. 1998. *Strangers to the Law*. Ann Arbor: University of Michigan Press.

Kelly, E. 1999. Theorizing corporate family policies: How advocates built "the Business Case" for "family-friendly" Policies. *Research in the Sociology of Work* 7:167–202.

———. 2003. The strange history of employer-sponsored child care: Interested actors, uncertainty, and the transformation of law in organizational fields. *American Journal of Sociology* 109:606–649.

Kelly, E. and F. Dobbin. 1999. Civil rights law at work: Sex discrimination and the rise of maternity leave policies. *American Journal of Sociology* 105(2):455–492.

Kelly, E. and A. Kalev. 2003. Flexible formalization and limited legalization: Managing flexible work arrangements in the new economy. Manuscript submitted for publication.

Kessler-Harris, A. 1982. *Out to Work: A History of Wage-Earning Women in the United States*. Oxford: Oxford University Press.

———. 2001. *In Pursuit of Equity: Women, Men and the Quest for Economic Citizenship in 20th-Century America*. Oxford: Oxford University Press.

Kim, M. 1999. Inertia and discrimination in the California State Civil Service. *Industrial Relations* 38:46–68.

Kinder, D. R. 1998. Opinion and action in the realm of politics. In D. T. Gilbert, S. T. Fiske, and G. Lindzey (Eds.), *Handbook of Social Psychology* (4th ed., Vol. 2, pp. 778–867). New York: McGraw-Hill.

Kirschenman, J. and K. M. Neckerman. 1991. "We'd love to hire them, but . . . ": The Meaning of Race for Employers. In C. Jencks and P. E. Peterson (eds.), *The Urban Underclass* (pp. 203–232). Washington, D.C.: Brookings Institution.

Kiser, E. and M. Hechter. 1991. The role of general theory in comparative-historical sociology. *American Journal of Sociology* 97:1–30.

Klawitter, M. M. and V. Flatt. 1998. The effects of state and local antidiscrimination policies on earnings for gays and lesbians. *Journal of Policy Analysis and Management* 17:658–686.

Kleiman, C. 2004. Bias against mothers: Then and now. *Chicago Tribune* July 20, 2004, p. 2.

Kleiman L. S. and K. J. Clark. 1984. An effective job posting system. *Personnel Journal*. 63:20–25.

Kleugel, J. R. and E. R. Smith. 1986. *Beliefs About Inequality: Americans' View of What is and What Ought to Be*. Hawthorne, NJ: Aldine de Gruyer.

Koch, J. V. and C. W. VanderHill. 1988. Is there discrimination in the 'black man's game'? *Social Science Quarterly* 69:83–94.

Kohlman, M. R. H. 2000. Locating sexual harassment within intersections of experience in the U.S. labor market, at 97. Unpublished PhD Dissertation (on file with author), University of Maryland College Park Department of Sociology.

Konrad, A. M. and J. Pfeffer. 1991. Understanding the hiring of women and minorities in educational institutions. *Sociology of Education* 64:141–157.

Konrad, A. M. and F. Linnehan. 1995. Formalized HRM structures: Coordinating equal employment opportunity or concealing organizational practices? *Academy of Management Journal* 38:787–829.

———. 1999. Affirmative action. In G. N. Powell (Ed.), *Handbook of Gender and Work* (pp. 429–452). Thousand Oaks: Sage.

Koppelman, A. 1988. The miscegenation analogy: Sodomy law as sex discrimination. *Yale Law Journal* 98:145–164.

———. 1994. Why discrimination against lesbians and gay men is sex discrimination. *New York University Law Review* 69(2):197–287.

———. 2001. Defending the sex discrimination argument for lesbian and gay rights: A reply to Edward Stein. *UCLA Law Review* 49:519–538.

Korenman, S. and D. Neumark. 1992. Marriage, motherhood, and wages. *Journal of Human Resources* 27(2):233–255.

Korn/Ferry. 1986. *Korn/Ferry International's Executive Profile: A Survey of Corporate Leaders in the Eighties*. New York: Korn/Ferry.

———. 1990. Korn/Ferry international's executive profile: 1990 *A Survey of Corporate Leaders*. New York: Korn/Ferry.

Kostiner, I. 2003. Evaluating legality: Toward a cultural approach to the study of law and social change. In *Law and Society Review* 37(2):323–368.

Kovel, J. 1970. *White racism: A psychohistory*. New York: Pantheon.

Krieger, L. 2000. Afterword: Socio-Legal Backlash. *Berkeley Journal of Employment and Labor Law* 21:475–519.

Krieger, L. H. 1995. The content of our categories: A cognitive bias approach to discrimination and equal employment opportunity. *Stanford Law Review* 47:1161–1248.

———. 1998. Civil rights perestroika: Intergroup relations after affirmative action. *California Law Review* 86:1251–1333.

———. 2000. Foreword—backlash against the ADA: Interdisciplinary perspectives and implications for social justice strategies. *Berkeley Journal of Employment and Labor Law* 21:1–19.

———. 2005. Naturalizing Disparate Treatment Theory. Unpublished manuscript, forthcoming in this edition, 7.

Kritzer, H. M. 1990. *The Justice Broker: Lawyers and Ordinary Litigation*. New York: Oxford University Press.

LaFree, G. 1989. *Rape and Criminal Justice: The Social Construction of Sexual Assault*. Belmont, CA: Wadsworth Publishing Co.

Lande, J. 1998. Failing faith in litigation? A survey of business lawyers' and executives' opinions. *Harvard Negotiation Law Review* 3:1.

Landrine, H. and E. A. Klonoff. 1996. The schedule of racist events: A measure of racial discrimination and a study of its negative physical and mental health consequences. *Journal of Black Psychology* 22:144–168.

Lane, J. D. and D. M. Wegner. 1995. The cognitive consequences of secrecy. *Journal of Personality and Social Psychology* 69:237–253.

Langer, E. 1975. The illusion of control. *Journal of Personality and Social Psychology* 32:311–328.

Latting, J. K. 1993. Soliciting individual change in an interpersonal setting: The case of racially or sexually offensive language. *Journal of Applied Behavioral Science*. Special Issue: Emerging developments in action research, 29:464–484.

Lawrence, C. 1997. The Id, the ego, and equal protection: Reckoning with unconscious racism. In J. Donahue (Ed.), *Foundations of Employment Discrimination Law* (p. 122). New York: Foundation Press.

Lee, M. D., S. M. MacDermid, and M. L. Buck. 2000. Organizational paradigms of reduced-load work: Accommodation, elaboration, and transformation. *Academy of Management Journal* 43:1211–1226.
Lempert, R. 1976. Mobilizing private law: An introductory essay. *Law and Society Review* 2:173–189.
———. 1998. A resource theory of the criminal law: Exploring when it matters. In B. G. Garth and A. Sarat (Eds.), *How Does Law Matter* (pp. 227–247). Evanston, IL: Northwestern University Press.
Leonhart, D. 2003. Gap between pay of men and women smallest on record. *New York Times* February 17, 2003, Al.
Lerner, M. J. 1980. *The Belief in a Just World: A Fundamental Delusion*. New York: Plenum Press.
Lerner, M. J. and D. T. Miller. 1978. Just world research and the attribution process: Looking back and ahead. *Psychological Bulletin* 85:1030–1051.
Levine, J. Z. 1994 Job posting practices. *Personnel* 61:48–52.
Levine, M. P. 1979. Employment discrimination against gay men. *International Review of Modern Sociology* 9:151–163.
Lewin, T. 1994. Men whose wives work earn less, studies show. *New York Times* October 12, 1994, Al.
Liebowitz, A. and J. A. Klerman. 1995. Explaining changes in married mothers' employment over time. *Demography* 32:365–378.
Lin, N. 2000. Inequality in social capital. *Contemporary Sociology* 29:785–795.
Lind, A. E. and T. R. Tyler. 1988. *The Social Psychology of Procedural Justice*. New York: Plenum.
Lindblom, C. 1977. *Politics and Markets*. New York: Basic Books.
———. 2001. *The Market System: What It is, How It Works, and What to Make of It, Yale ISPS Series*. New Haven: Yale University Press.
Litras, M. F. X. 2000. "Civil Rights Complaints in U.S. District Courts 1990–98." U.S. Department of Justice, Bureau of Justice Statistics (Federal Justice Statistics Program, NCJ 173427).
———. 2002. "Civil Rights Complaints in U.S. District Courts 2000." U.S. Department of Justice, Bureau of Justice Statistics (Federal Justice Statistics Program, NCJ 193979).
Lord, C. G. and D. S. Saenz. 1985. Memory deficits and memory surfeits: Differential cognitive consequences of tokenism for tokens and observers. *Journal of Personality and Social Psychology* 49:918–926.
Loy, P. H. and L. P. Stewart. 1984. The extent and effects of sexual harassment of working women. *Sociological Focus* 17:31–43.
Lucas, S. R. 1994. Effects of race and gender discrimination in the United States, 1940–1980. Unpublished Doctoral Dissertation Thesis Thesis, Sociology, University of Wisconsin, Madison.
Lugones, M. C. and E. V. Spelman. 1983. Have we got a theory for you! Feminist theory, cultural imperialism and the demand for the 'woman's voice'. *Women's Studies International Forum* 6:573–581.
Lukes, S. 1974. *Power: A Radical View*. London: Macmillan Press.
Lundberg, S. and E. Rose. 2000. Parenthood and the earnings of married men and women. *Labour Economics*. 7:689–710.
Lye, L. C. Y. 1998. Title 7's tangled tale. *Berkeley Journal of Employment and Labor Law* 19:315–361.
Macaulay, S. 1963. Non-contractual relations in business: A preliminary study. *American Sociological Review* 28:55–68.
———. 1979. Lawyers and consumer protection laws. *Law and Society Review* 14:115–171.
MacIver, R. M. 1942. *Social Causation*. New York: Harper Torchbooks.
MacKinnon, C. A. 1979. *Sexual Harassment of Working Women: A Case of Sex Discrimination* (Vol. 53). New Haven, CT: Yale Univ. Press.
———. 1989. *Toward a Feminist Theory of the State*. Cambridge: Harvard University Press.
Macrae, C. N. and G. V. Bodenhausen. 2000. Thinking categorically about others. In S. T. Fiske, D. L. Schacter, and C. Zahn-Waxler (Eds.), *Annual Review of Psychology* (Vol. 51, pp. 93–120). Palo Alto, CA: Annual Reviews.

Magley, V. J., C. L. Hulin, L. F. Fitzgerald, and M. DeNardo. 1999. Outcomes of self-labeling sexual harassment. *Journal of Applied Psychology* 84(3):390–402.

Major, B. 1989. Gender differences in comparisons and entitlement. *Journal of Social Issues* 45:99–115.

Major, B. 1994. From social inequality to personal entitlement: The role of social comparisons, legitimacy appraisals, and group membership. In M. P. Zanna (Ed.), *Advances in Experimental Social Psychology* (Vol. 26, pp. 293–348). San Diego: Academic Press.

Major, B., C. Kaiser, and S. K. McCoy. 2003. It's not my fault: When and why attributions to prejudice protect self-esteem. *Personality and Social Psychology Bulletin* 29:772–781.

Major, B. N. and L. T. O'Brien. 2005. The social psychology of stigma. In. S. T. Fiske, D. L. Schacter, and C. Zahn-Waxley (Eds.), *Annual Review of Psychology* Palo Alto, California: Annual Review Inc. 56:393–421.

Major, B. and W. J. Quinton. 2001. Relationship between feminist self-labeling and perceptions of personal discrimination. Unpublished manuscript, University of California at Santa Barbara.

Major, B., R. H. Gramzow, S. K. McCoy, S. Levin, T. Schmader, and J. Sidanius. 2002. Perceiving personal discrimination: The role of group status and legitimizing ideology. *Journal of Personality and Social Psychology* 82:269–282.

Major, B., S. McCoy, C. R. Kaiser, and W. J. Quinton. 2003. Prejudice and self-esteem: A transactional model. *European Review of Social Psychology* 14:77–104.

Major, B., W. J. Quinton, and S. K. McCoy. 2002. Antecedents and consequences of attributions to discrimination: Theoretical and empirical advances. In M. P. Zanna (Ed.), *Advances in Experimental Social Psychology* (Vol. 34). New York: Academic Press.

Major, B., W. J. Quinton, and T. Schmader. 2003. Reconsidering the antecedents and consequences of attributions to discrimination. *Journal of Experimental Social Psychology* 39:220–231.

Mangione-Lambie, M. G. 1994. Sexual harassment: The effects of perceiver gender, race and rank on attitudes and actions, at 104. Unpublished PhD Dissertation (on file with author), California School of Professional Psychology at San Diego.

Margolis, B. and J Piliavin. 1999. Stacking in major league baseball: A multivariate analysis. *Sociology of Sport Journal* 16:16–34.

Markham, W. S. Harlan, and E. Hackett. 1987. Promotional opportunity in organizations: Causes and consequences. In K. Rowland and G. Ferris (Eds.), *Research in Personnel and Human Resources Management* (pp. 223–287). Stanford, CT: Jai Press.

Markham, W. T., S. L. Harlan, and E. J. Hackett. 1987. Promotion opportunity in organizations: Causes and consequences. *Research in Personnel and Human Resource Management* 5:223–287.

Marks, J. H. 2002. Smoke, mirrors, and the disappearance of "vicarious" liability: The emergence of a dubious summary-judgement safe harbor for employers whose supervisory personnel commit hostile environment workplace harassment. *Houston Law Review* 38:1401.

Marsden, P. V., A. L. Kalleberg, and C. R. Cook. 1993. Gender differences in organizational commitment: Influences of work positions and family roles. *Work and Occupations* 20:367–390.

Marsden, P. V. and E. H. Gorman. 1998. Social capital in internal staffing practices. In R. T. A. J. Leenders and S. Gabbay (Eds.), *Corporate Social Capital* (pp. 167–183). Amsterdam: Kluwer.

Marsden, P. V. and E. Gorman. 2001 Social networks, job changes, and recruitment. In I. Berg and A. L. Kalleberg (Eds.), *Sourcebook on Labor Markets: Evolving Structures and Processes* (pp. 467–502). New York: Plenum Publishing.

Marshall, A.-M. 1998. Closing the gaps: Plaintiffs in pivotal sexual harassment cases. *Law and Social Inquiry* 23:761–793.

———. 2003. Injustice frames, legality, and the everyday construction of sexual harassment. *Law and Social Inquiry* 28(3):659–690.

———. 2005. Idle rights: Employees' legal consciousness and the construction of sexual harassment policies. *Law and Society Review* 39(1):83–124.

Marx, K. and F. Engels. 1846/1970. The German ideology. In C. J. Arthur (Ed.), New York: International Publishers.

———. 1978. The Marx-Engels reader. In R. Tucker (Ed.), New York: W. W. Norton.

Mason, M. A. and M. Goulden. 2002. Do babies matter: The effect of family formation on the life long careers of women. Academe, available at http://www.aaup.org/publications/Academe/2002/02nd/02ndmas.htm (visited on May 19, 2005).

Massaro, T. M. 1996. Gay rights, thick and thin. *Stanford Law Review* 49:45.

Maume, D. J., A. S. Cancio, and T. D. Evans. 1996. Cognitive skills and racial wage inequality: Reply to Farkas and Vicknair. *American Sociological Review* 61:561–564.

McCall, L. 2001. Sources of racial wage inequality in metropolitan labor markets. *American Sociological Review* 66:520–541.

McCall, L. 2001a. Managing Complexity: Methodologies for the Analysis of Multiple Categories," paper presented at the Regular Session on Feminist Theory, 2001 American Sociological Association Meetings, Anaheim Ca (unpublished manuscript, on file with author).

———. 2001b. *Complex Inequality: Gender, Class, and Race in the New Economy*. London: Routledge.

McCann, M. 1986. *Taking Reform Seriously*. Ithaca: Cornell University Press.

McCann, M. 1994. *Rights at Work: Pay Equity Reform and the Politics of Legal Mobilization*. Chicago: University of Chicago Press.

———. 1998. How does law matter for social movements? In B. Garth and A. Sarat (Eds.), *How Does Law Matter?* Evanston, Illinois: Northwestern University Press.

McConahay, J. B. 1986. Modern racism, ambivalence, and the modern racism scale. In J. F. Dovidio and S. L. Gaertner (Eds.), *Prejudice, Discrimination, and Racism* (pp. 91–125). Thousand Oaks, CA: Academic Press.

McCreery, P. 1999. Beyond gay: 'Deviant' sex and the politics of the ENDA workplace. *Social Text* 17(4):39–58.

McDermott, P., R. O'Barr, A. Jose, and M. Bowers. 2000. An evaluation of the equal opportunity commission mediation program. http://www.eeoc.gov/mediate/report/index.html.

McEvoy, A. 1998. Freedom of contract, labor, and the administrative state. In H. N. Scheiber (Ed.), *The State and Freedom of Contract* (pp. 198–235). Stanford: Stanford University Press.

Meares, T. and H. Bernard. 2000. Foreword: Transparent adjudication and social science research in constitutional criminal procedure. *Journal of Criminal Law and Criminology* 90:733, 1264.

Medoff, M. 1975. A reappraisal of discrimination against blacks in professional baseball. *Journal of Black Political Economy* 5:259–268.

Mendoza-Denton, R., V. J. Purdie, G. Downey, A. Davis, and J. Pietrzac. 2002. Sensitivity to status-based rejection: Implications for African-Americans students' college experience. *Journal of Personality and Social Psychology* 83:896–918.

Mendoza-Denton et al. 2002.

Menkel-Meadow, C. 1984. Toward another view of legal negotiation: The structure of problem-solving. *UCLA Law Review* 31:754–842.

Merit Systems Protection Bd. 1981. Sexual harassment in the federal workplace: Is it a problem? In L. W. Stein (Ed.), *Sexual Harassment in America: A Documentary History* (pp. 19–22, 21). 1999. Westport, CT: Greenwood Press.

Merry, S. E. 1990. *Getting Justice and Getting Even: Legal Consciousness Among Working Class Americans*.

Merry, S. E. 2000. *Colonizing Hawai'i: The Cultural Power of Law*. Princeton: Princeton University Press.

Meyer, J. W. and B. Rowan. 1977. Institutionalized organizations: Formal structure as myth and ceremony. *American Journal of Sociology* 83:340–363.

Meyer, J. W. and W. R. Scott. 1983. *Organizational Environments: Ritual and Rationality*. Beverly Hills: Sage Publications.

Milkman, R. 1987. *Gender at Work.* Urbana: University of Illinois.
Miller, R. E. and A. Sarat. 1981. Grievances, claims and disputes: Assessing the adversary culture. *Law and Society Review* 15:525–566.
Mincer, J. and H. Ofek. 1982. Interrupted work careers. *Journal of Human Resources* 17:3–24.
Minow, M. 1987. Interpreting rights: An essay for Robert Cover. *Yale Law Journal* 96:1860–1915.
———. 1987. Justice engendered. *Harvard Law Review* 101(10):88–89.
———. 1990. *Making All the Difference: Inclusion, Exclusion, and American Law.* Ithaka, NY: Cornell University Press.
Minter, S. 2000. Do transsexuals dream of gay rights? Getting real about transgender inclusion in the gay rights movement. *New York Law School Journal of Human Rights* 17:589–620.
Mirels, H. and J. Garrett. 1971. The Protestant ethnic as a personality variable. *Journal of Consulting and Clinical Psychology* 36:40–44.
Mnookin, R. and L. Kornhauser. 1979. Bargaining in the shadow of the law: The case of divorce. *Yale Law Journal* 88:950–997.
Mnookin, R. H. and L. Kornhauser. 1979. Bargaining in the shadow of the law: The case of divorce. *Yale Law Journal* 88:950.
Moen, P. 2003. *It's About Time: Couples and Careers.* Ithaca, NY: ILR Press.
Moen, P. and P. Roehling. 2005. *The Career Mystique: Cracks in the American Dream.* New York: Rowman and Littlefield.
Molot, J. 2003. An old judicial role for a new litigation era. Forthcoming in *Yale Law Journal* 113:27–118. at __, http://ssrn.com/abstract=394100.
Monahan, J. and L. Walker. 1998. *Social Science in Law: Cases and Materials. Chapter Five Social Science Used to Provide Context* (4th Ed.), New York: Foundation Press.
Monteith, M. J. 1993. Self-regulation of prejudiced responses: Implications for progress in prejudice-reduction efforts. *Journal of Personality and Social Psychology* 65:469–485.
Monteith, M. J., J. W. Sherman, and P. G. Devine. 1998. Suppression as a stereotype control strategy. *Personality and Social Psychology Review* 2:63–82.
Montgomery, D. 1976. Workers' control of machine production in the nineteenth century. *Labor History* 17:485–509.
———. 1987. *The Fall of the House of Labor: The Workplace, The State and American Labor Activism, 1865–1925.* Cambridge: Cambridge University Press.
Morgan, P. 1999. Risking relationships: Understanding the litigation choices of sexually harassed women. *Law and Social Review* 33(1):67–93.
Morgan, P. A. 1999. Risking relationships: Understanding the litigation choices of sexually harassed women. *Law and Society Review* 33:67–91.
Morrill, C. 1995. *The Executive Way: Conflict Management in Corporations.* Chicago: University of Chicago Press.
Morris, C. 1994. *Bearing Witness: Sexual Harassment and Beyond—Every Woman's Story.* Boston, MA: Little, Brown and Co.
Morris, R. 1996. Configuring the bo(u)nds of marriage: The implications of Hawaiian culture and values for the debate about homogamy. *Yale Journal of Law the Humanities* 8:105–159.
Moskowitz, G. B., A. R. Salomon, and M. Constance. 2000. Preconsciously controlling stereotyping: Implicitly activated egalitarian goals prevent the activation of stereotypes. *Social Cognition* 18: 151–177.
Moskowitz, G. B., P. M. Gollwitzer, W. Wasel, and B. Schaal. 1999. Preconscious control of stereotype activation through chronic egalitarian goals. *Journal of Personality and Social Psychology* 77:167–184.
Moss, P. and C. Tilly. 1996. Soft skills and race: An investigation of black men's employment problems. *Work and Occupations* 23:252–276.
Mueller, C. W., M. Mulinge, and J. Glass. 2002. Interactional processes and gender workplace inequalities. *Social Psychology Quarterly* 65:163–185.

Mullen, B. 1991. Group composition, salience, and cognitive representations: The phenomenology of being in a group. *Journal of Experimental Social Psychology* 27:297–323.

Mullen, B. and L. Hu. 1989. Perceptions of ingroup and outgroup variability: A meta-analytic integration. *Basic and Applied Social Psychology* 10:233–252.

Murray, C. 1999. The Secular Increase in IQ and Longitudinal Changes in the Magnitude of the Black–White Difference: Evidence from the NLSY, paper presented to the Behavior Genetics Association Meeting.

Murrell, A. J. 1996. Sexual harassment and women of color: Issues, challenges, and future directions. In M. S. Stockdale (Ed.), *Sexual Harassment in the Workplace: Perspectives, Frontiers, and Response Strategies* (pp. 51–66). Thousand Oaks, CA: Sage Publishers.

Nardinelli, C. and C. J. Simon. 1990. Customer racial discrimination in the market for memorabilia: The case of baseball. *The Quarterly Journal of Economics* 105:575–595.

Neal, D. 2004. The measured black-white wage gap among women is too small. *Journal of Political Economy* 112(1, part 2):S1–S28.

Neal, D. and W. Johnson. 1996. The role of premarket factors in black–white wage differences. *Journal of Political Economy* 104(5):869–895.

Neal, D. and W. R. Johnson. 1998. Basic skills and the black–white earnings gap. In C. Jencks and M. Phillips (Eds.), *The Black–White Test Score Gap*. Washington, D.C.: Brookings Institution Press.

Neckerman, K. M. and J. Kirschenman. 1991. Hiring strategies, racial bias, and inner-city workers: An investigation of employers' hiring decisions. *Social Problems* 38:433–447.

Nelson, R. L. 1994. The future of American lawyers: A demographic profile of a changing profession in a changing society. *Case Western Reserve Law Review* 44:345–406.

Nelson, M. A. and M. Manis. 1996. Irrepressible stereotypes. *Journal of Experimental Social Psychology* 32:13–38.

Nelson, R. and W. P. Bridges. 1999. *Legalizing Gender Inequality: Courts, Markets, and Unequal Pay for Women in America*. New York: Cambridge University Press.

Nelson, R. L. and W. P. Bridges. 1999. *Legalizing Gender Inequality*. New York: Cambridge University.

Nelson, R. L. and L. B. Nielsen. 2000. Cops, counsel, or entrepreneurs: The shifting roles of lawyers in large business corporations. *Law and Society Review* 34:457–494.

Neuberg, S. L. and S. T. Fiske. 1987. Motivational influences on impression formation: Outcome dependency, accuracy-driven attention, and individuating processes. *Journal of Personality and Social Psychology* 53:431–444.

Neuman, W. L. 1992. Gender, race, and age differences in student definitions of sexual harassment. *Wisconsin Sociologist* 29:63–75.

Neumark, D. 1996. Sex discrimination in the restaurant industry: An audit study. *Quarterly Journal of Economics* 111:915–941.

Ng, S. H. 1984. Equity and social categorization effects on intergroup allocation of rewards. *British Journal of Social Psychology* 165.

Nicholson, L. 1997. The myth of the traditional family. In H. Nelson (Ed.), *Feminism and Families*. New York: Routledge. p. 27–42.

Nielsen, L. B. 1999. Paying workers or paying lawyers: Employee termination practices in the United States and Canada. *Law and Policy* 21:247–282.

———. 2000. Situating legal consciousness: Experiences and attitudes of ordinary citizens about law and street harassment. *Law and Society Review* 34:201–236.

Nielsen, L. B. and A. Beim. 2004. Media misrepresentation: Title VII, print media, and public perceptions of discrimination litigation. *Stanford Law and Policy Review* 15(1):237–265.

Nier, J. A., S. L. Gaertner, J. F. Dovidio, B. S. Banker, and C. M. Ward. 2001. Changing interracial evaluations and behavior: The effects of a common group identity. *Group Processes and Intergroup Relations* 4:299–316.

Nieva V. F. and B. A. Gutek. 1980. Sex effects on evaluation. *Academy of Management Review* 5:267–275 (especially pages 270–274).

Noonan, M. C. 2001, The impact of domestic work on men's and women's wages. *Journal of Marriage and the Family.* 63:1134–1145.

———. 2002. How much does the long-term cost of a work interruption influence women's employment behavior surrounding first birth? Manuscript Submitted for Publication.

Note. 1996. Employment discrimination. *Harvard Law Review* 109:1568.

Obermayer, J. L. 2001. Women of Color and White Women's Resistance to Sexual Harassment. Unpublished PhD Dissertation (on file with author), American University Sociology Department, 1–142.

O'Connor, A., C. Tilly, and L. Bobo. (Eds.). 2001. *Urban Inequality: Evidence from Four Cities.* New York: Russell Sage.

Okamoto, D. and P. England. 1999. Is there a supply side to occupational sex segregation? *Sociological Perspectives* 42(4):557–582.

Okin, S. M. 1989. *Justice, Gender and the Family*. New York: Basic Books, Inc.

Oliver, M. 1990. *The Politics of Disablement: A Sociological Approach*. New York: St. Martin's Press.

———. 1996. *Understanding Disability: From Theory to Practice*. London: Macmillan.

Oliver, M. L. and T. M. Shapiro. 1997. *Black Wealth/White Wealth: A New Prespective on Racial Inequality*. New York: Routledge.

Olson, J. and C. L. Hafer. 2001. Tolerance of personal deprivation. In J. T. Jost and B. Major (Eds.), *The Psychology of Legitimacy: Emerging Perspectives on Ideology, Justice, and Intergroup Relations* (pp. 157–175). New York: Cambridge University Press.

Olson, W. K. 1991.*The Litigation Explosion: What Happened When America Unleashed the Lawsuit.* New York: Dutton.

———. 1997. *The Excuse Factory: How Employment Law is Paralyzing the American Workplace*. New York: Martin Kessler Books.

Ontiveros, M. L. 1993. Three perspectives on workplace harassment of women of color. *Golden Gate University Law Review* 23:817–828.

Operario, D. and S. T. Fiske. 2001. Ethnic identity moderates perceptions of prejudice: Judgments of personal versus group discrimination and subtle versus blatant bias. *Personality and Social Psychology Bulletin* 27:550–561.

Oppenheimer, D. B. 1993. Negligent discrimination. *University of Pennsylvania Law Review* 14:899–972.

Oppenheimer, D. B. 2003. Verdicts matter: An empirical study of California employment discrimination and wrongful discharge jury verdicts reveals low success rates for women and minorities. *University of California Davis Law Review* 37.

Oskamp, S. (Ed.). 2000. *Reducing Prejudice and Discrimination*. Mahwah NJ: Erlbaum.

Otten, S. and G. B. Moskowitz. 2000. Evidence for implicit evaluative in-group bias: Affect-based spontaneous trait inference in a minimal group paradigm. *Journal of Experimental Social Psychology* 36:77–89.

Padilla, L. 1997. Intersectionality and positionality: Situating women of color in the affirmative action dialogue. *Fordham Law Review* 66:843–929.

Pascal, A. and L. Rapping. 1972. The economics of discrimination in organized baseball. In Anthony Pascal (Ed.), *Racial Discrimination in Economic Life* (pp. 119–156). Lexington, MA: D.C. Heath.

Pateman, C. 1988. *The Sexual Contract*. Stanford: Stanford University Press.

Patterson, O. 1998. *The Ordeal of Integration: Progress and resentment in America's "racial" crisis.* Washington, D.C.: Civitas/Counterpoint.

Patton, C. 1995. Refiguring social space. In L. Nicholson and S. Seidman (Eds.), *Social Postmodernism: Beyond Identity Politics*. P. 216–249 Cambridge: Cambridge University Press.

———. 1997. Queer space/God's space: Counting down to the apocalypse. *Rethinking Marxism* 9(2):1–23.

Perlow, L. 1997. *Finding Time: How Corporations, Individuals, and Families Can Benefit from New Work Practices*. Ithaca, NY: ILR Press.

Perry, E. L., A. Davis-Blake, and C. T. Kulik. 1994. Explaining gender-based selection decisions. *Academy of Management Review* 19:786–820.

Petersen, T. and L. A. Morgan. 1995. Separate and unequal: Occupation-establishment sex segregation and the gender wage gap. *American Journal of Sociology* 101:329–365.

Petersen, T., I. Saporta, and M.-D. L. Seidel. 2000. Offering a job: meritocracy and social networks. *American Journal of Sociology* 106:763–816.

Pettigrew, T. F. 1959. Regional differences in anti-Negro prejudice. *Journal of Abnormal and Social Psychology* 59:28–36.

———. 1979. The ultimate attribution error: Extending allport's cognitive analysis of prejudice. *Personality and Social Psychology Bulletin* 5:461–476.

———. 1998a. Intergroup contact theory. In J. T. Spence, J. M. Darley, and D. J. Foss (Eds.), *Annual Review of Psychology* (Vol. 49, pp. 65–85). Palo Alto, CA: Annual Reviews.

———. 1998b. Reactions toward the new minorities of western Europe. In J. Hagan and K. S. Cook (Eds.), *Annual Review of Sociology* (Vol. 24, pp. 77–103). Palo Alto, CA: Annual Reviews.

Pettigrew, T. F. and J. Martin. 1987. Shaping the organizational context for Black American inclusion. *Journal of Social Issues* 43:41–78.

Pettigrew, T. F. and R. W. Meertens. 1995. Subtle and blatant prejudice in Western Europe. *European Journal of Social Psychology* 25:57–76.

Pfeffer, J. and G. R. Salancik. 1978. *The External Control of Organizations*. New York: Harper and Row.

Phelps, E. S. 1972. The statistical theory of racism and sexism. *American Economic Review* 62:659–661.

Phelps, E. A., K. J. O'Connor, W. A. Cunningham, E. S. Funayama, J. C. Gatenby, J. C. Gore, and M. R. Banaji. 2000. Performance on indirect measures of race evaluation predicts amygdala activation. *Journal of Cognitive Neuroscience* 12:729–738.

Phillips, K. P. 2002. *Wealth and Democracy: A Political History of the American Rich* (1st ed.). New York: Broadway Books.

———. 1998. *Gender Trials: Emotional Lives in a Contemporary Law Firm*. Berkeley: University of California.

Pinel, E. C. 1999. Stigma consciousness: The psychological legacy of social stereotypes. *Journal of Personality and Social Psychology* 76:114–128.

Player, M. A. 1992. *Federal Law of Employment Discrimination in a Nutshell* (3rd ed.). St. Paul, MN: West.

Pleck, J. 1993. Are "family supportive" employer policies relevant to men? In J. Hood (Ed.), *Men, Work, and Family* (pp. 217–327). Thousand Oaks, CA: Sage Publications.

Post, R. 2000. Prejudicial appearances: The logic of American antidiscrimination law. *California Law Review* 88:1, 17, 30.

Post, R. C. and R. B. Siegel. 2000. Equal protection by law: Federal antidiscrimination legislation after Morrison and Kimel. *Yale Law Journal* 110:441–526.

Priest, G. and B. Klein. 1984. The selection of disputes for litigation.*Journal of Legal Studies* 13:1.

Pugh, M. D. and R. Wahrman. 1983. Neutralizing sexism in mixed-sex groups. *American Journal of Sociology* 88:746–762.

Pyszczynski, T., J. Greenberg, and S. Solomon. 1997. Why do we need what we need? A terror management perspective on the roots of human social motivation. *Psychological Inquiry* 8(1):1–20.

Quinn, B. A. 2000. The paradox of complaining: Law, humor and harassment in the everyday work world. *Law and Social Inquiry* 25(4):1151–1185.

Radin, M. J. 1990. The pragmatist and the feminist. *Southern California Law Review* 63:1699–1726.

Ragins, B. R. and J. M. Cornwell. 2001. Pink triangles: Antecedents and consequences of perceived workplace discrimination against gay and lesbian employees. *Journal of Applied Psychology* 86:1244–1261.

Rapoport, R., L. Bailyn, J. K. Fletcher, B. H. Pruitt. 2001. *Beyond Work-Family Balance: Advancing Gender Equity and Workplace Performance.* San Francisco: Jossey-Bass.

Raudenbush, S. and R. Kasim. 1998. Cognitive skill and economic inequality. *Harvard Educational Review* 68:33–79.

Raustiala, K. and S. Anne-Marie. 2002. International law, international relations, and compliance. In Carlsnaes, et al. (Eds.), *Handbook of International Relations* (p. 538), available at http://ssrn.com/abstract_id=347260.

Reinarman, C. 1987. *American States of Mind: Political Beliefs and Behavior Among Private and Public Workers*. New Haven: Yale University Press.

Reskin, B. F. 1988. Bringing the men back in. *Gender and Society* 2:58–81.

———. 1998. *The Realities of Affirmative Action in Employment.* Washington, D.C.: American Sociological Association.

Reskin, B. and P. Roos. 1990. *Job Queues, Gender Queues: Explaining Women's Inroads into Occupations*. Philadelphia: Temple University Press.

Reskin, B. F. and C. Ross. 1992. Jobs, authority, and earnings among managers: The continuing significance of sex. *Work and Occupations* 19:342–365.

———. 2001. Employment discrimination and its remedies. In I. Berg and A. L. Kallberg (Eds.), *Sourcebook of Labor Markets: Evolving Structures and Processes*. New York: Kluwer Academic/Plenum Publishers.

Reskin, B. F., D. B. McBrier, and J. A. Kmec. 1999. The determinants and consequences of workplace race and sex composition. *Annual Review of Sociology* 25:335–361.

Reskin, B. F. and C. Z. Charles. 1999. Now you see 'em, now you don't: Theoretical approaches to race and gender in labor markets. In I. Browne (Ed.), *Latinas and African American Women in the Labor Market* (pp. 380–407). New York: Russell Sage.

Reskin, B. 2000. The proximate causes of discrimination. *Contemporary Sociology* 29:319–329.

Reskin, B. 2002. Retheorizing employment discrimination. In M. F. Guillen, R. Collins, P. England, and M. Meyer (Eds.), *The New Economic Sociology: Developments in an Emerging Field* (pp. 218–244). New York: Russell Sage.

Reskin, B. F. and D. B. McBrier. 2000. Why not ascription? Organizations' employment of male and female managers. *American Sociological Review* 65:210–233.

Reskin, B. F. 2003. Putting mechanisms in our models of ascriptive inequality. *American Sociological Review.*

Richards, D. 1999. *Identity and the Case for Gay Rights: Race, Gender, Religion as Analogies*. Chicago: University of Chicago Press.

Richtel, M. 2000. Online revolution's latest twist: Computers screening job seekers. *New York Times*.

Ridgeway, C. 1997. Interaction and the conservation of gender inequality. *American Sociological Review* 62:218–235.

Rimmerman, C. A. 2002. *From Identity to Politics: The Lesbian and Gay Movements in the United States*. Philadelphia: Temple University Press.

Rock, E. B. and M. L. Wachter. 1996. The enforceability of norms and the employment relationship. *University of Pennsylvania Law Review* 144:1913.

Rodgers, W. M., III and W. E. Spriggs. 1996. What does the AFQT really measure. *Review of Black Political Economy* Spring:13–46.

Rodin, M. J., J. M. Price, J. B. Bryson, and F. J. Sanchez. 1990. Asymmetry in prejudice attribution. *Journal of Experimental Social Psychology* 26:481–504.

Rogers, R. W. and S. Prentice-Dunn. 1981. Deindividuation and anger-mediated interracial aggression: Unmasking regressive racism. *Journal of Personality and Social Psychology* 41:63–73.

Rohlen, T. 1974. *For Harmony and Strength*. Berkeley, LA: University of California Press.

Rose, N. 1987. Beyond the public/private division: Law, power and the family. *Journal of Law and Society* 14(1):61–76.

———. 1996. Governing "advanced" liberal democracies. In A. Barry, T. Osborne, and N. Rose (Eds.), *Foucault and Political Reason*. Chicago: University of Chicago Press p. 37–64.

Rose, N. and P. Miller. 1992. Political power beyond the state: Problematics of government. *British Journal of Sociology* 43(2):173–205.

Rosenbloom, D. H. 1977. *Federal Equal Employment Opportunity: Politics and Public Personnel Administration.* New York: Praeger.

Rosenberg, G. N. 1991. *The Hollow Hope: Can Courts Bring About Social Change?* Chicago: University of Chicago Press.

Rosenberg, M. and R. G. Simmons. 1972. *Black and White Self-Esteem: The Urban School Child.* Washington, D.C.: American Sociological Association.

Rosen, R. E. 1989. The inside counsel movement, professional judgment, and organizational representation. *Indiana Law Journal* 64:479–553.

Rosenthal, R. 1994. Interpersonal expectancy effects: A 30-year perspective. *Current Directions in Psychological Science* 3:176–179.

Rospenda, K. M., J. A. Richman, and S. J. Nawyn. 1998. Doing power: The confluence of gender, race, and class in contrapower sexual harassment. *Gender and Social* 12(40–60):54 (citing Cortina, L. M. et al. 1996.? 'Dios mío... qué hacer?" Hispanic Women's Responses to Sexual Harassment. Unpublished paper presented at the 1995 Annual Meeting of the Midwestern Psychological Association in Chicago, Illinois).

Ross v. Kansas City Power and Light Company. 2002. U.S. Court of Appeals for the Eighth Circuit 293 F.3d 1041; 2002 U.S. App.

Rubenfeld, J. 1998. Textualism and democratic legitimacy: The moment and the millennium. *George Washington Law Review* 66:1085–1111.

Rubenstein, W. B. 1998. Some reflections on the study of sexual orientation bias in the legal profession. *UCLA Women's Law Journal* 8:379–403.

———. 2001. Do gay rights laws matter? An empirical assessment. *Southern California Law Review* 75:65–119.

Rudd, E. 2001. Framing Family Leave: Gender Equality, Personal Choice, and Crisis Response, paper presented at the American Sociological Association meeting, Anaheim, CA, August 18–21, 2001.

Rudin J. P. and J. W. Boudreau. 1996. Information acquisition in promotion decisions. *Human Relations* 49:313–325.

Sackett, P., C. Hardison, and M. Cullen. 2004. On interpreting stereotype threat as accounting for African American–White differences in congitive tests. *American Psychologist* 59(1):7–13.

Salancik, G. R. and J. Pfeffer. 1978. Uncertainty, secrecy, and the choice of similar others. *Social Psychology* 41:246–255.

Sampson, R. J. and J. L. Lauritsen. 1997. Racial and ethnic disparities in crime and criminal justice in the United States. In M. H. Tonry (Ed.), *Ethnicity, Crime, and Immigration: Comparative and Cross-National Perspectives*, *Crime and Justice Series* (Vol. 21, pp. 311–374). Chicago: University of Chicago Press.

Sanders, J. and V. L. Hamilton. 2001. *Handbook of Justice Research in Law*. New York: Kluwer Academic/Plenum Publishers.

Santora, T. 2001. What's good for the goose: A critical review of unions as employers and the continuing struggle toward equal benefits in the workplace. *Working USA* 4(4):98–123.

Sarat, A. and T. S. Kearns. 1993. Beyond the great divide: Forms of legal scholarship and everyday life. In A. Sarat and T. R. Kearns (Eds.), *Law in Everyday Life.* Ann Arbor: University of Michigan Press. p. 21–62.

Scales-Trent, J. 1989. Black women and the constitution: Finding our place, asserting our rights. *Harvard Civil Rights and Civil Liberties Law Review* 24:9–40.

Scarborough, C. 1989. Note, conceptualizing black women's employment experiences. *Yale Law Journal* 98:1457–1478.

Schacter, J. 1997. Skepticism, culture and the gay civil rights debate in a post-civil-rights era. *Harvard Law Review* 110:684.
Schacter, J. S. 1994. The gay civil rights debate in the states: Decoding the discourse of equivalents. *Harvard Civil Rights—Civil Liberties Law Review* 29:283–317.
Scheingold, S. A. 1974. *The Politics of Rights*. New Haven: Yale University Press.
Schelling, T. C. 1978. *Micromotives and Macrobehavior.* New York: Norton.
Schor, J. B. 1992. *The Overworked American: The Unexpected Decline of Leisure*. New York: Basic Books.
Schowengerdt, D. 2001/2002. Defending marriage: A litigation strategy to oppose same-sex 'marriage'. *Regent University Law Review* 14:487–511.
Schultz, V. 1998. Reconceptualizing sexual harassment. *The Yale Law Journal* 107:1683–1805.
Schultz, V. 1990. Telling stories about women and work: Judicial interpretations of sex segregation in the workplace in title VII cases raising the lack of interest argument. *Harvard Law Review* 103:1749.
Schultz, V. and S. Petterson. 1992. Race, gender, work, and choice: An empirical study of lack of interest defense in title 7 cases challenging job segregation. *University of Chicago Law Review* 59:1073–1181.
Schuman, H., C. Steeh, L. Bobo, and M. Krysan. 1997. *Racial Attitudes in America: Trends and Interpretations*. Cambridge, MA: Harvard University Press.
Schwartz, D. 2002. When is sex because of sex? The causation problem in sexual harassment law. *University of Pennsylvania Law Review* 150:1697–1794.
Scotch, R. 2001. *From Good Will to Civil Rights: Transforming Federal Disability Policy*. Philadelphia: Temple University Press.
Scott, J. and D. M. Trubek. 2002. Mind the gap: Law and new approaches to governance in the European union. *European Law Journal* 8:1.
Scott, M. F., F. Zettelmeyer, and J. Silva-Risso. 2002. *The Effect of Information and Institution on Price Negotiations: Evidence from Matched Survey and Auto Transaction Data*. Unpublished Working paper.
———. 2003. Consumer information and discrimination: Does the internet affect the pricing of new cars to women and minorities? *Quantitative Marketing and Economics* 1(1):65–92.
Scott, W. R. 2003. *Organizations: Rational, Natural, and Open Systems*. New Jersey: Prentice Hall.
Scully, G. W. 1974. Pay and performance in major league baseball. *American Economic Review* 64:915–930.
Sears, D. O. 1988. Symbolic racism. In P. A. Katz and D. A. Taylor (Eds.), *Eliminating Racism: Profiles in Controversy* (pp. 53–84). New York: Plenum Press.
Sears, D. O., P. J. Henry, and R. Kosterman. 2000. Egalitarian values and contemporary racial politics. In D. O. Sears, J. Sidanius, and L. Bobo (Eds.), *Racialized Politics: The Debate About Racism in America* (pp. 75–117). Chicago, IL: University of Chicago Press.
Sekigawa, H. 1998. *ADA, soshite JDA e* [from the ADA to the JDA]. In *JB—Joyful Begin* 9:97–108.
Selmi, M. 1996. The value of the EEOC: Reexamining the agency's role in employment discrimination law. *Ohio St. Law Journal* 57:1, 1.
———. 1998. Public vs. private enforcement of civil rights. *UCLA Law Review* 45:1401–1459.
Selmi, M. L. 2003. The price of discrimination: The nature of class action employment discrimination and its effects. *Texas Law Review* 81.
Selznick, P. 1969. *Law, Society, and Industrial Justice*. New York: Russell Sage Foundation.
Sewell, W. H. 1992. A theory of structure: Duality, agency, and transformation. *American Journal of Sociology* 98:1.
Shapiro, M. 2001. *For Moral Ambiguity: National Culture and the Politics of the Family*. Minneapolis: University of Minnesota Press.
Shelton, J. N. and S. Stewart. 2004. Confronting Perpetrators of Prejudice: The inhibitory role of social costs. *Psychology of Women Quarterly* 28(3):215–224.
Sherman, J. 2001. Domestic partnership and ERISA preemption. *Tulane Law Review* 76:373–429.

Sidanius, J. and F. Pratto. 1993. The dynamics of social dominance and the inevitability of oppression. In P. Sniderman and P. E. Tetlock (Eds.), *Prejudice, Politics, and Race in America Today*. Stanford, CA: Stanford University Press.

———. 1999. *Social Dominance: An Intergroup Theory of Social Hierarchy and Oppression*. New York: Cambridge University Press.

Sidanius, J., P. Singh, J. J. Hetts, and C. Federico. 2000. It's not affirmative action, it's the blacks: The continuing relevance of race in American politics. In D. O. Sears, J. Sidanius, and L. Bobo (Eds.), *Racialized Politics: The Debate About Racism in America* (pp. 191–235). Chicago: University of Chicago Press.

Siegelman, P. 1999. Racial discrimination in "everyday" commercial transactions: What do we know, what do we need to know, and how can we find out? In M. Fix and M. A. Turner (Eds.), *A National Report Card on Discrimination in America: The Role of Testing*. Washington, D.C.: Urban Institute.

Siegelman, P. and J. J. Donohue III. 1991. Studying the Iceberg from its tip? An analysis of differences between published and unpublished federal employment discrimination cases.*Law and Social Review* 24:1133.

Siegelman, P. and J. J. Donohue III. 1995. "The Selection of Employment Discrimination S for Lifecation: Clsmy Business Cycle Effects to Test the Priest/Klern Hypothesis," *Journal of Legal Studies*, 24:427.

———. 1995. The selection of employment discrimination disputes for litigation: Using business cycle effects to test the Priest/Klein hypothesis. *Journal of Legal Studies* 24:427.

Silbey, S. and A. Sarat. 1989. Dispute processing in law and legal scholarship: From institutional critique to the reconstruction of the juridical subject. *Denver University Law Review* 66:437, 498.

Silvers, A., D. Wasserman, and M. B. Mahowald (Eds.). 1998. *Disability, Difference, Discrimination: Perspectives on Justice in Bioethics and Public Policy*. Lanham, Maryland: Rowman and Littlefield.

Simmons, T. and M. O'Connell. 2003. *Married-Couple and Unmarried-Partner Households: 2000. Census 2000 Special Reports. CENSR-5*. Washington, D.C.: U.S. Census Bureau.

Smedley, B. D., A. Y. Stith, and A. R. Nelson. 2002. *Unequal Treatment: Confronting Racial and Ethnic Disparities in Health Care*. Washington, D.C.: The National Academies Press.

Smelser, N., W. J. Wilson, and F. Mitchell. (Eds.). 2001. *American Becoming*. Washington, D.C.: National Academy Press.

Smith, J. P. and F. R. Welch. 1983. Longer Trends in Black/White Economic Status and Recent Effects of Affirmative Action, paper prepared for Social Science Research Council conference at the National Opinion Research Center, Chicago.

———. 1986. *Closing the Gap: Forty Years of Economic Progress for Blacks*. Santa Monica, CA: Rand Corporation.

Smith, J. P. 1984. race and human capital. *American Economic Review* 4:685–698.

Smith, T. W. 2000. *Taking America's Pulse: NCCJ's 2000 Survey of Intergroup Relations in the United States*. New York: National Conference for Community and Justice.

Smith, R. A. 2001. Particularism in control over monetary resources at work. *Work and Occupations* 28:447–468.

———. 2002. Class, gender, and race in authority outcomes at work. *Annual Review of Sociology* 28:509–542.

———. 2002. *Measuring Racial and Ethnic Discrimination*. Chicago: National Opinion Research Center, University of Chicago.

Snow, D. A. a. R. D. B. 1992. Master Frames and Cycles of Protest. Frontiers in Social Movement Theory. A. D. M. a. C. M. Mueller. New Haven, Yale University Press.

Snow, D. A. Jr., E. B. Rochford, S. K. Worden, and R. D. Benford. 1986. Frame alignment processes, micromobilization, and movement participation. *American Sociological Review* 51:464–481.

Snyder, M. 1984. When belief creates reality. In L. Berkowitz (Ed.), *Advances in Experimental Social Psychology* (Vol. 18, pp. 247–305). New York: Academic Press.

Sørensen, A. B. 1998. Theoretical mechanisms and the empirical study of social processes. In P. Hedström and R. Swedberg (Eds.), *Social Mechanisms* (pp. 238–266). New York: Cambridge University.

Sorenson, R. C., M. Mangione-Lambie, and R. Luzio 1998. Solving the chronic problem of sexual harassment in the workplace: An empirical study of factors affecting employee perceptions and consequences of sexual harassment. *California W. Law Review* 34(457–491):470, 475.

South, S. J. and G. D. Spitze. 1994. Housework in marital and nonmarital households. *American Sociological Review* 59(3):327–347.

Sowell, T. 1981. *Ethnic America: A History*. New York: Basic Books.

Spelman, E. V. 1988. *Inessential Woman: Problems of Exclusion in Feminist Thought*. Boston, MA: Beacon Press.

Squires, G. D. and S. O'Connor. 2001. *Color and Money: Politics and Prospects for the Community Reinvestment Movement in Urban America*. Albany: SUNY Press.

Stacey, J. 1996. *In the Name of the Family: Rethinking Family Values in the Postmodern Age*. Boston: Beacon Press.

Stafford, F. K. and M. Sundstrom. 1996. Time out for childcare: Signalling and earnings rebound effects for men and women, *Labour* 10(3):609–629.

Stangor, C., J. K. Swim, G. B. Sechrist, J. Decoster, K. L. VanAllen, A. Ottenbreit. 2003. Ask, answer, and announce: Three stages in perceiving and responding to prejudice. *European Review of Social Psychology* 14:277–311.

Stangor, C., J. K. Swim, K. L. Van Allen, and G. B. Sechrist. 2002. Reporting discrimination in public and private contexts. *Journal of Personality and Social Psychology* 82:69–74.

Statistical Abstract of the United States. 1997. U.S. Census bureau.

Steele, C. and J. Aronson. 1998. Stereotype threat and the test performance of academically successful African Americans. In C. Jencks and M. Phillips (Eds.), *The Black–White Test Score Gap* (pp. 401–427). Washington, D.C.: The Brookings Institution.

Steele, C. M., S. Spencer, and J. Aronson. 2002. Contending with group image: The psychology of stereotype and social identity threat. In M. Zanna (Ed.), *Advances in Experimental Social Psychology* (Vol. 34, pp. 379–440). San Diego, CA: Academic Press.

Stein, E. 2001. Evaluating the sex-discrimination argument for lesbian and gay rights. *UCLA Law Review* 49:471.

Steinberg, R. J. 1992. Gendered instructions. *Work and Occupations* 19:387–423.

Stephan, W. G. and C. W. Stephan. 1985. Intergroup anxiety. *Journal of Social Issues* 41:157–175.

Stier, H., N. Lewis-Epstein, and M. Braun. 2001. Welfare regimes, family supportive policies, and women's employment along the life course. *American Journal of Sociology* 106:1731–1760.

Stigler, G. J. 1971. The theory of economic regulation. *Bell Journal of Economics and Management Science* 2:3–21.

Stinchcombe, A. 1965. Social structure and organizations. In J. G. March (Ed.), *Handbook of Organizations* (pp. 142–193). New York: Rand McNally.

Stinchcombe, L. 1965. Social structure and organizations. In J. G. March and R. McNally (Eds.), *Handbook of Organizations* (pp. 142–93). Chicago: Rand McNally

Stone, D. A. 1984. *The Disabled State*. Philadelphia: Temple University Press.

Stone, P. and M. Lovejoy. 2004. Fast-track women and the "choice" to stay home. *The Annals of the American Academy of Political and Social Science* 596:62–83.

Stryker, R. 2001. Disparate impact and the quota debates. *Sociological Quarterly* 42:13–46.

———. 1994. Rules, resources, and legitimacy processes: Some implications for social conflict, order, and change. *American Journal of Sociology* 99:847–910.

Stryker, R., M. Scarpellino, and M. Holtman. 1999. Political culture wars 1990s style: The drum beat of quotas in media framing of the Civil Rights Act of 1991. *Research in Social Stratitication and Mobility* 17:33–106.

Stryker, R., S. Eliason, and E. Tranby. 2004. The Welfare State, Family Policies, and Women's Labor Force Participation: A Fuzzy-set Analysis, paper presented at the RC-19 Annual Meeting, Paris, France, September 3–7, 2004.

Sturm, S. 2001. Second generation employment discrimination: A structural approach. *Columbia Law Review* 101:458–568.

———. 1990. Resolving the remedial dilemma: Strategies of judicial intervention in prisons. *University of Pennsylvania Law Review* 138:305.

Stychin, C. 1995. *Law's Desire: Sexuality and the Limits of Justice*. London: Routledge.

Subcommittee on Select Education and Civil Rights of the Committee on Education and Labor, House of Representatives. 1994. *Employment Discrimination Against Gay Men and Lesbians*. Washington, D.C.: U.S. Government Printing Office.

Suchman, M. and Edelman, L. 1996. Legal rational myths: The new institutionalism and the law and society tradition. *Law and Social Inquiry* 21:903.

Sugarman, D. 1994. Blurred Boundaries: The Overlapping Worlds of Law, Business, and Politics, in Lawyers in a Post-Modern World (p. 115) in Cain. M. and C. Harrington. *Lawyers in a Postmodern World: Translation and Transgression*. Buckingham: Open University Press.

Suh, S. A. 2000. Women's perceptions of workplace discrimination: Impacts of racial group, gender, and class. In M. L. Oliver, L. D. Bobo, J. H. Johnson, and A. Valenzuela (Eds.), *Prismatic Metropolis: Inequality in Los Angeles* (pp. 561–596). New York: Russell Sage Foundation.

Sullivan, A. 1995. *Virtually Normal: An Argument About Homosexuality*. New York: Vintage.

Sunstein, C. R. 1994. Homosexuality and the constitution. *Indiana Law Journal* 70(1):1.

Sutton, J. R., F. Dobbin, J. W. Meyer, and W. R. Scott. 1994. Legalization of the workplace. *American Journal of Sociology* 99(4):944–971.

Sutton, J. R. and F. Dobbin. 1996. The two faces of governance: Responses to legal uncertainty in U.S. Firms, 1955 to 1985. *American Sociological Review* 61:794–811.

Swain, C. M., K. R. Greene, and C. M. Wotipka. 2001. Understanding racial polarization on affirmative action: The view from focus groups. In J. D. Skrentny *Color Lines* (pp. 214–237). Chicago: University of Chicago.

Swidler, A. 1986. Culture in action: Symbols and strategies. *American Sociological Review* 51:273–286.

Swim, J., E. Borgida, G. Maruyama, and D. G. Myers. 1989. Joan McKay versus John McKay: Do gender stereotypes bias evaluations? *Psychological Bulletin* 105:409–442.

Swim, J. K. and L. L. Hyers. 1999. Excuse me–What did you say?! Women's public and private responses to sexist remarks. *Journal of Experimental Social Psychology* 35:68–88.

Swim, J. K., L. L. Hyers, L. L. Cohen, and M. J. Ferguson. 2001. Everyday sexism: Evidence for its incidence, nature, and psychological impact from three daily diary studies. *Journal of Social Issues* 57:31–53.

Swim, J. K. and L. J. Sanna. 1996. He's skilled, she's lucky: A meta-analysis of observers' attributes for women's and men's successes and failures. *Personality and Social Psychology Bulletin* 22:507–519.

Szymanski, S. and C. Pullman. 1994. *Sexual Harassment At Work: A Training Workbook for Working People*. New York: Labor Institute.

Tajfel, H. and J. C. Turner. 1979. The social identity theory of intergroup behavior. In W. G. Austin and S. Worchel (Eds.), *The Social Psychology of Intergroup Relations* (pp. 7–24). Chicago, IL: Nelson-Hall.

———. 1986. The social identity theory of intergroup behavior. In S. Worchel and W. G. Austin (Eds.), *The Psychology of Intergroup Relations* (pp. 7–24). Chicago, IL: Nelson-Hall.

Taylor, D. M., S. C. Wright, and L. E. Porter. 1994. Dimensions of perceived discrimination: The personal/group discrimination discrepancy. In M. P. Zanna and J. M. Olson (Eds.), *The Psychology of Prejudice: The Ontario Symposium* (Vol. 7, pp. 233–255). Hillsdale, NJ: Lawrence Erlbaum Associates, Inc.

Taylor, S. E. 1981. A categorization approach to stereotyping. In D. L. Hamilton (Ed.), *Cognitive Processes in Stereotyping and Intergroup Behavior* (pp. 83–114). Mahwah, NJ: Erlbaum.

Taylor, S. E. and J. D. Brown. 1988. Illusion and well-being: A social psychological perspective on mental health. *Psychological Bulletin* 103:193–210.

Taylor, S. E., S. T. Fiske, N. L. Etcoff, and A. J. Ruderman. 1978. Categorical and contextual bases of person memory and stereotyping. *Journal of Personality and Social Psychology* 36:778–793.

Taylor, V. and N. C. Raeburn. 1995. Identity politics as high-risk activism: Career consequences for lesbian, gay and bisexual sociologists. *Social Problems* 42:252–273.

Tetlock, P. E. 1983. Accountability and complexity of thought. *Journal of Personality and Social Psychology* 45:47–83.

Tetlock, P. E. 1992. The impact of accountability on judgment and choice. In M. P. Zanna (Ed.), *Advances in Experimental Social Psychology* (Vol. 23, pp. 331–376). New York: Academic Press.

Tilly, C. 1998. *Durable Inequality*. Berkeley: University of California Press.

Time. June 18, 2001. Rank and fire: Attrition isn't working, so best-to-worst grading is gaining." *Time* 157(24):38.

Theodore, N. C. and D. G. Taylor. 1991. *The Geography of Opportunity: The Status of African Americans in the Chicago Area Economy*. Chicago: Chicago Urban League.

Thernstrom, S. and A. Thernstrom. 1997. *America in Black and White, One Nation, Indivisible*. New York: Simon and Schuster.

Thompson, E. P. 1967. Time, work-discipline, and industrial capitalism. *Past and Present* 38:56–97.

Tolbert, P. S. and L. G. Zucker. 1983. Institutional sources of change in the formal structure of organizations: The diffusion of Civil Service reform, 1880–1935. *Administrative Science Quarterly* 28:22–9.

Tomaskovic-Devey, D. 1993. *Gender and Racial Inequality at Work: The Sources and Consequences ofJob Segregation*. Ithaca, NY: ILR Press.

Tomaskovic-Devey, D., A. L. Kalleberg, and P. V. Marsden. 1996. Organizational patterns of gender segregation. In A. L. Kalleberg, D. Knoke, P. V. Marsden, and J. L. Spaeth (Eds.), *Organizations in America* (pp. 276–301). Newbury Park: Sage.

Tomlins, C. L. 1993. *Law, Labor and Ideology in the Early American Republic*. Cambridge: Cambridge University Press.

Townsend, N. 2002. *The Package Deal: Marriage, Work, and Fatherhood in Men's Lives*. Philadelphia: Temple University Press.

Travis, M. A. 2003. Equality in the virtual workplace. *Berkeley Journal of Employment and Labor Law* 27:283–376.

Tucker, J. 1993. Everyday forms of employee resistance. *Sociological Forum* 8:25–45.

Turner, A. 2002. The denial of benefits to the same-sex domestic partners of state employees: How do claims of discrimination fare outside the shadow of ERISA preemption? *University of Pennsylvania Journal of Labor and Employment Law* 4:669–693.

Turner, J. C. 1985. Social categorization and the self-concept: A social cognitive theory of group behavior. In E. J. Lawler (Ed.), *Advances in Group Processes* (Vol. 2, pp. 77–122). Greenwich, CT: JAI Press.

United States Department of Labor. 2000. *Current Population Survey: 2000 Annual Averages*. Washington, D.C.: Bureau of Labor Statistics.

Upham, F. 1987. *Law and Social Change in Postwar Japan*. Cambridge: Harvard University Press.

Urzua, S. 2003. The Educational White–Black Gap: Evidence on Years of Schooling. Unpublished manuscript, University of Chicago, Department of Economics.

U.S. Bureau of the Census. 1993. U.S. Dep't of Commerce, Statistical Abstract of the United States: 1993, at 409.

U.S. Equal Employment Opportunity Comm'n. 1988. Notice N-915-035, Policy Guidance on Current Issues of Sexual Harassment.

U.S. Equal Employment Opportunity Comm'n. 1990. Notice N-915-050, Policy Guidance on Current Issues of Sexual Harassment.

U.S. Equal Employment Opportunity Comm'n. 1992. Questions and Answers About Sexual Harassment 1.
U.S. Department of Labor. 1999. Labor force participation of fathers and mothers varies with children's ages. *Monthly Labor Review, available* at http://www.bls.gov/opub/ted/1999/Jun/wkl/art03.html.
U.S. Merit Systems Protection Board. 1992. *A Question of Equity: Women and the Glass Ceiling in the Federal Government.* Washington, DC: The Board.
U.S. Equal Employment Opportunity Comm'n. 2001. Sexual Harassment Charges EEOC and FEPAs Combined: FY 1992–FY 2000, available at http://www.eeoc.gov/stats/harass.html (visited on January 18, 2001).
U.S. General Accounting Office. 2002. Sexual Orientation-Based Employment Discrimination: States' Experience with Statutory Prohibitions. GAO-02-878R. Washington, D.C. July 9.
U.S. Merit Systems Protection Board. 1981. *Sexual Harassment of Federal Workers: Is It a Problem?* Washington D.C.: U.S. Government Printing Office.
Vaid, U. 1995. *Virtual Equality: The Mainstreaming of Gay and Lesbian Liberation.* New York: Anchor Books.
Vanneman, R. and L. W. Cannon. 1987. *The American Perception of Class, Labor and Social Change.* Philadelphia: Temple University Press.
Van Wezel Stone, K. 2001. Dispute resolution in the boundaryless workplace. *Ohio State Journal on Dispute Resolution* 16:467.
von Sternberg, B. 2003. "Climate has changed on gay-rights issues." Star-Tribune (Minneapolis), 10 August, metro edition.
Vorauer, J. D. and M. Ross. 1993. Making mountains out of molehills: An informational goals analysis of self- and social perception. *Personality and Social Psychology* 19:620–632.
Vorauer, J. and S. M. Kumhyr. 2001. Is this about you or me? Self-versus other-directed judgments and feelings in response to intergroup interaction. *Personality and Social Psychology Bulletin* 27:706–719.
Vuocolo, J. 2004. Courts protect working moms from perception bias. *Wall Street Journal Online*, April 30, 2004, available at http://www.careerjournal.com/myc/workfamily/20040430-vuocolo.html (viewed on July 30, 2004).
Waddington, L. 1994. Legislating to employ people with disabilities: The European and the American way. *Maastricht Journal of European and Comparative Law* 1(4):367–395.
Wald, K. D., J. W. Button, and B. A. Rienzo. 1996. The politics of gay rights in American communities: Explaining antidiscrimination ordinances and policies. *American Journal of Political Science* 40:1152–1178.
Waldfogel, J. 1997. The effect of children on women's wages. *American Sociological Review* 62:209–217.
———. 1998a. Understanding the "family gap" in pay for women with children. *Journal of Economic Perspectives* 12:137–156.
———. 1998b. The family gap for young women in the United States and Britain: Can maternity leave make a difference? *Journal of Labor Economics* 16:505–546.
Waldfogel, J. 1997. The effect of children on women's wages. *American Sociological Review* 62:209–218.
Walker, L. and M. John. 1988. Social facts: Scientific methodology as legal precedent. *California Law Review* 76:877.
Waller, M. R. 2002. My *Baby's Father: Unmarried Parents and Paternal Responsibility.* Ithaca: Cornell University Press.
Walters, S. D. 2001. *All the Rage: The Story of Gay Visibility in America.* Chicago: University of Chicago Press.
Walton S. and J. Huey. 1992. *Sam Walton: Made in America* (p. 218). My Story, Bantam Books. New York: Doubleday.
Washington, R. E. and K. David. 2001. Sport and society. *Annual Review of Sociology* 27:187–212.
Waters, M. C. 1999. *Black Identities.* New York: Russell Sage.
Watkins, S. 1993. Racism *du Jour* at Shoney's. *The Nation* 257:424–428, October 18.

Wax, A. 1999. Discrimination as accident. *Indiana Law Review* 74:1129.

Waxman, E. and S. Lambert. 2002. Opportunity in Lower-Level Jobs: Structured, Realized, and Experienced, paper presented at the Association for Public Policy Analysis and Management meeting, Dallas, TX, November 7, 2002.

Weber, M. 1947. In A. M. Henderson and T. Parsons (Eds.), *The Theory of Social and Economic Organization*. New York: Oxford University Press.

———. 1968. *Economy and Society*; ed. G. Roth and C. Wittich. New York: Bedminster.

Wegner, D. M. 1994. Ironic processes of mental control. *Psychological Review* 101:34–52.

Weiner, B. 1995. *Judgments of Responsibility: A Foundation for a Theory of Social Conduct*. New York: The Guilford Press.

Weiner, B., R. P. Perry, and J. Magnusson. 1988. An attributional analysis of reactions to stigmas. *Journal of Personality and Social Psychology* 55:738–748.

Werum, R. and B. Winders. 2001. Who's 'in' and who's 'out': State fragmentation and the struggle over gay rights, 1974–1999. *Social Problems* 48:386–410.

West, C. and D. H. Zimmerman. 1987. Doing gender. *Gender and Society.* 1(2):125–151.

West, J. 1993. *The Evolution of Disability Rights. Implementing the Americans With Disabilities Act. L. O. G. a. H. A. Beyer* (pp. 3–15). Baltimore: Paul H. Boorkes Publishing Co.

Wheeler, M. E. and S. T. Fiske. 2001. *fMRI Study of Three Cognitive Tasks that Differentially Modulate Stereotype Accessibility and Human Amygdala Response to Racial Outgroup Faces.* Poster presented at Society for Neuroscience meetings, San Diego, CA.

———. 2005. Controlling racial prejudice and stereotyping: Social cognitive goals affect amygdala and stereotype activation. *Psychological Science* 16:56–63.

Whorf, B. L. 1941. Languages and logic. *In Language, Thought, and Reality: Selected Writings.* Cambridge: Massachusetts Institute of Technology Press [1956].

Wilkins, D. B. and G. M. Gulati 1996. Why are there so few black lawyers in corporate law firms? An institutional analysis. *California Law Review* 84:496.

Williams, J. 1989. Deconstructing gender. *Michigan Law Review* 87:797.

———. 2000. *Unbending Gender: Why Families and Work Conflict and What to Do About It.* Oxford: Oxford University Press.

Williams, P. 1991. *The Alchemy of Race and Rights*. Cambridge: Harvard University Press.

Williams, R. M. Jr. 1947. *The Reduction of Intergroup Tensions*. New York: Social Science Research Council.

Williams, J. C. and N. Segal. 2003. Beyond the maternal wall: Relief for family caregivers who are discriminated against on the job. *Harvard Women's Law Journal* 26:77–162.

Wilson, T. D. and N. Brekke. 1994. Mental contamination and mental correction. *Psychological Bulletin* 116:117–142.

Winston, K. 2002. Lessons from the Right of Silence, in Legality and Community, supra, at 389, 392.

Wisconsin Law Review. 2002. Symposium Issue. Lawyers and the practice of workplace equity. *Wisconsin Law Review.*

Wolfe, A. 1998. *One Nation, After All: How Middle-Class Americans Really Think About: God, Country, Family, Racism, Welfare, Immigration, Homosexuality, Work, the Right, the Left, and Each Other*. New York, NY: Viking.

Women Pub. Service, Ctr. for Women in Gov't, Univ. of Albany, Albany, N.Y. 1994. Cost of Sexual Harassment to Employers Up Sharply: More Employees are Bringing Charges and Receiving Compensation for Damages, Spring 1994.

Woods, J. D. 1993. *The Corporate Closet: The Professional Lives of Gay Men in America*. New York: Free Press.

Woods, S. E. and K. M. Harbeck. 1991. Living in two worlds: The identity management strategies used by lesbian physical educators. *Journal of Homosexuality* 22(3–4):141–66.

Woodzicka, J. A. and M. LaFrance. 2001. Real versus imagined gender harassment. *Journal of Social Issues* 57:15–30.
Word, C. O., M. P. Zanna, and J. Cooper. 1974. The nonverbal mediation of self-fulfilling prophecies in interracial interaction. *Journal of Experimental Social Psychology* 10:109–120.
Wright, S. C., A. Aron, T. McLaughlin-Volpe, and S. A. Ropp. 1997. The extended contact effect: Knowledge of cross-group friendships and prejudice. *Journal of Personality and Social Psychology*, 73:73–90.
Yang, A. S. 1997. Attitudes toward homosexuality. *Public Opinion Quarterly* 61:477–507.
———. 2001. *The 2000 National Elections Study and Gay and Lesbian Rights: Support for Equality Grows*. Washington, D.C.: National Gay and Lesbian Task Force Policy Institute.
Yamagata, H., K. S. Yeh, S. Stewman, and H. Dodge. 1997. Sex segregation and glass ceilings. *American Journal of Sociology* 103:531–565.
Yinger, J. 1997. Cash in your face. *Journal of Urban Economics* 42:339–365.
Yngvesson, B. 1985. Law, private governance, and continuing relationships. *Wisconsin Law Review* 1985:623–646.
———. 1988. Making law at the doorway: The clerk, the court, and the construction of community in a New England town. *Law and Society Review* 22:409–448.
Yoshino, K. 2002. Covering. *Yale Law Journal* 111:769–939.
Yzerbyt, V., O. Corneille, and C. Estrada. 2001. The interplay of subjective essentialism and entitativity in the formation of stereotypes. *Personality and Social Psychology Review* 5:141–155.
Zald, M. N. 1970. Political economy: A framework for comparative analysis. In M. N. Zald (Ed.), *Power in Organizations* (pp. 221–261). Nashville: Vanderbilt University Press.

CASES CITED

Adams v. Florida Power Corp. 255 F.3d 1322 (11th Cir. 2002).
Adarand Constructors, Inc. v. Pena. 515 U.S. 200 (1995).
Alabama v. Garrett. 531 U.S. 356 (2001).
Albertson's, Inc. v. Kirkingburg. 527 U.S. 555 (1999).
Alexander v. Sandoval. 532 U.S. 275 (2001).
Beck v. Boeing. 203 F.R.D. 459 (W.D. Wash. 2001).
Burlington Industries, Inc. v. Ellerth. 524 U.S. 742 (1998).
Butler v. Home Depot, Inc. 1996. U.S. Dist. LEXIS 3370 (N.D. Cal. 1996).
Butler v. Home Depot, Inc. 984 F. Supp. 1257 (N.D. Cal. 1997).
Castaneda v. Partida. 430 U.S. 482, 497 n.17 (1977).
Circuit City v. Adams. 532 U.S. 105 (2001).
City of Richmond v. Croson. 488 U.S. 469 (1989).
Coleman v. General Motors Acceptance Corp. No. 3-98-0211, 2000 U.S. Dist. LEXIS 13236 (M.D. Tenn. Aug. 28, 2000).
Collier v. Bradley University. 113 F. Supp. 2d 1235 (C.D. Ill. 2000).
DeGrace v. Rumsfeld. 614 F.2d 796 (1st Cir. 1980).
DeGraffenreid v. General Motors. 413 F. Supp. 142 (E.D. Mo. 1976), aff'd in part, rev'd in part and remanded, 558 F.2d 480 (8th Cir. 1977).
Dukes v. Wal-mart Stores, Inc.
EEOC's ADR Policy Statement (1995) http://www.eeoc.gov/policy/docs/adrstatement.html
Ellis v. United Airlines, Inc. 73 F.3d 999 (10th Cir. 1996).
Farragher v. City of Boca Rotan. 524 U.S. 775 (1998).
Ford Motor Co. v. EEOC. 458 U.S. 219 (1982).

Fortino v. Quasar Co. 751 F. Supp. 1306 (N.D. I11. 1990).
Gilmer. v. Interstate/Johnson Lane Corporation. 500 U.S. 20 (1991).
Griggs v. Duke Power Co. 401 U.S. 424 (1971).
Harrington v. Vandalia-Butler Bd. of Educ. 585 F.2d 192 (6th Cir. 1978).
Harris v. Forklift Systems, Inc. 510 U.S. 17 (1993).
Hazen Paper v. Biggins. 507 U.S. 604 (1993).
Hicks v. Gates Rubber Co. 833 F.2d 1406 (10th Cir. 1987).
Int'l Bd. of Teamsters v. United States. 431 U.S. 324, 358 (1977).
Jefferies v. Harris Community Action Ass'n. 615 F.2d 1025 (5th Cir. 1980).
Johnson v. Railway Express Agency. 421 U.S. 454 (1975).
Johnson v. Santa Clara County. 480 U.S. 616 (1987).
Judge v. Marsh. 649 F. Supp. 770 (D.D.C. 1986).
Latino Officers Association City of New York v. City of New York. 209 F.R.D. 79 (S.D.N.Y. 2002).
Lawrence v. Texas. 539 U.S. 558 (2003).
Lorance v. ATT Technologies. 490 U.S. 900 (1989).
Martin v. Wilkes. 490 U.S. 755 (1989).
McDonnell Douglas Corp. v. Green. 411 U.S. 792, 802 (1973).
Meritor Savings Bank FSB v. Vinson. 477 U.S. 57 (1986).
Molski v. Gleich. 318 F.3d 937 (9th Cir. 2002).
Murphy v. United Parcel Service. 527 U.S. 516 (1999).
Patterson v. McLean Credit Union. 491 U.S. 164 (1989).
Pearson v. W. Elec. Co. 542 F.2d 1150 (10th Cir. 1976).
Pennsylvania State Police v. Suders 542 U.S. 129 (2004).
Price Waterhouse v. Hopkins. 490 U.S. 228 (1989).
Romer v. Evans. 517 U.S. 620 (1996)
Reid v. Lockheed Martin Aeronautics. 205 F.R.D. 655 (N.D. Ga. 2001).
Scott v. Macy. 121 U.S. App. D.C. 205 (1965).
Steelworkers v. Weber. 443 U.S. 193 (1979).
Stender v. Lucky Stores. 803 F.Supp. 259, 335 (N/D/ Cal 1992).
Sutton v. United Air Lines. 527 U.S. 471 (1999).
United States v. Burke. 504 U.S. 229 (1992).
United States v. Lopez. 514 U.S. 549 (1995).
U.S. v. Morrison. 120 S.Ct. 1740 (2000).
Wards Cove Packing Co. v. Atonio. 490 U.S. 642 (1989).
Ward's Cove Packing v. Atonio. 490 U.S. 642 (1989).
Webb v. Merck and Co. 206 F.R.D. 399 (E.D. Pa. 2002).
Wygant v. Jackson Board of Education. 476 U.S. 267 (1986).

FEDERAL STATUTES CITED

Age Discrimination in Employment Act of 1967. 81 Stat. 602, Dec. 15, 1967.
Americans with Disabilities Act of 1990. 104 Stat. 327, July 26, 1990; 105 Stat. 1071, Nov. 21, 1991.
Civil Rights Act of 1964. 42 U.S.C. Sections 2000E–2000E-17, July 2, 1964, amended in 1966, 1972, 1978, 1991.
Civil Rights Act of 1991. 105 Stat. 1071, Nov. 21, 1991.
Equal Credit Opportunity Act, 15 U.S.C. §§1691-1691f (1994 and Supp. IV 1998).
Rule 23, F.R.C.P.
Family and Medical Leave Act of 1993. 107 Stat. 6, Feb.3, 1993.

About the Authors

Laura Beth Nielsen
American Bar Foundation and Sociology, Northwestern University

Robert L. Nelson
American Bar Foundation and Sociology, Northwestern University

Susan Sturm
Law, Columbia University

Susan T. Fiske
Psychology, Princeton University

Barbara F. Reskin
Sociology, University of Washington

Pedro Carneiro
Economics, University College London

James J. Heckman
Economics, University of Chicago and American Bar Foundation

Dimitriy V. Masterov
Economics, University of Chicago

Ian Ayres
Law and Economics, Yale University

William Bridges
Sociology, University of Illinois, Chicago

Kathleen E. Hull
Sociology, University of Minnesota

Sharon M. Collins
Sociology, University of Illinois, Chicago

Mary L. Dudziak
Law, History and Political Science, University of Southern California Law School

Jonathan Goldberg-Hiller
Political Science, University of Hawai'i

Katharina Heyer
Political Science, University of Hawai'i

John J. Donohue III
Law and Economics, Yale University

Brenda Major
Psychology, U.C. Santa Barbara

Catherine R. Albiston
Jurisprudence and Social Policy, University of California, Berkeley

Tanya Katerí Hernández
Law, Rutgers University-Newark

Lauren Edelman
Jurisprudence and Social Policy, U.C. Berkeley

Erin L. Kelly
Sociology, University of Minnesota

Samuel L. Gaertner
Psychology, University of Delaware

William T. Bielby
Sociology, University of Pennsylvania

Cheryl R. Kaiser
Psychology, Michigan State University

Peter Siegelman
Law and Economics, University of Connecticut

John F. Dovidio
Psychology, Colgate University

Jason A. Nier
Psychology, Connecticut College

Gordon Hodson
Psychology, Brock University

Melissa A. Houlette
Business Administration and Behavioral Sciences, College of Mount St. Joseph

Index

§1981, 12, 265–268, 271, 272
11th Amendment, 12–14
Abraham, K.S., 19, 54, 342
Abraham v. Graphic Arts International, 369
Abrahamson, E., 347
Abrams, D., 386
Abrams, K., 329
Adam, B.D., 173
Adams v. Florida Power Corp., 14, 15
Adams, J.H., 332
adolescent, 106, 126
Adorno, T.W., 379, 381
adult, 18, 99, 104, 119, 136, 354, 360
affirmative action, 13, 14, 33, 90, 100, 135, 150, 189, 191, 196, 199, 214, 219, 229, 252, 256, 327, 340, 346, 395
AFQT, 81, 82, 100–103, 110, 112, 113, 115, 118–125, 131, 132, 134
African American, 5, 6, 17–19, 30–32, 90, 94, 100, 140, 143, 147, 151–154, 156–159, 161–165, 169, 181, 189, 190–192, 195, 196, 206, 225, 280, 284, 288, 290, 292, 295–298, 325, 330
Age Discrimination in Employment Act (ADEA), 14, 15, 265, 272
age, 4, 18, 20, 21, 82, 87, 88, 100, 101, 105, 107–112, 113, 118, 120, 125, 132, 133
Alabama v. Garrett, 14
Albertson's, Inc. v. Kirkingburg, 254, 269
Albiston, C., 32, 50, 51, 301, 302, 304, 306, 308, 310, 312, 314, 316, 318, 320, 322, 349, 364, 371, 373
Alexander v. Sandoval, 15
allocation mechanism, 85, 96
Allport, G., 60, 70, 80, 288, 385, 387
Altonji, J., 100
ambivalence, 63, 176, 185, 219, 226, 231, 378
Americans with Disabilities Act (ADA), 11–14, 20, 21, 179, 237, 238, 239, 241, 242, 244–247, 252, 254–257, 261, 264, 269–272, 274, 276, 278, 373
amicus curia, 214
Anastasio, P.A., 381, 386, 387
anti-social behavior index, 132
Aron, A., 390
Aronson, J., 104, 116, 117, 288
ascription
  ascriptive characteristics, concealing, 91
  ascriptive inequality, 75–97
ATA v. San Francisco, 233
attributional ambiguity, 287
Australia, 241, 370
aversive racism, 377–393

Bachman, B.A., 386, 387
Back v. Hastings-on-Hudson Union Free School District, 368, 372
Baehr v. Lewin, 230
Baehr v. Miike, 226, 232
Baker v. Vermont, 233
Baldi, S., 82, 93
Banaji, M.R., 7, 60, 71, 86, 287, 398, 399
Banker, B.S., 387, 388
Bargh, J.A., 60, 69, 86, 87, 88, 398
Barnes, J., 10, 12
Baron, J.N., 92, 94, 149, 289, 346, 399, 404
Beck v. Boeing, 52
Becker, G., 77
Beim, A., 4, 15, 29
Bellinger, N., 13
Berg, N., 172, 225
Berg, P. 255
Berger, J., 3
Berger, P.L., 303
Bernstein, L., 44
Bersoff, D.N., 7, 68
Betty Dukes et al. v. Wal-Mart Stores, Inc. See *Dukes Wal-Mart Stores, Inc.*
bias
  overt, 381, 390
  subtle, 7, 59, 67, 379–81, 383, 385, 388

Bielby, D.D., 361, 398, 399, 400
Bielby, W.T., 4, 28, 90, 93, 361, 395, 396, 398, 399, 400, 402, 404, 405, 406, 408
Bisom-Rapp, S., 4, 10, 55, 90, 91, 342, 373
Blalock, H.M., 92
Blank, R.M., 100
Blau, F.D., 77, 78
Blau, P.M., 86
Blumrosen, A.W., 88, 89
Board of Trustees v. Garrett, 217
Bobo, L., 7, 17, 64, 82, 378
Boddie v. Connecticut, 227
Bodenhausen, G.V., 60, 391, 399
Bone, R., 52
Borgida, E., 7, 68, 400
Bourdieu, P., 9, 303, 305, 401
Bourgeois, M., 4, 28, 90
Bourke, J., 370
Bowers, M., 54
Bowers v. Hardwick, 221, 228
Brekke, N., 79, 91
Brewer, M.B., 62, 85, 86, 379
Bridges, W.P., 4, 6, 7, 8, 91, 93, 149, 150, 152, 154, 158, 160, 164, 304, 351, 369, 373
Brigham, J.C., 7
Brooks-Gunn, J., 106
Broschak, J.P., 93
Brown, R.J., 62, 85, 86, 205, 287
Brown v. Board of Education, 205
Bumiller, K., 4, 18, 32, 303, 308, 349
bureaucracy, 94, 338
Burgess, D., 298, 400
Burke, T., 9, 12, 31, 207, 208, 270
Burlington Industries v. Ellerth, 54, 46, 351
Burrows, L., 60
Burstein, P., 88, 89, 303
Butler, J., 221
Butler v. Home Depot, 52, 53

Cain, M., 37, 168
Cancio, A.S., 82, 94, 97
capacity-building work, 366
career track, 356, 362, 363, 369
Carneiro, P., 99, 100, 102, 104, 106, 108, 110, 112, 114, 116, 117, 118, 119, 122, 126, 128, 130, 131, 132, 134, 136
Carroll, G.R., 80
Castilla, E.J., 85
Charny, D., 36, 44, 50, 54
Chen, D.W., 283
Chen, M., 60, 86, 88
childhood, 106, 132
Christian Right, 167, 180, 181, 182
City of Richmond v. Croson, 14
civil litigation, 24, 29
civil rights, 5, 9, 10, 20, 24, 26, 27, 37, 100, 135, 176, 177, 182, 191, 203–209, 213, 214, 215, 216, 220, 221, 224, 226, 228, 230, 237, 239, 240, 241, 245, 253–254, 256, 284, 302, 308, 319, 329, 339, 346
Civil Rights Act of 1964, 4, 11, 19, 88, 204, 205, 208, 216, 325, 368, 371
Civil Rights Act of 1991, 4, 10, 11–15, 28, 261, 266–271, 331
claiming, 6–8, 15–16, 285–286
Clark, K.J., 401
Clermont, K., 4
CNLSY, 106, 107, 110, 114, 116, 117, 119, 129, 132
Cockburn, C., 94
cognitive
  and ability, 82, 110
  and skill, 82, 106
Cole, J., 48, 251
Cole, R., 251
Coleman v. General Motors Acceptance Corp., 147
Colker, R., 4, 28
Collier v. Bradley University, 53
Collins, P.H., 327
Collins, R., 78
Collins, S.M, 189–200
collusion, 152, 155, 160
Common Ingroup Identity Model, 377, 378, 386–389, 391, 392
competition, 9, 63, 65, 81, 149, 150, 151, 152, 153, 160, 164, 196, 199
complementarity, 119
compliance
  compliance professionals, 340, 341, 343, 344, 349
  symbolic compliance, 341
Conley, D., 6
Conley, F.K., 356
Constance, M., 61, 333
contact hypothesis, 387
contextual effects, 93
Cooper, D., 221

Cooper, M., 355
Cordova, D.I., 92
Cox, P.N., 12, 265
Crary, D., 368, 372
Crosby, F., 62, 63, 92, 287, 291, 296
Cuddy, A.J., 7, 63, 69
Curran, B.A., 18, 32

Davis-Blake, A., 93
Deaux, K., 7, 62, 68, 399
DeGrace v. Rumsfeld, 265
DeGraffenreid v. General Motors, 326
Delgado, R., 45, 327
Devine, P.G., 60, 61, 64, 287, 391, 404
Dijksterhuis, A., 60, 61
disability
  disability activism, 238, 245, 247–249
  disability law, 244, 256, 257
  disability rights, 237–239, 241, 246–249, 251, 253, 256, 257
  medical model of disability, 240
  social model of disability, 246
discrimination
  and age, 4, 261, 272
  and disability, 4, 237, 247, 255, 261, 264, 272, 280
  and gender, 4, 138, 168, 329, 334, 367, 368, 395
  and race, 6, 30, 82, 139, 169, 203–205, 207, 208, 210, 216, 266–269, 325, 326, 327, 329
  and sex, 12, 20, 22, 77, 95, 230, 266–268, 271–273, 291, 326, 327, 329, 367, 370, 372
  and sexual orientation, 167, 168, 174
  market discrimination, 6, 100, 102, 104, 105, 106, 122, 129, 135, 149
  non-market discrimination, 152
  perceived discrimination, 5, 17, 170
disparate impact, 10, 13–15, 89, 92, 139, 147, 179, 266–268, 368–370
disparate treatment, 66, 137, 139, 140, 148, 193, 266, 268, 345, 367, 368, 370, 377
dispute pyramid, 16, 17, 29, 30
diversity, 4, 90, 170, 192, 196, 229, 235, 290, 296, 347, 348, 371, 373, 395, 396, 405–408
Dixon, K.A., 4, 7, 18, 19
Dobbin, F., 91, 344, 369, 371, 372
Doeringer P., 404
domestic partnership, 220, 225, 233, 234
Donohue, J.J., 4, 6, 15, 20, 23, 26, 89, 261, 262, 264, 265, 266, 268, 270, 272, 274, 276, 277, 278, 280, 282, 284
Dorf, M.C., 56
Dovidio, J.F., 7, 60, 62–64, 173, 377–379, 381–388, 390, 391, 393
Duckitt, J., 65, 379
Dukes v. Wal-mart Stores, Inc., 48, 52, 395
Duncan, G., 106

Eagly, A.H., 70, 398
Eberhardt, J.L., 404
Edelman, L.B., 4, 10, 19, 38–40, 43–55, 56, 91, 302, 304, 310, 319, 337–339, 340, 342–350, 352, 367, 371, 372, 373, 404
Edwards, H.T., 54
Edwards, M.E., 88
Edwards, R., 304
Edwards, W., 251, 326
EEOC, 3, 4, 5, 9, 11, 12, 15, 16, 19, 20–22, 28–33, 88, 89, 90, 150, 165, 169, 191, 262, 265, 267, 272, 273, 284
EEOC v. Premier Operator Services, 90
EEOC v. RD's Drive-In, 90
EEOC v. Warshawsky & Co., 369
Eisenberg, T., 4, 28
Elana Back v. Hastings-on-Hudson UnionFree School District. See *Back v. Hastings-on-Hudson UnionFree School District*
elder care, 354, 359
Ellis v. United Airlines Inc., 15
Employment Non-Discrimination Act (ENDA), 178, 179, 184, 220, 224, 234
endogenous, 337–339, 350–352
Equal Employment Opportunity Commission (EEOC), 3, 21, 22, 56, 372
Erlanger, H.S., 4, 19, 39, 40, 43, 44, 45, 55, 56, 302, 304, 342, 343, 346, 404
Estreicher, S., 12
Evans v. Romer, 227
expert testimony, 48, 53, 56
explaining inequality, 84

family, 12, 17–19, 32, 81, 91, 99, 102, 106, 107, 110, 112–114, 118, 119, 132, 134, 168, 172, 180, 184, 222, 230, 232, 233, 295, 301, 302, 304–307, 310, 311–321, 353–368, 370–372, 383, 389, 398, 403, 404

Family and Medical Leave Act (FMLA), 12, 301–305, 307–314, 317, 319, 321, 322, 357
family leaves, 357, 363, 364, 371
family-friendly, 363–365, 371, 372
Faragher v. City of Boca Raton, 14, 43, 54, 118
Farkas, G., 82, 97
fathers, 354, 355, 356, 359, 360, 367, 368
Feagin, J.R., 17, 296
Federico, C., 7
Feeley, M., 49
Fein, S., 61
Ferguson, R., 106, 107, 292
Fernandez, R., 84, 85, 94
field
  and legal, 343, 349, 350, 352
  and logics, 341
  and organizational, 342
Fischer, H., 60
Fischer, K., 295
Fiske, M.L., 404
Fiske, S.T., 7, 59–71, 85, 86, 290, 291, 295, 398, 399
Fiss, O., 41–43, 54
Flack, M., 91
flextime, 363
Foddy, M., 91
Ford Motor Co. v. EEOC, 265
Fordham, E.W., 76, 261
Fortino v. Quasar Co., 265
free agent, 151, 158, 160
Freeman, A.D., 13, 404
Freeman, R., 191
Frenkel-Brunswik, E., 379
Freshman, C., 80, 92
Friedman, J.J., 347
Friedman, L.M., 8
Friedman, S.D., 364
Fryer, R., 106, 107

Gaertner, S. L., 7, 60, 62, 64, 377–388, 390–393
Galanter, M., 5, 9, 16, 17, 52, 88, 303, 307, 347
Garst, 399
gay rights, 167, 168, 175–182, 184–186, 222, 224, 227, 228
gays and lesbians, 167–177, 181
gender
  discrimination, 4, 138, 168, 329, 334, 367, 368, 395
  segregation, 396
General Education Development (GED), 131
General Electric v. Gilbert, 372
Germany, 237–239, 242–245, 247–249, 252, 257
Gilbert, D.T., 61
Gilmer v. Interstate/Johnson Lane Corporation, 54
Glaser, J., 65
glass ceilings, 355
Glick, P., 7, 63, 67, 69, 399, 400
Goldin, C., 91
Gonzales v. Raich, 217
Gorman, E.H., 84, 398
Graham, H.D., 88, 204, 232
Green, D.P., 65
Greenwald, A.G., 60, 86
grievance, 16, 32, 43, 149, 343, 344, 346, 349, 350, 351, 371
Griffin v. Illinois, 231
Griggs v. Duke Power Co., 13
Grillo, T., 45, 54, 55, 327
Grodsky, E., 7, 93
group differences, 78, 83, 92, 96
Grutter v. Bollinger, 214
Gulati, G.M., 36
Gutek, B., 333, 399, 400

Hackett, E.J., 400
Hamilton, V.L., 8
Hannan M.T., 80, 404
Harcourt, B., 53, 56
Hardin, C.D., 7, 398, 399
Harlan, S.L., 227, 373, 400
Harper, M.C., 12, 401, 405
Harper v. Virginia, 231
Harrington v. Vandalia-Butler Bd. of Educ, 265
Harris, A.P., 206, 305
Harris v. Forklift Systems, Inc., 43
Harris Poll, 176, 208, 220
Hart, A.J., 60, 214
Hass, R.G., 62, 63, 64, 378
Hazen Paper v. Biggins, 15
Head Start, 104
Heart of Atlanta Motel v. United States, 205
Heckman, J. J., 6, 88, 99, 100, 102, 104, 106, 108, 110, 112, 114, 116–119, 122, 126, 128, 130–132, 134–136, 138, 146–148
Heilman, M.E., 7, 68
Heneman, H.G., 401
Henry, P.J., 216, 380
Herrnstein, R., 102

Hetts, J.J., 7
Hicks v. Gates Rubber Co., 329
Hispanic, 18, 99, 100–104, 107–118, 120–126, 128–135, 143, 192, 323
Hixon, J.G., 61
Hodgins, H.S., 399
Hollins v. Atlantic Co., 90
Holzer, H.H., 82
housework, 354, 359, 360
Howard, J. M., 386
Howard, P. K., 4
Huey, J., 399
Huffman, M.L., 82
human capital, 6, 119, 126, 193, 353, 354, 359–362
Hunter v. Allis–Chalmers, 351

ideology, 294, 312, 314
income
  and family, 112, 113, 114, 132, 134, 383
  and permanent, 110
inequality, 4–8, 13, 14, 35–37, 45, 48, 57, 75–97, 136, 189, 190, 192, 193, 198, 200, 226, 231, 287, 305, 335, 338, 351, 353, 354, 356, 368, 396
ingroup
  and favoritism, 65, 68, 379, 385, 391, 393
institutional, 9, 35, 36, 38, 43, 46, 48, 49, 50, 51, 53, 55, 88, 93, 151, 155, 194, 200, 226, 254, 257, 338, 339
Int'l Bd. of Teamsters v. United States, 325
interpersonal mechanisms, 85, 87
intervention, 116, 132, 136, 196, 276, 373, 381, 385, 387, 393
intradisciplinarity, 95
intrapsychic mechanisms, 85
investment, 96, 126, 163, 197, 199, 363, 365
Issachoroff, S., 52

Jacobs, J. A., 4, 7, 83, 356, 363
Japan, 237, 238, 239, 242, 243, 244, 245, 246, 248, 249, 251, 252, 257
Jefferies v. Harris Community Action Center, 326
Jencks, C., 82, 106, 131
Johnson v. Santa Clara County, 14
Jones, J.M., 377
Jose, A., 54
Jost, J.T., 71, 287, 298
Judge v. Marsh, 326
judicial deference, 340

Kagan, R.A., 9
Kaiser, C.R., 17, 32, 285, 286, 288, 289, 290, 292, 294, 296, 297, 298
Kalev, A., 364, 373
Kalin, R., 399
Kalleberg, A.L., 82, 83, 305, 356, 398
Kanter, R.M., 68, 78, 86, 87, 193, 361, 362, 399
Karau, J., 398
Kasim, R., 82
Katz, I., 62, 63, 64, 378
Katzenbach v. McClung, 205
Kawakami, K., 60, 391, 393
Kelly, E., 353, 354, 356, 358, 360, 362, 363, 364, 366, 368, 369, 370, 371, 372, 373, 374
Kessler-Harris, A., 305, 368, 370
Kim, M., 94
Kimel v. Florida Board of Regents, 14
Kirschenman, J., 7, 193
Kleiman, L.S., 401
Kleiman, C., 368, 372
Klonoff, E.A., 17
Kmec, J.A., 399
Konrad, A.M., 90, 94
Kornhauser, L., 37, 44, 306
Kosterman, R., 380
Krieger, L., 13, 36, 37, 39, 41, 42, 302, 367, 377, 393, 399
Kritzer, H.M., 8
Krysan, M., 378
Kulik, T., 93

labor market
  competition, 149
  discrimination, 149
Lande, J., 4, 39, 40, 55, 302, 346
Landrine, H., 17
Lane, J.D., 391
Langer, E., 287, 293
Larenas, M., 99, 104
Latino Officers Association City of New York v City of New York, 52
Lauritsen, J.L., 6
Lawrence, C., 36, 37, 332
Lawrence v. Texas, 176, 228
lawsuits, 3, 4, 5, 15, 16, 19, 23, 28, 29, 30, 31, 33, 89, 94, 342
legal consciousness, 348
legal endogeneity, 337
Lepinasse, V., 61
Lerner, M.J., 287, 293

Levine, J.Z., 355, 401
Levine, M.P., 173
Levinson, D.J., 379
lifecycle, 104, 105, 106, 110, 131, 132
Lind, A.E., 8
Linnehan, F., 90
Litras, M.E.X., 4, 20, 23
Lorance v. AT&T Technologies, 266, 268

M. v. H., 232
Macaulay, S., 8, 302, 304, 339
MacIver, R. M., 79
Macrae, C.N., 60, 391, 399
Major, B.N., 11, 32, 71, 92, 150, 206, 285, 286, 287, 288, 289, 290, 291, 292, 293, 294, 296, 298
managerialization of law, 43, 340, 341, 345, 346, 348
Mann, J.A., 387
Markham, W.T., 400, 401
Marks, J.H., 14
Marsden, P.V., 82, 84, 398
Marshall, A.-M., 9, 17, 207, 208, 303, 331, 349
Martin, J., 7, 189, 204, 207, 217
Martin v. Wilkes, 11, 266, 268
maternal wall, 372
maternity leave, 315, 357, 368, 372
Maume, D.J., 82
McBrier, D.B., 82, 93, 94, 373, 399
McCann, M., 37, 44, 303, 304, 312, 371
McConahay, J.B., 62, 380, 381
McCoy, S.K., 32, 286, 289, 293
McDermott, P., 54
McDonnell Douglas Corp. v. Green, 325
McGhee, D.E., 60
McInerney, S.C., 60
McLaughlin-Volpe, T., 390
Meares, T., 53, 56
mechanisms, 54, 75–80, 83–7, 185, 199, 226, 230, 345, 353, 354
Meertens, R.W., 378
Meritor Savings Bank v. Vinson, 12, 350
Merry, S.E., 37, 235
Miller, R.E., 3, 5, 15, 16, 17, 32, 227, 231, 287, 290, 292, 294, 296, 297, 303, 349
Mincer, J., 6
Minow, M., 36, 37, 41, 42, 44, 253, 307
Mnookin, R., 37, 44, 306
mobilization, 37, 180, 247, 248, 256, 257, 263, 302–312, 321, 340, 341, 393
models of inequality, 84
Moen, P., 361, 362, 371
Molski v. Gleich, 53
mommy track, 356
Monahan, J., 53, 56, 396
Monteith, M.J., 61, 391
Moore, W.E., 85
Moore vs. Alabama State University, 367
Morasch, B., 400
Morgan, P.A., 4, 32, 83, 303, 307, 308, 333
Moskowitz, G.B., 61, 386
Moss, P., 81
motives, 61, 75–5, 95, 96, 268, 374, 386
Mueller, C.W., 93
Mulinge, M., 93
Murphy v. United Parcel Service, 254
Murray, C., 102, 117
Murrell, A.J., 332, 387

Neal, D., 99, 100, 102, 104–06, 118, 119, 121, 122, 126, 130, 135, 224, 283
Neckerman, K.M., 7, 193
Nelson, C., 399
Nelson, M.A., 404
Nelson, R.L., 3–34, 304, 347, 351, 369, 373
neo-institutional theory, 338
Neuberg, S.L., 61, 404
Neumark, D., 7
Nielsen, L.B., 3, 4, 6, 8, 9, 10, 12, 14–6, 18, 20, 22, 24, 26, 28, 29, 30, 32, 34, 59, 75, 99, 137, 149, 167, 169, 186, 189, 203, 219, 237, 261, 285, 301, 325, 337, 347, 348, 353, 377, 395
Nieva, V.F., 399
NLSY79, 100, 103, 106, 107, 108, 109, 112, 118, 122, 123, 129, 130, 133, 134
noncognitive
  ability, 99
  skills, 106, 131, 132, 135
  norms, 8, 32, 35, 36, 37, 38, 39, 40, 41, 42, 43, 44, 45, 46, 47, 48, 49, 50, 51, 53, 54, 55, 56, 57, 62, 64, 67, 70, 93, 170, 190, 223, 225, 228, 230, 232, 239, 247, 248, 249, 303, 304, 307, 309, 311, 314, 315, 316, 317, 318, 319, 320, 321, 322, 339, 345, 350, 367, 379, 390, 392, 393

O'Barr, R., 54
O'Connor, A., 6, 60, 82, 214
Ofek, H., 6
Office of Federal Contract Compliance Programs (OFCCP), 9, 92
Oliver, M.L., 6, 239, 305
Olson, J., 293
Olson, W.K., 4
Oppenheimer, D.B., 20, 37, 39, 41, 94
organizational field, 10, 295
organizations
  organizational inequality, 94
  organizational inertia, 94
Otten, S., 386
outgroup, 60, 62, 63, 64, 66, 67, 69, 86, 290, 296, 379, 386, 387, 388, 390, 391, 404
overtime, 362, 366, 369, 370

Pager, D., 7, 93
Parts of the Body Test, 107
part-time
  and experience, 358, 359
  and work, 269, 358, 359, 362, 364, 369, 370
  and workers, 358, 365, 369
Patterson v. McLean Credit Union, 266, 268
pay gaps, 78, 93
Pearson v. W. Elec. Co., 265
Pennsylvania State Police v. Suders, 351
perceived injurious experiences, 16
performance evaluation, 364, 365, 366, 401, 406
perpetrator model, 13
Petersen, T., 82, 83, 94
Pettigrew, T.F., 7, 62, 63, 64, 66, 378, 380, 390
Pfeffer, J., 91, 94
Phelps, E.A., 60
Phelps, E.S., 78
Phillips, K.P., 82, 106, 131, 226, 234
Phillips v. Martin, 367
PIAT Math, 107
Piore, M., 404
policy, 6, 8, 9, 10, 14, 49, 54, 62, 90, 94, 96, 97, 100, 104, 106, 132, 136, 174, 179, 180, 182, 204, 206, 208, 209, 210, 211, 212, 213, 220, 222, 223, 227, 229, 237, 238, 239, 240, 243, 244, 245, 246, 249, 250, 251, 252, 301, 340, 342, 350, 351, 352, 395, 396, 400, 401, 402, 404, 405, 406, 407, 408
Pomare, M., 387
Post, R.C., 13, 36, 37, 39, 41, 42, 44, 171, 205, 209, 217, 221
pregnancy, 88, 113, 301, 309, 313, 316, 323
preschool, 99
Price-Waterhouse v. Hopkins, 11, 266, 268
priming, 290
productivity, 78, 82, 119, 126, 160, 168, 233, 269, 305, 347, 360, 362, 365, 366
Pryor, J.B., 60
public opinion, 6, 7, 168, 248
Pugh, M. D., 91

racism
  modern, 380
  subtle, 388
  symbolic, 380
Rauch, S.L., 60
Raudenbush, S., 82
Raymond, P., 60
reading, 106, 113, 115, 203, 212, 341, 344
reasonable accommodation, 13, 256, 269, 367, 370
Reskin, B.F., 4, 7, 75, 76, 78, 80, 82, 83, 84, 85, 86, 88, 90, 92, 93, 94, 96, 193, 373, 374, 399
Rich, A., 65
rights, 3, 5, 8, 9, 10, 11, 12, 14, 15, 19, 20, 24, 26, 27, 32, 33, 34, 36, 37, 39, 43, 47, 100, 135, 150, 167, 168, 175–86, 190, 191, 203–35, 237–242, 244–266, 268, 282, 284, 301–322, 326, 329, 337, 338, 339, 340, 343, 345, 346, 348, 349, 350, 393
Robert, P.M., 3, 4, 6, 8, 10, 12, 14, 16, 18, 20, 22, 24, 26, 28, 30, 32, 34, 44, 204, 205, 209, 217, 219, 229, 373
Rock, E.B., 44
Rodgers, W.M., 82
Romer v Evans, 182, 221, 226
Ropp, S.A., 390
Rosenbloom, D.H., 91
Ross, S.A., 83, 288
Ross v. Kansas City Power Light, 87
Rothman, A.J., 7, 399
Rouse, C., 91
Rubin, E., 49
Rudin, J.P., 401
Rust, M., 386, 387

Sabel, C.F., 56
Salancik, G.R., 91

salary
  and arbitration, 150
Salomon, 61
Sampson, R.J., 6
San Antonio Indep. Sch. Dist. v. Rodriguez, 231
Sanders, J., 8, 172
Sanford, R.N., 379
Sanitioso, 381
Sanna, L.J., 398
Santiago-Ramos v. Centennial P.R. Wireless Corp, 367
Sarat, A., 3, 5, 15, 16, 45, 47, 303, 304, 349
schooling
  and attainment, 99
Schultz, V., 36, 37, 39, 41, 94, 303, 331, 361
Schuman, H., 378, 384
Schwartz, D., 60, 205, 223
Scott, J., 47
Scott, M.F., 140–147
Scott, W.R., 338, 344
Scott v. Macy, 178
Sears, D.O., 242, 378, 380
second generation discrimination, 373
segregation
  and position, 165
Seidel, M.-D.L., 82
Selmi, M.L., 39, 88, 89, 272
Selznick, P., 8, 339
sex
  and composition, 93
sexual harassment
  hostile work environment, 14
sexual orientation
  and discrimination, 167, 168, 174
  and form, 168
  and indirect, 169
Shapiro, M., 6, 235, 254
Sherman, J., 61, 233, 391
Shin, L.M., 60
Sidanius, J., 7, 65, 287, 293
Siegel, R.B., 13, 205
Siegelman, P., 4, 6, 15, 20, 23, 26, 89, 138, 141, 261, 262, 264, 266, 268, 270, 272, 274, 276, 277, 278, 280, 282, 283, 284
Silbey, S., 45, 47, 303, 348
Singh, P., 7
skill, 82, 94, 99, 100, 102, 105, 106, 110, 119, 121, 129, 132, 136, 200, 269, 397
Smedley, B.D., 6
Smelser, N., 64, 67
Smith, E.R., 287
Smith, J.P., 192
Smith, M.D., 333
Smith, R.A., 94
Smith, T.W. 17
Smithson, M., 91
social change, 246, 247, 248, 257, 302, 303, 306, 319, 322, 338, 352
social psychology, 375, 379, 381, 383, 385, 387, 389, 391, 393, 397, 399, 401, 403, 405, 407
soft skill, 81, 199
Sørensen, A.B., 82, 84, 93
Spears, R., 61, 393
Spencer, S.J., 61, 288
Spriggs, W.E., 82
Squires, G.D., 6
stacking hypothesis, 152
Steele, C., 104, 116, 117, 288, 378
Steelworkers v. Weber, 14
Stephan, W.G., 391
Stinchcombe, A.L., 80, 404
Stith, A.Y., 6
Storen, D., 4, 7
Strack, F., 60
structural effects, 193
Stryker, R., 80, 358, 371
Sturm, S., 10, 35, 36, 38, 40, 42, 44, 46, 48, 49, 50, 52, 54, 55, 56, 89, 91, 94, 95, 373
Suchman, M., 4, 38, 339, 345, 347
Sugarman, D., 37
Suh, S.A., 17
Sutton v. United Air Lines, 254, 269
Swedberg, R., 84, 95
Swim, J., 91, 287, 288, 292, 294, 295, 296, 398
system-justifying beliefs, 293

Tajfel, H., 62, 289, 291, 293, 385, 386
Taylor, D.M., 62, 68, 171, 172, 175, 192, 207, 287
telecommuting, 364, 366, 370, 374
Tennessee v. Lane, 205
test score
  and home, 110, 112, 113, 116, 132, 134
Tetlock, P.E., 67, 91
Tilly, C., 77, 78, 79, 81, 82

Title VII, 6, 12, 14, 20, 21, 42, 150, 179, 265, 267, 268, 269, 270, 272, 273, 280, 281, 282, 283, 325, 329, 368, 370, 393
Todd, 100
Tomaskovic-Devey, D., 78, 82, 84, 94
Toyota v. Williams, 255
Travis, M.A., 368, 369, 370, 373
Trubek, D.M., 47
Turner, A., 62, 233, 289, 291, 293, 386
Tyler, R.B., 60
Tyler, T.R., 8

Uggen, C., 43, 44, 45, 56, 304, 343
Ullman, J.C., 399
United States v. Burke, 270
United States v. Carolene Products, 222
United States v. Lopez, 13, 217
United States v. Morrison, 13, 217
Urzua, S., 102, 104

Van Horn, C.E., 7
Van Wezel Stone, K., 54
Velasco, S.C., 82
Vicknair, K., 82, 97
Vuocolo, J., 368, 372

Wachter, M.L., 44
Wackenhut, J., 378
wage
  Black–White wage gap, 105, 121
  wage gap, 6, 7, 8, 82, 101, 102, 105, 120, 121, 123, 124, 135, 357, 360, 364
Walker, L., 53, 56, 396
Wal–Mart, 395, 396, 398, 399, 400, 401, 402, 404, 405, 406, 407, 408
Walton, S., 399, 400, 404
Ward, C.M., 226, 387, 388
Ward's Cove Packing v. Atonio, 10, 11, 13, 94, 266, 268
Watkins, S., 90
Wax, A., 37, 39
Webb v. Merck & Co., 2002, 52
Weber, M., 14, 84, 93
Wegner, D.M., 61, 391
Weinberg, N., 84, 85
Whalen, P.J., 60, 291
Wheeler, M.E., 61
Whorf, B.L., 95
Wickard v. Filburn, 216, 217
Wilkins, D.B., 36, 206
Williams, J. C., 305, 354–357, 361, 362, 367, 369, 371
Williams, P., 303, 307
Williams, R.M., 387
Wilson, T. D., 64, 75, 79, 91, 207
Winston, K., 51, 275
Word, C.O., 87
work hours, 249, 363, 401
Wright, S.C., 287, 390

Xing Zhong, 99
Xu, J., 7, 63

Yamagata, H., 92
Yngvesson, B., 32, 44
Yoshino, K., 36, 174, 175, 223, 228

Zion, C., 399